1 MONTH OF
FREE
READING

at

www.ForgottenBooks.com

By purchasing this book you are eligible for one month membership to ForgottenBooks.com, giving you unlimited access to our entire collection of over 1,000,000 titles via our web site and mobile apps.

To claim your free month visit:
www.forgottenbooks.com/free43854

ISBN 978-1-5283-5385-4
PIBN 10043854

TREATY-MAKING POWER

OF THE

UNITED STATES

BY

CHARLES HENRY BUTLER

OF THE NEW YORK BAR

VOL. I.

PART I. THE UNITED STATES IS A NATION.
PART II. HISTORICAL REVIEW OF THE TREATY-MAKING POWER OF THE
UNITED STATES.

———

THE BANKS LAW PUBLISHING CO.
21 MURRAY STREET, NEW YORK
1902

These volumes are dedicated
with affection and respect
to the memory of my grandfather
BENJAMIN FRANKLIN BUTLER
whom the Historian Bancroft described
as "ever the upright statesman."
He was born at Kinderhook Landing (Stuyvesant)
New York, December 14, 1795, and
died at Paris, France, November 8, 1858.
He was appointed in 1824 a Commissioner to Revise the
Statute Laws of the State of New York.
He was Attorney-General of the United States from 1833
to 1838 during the administrations of ANDREW
JACKSON and MARTIN VAN BUREN, and for a part of
that period he was also Secretary of War.
On more than one occasion, while he was Attorney-
General, he sustained
THE TREATY-MAKING POWER OF THE UNITED STATES
before the
SUPREME COURT
while JOHN MARSHALL was the CHIEF JUSTICE
and JOSEPH STORY an ASSOCIATE JUSTICE
of that august tribunal.

" There were giants in the earth in those days."

PREFACE

A little over a year ago the original manuscript of this work, upon which nearly three years had then been spent, was handed to the publisher with the hope and expectation that the single volume then in contemplation would be completed and offered to the reading public within the following sixty days. Such hope and expectation, however, failed to be realized as the necessity for revision of, and additions to, the original manuscript and the pages as they returned from the printer, resulted in expanding the work to its present proportions, and in delaying its publication until the present time. The increased bulk of these volumes it is hoped, is, to some extent, atoned for by the thoroughness with which they have been indexed, for that part of the work can be referred to without egotism as it has been done almost, if not entirely, by Mr. E. E. Treffrey whose ability as an analyzer and indexer of works of this nature has earned for him a well deserved reputation.

The selection of the subject-matter of these volumes was the natural outcome of my investigations into the nature and extent of the treaty-making power of the United States during my connection in 1898 with the Anglo-American Joint High Commission, particularly in regard to the extent of the power of the United States to enforce, by appropriate Federal legislation, treaty stipulations in regard to matters which, in the absence of treaty relations, would be wholly

within State jurisdiction. The result of such investigations
appears in chapter XV of volume II, but after the conclusions there stated had been reached and even after my connection with the Commission had ceased, the subject continued to interest and fascinate me, and so held my attention
that I determined to make it the basis of a work in which
the treaty-making power of the United States in all of its
varied phases and aspects should be the principal subject instead of being, as until the present time it generally has
been, the subject merely of a subdivision, or of a chapter, in
works on constitutional and international law.   It has been
impossible, however, to cover the subject as thoroughly
as was originally intended, because, as the work has progressed, new branches and subdivisions have constantly appeared, and doubtless if they had not been brought to an
abrupt close these volumes might have been indefinitely increased in size, and delayed in publication.

The expansion of the work has to a great extent been caused
by the addition to volume I of the Insular Cases Appendix
which contains an abstract of all of the decisions and opinions
of the Supreme Court of the United States in the cases decided
in May and December, 1901, which involved the status, so far
as the revenue provisions of the Constitution are concerned,
of our newly acquired possessions ; and also of the Treaties
Appendix to volume II which contains a list of treaties and
agreements, and proclamations affecting our relations, with
foreign countries, arranged alphabetically according to countries, and which, owing to the great pains and labor of
Captain Osgood Smith of the New York Bar and now of
Havana, who assisted me in its preparation, is probably more
complete than any other published list of treaties and proclamations.

The delay in publication has largely been on account of
the rapidity with which " history-making " has progressed

during the preparation of these volumes. The deaths of Queen Victoria and President McKinley were undoubtedly the two most important historical events of 1901, but those having the most important bearing upon the treaty-making power were the decisions on May 27th and December 2d, of the Supreme Court in the Insular Cases which have already been referred to, and the negotiation and ratification of the Hay-Pauncefote treaty by which the Clayton-Bulwer treaty of 1850 was superseded and abrogated. As these, and other, events happened after much of the matter was actually "in plate" they necessitated changes and delay. Even now, as this book goes to press, and it is too late to make more than a brief mention thereof, (p. 457, vol. I) the irrepressible conflict between the Senate and the House of Representatives as to the necessity of legislation to make treaty stipulations not only obligatory as contracts, but also effectual as laws, has been reopened; and the question which, as Senator Cullom declared, has been debated for over a century in both Houses of Congress without reaching any decision, has once more assumed serious and practical importance. It has, indeed, been a temptation to delay the publication until some definite conclusion shall have been reached in the pending contest, but it has been resisted, and should any additional treaty history be made, or treaty law be newly expounded, reference thereto will have to await the publication of further editions, if any shall ever be warranted by the reception accorded to this.

That which has most impressed itself upon me as I have prepared these pages is the magnitude of any element of constitutional law; indeed the grandeur of the Constitution itself, not only as the subject of study but as the "great charter of our liberties" as it was fitly called by Justice Story in his opinion in the great case of *Martin* vs. *Hunter* must steadily grow upon any one who carefully studies it; the

words then uttered by that great jurist have a lasting significance, and they will be as applicable in the future as they
are to-day and were in 1816 when he declared: "The instrument was not intended to provide merely for the exigencies
of a few years, but was to endure through a long lapse of
ages, the events of which were locked up in the inscrutable
purposes of Providence"; and who can fail to be impressed
with the wisdom of its framers who "foreseeing that it
would be a perilous and difficult, if not an impracticable,
task to provide for minute specification of its powers, expressed them in general terms, leaving to the legislature from
time to time, to adopt its own means to effectuate legitimate
objects, and mould and model the exercise of its powers as
its wisdom and the public interests should demand." Surely
the temptations which those men in Philadelphia resisted to
insert specifications and details applicable to then existing
circumstances must have been strong indeed, and all praise
must be given to them, in that they were able to rise above
local and temporary exigencies and frame an instrument
which is to-day as true a chart and compass for a great
world power as it was then for an infant nation struggling
for existence.

In presenting this my first work of any magnitude, I acknowledge that it must contain many errors and that much
has been omitted which should have found a place therein,
and indulgence is asked for all these faults. I also know that
some of the opinions which have been expressed differ from
those held by men whom no one respects more than I do.
Questions involving the construction of our Constitution always have been, and always will be, debatable; it is well for
our country that it is so, as it is only by the earnest presentation of both sides of every question that truth is finally reached
and safe methods adopted. In expressing my own opinions, however, an effort has been made to place the reader in

possession of the views of others and to furnish such references as will enable them to form their own conclusions.

These volumes have been dedicated to my grandfather, but, in order that the name of my father, William Allen Butler, may also in some manner be linked with them, they will make their first appearance on that anniversary of his birth (February 20, 1825), on which he completes the seventy-seventh year of his life. For more than fifty-five years he has been a member of the New York Bar in active practice; he has been President of the American Bar Association and also of the Association of the Bar of the City of New York. On this day, and under these circumstances, it certainly is justifiable for me to refer to the words uttered on an appropriate occasion by the Honorable Joseph H. Choate a few weeks ago, just before he left this country to resume those duties as our ambassador at the Court of St. James, which he is so gracefully and efficiently performing, in which he described my father as " the very Dean of our profession and entitled to be so called not only by reason of his seniority, but also from his character, and the manner in which, during his more than half century of practice, he has constantly upheld the honor and dignity of the Bar."

Had these volumes been dedicated to any person other than my father or grandfather, two names would have presented themselves to me between which it would have been hard for me to have chosen.

Delivering the manuscript to the publishers about a year ago, while the members of our profession were universally preparing for the appropriate celebration of the centennial anniversary of his appointment as Chief Justice of the Supreme Court of the United States, the name of that great jurist, John Marshall, naturally presented itself to my mind, and as my work has progressed, my veneration and respect for him whom John Randolph used affectionately to call "the Great Lord Chief" has constantly increased, for it is perhaps more to him than to any other single man that this country owes to-day its ability to stand among the other nations on an equal footing as a fully sovereign power, unshorn of any element of national strength or trammelled with the fetters of strict construction by which at one time it was threatened to be strangled. In fact, Mr. Garfield might well have added to that eloquent passage in his memorial address, in which he declared that Marshall found the Constitution a skeleton and clothed it with flesh and blood, that the Chief Justice also breathed into the body, which he thus really created, the breath of national life and sovereign power without which it would have remained an inert mass, but through the possession whereof it has been able to live and move and have its being.

It is hardly necessary to mention the other name for that of William McKinley must naturally suggest itself to the reader. It was largely due to his kindly inspiration and the friendly interest which he ever expressed in this and other work undertaken by myself that this book was conceived in its concrete form and the earlier portions thereof completed. During our last interview the plan and scope of these volumes were discussed and the desire which he expressed to see them completed was one of the inspiring influences which sustained me while the work was in progress.

That Mr. McKinley was pre-eminently appreciative of the value and extent of the treaty-making power of our government, was evidenced by those utterances in his Buffalo speech which, in view of the tragic events of the following day, were strangely mystical and prophetic; and surely it was not by chance, for the hand of God was clearly discernible, that on the very last day on which it could possibly have occurred, he declared that the day of reprisals was past, and the day of reciprocity treaties had come, that God and man had joined the nations together, that our ships of war must now be white winged messengers of peace. Surely it can well be said of him that this country is the greater from the way in which he lived and did his work, and is the better for the noble, Christian manner in which he passed from this earth unto his lasting reward, leaving precious memories in the hearts of all his fellow citizens whom he loved and served so well.

But his words must be heeded and no monument erected to the memory of William McKinley, no matter how great or how grand it may be, can ever atone for the insult which will be offered to his memory if the pledges made to Cuba during his administration shall not be carried out in letter and in spirit. He, to whom the great industries of this country owe so much and who could never have had one thought which could do them harm, stood pledged to give assistance as well as freedom to that island whose nearness to our coasts made us her natural protector; and now that he has gone a double duty rests upon us to fulfil those pledges, not only for the sake of Cuba but for his honor and our own.

Before closing this preface it is my great pleasure to gratefully acknowledge the assistance which has been received during the preparation of these volumes from many kind friends; it is impossible to enumerate them all but I wish especially to thank the Honorable Orville H. Platt, United States Senator from Connecticut, the Honorable Elihu Root, Secretary of War, Dr. David J. Hill and Mr. Alvey A. Adee, Assistant Secretaries of State, Mr. Andrew H. Allen, keeper of the Rolls and Archives in the State Department and Mr. Charles G. Phelps Secretary of the Senate Committee on Relations with Cuba, for the many courtesies extended to, and documents obtained for me.

This work was commenced in Washington during my sojourn there of 1898–1899, but for the past two years it has been carried on in New York almost entirely in the building of the Association of the Bar of the City of New York and it is not only my duty, but also my pleasure, to express in more than a merely perfunctory manner my appreciation of the great assistance rendered to me by the Librarian and the entire staff of the Association. As an almost daily visitor to the library for over two years I have had every opportunity of testing the efficiency of the staff in charge of the building and the library and in every respect it has been tried and not found wanting.

My work for the present is finished. That of my readers now commences—my greatest hope is that they will not find their task in perusing these pages less interesting than mine has been in writing them.

C. H. B.

Bar Association Library, New York City,

February 20, 1902.

TABLE OF CONTENTS

OF

VOLUME I.

INTRODUCTION.

VIEWS OF THE AUTHOR ON THE TREATY-MAKING POWER OF THE UNITED STATES, AND THE METHOD OF ITS DISCUSSION AS THE SUBJECT-MATTER OF THIS VOLUME. PAGES 1-14.

PART I.

THE UNITED STATES IS A NATION.

CHAPTER I.

THE NATIONALITY AND SOVEREIGNTY OF THE UNITED STATES.
PAGES 15-70.

CHAPTER II.

THE NATIONALITY AND SOVEREIGNTY OF THE UNITED STATES AS EVI-
DENCED BY ACQUISITION OF TERRITORY. PAGES 71-136.

CHAPTER III.

THE NATIONALITY AND SOVEREIGNTY OF THE UNITED STATES AS RECOGNIZED BY OTHER SOVEREIGN POWERS. PAGES 137–190.

PART II.

HISTORICAL REVIEW OF THE TREATY-MAKING POWER OF THE UNITED STATES.

CHAPTER IV.

THE TREATY-MAKING POWER AS AN ATTRIBUTE OF SOVEREIGNTY AND AS EXERCISED BY CENTRAL GOVERNMENTS OF CONFEDERATED POWERS. PAGES 191—234.

CHAPTER V.

TREATIES, AND THE TREATY-MAKING POWER OF THE UNITED STATES AS
EXERCISED PRIOR TO AND UNDER THE CONFEDERATION. PAGES 235–
284.

CHAPTER VII.

PROCEEDINGS OF THE CONSTITUTIONAL CONVENTIONS OF THE SEVERAL STATES, IN SO FAR AS THEY RELATE TO THE TREATY-MAKING POWER OF THE NATIONAL GOVERNMENT. PAGES 339–370.

B

CHAPTER VIII.

THE TREATY-MAKING POWER AS A FACTOR IN THE GREAT NATIONAL DEBATE OF 1787–8. PAGES 371–392.

CHAPTER IX.

OPINIONS OF PUBLICISTS, HISTORIANS AND EXPOUNDERS OF THE CONSTITUTION IN REGARD TO THE EXTENT AND SCOPE OF THE TREATY-MAKING POWER OF THE UNITED STATES. PAGES 393–416.

CHAPTER X.

THE TREATY-MAKING POWER AND THE RELATIONS OF BOTH HOUSES
OF CONGRESS THERETO, AS THE SAME HAS BEEN THE SUBJECT OF
CONGRESSIONAL DEBATE AND ACTION. 417–458.

INSULAR CASES APPENDIX.

TABLE OF CONTENTS OF VOLUME II.

PART III.

JUDICIAL DECISIONS AFFECTING THE TREATY-MAKING POWER OF THE UNITED STATES, ITS EXTENT AND APPLICATION.

CHAPTER XI.

CHAPTER XII.

CHAPTER XIII.

CHAPTER XIV.

CHAPTER XV.

CHAPTER XVI.

TREATIES APPENDIX.

INDEX.

TABLE OF AUTHORITIES REFERRED TO.

In preparing this list of authorities the author has not intended to simply preface his work with a bibliography of the various subjects discussed in the volume; had he intended to do so the following list would have been very incomplete as it simply includes most of the books from which quotations have been made in the text, or which have been consulted, and relied upon, by the author. This list, of course, does not include any official reports or digests of Federal or State courts, opinions of the Attorney-General, or publications containing the statutes of Federal and State legislative bodies.

In specifying editions the author has not intended to express any preference for those particularly referred to, but simply to indicate that such edition was used by him because it was the most accessible; in all cases, however, he has endeavored to use the latest edition of standard works. Almost all of the books referred to can be found in the library of The Association of the Bar of New York City. Biographies are classed under the name of the subject, other books with few exceptions under the name of the author; subjects and authors are indexed in detail in the general index to the volume. The description of the book is as a general rule the title page of the first volume. Only a few of the Government publications consulted are referred to in this list.

H. C. ADAMS; PUBLIC DEBTS.

Public Debts; An Essay in the Science of Finance, by Henry C. Adams, Ph. D., of the University of Michigan, and Cornell University, New York, D. Appleton & Co., 1890.

LIFE OF SAMUEL ADAMS; JAMES K. HOSMER.

American Statesmen Series. Samuel Adams, by James K. Hosmer, Professor in Washington University, St. Louis, Missouri. 7th edition. Boston and New York, Houghton, Mifflin & Co., The Riverside Press, Cambridge, 1888.

SHELDON AMOS; FIFTY YEARS OF THE ENGLISH CONSTITUTION.

Fifty Years of the English Constitution, 1830–1880, by Sheldon Amos, M. A., Barrister-at-Law, late Professor of Jurisprudence in University College, London; and of Jurisprudence and Constitutional Law and Legal History to the Inns Courts; Late Examiner in the Constitutional History of England to the University of London; author of "A Primer of the English Constitution," "A Systematic View of the Science of Jurisprudence," etc. Boston, Little, Brown & Co., 1880.

SIR WILLIAM R. ANSON; ANSON'S LAW OF THE CONSTITUTION; PART II, THE CROWN.

The Law and Custom of the Constitution, Part II, The Crown, by Sir William R. Anson, Bart., D. C. L., of the Inner Temple, Barrister-at-Law, Warden of All Soul's College, Oxford. Second edition. Oxford, at the Clarendon Press, London, Henry Frowde and Stevens & Sons, Limited, 1896.

WALTER BAGEHOT; FOREST MORGAN'S EDITION OF BAGEHOT'S WORKS.

The Works of Walter Bagehot, M. A., and Fellow of University College of London, with memoirs by R. H. Hutton, now first published in full by The Traveller's Insurance Company of Hartford, Conn., edited by Forest Morgan, in 5 volumes, Hartford, 1891.

SIR SHERSTON BAKER; HALLECK'S INTERNATIONAL LAW.

Halleck's International Law, or Rules Regulating the Intercourse of States in Peace and War. Third edition thoroughly revised and in many parts rewritten. By Sir Sherston Baker, Bart., of Lincoln's Inn, and of the Western Circuit, Barrister-at-Law; author of "The Laws Relating to Quarantine," "The Office of the Vice-Admiral," etc., 2 volumes, London, Kegan, Paul, Trench, Trubner & Co., Limited, 1893.

GEORGE BANCROFT; HISTORY OF THE UNITED STATES.

History of the United States of America, from the Discovery of the Continent, by George Bancroft. The author's last revision. In six volumes. New York, D. Appleton & Co. 1892.

GEORGE BANCROFT; HISTORY OF THE CONSTITUTION.

History of the Formation of the Constitution of the United States of America, by George Bancroft. In two volumes. Sixth edition. New York, D. Appleton & Co., 1893.

THOMAS H. BENTON; THIRTY YEARS IN THE UNITED STATES SENATE.

Thirty Years' Views, or a History of the Working of the American Government for Thirty Years, from 1820 to 1850. Chiefly taken from the Congress Debates, the private papers of General Jackson and the speeches of ex-Senator Benton, with his actual view of men and affairs; with historical notes and illustrations, and some notices of eminent deceased contemporaries, by a Senator of Thirty Years. In two volumes. Vol. I. New York and London, D. Appleton & Company, 1854. (Vol. II. New York, D. Appleton & Company; Cincinnati, W. A. Clarke & Co., 1856.)

SIR WILLIAM BLACKSTONE; see CHASE and TUCKER.

JAMES G. BLAINE; TWENTY YEARS OF CONGRESS, 1861–1881.

Twenty Years of Congress, from Lincoln to Garfield. With a review of the events which led to the political revolution of 1860, by James G.

Blaine. In two volumes; volume I, Norwich, Conn., The Henry Bill Publishing Company, 1884. (Vol. II, 1886.)

PHILEMON BLISS; Bliss on Sovereignty.

Of Sovereignty. By Philemon Bliss, LL.D., Professor of Law in the State University of Missouri; author of "Bliss on Code Pleading." Boston, Little, Brown & Company, 1885.

J. K. BLUNTSCHLI; The Theory of the State.

The Theory of the State, by J. K. Bluntschli, late Professor of Political Sciences in the University of Heidelberg. Authorized English translation from the sixth German edition. Oxford, at the Clarendon Press, 1885.

GEORGE S. BOUTWELL; The Constitution of the United States at the End of the First Century.

The Constitution of the United States at the End of the First Century, by George S. Boutwell. Boston, U. S. A., D. C. Heath & Co., 1895.

A. C. BOYD; Wheaton's International Law.

Elements of International Law, by Henry Wheaton, LL.D., Minister of the United States at the Court of Prussia; Corresponding Member of the Academy of Moral and Political Sciences in the Institute of France; Honorary Member of the Royal Academy of Sciences at Berlin, etc. Third English edition, edited with Notes, and an Appendix of Statutes and Treaties, bringing the work down to the present time. By A. B. Boyd, Esq., LL.B. (Camb.), J. P., Barrister-at-Law of the Inner Temple and Midland Circuit, author of "The Merchant Shipping Laws." London, Stevens and Sons, Limited, 1889.

JAMES BRYCE; The American Commonwealth.

The American Commonwealth, by James Bryce, author of "The Holy Roman Empire," M. P. for Aberdeen. In two volumes. London, Macmillan and Co., and New York, 1889.

JOHN W. BURGESS; Political Science and Constitutional Law.

Political Science and Comparative Constitutional Law; volume 1, Sovereignty and Liberty; volume 2, Government. By John W. Burgess, Ph. D., LL.D., Professor of History, Political Science and International Law, Dean of the University Faculty of Political Science in Columbia College. Boston, U. S. A., and London, Ginn & Company, 1891.

JOHN L. CADWALADER; Digest of Opinions and Leading Cases on International Law.

Digest of the published Opinions of the Attorneys-General, and of the Leading Decisions of the Federal Courts, with reference to International Law, Treaties, and Kindred Subjects. By John L. Cadwalader, Washington, Government Printing Office, 1877.

JOHN C. CALHOUN; Works of; see R. C. Cralle, Editor.

JAMES MORTON CALLAHAN; Cuba and International Relations.
An Historical Study in American Diplomacy, by James Morton Callahan, Ph. D. Albert Shaw, Lecturer in Diplomatic History, Johns Hopkins University. The Johns Hopkins Press, Baltimore, 1899.

HAMPTON L. CARSON; 100th Anniversary of the Constitution of the United States.
History of the Celebration of the One Hundredth Anniversary of the promulgation of the Constitution of the United States, edited by Hampton L. Carson, Secretary of the Constitutional Centennial Commission. In two volumes, with illustrations. Published under the direction and by the authority of the Commission, by J. B. Lippincott Company, Philadelphia, 1889.

HAMPTON L. CARSON; History of the Supreme Court of the United States.
The Supreme Court of the United States: Its History by Hampton L. Carson of the Philadelphia Bar, and Its Centennial Celebration, February 4, 1890. Prepared under direction of The Judiciary Centennial Committee. Philadelphia, John Y. Huber Company, 1891.

GEORGE CHASE; Blackstone's Commentaries.
Commentaries on The Laws of England; In Four Books, by Sir William Blackstone, Knight, one of the Justices of the Court of Common Pleas. So abridged as to retain all portions of the original work which are of historical or practical value. With notes, and references to American decisions; for the use of American students. By George Chase, LL. B., Professor of Law in the Law School of Columbia College, N. Y. Editor of Stephen's Digest of the Law of Evidence (American edition). Third edition. New York and Albany, Banks and Brothers, 1890.

SIR EDWARD CLARKE; Clarke's Law of Extradition.
A Treatise upon the Law of Extradition. With the Conventions upon the Subject existing between England and Foreign Nations, and the Cases decided therein. By Sir Edward Clarke, Knt., Her Majesty's Solicitor General; formerly Tancred Student of Lincoln's Inn. Third edition. London, Stevens and Haynes, 1888.

LIFE OF HENRY CLAY; Carl Schurz.
American Statesmen Series. Life of Henry Clay, by Carl Schurz, in two volumes. Boston and New York, Houghton, Mifflin & Co., The Riverside Press, Cambridge, 1888.

CLAYTON–BULWER TREATY.

Correspondence in relation to the Proposed Interoceanic Canal between the Atlantic and Pacific Oceans, The Clayton-Bulwer Treaty and the Monroe Doctrine; being a reprint of Senate Executive Documents No. 112, 46th Congress, 2d Session; No. 194, 47th Congress, 1st Session; and No. 26, 48th Congress, 1st Session. Washington, Government Printing Office, 1885.

THOMAS M. COOLEY; COOLEY'S CONSTITUTIONAL LIMITATIONS.

A Treatise on the Constitutional Limitations which rest upon the Legislative Power of the States of the American Union. By Thomas M. Cooley, LL. D., formerly one of the Justices of the Supreme Court of Michigan, and Jay Professor of Law in the University of Michigan; now Chairman of the Interstate Commerce Commission. Sixth edition, with large additions, giving the results of the recent cases, by Alexis C. Angell, of the Detroit Bar. Boston, Little, Brown & Company, 1890.

THOMAS M. COOLEY; PRINCIPLES OF CONSTITUTIONAL LAW.

Student's Series. The General Principles of Constitutional Law in the United States of America, by Thomas M. Cooley, LL. D., author of "Constitutional Limitations," etc. Third edition by Andrew C. McLaughlin, A. M., LL. B., Professor of American History, University of Michigan. Boston, Little, Brown & Company, 1898.

HOMERSHAM COX; THE INSTITUTIONS OF THE ENGLISH GOVERNMENT.

The Institutions of the English Government: being an account of The Constitution, Powers, and Procedure, of its Legislative, Judicial, and Administrative Departments. With copious references to ancient and modern authorities. By Homersham Cox, M. A., Barrister-at-Law. author of "The British Commonwealth," etc. London, H. Sweet, 1863.

BRINTON COXE; JUDICIAL POWER AND UNCONSTITUTIONAL LEGISLATION.

An Essay on Judicial Power and Unconstitutional Legislation, being a Commentary on Parts of the Constitution of the United States, by Brinton Coxe, of the Bar of Philadelphia; Kay and Brother, Philadelphia, 1893.

RICHARD K. CRALLE; WORKS OF JOHN C. CALHOUN.

A Disquisition on Government and a Discourse on the Constitution and Government of the United States, by John C. Calhoun. In six volumes. Edited by Richard K. Cralle. New York, D. Appleton & Company, 1888.

SIR EDWARD CREASY; THE CONSTITUTIONS OF THE BRITANNIC EMPIRE.

The Imperial and Colonial Constitutions of the Britannic Empire including Indian Institutions, by Sir Edward Creasy, M. A., author of "The Rise and Progress of the English Constitution," "The History of England," etc. London, Longmans, Green and Co., 1872.

SIR EDWARD CREASY; HISTORY OF THE ENGLISH CONSTITUTION.

The Rise and Progress of the English Constitution by Sir Edward Creasy, M. A., late Chief Justice of Ceylon, author of "The Fifteen Decisive Battles of the World," etc. Fourteenth edition. London: Richard Bently & Son, Publishers in Ordinary to Her Majesty the Queen, 1880.

GEORGE TICKNOR CURTIS; CONSTITUTIONAL HISTORY OF THE
UNITED STATES.

Constitutional History of The United States from their Declaration of Independence to the close of their Civil War, by George Ticknor Curtis. In two volumes, New York, Harper & Brothers, 1889. (Vol. II edited by Joseph Culbertson Clayton, 1896.)

R. H. DANA, JR.; WHEATON'S INTERNATIONAL LAW.

Elements of International Law. By Henry Wheaton, LL. D., Minister of the United States at the Court of Prussia; Corresponding Member of the Academy of Moral and Political Sciences in the Institute of France; Honorary Member of the Royal Academy of Science at Berlin, etc. Eighth edition. Edited, with notes, by Richard Henry Dana, Jr., LL. D. Boston, Little, Brown & Company, 1866.

J. C. BANCROFT DAVIS; see SAMUEL F. MILLER.

HENRY B. DAWSON; THE FŒDERALIST.

The Fœderalist; a Collection of Essays, written in favor of the new Constitution, as agreed upon by the Federal Convention, September 17, 1787. Reprinted from the original text, under the editorial supervision of Henry B. Dawson. University edition New York, Charles Scribner & Company, 1870.

A. V. DICEY; DICEY ON THE CONSTITUTION.

Introduction to the study of The Law of the Constitution, by A. V. Dicey, B. C. L., of the Inner Temple: Vinerian Professor of English Law, Fellow of All Soul's College, Oxford, Hon. LL. D., Glasgow and Edinburgh. Fourth edition. London and New York, Macmillan & Co., 1893.

WILLIAM ALEXANDER DUER; DUER'S CONSTITUTIONAL JURIS-
PRUDENCE.

A Course of Lectures on the Constitutional Jurisprudence of the United States; delivered annually in Columbia College, New York, by William Alexander Duer, LL. D., Late President of that Institution, The second edition, revised, enlarged and adapted to professional, as well as general, use. Boston, Little, Brown & Company, 1856.

JONATHAN ELLIOTT; ELLIOTT'S DEBATES.

The Debates in the several State Conventions, on the adoption of the Federal Constitution, as recommended by the General Convention at Philadelphia, in 1787, together with the Journal of the Federal Convention, Luther Martin's Letter, Yate's Minutes, Congressional Opinions, Virginia and Kentucky Resolutions of '98–'99, and other illustrations of the Constitution. In five volumes, second edition, with considerable additions. Collected and Revised from Contemporary Publications, by Jonathan Elliot. Published under the sanction of Congress. Philadelphia, J. B. Lippincott & Co., Washington, Taylor & Maury, 1866.

JONATHAN ELLIOT; ELLIOT'S DEBATES ON THE FEDERAL CONSTITUTION; SUPPLEMENT—THE MADISON PAPERS.

Debates on the Adoption of the Federal Constitution, in the Convention held at Philadelphia, in 1787; with a Diary of the Debates of The Congress of the Confederation; as reported by James Madison a Member and Deputy from Virginia. Revised and newly arranged by Jonathan Elliott. Complete in one volume. Vol. V. Supplementary to Elliot's Debates. Published under the sanction of Congress. Philadelphia, J. B. Lippincott & Co., Washington, Taylor & Maury, 1866.

THE FEDERALIST; see DAWSON, J. C. HAMILTON and LODGE.

JOHN FISKE; THE CRITICAL PERIOD OF AMERICAN HISTORY.

The Critical Period of American History, 1783–1789, by John Fiske. Boston and New York, Houghton, Mifflin & Company, The Riverside Press, Cambridge, 1899.

PAUL LEICESTER FORD; ESSAYS ON THE CONSTITUTION, 1787–8.

Essays on the Constitution of the United States, published during its discussion by the people, 1787–1788. Edited by Paul Leicester Ford. Brooklyn, N. Y., Historical Printing Club, 1892.

PAUL LEICESTER FORD; PAMPHLETS ON THE CONSTITUTION, 1787–8.

Pamphlets on the Constitution of the United States, published during its discussion by the people, 1787–1788. Edited with notes and a bibliography, by Paul Leicester Ford. Brooklyn, N. Y. 1888.

JOHN W. FOSTER; A CENTURY OF AMERICAN DIPLOMACY.

A Century of American Diplomacy, being a brief review of the Foreign Relations of the United States, 1776–1876, by John W. Foster, Boston and New York, Houghton, Mifflin & Company, Riverside Press, Cambridge, 1901.

EDWARD A. FREEMAN; GROWTH OF THE ENGLISH CONSTITUTION.

The Growth of the English Constitution from the earliest times by Edward A. Freeman, M. A., Hon. D. C. L., Late Fellow of Trinity College, Oxford. London, Macmillan & Co., 1872.

DANIEL GARDNER; GARDNER'S INSTITUTES, AMERICAN INTERNATIONAL LAW.

Institutes of International Law, Public and Private, as settled by the Supreme Court of the United States, and by our Republic. With references to Judicial Decisions. By Daniel Gardner, Esq., Counsellor at Law, of the New York Bar. New York, John S. Voorhies, 1860.

JAMES W. GERARD; THE PEACE OF UTRECHT.

The Peace of Utrecht. An Historical Review of the Great Treaty of 1713–14, and of the Principal Events of the War of the Spanish Succession. By James W. Gerard. New York and London, G. P. Putnam's Sons, The Knickerbocker Press, 1885.

EDWIN F. GLENN; GLENN'S INTERNATIONAL LAW.

Hand Book of International Law by Captain Edwin F. Glenn, Acting Judge Advocate United States Army. St. Paul, Minn., West Publishing Co., 1895.

RUDOLPH GNEIST; GNEIST'S HISTORY OF THE ENGLISH CONSTITUTION.

The History of the English Constitution by Dr. Rudolph Gneist, Professor of Law at the University of Berlin. Translated by Phillip A. Ashworth, of the Inner Temple, Esq., Barrister-at-law. Second edition revised and enlarged. In two volumes. London, William Clowes and Sons, Limited, 1889.

WILLIAM D. GUTHRIE; THE FOURTEENTH AMENDMENT TO THE CONSTITUTION OF THE UNITED STATES:

Lectures on the Fourteenth Article of Amendment to the Constitution of the United States delivered before the Dwight Alumni Association, New York, April–May, 1898. By William D. Guthrie, of the New York Bar. Boston, Little, Brown & Company, 1898.

WILLIAM EDWARD HALL; HALL'S INTERNATIONAL LAW.

A Treatise on International Law by William Edward Hall, M. A. Fourth edition. Oxford, at the Clarendon Press, London, Henry Frowde, Oxford, University Press Warehouse, Amen Corner and Stevens & Sons, Limited, 1895.

WILLIAM EDWARD HALL; HALL'S FOREIGN JURISDICTION OF THE BRITISH CROWN.

A Treatise on the Foreign Powers and Jurisdiction of the British Crown by William Edward Hall, M. A., Barrister-at-law. Oxford at the Clarendon Press, London: Henry Frowde and Stevens & Sons, Limited, 1894.

HALLECK; see SIR SHERSTON BAKER.

ALEXANDER HAMILTON; see DAWSON, J. C. HAMILTON and LODGE, EDITORS OF FEDERALIST.

JOHN C. HAMILTON; The Federalist.

The Federalist. A Commentary on the Constitution of the United States. A collection of essays by Alexander Hamilton, Jay and Madison. Also the Continentalist and other papers, by Hamilton. Edited by John C. Hamilton, Author of the History of the Republic of the United States. Philadelphia, J. B. Lippincott Company, 1888.

SAMUEL BANNISTER HARDING; The Federal Constitution in Massachusetts.

Harvard Historical Studies, II. The Contest over the Ratification of the Federal Constitution in the State of Massachusetts, by Samuel Bannister Harding, A. M.; sometime Morgan Fellow in Harvard University; Assistant Professor of History in Indiana University. New York, London and Bombay, Longmans, Green and Co., 1896.

JOHN H. HASWELL; see Treaties of United States.

BINGER HERMANN; The Louisiana Purchase.

The Louisiana Purchase and Our Title West of the Rocky Mountains, with a Review of Annexation by the United States, by Binger Hermann, Commissioner of the General Land Office. Washington, Government Printing Office, 1898.

WILLIAM HICKEY; The Constitution of the United States.

Hickey's Constitution of the United States of America, with an alphabetical analysis; Proceedings of the Contintental Congress; Non-Importation Agreement; Address to the Crown and People of Great Brittain; The Declaration of Independence, etc., etc., by William Hickey. New and enlarged edition. Revised and brought down to the 4th of March, 1877, by Alexander Cummings, Counsellor at Law. Baltimore, John Murphy & Co., for the benefit of the heirs of William Hickey, 1878.

FREDERICK W. HOLLS; The Peace Conference at The Hague.

The Peace Conference at The Hague and its Bearings on International Law and Policy by Frederick W. Holls, D. C. L., a member of the Conference of the United States of America. New York, The Macmillan Company; London, Macmillan & Co., Ltd., 1900.

DAVID FRANKLIN HOUSTON; A Study of Nullification in South Carolina.

Harvard Historical Studies, III. A Critical Study of Nullification in South Carolina by David Franklin Houston, A. M., Adjunct Professor of Political Science in the University of Texas; sometime Morgan Fellow of Harvard University. Longmans, Green and Co., New York, London and Bombay, 1896.

JOHN C. HURD; The Theory of our National Existence.

The Theory of our National Existence, as shown by the action of the Government of the United States since 1861. John C. Hurd, LL. D., author of " The Law of Freedom and Bondage in the **United States.**" Boston, Little, Brown & Company, 1881.

E. P. HURLBUT; ESSAYS ON HUMAN RIGHTS.

Essays on Human Rights and their Political Guaranties, by E. P. Hurlbut, Counsellor at Law in the City of New York, with notes by George Combe. Sixth thousandth. New York, Fowlers and Wells, 1850.

INDIAN LAWS; UNITED STATES INDIAN LAWS.

Laws of the United States relating to Indian Affairs, compiled from the Revised Statutes of the United States enacted June 22, 1874, and from Statutes at Large from that date to March 4, 1893; also, Special Acts and Resolutions previous to the enactment of the Revised Statutes, not embraced in or repealed by the Revision; also, List of all Ratified Treaties and Agreements made with the several Indian Tribes. Third Edition. Compiled by the Indian Bureau. Washington, Government Printing Office, 1884.

INDIAN TREATIES; REVISION OF INDIAN TREATIES, 1873.

A Compilation of all the Treaties between the United States and the Indian Tribes now in force as Laws. Prepared under the provisions of the act of Congress, approved March 3, 1873, entitled " An Act to provide for the preparation and presentation to Congress of the Revision of the laws of the United States, consolidating the Laws relating to the Postroads, and a Code relating to Military Offenses, and the Revision of Treaties with the Indian Tribes now in force." Washington, Government Printing Office, 1873.

F. J. KIRCHNER; L'EXTRADITION.

L'Extradition; Recueil Renfermant in extenso tous les Traités conclus jusqu'an 1er Janvier, 1883, entre les Nations Civilisées, et donnant la solution précise des difficultés qui peuvent surgir dans leur application; avec une préface de M. Georges Lachaud, avocat à la Cour D'appel des Paris; Publié sous les Auspices de M. C. E. Howard Vincent, Directeur des Affaires Criminelles de la Police Métropolitaine de Londres; membre de la Faculté de Droit et de la Société Générale des Prisons de Paris; avec le Concours Beinveillant du Corps Diplomatique, par F. J. Kirchner, attaché à la Direction des Affaires Criminelles. London; Stevens and Sons, Chancery Lane, 1883.

LINDLEY MILLER KEASBEY; THE NICARAGUA CANAL AND THE MONROE DOCTRINE.

A Political History of Isthmus Transit, with special reference to the Nicaragua Canal Project and the Attitude of the United States Government thereto, by Lindley Miller Keasbey, Ph. D., R. P. D., Associate Professor of Political Science, Bryn Mawr College. G. P. Putnam's Sons, New York and London, 1896.

JUDSON S. LANDON; The Constitutional History and Government of the United States.

The Constitutional History and Government of the United States by Judson S. Landon, LL. D., Revised edition. Boston and New York, Houghton, Mifflin & Company, The Riverside Press, Cambridge, 1900.

T. J. LAWRENCE; The Principles of International Law.

The principles of International Law by T. J. Lawrence, M. A., LL. D., Rector of Girton, and Lecturer in Downing College, Cambridge, England: Associate of the Institute of International Law, etc. Boston, U. S. A. D. C. Heath & Co., 1895.

WILLIAM LAWRENCE; Law of Claims against Governments.

The Law of Claims against Governments including the mode of adjusting them and the Procedure adopted in their investigation. Credited to Hon. William Lawrence, Comptroller of the Treasury. Published by order of the Congress of the United States of America, Washington Government Printing Office, 1875.

WILLIAM BEACH LAWRENCE; Lawrence's Wheaton on International Law.

Elements of International Law. By Henry Wheaton, LL. D., Minister of the United States at the Court of Prussia; Corresponding Member of the Academy of Moral and Political Sciences in the Institute of France. Honorary Member of the Royal Academy of Sciences at Berlin, etc., Second annotated edition by William Beach Lawrence, author of "Visitation and Search," etc. Boston, Little, Brown & Company; London, Sampson Low, Son and Company, 1863.

HENRY CABOT LODGE; The Federalist.

The Federalist, A Commentary on The Constitution of the United States, being a Collection of Essays written in support of the Constitution agreed upon September 17, 1787, by The Federal Convention. Reprinted from the original text of Alexander Hamilton, John Jay, and James Madison. Edited by Henry Cabot Lodge, Author of "Life and Letters of George Cabot," "A short History of the English Colonies in America," "Alexander Hamilton," and "Daniel Webster" (in "American Statesmen" Series), and "Studies in History." New York and London, G. P. Putnam's Sons, 1894.

JOHN BACH McMASTER; A History of the People of the United States.

A History of the People of the United States, from the Revolution to the Civil War. By John Bach McMaster. In five volumes. Volume I, New York, D. Appleton and Company, 1893. Other volumes issued subseqently.

JOHN BACH McMASTER; Monroe Doctrine.

The Origin, Meaning and Application of the Monroe Doctrine by Professor John Bach McMaster and Henry Altemus. Philadelphia, 1896.

c

McMASTER AND STONE; Pennsylvania and the Federal Constitution, 1787–1788.

Pennsylvania and the Federal Constitution 1787–1788. Edited by John Bach McMaster and Frederick D. Stone. Published for the subscribers by The Historical Society of Pennsylvania, 1888.

WILLIAM MACDONALD; Select Charters Illustrative of American History, 1606–1775.

Select Charters and Other Documents illustrative of American History 1606–1775. Edited with notes by William Macdonald, Professor of History and Political Science in Bowdoin College. Editor of " Select Documents Illustrative of the History of the United States, 1776–1861.'' New York, The Macmillan Company, 1899.

JAMES MADISON; Madison Papers.

The Papers of James Madison, Purchased by Order of Congress, being his Correspondence and Reports of Debates during the Congress of the Confederation and his Report of Debates in the Federal Convention; now published from the original manuscripts, deposited in the Department of State, by direction of the Joint Library Committee of Congress under the superintendence of Henry D. Gilpin. Washington, Langtree & O'Sullivan, 1840. (In three volumes.)

CHARLES E. MAGOON; Congressional Document.

Senate Document, No. 234, LVI Congress; first session; Report on legal status of the territory and inhabitants of the islands acquired by the United States during the war with Spain, considered with reference to territorial boundaries, the Constitution and laws of the United States, by Charles E. Magoon, Law Office, Division of Insular Affairs, War Department, submitted to Secretary of War Elihu Root, February 12, 1900, presented to the Senate by Cushman K. Davis, chairman of the Committtee on Foreign Relations, March 20, 1900.

SIR HENRY SUMNER MAINE; Popular Government.

Popular Government, Four Essays, by Sir Henry Sumner Maine, K. C. S. I., LL. D., F. R. S. Foreign Associate of the Institute of France, author of " Ancient Law.'' London, John Murray, 1885.

JOHN MARSHALL; On the Federal Constitution.

The Writings of John Marshall late Chief Justice of the United States upon The Federal Constitution. Boston, James Munroe & Company, 1839.

WILLIAM M. MEIGS; The Growth of the Constitution.

The Growth of the Constitution in the Federal Convention of 1787. An effort to trace the origin and development of each separate clause from its suggestion in that body to the form finally approved, containing also a fac-simile of a heretofore unpublished manuscript of the first draft of the instrument made for use in the committee of detail, by

William M. Meigs, author of "The Life of Charles Jared Ingersoll."
Second edition. Philadelphia and London, J. B. Lippincott Company, 1900.

SAMUEL FREEMAN MILLER; MILLER'S LECTURES ON THE UNITED STATES CONSTITUTION.

Lectures on the Constitution of The United States by Samuel Freeman Miller, LL. D., late an Associate Justice of the Supreme Court of the United States. New York and Albany, Banks and Brothers, 1891. With notes by J. C. Bancroft Davis and Gheradi Davis.

LIFE OF JAMES MONROE; DANIEL C. GILMAN.

American Statesman Series. James Monroe in his relations to the Public Service during half a Century, 1776–1826, by Daniel C. Gilman, President of the Johns Hopkins University, Baltimore. Ninth edition. Boston and New York, Houghton, Mifflin & Co., Riverside Press, 1888.

JOHN BASSETT MOORE; INTERNATIONAL ARBITRATIONS.

History and Digest of the International Arbitrations to which the United States has been a Party, together with Appendices containing the Treaties relating to such Arbitrations, and Historical and Legal Notes on other International Arbitrations Ancient and Modern, and on the Domestic Commissions of the United States for the Adjustment of International Claims. By John Bassett Moore, Hamilton Fish Professor of International Law and Diplomacy, Columbia University, New York; Associate of the Institute of International Law; sometime Assistant Secretary of State of the United States; author of a work on Extradition and Interstate Rendition, of American notes on the Conflict of Laws, etc. In six volumes. Washington, Government Printing Office, 1898.

JOHN BASSETT MOORE; MOORE ON EXTRADITION; EXTRADITION AND INTERSTATE RENDITION.

A Treatise on Extradition and Interstate Rendition. With Appendices containing the Treaties and Statutes relating to Extradition; the Treaties relating to the Desertion of Seamen; and the Statutes, Rules of Practice, and Forms, in force in the several States and Territories, relating to Interstate Rendition. By John Bassett Moore, Third Assistant Secretary of State of the United States; Author of a work on "Extra Territorial Crime," of a report on Extradition to the International American Conference, etc. In two volumes. Boston, The Boston Book Company, 1891.

JOSEPH WEST MOORE; THE AMERICAN CONGRESS.

The American Congress. A History of National Legislation and Political Events, 1774–1895, by Joseph West Moore, New York, Harper & Brothers, 1895.

G. Reynolds, United States Attorney for the Court of Private Land Claims. (Containing also Rules of Court of Private Land Claims.) St. Louis, Mo., 1895.

RHODES; History of the United States.

History of the United States from the Compromise of 1850, by James Ford Rhodes. Four volumes. New York, Harper Brothers, 1893.

WILLIAM C. RIVES; Life and Times of James Madison.

History of the Life and Times of James Madison, by William C. Rives. Two volumes. Boston, Little, Brown & Co., 1859.

ALPHONSE RIVIER: Principes du Droit des Gens.

Principes du Droit des Gens par Alphonse Rivier, Consul Général de la Confédération Suisse. Professeur a L'Université de Boutelles, Professeur Honoraire a L'Université de Lausanne. Duex tomes. Paris Litrairie Nouvelle de Droit et de Jurisprudence. Arthur Rousseau, Editeur, 1896.

THEODORE ROOSEVELT; The Winning of the West.

The Winning of the West, by Theodore Roosevelt, author of "Naval War of 1812," "Life of Thomas Hart Benton," "Life of Governor Morris," "Hunting Trips of a Ranchman," "Ranch Life and the Hunting Trail," "Essays on Practical Politics," etc. Four volumes. Volumes I and II, 1889, From the Alleganies to the Mississippi; volume III, 1894, The Founding of the Trans-Alleghany Commonwealth; volume IV, 1896, Louisiana and the Northwest. C. P. Putnam's Sons, New York and London.

SAMUEL T. SPEAR; Spear on the Law of Extradition.

The Law of Extradition, International and Interstate with an Appendix, containing the Extradition Treaties and Laws of the United States, the Extradition Laws of the States, several sections of the English Extradition Act of 1870, and the Opinion of Governor Cullom. By Samuel T. Spear, author of "The Law of the Federal Judiciary;" "The Constitutionality of the Legal Tender Acts," etc. Second edition. Albany, Weed, Parsons & Co., 1884.

JOSEPH STORY; Commentaries on the Constitution.

Commentaries on the Constitution of the United States; with a Preliminary Review of the Constitutional History of the Colonies and States before the adoption of the Constitution. By Joesph Story, L. L. D. In two volumes. Fifth edition by Melville M. Bigelow, Ph. D. Boston, Little, Brown & Co., 1891.

HANNIS TAYLOR; The Origin and Growth of the English Constitution.

The Origin and Growth of the English Constitution. An Historical Treatise in which is drawn out, by the light of the most recent researches, the gradual development of the English Constitutional system, and the growth out of that system of the Federal Republic of the United States. By Hannis Taylor. In two parts. Part I. The Making of the Constitution. Part II. Boston and New York, Houghton, Mifflin & Company; London, Sampson, Low, Marston, Searle & Rivingston; The Riverside Press, Cambridge, 1889.

R. W. THOMPSON; HISTORY OF THE TARIFF.

The History of Protective Tariff Laws by R. W. Thompson, Ex-Secretary of the U. S. Navy.   Third edition.   Chicago, R. S. Peale & Co., 1888.

C. G. TIEDEMAN; THE UNWRITTEN CONSTITUTION OF THE UNITED STATES.

The Unwritten Constitution of the United States, a Philosophical Inquiry into the Fundamentals of American Constitutional Law, by Christopher G. Tiedeman, A. M., LL. B., Professor of Law in the University of Missouri, author of treatises on "The Limitation of Police Power," "The Law of Real Property," and "Law of Commercial Paper." C. P. Putnam's Sons, New York and London, 1890.

ALPHEUS TODD; PARLIAMENTARY GOVERNMENT IN THE BRITISH COLONIES.

Parliamentary Government in the British Colonies.   By Alpheus Todd, Librarian of Parliament, Canada; author of " Parliamentary Government in England," etc.   Boston, Little, Brown & Company.   1880.

TREATIES; TREATIES AND CONVENTIONS BETWEEN UNITED STATES AND OTHER POWERS.   1776-1887.

Treaties and Conventions concluded between the United States of America and other Powers, since July 4, 1776, complied by John H. Haswell, containing notes, with References to negotiations preceding the several treaties, to the executive, legislative, or judicial construction of them, and to the causes of the abrogation of some of them; a chronological list of treaties; and an analytical index.   Washington, Government Printing Office, 1889.

TREATIES IN FORCE, 1899—BRYAN.

Compilation of Treaties in Force.   Prepared under Act of July 7, 1898, by Henry L. Bryan.   Washington, Government Printing Office, 1899.

SEE ALSO INDIAN TREATIES.

GEORGE F. TUCKER; THE MONROE DOCTRINE.

The Monroe Doctrine.   A Concise History of its Origin and Growth, by George F. Tucker, of the Boston Bar (author of " Manual of Wills "). Boston, George B. Reed, 1885.

JOHN RANDOLPH TUCKER; THE CONSTITUTION OF THE UNITED STATES.

The Constitution of the United States; A Central Discussion of its

Genesis, Development, and Interpretation, by John Randolph Tucker, LL. D., Late Professor of Constitutional and International Law and Equity, Washington and Lee University. Edited by Hon. St. George Tucker, Professor of Constitutional and International Law and Equity in Washington and Lee University. Four volumes. Chicago, Callaghan & Co., 1899.

ST. GEORGE TUCKER; TUCKER'S BLACKSTONE.

Blackstone's Commentaries with notes of Reference to the Constitution and Laws of the Federal Government of the United States; and of the Commonwealth of Virginia. In five volumes. With an appendix to each volume, constituting short tracts upon such subjects as appeared necessary to form a connected view of the laws of Virginia, as a member of the Federal Union. By St. George Tucker, Professor of Law in the University of William and Mary, and one of the Judges of the General Court in Virginia. Philadelphia, William Young Birch, and Abraham Small, 1803.

DR. H. VON HOLST; CONSTITUTIONAL HISTORY OF THE UNITED STATES, 1750–1861.

The Constitutional and Political History of the United States, by Dr. H. Von Holst, Professor of the University of Freiburg. Translated from the German by John J. Lalor and Alfred B. Mason. 1750–1833. State Sovereignty and Slavery. Chicago, Callaghan and Company, 1876.

DR. H. VON. HOLST; CONSTITUTIONAL LAW OF THE UNITED STATES.

The Constitutional Law of the United States of America, by Dr. H. Von Holst, Privy Councilor and Professor in the University of Freiburg. Authorized edition. Translated by Alfred Bishop Mason. Chicago, Callaghan & Co., 1887.

THOMAS ALFRED WALKER; A HISTORY OF THE LAW OF NATIONS.

A History of the Law of Nations by Thomas Alfred Walker, M. A., LL. D., Fellow and Tutor of and Lecturer in History in Peterhouse, Cambridge. Vol. I. From the Earliest Times to the Peace of Westphalia, 1648. Cambridge, at The University Press, 1899.

ROBERT WARD; WARD'S LAW OF NATIONS.

An Inquiry into the Foundation and History of the Law of Nations in Europe, from the time of the Greeks and Romans, to the Age of Grotius. By Robert Ward, of the Inner Temple, Esq., Barrister-at-Law. In two volumes. Vol. II. London. A. Strahan and W. Woodfall, 1795.

DANIEL WEBSTER; THE WORKS OF DANIEL WEBSTER.

In six volumes. Twentieth edition. Boston, Little, Brown & Co., 1890. First volume contains Biographical Memoir of the Public Life of Daniel Webster, by Edward Everett.

FRANCIS WHARTON; INTERNATIONAL LAW DIGEST.

A Digest of The International Law of the United States, taken from

Documents issued by Presidents and Secretaries of State, and from Decisions of Federal Courts and Opinions of Attorneys-General. Edited by Francis Wharton, LL. D., author of a treatise on Conflict of Laws, and of Commentaries on American Law. In three volumes (second edition). Washington, Government Printing Office, 1887.

HENRY WHEATON; WHEATON'S INTERNATIONAL LAW. See BOYD, DANA and LAWRENCE.

HENRY WHEATON; HISTORY OF THE LAW OF NATIONS.
History of the Law of Nations in Europe and America; from the earliest times to the Treaty of Washington, 1842. By Henry Wheaton, LL. D., Minister of the United States at the Court of Berlin, Corresponding Member of the Academy of Moral and Political Sciences in the Institute of France. New York, Gould, Banks & Co., Wm. & A. Gould & Co., Albany; and Andrew Milliken, Dublin, Ireland, 1845.

HENRY WILSON; RISE AND FALL OF THE SLAVE POWER IN AMERICA.
History of the Rise and Fall of the Slave Power in America, by Henry Wilson, in three volumes, Ninth edition. Boston and New York, Houghton, Mifflin & Company, The Riverside Press, Cambridge.

THEODORE DWIGHT WOOLSEY; INTERNATIONAL LAW.
Introduction to the study of International Law designed as an aid in teaching and in historical studies by Theodore Dwight Woolsey. Sixth edition, revised and enlarged by Theodore Salisbury Woolsey. New York, Charles Scribner's Sons, 1891.

THEODORE SALISBURY WOOLSEY; AMERICA'S FOREIGN POLICY.
America's Foreign Policy; Essays and Addresses by Theodore Salisbury Woolsey, M. A., Professor of International Law in the Law School of Yale University. New York, The Century Co., 1898.

HEZEKIAH BUTTERWORTH.
South America, a Political History of the Struggle for Liberty in the American Republics and Cuba, by Hezekiah Butterworth, author of Over the Andes, Zizzag Journeys. New York, Doubleday & McClure Co., 1898.

JAMES MORTON CALLAHAN.
Agreement of 1817. Reduction of naval forces upon the lakes. By James Morton Callahan, Ph. D., sometime Assistant and Fellow in History, Johns Hopkins University. Series XVI of Johns Hopkins University Studies in historical and political science, 1898.

CONSTITUTIONAL MANUAL.
The Conventional Manual of the Sixth New York State Constitutional Convention, 1894. Foreign Constitutions, comprising The Constitutions of Argentine, Belgium, Brazil (Empire and Republic), Colombia, Ecuador, France, Germany, Honduras, Japan, Mexico, Prussia, Switzerland

and Venezuela. Prepared in pursuance of chapter 8, of Laws of 1893, and chapter 228 of Laws of 1894. Under the direction of John Palmer, Secretary of State, James A. Roberts, Comptroller, Theo. E. Hancock, Attorney-General. By George A. Glynn, Syracuse, Compiler. Part 2, vol. 3, Albany, The Argus Company, Printers. 1894.

PAUL LEICESTER FORD; THE FEDERALIST.

The Federalist, a Commentary on the Constitution of the United States, by Alexander Hamilton, James Madison, and John Jay. Edited, with notes, illustrative documents, and a copious index by Paul Leicester Ford, Editor of Pamphlets and Essay on the Constitution. New York, Henry Holl and Co., 1898.

ALBERT BUSHNELL HART; THE FOUNDATIONS OF AMERICAN FOREIGN POLICY.

With a Working Bibliography. By Albert Bushnell Hart, Professor of History in Harvard University. The Macmillan Company, 1901.

JOSEPH ROGERS HEROD; FAVORED NATION TREATMENT.

An Analysis of the Most Favored Nation Clause, with Commentaries on its uses in Treaties of Commerce and Navigation, by Joseph Rogers Herod, M. A., formerly Secretary of Legation and Chargé d'Affaires of the United States to Japan. Banks Law Publishing Co., New York, 1901.

JOHN H. LATANE.

The Albert Shaw Lectures on Diplomatic History, 1899. The diplomatic relations of the United States and Spanish America, by John H. Latané, Ph. D., Professor of History in Randolph-Macon Woman's College. Baltimore, The Johns Hopkins Press, 1900.

WILLIAM H. MICHAELS.

History of the Department of State of the United States. Its formation and duties, together with biographies of its present officers and secretaries from the beginning. Washington, Government Printing Office, 1901.

E. PARMALEE PRENTICE AND JOHN G. EGAN.

The commerce clause of the Federal Constitution, by E. Parmalee Prentice and John G. Egan of Chicago. Chicago, Callaghan and Company, 1898.

FRANCIS NEWTON THORPE.

The constitutional history of the United States. By Francis Newton Thorpe. In three volumes, 1765–1895. Chicago, Callaghan & Company, 1901.

SIDNEY WEBSTER; TWO TREATIES OF PARIS.

Two Treaties of Paris and the Supreme Court, by Sidney Webster. New York and London, Harper & Bros., 1901.

TABLE OF CASES.

xliii

E

Page | Page

F

Page | Page

Page | Page

TABLE OF CASES.

THE

TREATY-MAKING POWER OF THE UNITED STATES.

BY

CHARLES HENRY BUTLER.

INTRODUCTION.

VIEWS OF THE AUTHOR ON THE TREATY-MAKING POWER OF THE
UNITED STATES, AND THE METHOD OF ITS DISCUSSION AS THE
SUBJECT-MATTER OF THIS VOLUME.

§ 1. **Government of United States one of enumerated powers.**—The Government of the United States is frequently, in fact generally, referred to, as one of delegated, limited or enumerated powers; it has been so described by the Supreme

1

Court,[1] and by eminent commentators; the Constitution undoubtedly expressly confers certain definite and prescribed powers upon the Federal, or as many prefer to call it, the National Government; it also expressly declares that the powers not delegated thereby are reserved to the States, or to the people.[2]   There can be no doubt, therefore, as a general proposition, applicable to the exercise of many of its prerogatives, that the National Government is limited to those powers which are so unequivocally expressed in, and conferred by, the Constitution as to be beyond peradventure or dispute; it must also be conceded that, in all controversies in which State sovereignty is involved, all questions as to the extent of those powers must, as far as possible, be answered in favor of extending the powers of the States, and of limiting the powers of the National Government as closely as possible to the lines laid down in the Constitution.   The rights of the States were guarded as earnestly, and with as much care, in 1787 as they have been at any time since then, even during the bitterest controversies over slavery and secession.

Questions, however, have frequently arisen, and are constantly arising, as to the extent of the powers vested by the people in, and surrendered by the States to, the Central Government;[3] able and distinguished expounders of the Constitution have found this element of its history and construction

§ 1.

[1] "The general government, though limited as to its objects, is supreme with respect to those objects.   This principle is a part of the Constitution; and if there be any who deny its necessity none can deny its authority."

Cohens vs. Virginia, 1821, 6 Wheaton, 264, p. 381, MARSHALL, Ch. J.

[2] "The powers not delegated to the United States by the Constitution, nor prohibited by it to the States, are reserved to the States respectively or to the people." Article X. of the Amendments to the Constitution.

[3] "This government is acknowledged by all to be one of enumerated powers.   The principle that it can exercise only the powers granted to it, would seem too apparent to have required to be enforced by all those arguments which its enlightened friends, while it was depending before the people, found it necessary to urge. That principle is now universally admitted.   But the question respecting the extent of the powers actually granted is perpetually arising, and will probably continue to arise, as long as our system shall exist."

McCulloch vs. State of Maryland, 1819, 4 Wheaton, 316, p. 405, MARSHALL, Ch. J.

a fertile field for academic investigation and discussion. It has also afforded the Supreme Court of the United States, the creation of which was the crowning evidence of the practical, as well as the theoretical, genius of the men who framed the Constitution,[4] the occasions for rendering some of its ablest decisions in the delimitation of the boundary line between State and Federal jurisdiction, upon which have been placed the monuments bearing the warning to Federal aggression—"Thus far shalt thou go and no farther."

[4] "The establishment of the Supreme Court of the United States was the crowning marvel of the wonders wrought by the statesmanship of America. In truth the creation of the Supreme Court with its appellate powers was the greatest conception of the Constitution. It embodied the loftiest ideas of moral and legal power, and although its prototype existed in the Superior Courts established in the various States, yet the majestic proportions to which the structure was carried became sublime. No product of government, either here or elsewhere, has ever approached it in grandeur. Within its appropriate sphere it is absolute in authority. From its mandates there is no appeal. Its decree is law. In dignity and moral influence it outranks all other judicial tribunals of the world. No court of either ancient or modern times was ever invested with such high prerogatives. Its jurisdiction extends over Sovereign States as well as over the humblest individual. It is armed with the right as well as the power to annul in effect the statutes of a State whenever they are directed against the civil rights, the contracts, the currency or the intercourse of the people. It restricts Congressional action to Constitutional bounds. Secure in the tenure of its Judges from the influence of politics, and the violence of prejudice and passion, it presents an example of judicial independence unattainable in any of the States and far beyond that of the highest Court in England. Yet its powers are limited and strictly defined. Its decrees are not arbitrary, tyrannical or capricious, but are governed by the most scrupulous regard for the sanctity of law. It cannot encroach upon the reserved rights of the States or abridge the sacred privileges of local self-government. Its power is never exercised for the purpose of giving effect to the will of the Judge, but always for the purpose of giving effect to the will of the legislature, or, in other words, to the will of the law. Its administration is a practical expression of the workings of our system of liberty according to law. Its Judges are the sworn ministers of the Constitution, and are the High Priests of Justice. Acknowledging no superior, and responsible to their consciences alone, they owe allegiance to the Constitution and to their own exalted sense of duty. Instructed and upheld by a highly educated bar, their judgments are the ripest fruits of judicial wisdom. Amenable to public opinion, they can be reached, in

§ 2. **Exceptions to general rule of limitations of power.** —There are, however, some exceptions to this general rule; there are certain instances in which the Federal Government not only possesses, and exercises, powers which have been delegated to it by the people, and which are portions of the delegated sovereignty as enumerated in the Constitution, but in which it also possesses, and exercises certain other powers, as inherent attributes of the sovereignty with which it is clothed, in the same manner as all other fully sovereign states possess and exercise such powers; one of the most notable instances of these inherent attributes of sovereignty is the treaty-making power, the basis of discussion in this work; it is undoubtedly one of the most far-reaching and important prerogatives possessed by the National Government, because through it not only the internal affairs of every State in the Union are affected, but relations are established between this nation and all the people composing it, with all the other nations and peoples of the world. Although the National Government possesses this power under the Constitution, as one of the powers expressly enumerated therein, the exercise thereof is controlled not only by constitutional limitations but also by the general rules of law applicable to all sovereign powers and to their exercise of this prerogative.[1]

§ 3. **Author's general views as to extent of treaty-making power.**—The author fully appreciates that any attempt to extend Federal jurisdiction to matters which are

case of necessity, by impeachment by the Senate of the United States. No institution of purely human contrivance presents so many features calculated to inspire both veneration and awe." Carson's History of the Supreme Court of the United States, pp. 6–8.

§ **2.**

[1] " By the law of nations, recognized by all civilized States, dominion of new territory may be acquired by discovery and occupation, as well as by cession or conquest; and when citizens or subjects of one nation, in its name, and by its authority or with its as-

sent, take and hold actual, continuous and useful possession, (although only for the purpose of carrying on a particular business, such as catching and curing fish, or working mines), of territory unoccupied by any other government or its citizens, the nation to which they belong may exercise such jurisdiction and for such period as it sees fit over territory so acquired. This principle affords ample warrant for the legislation of Congress concerning Guano Islands. Vattel, lib. 1, c. 18; Wheaton on International Law (8th ed.), §§ 161, 165, 176, note

4

not clearly expressed in the Constitution carries with it the *onus probandi* to its fullest extent. He is, however, so firmly convinced that the government of the United States is completely endowed with all the essential attributes of nationality and sovereignty in regard to National affairs that he feels fully justified in expressing the following opinion:

First: That the treaty-making power of the United States, as vested in the Central Government, is derived not only from the powers expressly conferred by the Constitution, but that it is also possessed by that Government as an attribute of sovereignty, and that it extends to every subject which can be the basis of negotiation and contract between any of the sovereign powers of the world, or in regard to which the several States of the Union themselves could have negotiated and contracted if the Constitution had not expressly prohibited the States from exercising the treaty-making power in any manner whatever and vested that power exclusively in, and expressly delegated it to, the Federal Government.

Second: That this power exists in, and can be exercised by, the National Government, whenever foreign relations of any kind are established with any other sovereign power, in regulating by treaty the use of property belonging to States or the citizens thereof, such as canals, railroads, fisheries, public lands, mining claims, etc.; in regulating the descent or possession of property within the otherwise exclusive jurisdiction of States; in surrendering citizens and inhabitants of States to foreign powers for punishment of crimes committed outside of the jurisdiction of the United States or of any State or territory thereof; in fact, that the power of the United States to enter into treaty stipulations in regard to all matters, which can properly be the subject of negotiation between sovereign states, is practically unlimited, and that in no case is the sanction, aid or consent of any State necessary to validate the treaty or to enforce its provisions.

Third: That the power to legislate in regard to all mat-

104; Halleck on International Law, c. 6, §§ 7, 15; 1 Phillimore on International Law (3d ed.), §§ 227, 229, 230, 232, 242; 1 Calvo Droit International (4th ed.), §§ 266, 277, 300; *Whiton* vs. *Albany Ins. Co.*, 109 Mass. 24, 31."

Jones vs. *United States*, U. S. Sup. Ct. 1890, 137 **U. S.** 202, p. 212, GRAY, J.

ters affected by treaty stipulations and relations is co-exten-sive with the treaty-making power, and that acts of Congress enforcing such stipulations which, in the absence of treaty stipulations, would be unconstitutional as infringing upon the powers reserved to the States, are constitutional, and can be enforced, even though they may conflict with State laws or provisions of State constitutions.

Fourth: That all provisions in State statutes or constitu-tions which in any way conflict with any treaty stipula-tions, whether they have been made prior or subsequent thereto, must give way to the provisions of the treaty, or act of Congress based on and enforcing the same, even if such provisions relate to matters wholly within State jurisdiction.

§ 4. **State legislation not necessary to carry out treaty stipulations.**—So far-reaching is this treaty-making power, that the author unhesitatingly condemns the policy, which has occasionally been adopted by the United States, of avoid-ing absolute treaty stipulations as to matters within the juris-diction of the several States, but at the same time stipulat-ing to urge the States to enact legislation necessary to obtain the desired results; such method is not only unnecessary, but is also undignified; in many cases the results are not only unsatisfactory, as no distinct obligations are created, but they are frequently productive of injustice, as general concessions for the benefit of the entire Union and all of the inhabitants thereof may be lost by the refusal of the legis-lature or people of a single State to adopt the necessary leg-islation; in fact, history shows that Article VI of the Con-stitution which makes treaties the supreme law of the land was undoubtedly framed and inserted in the Constitution for the special purpose of preventing exactly that class of treaty stipulations which, under the Confederation, had been tried on several occasions and found wanting in every instance.[1]

§ 5. **Treaties made by United States Government bind-ing on all States.**—The authorities bearing upon this sub-ject also show that the United States Government, when it exercises the treaty-making power in regard to matters which

§ 4.
[1]See sec. 159, chap. V; sec. 211, chap. VII; secs. 266–72, chap. IX, and cases cited, and opinions re-ferred to, in those sections.

are otherwise within the exclusive jurisdiction of one or more States, does so as the agent, as it were, for and on behalf of the people of the State or States affected by the treaty, and as such agent is clothed with full power to represent and bind them. As the States are absolutely deprived of all treaty-making power by express Constitutional limitations, it is only through the intervention of the Federal Government, thus exercised on their behalf, that the rights of the States and their citizens, in their relations with foreign nations can be protected and conserved.

§ 6. **Treaties the Supreme law of the land.**—The decisions of the Supreme Court show that whenever this power has been exercised, even to its fullest extent in regulating by international agreement matters which otherwise are exclusively within the control of any State, those provisions of the treaty itself, as well as all Congressional legislation subsequently enacted to carry them into effect, have been sustained by that court of highest power and of last resort as being within the sense and meaning of Article VI. of the Constitution which declares that "this Constitution, and the Laws of the United States which shall be made in Pursuance thereof; and all Treaties made or which shall be made, under the Authority of the United States shall be the supreme Law of the Land; and the judges in every State shall be bound thereby, any Thing in the Constitution or Laws of any State to the Contrary notwithstanding."[1]

§ 7. **Sources of author's information and grounds of his**

§ 6.

[1] "This brief and comprehensive declaration proposed in the convention on July 17, 1787, by Luther Martin, of Maryland, and passed unanimously, stands in the Constitution as the Bill of Rights of the Federal Judiciary. It is a nail fastened in a sure place. It would have been wholly in vain to grant the supreme judicial power to the Federal Courts without this solemn guaranty · against any remaining power in the State Courts, or Judges, to nullify or impede its exercise. The supreme power must reside somewhere, and the basis of the American constitutional supremacy is nowhere better described than in Washington's terse phrase, in his letter as President of the Convention, commending the work to the approval of the States, as the 'giving up a share of liberty to preserve the rest.'" Address of Mr. William Allen Butler on "The Origin of the Supreme Court of the United States and its place in the Constitution," delivered at the Centennial Celebration of the or-

opinion.—Although the author's opinion, that the treaty-making power is undoubtedly the most far-reaching in its scope of any of the powers possessed by the Federal Government, is very broadly expressed, it is based upon an examination of the history and construction of treaties made prior to the Confederation and the adoption of the Constitution, as well as subsequently thereto; of the proceedings of the Federal Convention in which the Constitution was framed, and of the conventions of the several States to which it was submitted for ratification; of the three hundred or more treaties which have been entered into by the United States with foreign powers and which relate in their various provisions to almost every conceivable subject which can be, or ever has been, the basis of international contract or agreement between Sovereign States, and which have frequently affected, and in many instances still affect, the individual interests of States and citizens; of the frequent utterances in Congress, by the great masters of constitutional law when these questions have been raised and debated, as they often have been, in both the Senate and the House of Representatives; of the opinions of students and expounders of the Constitution including some of the most eminent legal historians of our Nation; and also of the opinions of the judges of our highest courts, both Federal and State, who have been called upon to construe the Constitution in this respect.   After careful consideration of these authorities the author feels confident that, notwithstanding the practice which at one time was pursued by the framers of our treaties of avoiding direct stipulations affecting matters within State control, and of relegating certain classes of treaty obligations to State legislation, the full power of the United States to make such stipulations absolutely, and also to enforce them by appropriate and consistent legislation of Congress is supported by such eminent authorities as Alexander Hamilton, James Madison, William A. Duer, Patrick Henry, William Henry Rawle, Chancellor Kent, George Ticknor Curtis, Thomas M. Cooley, John Norton Pomeroy; by many distinguished Justices of the Supreme Court,

ganization of the Supreme Court of the United States, New York, February 4, 1890, and found in | Carson's History of the Supreme Court, p. 615.

including Jay, Field, Bradley, Miller, Harlan, Gray, and Fuller, and many others too numerous to mention ; and it has also been sustained in its most far-reaching extent by those great legal luminaries, John Marshall, and Joseph Story, whose opinions, like beacon lights, have so often guided the Ship of State through dangerous and intricate passages of constitutional construction, and which so far from growing dimmer with age, have constantly increased in brilliancy and strength from the respect and reverence which have ever been accorded to the genius and integrity of their authors, not only in this country, but in every land where law and justice are synonymous.[1]

To thoroughly consider the subject under discussion, the history of treaties in general and the vesting of the treaty-making power in the Central Government of this country must be examined from a period anterior to the adoption of the Constitution ; the proceedings of the Constitutional Convention by which the Constitution was framed, as well as the conventions of the several States which considered and ratified it, must also be carefully investigated, as well as the expressions of the then leaders of public opinion, as they were contained in the numerous pamphlets which appeared upon both sides of the question during the period that the adoption or rejection of the Constitution was the chief subject of thought throughout the country. Such an investigation will show how the people generally regarded, and how thoroughly they understood, this subject at the time of the adoption of the Constitution ; it will also develop the causes for, and the method of, the adoption of the rule by which this great power was vested in the Central Government. In addition it will be necessary to examine the opinions of the judges, both State and Federal, who have since then expounded and defined the exact meaning of these and other cognate and analogous clauses in the Constitution. It is the result of such an investigation that the author desires to present to the readers of this volume.

§ 8. **Nationality and sovereignty of the United States to**

§ 7.
[1] The opinions of these statesmen, authors and jurists, as they have been quoted in this work, can be found by referring to the index at the end of volume II.

be first considered.—It is impossible, however, to enter upon any discussion of the subject without first thoroughly examining the nature of the Government of the United States and realizing to its fullest extent one great fact which such an examination makes apparent,—the completeness of the nationality and sovereignty of the United States. It is only through the exercise of those inherent qualities of nationality and sovereignty that the United States Government is able to exercise its great powers for the general benefit and protection of the whole nation and all of the territory under its jurisdiction, as well as for the benefit and protection of the several States and the citizens thereof; of all these great powers the treaty-making power is probably the greatest and the most far-reaching; at all events it is the one by which the interests of all those who owe allegiance to the Central Government, and over whom that Government extends protection, have often been conserved, and through which those great results have been obtained which have placed the United States in the foremost rank of the nations of the world.

§ 9. **Plan of discussion of subject.**—The subject-matter will, therefore, be divided into three parts and sixteen subdivisions or chapters, as follows:

Part I. The United States is a Nation;—consisting of three chapters (I–III) in which the nature of the Government of the United States will be considered especially in regard to its relations with foreign powers and its attributes of nationality and sovereignty as follows:

I. The nationality and sovereignty of the United States, showing that the Central Government possesses not only those powers which are delegated to it by the Constitution in regard to internal affairs, but that it also possesses all the attributes of sovereignty possessed by any other sovereign nation of the world in regard to external relations.

II. The nationality and sovereignty of the United States as evidenced by the acquisition and government of territory, showing that it is only by the possession of the great attributes of sovereignty that the United States has been able to acquire, and govern, the territory which has been added

10

to the domain of the original thirteen States and of the Nation, as they existed in 1787.

III. The nationality and sovereignty of the United States, as recognized by every other sovereign power, showing that every other nation recognizes, and always has recognized, the Government of the United States as being equally sovereign with any other government in the world.

Part II. Historical review of the treaty-making power of the United States;—consisting of seven chapters (IV–X) as follows:

IV. Treaty-making power in general, and especially as an attribute of sovereignty, as exercised by central governments of federated powers, showing that in nearly, if not all, instances of federations it has been necessary to vest the Central Government with full and complete power in regard to the external relations of all the constituent States of the Federation, even as to those matters which otherwise would be exclusively under State jurisdiction.

V. The treaty-making power, as it was exercised for, and on behalf of, the colonies prior to, and under, the Articles of Confederation, showing that from the earliest inception of the ideas of independence and union it was a conceded fact that all relations with foreign powers must be controlled by, and carried on through, the Central Government; also showing the co-ordinate development of the twin ideas of the National unity, and the independence, of the colonies and States.

VI. Proceedings of the Constitutional Convention of 1787, in so far as they relate to treaties, and the vesting of the treaty-making power in the Federal Government, showing that it was the unanimous opinion of the members of that Convention that the Central Government should have the widest scope in exercising this power, and that it was essential for the safety of the Union that the making of treaties, and the enforcement thereof, should be placed, practically without limitation, in the hands of the Federal Government.

VII. Proceedings of the constitutional conventions of the several States by which the Constitution was ratified, in so far as they relate to the provisions vesting the treaty-

11

making power in the Federal Government, showing that the great extent of that power was fully appreciated by the representatives of the people and of the States, and that it was acknowledged by them that the safety of the several States demanded its exercise by the Central Government, to the complete exclusion of the States themselves.

VIII. The treaty-making power as a factor in the great National debate of 1787–8, showing that the great extent and scope of the power was thoroughly discussed, and understood, by the people prior to the adoption of the Constitution.

IX. Opinions of publicists, historians and expounders of the Constitution as to the extent and scope of the treaty-making power of the United States, showing that the more this subject has been considered, the wider have become the views of those who have studied it, and who have expressed their views in regard thereto.

X. The treaty-making power in Congress, the extent and effect of ratification by the Senate, and the participation by the House of Representatives in such ratification, and in legislation based upon treaties, as the same has been the subject of Congressional debate and Congressional action.

Part III. Judicial decisions affecting the treaty-making power of the United States, its extent and application;—consisting of six chapters (XI–XVI), as follows:

XI. Decisions of the Federal and State courts in regard to treaties made by the United States, and provisions therein, affecting rights and matters which, in the absence of treaty stipulations, are wholly within State jurisdiction, showing that in all such cases the courts of last resort, both State and Federal, have sustained the treaty-making power of the United States, and held that such stipulations are paramount and, of necessity, supersede all State laws which in any manner conflict therewith.

XII. Decisions of the Federal courts as to the relative effects of treaties and United States statutes, showing to what extent Congressional legislation is necessary to enforce treaties, how far it can supersede them, and how treaties and United States statutes must be construed when they are in conflict with each other.

XIII. Treaties of cession, involving change of sovereignty

12

over the ceded territory, and the effect thereof on laws, persons and property.

XIV. The treaty-making power as it has been exercised with Indian tribes, and the relative effect of statutes, State and Federal, and Indian treaties, with some reference to the status of the Indian tribes in the United States, and the rights which the Indians originally possessed, and which they have since acquired under treaties.

XV. Special instances in which the treaty-making power has been exercised by the United States, showing that in the instances referred to, both as to the treaties themselves, and the subsequent legislation of Congress based thereon, the United States has exercised the power to the widest extent, and far beyond the domain of Congressional legislation in the absence of treaties.

XVI. Limitations on the treaty-making power of the United States as the same have been suggested by publicists, and in the opinions of the Supreme Court, and the conclusions which can be deduced therefrom.

§ 10. **This work confined to United States law and decisions ; other work contemplated by author.**—In discussing the subject-matter of this work only authorities of Federal and State Courts of the United States will be cited and relied upon. The question of the extent of the power to be exercised by the United States Government in making and enforcing treaties, is one wholly within our own municipal law, and is not one of international law, or even the subject of diplomatic correspondence ; in fact, it is not the intention of the author in this volume to discuss treaties in any aspect except as to the power of the United States Government to make them with foreign powers, and their effect when so made upon State and Federal legislation. As to all foreign countries the United States must be considered as possessing plenary powers, otherwise foreign nations would not negotiate, or conclude treaties with it ; how our treaties shall be enforced within the United States—the subject-matter of this work—is wholly within the jurisdiction of the Federal courts. To exceed these limits would be to extend the work to other fields which are sufficiently extensive to require individual consideration.

There are more than a thousand statutes, and a far greater number of judicial decisions which affect the treaty and foreign relations of the United States, and which must be examined and classified in order to fully cover the entire domain of what may properly be called "treaty law."

The author hopes to publish at a not far future date a third volume which is now in course of preparation, and to some extent cover treaty law of the United States, including rules as to construction of treaties, and the rights of States and individuals, created and affected thereby. For the present, however, the attention of the reader will be confined to the questions referred to in the previous section, especially those relating to the power and capacity of the Central Government of the United States to negotiate and conclude those agreements with foreign nations, which are so essential to the prosperity and happiness of our neighbors and ourselves, and which, in view of the far-reaching extent of American commerce and enterprise, are daily becoming of more and more importance.

14

PART I.

THE UNITED STATES IS A NATION.

CHAPTER I.

THE NATIONALITY AND SOVEREIGNTY OF THE UNITED STATES.

§ 11. Definition of Terms used in Title of Chapter.— The terms used in the title of this chapter would, in themselves, afford sufficient matter for an entire volume; if the author desired to wander from the main course of his subject

15

he could, at the very outset, find an intersecting pathway which would lead him far from the ultimate goal.

In this discussion, however, all of the terms are used in their broadest signification, and the subtle distinctions which can be drawn between the various uses of the terms do not form a part of the general subject-matter of this volume; the author has, however, expressed his own views and collated some of the views of authors and jurists in regard to these terms in the footnote to this section.[1]

NOTE BY THE AUTHOR ON DEFINITIONS OF TERMS USED.

§ 11.

[1] The definition of the three terms used in the title of this chapter, to-wit: nationality, sovereignty and United States, are more within the domain of a work on political science than of one on the legal principles under consideration; the author does not intend, therefore, to enter into any elaborate dissertation upon the exact meaning of the terms, which are simply used in their generally accepted sense. It may not be out of place, however, to give in these notes the author's conceptions of those terms, as of course differences of opinion exist as to their meaning.

Nationality.—Nationality is used in the sense that the people of the United States constitute one nation, as stated in the decisions of Chief Justice Marshall in *Cohens* vs. *Virginia*, and Mr. Justice Gray in the *Legal Tender* and *Chinese Exclusion* cases, referred to hereafter, as distinguished from the federal element of citizenship; there is no nationality of New York, Pennsylvania or California, although those States in many respects are sovereign States; since the Civil War there is no doubt that, while there is an allegiance growing out of State citizenship, the allegiance owed by the people of the United States to the United States is paramount to every other tie of citizenship or allegiance. Nor is the word "nationality" used to distinguish the people of the United States as a people rather than as a race; the people of the United States forming, as they do, a nation, are necessarily composed of many races —Christian and Mohammedan—Anglo-Saxon, Teutonic and Latin—Jew and Gentile—all of these, as well as other *racial* elements, unite in forming one people as a nation; in this sense, therefore, "nationality" signifies as to the people, the element of homogeneity by which all these people are united, regardless of internal and sectional differences, into one great nation owing allegiance to a common government as against all of the other governments of the world; and that such government and the various departments composing it, is the only medium through which this great nation, and all of those elements composing it, can deal with any external government, influence or power.

Sovereignty.—This is a word which has generally been discussed more

16

§ 12. **The United States is a Nation.**—It is impossible to appreciate the scope of the treaty-making power of the Gov-

from the standpoint of political science than of legal application. The various theories as to the existence of sovereignty, its nature, and how it is exercised and controlled, are numerous and diverse; some of them, in fact, are diametrically opposite to each other, although they are supported respectively by eminent authorities on the subjects of political science and jurisprudence; these theories, however, can be divided in two great classes, one of which, based on the divine right of kings, places sovereignty in the rulers and permits them to exercise over their subjects authority which they possess inherently, owing to the fact that they are rulers, and have so become, by the principles recognized in the country over which they rule; under this theory the great residuum of power or sovereignty remains in the ruler, and any limitations must be construed adversely to the people ruled over and favorably to the ruling power. The other class includes what may be called the Anglo-Saxon theory, which is that complete sovereignty originally exists in its entirety in the people, and that only such portion of sovereignty has been vested in the rulers as the people themselves have expressly delegated to the ruling power, the residuum remaining in the people.

There can be no doubt that the American principle is that complete sovereignty is vested in the people of a nation, and that the people of the United States possess sovereignty in its entirety. In adopting, as we have, a dual system of government, the sovereignty of the people has been partly delegated to the State governments, and partly to the Central Government, and the people retain only that portion of sovereignty which has not been vested in the ruling power of the States respectively, or of the United States in its national capacity. This sovereignty of the people is a part of the heritage of the Anglo-Saxon race; as such it naturally exists in all nations composed of Anglo-Saxons; it does not, however, necessarily exist naturally in people of other races; it may be that the sovereignty exercised by governmental powers of the nations of the Latin races over their people, and especially their colonies, has been, by long usage and prescription, recognized by those people and colonists as proceeding from the ruling class downward, instead of from the ruled classes upwards; in this way an apparent difficulty in handling our recently acquired possessions may be completely overcome. By the Treaty of Paris of 1898, the sovereignty over Spanish possessions was transferred to the United States; the United States succeeds to the sovereignty, as it was recognized by the subjects of Spain; it remains for the United States to clothe the people of the ceded possessions, as it has done in many respects as to the people of Porto Rico, with the same degree of autonomy as other portions of our people possess; although the change may be made gradually the people of the new possessions will finally succeed to all of the rights possessed by other people of the United States. There is no inconsistency with historical precedents in thus gradually admitting those people to privileges which they have never had before; a rule of international law which has been uni-

2

ernment of the United States without taking into consideration the great cardinal fact that the UNITED STATES IS A

versally recognized is that the governmental conditions of inhabitants of
ceded territory remain the same until altered by the new sovereignty,
there are no legal difficulties, therefore, in recognizing that the sovereignty transferred by the former rulers may be of a different nature
from the sovereignty existing in the new ruling power.

The expressions of some of the leading authorities on international
law in regard to the term sovereignty are appended to this note.

BLUNTSCHLI'S VIEWS.

Bluntschli, in his Theory of State which has been translated and published in English, devotes the whole of chapters I. to IV., pages 463–481,
to the discussion of the word sovereignty.   On pages 464-5 he states
that Sovereignty implies:

"1. Independence of the authority of any other State.   Yet this independence must be understood as only relative.   International law,
which binds all States together, no more contradicts the Sovereignty
of States than constitutional law, which limits the exercise of public
authority within.   Even the separate States (*Länderstaten*) in a com-
posite State may be regarded as sovereign, although dependent in essential matters, e. g., foreign policy and control of the army.

"2. Supreme public dignity—what the Romans called *majestas*.

"3. Plenitude of public power, as opposed to mere particular powers.   Sovereignty is not a sum of particular isolated rights, but is a
general or common right: it is a 'central conception,' and is as important in Public as that of property is in Private Law.

"4. Further, it is the highest in the State.   Thus there can be no
political power above it.   The French Seigneurs of the middle ages
ceased to be sovereign when they were compelled to submit in all essential matters to the king as their feudal lord.   The German Electors were
able to maintain sovereignty in their own dominions from the fourteenth
century, because they exercised supreme authority in them as their
proper right.

"5. Unity, a necessary condition in every organism.   The division of
sovereignty paralyses and dissolves a State, and is therefore incompatible with its healthy existence."   The Theory of the State, by Bluntschli, pp. 464–465.

Chapter II., page 467, is devoted to answering the question to whom
sovereignty belongs.   He refers to the difference between the sovereignty in the people and the sovereignty in the State, and in a note,
page 473, he discusses what the sovereignty of the people means as follows:

"The phrase 'sovereignty of the people' is sometimes used to express,
not the supremacy of the majority, but only the idea that a form of
State or a manner of government, which is incompatible with the existence and welfare of the majority of the people, cannot be maintained,

NATION; that as to all matters connected with foreign relations it is not *federal* in its character, but *national*, and that

or, that the form of the State and the government are there *for* the people—an idea which is true, but badly expressed.

"Again, if by 'sovereignty of the people' it is meant that the authority of the State is *derived originally* from the will of the majority, we must indeed admit that many democratic constitutions, and even some monarchical (e. g., the Roman Empire, the French Empire), are based, in theory or principle at least, on the voluntary act of the majority of the people. In the same way the constitutions of several Swiss Cantons declare, not that the people (*Volk*) is sovereign, but that 'the sovereignty resides in the people as a whole (*auf der Gesammtheit des Volks beruhe*), and is exercised by the Great Council,' (e. g., the Zurich Constitution of 1831, sec. 1). But even this principle would not be applicable to all States, and the term 'sovereignty,' which expresses a permanent right, is inappropriate when applied to particular and transitory acts.

"Finally, if the phrase 'sovereignty of the people' be understood, as has often happened in practice, to imply that the people, as distinct from the government, or even any powerful and excited multitude, is justified in arbitrarily overthrowing the government or destroying the constitution, this is an idea which is altogether to be condemned, and which is irreconcilable even with democratic principles.

"(In England, the question of sovereignty has in recent times been chiefly discussed in connection with the famous definition of Austin, *Jurisprudence*, Lect. vi.: 'If a determinate human superior, not in a habit of obedience to a like superior, receive habitual obedience from the bulk of a given society, that determinate superior is Sovereign in that society, and the society, including the superior, is a society political and independent.' This abstract analysis of the conception of sovereignty, which is quite unhistorical and difficult to apply in practice, is criticised by Maine, *Early History of Institutions*, Lect. xii, xiii. See also F. Harrison on *The English School of Jurisprudence*, in *Fortnightly Review*, vol. 30 (1878); *Clark's Practical Jurisprudence, a Comment on Austin*, Part I., ch. xiv.; *Holland's Jurisprudence*, ch. iv.)" The Theory of the State, by Bluntschli, pp. 473–474.

JUDGE COOLEY'S VIEWS.

"A state is a body politic, or society of men, united together for the purpose of promoting their mutual safety and advantage by the joint efforts of their combined strength. The terms *nation* and *State* are frequently employed, not only in the law of nations, but in common parlance, as importing the same thing, but the term *nation* is more strictly synonymous with *people*, and while a single State may embrace different nations or peoples, a single nation will sometimes be so divided politically as to constitute several States.

"In American constitutional law the word *State* is applied to the several members of the American Union, while the word *nation* is applied

as such it possesses, and exercises, every function exercisable by any other sovereign government in the world.

to the whole body of the people embraced within the jurisdiction of the federal government.

"*Sovereignty*, as applied to States, imports the supreme, absolute, uncontrollable power by which any State is governed. A State is called a sovereign State when this supreme power resides within itself, whether resting in a single individual, or in a number of individuals, or in the whole body of the people. In the view of international law, all sovereign States are and must be equal in rights, because from the very definition of sovereign State, it is impossible that there should be, in respect to it, any political superior.

"The sovereignty of a State commonly extends to all the subjects of government within the territorial limits occupied by the associated people who compose it; and, except upon the high seas, which belong equally to all men, like the air, and no part of which can rightfully be appropriated by any nation, the dividing line between sovereignties is usually a territorial line. In American constitutional law, however, there is a division of the powers of sovereignty between the national and State governments by subjects; the former being possessed of supreme, absolute, and uncontrollable power over certain subjects throughout all the States and Territories, while the States have the like complete power, within their respective territorial limits, over other subjects. In regard to certain other subjects, the States possess powers of regulation which are not sovereign powers, inasmuch as they are liable to be controlled, or for the time being to become altogether dormant, by the exercise of a superior power vested in the general government in respect to the same subjects." Cooley's Constitutional Limitations, 6th edition pp. 3–4, and also see cases cited in footnotes.

GEORGE TICKNOR CURTIS' DEFINITION.

"Lest, however, the controversy may degenerate into a dispute about the meaning of a word, it may be well to define here what I mean by 'sovereignty,' and what Mr. Tyler appears to mean. He says (Tyler I., 285): 'Sovereignty is the *will* of the sovereign people, and government which is a mere servant or trustee can never be sovereign, for it wields delegated powers only. The people might have a *hundred* governments, each a specific power, without surrendering an atom of sovereignty. Sovereignty being the will of the people, is spiritual and indivisible. It may grant powers for the common *good*, but the invocation of those powers is of the essence of free will. Accordingly, all that talk of the Jackson-Webster-Madison school of sovereignty, part delegated to the Federal Government and part to the State Government, is the merest clap-trap ever devised.' He adds in a note, 'The error lies in confusing *powers*, which are capable of division, with sovereignty, which is not.'

"'Sovereignty' as I use the term, as it is used by other American publicists, means simply the right to govern. Undoubtedly, sovereignty is the will of the sovereign people; and in our American sense all gov-

This is perfectly consistent with the fullest retention by the State Governments of the control of all matters pertain-

ernment is derived from that will. But when it is said that government can never be sovereign, there is a begging of the question, for it may be the will of the people that a particular government shall exercise the powers of sovereignty, or, in other words, shall hold and exercise the power of governing. I have elsewhere said that the framers of the Constitution of the United States made a great discovery in the science of government, which was that political powers, or the powers of government, may be distributed by the sovereign people among different governments, part of them being assigned to one class of public servants or trustees, and the residue being retained by the sovereign people, and bestowed according to their pleasure, on another class of public servants and trustees. It is therefore just as correct to speak of the sovereignty of the Federal Government as it is to speak of the sovereignty of the States; for in either case what is meant is the right to govern on certain subjects and relations. This idea of sovereignty is entirely different from the European idea. Vattel, who is quoted by Mr. Tyler, was entirely right, in the European sense, in saying, 'that every sovereignty properly so called, is, in its own nature, one and indivisible.' It is so in the European sense, but not in the American. In Great Britain, for example, the sovereignty is held by the king and the two houses of Parliament, and the people have no power, save by a revolution, to do anything but what the king, lords, and commons in Parliament assembled prescribe and ordain. The chief executive ruler, who is called *the sovereign*, is so designated because he or she *is* the chief executive ruler, and not because he or she has any sovereign powers separate from the conjoint action of the reigning monarch and the two houses of Parliament. In some of the other European countries the sovereignty is held by the monarch alone; in others, in recent times especially, the sovereignty is held and exercised by the conjoint action of the executive head and other bodies; but in none of them is there the same sovereignty of the people that there is in the American system. For this reason, among others, it is rare to find a European writer of a former period or of later times who has a correct understanding of our system of government. I once had an amusing but very instructive proof of this. Fifty years ago, being in England, I was told by a very eminent English judge (no less a person than the late Lord Campbell, then Chief-Justice of the Queen's Bench, afterwards Lord Chancellor) that he could not understand the distinction between the jurisdiction of our Federal and our State Courts. When I explained to him that it is founded on the fact that the Federal Government has the exclusive right to govern on certain subjects and relations, and that as to other subjects and relations the separate States have the exclusive right to govern, he replied that I had given him information which he never had before. At the same time, he owned that this was contrary to all English ideas, inasmuch as their system does

ing to their internal affairs, and also with the well established rule and Constitutional provisions, that, as to those

not admit of such a partition of the powers of sovereignty." Curtis' Constitutional History of the United States, vol. 2, pp. 520–521.

J. R. TUCKER'S VIEWS.

" The two rival theories of government may therefore be described as follows: The polity of individualism and the polity of paternalism.

" In the ancient world the system of paternalism was most prevalent, and, as a late writer has very strongly said, ' the Hellenic State, like the ancient State in general, because it was considered all-powerful, actually possessed too much power. It was all in all. The citizen was nothing, except as a member of the State. His whole existence depended on and was subject to the State. . . . The independence of the family, home-life, education, even conjugal fidelity, were in no way secure from State interference; still less, of course, the private property of the citizens. The State meddled in everything, and knew neither moral nor legal limits to its power. It disposed of the bodies, and even of the talents, of its members.' (Bluntschli's Theory of the State, page 37.)

" The ideal republic of Plato was a system under which all individualism was merged in the State, and everything was regulated by it, as the parent of its citizens; and while he clearly held the governor should not consider his own good, but only the good of the government for whom he was steward, yet he held that the State was created so that all might be happy to the fullest extent by the State giving happiness to every one.

" The history of this system of political thought repeated itself about two centuries ago in the *Patriarcha* of Sir Robert Filmer, the champion of the House of Stuart. In this work he maintained that, by derivative title from God through Adam, there had been transferred to the king the original *patria potestas* of the family, and that to this royal *patriarcha* absolute obedience was due by all and to him were confided the care and training of his children—the men and women of the Nation. This was the *patriarcha* of the Stuarts, which had its first condemnation on the scaffold where Charles I. was beheaded, and in the abdication of the last of the Stuarts in 1688.

" The paternal government, the *patriarcha*, is based on falsehood and is a political fraud. It takes the paternal name to sanction its absolute authority, but discards the paternal duty in administering government. A father in name, it is without his natural love to mitigate tyranny, or to do equal justice among its people. It claims unlimited power to dispense blessings or cursings at its will. It has petted parasites attached to itself, because they feed upon it, and it draws the resources with which to supply them from the disinherited mass of its children, whom it exhausts, but never helps. It has its foster children and its foundlings—its favorites and its victims—and burdens many for the benefit of the few." Tucker on the Constitution, vol. 1, § 61.

22

matters, the Central Government is one of delegated or enumerated powers only, with the residuum of control remaining in the States and in the people.

PROFESSOR BLISS ON SOVEREIGNTY.

Professor Bliss in a brief treatise on Sovereignty published by Little, Brown & Co., 1885, has collated numerous opinions as to the definition of the word "sovereignty," both in its general use and in its particular use as to Federal States.

He collates the arguments and quotes liberally from text-book writers; in regard to the United States he declares on page 72 that the Federal Union forms a body politic, a State, a nation, and that while the term United States is " geographical and indicates a union of societies called States, it is also the name of an organized body created by the people for governmental purposes. It is itself a State. . . . That with us there is such a Union, such a State, is matter of fact and matter of law. Its existence is a fact; its character, the nature and extent of its powers, involve questions of law. The Union embraces every characteristic of a State except the general, the unlimited power, except the idol of sole sovereignty.

" The national name has been the occasion of much quibbling and word-jingling. The Congress of United Colonies became a Congress of United States, and in the treaty of peace one party was called the United States of America. This name was continued when the Articles of perpetual Confederation were changed for a Constitution of government, when a State was organized. Had a new name—as Alleghania, or some other —been adopted, the fact of a body politic might have more clearly appeared; but the name so naturally used seems to suggest a co-operation of States rather than an organic State formed by union. But a name proves nothing. We seldom invent words even for new things; they are suggested by likes, are more or less figurative, are used in divers senses; only in mathematics, and not always there, are they found of exact meaning. In a given case we must know the connected facts before we can see their sense. Contemporaneous history is a part of a constitution; the thing done, the actual organization and powers, rather than a phrase, decides the character of a political society. By knowing that history, by seeing what was done,—the new framework of the Union, and what it was to do,—we can understand the term ' State' as applied to the local bodies, and the term ' United States ' as applied to the whole." Bliss on Sovereignty, pp. 73–74.

TUCKER'S BLACKSTONE.

"9. Since, according to the fundamental principles of both the Federal and State Constitution, and Government, the supreme power (or *Jura summi imperii*) resides in the people, it follows that it is the right of the people to make laws. But as the exercise of that right by the people at large would be equally inconvenient and impracticable, the constitution of the State has vested that power in the General Assembly of the Commonwealth; and the Constitution of the United

The moment, however, that the local individual interests of any, or all, of the States are eliminated, the Central Gov-

States has reposed the exercise of the same power as it relates to the Federal Government, in the Congress of the United States; a body composed either immediately, or mediately, of Representatives of the People; the House of Representatives being the immediate delegates of the people in their individual capacity; the Senate representing them in their political capacity, as forming different States; the latter although not chosen by the people, themselves, yet being chosen by the State Legislatures, which have no rights, nor authority, nor even an existence, but from the people, must be considered in the same light as the Representatives who are immediately chosen by them. It is from these express provisions both in the State, and Federal Constitution, and not from metaphysical deduction, that the State, and Federal Legislatures derive the power of making laws. See Constitution of Virginia, Art. 8, C. U. S. Art. 1.'' Tucker's Blackstone, vol. 1, p. 52, *note.* See also Von Holst's Constitutional Law of the United States, § 15 *et seq.*

United States.—The term UNITED STATES has given rise to a great deal of discussion; the words are used sometimes as meaning States that are united, either in their individual capacity as separate States, or collectively as a federation; at other times the term is used as the name of a government exercising either federal or national powers, as the case may be; it is also used as a geographical expression for the territory composed of, and owned by, the various States and the Federal Government, within the limits over which the United States Government exercises jurisdiction.

This interchangeable use of one term necessarily gives rise to many peculiar questions, which can only be decided by determining the sense in which the words are used on the particular occasion. If, instead of United States of America, a name had been given, such as Columbia, or America, to the country as a whole, many of these difficulties would have been obviated; in fact, in other countries this difficulty does not arise as each separate element is represented by a different name, for instance, with Great Britain, the United Kingdom refers to England, Scotland, Ireland and Wales; British Empire, on the other hand, comprehends the United Kingdom and its colonies and dependencies, while the government is expressed by a term such as Her (now His) Britannic Majesty's Government. The single word England, or Great Britain, has never been used indiscriminately to indicate a combination of different territories, the government thereof, and the geographical limits of the whole.

In fact, so various have the uses of the term United States been that there does not seem to be any settled and uniform rule as to whether it is to be grammatically construed in the singular, or in the plural number; the author has stated in the text that if one of the two words is to be construed as an adjective and the other as a noun, they must be con-

ernment passes from its Federal character into that of its
National character, and represents in that capacity, not a col-

sidered as requiring a plural construction, but if the expression is used
as indicating either the country itself, or the government exercising
jurisdiction thereover, the two words should certainly be used as a
single name, and construed as a proper noun, singular, and the author
has endeavored to adhere consistently to this rule.

This construction seems now to be generally adopted; in many of the
decisions of the Supreme Court, however, the term United States in all
of its different significations will be found followed by a verb in the
plural number; even Mr. Justice Gray, whose theories of nationality
and unity are perhaps the most pronounced of any Justice who ever sat
upon the Supreme Court bench, has declared that the United States *are*
a nation, and in this respect he has followed Chief Justice Marshall,
who made a similar declaration.

The author, however, considers that wherever the words United
States are used in the sense that the framers of the Constitution might
have used the word Columbia, or the word America, had that corporate
title been adopted, should be followed by *is* instead of *are* exactly as
the names France, England, Germany or The Argentine Confederation
are all used in the singular number.

ATTORNEY GENERAL GRIGGS' POSITION.

The definition, and proper use, of the term United States are involved
in the suits now pending before the Supreme Court of the United States
in which the status of our newly acquired territory is involved, and the
position taken by the United States Government in regard to the term
United States is set forth in the brief submitted by Attorney General
John W. Griggs, in the case of *Goetze* vs. *United States*, which was argued
in December, 1900. On pages 128 to 132 his views are stated as follows
under the points entitled " Meanings of the term 'United States,'" and
" The Source of Political Power " :

" This designation is first used in the Declaration of Independence, is
continued in the Articles of Confederation, and in the present Constitution.

" It has different significations, according to the connection and the
sense in which it is used. It may signify:

" 1· The corporate name of the nation or governmental entity, the
same as was provided in the Articles of Confederation, which declared
' the stile of this Confederacy shall be the United States of America.'

" 2. The States united—referring to the several States composing the
Union.

" In this sense, of course, it excludes Territories.

" 3. The international sense, designating the extent of our domain as
a sovereign nation.

" In this sense it includes all territory under our dominion wherein no
other nation has sovereignty even such as may be under our control by
temporary conquest, as Tampico, Mexico, during the Mexican war (*Flem-*

25

lection of States as a federation, but the entire country as a
National unit, without regard to the internal boundaries of
States or territories.

ing vs. *Page*); while in a domestic sense it includes geographically the
States of the Union and such territory as the President and Senate have
by treaties expressly annexed to and made part of the United States,
and such as Congress and the President, by act or resolution, have expressly annexed to and made part of the United States, as the Hawaiian
Islands.

"Under the first head are classed such expressions as:
>   The Treasury of the United States,
>   Service of the United States,
>   Coin of the United States,
>   Seat of government of the United States,
>   President of the United States,
>   Government of the United States,
>   Office of honor, profit, or trust under the United States,
>   Office under the authority of the United States,
>   Credit of the United States.

"Under the second head are such expressions as:
>   We, the people of the United States,
>   Congress of the United States,
>   Senate of the United States,
>   To establish a uniform rule of naturalization and uniform laws on
>   the subject of bankruptcy *throughout the United States,*
>   Time of choosing electors, etc., to be the same *throughout the
>   United States,*
>   Duties, imposts, and excises shall be uniform *throughout the
>   United States.*

"All the authority of the United States is derived from the people of
the States. The people of the Territories do not and 'cannot share or
contribute to that authority. The people of the States alone elect Con-
gressmen; the States choose Senators and electors. Congress alone,
composed of Senators and Representatives from the States, can make
laws for the government of the whole nation. No Territorial legislature
can possibly be empowered to legislate for any portion of the United
States. Government by the people under our system means by the people of the several States. A republican form of government is guaranteed to the States, but not to Territories. Outside the area of the
United States considered as a union of States there is no political power,
no guaranty of republican government, no pledge against local discrim-
inations by way of port charges, or regulations of commerce, or revenue,
or tax on exports; nor any rule of uniformity as to duties, imposts, and
excises.

"The judicial power of the United States as defined by the Constitution
does not extend to territory. Territorial courts are established under
the clause which authorizes Congress to make all needful rules and reg-

26

To sum it up in a single sentence, as to State matters and internal affairs, the United States *are* a federation, as to gen-

ulations respecting the territory belonging to the United States: *Insurance Co.* vs. *Canter*, 1 Peters, 511; *Clinton* vs. *Englebrecht*, 13 Wall. 447.

"In *Hepburn* vs. *Ellzey* (2 Cranch, 445, 1805), Chief Justice Marshall held that a citizen of the District of Columbia could not maintain an action as a citizen of a State within the meaning of the Constitution against a citizen of Virginia. In support of the jurisdiction Mr. Lee insisted that to give the term State a limited construction would deprive the citizens of the District of general rights of citizens of the United States and put them in a worse condition than aliens. He put the question whether in view of the provision that 'No tax or duty shall be laid on articles exported from any State' Congress can lay a tax or duty on articles exported from the District; and also whether Congress can constitutionally give a preference to the ports of the District. The Chief Justice said, page 452:

"'But as the act of Congress obviously uses the word "State" in reference to that term as used in the Constitution, it becomes necessary to inquire whether Columbia is a State in the sense of that instrument. The result of that examination is a conviction that the members of the American confederacy only are the States contemplated in the Constitution.'

"'The House of Representatives is to be composed of members chosen by the people of the several States; and each State shall have at least one Representative.

"'The Senate of the United States shall be composed of two Senators *from* each State.

"'Each State shall appoint, for the election of the Executive, a number of electors equal to its whole number of Senators and Representatives.

"'These clauses show that the word State is used in the Constitution as designating a member of the Union, and excludes from the term the signification attached to it by writers on the law of nations.'

"In *New Orleans* vs. *Winter* (1 Wheaton, 91, 1816), it was held that a citizen of the Mississippi Territory could not sue a citizen of a State. Chief Justice Marshall said, page 94:

"'It has been attempted to distinguish a *Territory* from the District of Columbia, but the court is of opinion that this distinction cannot be maintained. They may differ in many respects, but neither of them is a State in the sense in which that term is used in the Constitution.'

"'In the recent case of *Hooe* vs. *Jamieson* (166 U. S. 395), Chief Justice Fuller followed Chief Justice Marshall, saying, page 397:

"'We see no reason for arriving at any other conclusion than that announced by Chief Justice Marshall in *Hepburn* vs. *Ellzey* (2 Cranch, 445), February term, 1805, "that the members of the American confederacy only are the States contemplated in the Constitution;" that the District of Columbia is not a State within the meaning of that instrument; and that the courts of the United States have no jurisdiction of cases between citizens of the District of Columbia and citizens of a State.'"

eral matters, affecting foreign affairs or territory held in common, the United States *is* a nation.

To deny this proposition is to assert that the United States is not a completely sovereign power, and therefore is not entitled to rank as one of the great and sovereign powers of the world; this indeed would be a mortifying position for a country with over seventy-five million inhabitants and a territorial area of over three million square miles.[1]

§ 13. **States' Rights School and Broad Constructionists.** —Notwithstanding the absolute necessity of clothing the Central Government with the fullest powers of sovereignty in this respect, advocates of the States' Rights School have persisted and to some extent, although not so much as formerly, still persist in maintaining the doctrine that no such complete condition of nationality and sovereignty either ex-

The converse of the Attorney General's proposition will be found in the briefs filed by the opposing counsel. See also views of ex-President Harrison on meaning of terms "United States" and "Sovereignty," in *North American Review*, January, 1901, referred to in § 37, p. 63, *post*.

Since this portion of this volume was completed the Supreme Court has decided several cases involving the status of some of the recently acquired possessions of the United States, notably Porto Rico and Hawaii. Those opinions are referred to at length under §§ 61a–61h, pp. 117, *et seq.*, and other sections there referred to. The status of territories and the extent of congressional power thereover are discussed at length in those opinions. See *DeLima* vs. *Bidwell, Downes* vs. *Bidwell,* and other *Insular Cases* decided **May 27, 1901,** and reported in volume 182, United States Reports, and abstracts of which are in appendix at end of this volume.

§ 12.
[1] *Cohens* vs. *Virginia*, U. S. Sup. Ct. 1821, 6 Wheaton, 264, MARSHALL, Ch. J., and see extract from opinion, section 29, *post*.

American Insurance Co. vs. *Canter*, U. S. Sup. Ct. 1828, 1 Peters, 511, MARSHALL, Ch. J.

Juilliard vs. *Greenman* (*Legal-Tender case*), 1884, 110 U. S. 421, GRAY, J.

In re Lau Ow Bew, U. S. Sup. Ct, 1891, 141 U. S. 583, FULLER, Ch. J. *Law Ow Bew* vs. *United States*, U. S. Sup. Ct. 1892, 144 U. S. 47, FUL-

LER, Ch. J., and see extract under note to sec. 379, Vol. II, pp. 98 *et seq.*

Fong Yue Ting vs. *United States,* U. S. Sup. Ct. 1893, 149 U. S. 698, GRAY, J.

Lem Moon Sing vs. *United States,* U. S. Sup. Ct. 1895, 158 U. S. 538, HARLAN, J., and see extract under sec. 379, Vol. II, p. 107.

See also the numerous cases cited in the opinions of the court in the above cases; also the cases collated in §§ 23, *et seq., post;* and the *Insular Cases* under § 61, pp. 117, *et seq.*

ists, or, under our form of government can exist, and that even as to the treaty-making power the Central Government is limited in scope, both as to the subject-matter which can be affected by treaties, and the method in which those subjects which are admittedly within its proper scope can be handled. Ever since the adoption of the Constitution there have been two parties as to its construction and the extent and nature of the powers of the Central Government; one of these parties has favored broad construction and wide powers, while the other has insisted upon narrow construction and limited powers.[1]

§ 13.

[1] The doctrine of the States' Rights School is expressed in the resolutions adopted in 1798, by the State Legislature of Kentucky on November 14th, and by the Legislature of Virginia on December 24th. The subsequent declarations of the Hartford Convention in 1814, and the nullification acts of South Carolina, in 1833, as well as the whole series of actions on the part of those States in which the States' Rights doctrine prevailed, were based on the declarations contained in the Kentucky and Virginia Resolutions.

It is not within the scope of this volume to enter into any discussion as to the authorship of those resolutions. The reader is referred to McMaster's History of the People of the United States, vol. II., chap. 11, p. 420; Von Holst's Constitutional History of the United States, vol. I., chap. IV.; Curtis' History of the Constitution, vol. II., chap. I., as well as other detailed histories of the United States in which the history of those resolutions, and the connection therewith of Thomas Jefferson, James Madison, the two Nicholases and others is discussed at length. While the Resolutions were the outcome of the Alien and Sedition Laws which had then been recently passed by Congress, as a matter of fact, they were simply the expression of the views of the then ultra anti-federalists and the enactment of those laws was made the excuse of uttering them. The sentiment contained in the first of the nine resolutions adopted by Virginia has always been the keynote of the view of the States' Rights party.

It is as follows:

"*Resolved*, that the several States composing the United States of America are not united on the principle of unlimited submission to their general Government; but that, by a compact under the style and title of a Constitution for the United States, and of Amendments thereto, they constituted a general Government for special purposes, delegated to that Government certain definite powers, reserving, each State to itself, the residuary mass of rights to their own self government; and that whensoever the general Government assumes undelegated powers, its acts are unauthoritative, void, and of no force; that to this compact each State acceded as a State, and is an integral party, its co-States forming, as to itself the other party; that the

§ 14. Eras of Constitutional History of the United States.

—There are two distinct periods or eras in the con-

Government created by this compact was not made the exclusive or final judge of the extent of the powers delegated to itself; since that would have made its discretion, and not the constitution, the measure of its powers; but that, as in all other cases of compacts among powers having no common judge, each party has an equal right to judge for itself as well of infractions as of the mode and measure of redress."

The Virginia and Kentucky resolutions were reiterated in 1838 in a series of resolutions introduced by John C. Calhoun in the Senate and adopted, some of which are quoted at length as they are a good expression of the ultra views of the States' Rights School before the Civil War. They refer particularly to slavery, which was natural in view of the necessity of maintaining that institution.

The resolutions were as follows:

On the 12th of January, 1838, Mr. Calhoun embodied the Southern position in certain resolutions which he introduced in the Senate of the United States. The first three of these resolutions were as follows:

" 1. *Resolved*, That, in the adoption of the Federal Constitution, the states adopting the same acted, severally, as free, independent and sovereign states; and that each for itself, by its own voluntary assent, entered the Union with the view to its increased security against all dangers, *domestic*, as well as foreign, and the more perfect and secure enjoyment of its advantages —natural, political, and social.

" 2. *Resolved*, That, in delegating a portion of their powers to be exercised by the Federal Government, the states retained, severally, the exclusive and sole right over their own domestic institutions and police, to the full extent to which those powers were not thus delegated, and are alone responsible for them; and that any intermeddling of any one or more states, or a combination of their citizens, with the domestic institutions and police of the others, on any ground, political, moral or religious, or under any pretext whatever, with the view to their alteration or subversion, is not warranted by the Constitution, tending to endanger the domestic peace and tranquillity of the states interfered with, subversive of the objects for which the Constitution was formed, and, by necessary consequence, tending to weaken and destroy the Union itself.

" 3. *Resolved*, That this government was instituted and adopted by the several states of this Union as a common agent, in order to carry into effect the powers which they had delegated by the Constitution for their mutual security and prosperity, and that, in fulfilment of this high and sacred trust, this government is bound so to exercise its powers as not to interfere with the stability and security of the domestic institutions of the states that compose the Union; and that it is the solemn duty of the government to resist, to the extent of its constitutional power, all attempts by one portion of the Union to use it as an instrument

30

stitutional history of the United States; the ante-bellum period from 1789 to 1861, and the post-bellum period from 1861 to the present time. The dividing line between these two eras is the Civil War; the removal of the two great elements of slavery and the right of secession from constitutional discussion, and the non-existence of those two causes of difference has naturally resulted in a material modification of the views of many who had adopted the most extreme position in order to sustain those two principles which are now fortunately only elements of constitutional history and not of present construction.[1]

§ 15. **Marshall, Story and Gray; Calhoun, Taney and Tucker.**—During both of these periods there have been many

to attack the domestic institutions of another, or to weaken or destroy such institutions."

The remaining resolutions related exclusively to the relations of the Federal Government to the institution of slavery in the Southern states.

The final vote upon the adoption of these resolutions was 35 yeas and 9 nays.

Massachusetts, Vermont and Rhode Island were the only states that voted in the negative.

These extracts are sufficient to show the basic doctrine of the States' Rights School which has also been expressed by John Randolph Tucker, whose opinion is quoted at length in the text of section 16. Fortunately these views have been confined to a part of the people of a part of the States, and the broader views of those who believe that the United States is a Nation will undoubtedly prevail, with the result that the United States will always remain, as it has been, a Nation possessed of national and sovereign powers.

§ 14.

[1] "The United States of Amer-ica, from the Atlantic to the Pacific, from the Canadian lakes to the Mexican border, appear destined to remain for an indefinite time under the same political institutions; and there is no evidence that these will not continue to belong to the popular type. Of these institutions, the most important part is defined by the Federal Constitution. The relative importance, indeed, of the Government of the United States, and of the State Governments, did not always appear to be as clearly settled as it appears at the present moment. There was a time at which the authority of the several States might be thought to be gaining at the expense of the authority of the United States; but the War of Secession reversed this tendency, and the Federation is slowly but decidedly gaining at the cost of the States. Thus, the life and fortunes of the most multitudinous and homogeneous population in the world will, on the whole and in the main, be shaped by the Constitution of the United States." Popular Government, Sir Henry Maine, p. 197.

advocates of extremely limited, and of extremely unlimited, powers in the Central Government. John C. Calhoun and Chief Justice Taney can fairly be taken as exponents of the States' Rights School of the ante-bellum period, while John Randolph Tucker occupies the same position in the post-bellum period; Chief Justice Marshall and Justice Story, before the war, and Justices Field, Miller and Gray, since the war, are the leading spirits of the broad constructionists during their respective periods of service on the bench of the Supreme Court of the United States. Many other able publicists, jurists and judges have arrayed themselves on one side or the other of these great questions during both periods of our constitutional history; those who have been named, however, have expressed the views of the schools to which they have respectively belonged so thoroughly and completely, that most of the opinions and decisions which will be referred to in the subsequent pages will be taken from their writings and opinions.

§ 16. **John Randolph Tucker's views.**—John Randolph Tucker of Virginia comes of a family which has produced a long line of strict constructionists and of eminent statesmen of the States' Rights School; his recently published book edited after his death by his talented son, Henry St. George Tucker, is the latest exposition of the theories of that faction; it is largely an answer, or more properly speaking, an attempted answer to the exposition of the broader principles of nationality and sovereignty contained in Mr. Justice Story's Commentaries on the Constitution.[1] Mr. Tucker, in acknowledging the existence of the two opposite schools of construction of the Constitution, says:

" On the nature of the Constitution of the United States and the relations of the States to the Union, there are two leading schools of thought:

" *First*. That the unit of sovereignty is the State, which is

---

§ 16.

[1] On the other hand Justice Story, in his Commentaries, had directly refuted many of the statements contained and arguments made in Tucker's Blackstone, the work of John Randolph Tucker's grandfather, St. George Tucker; the recently published book of John Randolph Tucker might be considered as a brief in reply to Judge Story, if not as a brief reply.

a Body-politic; that the Constitution of the United States is a compact between these sovereign units and Bodies-politic, making a Federal Union between the States; that the organic Federal force of the Federal Union is the Federal Government, to which, by the Constitution of the United States, the States, separately and in combination, have delegated powers, reserving the residuum of powers not so delegated to the United States, nor prohibited to the States, to the State governments, or to the people of the States, respectively.

"*Second.* The second school holds that the Union is itself the unit of sovereignty, of which the States are subordinate parts, to which certain powers belong under the Constitution of the United States, while the main powers belong to the National Government.

"Under the first view the Union is a multiple of units; under the second, the Union is a unit of which the States are fractions. At the head of the second school, Judge Story is *primus inter pares,* and following him we have, in the present day, Von Holst, Burgess, Hare, Pomeroy, and a number of others."[2]

Mr. Tucker's views as to the extent and limitations of the treaty-making power of the United States found official utterance in a report made by the Judiciary Committee of the House of Representatives, of which he was Chairman in 1887, and to which more extended reference will be made later.[3]

§ 17. **Discussion limited to the Treaty-Making Power.—** It is not the purpose of this volume to enter into a general discussion of the theories of the delegated, or general, powers of the Government of the United States, except so far as they affect the treaty-making power; in this respect, it seems not only possible to reconcile the two conflicting doctrines of construction, but also to harmonize them in sustaining to the fullest extent this great and necessary power of the Federal or National Government, whichever it may be called.

§ 18. **Duality of Government of United States.—**The

[2] Tucker on the Constitution, vol. I., sec. 106, p. 178.

[3] Cong. Doc. 49th Congress, 2d Session, House of Rep., Report No. 4177 on Treaty with Hawaiian Islands, March 3, 1887.

3

question which is so often asked whether the Government of the United States is National or Federal can be consistently answered by the declaration that it is both.   While the two words from the standpoint of the lexicographer may be exclusive of each other as to certain matters, they are not necessarily so when considered as to the different capacities of governmental action and control over people who have delegated different portions of sovereignty to the State and Central Governments respectively.   In fact, those separate phases so exist that the diverse nature of the government not only necessarily exists, but it would be an impossibility for the government to survive without its existence.   Although this duality in nature of the Government of the United States in its Federal and National capacities has existed from its very inception, it had to be thoroughly understood and appreciated, not only in theory but also in practice, before this question was, as it certainly has been, settled by the Supreme Court of the United States, which has finally, and beyond all doubt, decided that the elements of nationality and sovereignty exist as to some matters, while the limitations which necessarily attend all delegated power where there is any residuum reserved, exist in regard to other matters.[1]

§ 19. **Extent of original State Sovereignty.**—Whatever State sovereignty existed at the time of the adoption of the Constitution, and was not delegated to the Central Government, was undoubtedly reserved to the States; such reservation, however, must necessarily have been in regard to those matters over which State sovereignty had been, or could have been, exercised; in all such respects this reservation of power and sovereignty must be construed as broadly as possible for the benefit of the States.   As to those subjects, however, over which it was neither proper nor practical for an individual State to exercise any control or sovereignty, but which required National action for the joint or equal benefit of every State, it is a self-evident proposition, that, as no power or sovereignty existed in regard thereto in any State, it was impossible for any one of the States separately, or all the States col-

§ 18.
[1] *United States* vs. *Cruikshank,* U. S. Sup. Ct. 1875, 92 U. S. 542, WAITE, Ch. J., and also see cases cited under § 12, *ante,* and §§ 35-6, *post.*

lectively, either to delegate to the newly formed government, or to reserve to themselves, elements of sovereignty which none of them possessed.[1] For the same reason it cannot be

§ 19.

[1] " The states were not ' sovereigns ' in the sense contended for by some. They did not possess the peculiar features of sovereignty— they could not make war, nor alliances, nor treaties. Considering them as political beings they were dumb, for they could not speak to any foreign sovereign whatever. They were deaf, for they could not hear any propositions from such sovereign. They had not even the organs of defense or offense, for they could not of themselves raise troops, nor equip vessels for war." (Mr. King, on June 19, 1787, in the Philadelphia convention, Madison papers; Elliot, Deb., V., p. 212, and see § 179 of chap. VI., *post.*) " Mr. Ruffin called attention in the debates of the peace convention at Washington, February, 1861, to the fact that during the Revolutionary War North Carolina had laid the foundation of a fleet, to which Orth of Indiana replied: ' There, then, we have a single instance of one of the States taking a step towards sovereignty.' None of the delegates from the Southern States could adduce another instance." Chittenden, Debates of the Peace Convention, p. 262. See also Von Holst, vol. I., chap. 1 p. 24, where the above appears as a footnote.

The complete lack on the part of any State government to perform any act which involves foreign relations is illustrated by the fact that no State can deliver up a fugitive to a foreign power except in pursuance of an act of Congress. In this regard Spear says (p. 18):

" The Constitution, in its first article, and in the first clause of the tenth section, declares that ' no State shall enter into any treaty, alliance or confederation;' and, in a subsequent clause of the same section, it declares that no State shall, without the consent of Congress, ' enter into any agreement or compact with another State, or with a foreign power.'

" The first of these prohibitions is absolute and unqualified, and completely excludes all power in the States to make treaties with foreign nations on any subject whatever. The States, of course, cannot make extradition treaties securing the right to demand fugitive criminals from foreign Governments, and contracting the obligation to deliver them up to such Governments.

" The second prohibition forbids the States, without the consent of Congress, to enter into any agreement or compact ' with a foreign power.' The 'agreement or compact,' as here referred to, is not identical with a formal treaty, which is absolutely forbidden in a previous clause of the section. The words mean any arrangement, negotiation, agreement or compact with a foreign power, though it should not amount to a treaty in the strict sense; and no State, unless with the prior consent of Congress, can enter into any arrangement, negotiation, agreement, or compact on any subject with another State or with a foreign power.

" The plain design of both prohibitions is to exclude the States

35

said that the people, in ratifying the Constitution, reserved any portion of sovereignty in regard to such matters to the States rather than to the Central Government.

from all official intercourse with foreign nations, and leave all such intercourse to be exclusively managed and conducted by the General Government. They cannot make a treaty, and they cannot, except with the consent of Congress, enter into *any* agreement or compact, either with each other or with a foreign power, even though it should not be a treaty in the technical sense.

"It follows that no State can, without such consent, agree in a specific case to deliver up a fugitive criminal to a foreign Government; and if it has no power to make such an agreement, then it has no power to do the thing itself. No state can do what it has no power to agree to do. The delivery of a fugitive criminal to a foreign Government, even without a regular and formal agreement beforehand, would be essentially the same thing as doing it with such an agreement. It would, in that case, be an affirmative response to the request or demand of the foreign Government, and an agreement to do the thing requested or demanded, accompanied with the actual doing of it, and would be just the thing in kind which it is the purpose of the Constitution to forbid and prevent.

"Moreover, the delivery of a fugitive criminal to a foreign Government by a State, even with the consent of Congress, supposing this consent to be obtained, would not be admissible, since the power to do so, as already shown, would be repugnant to a similar power vested in the General Government. The agreement or compact with a foreign power which, with the consent of Congress, is admissible, is evidently not of the kind that embraces the extradition of fugitive criminals, since this is provided for in the powers of the General Government, and since it is a part of the foreign intercourse of the United States intended to be exclusively confided to that Government, and especially to the President in the exercise of the treaty-making power. The framers of the Constitution evidently did not mean that Congress, by simply giving its consent, should be able to endow a State with any such power."

In speaking of the case of *Holmes* vs. *Jennison*, Spear says on p. 21:

"This decision (of the Supreme Court of the State of Vermont) affirmed and sustained the power of the Governor of Vermont to issue the warrant for the arrest, detention and delivery of Holmes to the Canadian authorities as a fugitive criminal, even without any express statute of the State providing therefor. It assumed that the State, through its executive authority, could make such an arrest and delivery, and that, too, notwithstanding the President of the United States for want of power had declined to act. The Governor of Vermont, in a matter of foreign intercourse, undertook to do what the President decided that he had no power to do; and the Supreme Court of the State affirmed the legality of his action. "The decision being rendered by the highest court of the State of Ver-

§ 20. Original nationality and sovereignty of Central Government.—In respect, therefore, to matters wholly with-

mont, Holmes, under the twenty-fifth section of the Judiciary Act of 1789 (1 U. S. Stat. at Large, 73), sued out a writ of error from the Supreme Court of the United States; and this court, being divided in opinion, was not able, as a court, to render any other judgment than that of dismissing the case for want of jurisdiction. *Holmes* vs. *Jennison*, 14 Pet. 540. There was, consequently, no positive decision by the court in regard to the specific question involved in the action of Governor Jennison, and decided by the Supreme Court of Vermont." Spear on the Law of Extradition, pp. 18–21.

That a State has no power to deliver to a foreign government, was, however, decided by the Court of Appeals of the State of New York in the case of *The People ex rel. Barlow* vs. *Curtis*, 50 N. Y. 321. The syllabus in that case says:

" By the Constitution of the United States the whole subject of foreign intercourse is committed to the Federal Government, and upon all questions relating thereto it alone can speak and act. It has the exclusive power to regulate, provide for and control the surrender of fugitives from justice from foreign countries. The provision, therefore, of the Revised Statutes (1 R. S. 164, §§ 8–11, 8th ed. p. 497) providing for such surrender, is unconstitutional, and a warrant issued by the governor in pursuance thereof is void." In this case, on the request of the Minister of Belgium, one Vogt charged with the crimes of murder, robbery and arson, was about to be delivered to the Belgian authorities, to the

end that he might be taken to Brussels and there tried for his crimes. This was in 1872; there was no extradition treaty between the United States and Belgium at that time, the President of the United States therefore had no authority to deliver up fugitive criminals to the Belgian government.

The Governor of New York acted under a statute, originally enacted in 1822, which provided that " the Governor may, in his discretion, deliver over to justice any person *found* within the State, who shall be charged with having committed, without the jurisdiction of the United States, any crime except treason, which by the laws of this State, if committed therein, is punishable by death or by imprisonment in the State prison." 1 R. S. of New York, 164. There is no doubt that this statute of the State of New York authorized the act of the Governor in ordering the arrest and delivery of Vogt. The only question, therefore, was whether the statute itself was consistent with the Constitution of the United States.

Vogt sued out a writ of *habeas corpus*, returnable before Judge Curtis, of the Superior Court of the city of New York, who discharged Vogt on the ground that the statute, and the warrant of arrest under it, were in conflict with the Constitution of the United States. This proceeding was reviewed and afterwards affirmed by the General Term of the Supreme Court, also by the New York Court of Appeals.

See views of Justice Samuel F. Miller on State Sovereignty, quoted in section 29 of this chapter *post.*

37

out the jurisdiction of any State the National Government was created by the original joinder of the colonies, at a time when unity of action was recognized as a prerequisite for independence, and the existence of its nationality dates from a period prior to the adoption of the Articles of Confederation. That National Government, the existence of which continued under those articles, and still continues under the Constitution, is necessarily not one of exclusively delegated powers; it undoubtedly possesses certain delegated powers, the source of which can be found in, and must necessarily be limited by, those great instruments which have, and always will, form such an important part of our organic law; it also, however, originally possessed, as it still must possess, complete nationality and sovereignty in many other respects in the same manner as they are possessed and can be exercised by other sovereign powers of the world.   It necessarily follows that this proposition relates with even greater force to the treaty-making power, and to the establishment and conduct of relations between this country and every part thereof with foreign countries than it does to almost any other existing governmental powers, because in no other respect is it so generally admitted, that the government of the United States is national in its character and scope.

The Constitution recognizes the distinction between the Federal and National sources of power; this is evidenced by the Tenth Amendment, which declares that the reservation of undelegated powers is " to the States, and to the people." The people in this respect are referred to, not only as inhabitants or citizens of the States, but also as the people of the entire country as a National unit.

§ 21. **Residuum of Power.**—This residuum of delegated power contains in itself a complete exposition of the sovereignty of the Central Government in national affairs.

It will be again referred to in the final chapter of this volume, but it requires a brief reference at this point also. As to matters affecting States in their individual capacities, all delegated power, except so far as it was reserved in the people themselves, vests in the State in the absence of specific delegation to the Central Government; as the power of the Central Government diminishes that of the State increases,

38

and *vice versa;* but full and complete sovereignty so far as the people have parted with it exists between the two governments, and there is never any loss of the whole amount of power so delegated. When, however, no State can possibly exert control over a matter, or exercise any jurisdiction owing to the nature of the subject-matter or to constitutional limitations, the entire power delegated must necessarily remain in, and be exercised solely by, the Central Government; hence it can, as it often has done, and often must do, exercise plenary power in regard to those matters, and in so doing it has been held that its power is unrestrained, except so far as it must be exercised in consonance with the fundamental principles which are intended as general securities for public liberty, and subject only to those natural limitations which are imposed upon all sovereign powers, no matter how absolute they may be, of equity, justice and truth.[1]

§ 22. **Powers reserved to States relate to internal affairs.**—It must also be remembered that the limitations upon the Central Government are those which reserve to the States the control of matters relating to their internal affairs; there are no express or implied limitations upon those matters which are within the purview of the national government. In fact while the treaty-making and some other powers are delegated to the Central Government in general terms, and without any specified limitations whatever, the Constitution expressly provides that "no State shall enter into any treaty, alliance or confederation; . . or, without the consent of Congress, enter into any agreement or compact with another State or with a foreign power,"[1] thus not only placing the power generally in the Central Government, but absolutely prohibiting any State from acquiring any additional territory, or performing any functions of sovereignty beyond its own boundaries, except through the medium of the Central Government; unless that government therefore is completely vested with the fullest powers in these respects, some portion of delegated sovereignty would neces-

§ 21.
[1] See cases cited under §§ 36–40, *post.*

§ 22.
[1] U. S. Const. Art. I, § 10.

sarily be lost, because no part of it would, for it could not, under the prohibitory clauses revert to the States individually or collectively ; under such circumstances this country would have to stand before the world in the mortifying position of not having any government, State or National, able to perform the most necessary and far-reaching of all governmental functions; the one which all other, and fully sovereign, powers are constantly performing, and in the absence of which, foreign relations could not be maintained with any dignity or satisfactory results whatever, either for the Central Government or for the States themselves.[2]

[2] In an opinion delivered to Secretary of State Marcy, on February 26, 1857, in regard to the right of the United States to regulate by treaty the succession of property in States of the Union as to citizens of another Country, Attorney General Caleb Cushing says: "Supposing engagement of this nature to exceed the Constitutional power of the Federal Government, that with Prussia does not the less exist: it is for the consideration of reciprocal benefits actually received by us; and, if it be unconstitutional, it will remain for us,—after pleading *mea culpa, mea culpa gravissima*, and begging pardon for entering into stipulations which we had no power to make,—then it will only remain for us to indemnify Prussia for our past shortcomings, and to negotiate a release from further obligation.

"But can it be, is there any good reason to think, that the Federal Government has no power to make such a stipulation? It may be inconvenient, because involving conflict with, or abrogation of, the laws of one or more of the States. Granted: but inconvenience is not unconstitutionality: question of which depends on the text of the Federal Constitution.

"The power, which the Constitution bestows on the President, with advice and consent of the Senate, to make treaties, is not only general in terms and without any express limitation, but it is accompanied with absolute prohibition of exercise of treaty-power by the States. That is, in the matter of foreign negotiation, the States have conferred the whole of their power, in other words, all the treaty-powers of sovereignty, on the United States. Thus, in the present case, if the power of negotiation be not in the United States, then it exists nowhere, and one great field of international relation, of negotiation, and of ordinary public and private interest, is closed up, as well against the United States as each and every one of the States. That is not a supposition to be accepted, unless it be forced upon us by considerations of overpowering cogency. Nay, it involves political impossibility. For, if one of the proper functions of sovereignty be thus utterly lost to us, then the people of the United States are but incompletely sovereign,—not sovereign,—nor in coequality of right with other admitted sovereignties of Europe and America."

§ 23. **Proposition supported by eminent jurists.**—This broad proposition may sound paradoxical, especially when it is accompanied by the statement that we are a constitutionally governed country; it is founded, however, upon opinions and decisions expressed by the ablest jurists and authorities upon constitutional law and construction which this country has ever produced, and who have been able to extend their vision beyond the bounds of a mere league of confederated semi-sovereignties, or states banded together for the selfish protection of individual interests, to the more expansive view of a great nation, exercising through a Central Government national functions, not only for internal protection and development, but far beyond the original limits, for the benefit of mankind and civilization.

Those who have recently had the temerity to affirm, for example, as a legal proposition, that our government has in any way exceeded, or is exceeding, its powers either in acquiring or in governing, our new possessions, would do well to examine the opinions and decisions of the Supreme Court, as they have been declared by Chief Justice Marshall and Justices Story, Curtis, Field, Bradley, Harlan and Gray[1] and other former and present members of that great tribunal, as well as the utterances of such statesmen as Caleb Cushing, Daniel Webster, Charles Sumner, William H. Seward and others noted no less for their prudence and conservatism than for their legal ability and political acumen; after weighing the expressed opinions of those eminent jurists and masters of political science, they may materially modify their own opinions; their doubts may be dispelled, and they may recognize that there has been no excess of power exerted in the recent actions of the Government, so far as treaty-making is concerned;[2] in every instance of territorial acquisition and the subsequent government of the acquired territory, the National Government has exercised powers which are only compati-

Opinions of Attorneys General, vol. VIII, 411, p. 415.

§ 23.

[1] For references to utterances of these jurists consult index at end of volume.

[2] For decisions of the court and the questions involved in the suits pending before the Supreme Court see §§ 61a–61h, *post*; see also § 101, chapter III, *post*.

ble with the inherent possession of complete sovereignty, and wholly incompatible with the delegated possession of incomplete sovereignty, and the Supreme Court has uniformly sustained the action of the Government whenever it has been based upon treaty stipulations, not only as to the treaty itself, but also as to the legislation subsequently enacted in pursuance thereof.

§ 24. **National Unity expressed in preamble of Constitution.**—This idea of national unity is also expressed in the preamble of the Constitution, which enumerates amongst the actuating motives for its adoption, provision for the *common* defence, promotion of the *general* welfare and security of the blessings of liberty for the *people* of the United States, referring unquestionably to the people at large in their National capacity. It must also be remembered that one of the greatest discussions in the Federal Convention was on the question whether the Constitution should be submitted for ratification to the various State legislatures, or to the people themselves, and that the latter course was adopted after an able dissertation upon the subject by Mr. Madison, the details of which are referred to at greater length in the subsequent chapter of this volume which is devoted to the proceedings of the Constitutional Convention of 1787.[1]

§ 25. **Ratification of Amendments by States result of delegation by People.**—The reason why amendments to the Constitution can now be ratified by the legislative bodies of the States, and not necessarily by the people either directly, or through conventions specially called for the purpose, is not because the States, as such, inherently possess any power or sovereignty to amend the Constitution of the Union, but because the people themselves, by a provision in the Constitution, clothed the state legislatures with the power of ratifying amendments whenever they were proposed by a two thirds vote of both houses of Congress, provided the legislatures of three fourths of the States accepted them; the people thus constitute the legislatures of the several States their agents, subject to the prescribed limitations for the purpose of ratifying such Amendments.[1]

§ 24.
[1] See § 195 chapter VI *post*.

§ 25.
[1] " The Congress, whenever two

§ 26. Supremacy of General Government as to objects within its domain.

— "The general government," said Chief Justice Marshall, "though limited as to its objects is supreme with respect to those objects, and this principle is a part of the Constitution."[1] He also asserted that no rule of narrow

thirds of both Houses shall deem it necessary, shall propose Amendments to this Constitution, or, on the Application of the Legislatures of two thirds of the several States, shall call a Convention for proposing Amendments, which, in either Case, shall be valid to all Intents and Purposes, as Part of this Constitution, when ratified by the Legislatures of three fourths of the several States, or by Conventions in three fourths thereof as the one or the other Mode of Ratification may be proposed by the Congress; Provided that no Amendment which may be made prior to the Year One thousand eight hundred and eight shall in any Manner affect the first and fourth Clauses in the Ninth Section of the first Article; and that no State, without its Consent, shall be deprived of its equal suffrage in the Senate."

Article V. Constitution of United States. (The first and fourth clauses of the Ninth Section of Article One, relating to the migration and importation of, and taxation on, slaves).

§ 26.

[1] "The American States, as well as the American people, have believed a close and firm Union to be essential to their liberty and to their happiness. They have been taught by experience, that this Union cannot exist without a government for the whole; and they have been taught by the same experience that this government would be a mere shadow, that must disappoint all their hopes, unless invested with large portions of that sovereignty which belongs to independent States. Under the influence of this opinion, and thus instructed by experience, the American people, in the conventions of their respective States, adopted the present constitution.

"If it could be doubted, whether from its nature, it were not supreme in all cases where it is empowered to act, that doubt would be removed by the declaration, that 'this constitution, and the laws of the United States, which shall be made in pursuance thereof, and all treaties made, or which shall be made, under the authority of the United States, shall be the supreme law of the land; and the judges in every State shall be bound thereby; anything in the constitution or laws of any State to the contrary notwithstanding.'

"This is the authoritative language of the American people; and, if gentlemen please, of the American States. It marks, with lines too strong to be mistaken, the characteristic distinction between the government of the Union, and those of the States. The general government, though limited as to its objects, is supreme with respect to those objects. This principle is a part of the constitution; and if there be any who deny its necessity, none can deny its authority.

"To this supreme government ample powers are confided; and if it were possible to doubt the great

or strict construction would be adopted as to the power of
the Central Government; when once the nail was found on
which to hang the authority to act, he declared, that the nail
is strong enough to hold any weight that could be suspended
therefrom.[2]

The rule of supreme power, as laid down by the eminent
Chief Justice, has been expanded rather than contracted by
subsequent decisions of the Supreme Court, which has always
upheld the sovereignty and nationality of our government.

purposes for which they were so
confided, the people of the United
States have declared, that they are
given 'in order to form a more perfect union, establish justice, ensure
domestic tranquillity, provide for
the common defense, promote the
general welfare, and secure the
blessings of liberty to themselves
and their posterity.'

"With the ample powers confided to this supreme government,
for these interesting purposes, are
connected many express and important limitations on the sovereignty of the States, which are
made for the same purposes. The
powers of the Union, on the great
subjects of war, peace, and commerce, and on many others, are in
themselves limitations of the sovereignty of the States; but in addition to these, the sovereignty of
the States is surrendered in many
instances where the surrender can
only operate to the benefit of the
people, and where, perhaps, no
other power is conferred on Congress than a conservative power
to maintain the principles established in the constitution. The
maintenance of these principles in
their purity, is certainly among
the great duties of the government.
One of the instruments by which
this duty may be peaceably performed, is the judicial department.

It is authorized to decide all cases
of every description, arising under
the constitution or laws of the
United States." *Cohens* vs. *Virginia*, U. S. Sup. Ct. 1821, 6
Wheaton, 264, p. 380, MAR-
SHALL, Ch. J.

[2] "This instrument (the Constitution) contains an enumeration of
powers expressly granted by the
people to their government. It has
been said, that these powers ought
to be construed strictly. But why
ought they to be so construed? Is
there one sentence in the constitution which gives countenance to
this rule? In the last of the enumerated powers, that which grants,
expressly, the means for carrying
all others into execution, Congress
is authorized 'to make all laws
which shall be necessary and
proper' for the purpose. But this
limitation on the means which may
be used, is not extended to the
powers which are conferred, nor is
there one sentence in the constitution, which has been pointed out
by the gentlemen of the bar, or
which we have been able to discern,
that prescribes this rule. We do
not, therefore, think ourselves justified in adopting it." *Gibbons* vs.
Ogden, U. S. Sup. Court 1824, 9,
Wheaton, 1, p. 187, MARSHALL,
Ch. J.

§ 27. **Meaning of "The People of the United States."**—
These words, which occur in the preamble of the Constitution, have been held by Calhoun, Tucker and other upholders
of States' rights and the theory of a collection of State units
instead of a single national unit, as meaning the people of
the different States, and not the people of the United States
as an entirety.

On the other hand, those who believe in the nationality
of our Government maintain that, although the Constitution was adopted in separate State conventions, the people
necessarily adopted such method as the only possible one
under which they could act at that time.

The theory of the nationalists is supported by the fact that
the State legislatures had no power to accede to a confederation, or to a national government, except by the consent of
the people themselves, and that in such respect the action
of the people was superior to the State governments.

Chief Justice Marshall, Mr. Justice Story and others have
discussed this question in their opinions, and commentaries
upon the Constitution, and some of their views are collated
in the footnote to this section. Chief Justice Marshall declared in the opinion quoted in the note that the people acted
upon the Constitution in the only manner in which they could
safely, effectively and wisely act upon such a subject, to
wit: by assembling in convention. Continuing he declared
that while no political dreamer was ever wild enough to
think of breaking down the lines which separated the States,
or of compounding the American people into one common
mass, the measures which were adopted in the separate State
conventions did not on that account cease to be the measures
of the people themselves, or become the measures of the
State governments. In fact, the Chief Justice said, that the
Government of the United States proceeded directly from
the people, was ordained and established in the name of the
people for the purposes stated in the preamble, and that the
assent of the States in their sovereign capacity was implied
in calling the conventions and submitting the instrument to
the people, but, he declared, "The people were at perfect
liberty to accept or reject it; their act was final;" it did not
require the affirmance and could not be negatived by the

States, and the Constitution as thus adopted, was a complete obligation and bound the State sovereignties.[1]

§ 27.

[1] VIEWS OF MARSHALL AND STORY AS EXPRESSED BY GEORGE TICKNOR CURTIS.

"When we turn to the views of the nature of the Constitution that have always been held and acted upon by the Supreme Court of the United States, it becomes at once apparent that they have admitted of no place for the doctrine which is implied in the idea of state resistance, or organized resistance of any kind. Beginning with the earliest judicial interpretations of the Constitution, and coming down to the latest, we shall find that they have been uniform and consistent.

"When the Supreme Court was composed of Marshall as chief justice, Bushrod Washington, Story, and their associates, it became necessary for them to speak positively concerning the nature of the Constitution, because it was then claimed, in the particular controversy which they had to decide, that the Constitution was established by the states in their sovereign capacities. This doctrine was distinctly negatived by the court in the following terms: 'The Constitution of the United States was ordained and established, not by the states in their sovereign capacities, but emphatically, as the preamble of the Constitution declares, by the *people* of the United States. There can be no doubt that it was competent to the people to invest the government with all the powers which they might deem proper and necessary, to extend or restrain those powers according to their own good pleasure, and to give them permanent and supreme authority.' (*Martin* vs. *Hunter*, STORY, J., 1 Wheaton, 304.)

"A few years later, Chief Justice Marshall, speaking for the whole bench, said: 'The government of the Union is a government of the *people;* it emanates from them; its powers are granted by them, and are to be exercised on them and for their benefit. . . . The government of the Union, though limited in its powers, is supreme within its sphere of action; and its laws, when made in pursuance of the Constitution, form the supreme law of the land.' (*McCulloch* vs. *The State of Maryland*, 4 Wheaton, 316.)

"Did Story, in referring to the preamble of the Constitution, or did Marshall, in speaking of the p*eople*, mean that the Constitution was ordained and established by the people of the United States regarded as a nation? It is quite apparent that the preamble, in using the words 'We, the people of the United States . . . do ordain and establish this Constitution for the United States of America,' meant that the people of the several states do this great political act. It is, too, made certain that the very eminent jurists and magistrates, whose language I am now considering, did not regard the Constitution as ordained and established by that mass of people of whom we commonly speak as the People of the United States when we refer to them as a nation. This is apparent from what was said by Chief Justice Marshall."

Mr. Curtis then quotes a long extract from *McCulloch* vs. *Maryland*,

§ 28. Views of Chancellor Kent and Joseph Story.—These views were held by Mr. Justice Story, who expressed them in

in the course of which the following occurs which seems to indicate that Chief Justice Marshall considered that, while the *people* acted as *people of the States*, they did so in a manner that was superior to the governments of the States themselves.

"'In discussing this question, the counsel for the state of Maryland have deemed it of some importance in the construction of the Constitution, to consider that instrument, not as emanating from the people, but as the act of sovereign and independent states. The powers of the general government, it has been said, are delegated by the states, who alone are truly sovereign, and must be exercised in subordination to the states, who alone possess supreme dominion. It would be difficult to sustain this proposition. The convention which framed the Constitution was, indeed, elected by the state legislatures. But the instrument when it came from their hands was a mere proposal, without obligation or pretensions to it. It was reported to the then existing Congress of the United States, with a request that it might ' be submitted to a convention of delegates, chosen in each state, by the people thereof, under the recommendation of its legislature for their assent and ratification.' This mode of proceeding was adopted; and by the Convention, by Congress, and by the state legislatures the instrument was submitted to the people.

"' They acted upon it, in the only manner in which they can safely, effectively, and wisely on such a subject, by assembling in convention. It is true, they assembled in their several states; and where else should they have assembled? No political dreamer was ever wild enough to think of breaking down the lines which separate the states, and of compounding the American people into one common mass. Of consequence, when they act, they act in their states. But the measures they adopt do not, on that account, cease to be the measures of the people themselves, or become the measures of the state governments. From these conventions the Constitution derives its whole authority. The government proceeds directly from the people; is ' ordained and established' in the name of the people; and is declared to be ordained 'in order to form a more perfect union, establish justice, insure domestic tranquillity, and secure the blessings of liberty to themselves and to their posterity.' The assent of the states, in their sovereign capacity, is implied in calling a convention, and thus submitting that instrument to the people. But the people were at perfect liberty to accept or reject it, and their act was final.

"' It required not the affirmance, and could not be negatived, by the state governments. The Constitution, when thus adopted, was of complete obligation and bound the state sovereignties.

"' It has been said that the people had already surrendered all their powers to the state sovereignties and had nothing more to give. But surely the question whether they may resume and modify the powers granted to government does not remain to be settled in this country.

47

Martin vs. *Hunter* as quoted at length in the foot-note to
the preceding section, to the effect that " the Constitution

Much more might the legitimacy of the general government be doubted
had it been created by the states. The powers delegated to the state
sovereignties were to be exercised by themselves, not by a distinct
and independent sovereignty created by themselves. To the formation of a league such as was the Confederation, the state sovereignties
were certainly competent. But when, 'in order to form a more perfect
union,' it was deemed necessary to change the alliance into an effective
government possessing great and sovereign powers and acting directly on
the people, the necessity of referring it to the people, and of deriving
its powers directly from them, was felt and acknowledged by all. The
government of the Union, then (whatever may be the influence of this
fact on the case), is emphatically and truly a government of the people.
In form and in substance it emanates from them. Its powers are
granted by them, and are to be exercised directly on them and for their
benefit.' " Curtis' Constitutional History of the United States, vol. II.,
pp. 71–74.

VIEWS OF PROFESSOR VON HOLST.

"Sec. 8. *The Doctrine of State Sovereignty.* The premise of the argument of the so-called state's-right school is that there never has been,
either in point of fact or in point of law, one people of the United States.
The argument proceeds as follows: The people of each state, without
being bound in any way by the action or the non-action of the other
states, decided for themselves, through their authorized representatives,
whether or not they would accept the draft of the Philadelphia convention. That the constitution is a work of states is, therefore, a fact which
cannot be gotten rid of on the plea that the constitution begins with the
words: ' We, the people of the United States.' If these words do not
contain an evident falsehood, then must the phrase ' United States ' be
read here as ' states united; ' but so read they say simply that the states,
in order to better protect their interests, have entered into a new compact to regulate everything in regard to those matters as to which they
wish to form one commonwealth. The political existence of the Union
was not changed. The states were sovereign afterwards as well as before, and they alone were sovereign because a partition of sovereignty
is impossible from its very meaning. It would be to turn nature upside
down if the creator were made subordinate to the creature. There was
no common judge standing above the federal powers and the states. If
a conflict of authority broke out between them, the decisive judgment
was left to the states, that is, to each of them for itself, as to what
rights they had reserved for themselves and what powers they had given
to the Union. If the federal government, in the opinion of a single
state, exceeded its constitutional authority, that state was justified in
declaring the particular law, so far as it came in question, to be null and
void. John C. Calhoun, of South Carolina, who with great logical acuteness developed into a complete system this so-called doctrine of nulli-

of the United States was ordained and established, not by the States in their sovereign capacities, but emphatically, as

fication, declared that nullification was an 'eminently conservative remedy,' and affirmed that it, and it alone, could prevent the dissolution of the Union. The younger school of the southern state's-right men did not stand by him in this. The doctrine of nullification was constantly pushed into the background and often completely rejected, and on the other hand, again and again and more unconditionally the last consequences were deduced from the premises of the state's-school. Since the constitution is a compact between sovereign states, they said, the states have the power to cut loose from the Union if the compact is broken, either by the national government or by the other states,—if it changes from a means of protection and of advancement into a source of destruction and certain ruin. Sovereignty is not only indivisible, but cannot be parted with, and the states, bound only through an act of their own free will, can be bound only as long as their will does not change; that is, as they wish to be bound. Secession is thus not a right *under* the constitution, that is, a constitutional right, but it is inherent in the nature of the states, and therefore could not possibly be given up by the adoption of the constitution. The attempt to prevent by force the secession of a state is not a suppression of a rebellion, but an international war. Others did not go as far, and thought they had found a middle course. They admitted that secession was a revolutionary act, but affirmed that the federal government was not empowered to use force against the sovereign states. This was the non-coercion theory. They claimed that the sovereign states had the right of neutrality; that is, that although they had not cut loose from the Union, they were justified in standing on one side as spectators during a conflict fought out with the sword between the federal government and the seceded states.

"The result of the civil war made this one of the dead and gone doctrines of history. After its champions had appealed to the *ultima ratio* and had been completely conquered, it had no more political vitality. And it will never again have it. The victorious north did not even consider it necessary to guard itself against the possibility of the revival of this doctrine by inserting in the constitution a new express declaration against it. The opposite doctrine is thus unquestionably valid constitutional law to-day, whatever one may think on the question as to what *originally* was constitutional law. There is no need here of any further critical examination of the doctrine of state sovereignty. This is involved in the statement of the opposite doctrine, which is the constitutional law of to-day.

"Sec. 9. The *People of the United States* of course did not act as one uniform whole when they gave themselves this constitution. The people, that is, the part of the population of each state endowed with full political rights, acted for themselves, and had absolute freedom of decision. They could accept the draft of the Philadelphia convention through their authorized representatives, or they could reject it, and therewith cut loose from the Union, if the projected organization of the

4

the preamble of the Constitution declares 'by the people of the United States.' " [1]

Chancellor Kent, in his Lectures on the Government and Constitutional Jurisprudence, which forms the second part

§ 28.
[1] *Martin* vs. *Hunter*, U. S. Sup. Ct. 18, 1816, 1 Wheaton, 304, p. 324,

STORY, J. See note 3 to preceding section and also see chap. V. § 138, *et seq.*

latter were accomplished. But their ratification did not make the draft a constitution. Their ratification was simply a declaration, binding in law, that if the people of at least eight other states came to the same conclusion, the organization of the Union should therewith become an accomplished fact; so that, for the states concerned, this draft should be good as a constitution given by the people of the United States to the United States. Only by and through the choice of its own people did each state become a constituent member of the Union. This, however, did not happen through an act of will of any single state, but the Philadelphia draft first became a constitution by the equal and co-operating consent of the people of nine states, and the states which ratified it afterwards evidently acquired by their ratification exactly the same legal *status* in the Union. Chief Justice Chase was unquestionably right when he said that 'the Union of the states never was a purely artificial and arbitrary relation.' This fact, however, did not settle the matter at issue. Whether the states were or were not sovereign from the time of the declaration of independence, by common consent every one of them decided as a sovereign upon the adoption of the constitution, that is, upon its own entrance into the Union. On the other hand, whatever their legal *status* in the confederation and their political nature up to this time might have been, they were not sovereign by common consent, that is, according to the constitution, as members of the new Union. The Philadelphia convention began its labor by the adoption of a resolution which declared 'that a *national* government ought to be established, consisting of a *supreme* legislative, executive and judiciary.' If a state adopted the draft, its people thereby declared that they, as far and as widely as this draft provided, should be fused with the people of the other states into one people of the United States; and by the concurrent decision of all, this declaration, put in this way, was placed at the beginning of the constitution, so that this proclaimed itself as the work of this one people of the United States.

" Sec. 10. *The Constitution* is not a compact between the states, but it is, as it declares itself to be, a constitution, and in truth, *the* constitution of the United States, that is, of the Union, of the commonwealth formed out of the states. Therefore, it is unconditionally binding, as well for the whole people as for the states as such. No room for doubt is left, for the second section of the sixth article reads: ' This constitution, and the laws of the United States which shall be made in pursuance thereof, and all treaties made or which shall be made under the authority of the United States, shall be the supreme law of the land,

of his Commentaries, says in regard to this element of nationality :

"The Government of the United States was erected by the free voice and joint will of the people of America, for their common defence and general welfare. Its powers apply to those great interests which relate to this country in its national capacity, and which depend for their stability and protection on the consolidation of the Union. It is clothed with the principal attributes of political sovereignty, and it is justly deemed the guardian of our best rights, the source of our highest civil and political duties, and the sure means of national greatness. The constitution and jurisprudence of the United States deserve the most accurate examination ; and an historical view of the rise and progress of the Union, and of the establishment of the present Constitution, as the necessary fruit of it, will tend to show the genius and value of the government, and prepare the mind of the student for an investigation of its powers.

"The association of the American people into one body politic, took place while they were colonies of the British empire, and owed allegiance to the British crown. That the union of this country was essential to its safety, its prosperity, and its greatness had been generally known, and frequently avowed long before the late revolution, or the claims of the British Parliament which produced it."[2]

---

[2] Kent's Comm. (14th ed.), Lecture X., p. 202.

and the judges in every state shall be bound thereby, anything in the constitution or laws of any state to the contrary notwithstanding.' The constitution is thus the law, and, moreover, the supreme law of the land. The constitutions of the separate states are their fundamental laws only in regard to those matters which are not submitted by the federal constitution to federal authority. This provision makes the constitution an integral part of the constitution of each state. If there is a conflict between them, then the provision of the state constitution opposed to the federal constitution is *ipso facto* null and void. All judges, and therefore, evidently, all other state officers, and all citizens of the state, are absolutely bound down to this fundamental principle. He who seeks to overthrow it lays hands on the fundamental law of the land. The federal government, which is bound to give the constitution life and being by law, is therefore not only empowered but directed to break down any opposition ;—if possible, by the ordinary and peaceful powers of the state as provided by the constitution, but in case of need, by

51

§ 29. **Samuel F. Miller's views.**—One of the strongest expositions of the completeness of the sovereignty of the United States is found in Justice Samuel F. Miller's "Lectures on the Constitution," which have been annotated and published since his death by Mr. J. C. Bancroft Davis. This volume is recognized as a text-book of high authority on the interpretation of the Constitution; and justly so, as the author was often called upon judicially to construe it while he was a member of the Supreme Court, and the annotator has had the greatest opportunity of studying that instrument, and the interpretation thereof by the Supreme Court, during his term as its reporter, which has extended over a period represented by more than seventy volumes of the reports, and during which time he has prepared the headnotes of nearly every important decision on constitutional questions. In the notes to Lecture I. it is stated that, after the fall of British sovereignty, the broad functions of general government were assumed by the Continental Congress and exercised without question, even before the adoption of the Federal Constitution or the Articles of Confederation; that this state of facts existed while the Constitution was being framed, and continued after its adoption. As to these great natural powers of sovereignty, the notes say: "They were never enjoyed or exercised by the States separately, and, consequently, as an historic fact, independently of theory, could not have been retained when the States conferred upon the General Government the other enumerated powers." In speaking of the acceptance of the Northwest Territory, the declaration is made that the "sovereignty over it was vested in the United States as one undivided and independent nation. The simple truth is, the United States existed as a sovereign power from the necessities of the emergency."[1]

In 1867 Mr. Justice Miller pronounced the opinion of the Court in a case in which it was decided that no State had the right to tax railroad and stage companies for passengers carried out of the State, or for the privilege of passing through

§ **29.**

[1] Miller's Lectures on the Constitution, pp. 38–58.

force." The Constitutional Law of the United States by Dr. H. Von Holst, §§ 8–10, pp. 39–44.

the State. He declined to concede that the question could be determined by the commerce clause of the Constitution but held that the tax was void because it interfered with *National* rights of the people of the United States.[2] But although he was an ardent upholder of the sovereign powers of the National Government, Mr. Justice Miller never lost sight of the extensive powers of the States, or of the boundary line between Federal or National and State jurisdiction, as was evidenced by his far-reaching opinion in the *Slaughter-house cases* which will be referred to at length hereafter.[3]

. § 30. **Justice Field's Opinion.**—In 1889, Mr. Justice Field,[1] after quoting these prior declarations of the court, declared that, "the United States formed for many and for important

[2] "The people of these United States constitute one nation. They have a government in which all of them are deeply interested. This government has necessarily a capital established by law, where its principal operations are conducted. Here sits its legislature, composed of senators and representatives from the States and from the people of the States. Here resides the President, directing through thousands of agents, the execution of the laws over all this vast country. Here is the seat of the supreme judicial power of the nation, to which all citizens have a right to resort to claim justice at its hands. Here are the great executive departments, administering the offices of the mails, of the public lands, of the collection and distribution of the public revenues, and of our foreign relations. These are all established and conducted under the admitted powers of the Federal government. That government has a right to call to this point any or all of its citizens to aid in its service, as members of the Congress, of the courts, of the executive departments, and to fill all its other offices; and this right cannot be made to depend upon the pleasure of a State over whose territory they must pass to reach the point wherein these services must be rendered. The government, also, has its offices of secondary importance in all other parts of the country. On the sea-coasts and on the rivers it has its ports of entry. In the interior it has its land offices, its revenue offices, and its sub-treasuries. In all these it demands the services of its citizens, and is entitled to bring them to those points from all quarters of the nation, and no power can exist in a State to obstruct this right that would not enable it to defeat the purposes for which the government was established." *Crandall* vs. *Nevada*, U. S. Sup. Ct. 1867, 6 Wallace, 35, p. 43, MILLER, J.

[3] The *Slaughter House Cases*, U. S. Sup. Ct. 1872, 16 Wallace, 36, MILLER, J., and see § 357, Chapter XI. Vol. II, pp. 52, *et seq.*

§ 30.

[1] *Chae Chan Ping* vs. *United States*, U. S. Sup. Ct. 1889, 130 U. S. 581, p. 604, FIELD, J.

purposes a single nation." Continuing, that gifted jurist, who longer than any other justice of the Supreme Court, occupied a seat upon its bench, re-stated as the rule of the Court the views expressed by Chief Justice Marshall sixty-eight years before as follows:[2] "In war, we are one people. In making peace we are one people. In all commercial regulations, we are one and the same people. In many other respects the American people are one, and the government which is alone capable of controlling and managing their interests in all these respects is the government of the Union. It is their government, and in that character they have no other. America has chosen to be, in many respects and to many purposes, a nation ; and for all these purposes her government is complete. To all these objects it is competent. The people have declared, that in the exercise of all powers given for these objects, it is supreme. It can, then, in effecting these objects, legitimately control all individuals or governments within the American territory."[3]

There is a significance in the use of the word "American" throughout this declaration of unity, for by that name the people of this country are essentially known in their national, as distinguished from their federal, capacity.

§ 31. **Views of Justices Gray and Bradley.**—The same rule was reaffirmed in 1893 by Mr. Justice Gray, who, reiterating statements made by Mr. Justice Bradley,[1] expressed the views of the court as follows: "The United States is not only a government, but a national government, and the only government in this country that has the character of nationality. It is vested with power over all the foreign relations of the country, war, peace and negotiations, and intercourse with other nations, all of which are forbidden to the State governments—for local interests the several states of our Union exist, but for international relations, with for-

[2] *Cohens* vs. *Virginia*, U. S. Sup. Ct. 1821, 6 Wheaton, 264, p. 413, MARSHALL, Ch. J.

[3] See also opinion of Justice FIELD, sustaining the jurisdiction of United States Consular Courts in foreign countries: *In re Ross*, U. S. Sup. Ct. 1891, 140 U. S. 453,

and referred to at length § 379, chapter XII. and §§ 448, 453, chapter XV, Vol. II.

§ 31.

[1] *Knox* vs. *Lee*, (*Legal-tender cases*) U. S. Sup. Ct. 1870, 12 Wallace, 457, p. 455, BRADLEY, J.

eign powers we are but one people, one nation, one power.[2]
. . . . The United States are a sovereign and independent nation, and are vested by the Constitution with the entire control of international relations, and with all the power of government necessary to maintain their control and to make it effective. The only government in this country which other governments recognize, or treat with, is the government of the Union. The only American flag known throughout the world is the flag of the United States. The Constitution speaks with no uncertain sound upon this subject."[3]

Mr. Justice Gray has also expressed the opinion of the Supreme Court as to the power of the United States to exercise the natural functions of sovereignty not referred to expressly in the Constitution, but which are exercisable because it is a nation, and its Government must, therefore, be a sovereign power endowed with every element of nationality and sovereignty.[4]

Judge Gray's opinion in the *Fong Yue Ting* case was referred to in a speech recently made by Senator O. H. Platt, of Connecticut, an extract from which is quoted in the notes.[5]

---

[2] Following *Chae Chan Ping* vs. *United States*, U. S. Sup. Ct. 1889, 130 U. S. 581, p. 606, FIELD, J.

[3] *Fong Yue Ting* vs. *United States*, U. S. Sup. Ct. 1893, 149 U. S. 698, pp. 705–707, GRAY, J.

[4] *Nishimura Ekiu* vs. *United States*, U. S. Sup. Ct. 1891, 142 U. S. 651, GRAY, J.

Jones vs. *United States*, U. S. Sup. Ct. 1890, 137 U. S. 202, GRAY, J.

[5] December 19, 1898 (Cong. Record, p. 288, *et. seq.*, and see numerous authorities referred to), after quoting from Judge Gray's opinion, Senator Platt continued in regard to the nationality of the United States as follows:

"The doctrine was denied by Hayne. It was triumphantly asserted by Webster in his great debate in which he first made it plain to the American people that the United States lacked no element of nationality. It was denied in the nullification acts. It was triumphantly asserted by Jackson when he threatened to hang John C. Calhoun, and so cowed the incipient rebellion. It was denied in the ordinances of secession; but it was again gloriously asserted by Abraham Lincoln when he issued his call for 75,000 volunteer troops to preserve the Nation, and the people gloriously responded. It has been written in the books. It has been written in the published utterances of statesmen from the time when the people of the States made our Constitution down to the present time.

"But Mr. President, it has been otherwise written. It has been

§ 32. Navassa Islands Case.

§ 32. **Navassa Islands Case.**— The ownership by the United States of the Navassa and other Guano Islands, over which it exercises governmental control, rests exclusively upon discovery and occupation and acts done in pursuance of, and in conformity with, the acts of Congress passed in regard to Guano Islands.[1]   These acts, in some respects, are

written in the blood which deluged the battlefields of the Civil War for four long years. It has been written with the sword upon the heart of every true American citizen. It has been written on the mourning weeds of the widows who lost husbands, of the mothers who lost children, of the children who lost fathers. It is too late to deny it, Mr. President; it is time to believe in it with a living, saving faith, from which all doubt is eradicated."

§ 32.

[1] TITLE LXXII.

REVISED STATUTES OF UNITED STATES—GUANO ISLANDS.

"Sec. 5570. Claim of United States to islands. Whenever any citizen of the United States discovers a deposit of guano on any island, rock, or key, not within the lawful jurisdiction of any other government, and not occupied by the citizens of any other government, and takes peaceable possession thereof, and occupies the same, such island, rock, or key may, at the discretion of the President, be considered as appertaining to the United States. (18 Aug. 1856, c. 164, s. 1, v. 11, p. 119.)

"Sec. 5571. Notice of discovery, and proofs to be furnished. The discoverer shall, as soon as practicable, give notice, verified by affidavit, to the Department of State, of such discovery, occupation, and possession, describing the island, rock, or key, and the latitude and longitude thereof, as near as may be, and showing that such possession was taken in the name of the United States; and shall furnish satisfactory evidence to the State Department that such island, rock, or key was not, at the time of the discovery thereof, or of the taking possession and occupation thereof by the claimants, in the possession or occupation of any other government or of the citizens of any other government, before the same shall be considered as appertaining to the United States.

"Sec. 5572. Completion of proof in case of death of discoverer. If the discoverer dies before perfecting proof of discovery or fully complying with the provisions of the preceding section, his widow, heir, executor, or administrator, shall be entitled to the benefits of such discovery, upon complying with the provisions of this Title; but nothing herein shall be held to impair any rights of discovery or any assignment by a discoverer heretofore recognized by the United States. (2 April, 1872, c. 81, s. 1, v. 17, p. 48.)

"Sec. 5573. Exclusive privileges of discoverer. The discoverer, or his assigns, being citizens of the United States, may be allowed, at the pleasure of Congress, the exclusive right of occupying such island, rocks, or

apparently repugnant to constitutional prohibitions and limitations; arbitrary rules and regulations, made for the gov-

keys, for the purpose of obtaining guano, and of selling and delivering the same to citizens of the United States, to be used therein, and may be allowed to charge and receive for every ton thereof delivered alongside a vessel, in proper tubs, within reach of ship's tackle, a sum not exceeding eight dollars per ton for the best quality, or four dollars for every ton taken while in its native place of deposit. (18 Aug. 1856, c. 164, s. 2, v. 11, p. 119.)

"Sec. 5574. Restrictions upon exportation. No guano shall be taken from any such island, rock, or key, except for the use of the citizens of the United States or of persons resident therein. The discoverer, or his widow, heir, executor, administrator, or assigns, shall enter into bond, in such penalty and with such sureties as may be required by the President, to deliver the guano to citizens of the United States, for the purpose of being used therein, and to none others, and at the price prescribed, and to provide all necessary facilities for that purpose within a time to be fixed in the bond; and any breach of the provisions thereof shall be deemed a forfeiture of all rights accruing under and by virtue of this Title. This section shall, however, be suspended in relation to all persons who have complied with the provisions of this Title, for five years from and after the fourteenth day of July, eighteen hundred and seventy-two. (28 July, 1866, c. 298, s. 3, v. 14, p. 328. 2 April, 1872, c. 81, s. 1, v. 17, p. 48.)

"Sec. 5575. Regulation of guano trade. The introduction of guano from such islands, rocks, or keys, shall be regulated as in the coasting-trade between different parts of the United States, and the same laws shall govern the vessels concerned therein. (18 Aug. 1856, c. 164, s. 3, v. 11, p. 120.)

"Sec. 5576. Criminal jurisdiction. All acts done, and offenses or crimes committed, on any such island, rock, or key, by persons who may land thereon, or in the waters adjacent thereto, shall be deemed committed on the high seas, on board a merchantship or vessel belonging to the United States; and shall be punished according to the laws of the United States relating to such ships or vessels and offenses on the high seas, which laws for the purpose aforesaid are extended over such islands, rocks, and keys.

"Sec. 5577. Employment of land and naval forces. The President is authorized, at his discretion, to employ the land and naval forces of the United States to protect the rights of the discoverer or of his widow, heir, executor, administrator, or assigns.

"Sec. 5578. Right to abandon islands. Nothing in this Title contained shall be construed as obliging the United States to retain possession of the islands, rocks, or keys, after the guano shall have been removed from the same."

See also the Guano Islands Acts of August 18, 1856, chapter 164; 11 U. S. Stat. at Large, 119; 28 July, 1868, c. 298, § 3, v. 14, p. 328; 2

ernment of the islands, and for commercial intercourse therewith, so far from being uniform with those in force in the States, and other Territories of the union, are applicable only to these islands.[2]

Three men who had committed murder in one of these islands were brought to this country, indicted, and tried in accordance with these statutory provisions; they were found guilty as charged, and sentenced. An appeal was taken to the Supreme Court where able counsel contended that nowhere in the Constitution could be found the power of the United States either to acquire these islands, or to govern them by the arbitrary and unequal rules which had been provided for them and their inhabitants; thus in the most solemn manner conceivable the court was called upon to determine the rights and powers of this government; under such circumstances it was bound by the principle of American and English jurisprudence, which is the birthright of our nation, that the benefit of the doubt must in every instance be given to the accused. If there had been any lack of sovereignty in the Government of the United States, in regard to the external affairs of the country the convictions could not have been sustained; the test was the most severe

April, 1872, c. 81, § 1, v. 17, p. 48, on which the above quoted sections of the Revised Statutes are founded.

[2] The sovereignty and jurisdiction of the United States have attached to the territory embraced in a number of islands, under the act of August 18, 1856, as will appear from the following correspondence on file in the Treasury Department:

TREASURY DEPARTMENT,
FIRST COMPTROLLER'S OFFICE,
Washington, D. C., September 16, 1893.

Hon. S. WIKE,
  Assistant Secretary of the Treasury.

SIR: In compliance with the request contained in your letter of the 15th instant, I have the honor to transmit herewith a list of the guano islands bonded under the act of August 18, 1856, as appears from the bonds on file in this office up to the present date. You will observe that the list is the same as that transmitted with letter from this office, dated December 22, 1885, no additional bonds having been received since that date.

Respectfully yours,
R. S. BOWLER,
Comptroller.

one that could be applied, but the principles of sovereignty and nationality withstood every argument brought against them; the judgments were affirmed on the ground that the United States, as a sovereign power, and possessing every element of nationality and sovereignty, had taken possession of the islands and governed them under and by virtue of the broad right, recognized by international law, of acquiring territory by discovery and occupation; that it possessed and exercised this right in the same manner and to the same extent as it is possessed, and can be exercised, by every other sovereign power, as a general attribute of sovereignty, and one which is given by the law of nations and of nature, and exercisable to the fullest extent recognized by those laws, and that it is not a merely delegated power under the Con-

Inclosed is a list of about 75 guano islands, appertaining to the United States, bonded under the act of August 18, 1856, as appears from bonds on file in the office of the First Comptroller of the Treasury, September 16, 1893, tabulated as follows:

Number of bond.	Date of bond.	Name of Island.	Latitude.	Longitude.

CIRCULAR—GUANO ISLANDS NOT APPERTAINING TO UNITED STATES.
[1894.—Department No. 176.—Bureau of Navigation.]
TREASURY DEPARTMENT,
OFFICE OF THE SECRETARY,
Washington, D. C., November 21, 1894.

To Collectors of Customs and others:

At the request of the Secretary of State, the following-named "guano-islands," specified in lists issued by this Department of guano islands appertaining to the United States, will be considered as stricken from said list, and no longer included among the guano islands bonded by the United States under the Act of August 18, 1856, viz:

Arenas,	Pajoras,	Arenas Key,
Perez,	Chica,	Western Triangles.

S. WIKE, *Assistant Secretary.*

[Extract from Report of Charles E. Magoun, Law Officer, Division of Insular Affairs, War Department, on legal status of islands acquired by the United States, February, 1900, and also see this report for collation of cases on nationality and sovereignty of United States and right to acquire territory.]

stitution, or limited by anything contained in the enumeration of powers granted to the Central Government.[3]

§ 33. **Right of the United States to acquire territory.**— The right of the United States to acquire territory, under its treaty-making power, and also by virtue of the power it possesses as a sovereign nation, will be the subject of a separate chapter devoted to that point in particular; no further reference, therefore, will be made to it in this chapter.[1] The extended reference to the acquisition, and government of the Guano Islands has been made at this point so as to bring prominently into view the regular method by which this attribute of sovereignty has been exercised and also in which it has been acknowledged by every department of the Government.[2]

[3] *Jones* vs. *United States*, U. S. Sup. Ct. 1890, 137 U. S. 202, GRAY, J.

See also *Duncan* vs. *Navassa Phosphate Co.*, U. S. Sup. Ct. 1891, 137 U. S. 647, GRAY, J. (syllabus as follows):

"The right conferred by the United States, under the Guano Islands Act of August 18th, 1856, c. 164, (Rev. Stat. tit. 72,) upon the discoverer of a deposit of guano and his assigns, to occupy, at the pleasure of Congress, for the purpose of removing the guano, an island determined by the President to appertain to the United States, is not such an estate in land as to be subject to dower, notwithstanding the act of April 2, 1872, c. 81, (Rev. Stat. sec. 5572,) extending the provisions of the act of 1856 'to the widow, heirs, executors or administrators of such discoverer' if he dies before fully complying with its provisions."

§ 33.

[1] Chap. II., and see especially for *Insular Cases*, §§ 61*a*, *et seq.* See also § 101, chapter III.

[2] On May 27, 1901, the Supreme Court decided *De Lima* vs. *Bidwell*,

Downes vs. *Bidwell*, and other *Insular Cases*, which will be reported in volume 182, United States Reports, in which the right of the United States to acquire and govern territory is discussed at length. Those cases are referred to more at length in §§ 61*a*,–61*h*, pp. 117, *et seq.*, and at other points in this volume there referred to; while the members of the Court differed among themselves as to the status of territory when acquired, and as to the relations of acquired possessions and the inhabitants thereof to States and citizens of the United States, the Court was unanimous as to the right of acquisition and that the United States is a sovereign nation, and possessed of every attribute of nationality and sovereignty. The former decisions of the Supreme Court as to the extent of congressional power, and of constitutional limitations thereon, over, and in regard to, territories which were cited in the arguments before, and opinions of the Court in the *Insular Cases* are collated in the INSULAR CASES APPENDIX at end of volume.

§ 34. General consensus of opinion in support of Nationality of United States.—A long line of other expressions of opinion from Alexander Hamilton to date could be quoted, but the precedents referred to, together with the decisions and opinions collated in the subsequent chapters, and referred to in the footnotes, should certainly be accepted as fully answering every question which has ever been raised as to the completeness of the sovereignty and nationality of the United States. It is almost inexplicable why any person or party should desire to limit those powers of the Federal Government, which are exercised exclusively in regard to matters not only wholly within its domain, but which are also wholly beyond the power or control of any State; although no party, person, state or faction would be benefited by imposing such limitations, yet from the earliest period of our national history there has always been a party which for unexplained and unaccountable reasons has taken for its watchword the curtailment of national power, not only as to those matters which relate to the States, and in which the power of the State increases relatively as the power of the Central Government diminishes, but also as to matters exclusively within the domain of the National Government and which require for their proper administration the fullest measure of nationality, sovereignty and power.

§ 35. Gradual development of theory of Nationality.—The theory of complete nationality and sovereignty of the United States has been gradually developed; its evolution commences with the early decisions of Chief Justice Marshall, notably in the *Florida* or *Canter* case[1] which will be alluded to in another chapter, in which he said that the right to acquire territory was derived from the war or treaty-making power under constitutional delegation, or as an attribute of sovereignty existing in the government; he declared, however, that it was unnecessary at that time, to decide under which head to classify it; its complete development is shown in the decision of Mr. Justice Gray in the *Navassa Island* case,[2] in which he unhesitatingly and broadly

§ 35.
[1] *American Insurance Co. vs. Canter,* U. S. Sup. Ct. 1828, 1 Peters, 511, MARSHALL, Ch. J., *post.*

[2] *Jones vs. United States,* U. S.

asserted that the right of acquisition of territory was beyond
doubt an attribute of the United States Government, not
under constitutionally delegated power, but an attribute
vested in it under the law of nations, in the same manner and
to the same extent as the power is possessed by the governments of other sovereign nations.

§ 36. **Limitations by fundamental principles.**[1]—Side by
side with the theory of complete nationality there has also
developed, as was necessary and proper, the theory that these

Sup. Ct. 1890, 137 U. S. 202,
GRAY, J., and see § 32 and notes
thereunder, *ante.*

§ 36.

[1] The cases referring to the limitation of governmental powers by
the fundamental principles on
which this government is based will
be found in the collation of cases
referred to in the arguments before,
and opinions of the Supreme Court
in the INSULAR CASES APPENDIX
at end of this volume, including:

Bank of Columbia vs. *Okely,* U. S.
Sup. Ct. 1819, 4 Wheaton, 235,
JOHNSON, J.;

Chicago, etc., Ry. Co. vs. *Tompkins,* U. S. Sup. Ct. 1900, 176 U. S.
167, BREWER, J.;

Cummings vs. *Missouri,* U. S. Sup.
Ct.1866, 4 Wall. 277, FIELD, J.;

Dartmouth College vs. *Woodward,* U. S. Sup. Ct.1819,4 Wheaton,
518, MARSHALL, Ch. J.;

Kemmler, In re, U. S. Sup. Ct.
1890, 136 U. S. 436, FULLER, Ch. J.;

Legal Tender Cases, (1) U. S. Sup.
Ct. 1869, 8 Wall. 603, CHASE, Ch. J.;
(2) 1870, 12 Wall. 457, STRONG, J;
(3) 1884, 110 U. S. 421, GRAY, J.;

Loan Association vs. *Topeka,*
U. S. Sup. Ct. 1874, 20 Wall. 655,
MILLER, J.;

Lord Bishop of Natal, Privy
Council 1864, 3 Moore Priv. Coun.
N. S. 115, WESTBURY, Lord Chan.;

Marbury vs. *Madison,* U. S. Sup.

Ct. 1803, 1 Cranch, 137, MAR-
SHALL, Ch. J.;

Maxwell vs. *Dow,* U. S. Sup. Ct.
1900, 176 U. S. 581, PECKHAM, J.;

Mormon Church Case, U. S. Sup.
Ct. 1890, 136 U. S. 1, BRADLEY, J.;

Murphy vs. *Ramsey,* U. S. Sup.
Ct. 1885, 114 U. S. 15, MAT-
THEWS, J.;

Sharpless vs. *The Mayor, &c.,* 21
Penn. St. Rep. 147, Sup. Ct. Pa.,
1853, BLACK, J.;

Slaughterhouse Cases, U. S. Sup.
Ct. 1872, 16 Wall. 36, MILLER, J.;

Weimar vs. *Bunbury,* Sup. Ct.
Mich.1874,30 Mich. 201, COOLEY, J.;

Yick Wo vs. *Hopkins,* U. S. Sup.
Ct. 1886, 118 U. S. 356, MAT-
THEWS, J.; and see p. 369, where
the court says, in holding one of
the anti-Chinese ordinances of San
Francisco as void under the Fourteenth Amendment, "But the fundamental rights to life, liberty and
the pursuit of happiness, considered as individual possessions, are
secured by those maxims of constitutional law which are the monuments showing the victorious progress of the race in securing to men
the blessings of civilization under
the reign of just and equal laws;
so that in the famous language of
the Massachusetts Bill of Rights,
the government of the commonwealth 'may be a government of
laws and not of men.'"

62

natural and inherent attributes of sovereignty possessed by the Government of the United States in its National character, are limited in their exercise, not by constitutional provisions, but by those fundamental principles upon which the Government of the United States, and of its people, is based.

This joint development of the two theories is not only perfectly consistent, but one necessarily grows and expands with the other, and in such development each furnishes to the other mutual support and strength.

§ 37. **Views of Ex-President Harrison.***—True it is that Ex-President Harrison, in his recent utterances at Ann Arbor and in the *North American Review*,[1] declares that the theory of limitations by fundamental principles is not in accord with American constitutional history; learned as he is, however, in constitutional and international law, for unquestionably Mr. Harrison is one of our leading authorities upon those great branches of jurisprudence, as was evidenced by his remarkable, and in many respects successful, argument before the Venezuelan arbitration tribunal, he evidently overlooks the fact that the doctrine of limitation by fundamental principles has been clearly enunciated and defined by the Supreme Court; in fact that court has made it a part of the doctrine of acquisition of, and sovereignty over, the territories, which Mr. Harrison himself admits has not only been thoroughly, but properly, established as part of the constitutional law of this country. He declares that our forefathers were not content with general and unwritten limitations, but forced into the Constitution written limitations as to the exercise of sovereignty by the ruling powers.[2] In

* These sections were written prior to the death of Mr. Harrison.

§ 37.

[1] "The Status of Annexed Territory and of its Free Civilized Inhabitants" by Benjamin Harrison, formerly President of the United States, North American Review, January, 1901, p. 110.

[2] "For themselves, our fathers, were not content with an assurance of these great rights that rested wholly upon the sense of justice and benevolence of the Congress. The man whose protection from wrong rests wholly upon the benevolence of another man or of a Congress, is a slave—a man without rights. Our fathers took security of the governing departments they organized; and that, notwithstanding the fact that the choice of all public officers rested with the people. When a man

this, however, so far as he refers to government of territories, he is clearly wrong ; the decision of the Supreme Court shows that fundamental, rather than constitutional, limitations are frequently the only check upon congressional action.

Undoubtedly, as the Supreme Court asserted in *Murphy* vs. *Ramsay*,[3] complete and unlimited power is repugnant to our institutions ; but it also declared in the *Mormon Church* case,[4] that those limitations in many instances are found, not in the Constitution, but in the fundamental principles upon which our government is established ; these two judicial declarations have been repeatedly followed in later decisions of the Supreme, and other courts, of the United States, reference to some of which have been collated in the next chapter.

§ 38. **Unsoundness of Mr. Harrison's views.**—Mr. Harrison takes a very gloomy view of the results of the doctrine of fundamental principles ; in fact, he refers to it somewhat sarcastically as one of the limitations, not by principles of government, but by *benevolence ;* he also seems to feel that the doctrine if accepted, necessarily implies that the only limitations which can be placed upon congressional action are such as may appeal to Congress in its existing mood at the time of the legislation.[1]

But if this doctrine of limitation is to be applied to congressional action in regard to those matters in which the

strictly limits the powers of an agent of his own choice, and exacts a bond from him, to secure his faithfulness, he does not occupy strong ground when he insists that another person, who had no part in this selection, shall give the agent full powers without a bond.

" If there is anything that is characteristic in American Constitutions, state and national, it is the plan of limiting the powers of all public officers and agencies. You shall do this; you may do this; you shall not do this—is the form that the schedule of powers always takes. This grew out of our experience as English colonies.

A government of unlimited legislative or executive powers is an un-American government. And, for one, I do not like to believe that the framers of the National Constitution and of our first State Constitutions were careful only for their own liberties."

[3] *Murphy* vs. *Ramsay*, U. S. Sup. Ct. 1885, 114 U. S. 15, MATTHEWS, J.

[4] *Mormon Church* vs. *United States*, U. S. Sup. Ct. 1890, 136 U. S. 1, BRADLEY, J., And see extract from opinion in § 60, chapter II, *post.*

§ **38.**

[1] This also applies to the article of ex-Senator Edmunds, No. Am. Rev. Aug., 1901.

Federal Government is supreme and national, there is no more danger of proper bounds being exceeded than has ever existed in the past; on this point we have the authority of Chief Justice Marshall and Mr. Justice Story that the doctrine of limitations *ab inconvenienti*, or the limitation of a general power for fear that the right to exercise it may lead to abuse, will not be considered.[2] The principles of broad construction of the Constitution as to the delegated powers conveyed in general terms must apply with equal, if not stronger force, to those powers which Congress possesses in its capacity as the single mouth-piece of, and the only medium through which, the people of the United States can speak and act as to those matters which they possess and control as a national unit.

§ 39. **Fundamental principles and the first ten amendments.**—The theory of fundamental principles had its inception as early as the framing of the Constitution ; to many the adoption of the first ten amendments, commonly known as the Bill of Rights, was wholly unnecessary ; there were members of the Constitutional Convention who considered that the enumeration of certain fundamental rights would be dangerous as it might result in the exclusion, and to the derogation, of other rights equally fundamental, but which might possibly be omitted in the enumeration. The first ten amendments, however, were added in order to satisfy the wishes of those who felt that the personal rights of freedom and liberty therein enumerated should be specifically preserved to the people.

It is doubtful, however, if any one in this country considers that his personal rights have any greater protection by reason of the adoption of those amendments, than though they had remained as a part of the fundamental principles, upon which the whole government was based, and unexpressed except as they are embodied in the law of the land and as they have always been recognized by the people and by the courts.

[2] "A power, given in general terms, is not to be restricted to particular cases merely because it may be susceptible of abuse, and if abused may lead to mischievous consequences." 1 Story's Comm. on the Const. § 425, 5th ed. p. 324.

The history of these amendments, as it is contained in Story's Commentaries, will be found in the footnote to this section.[1] *

*For the Constitution and Amendments in full see pp. 519, et seq., post.

§ 39.

[1] " Another class of objections urged against the Constitution was founded upon its deficiencies and omissions. It cannot be denied that some of the objections on this head were well taken, and that there was a fitness in incorporating some provision on the subject into the fundamental articles of a free government. There were others, again, which might fairly enough be left to the legislative discretion and to the natural influences of the popular voice in a republican form of government. There were others, again, so doubtful, both in principle and policy, that they might properly be excluded from any system aiming at permanence in its securities as well as its foundations.

" Among the defects which were enumerated, none attracted more attention, or were urged with more zeal, than the want of a distinct bill of rights which should recognize the fundamental principles of a free republican government, and the right of the people to the enjoyment of life, liberty, property, and the pursuit of happiness. It was contended that it was indispensable that express provision should be made for the trial by jury in civil cases, and in criminal cases upon a presentment by a grand jury only; and that all criminal trials should be public, and the party be confronted with the witnesses against him; that freedom of speech and freedom of the press should be secured; that there should be no national religion, and the rights of conscience should be inviolable; that excessive bail should not be required, nor cruel and unusual punishments inflicted; that the people should have a right to bear arms; that persons conscientiously scrupulous should not be compelled to bear arms; that every person should be entitled of right to petition for the redress of grievances; that search-warrants should not be granted without oath, nor general warrants at all; that soldiers should not be enlisted, except for a short, limited term, and not be quartered in time of peace upon private houses without the consent of the owners; that mutiny bills should continue in force for two years only; that causes once tried by a jury should not be re-examinable upon appeal, otherwise than according to the course of the common law; and that the powers not expressly delegated to the general government should be declared to be reserved to the States. In all these particulars the Constitution was obviously defective; and yet, it was contended, they were vital to the public security.

" Besides these, there were other defects relied on, such as the want of a suitable provision for a rotation in office, to prevent persons enjoying it for life; the want of an executive council for the President; the want of a provision limiting the duration of standing armies; the want of a clause securing to the people the enjoyment of the common law; the want of security for proper elections of public officers; the want of a pro-

§ 40. **Congress compared, as to powers in national matters, with Parliament of Great Britain.**—To the author, it seems as though Congress, being the only medium of action

hibition of members of Congress holding any public offices, and of judges holding any other offices; and finally, the want of drawing a clear and direct line between the powers to be exercised by Congress and by the States.

"Many of these objections found their way into the amendments, which, simultaneously with the ratification, were adopted in many of the State conventions. With the view of carrying into effect popular will, and also of disarming the opponents of the Constitution of all reasonable grounds of complaint, Congress, at its very first session, took into consideration the amendments so proposed; and by a succession of supplementary articles provided, in substance, a bill of rights and secured by constitutional declarations most of the other important objects thus suggested. These articles (in all twelve) were submitted by Congress to the States for their ratification, and ten of them were finally ratified by the requisite number of States, and thus became incorporated into the Constitution. It is a curious fact, however, that, although the necessity of these amendments had been urged by the enemies of the Constitution and denied by its friends, they encountered scarcely any other opposition in the state legislatures than what was given by the very party which had raised the objections. The friends of the Constitution generally supported them upon the ground of a large public policy, to quiet jealousies and to disarm resentments.

"It is perhaps due to the latter to state that they believed that some of the objections to the Constitution existed only in imagination, and that others derived their sole support from an erroneous construction of that instrument. In respect to a bill of rights, it was stated that several of the State constitutions contained none in form, and yet were not on that account thought objectionable. That it was not true that the Constitution of the United States did not, in the true sense of the terms, contain a bill of rights. It was emphatically found in those clauses which respected political rights, the guaranty of republican forms of government, the trial of crimes by jury, the definition of treason, the prohibition against bills of attainder and *ex post facto* laws and titles of nobility, the trial by impeachment, and the privilege of the writ of *habeas corpus*. That a general bill of rights would be improper in a Constitution of limited powers like that of the United States, and might even be dangerous, as by containing exceptions from powers not granted it might give rise to implications of constructive power. That in a government like ours, founded by the people and managed by the people, and especially in one of limited authority, there was no necessity of any bill of rights; for all powers not granted were reserved, and even those granted might at will be resumed or altered by the people. That a bill of rights might be fit in a monarchy, where there were struggles between the crown and the people about prerogatives and privileges.

67

in those respects, must, as to national matters committed to it, possess powers co-ordinate with those of the Parliament of Great Britain, and that the possession of such powers cannot in any way tend to produce the dangerous results predicted by Mr. Harrison.

It is England's boast that the Anglo-Saxon heritage of personal freedom is nowhere so thoroughly protected as it is in Great Britain; there are, however, no written limitations upon Parliamentary action of any kind—in fact, Parliament, being the mouthpiece of the people, is necessarily supreme. The notes to section 11 of this chapter show that the sovereignty of the British Constitution is lodged, as declared by Blackstone, in Parliament; Professor Chase's note on this statement in his American edition of Blackstone's Commentaries, which is appended to this section, shows the difference between an act of Congress and an act of Parliament as to matters which are *covered* by the Constitution;[1]

But here the government is the government of the people; all its officers are their officers, and they can exercise no right or powers but such as the people commit to them. In such a case the silence of the Constitution argues nothing. The trial by jury, the freedom of the press, and the liberty of conscience are not taken away, because they are not secured. They remain with the people among the mass of ungranted powers, or find an appropriate place in the laws and institutions of each particular State.

"Notwithstanding the force of these suggestions, candor will compel us to admit that, as certain fundamental rights were secured by the Constitution, there seemed to be an equal propriety in securing in like manner others of equal value and importance. The trial by jury in criminal cases was secured; but this clause admitted of more clear definition and of auxiliary provisions. The trial by jury in civil cases at common law was as dear to the people, and afforded at least an equal protection to persons and property. The same remark may be made of several other provisions included in the amendments. But these will more properly fall under consideration in our commentary upon that portion of the Constitution. The promptitude, zeal and liberality with which the friends of the Constitution supported these amendments evince the good faith and sincerity of their opinions, and increase our reverence for their labors, as well as our sense of their wisdom and patriotism." 1 Story's Com. on the Cons. of the U. S. 5th ed. §§ 300 –305, pp. 217–220.

See also Thorpe's Constitutional History of the United States, vol. 2, chap. VI, p. 199, *et seq.*

§ 40.

[1] "There is a fundamental difference between the power and authority of the legislative branch of the Government in England and in the United States. The English Par-

the same difference cannot exist, however, as to matters which are lodged generally in the National Government or which it possesses not by delegation but as the attributes of sovereignty of a national government. Blackstone, however, and other writers upon the fundamental law of England, trace the British Constitution, unwritten as it is, from the earliest sources, showing that personal liberty and personal rights are amply protected from legislative aggression, and that no person can be deprived of them in any manner whatsoever. Undoubtedly the Supreme Court of the United States can be entrusted with the protection of personal rights of Americans, and of the inhabitants of any territory under the jurisdiction of the United States, to the same extent that the English courts can be trusted with the similar protection of citizens and subjects of Great Britain.

§ 41. **Simultaneous development of nationality and limitations by fundamental principles of natural and healthy growth.**—The simultaneous development of the two theories of complete nationality and sovereignty, and of the limitation of congressional action in regard to national matters by

liament is not limited, as regards the scope and extent and subject-matter of legislation, by a written constitution defining and restricting its powers, and its enactments therefore constitute the supreme law of the land and are absolutely binding upon the courts, which have no option but to appropriately enforce them. It is for this reason that Parliament is sometimes said to be "omnipotent." What is spoken of as the "English Constitution" embraces the body or system of laws, rules, principles and established usages, upon which is based the organization of the Government, the relation of its various departments or branches to each other, and the nature of their functions, and in accordance with which the administration of the Government is regularly conducted. But this Constitution, based as it is upon previous acts of Parliament, upon custom and tradition, is subject to change and modification by other acts of Parliament, though it is undoubtedly true, that it has, by force of precedent, and by the natural effect of ordinary usage upon the habits and ideas of people, great controlling and restrictive power upon the course of legislation. But in the United States, legislation is uniformly controlled by written constitutions adopted by the people in their sovereign capacity. The United States Constitution limits and defines the powers of Congress, and is also binding upon the legislatures of the several States, so that their enactments cannot violate its provisions. The legislation of the States is also further controlled by the special Constitution which each has adopted. To the courts is com-

fundamental principles, has up to the present time inured to the advantage and mutual benefit alike of the powers that govern, and of the people who are governed; this same development will undoubtedly continue in the spirit of Anglo-Saxon liberty without danger to the personál rights of individuals, or the enactment of any such grotesque legislation as is feared by the ex-President; in this respect it must be remembered that the combined action of the three departments of the American Government is always subject to the control of the people by the frequent recurrence of elections; the reversal or repeal of congressional action always follows when it appears that the legislation enacted is not in accord with the spirit of liberty as it is understood by the people, who must eventually be the sole judges as to whether or not the powers of sovereignty lodged in the National Government, great as they are, are being properly exercised. Not until the spirit of the people changes can Congress act with the spirit of despotism. If, however, the minds of the American people can ever become so perverted as to favor despotism in any form, that degeneracy will be reflected in Congress, and no constitutional provisions, or fundamental principles of liberty, will suffice to prevent the enactment of legislation which will accord with the popular sentiment as to those matters which are wholly within the domain of the National Government, and therefore under the control of the people themselves.

No such danger exists to-day; let us hope that it never will exist.

mitted the power and duty of determining whether particular enactments are in conformity with Constitutional provisions; and if it is adjudged that they are not, such laws are pronounced null and void, either in whole or in part (*Civil Rights* cases, 109 U. S. 3; *Baldwin* vs. *Franks*, 120 U. S. 678; *Duryee* vs. *Mayor of N. Y.* 96 N. Y. 477). This is not, however, done by the courts of their own motion, but only in the course of decision of actually litigated causes in which the Constitutionality of the statute is essentially involved. But all statutes not in conflict with the provisions of the Constitution of the State or of the United States are as supreme and absolute, within their appropriate sphere, as the acts of the English Parliament." Chase's Blackstone (3d ed.), p. 15, note.

CHAPTER II.

THE NATIONALITY AND SOVEREIGNTY OF THE UNITED STATES AS EVIDENCED BY ACQUISITION OF TERRITORY.

71

§ 42. **Development of United States from a Confederation into a Nation ; recognition of Sovereignty.**—We have already seen, in the last chapter, that the Government of the United States has developed from the mere central government of a confederation into a great national government possessing and exercising, as to all national matters, every sovereign power which any other sovereign nation of the world possesses and exercises ; also that this nationality and sovereignty has been recognized by our own people and our own courts.   It is purposed in this and the succeeding chapter to show that these attributes of sovereignty and nationalty have been exercised in adding to our domain vast tracts of territory, over which the Government of the United States has extended in its national and sovereign capacities, and also that the nationality and sovereignty of the United States have been continuously recognized by every other sovereign nation.

§ 43. **Right of sovereign powers to acquire territory.**— The right of sovereign powers to cede territory to, and to acquire territory from, other sovereign powers, with the accompanying transfer of sovereignty thereover, is one of the elementary principles of international law.   It is essential, however, that the contracting powers should be fully sovereign in order to act either as transferrer or transferee.[1]

§ 43.

[1] TRANSFER OF TERRITORY; VIEWS OF PUBLICISTS.

PROFESSOR POMEROY.

" It may be laid down as an universal doctrine of the international law, that every sovereign independent state may transfer or acquire territorial or other possessions.   I say this is a doctrine of the international law, which does not concern itself with the internal organization of countries, and the powers committed to governments, or to any departments thereof.   Whether, therefore, any particular nation may transfer its territory or acquire territory from another is a question to be answered by examining the constitution of that country, the functions and capacties conferred upon its rulers.   This belongs entirely to public and not to international law.   The same is true of the subordinate inquiry, what department of a government may effect the transfer or receive the acquisition?   Whether the king or other executive, the legislature, or the people assenting and ratifying the acts of their governmental agents. We are not called upon to discuss this subject; and although Vattel devotes a large space in his treatise to its consideration, he has therein

A government that is not fully sovereign has no right to extend its territorial possessions, and conversely one that

plainly departed from the legitimate scope of a writer upon international law.

"Sec. 116. To illustrate these statements: Whether the United States may acquire new territory by gift, purchase, or cession from another country, must be determined by the Constitution, and the powers of the general government erected by that organic law. The Constitution itself is silent upon this particular topic; yet the power has been exercised several times: in the purchase of Louisiana and of Florida, the annexation of Texas, and the cession of California and New Mexico. The people have acquiesced, although Jefferson thought it needed a constitutional amendment to ratify his act in acquiring Louisiana. But whether the United States may transfer any of its territory, so as to cede away its paramount dominion therein, is an entirely different question, which has never, thus far in our history, been raised or discussed.

"Sec. 117. By Grotius and the earlier writers upon public law kingdoms were divided into patrimonial or proprietary and usufructuary. The patrimonial, as it were, belonged to the monarch as a kind of private domain which he might alienate or dispose of at will. The usufructuary included all others, in which the rulers were looked upon as the representatives of a body politic behind them, and not as themselves constituting the state. Whatever might have been true in earlier times, it is certain that there is no such patrimonial kingdom or nation at the present day in Europe, and of course not in America.

"The general proposition of the international law, therefore, is, that by its proper, constituted authorities, whatever they may be,—king, president, legislature, people,—a nation may alienate to, or acquire from, another nation, territory or other things which are the objects of property. 'It is, moreover, of the last importance to remember that a nation which allows its ruler, either in his own person or through his minister, to enter into negotiations respecting the alienation of property with other nations, must be held to have consented to the act of the ruler; unless, indeed, it can be clearly proved that the other contracting party was aware at the time that the ruler in so doing was transgressing the fundamental laws of his state.'" Pomeroy's International Law, edited by Theodore S. Woolsey, pp. 132–134.

GENERAL HALLECK'S VIEWS.

"Sec. 6. Right of a State to own property. A state being regarded in public law as a body politic, or distinct moral being, naturally sovereign and independent, it is considered as capable of the same rights, duties and obligations, with respect to other States, as individuals with respect to other individuals. Among the most important of these natural rights is that of acquiring, possessing, and enjoying property. And this right applies not only to property of the State, as exclusive of other States, but to such property as exclusive of individuals. But international law generally considers only the former kind of property, or in-

73

cannot extend them does not possess the full measure of sovereignty. It is subject, by some limitation, to some other

ternational domain. When, however, we consider the rights of conquest and cession, the rights of maritime capture and of capture on land, it becomes necessary to consider the interior or municipal rights of property in the State, and to distinguish between the absolute and paramount rights of the State, in respect to property considered in its interior relations under municipal laws, rather than its exterior relations under international laws. As a general rule, the property of a State, of whatsoever description, is marked by the same characteristics relatively to other States, as the property of individuals, relatively to other individuals ; that is to say, ' it is exclusive of foreign interference, and susceptible of free disposition.'

"Sec. 7. Modes of acquisition. A State may acquire property or domain in various ways : its title may be acquired originally by mere occupancy and confirmed by the presumption arising from the lapse of time ; or by discovery and lawful possession ; or by conquest, confirmed by treaty or tacit consent ; or by grants, cession, purchase, or exchange; in fine, by any of the recognized modes by which private property is acquired by individuals. It is not our object to enter into any general discussion of these several modes of acquisition, any further than may be necessary to distinguish the character of certain rights of property which are the peculiar objects of international jurisprudence.

"Sec. 8. Right of disposition of territory. A sovereign State has the same absolute right to dispose of its territorial or other public property as it has to acquire such property, but it depends upon its own municipal constitution and laws how, and by what department of its government, the disposition shall be made. This is sometimes a question of peculiar interest to foreign States, who may acquire such property by purchase, exchange, cession, conquest, and treaties of confirmation and especially where such acquisitions are made from States continually subject to revolutions and fluctuations in the character of its government and in the powers of its rulers. The act of a government *de facto*, a government which is submitted by the great body of the people, and recognized by other States, is binding as the act of the State ; and it is not necessary for others to examine into the origin, nature, and limits of that authority. If it is an authority *de facto*, and *sufficient* for the purpose, others will not inquire how that authority was obtained.

"Sec. 9. Authority to make a valid transfer. Nevertheless, in order to make such transfer valid, the authority, whether *de facto* or *de jure*, must be competent to bind the State. Hence the necessity of examining into and ascertaining the powers of the rulers, as the municipal constitutions of different States throw many difficulties in the way of alienations of their public property, and particularly of their territory. Especially, in modern times, the consent of the governed, express or implied, is necessary, before the transfer of their allegiance can regularly take place. But formerly, what Grotius calls *patrimonial kingdoms* were considered in the light of absolute property of particular families, who,

power, which must be superior to it in that respect; when any government is in that condition owing to any cause what-

having received the blind submission of their subjects, sold and bartered them away, like any other property which they possessed. And such transfers of sovereignty included, not only the right of *eminent domain* and the absolute property of the sovereign or State, but all private lands, and the property, and services of the subjects, who were transferred with the soil, in the same manner as a slaveholder may transfer his slaves and all they possess, together with the title to his plantation.

"Sec. 10. Patrimonial kingdoms. There are numerous examples of such treaties of sale. In 1301, Theodoric, Landgrave of Thuringia, sold the Marquisate of Lusatia to Burchard, Archbishop of Magdeburg, for 600 marks of silver—'*in super cum ministerialibus vassalis et mancipiis, et aliis hominibus, cujuscumque conditionis in jam dicta terra commorantibus,*' etc. In the same manner, in 1311, Dantzic, Derschovia and Swiecae were sold by the Margrave of Brandenburg to the Grand Master of the Teutonic Order, for 10,000 marks. In 1333, the city and territory of Mechlin, was transferred for one hundred thousand reals of gold, by a treaty of sale between its Sovereign and the Earl of Flanders, the fealty being reserved. About the same time the city and county of Lucques were sold by John of Luxemburg to Philip of Valois, for 180,000 florins; and a few years after, the sovereignty of Frankenstein was sold by the Duke of Silesia, for 2,000 marks, to the King of Bohemia. The sovereignty which the Popes so long held over Avignon was purchased by Clement VI., for 80,000 florins, from Jane, Queen of Naples and Countess of Provence. Alaska was purchased from Russia by the United States, by treaty of March 13, 1867.

"Sec. 11. Inhabitants of such kingdoms. The practice also extended to the mortgaging of sovereignties, and the sales of reversionary interests in kingdoms. Thus, Robert, Duke of Normandy, in order to raise money to engage in the first crusade, mortgaged his duchy for 666 lbs. weight of silver to his brother William, and transferred the possession before his departure for the Holy Land. In 1479, Louis XI. bought the right of the house of Penthièvre, the next male heir in reversion, to Brittany. And fifteen years later Charles VIII. purchased, for an annual pension of 4,300 ducats, an estate of 5,000 in lands in France or Italy, and the disposition of the Morea (when conquered), of Paleologus, the nephew of Constantine, the last Christian Emperor, his right to the whole Empire of Constantinople. The act of sale being drawn up by two notaries, and ratified, Charles assumed the robes, and ornaments of the imperial dignity, and made no scruples in claiming the imperial rights vested in him by virtue of this purchase.

"Sec. 12. Modern Transfers. It was also the custom to dispose of sovereignties and dominions by deeds of gift, and by bequests. The Emperor Lewis V. created the dauphin Humbert *king*, with the full privilege of disposing of his sovereignty at will, during life, or at his death. In 1343, Humbert ceded his dominions to Philip of Valois, by solemn deed of gift. By similar deeds, and upon a like principle, the

ever, it must acknowledge that it lacks complete sovereignty,

Emperor Henry VI. conferred upon Richard I. the kingdom of Arles, and the Emperor Baldwin gave to the Duke of Burgundy the kingdom of Thessalonia. By bequests, not only were whole sovereignties dis posed of, but the orders of succession were frequently changed. Thus Charles II., King of Sicily and Count of Provence, changed by will the order of succession to the county, and the claims of Charles VIII. to the throne of Naples were founded upon the adoption of Louis of Anjou, by Jane, Queen of Naples, 1380, which was evidenced to all Europe by a solemn and public deed. In 1544 the English Parliament declared the succession to the Crown, but omitted to make any arrangement in the case of failure of issue of the children of Henry VIII. The King, *by his will*, named the descendants of his sister Mary, Duchess of Suffolk, as heirs in case of such failure." Halleck's International Law, third London edition, vol. 1, 1893, pp. 153—157.

PROFESSOR LAWRENCE'S VIEWS ON TITLE BY CESSION.

" Among the titles it is possible to obtain through the transfer of territories already in the possession of civilized states, the most important is title by cession.

" Cession is the formal handing over by agreement of territorial possessions from one state to another. The agreement is embodied in a treaty which usually contains stipulations as to the transfer along with the ceded district of a proportionate share of the public debt of the ceding state. Moreover, questions connected with the rights of citizenship of its inhabitants and rights over the state domains within it are usually settled in the treaty; but no general rule can be laid down as to these matters. The stipulations respecting them will vary with the circumstances of each case.

"Since cession is the usual method whereby changes are effected in the distribution of territory among states which are subjects of International Law, it follows that cessions may take place in consequence of transactions of various kinds. Of these we will consider first *Sale*. It is not very frequent; but cases of it are to be found even in modern times, as when in 1867 the United States purchased Russian America for $7,200,000. The next ground of cession is *Gift*. Free gifts of territory are not altogether unknown, though as a rule the intercourse of states is not conducted on principles of lavish generosity. Yet a government that desired for special purposes to retain another's good-will has been known to make a gift of territory by treaty of cession. Thus in 1762, France ceded to Spain the colony of Louisiana, in order to indemnify her for the loss of Florida, which had been transferred to England by the Treaty of Paris; and in 1850 Great Britain ceded to the United States a portion of the Horseshoe Reef in Lake Erie, in order that the government of Washington might erect a lighthouse thereon. But in matters of transfer of territory the gift is far more often forced than free. A state beaten in a war is sometimes obliged to make over a province or a colony to the victor as one of the conditions of peace. In-

and that it cannot rank among the great and independent powers of the world.[2]

Such is the condition of every State of this Union. No one of them is completely sovereign, because the people have either delegated certain elements of sovereignty to the Central Government, viewing it from a federal standpoint, or viewing it from a national standpoint, they have vested the Central Government with certain elements of sovereignty to the exclusion of the States. One of the elements of sovereignty which the States do not possess is this right of acquisition of additional territory. No one of them can extend its borders without the consent of the Central Government.[3]

Not having surrendered any of its fully sovereign powers, as to the matters wholly within its own domain, the United States therefore possesses, in common with every other sovereign power, this right of acquisition of territory which, in the light of international law as we are now viewing it, includes the right to acquire, and to exercise sovereignty

---

deed, most cessions are the results of warfare and come under the head of forced gifts. One of the most recent instances is to be found in the cession of Alsace and part of Lorraine by France to Germany. This was done by the Treaty of Frankfort of 1871, and was one of the results of the defeat and downfall of France in the war of that and the preceding year. The last ground of cession we will mention is *Exchange.* It was common enough in times when territories were cut and carved in order to make provision for the scions of ruling families, but the growth of the principle that populations should have a voice in the settlement of their political destiny has made it comparatively rare. We can, however, find one instance in recent European history. By the Treaty of Berlin of 1878 Roumania ceded to Russia that portion of Bessarabia given to it at Russia's expense in the Treaty of Paris of 1856, and received in exchange the Dobroutcha, which was taken from Turkey." Lawrence's Principles of International Law, section 97, pp. 156-157.

See also Woolsey's Int. Law, § 53, p. 62; Hall's Int. Law, § 7, p. 45; Glenn's Int. Law, § 37, p. 49; Phillimore's Int. Law, vol. 1, §§ 268-270, and 275; Calvo's Int. Law, vol. 1, §§ 291-299.

[2] "*Semi-Sovereign States* do not possess all the essential rights of sovereignty, and therefore, can be regarded as subjects of international law only indirectly, or at least in a subordinate degree." Halleck's Int. Law (Baker's 3d English Edition), § 17, p. 74, Vol. I.

See Hall's Int. Law, p. 31; Woolsey's Int. Law, p. 35; Glenn's Int. Law, § 9, p. 17, and see citations collected in footnote, Glenn, p. 17.

[3] U. S. Const. Art. I., § 10 and see § 19 of this volume, *ante.*

over, whatever territory it may desire and can obtain by any method recognized by international law, and also to extend such sovereignty over all of the inhabitants thereof.[4]

§ 44. **Methods of acquisition of Territory.**—There are various ways in which a sovereign power may increase its territory and extend its sovereignty. Those recognized by international law (besides accretion by the acts of the elements) are as follows:[1]

I. DISCOVERY AND OCCUPATION.—The original title to all of North and South America is based upon this method of acquisition. The United States added the Oregon district to its domain by the discovery of the mouth of the Columbia River by Captain Gray, the expedition of Lewis and Clarke, and the Astoria settlement. The title of the United States to the Guano and Midway Islands also rests upon discovery and occupation.

II. CONQUEST.—The right of the victorious nation to retain the ownership of invaded and conquered territory is still recognized by international law. Few recent titles rest exclusively upon conquest, however, as it has practically become a universal custom to settle ownership of territory and boundary lines after every war by a treaty; the conquering power generally, and properly, insists upon an unequivocal cession of the territory which it accepts as indemnity, or retains as conquered, so as to avoid all subsequent questions of ownership and sovereignty. For this reason it is sometimes difficult to determine whether territory so acquired is conquered or ceded; this applies to our Mexican territory acquired in 1848, as well as to our latest acquisitions. In both instances we held, and could have retained, them as conquered, but we obtained cessions thereof in the treaties of peace concluded on terminating the wars.

---

[4] *American Ins. Co.* vs. *Canter,* U. S. Sup. Ct. 1828, 1 Peters, 511, MARSHALL, Ch. J.

Jones vs. *United States,* U. S. Sup. Ct. 1890, 137 U. S. 202, GRAY, J.

§ 44.

[1] See report of Charles E. Magoon, law officer, Division of Insular Affairs, War Department February, 1890. Senate Document 234, 56th Congress, 1st session, for the legal aspects of the territorial acquisitions of the United States.

III. CESSION BY ONE SOVEREIGN POWER TO ANOTHER.—This may be either,

a. For a monetary consideration, without the element of conquest or coercion, as was the case when we purchased Louisiana from France in 1803, Florida from Spain in 1819, Arizona from Mexico in 1853, and Alaska from Russia in 1867.

b. By exchange of territory, which, to some extent was an element of our purchase of Florida, when we ceded to Spain a part of Texas, which, up to that time, we had claimed was included in the Louisiana purchase.

c. At the end of a war, partly for indemnity and partly for other considerations, as was the case when California and other Mexican territory was ceded in 1848, and the Philippines, Porto Rico and Guam were transferred to us in 1898.

d. Without any consideration except good-will, as was the case when Great Britain ceded Horse Shoe Reef in Lake Erie to the United States in 1850.

IV. BY ANNEXATION, WHEN TWO GOVERNMENTS BY TREATY OR RECIPROCAL LEGISLATION, UNITE UNDER THE GOVERNMENT OF ONE OR THE OTHER.—This was the case when Texas was admitted to the Union as a State and surrendered her independent government for the conditions of statehood in the United States in 1845, and also when Hawaii became a part of the territory of the United States under congressional resolution in 1898.

The title of the present domain of the United States, therefore, rests upon every different method of acquisition known to international law, but as to every portion thereof the title is clear and recognizable by that law as well as by our own laws, as they have been defined and construed by the Supreme Court.[2]

[2]NOTE BY AUTHOR ON ACQUISITIONS OF TERRITORY BY
UNITED STATES.

In December, 1898, immediately after the conclusion of the Treaty of Paris between the United States and Spain, the author published a pamphlet entitled "OUR TREATY WITH SPAIN," in which the various territorial annexations of the United States were enumerated as follows (The treaty volume referred to is the edition of 1889):

The right of the United States to acquire territory has been the sub-

§ 45. Cessions of Territory to other powers than United States.—All the instances of transfer given above relate to

ject of a vast amount of debate in Congress and in the papers. There are some who deny the right, but it is difficult to conceive on what authority. The Supreme Court has decided that the *United States is a nation*, and as such has all the rights of sovereignty that every other sovereign nation has, and can exercise them just as broadly, including the right of acquisition of territory. . . .

As to right of acquisition and the right to govern territory when acquired, see also, Pomeroy's Constitution, 494–498, *Jones* vs. *U. S.* (the *Navassa Islands case*), 137 U. S. pp. 202–212; Justice Miller's Lectures on the Constitution, 35, 36, 55, 57; Justice Curtis's Opinion (*Dred Scott case*), 19 Howard, 612–614.

These cases and opinions are all based upon the broad declaration made by Chief Justice Marshall, in 1824, in *American Ins. Co.* vs. *Canter*, 1 Peters, 511, p. 542: "The Constitution confers absolutely on the Government of the Union the power to make war and to make treaties; consequently that government possesses the power of acquiring territory either by conquest or by treaty."

Cessions of Territory made to the United States.—This (the cession of territory in the treaty of Paris of 1898) is the second cession of territory made by Spain to the United States, and, at least the eleventh acquisition of territory, by the United States, increasing its original area of less than a million square miles to its present magnificent domain three times as large in area and over fifteen times as great in population; the first cession made by Spain was in 1819 under the Adams-de Onis Treaty, by which Spain ceded Florida to the United States, in consideration of $5,000,000, which was the liquidated amount of the claims owed by Spain to citizens of the United States for depredations upon our commerce and in territory adjoining Florida.

The United States has acquired Territory as follows:

By the Treaty of Peace with Great Britain after the Revolutionary War, when the original boundaries of the United States were fixed, and Great Britain renounced all jurisdiction over the territory therein, which included not only the thirteen original States themselves, but also a part of what was afterwards included in the Northwest Territory; the original territory extended from what is now Canada on the north—the boundary line between which and the United States has been fixed by several subsequent treaties and arbitrations—to the northerly line of Florida on the south; from the Atlantic on the east, to the Mississippi on the west, containing about eight hundred and twenty-five thousand square miles. (U. S. Treaty Volume, p. 375.)

The acquisitions of territory since that time have been:

(1) *Louisiana*, consisting, including Oregon the discovery and occupation of which grew out of this acquisition, of over a million square miles, ceded by France to the United States under treaty of April 30, 1803, ratified October 21, 1803, by which France, under Napoleon Bonaparte as First Consul, through Barbé Marbois, ceded the territory for 60,000,000

our own acquisitions. Numerous examples could be given of similar transfers in every part of the world, and under

francs, and the relinquishment of claims amounting to 20,000,000 francs, (U. S. Treaty Volume, pp. 331-342). Well did Mr. Livingston exclaim to Mr. Monroe, as they arose from signing the treaty: "We have lived long, but this is the noblest work of our lives."

(2) *Florida*, consisting of about sixty thousand square miles, under the treaty with Spain in 1819, above referred to. (U. S. Treaty Volume, p. 1016.)

(3) *Oregon* and adjoining territory was acquired by the United States under the general rules of discovery and occupancy, based upon the discovery of the mouth of the Columbia River by Captain Gray, master of the good ship Columbia, entering from the Pacific in 1797; by Lewis and Clarke as explorers in an expedition fitted by the United States proceeding from the east about 1804; and by the erection of the furring post by John Jacob Astor at Astoria in 1811. The title to Oregon was subsequently confirmed by treaty with Spain in 1819, so far as the northerly line of the Spanish possessions was concerned, not, however, in the nature of cession, but only of quitclaim. (U. S. Treaty Volume, p. 1016.) The area of territory north of California and east of the Rockies is about three hundred and fifty thousand square miles.

(4) *Texas*, with an area of over a quarter of a million square miles, in 1845, by joint resolution, adopted by both Houses of Congress, after a proposed treaty had failed, was admitted as a State, the legislature of the Republic of Texas having accepted the terms and conditions contained in a joint resolution adopted by Congress. (For resolution and proclamation, see U. S. Statutes at Large for 1845.)

(5) *California, Colorado, Nevada, Utah, New Mexico,* and parts of Arizona and other States, over five hundred thousand square miles in all, were acquired under the Treaty of Guadalupe-Hidalgo with Mexico in 1848, at the termination of the Mexican War, and in consideration of $15,000,000 paid to Mexico under somewhat similar circumstances as the $20,000,000 is to be paid to Spain under the present treaty. (U. S. Treaty Volume, p. 687.)

(6) *Horse Shoe Reef in Lake Erie* was ceded to the United States by Great Britian in 1850, without any actual consideration, but under agreement that the United States would erect and maintain a lighthouse thereon. (U. S. Treaty Volume, p. 444.)

(7) *The Navassa Islands*, near Hayti, and the other *Guano Islands* in the Pacific Ocean, have been taken and occupied by the United States by discovery in pursuance of statutes of the United States made in regard thereto (U. S. Revised Statutes, secs. 5770-5778); *The Midway Islands*, situated in the Pacific Ocean, about half way between Hawaii and Japan, were discovered by citizens, and afterwards formally occupied in 1867 by the naval forces of the United States under the direction of Secretary Gideon Welles. (See Senator Platt's Speech, Senate, December 19, 1898, Congress. Rec. p. 325.)

(8) *Part of Arizona and New Mexico*, consisting of nearly fifty thou-

6

every method, showing that they have all been recognized as legal, and have been acted upon universally and constantly for centuries.

Canada was transferred by France to Great Britain in 1763 ; Spain and France several times exchanged Louisiana before it was finally ceded to the United States; Cuba and the Philippines were ceded by Spain to England in 1762, and by England back to Spain in 1764; in recent times Germany acquired Alsace and Lorraine from France by conquest and treaty cession; Savoy was ceded to France, the Ionian Islands

sand square miles, were acquired under treaty negotiated by James Gadsden in 1853, and for which the sum of $10,000,000 was paid to Mexico. (U. S. Treaty Volume, p. 694.)

(9) *Alaska*, in 1867, became United States territory by a treaty negotiated between William H. Seward, as Secretary of State, and Edward Stoekl, Russian Ambassador to the United States, and which conveyed to this Government all of the Russian possessions in America, consisting of over half a million square miles, and to which the name of Alaska has since been applied, for $7,200,000. (U. S. Treaty Volume, p. 939.)

(10) *Hawaii* was annexed by a joint resolution adopted by the Congress of the United States, and approved July 7, 1898, the terms of which were accepted by the legislative body of Hawaii shortly thereafter, and by which joint action all of the islands forming the sovereignty of Hawaii, and which were formerly known as the Sandwich Islands, became a part of the territory, but not as a State of the United States, and subject to the terms of the joint resolution. (30 Stat. at L., p. 750.)

(11) *The Philippines, Porto Rico and Guam* were annexed by the treaties with Spain of December 10, 1898, (30 Stat. at L., p. 1754; *see also* INSULAR CASES APPENDIX, p. 000, *post*) and of November 7, 1900 (31 Stat. at L., p. 1942). This latter treaty transferred a part of the Philippine Islands not included in the boundaries set by the treaty of 1898.

(12) The United States has also acquired the island of Tutuila, one of the group of the Samoan Islands, which contains the harbor of Pago-Pago. (See treaty with Samoa, U. S. Treaty Volume, ed. 1899, p. 551.)

(See the last map of the United States, published by the Government, for most of these additions of territory, showing their area and geographical location).

See also for details of acquisition of territory prior to 1898, The Louisiana Purchase, by Binger Hermann U. S. Land Commissioner, published by the Department of the Interior, Washington, Government Printing Office, 1898.

Volume I of James G. Blaine's Twenty Years in Congress contains an exhaustive review of the causes leading to annexation of territory and the effect of annexation.

to Greece, Venetia to Italy; in fact, an examination of the map of Europe will show constant and numerous changes of sovereignty, all of which have been recognized as valid by the powers to, and from, which the transfers have been made, by the inhabitants of the transferred territory, and by all the other powers of the world.[1]

§ 46. **Consent of governed not required under international law.**—The principle of international law, that the consent of the inhabitants of territory, ceded by one sovereign power to another, is not required to validate the transfer, either of the territory or the sovereignty thereover, is as well established as the principle of municipal law, as it is generally administered, has been established, that the consent of a tenant is not necessary to enable the owner of the fee to dispose of it.

This rule has been recognized and adopted not only in the United States, but the world over. There was no plebiscite in Alsace or Lorraine when the borderland Frenchmen became the subjects of Germany. The French colonists of Quebec could not speak English when by the treaty of 1763 they were transformed into British subjects. The Spanish and native population of Cuba and the Philippines were not consulted in 1762 or 1764.[1]

§ 45.
[1] See the instances of transfer of territory referred to in notes to § 43, *ante.*

§ 46.
[1] "§ 1. *Right of One Sovereign Power to Cede Territory to Another Sovereign Power.*—This right is discussed in Hall's International Law, section 9, pages 47–50. He defines it as follows (p. 47):

"'The rights of a state with respect to property consist in the power to acquire territory, . . . in being entitled to peaceable possession and enjoyment of that which it has duly obtained, and in the faculty of using its property as it chooses and alienating it at will. . . . The principle that the wishes of a population are to be consulted when the territory which they inhabit is ceded, has not yet been adopted into international law, and cannot be adopted into it until title by conquest has disappeared.'

"He cites the cessions of Savoy to France, the Ionian Islands to Greece, Venetia to Italy, and other European cessions, and further says (p. 49):

"'States being the sole international units, the inhabitants of a ceded territory, whether acting as an organized body or as unorganized mass of individuals, have no more power to confirm or reject the action of their state than is possessed by a single individual. An

§ 47. The United States has never asked the consent of the inhabitants of ceded territory.

§ 47. The United States has never asked the consent of the inhabitants of ceded territory.—The United States has never asked the inhabitants of any of its purchased territory

act, on the other hand, done by the state as a whole is, by the very conception of a state, binding upon all the members of it.'

"The following is a citation from an eminent authority:

"'I need not dwell upon the right to transfer territory, or in other words, to put an end to all dominion over them, for acquisition on the part of one nation implies transfer, or end of dominion, by another.'—John Norton Pomeroy's Lectures on International Law, edited by Theo. S. Woolsey, Boston, 1886, p. 198.

"In Halleck's International Law, San Francisco edition, 1861, at page 125, the rule is stated:

"'A state being regarded in our law as a body politic or distinct moral being, naturally sovereign and independent, it is considered capable of the same rights, duties and obligations with respect to other states as individuals with respect to other individuals. Among the most important of these natural rights is that of acquiring, possessing, and enjoying property. . . . A sovereign has the same absolute right to dispose of its territorial, or rather public, property, as it has to acquire such property.'

"Halleck thinks that in some cases the consent of the governed is necessary before the transfer of allegiance can take place, but he shows, however, that there are numerous examples of treaties of sale, and cites a number of them on pages 128 and 129, and states that in some instance territories have even been mortgaged, and bought in thereafter, and that furthermore, it has been the custom 'to dispose of sovereignties and dominions by deeds of gift and bequests.'"—From "Our Treaty with Spain," referred to in note under § 44 ante.

Professor Woolsey says:

"Sec. 54. There is a tendency, in quite recent times, to act, in international arrangements, upon the principle here stated, that the consent of the inhabitants of a ceded territory ought to be obtained. In the treaty of Prague of 1866 (see Append. ii., sub anno), it is provided that the rights of Austria to Schleswig-Holstein are ceded to Prussia, '·with the reservation that the inhabitants in northern Schleswig shall be united anew to Denmark, if they express the desire for it in a free vote.' (This, however, has never been taken.) Here, however, the Danish nationality of that part of the duchy was, without doubt, of weight, and of the more weight, as the Germans had insisted on the German nationality of both duchies in their contest with Denmark. In 1860 the Neapolitan provinces,—Sicily, the Marches, and Umbria,—were annexed to the kingdom of Italy in the same way by direct and universal suffrage. The decree of December 17, which declares the Neapolitan provinces to form thenceforth an integral part of the kingdom, is based on the submission of a *plebiscitum* to the people, on the proof that it was presented to them and accepted, and on a law authorizing the government to ratify the transfer. It has always acted on the basis that it had the right to acquire the territory if the other sovereign had the right to cede it. There was no plebiscite in 1803 in Louisiana, where the inhabitants were subjects of Spain, of France and of the United States, within the brief space of a single month. No consent was asked of the inhabitants of Florida in 1819, of the Mexicans in 1848 or 1853, or of the Alaska Indians or Russian colonists in 1867; no reason now exists why the consent of the inhabitants, Spanish or native, of the Philippines, Porto Rico or Guam, should be asked, expected, or in any manner regarded as requisite, to complete our title under the treaty of 1898.

Had the inhabitants of Louisiana refused their consent to the transfer of that province from Spain to France, or from France to the United States, would we have been forced to permit the mouth of the Mississippi, to obtain the control of which the purchase was made, to remain in the hands of a foreign power, and thus have lost, not only the territory we had paid for, but also all access to the sea, which was absolutely essential for our commercial salvation?

Had the inhabitants of Florida in 1819, as might possibly have been the case, insisted upon their consent being obtained,

'to accept, and by royal decrees establish, the annexation to the state of those provinces of central and southern Italy in which there shall be manifested freely, by direct, universal suffrage, the will to become an integral part of the constitutional monarchy,' of Italy. In this way, doubtless, it was intended to turn a half right into a whole one, or to sanctify unjust conquest by popular consent. The principle would be a good and beneficial one as between two states that such consent should be necessary before a transfer of allegiance. But, to make a desire on the part of the inhabitants of a district a ground for interfering on their behalf to disconnect them from one state, and to connect them with another, would go beyond any interference now known to international law in its disintegrating tendency, and would give rise to any amount of intrigue and unjust influence.

"In the Treaty of Turin, uniting Savoy and Nice to France, the first article provides that 'this union shall be effectuated without constraining the will of the inhabitants, and that the governments of the Emperor of the French and of the King of Sardinia will agree as soon as possible as to the best means of estimating and certifying the demonstrations of this will.' (Martens, N. Rec. Gen. XVI. 2, 539. Comp. App. ii., under 1859.)" Woolsey's Int. Law, pp. 63–65.

had the tribes of Indians, and hordes of buccaneers composing the population of that colony of Spain objected to the
strong arm of the United States being extended over them,
and their consent had been required, not only would we
never have been able to collect the indemnity due to us from
Spain, and which was represented by the value of that cession; but, according to the doctrines announced two years
ago by a minority in the Senate, we might still have a foreign
power between our southern boundary and the Gulf of Mexico.   The extension of our sovereignty from the western
boundary of the Louisiana purchase to the Pacific might
have been prevented in 1848, had it been necessary to obtain the consent of the then far scattered inhabitants of the
ceded territory.

The same conditions prevail in regard to the territory ceded
under the treaty of 1898.   The legal principles are exactly
the same; so far as they are concerned, the number of inhabitants, and their race, color and condition make no difference whatever.

§ 48. **Impracticability of ascertaining consent.**—The impracticability of ascertaining such consent after a ceding
government has ceded, and the receiving government has accepted, territory, can be most plainly shown by assuming for
a moment that such consent is required, and then ascertaining
how the consent must be evidenced, and what the result
would be if the inhabitants should not give their consent.
It would probably be beyond the ability of any expert in
municipal or international law to answer the following questions in regard to the recent acquisitions of the United
States :

1. Whose consent is necessary ; in this respect, bearing in
mind that until the extension of our laws over the territory
there is no basis for suffrage—men, women, children, black,
white, Spanish, Chinese, native, all are alike—and also how
can they express this consent ? 2. In what manner, and under
whose supervision, must this consent be expressed; in this
respect, bearing in mind that one of the highest acts of sovereignty is permitting the exercise of suffrage, and controlling the manner in which it may be exercised ? 3. What
would be the effect of the expression in case it were not, as

must inevitably be the case, unanimous; taking into consideration whether or not any power exists under those circumstances, by which the majority could coerce a minority until after some law to that effect had been established? 4. In case the consent were withheld, who is to enforce law and order, and how could the United States avoid national responsibility for disorder if it should now withdraw and leave the peaceable inhabitants to their fate?

Of course it is simply a *reductio ad absurdum* to say that we must exercise over any territory the very highest acts of sovereignty in order to find out if we have the right to exercise any sovereignty whatever.

§ 49. Special instances in which obtaining consent might be practicable.—There are, however, instances, as in the cases of Texas and Hawaii, where the inhabitants can express their consent, and the annexation can be made as the result of the voice and the wish of the inhabitants; it would be just as reasonable, however, to require that the inhabitants of the United States should be called upon to express, by a popular plebiscite, their acceptance of the annexation as to require the plebiscite of the other country, after the ruling powers, properly exercising sovereignty thereover, had consented to the annexation. Had the proposed annexations of Texas or Hawaii been rejected by a popular vote, they might have been prevented, although the author is not prepared to admit that such would have been the case if the ruling powers had assented thereto. Those annexations, however, were entirely different from the transfers of territory from sovereign powers that have been compelled to make the transfers either for reasons of political convenience or under duress of conquest; in such cases, of course, the refusal on the part of the inhabitants to assent to the transfer has no effect whatever except, as has been evidenced in the Philippine Islands, to place such of the non-consenting inhabitants who have attempted to express their dissent by force, in the category of insurgents.

§ 50. Restrictions on acquisitions of territory by European powers under " balance of power " theory.—While international law places no restraint upon any sovereign power from acquiring territory, there have been some restrictions placed thereon as between some of the great European powers; these restrictions, however, are not based upon any lack of power either to acquire territory or to cede it, but are based upon the political necessity of maintaining the equilibrium between those governments. This is known as the "balance of power" theory. Restrictions have also been placed on the acquisition by European powers of territory, on this side of the Atlantic, which are also based on political grounds but of a different nature, as will be stated in the next section.[1]

§ 51. **Acquisitions of United States never objected to by other powers.**—These points are referred to here for the purpose of calling attention to two remarkable facts. The first is, that of all the great powers of the world the United States alone has exercised the right to acquire territory without any restraint being imposed upon it, or protest being uttered against its course, by any other power great or small; the second is, that during the past seventy-five years the United States has prevented nearly every European power from exercising the right of acquisition, simply by protesting that the United States would consider the contemplated act as prejudicial to its own interests, and contrary to the policy which it has declared must govern the conditions of the Western Hemisphere.

When Russia forced Turkey in 1878 to cede vast tracts of territory to her in the nature of indemnity, the Congress of Berlin over which Bismarck presided not only protested against Russia's great accessions as being dangerous to the peace of Europe, but forced her to restore a large amount of the territory which she had acquired under the treaty of San Stephano.[1]

§ 50.
[1] The political doctrine known as "the balance of power," is referred to, and supported as one founded on natural principles, by James W. Gerard in his "Peace of Utrecht," chap. I., pp. 1–4.

§ 51.
[1] The treaty of San Stefano was concluded on March 3, 1878; by it the frontier line between Russia and Turkey was pushed so far to the south that the other European powers became alarmed at the great additional power acquired by Russia; Lord Salisbury at once gave notice that England could not look upon this with indifference and Count Münster on behalf of the Emperor of Germany invited

In the dismemberment of Turkey, the break-up of China, the parceling of Africa into colonies and spheres of influence, each power has jealously watched events so that all apparent advantages have been immediately equalized, either by the reduction of one or the increase of the other, as was the case when the seizure by the Germans of Foo Chow in China resulted immediately in Russia occupying Port Arthur, and Great Britain taking possession of Wei Hai Wei.

Against the steady increase, however, of the United States no protest has been raised, no equalizations have been demanded. We have negotiated, and carried into effect, every treaty involving cessions of territory without the intervention or interference of any other power.

No other government could have acquired the Philippine Archipelago without raising a storm of protest from all the other powers of the world; an attempt on the part of any European power to have acquired those islands would unquestionably have resulted in a congress being held at Berlin, Vienna, or some other European capital, to determine how the islands should be distributed between the different powers of Europe, or otherwise disposed of.

§ 52. **Acquisition of European powers prevented by United States under Monroe Doctrine.**—On the other hand the United States has, whenever it deemed it advisable, protested against the acquisitions of American territory by other powers, and has always been able to maintain its position. The Monroe Doctrine, dear to the heart of every American, and the keystone of our impregnable position on this hemisphere, could never have been promulgated and insisted upon by

the Powers to send representatives to a congress which should meet in Berlin to "discuss the stipulations of the Preliminary treaty between Russia and Turkey signed at San Stefano on the 3d of March, 1878." The invitation was addressed to all the powers which were signatory to the treaties of Paris of 1856 and of London of 1871. The Congress met on June 13, 1878, and Prince Bismarck was elected President; a treaty was concluded on July 13th by which a large part of the territory ceded under the treaty of San Stefano was restored to Turkey.

The signatory powers were Great Britain, Germany, Austria, France, Italy, Russia and Turkey.

The Treaty of San Stefano, the Protocols of the Berlin Congress and the Treaty of Berlin with maps showing the territory restored appear in vol. IV., Hertslet, Map of Europe by Treaty, pp. 2672–2799.

ourselves, nor indeed would any attention have been paid
thereto by any other government, had it not been the declaration of a nation that was as absolutely sovereign as any
other power in the world.[1]

§ 52.

[1] AUTHOR'S NOTE ON THE MONROE DOCTRINE.

THE MONROE DOCTRINE AS ENUNCIATED BY PRESIDENT MONROE, DECEM-
BER 2, 1823.

" At the proposal of the Russian Imperial Government, made through
the minister of the Emperor residing here, a full power and instructions
have been transmitted to the minister of the United States at St. Peters-
burg to arrange by amicable negotiation the respective rights and interests of the two nations on the Northwest coast of this Continent. A
similar proposal has been made by His Imperial Majesty to the Government of Great Britain, which has likewise been acceded to. The Government of the United States has been desirous by this friendly proceeding
of manifesting the great value which they have invariably attached to
the friendship of the Emperor and their solicitude to cultivate the best
understanding with his Government. In the discussions to which this
interest has given rise and in the arrangements by which they may terminate the occasion has been judged proper for **asserting, as a principle
in which the rights and interests of the United States are involved,
that the American Continents, by the free and independent condition
which they have assumed and maintain, are henceforth not to be
considered as subjects for future colonization by any European
powers. . .**

" It was stated at the commencement of the last session that a great
effort was then making in Spain and Portugal to improve the condition
of the people of those countries, and that it appeared to be conducted
with extraordinary moderation. It need scarcely be remarked that the
result has been so far very different from what was then anticipated.
Of events in that quarter of the globe with which we have so much intercourse and from which we derive our origin, we have always been
anxious and interested spectators. The citizens of the United States
cherish sentiments the most friendly in favor of the liberty and happiness of their fellow-men on that side of the Atlantic. In the wars of
the European powers in matters relating to themselves we have never
taken any part, nor does it comport with our policy so to do. It is
only when our rights are invaded or seriously menaced that we resent
injuries or make preparation for our defense.

" With the movements in this hemisphere we are of necessity more immediately connected, and by causes which must be obvious to all enlightened and impartial observers. The political system of the allied
powers is essentially different in this aspect from that of America.
This difference proceeds from that which exists in their respective Governments; and to the defense of our own, which has been achieved by

Protests indeed have been made against our right to maintain the Monroe Doctrine, but, notwithstanding the protests,

the loss of so much blood and treasure, and matured by the wisdom of their most enlightened citizens, and under which we have enjoyed unexampled felicity, this whole nation is devoted. We owe it, therefore, to candor and to the amicable relations existing between the United States and those powers to declare that we should consider any attempt on their part to extend their system to any portion of this hemisphere as dangerous to our peace and safety. **With the existing colonies or dependencies of any European power we have not interfered and shall not interfere. But with the Governments who have declared their independence and maintained it, and whose independence we have, on great consideration and on just principles, acknowledged, we could not view any interposition for the purpose of oppressing them, or controlling in any other manner their destiny, by any European power in any other light than as the manifestation of an unfriendly disposition toward the United States.** In the war between those new Governments and Spain we declared our neutrality at the time of their recognition, and to this we have adhered, and shall continue to adhere, provided no change shall occur which, in the judgment of the competent authorities of this Government, shall make a corresponding change on the part of the United States indispensable to their security.

" The late events in Spain and Portugal show that Europe is still unsettled. Of this important fact no stronger proof can be adduced than that the allied powers should have thought it proper, on any principle satisfactory to themselves, to have interposed by force in the internal concerns of Spain. To what extent such interposition may be carried, on the same principle, is a question in which all independent powers whose Governments differ from theirs are interested, even those most remote, and surely none more so than the United States. Our policy in regard to Europe, which was adopted at an early stage of the wars which have so long agitated that quarter of the globe, nevertheless remains the same, which is, not to interfere in the internal concerns of any of its powers; to consider the Government *de facto* as the legitimate Government for us; to cultivate friendly relations with it, and to preserve those relations by a frank, firm, and manly policy, meeting in all instances the just claims of every power, submitting to injuries from none. But in regard to those continents circumstances are eminently and conspicuously different. It is impossible that the allied powers should extend their political system to any portion of either continent without endangering our peace and happiness; nor can any one believe that our southern brethren, if left to themselves, would adopt it of their own accord. It is equally impossible, therefore, that we should behold such interposition in any form with indifference. If we look to the comparative strength and resources of Spain and those new Governments, and their distance from each other, it must be obvious that she can never subdue them. It is still the true policy of the United States to leave the parties to themselves, in the hope that other powers will pur-

our warnings have been respected in every instance in which
we have uttered them in accord with the spirit in which the

sue the same course." [Extract from the Seventh Annual Message
transmitted to the Congress of the United States by James Monroe,
fifth President of the United States, on December 2, 1823. Richardson's
Messages and Papers of the Presidents, vol. II., pp. 209, 217–219. The
paragraphs in bold face type in the preceding and subsequent quotations are those which are generally quoted as the "Monroe Doctrine,"
and which constitute the best existing exposition of the principle of
non-interference of European powers in American affairs.]

The neutral position which the United States had maintained in regard
to the relations of Spain and the Spanish-American Colonies was referred
to at length in President Monroe's Sixth Annual Message transmitted
to Congress on December 3, 1822, as follows:

"A strong hope was entertained that peace ere this would have been
concluded between Spain and the independent governments south of
the United States in this hemisphere. Long experience having evinced
the competency of those governments to maintain the independence
which they had declared, it was presumed that the considerations which
induced their recognition by the United States would have had equal
weight with other powers, and that Spain herself, yielding to those magnanimous feelings of which her history furnishes so many examples,
would have terminated on that basis a controversy so unavailing and at
the same time so destructive. We still cherish the hope that this result
will not be long postponed.

"Sustaining our neutral position and allowing to each party while
the war continues equal rights, it is incumbent on the United States to
claim of each with equal rigor the faithful observance of our rights according to the well-known law of nations. From each, therefore, a like
co-operation is expected in the suppression of the piratical practice
which has grown out of this war and of blockades of extensive coasts on
both seas, which, considering the small force employed to sustain them,
have not the slightest foundation to rest on.

"Europe is still unsettled, and although the war long menaced between Russia and Turkey has not broken out, there is no certainty that
the differences between those powers will be amicably adjusted. It is
impossible to look to the oppressions of the country respecting which
those differences arose without being deeply affected. The mention of
Greece fills the mind with the most exalted sentiments and arouses in
our bosoms the best feelings of which our nature is susceptible. Superior skill and refinement in the arts, heroic gallantry in action, disin-
terested patriotism, enthusiastic zeal and devotion in favor of public
and personal liberty are associated with our recollections of ancient
Greece. That such a country should have been overwhelmed and so
long hidden, as it were, from the world under a gloomy despotism has
been a cause of unceasing and deep regret to generous minds for ages
past. It was natural, therefore, that the reappearance of those people
in their original character, contending in favor of their liberties, should

doctrine was originally announced, and has ever since been, as it always should be, maintained.[2]

2 See reference to Lord Salis- | bury's letter in note 1 on page 107, *post.*

produce that great excitement and sympathy in their favor which have been so signally displayed throughout the United States. A strong hope is entertained that these people will recover their independence and resume their equal station among the nations of the earth.

"A great effort has been made in Spain and Portugal to improve the condition of the people, and it must be very consoling to all benevolent minds to see the extraordinary moderation with which it has been conducted. That it may promote the happiness of both nations is the ardent wish of this whole people, to the expression of which we confine ourselves; for whatever may be the feelings or sentiments which every individual under our Government has a right to indulge and express, it is nevertheless a sacred maxim, equally with the Government and the people, that the destiny of every independent nation in what relates to such improvements of right belongs and ought to be left exclusively to themselves.

"Whether we reason from the late wars or from those menacing symptoms which now appear in Europe, it is manifest that if a convulsion should take place in any of those countries it will proceed from causes which have no existence and are utterly unknown in the States, in which there is but one order, that of the people, to whom the sovereignty exclusively belongs. Should war break out in any of those countries, who can foretell the extent to which it may be carried or the desolation which it may spread? Exempt as we are from these causes, our internal tranquillity is secure; and distant as we are from the troubled scene, and faithful to first principles in regard to other powers, we might reasonably presume that we should not be molested by them. This, however, ought not to be calculated on as certain. Unprovoked injuries are often inflicted, and even the peculiar felicity of our situation might with some be a cause for excitement and aggression. The history of the late wars in Europe furnishes a complete demonstration that no system of conduct, however correct in principle, can protect neutral powers from injury from any party; that a defenceless position and distinguished love of peace are the surest invitations to war, and that there is no way to avoid other than by being always prepared and willing for just cause to meet it. If there be a people on earth whose more especial duty it is to be at all times prepared to defend the rights with which they are blessed, and to surpass all others in sustaining the necessary burthens, and in submitting to sacrifices to make such preparations, it is undoubtedly the people of these States.

"When we see that a civil war of the most frightful character rages from the Adriatic to the Black Sea; that strong symptoms of war appear in other parts, proceeding from causes which, should it break out, may become general and be of long duration; that the war still continues between Spain and the independent governments, her late Provinces,

§ 53. Russia's colonization on the Pacific Coast stopped.—
In 1823, even prior to the delivery of President Monroe's mes-

in this hemisphere; that it is likewise menaced between Portugal and
Brazil, in consequence of the attempt of the latter to dismember itself
from the former, and that a system of piracy of great extent is maintained in the neighboring seas, which will require equal vigilance and
decision to suppress it, the reasons for sustaining the attitude which we
now hold and for pushing forward all our measures of defence with the
utmost vigor appear to me to acquire new force.

"The United States owe to the world a great example, and, by means
thereof, to the cause of liberty and humanity a generous support. They
have so far succeeded to the satisfaction of the virtuous and enlightened
of every country. There is no reason to doubt that their whole movement will be regulated by a sacred regard to principle, all our institutions being founded on that basis. The ability to support our own
cause under any trial to which it may be exposed is the great point on
which the public solicitude rests. It has been often charged against
free governments that they have neither the foresight nor the virtue to
provide at the proper season for great emergencies; that their course is
improvident and expensive; that war will always find them unprepared,
and, whatever may be its calamities, that its terrible warnings will be
disregarded and forgotten as soon as peace returns. I have full confidence that this charge so far as relates to the United States will be
shown to be utterly destitute of truth." Richardson's Messages and
Papers of the Presidents, vol. II., pp. 192–195.

A year after the doctrine had been announced, President Monroe, in
his last annual message transmitted to Congress, December 7, 1824, referred to the effect of the announcement as follows:

"In turning our attention to the condition of the civilized world, in
which the United States have always taken a deep interest, it is gratifying to see how large a portion of it is blessed with peace. The only
wars which now exist within that limit are those between Turkey and
Greece, in Europe, and between Spain and the new Governments, our
neighbors, in this hemisphere. In both these wars the cause of independence, of liberty and humanity, continues to prevail. The success
of Greece, when the relative population of the contending parties is
considered, commands our admiration and applause, and that it has
had a similar effect with the neighboring powers is obvious. The feeling of the whole civilized world is excited in a high degree in their
favor. May we not hope that these sentiments, winning on the hearts
of their respective Governments, may lead to a more decisive result;
that they may produce an accord among them to replace Greece on the
ground which she formerly held, and to which her heroic exertions at
this day so eminently entitle her?

"With respect to the contest to which our neighbors are a party, it
is evident that Spain as a power is scarcely felt in it. These new States
had completely achieved their independence before it was acknowledged
by the United States, and they have since maintained it with little for-

sage to Congress, it had been quietly communicated by Secretary John Quincy Adams to Russia, and Russian coloniza-

eign pressure. The disturbances which have appeared in certain portions of that vast territory have proceeded from internal causes, which had their origin in their former Governments and have not yet been thoroughly removed. It is manifest that these causes are daily losing their effect, and that these new States are settling down under Governments elective and representative in every branch, similar to our own. In this course we ardently wish them to persevere, under a firm conviction that it will promote their happiness. In this, their career, however, we have not interfered, believing that every people have a right to institute for themselves the government which, in their judgment, may suit them best. Our example is before them, of the good effect of which, being our neighbors, they are competent judges, and to their judgment we leave it, in the expectation that other powers will pursue the same policy. The deep interest which we take in their independence, which we have acknowledged, and in their enjoyment of all the rights incident thereto, especially in the very important one of instituting their own Governments, has been declared, and is known to the world. **Separated as we are from Europe by the great Atlantic Ocean, we can have no concern in the wars of the European Governments nor in the causes which produce them. The balance of power between them, into whichever scale it may turn in its various vibrations, cannot affect us. It is the interest of the United States to preserve the most friendly relations with every power and on conditions fair, equal, and applicable to all. But in regard to our neighbors our situation is different. It is impossible for the European Governments to interfere in their concerns, especially in those alluded to, which are vital, without affecting us; indeed, the motive which might induce such interference in the present state of the war between the parties, if a war it may be called, would appear to be equally applicable to us. It is gratifying to know that some of the powers with whom we enjoy a very friendly intercourse, and to whom these views have been communicated, have appeared to acquiesce in them."** Richardson's Messages and Papers of the Presidents, Vol. II., pp. 259, 260.

THE MONROE DOCTRINE.

It is an absolute impossibility to successfully attempt to write upon any branch of the political history of the United States without making more or less extended reference to the original announcement of the Monroe Doctrine and the subsequent application thereof. The famous enunciation, although contained in a few brief paragraphs of an annual message of one of the Presidents, has been the basis of hundreds of articles, speeches, and even entire volumes which have been devoted to discussing "the origin, meaning, and application of the Monroe Doctrine"; the last sentence is quoted as it is the title of a brochure upon the subject published by Professor John Bach McMaster in 1896. Nor

tion upon the Pacific Coast was thenceforth confined to its then existing limits.[1]

§ 53.
[1] See references to correspond- | ence between Secretary Adams and our Minister to Russia, p. 97, *post.* has this discussion been confined to Americans, or to the United States; reference to it will be found in nearly all of the works on international law; and varied opinions have been delivered in regard to it by American, English and Continental authorities.

The question whether or not the Monroe Doctrine actually exists and is as applicable to-day to similar cases, as it was in 1823, has been presented to the American people on several occasions. One of these was in December, 1895, when Mr. Cleveland's message and Lord Salisbury's letter in regard to the Venezuela boundary brought the issue forward in a more practical manner than it had been presented for many years.

In the brochure above referred to Professor McMaster said: "The crisis is certainly a serious one, and an examination of these views is not untimely. The hour has come for the people of the United States to decide once for all whether there is or is not a Monroe Doctrine. If there is, it should be stated as clearly and precisely as possible. If there is not, then it becomes us to say so frankly and at once."

Since that time if any answer has been given to Professor McMaster's question it certainly is to the effect that the Monroe Doctrine does exist; that it is recognized as existing not only by the people of the United States, but also by the governing powers of other nations; and also that it has been reannounced, and so reaccepted, as "the traditional policy of the United States in regard to affairs of the Western Hemisphere" as was evidenced by the reservation under which the United States acceded to The Hague Treaties. (§ 58 *post* and footnotes thereto containing extract from Holl's Peace Conference at The Hague.)

The Monroe Doctrine, properly so-called, ever since December 2, 1823, when it was formally announced (in the form above quoted) in the seventh annual message transmitted to Congress by President James Monroe, was not the formulation of any new discovery of the political rights and power of the United States, but was the enunciation of principles which had already been adopted by the administration and which had been communicated to the other powers, who had acknowledged them as reasonable and proper in view of the unique position which the United States then occupied in this hemisphere, which it has ever since occupied, and which it will continue to occupy so long as the American people themselves recognize the wisdom and justice of the policy, our right to assert which no other power dares to directly deny, and few even dare to indirectly question.

It would be far beyond the scope of a footnote to give even a brief review of the causes leading up to the announcement of the Monroe Doctrine and of the occasions on which it has been applied since it was first uttered as an effective warning of "hands off" to the allied powers who were then masquerading under the *quasi*-religious, but wholly hypocritical guise of the Holy Alliance. A few dates and facts will be collated,

§ 54. England, Central and South America, and the Monroe Doctrine.—During the fifties, when England's protecto-

and references given to the original documents, and to the writings of those who have discussed the subject at length.

I. ANNOUNCEMENT OF THE MONROE DOCTRINE.

The Monroe Doctrine cannot be understood, nor can its full force and effect be appreciated without a thorough knowledge of the political conditions existing in the first quarter of the nineteenth century in Europe and America, both North and South.

The doctrine as enunciated in President Monroe's message was neither new nor unfamiliar, nor was it announced without premonition and warnings.

It had been foreshadowed in the President's annual message of the year previous, as appears by the paragraph quoted from the message of 1822, as well as in the correspondence which John Quincy Adams as Secretary of State had conducted with Russia in regard to Russian colonization on the northwest Pacific coast, and with England in regard to the recognition of the South American Republics, over which Spain first claimed dominion, although she could not exercise it. (See Professor Snow's article and John Quincy Adams' diary.)

The attitude of the European Powers in regard to those Republics and their relations with Spain forced the United States into taking a corresponding attitude; it is to the lasting credit of the United States that, earlier than any other country, it enacted strict neutrality laws and vigorously enforced them; in fact, the neutrality laws of 1790, 1818, and 1838 were not only the first crystallization into statutory form of the principles of neutrality, which had been recognized as elements of international law, but they have been taken as the models for the neutrality laws of many other countries. (See also §§ 5281 *et seq*. U. S. Rev. St.)

The neutrality of the United States in the Spanish-American wars had been maintained at great cost, and in spite of the sympathy which a majority of the people felt towards our struggling and weaker sisters who were following in our own footsteps and whose desires for freedom as a general rule found utterance in proclamations which were simply paraphrases of the Declaration of Independence.

No one championed the cause of these junior members of the American family of republics so earnestly or as ably as Henry Clay, whose speech in the Senate of the United States on March 25, 1818, in favor of recognizing the Republics of Buenos Ayres and of La Plata, is not only one of the most eloquent addresses ever delivered by that gifted statesman, but one which ranks among the masterpieces of American oratory.

Neutrality was also ostensibly preserved by the European countries, but the emotions of the people were suppressed by governmental espionage and the sympathy of the governing powers was entirely with Spain.

Alarmed by the rapid spread of republican tendencies in Europe as well as in America, "their Majesties, the Emperor of Austria, the King

7

rate of the Mosquito Coast and other portions of Central America created some anxiety in our minds, the Monroe

of Prussia and the Emperor of Russia," met at Paris to consider some method of averting the further spread of the desire for liberty which by them was considered as a disease. On September 26, 1815, they signed personally an agreement which from its first invocatory clause, "In the name of the Holy and Invisible Trinity," and its final words, "this Holy Alliance," has ever since that date been known as the " Treaty of the Holy Alliance."

The objects of this remarkable treaty, which, according to Capefigue, and as quoted by Professor Snow, is entirely in the handwriting of the Emperor Alexander, with corrections made by Madame Crudner, were stated in Articles 1, 2 and 3 as follows:

"Article I. In conformity to the words of the Holy Scriptures, which command all men to regard one another as brethren, the three contracting monarchs will remain *united*, by the bonds of a true and indissoluble fraternity; and, considering each other as compatriots, they will lend one another, on every occasion, and in every place, assistance, aid, and support; and, regarding the subjects and armies, as the fathers of their families, they will govern them in the spirit of fraternity with which they are animated, for the protection of *religion, peace and justice*.

"Article II. Therefore, the only governing principles between the above-mentioned governments and their subjects, shall be that of rendering *reciprocal services;* of testifying, by an unalterable beneficence, the mutual affection with which they ought to be animated; of considering all as only the members of one Christian nation, the three allied powers *looking upon themselves as delegated by* Providence to govern three branches of the same family, to wit: Austria, Prussia, and Russia, confessing, likewise, that the Christian nation, of which they and their people form a part, have really no other sovereign than Him to whom alone power belongs of right, because in Him alone are found all the treasures of love, of science and of wisdom, that is to say, God, our Divine Saviour, Jesus Christ, the word of the Most High, the word of Life.

" Their Majesties, *therefore*, recommend, with the most tender solicitude, to their people, as the only means of enjoying that peace which springs from a good conscience, and which alone is durable, to fortify themselves every day more and more in the principles and exercise of the duties which the divine Saviour has pointed out to us.

"Article III. All powers which wish solemnly to profess the sacred principles which have delegated this act, and who shall acknowledge how important it is to the happiness of nations, too long disturbed, that *these truths* shall henceforth exercise upon human destinies, all the influence which belongs to them, shall be received with as much readiness as affection, into this *holy alliance.*"

Other Continental Powers were asked to accede to the treaty; on November 22, 1822, an additional secret treaty was entered into at Verona by representatives of Austria, France, Prussia and Russia, in which the

98

Doctrine was asserted, with the desired effect that the protectorate was withdrawn, although that result was not ac-

vague expressions of the Treaty of Paris of 1815 were expressed in a somewhat more practical form.

This was signed on behalf of their respective sovereigns by four of the most famous diplomats that Europe has ever known, to wit: Metternich for Austria, Chateaubriand for France, Bernstet for Prussia, and Nesselrode for Russia.

The original treaty to provide for the peace of Europe had been signed at Chamont, France, on March 1, 1814. England, Austria, Russia and Prussia were the signatory Powers; it was aimed largely at the great ascendency over European matters which France was then aspiring to, and also to suppress the liberal ideas awakened by the French Revolution and the wars of Napoleon. It was renewed at Vienna, March 25, 1815, at the commencement of the "One Hundred Days," just after Napoleon had landed on his return from Elba.

It was again renewed at Paris, November 20, 1815, after the battle of Waterloo had forever removed Napoleon as a factor in European politics.

These last mentioned treaties, especially that of March, 1815, have sometimes been erroneously referred to as the "Holy Alliance;" the combination existing under that title, however, was confined to the treaties of Paris of September, 1815, and of Verona of November, 1822.

The treaty of November 20, 1815, provided for frequent congresses of the European Powers to regulate the affairs of Europe; pursuant thereto a Congress was held at Aix-la-Chapelle, in October, 1818. Great efforts were made by the Continental Powers to induce Great Britain to join in the "Holy Alliance," but the terms were too vague, and as the Duke of Wellington told the Emperor Alexander, there was no definite basis which justified the sovereign of Great Britain in acceding to it in such manner that his action would be understood or ratified by Parliament.

Meanwhile, however, Louis XVIII. joined the alliance on behalf of France, and many secondary Powers of Europe also acceded to the treaty. Thus the whole of continental Europe was a unit in sustaining monarchical institutions; in 1823, after the Kings of Spain and Portugal had been restored to their thrones, principally through French intervention, the question of aiding Spain in a last effort to reconquer her rebellious provinces in America was brought up and a meeting of the Powers to consider the advisability of joint action in that respect was proposed. It was this proposition, the knowledge of which was acquired by the Monroe administration, that furnished the occasion for announcing the principles by which this country would be guided in case the Powers of Europe united in intervening in the contest between Spain and her provinces, in regard to which all of those Powers, as well as the United States, had up to that time remained neutral.

Separate contests were being waged for independence in Venezuela, New Guiana, Mexico, Chile and Peru. It would be interesting to review

complished without a muttered protest.[1] In 1896, Lord
Salisbury expressed his doubts as to our right to interfere

§ 54.

[1] Central American affairs and the
Enlistment Question, Washington,
1856; see also other congressional
documents relating to this subject
referred to in Chapter XI. entitled
The Central American Imbroglio,

pp. 217 *et seq.* of Lindley Miller
Keasbey's book on the Nicaragua
Canal and the Monroe Doctrine,
G. P. Putnam, 1896. See also ref-
erences in footnote 1 to § 52 of this
chapter, page 103.

these wars for independence—to recount the deeds of valor and patriotism of Miranda, Bolivar, San Martin and the other heroes struggling for
liberty in South America, but this is not the place for such an extended
history. We can only consider the effects of those wars as they affected
our political and diplomatic relations with the other Powers. For an
interesting history of these wars the reader is referred to Hezekiah Butterworth's Political History of South America (N. Y., Doubleday & Mc-
Clure, 1898), which also contains a bibliography which will greatly aid
any one desiring to pursue this branch of the subject in more extended
research. The result of the announcement that the United States would
take up the defence of the South American Republics in case the European powers abandoned their position of neutrality, had the desired
effect. England recognized the Republics as well as the United States,
and before long commercial and diplomatic relations were established
which have ever since been maintained with occasional, but fortunately
not serious, interruptions. The announcement was received with satisfaction not only in the United States, but also in England. In fact,
Canning, who was then in the Foreign Office of Great Britain, claimed to
have originated the idea himself and to have urged the announcement
through Mr Rush. our then minister to England; he is even credited with
having said that he called the New World into existence to redress the
balance of the Old.

Undoubtedly he greatly favored the announcement and was glad of
the opportunity of recognizing the Republics. Both Professor Snow and
ex-Secretary of State, John W. Foster (A Century of American Diplomacy, 1900, Chapter XII., on The Monroe Doctrine) have shown that the
Monroe Doctrine was essentially of American origin and American con-
summation. Mr. Foster says in regard to effect of the announcement,
and as to Mr. Canning's connection therewith (on pp. 447–449) as follows:

"While the declaration is very broad in its application, it is very precise and restricted as to its cause. It is America for the Americans,
because otherwise (the peace and safety of) the United States would be
endangered.

"President Monroe might have communicated this declaration to the
allied powers in the usual diplomatic form, through the Department of
State, to our Ministers at the various European capitals, but he wisely
adopted the form of its promulgation in his annual message to Congress.
It thus became a notice, not to the Holy Alliance only, but to the whole
world, of the policy of the United States.

with England's arbitrary occupation of the disputed territory between Venezuela and British Guiana; the question how-

"Few, if any, official utterances of the century have had such general and lasting influence. When the Message was published in London it received universal commendation. Said one of the journals: 'We shall hear no more of a Congress to settle the fate of the South American States;' another: 'It is worthy the occasion and of the people destined to occupy so large a space in the future history of the world.' Mr. Canning's biographer, in recording the effect of its publication in Europe, says that, coupled with the refusal of England to take part in the proposed Congress to discuss Spanish-American affairs, it effectually put an end to the project. Mr. Brougham, the English statesman, said: 'The question with regard to South America is now disposed of, or nearly so, for an event has recently happened than which no event has dispensed greater joy, exultation, and gratitude over all the freemen of Europe; that event, which is decisive on the subject in respect of South America, is the message of the President of the United States to Congress.' It is further reported that 'the South American deputies in London were wild with joy, and South American securities of every sort rose in value.'

"The manner in which it was received in the United States was described by Mr. Webster, in a speech delivered in the Senate three years later, as follows: 'It met, sir, with entire concurrence and hearty approbation of the country. One general glow of exultation, one universal feeling of gratified love of liberty, one conscious and proud perception of the consideration which our country possessed, and of the respect and honor which belonged to it, penetrated all bosoms.' (3 Webster's Works, 178.) An undue share of credit has been assigned to Mr. Canning for the promulgation of the Monroe Doctrine, and to him has even been ascribed the origin or first suggestion of the idea. But it has been seen that fifteen years before, President Jefferson had set forth the policy in much broader terms than those contained in Canning's proposal to Rush. The published diplomatic correspondence shows that Secretary Adams was fully informed as to the designs of the Holy Alliance, and that six months before that proposal was broached he had given instructions to our Minister in Spain to make known at the proper time that our government would oppose any forcible intervention in American affairs or the transfer of any of the Spanish possessions to the European powers. Canning's proposal went no further than a protest against the transfer of any of the colonies to other powers, which was much narrower than Monroe's message; and the correspondence makes it plain that Great Britain was wholly influenced by a desire to retain and enlarge its trade and by its jealousy of France."

See also, as to effect of announcement and extracts from European publications, Professor McMaster's Origin, Meaning and Application of the Monroe Doctrine, Philadelphia, 1896.

The Monroe Doctrine has been asserted on numerous occasions between the time when it was first enunciated as a principle of American international diplomacy until its recent reaffirmance at The Hague un-

ever was finally, on our insistence, referred to the Arbitration Tribunal, which has recently rendered its award, and

der the style of "Traditional policy of the United States in regard to American affairs."

The occasions upon which it has been asserted can be divided into two classes. First, when it has been asserted in regard to the efforts of European powers to obtain a foothold or to increase their colonial possessions in North, South or Central America; second, when it has been asserted in regard to the relations between the United States and other republics of the Western Hemisphere, and the right of the United States, as the most powerful Government in America, to regulate affairs for the purpose of maintaining peace and averting the evils of war.

A few of these instances only can be referred to in this note. The reader is referred for a more detailed history of the application of the Monroe Doctrine to the authorities referred to at the end of this note; special reference is made at this point to Professor Freeman Snow's Treatise on American Diplomacy, published in 1894, over two hundred pages of which are devoted to a critical review of the Monroe Doctrine in its various aspects both as to origin and application, and which has greatly aided the author in making his own investigations in regard to this subject.

THE PANAMA CONGRESS.

Within a very brief period after the Monroe Doctrine was enunciated occasions arose for its practical application. In 1826 invitations were extended by some of the South American Republics to the United States to meet representatives of the other Republics in a Congress which was to be held at Panama to effect a general union of all the Republics. It was suggested that the Congress would consider, amongst other things, the desirability of "combining the forces of the Republics, to free the Islands of Puerto Rico and Cuba from the yoke of Spain . . . to take measures for joining in a prosecution of the war at sea and on the coasts of Spain, and to determine whether these measures should also be extended to the Canary and Philippine Islands." These objects were wholly beyond the objects, desires or rights of the United States, and were entirely inconsistent with one of the other objects stated in the call for the Congress; to wit, " to take into consideration the means of making effectual the declaration of the President of the United States, respecting any ulterior design of a foreign power to colonize any portion of this continent, and also the means of resisting all interference from abroad with the domestic concerns of the American Governments."

President John Quincy Adams, Mr. Monroe's successor, however accepted the invitation and stated in a message to Congress that ministers on the part of the United States " would be commissioned to attend at those deliberations and to take part in them so far as may be compatible with that neutrality, from which it is neither our intention nor the desire of the other American States that we should depart."

The president had power to appoint commissioners, but the appropria-

thus amicably settled a question which for a quarter of a century has threatened from time to time to plunge at least three countries into war.[2]

2 See reference to Lord Salis- | bury's letter in footnote 1 to § 52, | pages 107-8.

tion for their expenses had to be made by Congress. When the special message was sent to the Senate nominating Richardson C. Anderson and John Sergeant as envoys to the Congress, a resolution was at once offered as follows: "Resolved, That it is not expedient at this time for the United States to send any ministers to the Congress of American nations assembled at Panama."

While this resolution was pending in the Senate, the following resolution was introduced in the House: "Resolved, That in the opinion of this House, it is expedient to appropriate the funds necessary to enable the President of the United States to send ministers to the Congress at Panama."

The appropriation finally passed Congress, and commissioners were appointed; on account of the delay, however, our representatives did not actually participate in the meeting. The Congress met at Panama, but without accomplishing any actual results; it adjourned to meet at Tacubaya the following year, but no adjourned meeting was held, and as Professor Snow says in concluding his chapter on this episode, "Thus ended the first attempt to form an alliance of American states. The Monroe Doctrine was forgotten for the time; and the Spanish-Americans were left to work out their destiny in their own way, and to acquire by long training in the school of experience the capacity for self-government which they lacked at that time."

The details of the entire history of the Panama Congress are very interesting, and, according to a note in Professor Snow's article (page 312) the following documents contain a complete history of the conference.

"The documents and details of the Panama Congress are given in full in the 4th volume (Historical Appendix) of the proceedings of the *International American Conference*. See also: Lyman's *Diplomacy of the United States*, II., 467; *American Review and Whig Journal*, January, 1846; A. W. Young: *American Statesman*, 352; *Am. State Pap.* VI., 834-910; Benton's *Debates*, VIII.; Benton's *View*, I.; Webster's *Works*, III., 178; Niles's *Register*."

OTHER CONGRESSES OF AMERICAN REPUBLICS.

There have been a number of American congresses since the attempt to hold one in 1825-26.

Professor Snow refers to them as follows: (1) The Congress of Lima, 1847; (2) the Continental Treaty of 1856, which to some extent showed "a spirit of hostility to the United States," resulting from the Walker expeditions into Central America; (3) the Congress of Lima, 1864; (4) proposed Congress of Panama, 1881; (5) the proposed Congress at Washington, 1882; the International American Conference, 1890.

§ 55. Spain, Cuba, and the Monroe Doctrine.—In 1852, when we had reason to suspect that Spain contemplated a

TRANS-ISTHMIAN COMMUNICATIONS AND THE MONROE DOCTRINE.

The Monroe Doctrine has always been asserted by the United States in regard to the right of transit over the Isthmus of Panama and through the territory of Nicaragua, and in fact generally as to any trans-Isthmian communication.

Reference to this will be found in Professor Snow's book, page 326, in Lindley Miller Keasbey's Nicaragua Canal and the Monroe Doctrine, ex-Secretary of State John W. Foster's Century of American Diplomacy, and Tucker's Monroe Doctrine.

In connection with trans-Isthmian communication, however, so far as Great Britain is concerned, the Clayton-Bulwer treaty of 1850 is considered by some as a modification of the Monroe Doctrine; but although that treaty created a joint protectorate between this country and Great Britain as to a trans-Isthmian canal, under certain then expected conditions which up to this time have never materialized, it did not weaken the right of the United States to prevent the extension of British dominion in Central America, as was evidenced by the firm position which was asserted and maintained in regard thereto by Mr. Webster.

Particular reference in this respect is made to Mr. Keasby's chapter "the Central American Imbroglio," in which he says that the Monroe Doctrine was asserted with the result that Great Britain was obliged to withdraw from her protectorate over the Mosquito Coast. See also the history of Central American Complications with Great Britain in Government Document, 1856, Central American Affairs and the Enlistment Question.

RELATIONS WITH CUBA.

The relations of the United States and Cuba have always been more or less affected by the Monroe Doctrine. In 1852 France and England suggested that those powers and the United States should enter into a joint disavowal of ever intending to acquire the Island of Cuba; this the United States refused to do. On the contrary, those powers were informed that events might necessitate the acquisition of Cuba by the United States, but whether that were so or not, under no circumstances would this country permit any other country to take possession of that island.

On December 1, 1852, Secretary of State Edward Everett, wrote identic notes to Great Britain and France, in which he expressed the position of the United States as follows (1 Wharton's Digest, § 60):

" The United States, on the other hand, would, by the proposed convention, disable themselves from making an acquisition which might take place without any disturbance of existing foreign relations and in the natural order of things. The Island of Cuba lies at our doors. It commands the approach to the Gulf of Mexico, which washes the shores of five of our States. It bars the entrance of that great river which

transfer of Cuba to some other power, we gave notice at once that no such transfer would be permitted.[1] On the

§ 55.

[1] For an extended history of the foreign relations of the United States affecting Cuba, see: Cuba and International Relations, by James Morton Callahan, John Hopkins Press, 1899.

drains half the North American continent, and with its tributaries forms the largest system of internal water communication in the world. It keeps watch at the doorway of our intercourse with California by the Isthmus route.   If an island like Cuba, belonging to the Spanish Crown, guarded the entrance of the Thames and the Seine, and the United States should propose a convention like this to France and England, those powers would assuredly feel that the disability assumed by ourselves was far less serious than that which we asked them to assume. The opinions of American statesmen, at different times and under varying circumstances, have differed as to the desirableness of the acquisition of Cuba by the United States.   Territorially and commercially it would in our hands be an extremely valuable possession.   Under certain contingencies it might be almost essential to our safety.   Still for domestic reasons, on which in a communication of this kind it might not be proper to dwell, the President thinks that the incorporation of the island into the Union at the present time, although effected with the consent of Spain, would be a hazardous measure; and he would consider its acquisition by force, except in a just war with Spain, should an event so greatly to be deprecated take place, as a disgrace to the civilization of the age." (Mr. Everett, Sec. of State, to Mr. Crampton, Dec. 1, 1852, MSS. Notes Gr. Brit. See Mr. Everett and the Cuban Question, by Mr. Trescot, 9 South, Quar. Rev., new series, April, 1854, 429.   For Mr. Everett's views in full, see 1 Wharton's Digest, § 72).

Mr. Everett, on December 3, 1852, wrote again to Mr. Crampton as follows:

"To enter into a compact with European powers to the effect that the United States, as well as the other contracting powers, would disclaim all intention, now or hereafter, to obtain possession of Cuba, would be inconsistent with the principles, the policy, and the traditions of the United States." 1 Wharton's Digest, § 60. (Mr. Everett, Sec. of State, to Mr. Crampton, Dec. 3, 1852, MSS. Notes, Gr. Brit.; see also 1 Wharton's Digest, § 72.)

See also the authorities cited in section 60 of Wharton's Digest under the head of Intervention in Cuba, including extract from President Filmore's third annual message in 1852.

As to the present relations of Cuba and the United States and the effect of the Monroe Doctrine thereon, see §§ 106 *et seq.*, chap. III, *post.*

MEXICAN INTERVENTION.

One of the most notable instances of the application of the Monroe Doctrine was in 1861–1865 during which period Louis Napoleon attempted to establish a monarchy in Mexico under French protection.

other hand, however, when France and England asked us
to unite with them in a mutual declaration that all of the

England, Spain and France had claims against Mexico amounting, possibly, to a million dollars, but the French bankers held bonds which had
been issued to the amount of fifteen millions, although, comparatively,
only a trifling sum had been advanced upon them.

Mexico refused to pay the debt, and in 1861 the three Powers signed
a convention by which they agreed to exercise coercive measure to enforce the payment of their debts.   Article 2 of the convention was as
follows:

" Art. II. The high contracting parties engage not to seek for themselves, in the employment of the coercive measures contemplated by the
present Convention, any acquisition of territory, nor any special advantage, and not to exercise in the internal affairs of Mexico any influence of a nature to prejudice the right of the Mexican nation to choose
and to constitute freely the form of its government."

The War of the Rebellion was raging at that time, but even in its
crippled condition, the Government of the United States remained unchanged in its adherence to the Monroe Doctrine; " From the moment "
as stated by Tucker, " when intervention seemed probable, explanations
were demanded of France, and the assurance was given that her sole
purpose was the enforcement of the claims of the subjects of the Emperor.   During the entire period of the French occupation of Mexico,
the Government of the United States recognized only the Government
of Juarez, and after the termination of the Civil War in the United States
the Government at Washington was more pronounced than ever in
warning the Government of France of the consequences likely to follow
the prolonged stay of the French troops in Mexico."

This attitude of the United States was necessitated by the attempt on
the part of France to establish an empire with a monarchical form of
government in Mexico; in fact, the placing of Maximilian upon the
throne was not for the purpose of obtaining the payment of a debt to
France, but for the purpose of establishing in America an ally of France.

England and Spain withdrew from the attempt to destroy republican
institutions in Mexico, and thus left the matter entirely in the hands of
France.

The final result of the opposition asserted by the Government of the
United States, as communicated by Secretary Seward to the French
Government, was that France withdrew from Mexico; on the 5th of
April, 1866, it was announced that the French troops would evacuate
Mexico, and in a little less than a year from that date they all departed.

While this matter was entirely settled through diplomatic correspondence, there is no doubt that the fact that General Sheridan, whose reputation as a military commander was as well known and respected in
France as it was in the United States, was at the head of an army of
veterans of the Civil War, encamped in the vicinity of Mexico; although
there is nothing in the records of the War Department or the State Department to connect the exact causes of his location with the French

uniting powers disclaimed any intention of ever acquiring that island, we promptly declined, declaring that although

troops in Mexico, that location might have proved to be very fortunate for the United States, had it become necessary to use our military forces in order to enforce our rights under the Monroe Doctrine.

In speaking of the results of the Mexican episode, Sir Edward S. Creasy, an eminent English authority on international law, says at page 122: "The United States (occupied by their own Civil War, which was then raging) did not actually send troops to oppose the French in Mexico, but they steadily refused to recognize Maximilian, or any government except a republican government in Mexico, and the language of their statesmen exhibited the fullest development of the Monroe Doctrine."

VENEZUELA BOUNDARY DISPUTE WITH GREAT BRITAIN.

The most notable instance of the enforcement of the principles enunciated by President Monroe was in 1895 and 1896, when President Cleveland asserted that "the Monroe Doctrine finds its recognition in those principles of international law which are based upon the theory that every nation shall have its rights protected and its just claims enforced."

This sentence was contained in his message transmitted to Congress on December 17, 1895, after Lord Salisbury had declared in a dispatch to the British Ambassador, and which had been left with the Secretary of State, that the Monroe Doctrine did not embody any principle of international law founded upon the general consent of nations. The exact words of Lord Salisbury will be found in his dispatch dated November 26, 1895, commencing at page 563, part I. of the Foreign Relations' Report, 1895. In the course of his dispatch he declared that he would not be understood as expressing any acceptance of the doctrine on the part of Her Majesty's Government; in fact, he said:

"It must always be mentioned with respect, on account of the distinguished statesman to whom it is due, and the great nation who have generally adopted it. But international law is founded on the general consent of nations; and no statesman, however eminent, and no nation, however powerful, are competent to insert into the code of international law a novel principle which was never recognized before, and which has not since been accepted by the Government of any other country. The United States have a right, like any other nation, to interpose in any controversy by which their own interests are affected; and they are the judge whether those interests are touched, and in what measure they should be sustained. But their rights are in no way strengthened or extended by the fact that the controversy affects some territory which is called American. Mr. Olney quotes the case of the recent Chilean war, in which the United States declined to join with France and England in an effort to bring hostilities to a close, on account of the Monroe Doctrine. The United States were entirely in their right in declining to join in an attempt at pacification if they thought fit; but Mr. Olney's principle that American questions are for American de-

we would not permit any other power to acquire or occupy it, we would not bind ourselves not to do so, as circumstances

cision, even if it receive any countenance from the language of President Monroe (which it does not), cannot be sustained by any reasoning drawn from the law of nations.

"The Government of the United States is not entitled to affirm as a universal proposition, with reference to a number of independent States for whose conduct it assumes no responsibility, that its interests are necessarily concerned in whatever may befall those States simply because they are situated in the Western Hemisphere. It may well be that the interests of the United States are affected by something that happens to Chili or to Peru, and that that circumstance may give them the right of interference ; but such a contingency may equally happen in the case of China or Japan, and the right of interference is not more extensive or more assured in the one case than in the other."

Lord Salisbury's instructions to Sir Julian Pauncefote, from which the above is quoted, were practically in reply to the instructions of Mr. Olney, then Secretary of State, to Mr. Bayard, our Minister in London, July 20, 1895 (Foreign Relations, 1895, Part 1, page 545 ; pp. 558, 560), in which the following occurred :

"The people of the United States have learned in the school of experience to what extent the relations of states to each other depend not upon sentiment nor principle, but upon selfish interest. They will not soon forget that, in their hour of distress, all their anxieties and burdens were aggravated by the possibility of demonstrations against their national life on the part of powers with whom they had long maintained the most harmonious relations. They have yet in mind that France seized upon the apparent opportunity of our civil war to set up a monarchy in the adjoining state of Mexico. They realize that had France and Great Britain held important South American possessions to work from and to benefit, the temptation to destroy the predominance of the Great Republic in this hemisphere by furthering its dismemberment might have been irresistible. From that grave peril they have been saved in the past and may be saved again in the future through the operation of the sure but silent force of the doctrine proclaimed by President Monroe. To abandon it, on the other hand, disregarding both the logic of the situation and the facts of our past experience, would be to renounce a policy which has proved both an easy defense against foreign aggression and a prolific source of internal progress and prosperity.

"There is, then, a doctrine of American public law, well founded in principle and abundantly sanctioned by precedent, which entitles and requires the United States to treat as an injury to itself the forcible assumption by an European power of political control over an American state. The application of the doctrine to the boundary dispute between Great Britain and Venezuela remains to be made and presents no real difficulty. Though the dispute relates to a boundary line, yet, as it is between states, it necessarily imports political control to be lost by one

might render it advisable, or even necessary, for us to take such action.[2]

[2] See dispatch of Secretary of State Everett in regard to proposed mutual disavowal of England, France and United States to acquire Cuba, December 1, 1852, and referred to in note 1 to § 52, page 104-5.

party and gained by the other. The political control at stake, too, is of no mean importance, but concerns a domain of great extent—the British claim, it will be remembered, apparently expanded in two years some 33,000 square miles—and, if it also directly involve the command of the mouth of the Orinoco, is of immense consequence in connection with the whole river navigation of the interior of South America. It has been intimated, indeed, that in respect of these South American possessions Great Britain is herself an American state like any other, so that a controversy between her and Venezuela is to be settled between themselves as if it were between Venezuela and Brazil or between Venezuela and Colombia, and does not call for or justify United States intervention. If this view be tenable at all, the logical sequence is plain.

" Great Britain as a South American State is to be entirely differentiated from Great Britain generally, and if the boundary cannot be settled otherwise than by force, British Guiana, with her own independent resources and not those of the British Empire, should be left to settle the matter with Venezuela—an arrangement which very possibly Venezuela might not object to. But the proposition that an European power with an American dependency is, for the purpose of the Monroe Doctrine, to be classed not as an European but as an American state, will not admit of serious discussion. If it were to be adopted, the Monroe Doctrine would be too valueless to be worth asserting. Not only would every European power now having a South American colony be enabled to extend its possessions on this continent indefinitely, but any other European power might also do the same by first taking pains to procure a fraction of South American soil by voluntary cession.

" The declaration of the Monroe message—that existing colonies or dependencies of an European power would not be interfered with by the United States—means colonies or dependencies then existing, with their limits as then existing. So it has been invariably construed, and so it must continue to be construed unless it is to be deprived of all vital force. Great Britain cannot be deemed a South American state within the purview of the Monroe Doctrine, nor, if she is appropriating Venezuelan territory, is it material that she does so by advancing the frontier of an old colony instead of by the planting of a new colony. The difference is matter of form and not of substance, and the doctrine, if pertinent in the one case, must be in the other also. It is not admitted, however, and therefore cannot be assumed, that Great Britain is in fact usurping dominion over Venezuelan territory. While Venezuela charges such usurpation, Great Britain denies it, and the United States, until the merits are authoritatively ascertained, can take sides with

§ 56. Louis Napoleon, Mexico, and the Monroe Doctrine.
—In 1862, the Emperor Louis Napoleon attempted to take

neither. But while this is so—while the United States may not, under existing circumstances at least, take upon itself to say which of the two parties is right and which wrong—it is certainly within its right to demand that the truth shall be ascertained. Being entitled to resent and resist any sequestration of Venezuelan soil by Great Britain, it is necessarily entitled to know whether such sequestration has occurred or is now going on. Otherwise, if the United States is without the right to know and have it determined whether there is or is not British aggression upon Venezuelan territory, its right to protest against or repel such aggression may be dismissed from consideration."

The result of the Venezuela controversy was an adjustment between Venezuela and Great Britain referring the boundary dispute to an arbitration tribunal, which definitely defined the boundary line, giving a part of the disputed territory to Venezuela and a part to Great Britain; in a large measure the claims advanced by Venezuela and supported by the United States were justified, for, although, a larger amount of territory as to area was awarded to Great Britain, both sides of the mouth of the Orinoco River were included in the territory awarded to Venezuela, thus establishing one of the principal points contended for by Venezuela.

THE MONROE DOCTRINE AND RECENT ACQUISITIONS.

During the last three years the question has been raised, principally by those opposed to the acquisition of additional territory, that it is impossible for the United States to acquire territory in the Eastern Hemisphere, and also to maintain its traditional policy as expressed in the Monroe Doctrine in regard to affairs of the Western Hemisphere.

The author considers that the acquisition of the Philippines and the Monroe Doctrine have absolutely no bearing upon each other. The message of President Monroe in which his doctrine was enunciated, declared that it was against the policy of the United States to interfere with the disputes of European powers in regard to European matters. At that time the European powers were not interested in Asiatic matters. Since that time, while the relations of the United States in regard to European matters, and the policy of non-intervention therewith may not have changed, and while it might be impossible to change that policy, and to intervene in European affairs, without altogether abandoning, or to a great extent jeopardizing, our right to maintain the Monroe Doctrine, our relations with Asiatic countries are so entirely different that the Monroe Doctrine has absolutely no application thereto.

The countries on the eastern side of the Pacific Ocean are nearer neighbors to America than they are to Europe, not only as to distance but also as to commerce. In a recent publication the Pacific Ocean has been described as a great American lake. (See Josiah Strong's Expansion, N. Y., 1900.) The United States have a perfect right to protect their interests in the Eastern Hemisphere, to establish footholds therein,

advantage of the then weak and disturbed condition of Mexico to establish an Empire in America under French auspices

or to acquire territory in payment of indemnity, otherwise uncollectible, without in any way either renouncing the Monroe Doctrine or interjecting itself into the affairs of Europe; the mere fact that European nations have acquired or attempted to acquire Asiatic territory, or to exercise control over Asiatic governments, does not necessarily transform Asiatic affairs into European affairs. The enunciation of the Monroe Doctrine never disclaimed the right which the United States always has had, and always will have, of exercising its sovereign rights wherever and whenever other sovereign powers can exercise similar rights of sovereignty.

SOME OPINIONS OF PUBLICISTS.

It is impossible to collate all the authorities upon the Monroe Doctrine. A few only will be referred to. John W. Foster, as expressed in his Century of American Diplomacy, has already been referred to; Professor Theodore Dwight Woolsey and his son, Professor Theodore Salisbury Woolsey, have expressed some doubt as to the principles of the Monroe Doctrine so far as the right to intervene merely because the territory is in the western hemisphere, although they sustain that right whenever such intervention is prejudicial to our material interests. Their views are expressed in section 48, Introduction to the Study of International Law by Theodore Dwight Woolsey (6th edition, revised by Theodore Salisbury Woolsey, N. Y., 1891), and in the chapter devoted to that subject in Theodore S. Woolsey's America's Foreign Policy (N. Y., 1898).

Doctor Francis Wharton devotes sections 56a to 61a, pages 268 to 416 of volume I. to a consideration of the Monroe Doctrine under the title, "III. Intervention of European sovereigns in the affairs of this continent disapproved. Monroe Doctrine."

He refers to the original enunciation of the doctrine in sections 56a and 57; in the following sections he refers to subsequent applications of the doctrine in regard to Yucatan, Mexico, Peru, Cuba, Hayti, San Domingo and the Danish West Indies.

There are numerous extracts from opinions of the Presidents, dispatches and notes of Secretaries of State, and of the replies from foreign offices of their governments in regard to the Monroe Doctrine and its application.

In regard to the Clayton-Bulwer treaty, he says on page 288: "The Clayton-Bulwer treaty is the only exception to the rule that the Government of the United States will decline to enter into combinations or alliances with European powers for the settlement of questions connected with the United States." See also bibliography of Monroe Doctrine contained in Gilman's Life of James Monroe, American Statesmen Series.

On the other hand, some of the eminent French authorities on international law have declared that the Monroe Doctrine cannot be consid-

and protection; in 1865, however, after our civil war was over, and we had time to devote, and military forces with

ered in any light as a principle of international law, but that it is the mere expression of opinion of an American statesman. In this respect Alphonse Rivier says (Droit des Gens, Paris, 1896, pp. 404-5, Vol. 1):

§ 88. LA DOCTRINE DE MONROE.—"La politique d'intervention de la Sainte-Alliance a provoqué une déclaration importante du cinquième président des États-Unis, James Monroe, dans son message présidentiel due 2 Septembre, 1823.

"D'après cette déclaration, les États-Unis d'Amérique ne s'ingéreront pas dans les affaires des nations européennes qui ont des colonies en Amérique; mais ils ne toléreront pas non plus que les États nouveaux, reconnus par eux comme indépendants, soient en butte aux attaques d'États européennes, et ils respousseront toute immixtion de l'Europe sur le continent américain. C'est là ce qu'on désigne communément sous le nom de doctrine de Monroe. . . .

" Le message contient une autre déclaration, motivée par les revendications ou prétentions de la Russie dans le Nord de l'Amérique. 'Les continents américains, d'après l'état de liberté et d'indépendance qu'ils se sont acquis et dans lequel ils se sont maintenus, ne peuvent être considérées à l'avenir comme susceptibles d'être colonisés par aucune puissance européenne.' Ceci veut dire que le sol de l'Amérique n'est plus sans maître, qu'une occupation nouvelle par un État d'Europe n'y est donc pas concevable.

" La doctrine de Monroe est une maxime ou règle de conduite, qui n'avait, dans l'origine, d'autre valeur que celle d'une opinion ou d'une résolution personelle de son auteur responsable, énoncée en quelque sorte *ex cathedra*. Les successeurs de James Monroe y sont restés fidèles. John Quincy Adams, président à son tour, l'a proclamée derechef à propos du congrès de Panama (1826), et les républiques de l'Amérique espagnole ont déclaré l'adopter au congrès de Lima (1865). Mais elle n'a jamais fait l'objet d'une convention, à laquelle des États non américains auraient consenti. Il va sans dire qu'elle ne saurait avoir aucune sorte de force obligatoire pour l'Europe. Son principe ne fait point partie des principes du droit des gens. La prétention émise plus d'une fois par les États-Unis de l'imposer plus ou moins aux États européens, est dénuée de tout fondement juridique.

"D'autre part, cette maxime n'implique pas, ainsi qu'on l'a cru parfois, une intention des États-Unis de se désintéresser de la politique générale de la Société des nations, et il n'est point inutile de constater que tout en écartant jalousement toute immixtion européenne sur les continents américains, ils s'arrogent eux-mêmes le droit d'y intervenir partout et à tout propos, si bien qu'aujourd'hui ce qu'ils appellent la doctrine de Monroe est en réalité l'affirmation d'une pretention permanente des États-Unis d'intervenir dans les affaires de tous les autres États d' Amérique."

Calvo devotes sections 147-167, pp. 284-300 of the first volume of his International Law (fifth edition, Paris, 1896) to a history of the Mon-

which to attend, to such matters, Secretary Seward explained the Monroe Doctrine to the Emperor, and French support was withdrawn from the ill-fated Maximilian, thus ending the last attempt on the part of any European power to make a new foothold in the western hemisphere.[1]

§ 57. **Germany and Samoa.**—Not under the Monroe Doctrine, but simply on general principles we cried halt to Germany in her efforts to acquire Samoa, and forced her to make an equitable arrangement with this country and Great Britain in regard to the control of that far-off Archipelago

roe Doctrine as announced, its subsequent application and the opinions of publicists in regard thereto. At the foot of pp. 248, 285 and 300 will be found three notes which refer to numerous authorities which he has consulted in preparing his matter. The authorities as they are collated in those notes are as follows: At the foot of page 284 : "Wheaton, *Elem.*, pte. 2, ch. 1, Sec. 11; Wheaton, *Hist.*, t. 1, pp. 110-114; t. II, pp. 219-239, 252-260; Vattel, *Le droit*, livre II, ch. iv, sec., 54, 56, 57; liv. III, ch. iii, Sec. 50; Martens, *Precis*, Sec. 74; Phillimore, *Com.*, vol. I, pte. 4, pp. 433-483; Kent, *Com.*, vol. I, pp. 22, 23; Kluber, *Droit*, Sec. 51; Heffter, Secs. 44-46; Bluntschli, *Le droit*, Sec. 474; Manning, pp. 97, 98; Wildmann, vol. I, p. 47; Bello, pte. I, cap. i, Sec. 7; Riquelme, lib. I, tit. 2, cap. xxiv; Halleck, ch. iv, Sec. 4; ch. xxiv, Sec. 12; Huber, *De jure*, lib. III, cap. vii, Sec. 4; Pando, p. 74; Dolloz, *Repertoire*, V. *Droit des gens*, ns. 86 et seq.; Verge, *Martens*, t. I, pp. 202 et seq.; Berriat Saint-Prix, *Theorie*, pp. 164 et seq.; Pinheiro Ferreira, *Vattel*, iv. II, ch. iv, Sec. 56; Guizot, *Memories*, t. IV, pp. 4, 5; Pradier-Fodere, *Vattel*, t. II, pp. 27 et seq., 308; Ott, *Kluber*, Sec. 51, note c; Hautefeuille, *Le principe de non-intervention*; Funck Brentano et Sorel, *Precis*, ch. xi, Hall; *int. law*, p. 242."

At the foot of p. 300:

"Dana, *Elem.*, by Wheaton, note 36; *British and foreign State papers*, v. I, pp. 662 et seq.; v. VII, pp. 585 et seq.; v. VIII, pp. 524 et seq.; v. XI, pp. 4 et seq.; v. XII, pp. 535 et seq.; v. XIII, pp. 390 et seq.; 483 et seq.; v. XXXIII, pp. 198 et seq. ; *United States laws*, v. X, p. 995; Calhoun, *Works*, vol. IV, p. 454; Mackintosh, *Works*, vol. III, pp. 433-478; Webster, *Works*, vol. III, p. 178; Torres Caicedo, *Union*, cap. xii, p. 63; Sarmiento, *A discourse*, p. 14; Sarmiento, *Vida de Lincoln*, int. p. xxiii; Lastari, *La America*, cap. xiv, p. 139; Valiente, *Reformas*, p. 211; Gervinus, t. x, pp. 125 et seq.; Ch. Calvo, *America latina*, periodo I°, t. III, p. 338; periodo 3°; Alaman, t. V, pp. 815-819; Lawrence, *Elem.*, by Wheaton, note 46; Buchanan, p. 276; Creasy, *First platform*, Secs. 303 et seq.; Woolsey, *Introd. to the study of int. law*, Sec. 74."

§ 56.

[1] See reference to Congressional documents and history of French

Intervention in Mexico in note 1 to § 52, page

in the Pacific Ocean, which is of such strategic value to our merchant, and our naval, marine.[1]

Certainly, so far as international law is concerned, there is no doubt that it has been determined, by the consent of every nation of the world, that the right of acquisition of additional territory exists in every sovereign power, and that it exists paramountly in the United States.

§ 58. **Monroe Doctrine and the Peace Conference at The Hague; 1899.**—As appears in the foot note to § 52, the Monroe Doctrine is an American enunciation, to which some other nations claim that they have never acquiesced; the instances already cited, however, demonstrate that although almost every government has had the opportunity of protesting against its enforcement, they have all practically admitted our right to assert it.

In 1899, at the Peace Conference at The Hague, a treaty was prepared in which the United States joined, but in doing so made the following reservation:

"Nothing contained in this Convention shall be so construed as to require the United States of America to depart from its traditional policy of not entering upon, interfering with, or entangling itself in the political questions or internal administration of any foreign state, nor shall anything contained in the said Convention be so construed as to require the relinquishment by the United States of America, of its traditional attitude toward purely American questions."

The effect of this is that a treaty has been accepted by all the other signatory powers containing a declaration of the Monroe Doctrine as it has been adopted by, and made a part of, the traditional policy of the United States, and that all those Signatory Powers have recognized without protest the existence of the policy, and the intention of the United States to adhere to it.

§ 57.

[1] Convention between the United States, Germany and Great Britain to adjust amicably the questions between the three governments in respect to the Samoan Group of Islands. Signed December 2, 1899; ratified by Senate January 16, 1900; ratifications exchanged and treaty proclaimed February 16, 1900. 31 U. S. Statutes at Large, 56th Congress, 1st Sess. 1899–1900, appx. Treaties, p. 70. See other Treaties in regard to Samoan Islands: U. S. Treaties in Force 1899, p. 551.

114

The history of this reservation, and some observations as to its effect, will be found in the Fifth Chapter of "The Peace Conference at The Hague," in which Mr. Frederick W. Holls, the able and efficient Secretary of the American Commission, has permanently recorded the transactions of the Conference; the extract from that interesting volume quoted in the note to this section shows what an important bearing the appending of that reservation to The Hague Treaty will always have upon our international relations.[1]

§ 58.

[1] "Reservation by the American Representative; Text of the American Declaration; The Monroe Doctrine; The Declaration accepted; its importance. According to this Article every Signatory Power recognizes a new international obligation, as a duty toward itself and every other Signatory Power. Next to the establishment of the Permanent Court of Arbitration this Article undoubtedly marks the highest achievement of the Conference, for no doubt the establishment of the court would have been incomplete, if not nugatory, without this solemn declaration, which is undoubtedly 'the crown of the whole work,' as it was declared to be by one of the American representatives in the Committee on Arbitration. At the same time there was just one Power whose vital interests might be directly and unfavorably affected by this Article, if adopted without qualification, and that Power was the United States of America. The declaration, for which Mr. Holls made a reservation in the *Comite d'Examen*, and which was afterward carefully formulated, is for the United States of America by no means the least important part of the entire convention, and reads as follows:

· "'Nothing contained in this Convention shall be so construed as to require the United States of America to depart from its traditional policy of not entering upon, interfering with, or entangling itself in the political questions or internal administration of any foreign state, nor shall anything contained in the said Convention be so construed as to require the relinquishment, by the United States of America, of its traditional attitude toward purely American questions.'

"The adoption of the treaty without any qualification of Article 27, would undoubtedly have meant, on the part of the United States, a complete abandonment of its time-honored policy known originally as the Monroe Doctrine. This is not the place to discuss the merits of that policy, or the truth and wisdom of that doctrine. It is, however, a fact that the United States of America is determined more firmly than ever before in its history, to maintain this policy and the Monroe Doctrine, in its later approved and extended form, carefully and energetically. Not even in the supposed interest of universal peace would the American people have sanctioned for one moment an abandonment or the slightest infraction of a policy which appeals to them as being founded,

§ 59. Opposition to territorial expansion from within, and not from without.—The only voices which have been raised in opposition to the right of the United States to acquire and to govern territory have come from within our own boundaries and not from without.

There has always been a faction which has opposed the extension of the boundaries of the United States. The Supreme Court has, however, decided that the United States may constitutionally acquire territory by conquest, by treaty, by annexation and by discovery and the cases referred to in

not only upon legitimate national desires and requirements but upon the highest interests of peace and progress throughout the world. To recognize the American Continents as proper objects of any kind of European expansion, or interference on the part of one or more Powers, would not promote or increase the peace, prosperity, or happiness of a single human being; and assuming, in ever so small a degree the responsibility for the status of so large a part of the earth's surface, it is only fair that the great peace power of the West should not be required to interfere against its will in any other quarrel. Nor is any meritorious interest in the world unfavorably affected by this attitude of the United States— an attitude assumed and maintained, not as a challenge, not boastfully toward Europe, nor patronizingly toward its sister States on the American Continent, but simply in pursuance of a wise and far-seeing recognition of obvious facts and their logical bearings.

"The declaration was presented in the full session of the Conference on July 25, read by the Secretary of the Conference, and unanimously directed to be spread upon the minutes, and added to the Convention by a reference opposite the signatures of the American plenipotentiaries.

"The importance of this proceeding, so far as the United States of America is concerned, will readily be seen. Never before that day had the Monroe Doctrine been officially communicated to the representatives of all the great Powers, and never before was it received with all the consent implied by a cordial acquiescence, and the immediate and unanimous adoption of the treaty upon that condition. An express acceptance or recognition was, of course, impossible, but there can be no doubt that the declaration, as presented, constitutes a binding notice upon every Power represented at the Conference, forever estopping each one of them from thereafter quoting the treaty to the United States Government in a sense contrary to the declaration itself. The greatest advantage of the latter, however, is the fact that it leaves to the United States absolute and perfect freedom of action, and this, in view of the recent extension of American power, especially in the far East, is of incalculable importance." The Peace Conference at The Hague, Holls, The MacMillan Co., 1900, chap. V. pp. 269, 272.

the appendix[1] are so conclusive that they place the matter beyond all controversy, so far as the legal elements are concerned; in fact, it must be conceded at the present time that questions relating to annexation of territory and extension of the boundaries of the United States belong exclusively to the political departments of the government, and the judicial department has no control whatsoever thereover.[2]

§ 60. **Right to acquire territory based on nationality and sovereignty.**—The right of the United States to acquire territory, and to govern it, is based upon the sovereign and national power which the government possesses and which has been sustained in all the cases cited in the notes under preceding sections; in fact, if it were not for the complete nationality and sovereignty of the United States it would have been impossible for its Government to have made the treaties under which it acquired from other nations those great possessions by which our territory has more than quadrupled since the power was asserted in the Declaration of Independence that "as free and independent States they (the United States) have full power to levy war, conclude peace, contract alliances, establish commerce, and do other rights and things which independent states may of right do."[1]

§ 61. **Power to govern acquired territory; the Insular Cases; 1901.**—Article IV, section 3, clause 2 of the Constitution declares that Congress shall have the power to dispose of, and make all needful rules and regulations respecting the territory or other property belonging to the United States.[1]

Under this section it has been held that the Central Government has power to regulate all territory which the United States acquires, and that in doing so it has absolute and plenary powers, and is not limited in its legislation in the same

§ 59.

[1] See classified cases, p. 535, *post.*

[2] As to matters within domain of judicial department or legislative department and rules of non-interference by one with the other, see § 460, chapter XVI, Vol. II, *post.*

§ 60.

[1] The right of the United States to acquire territory was one of the questions involved in the *Insular Cases,* which will be discussed in the succeeding sections. The cases bearing on the subject are collected in the INSULAR CASES APPENDIX at the end of this volume.

§ 61.

[1] "The Congress shall have Power to dispose of and make all needful Rules and Regulations respecting the Territory or other Property be-

manner as it is limited in its legislation in regard to matters affecting the States, or territory wholly under State jurisdiction. In a case decided in 1894 the Supreme Court held that, "by the Constitution, as is now well settled, the United States, having rightfully acquired the Territories and being the only government which can impose laws upon them, have the entire dominion and sovereignty, national and municipal, Federal and State, over all the Territories so long as they remain in a territorial condition."[2]

The controversy as to whether the Constitution *ex proprio vigore* follows the flag, reached the Supreme Court in a concrete form in the *Insular Cases* which have already been referred to as pending before that Court and in which many questions were discussed, some of which have been settled, in regard to the extent of the limitations upon Congressional action in legislating for the territories, especially those recently acquired from Spain under the Treaty of Paris.

§ 61*a*. **The Insular Cases; status of New Possessions.** —These cases, so-called because they involved the status of the insular possessions acquired by the United States by treaty from Spain, and of the Hawaiian Islands annexed by resolution of Congress of July 7, 1898, were argued before the Supreme Court of the United States during the October term of 1900. Nine cases were argued, all but one of which were for refunds of customs duties exacted under the various tariff laws and orders either on goods brought from Porto Rico, the Philippines and Hawaiian Islands into other ports of the United States, or on goods brought from other ports of the United States into Porto Rico. The cases will be briefly considered in the order indicated in the notes hereto.[1]

longing to the United States; and nothing in this Constitution shall be so construed as to Prejudice any Claims of the United States, or of any particular State." U. S. Const. Art. IV, § 3, cl. 2.

[2] *Shively* vs. *Bowlby*, U. S. Sup. Ct. 1894, 152 U. S. 1, p. 48, GRAY, J., citing numerous cases. See also cases cited and collated in INSULAR CASES APPENDIX at end of this volume.

§ 61*a*.
[1] The titles to the *Insular Cases*, the order in which they will be considered, and the points involved in each case are as follows (see 182 U. S. Reports when published):

1 (61*b*). *De Lima* vs. *Bidwell*. For the return of duties exacted under the Dingley act on goods brought from Porto Rico to New York after the ratification of the treaty and prior to the Foraker act.

Opinions were delivered on May 27, 1901, in all of the cases except those involving the status of the Philippines and the validity of duties collected in Porto Rico under the Foraker Act.[2] The cases were decided after most of this volume was completed and "in plate." They, therefore, can only be referred to briefly at this point where a space was left in case the decisions were rendered before the volume was actually in press. They are more fully discussed at other points in this volume, and also in an appendix.

§ 61b. **The Insular Cases; Porto Rico and the Dingley Act.**—Two of the *Insular Cases*[1] were brought to recover duties on goods brought from Porto Rico to New York after the ratification of the treaty of Paris,[2] and prior to the

2 (61b). *Goetze* vs. *United States.* Same.

3 (61c). *Fourteen Diamond Rings, Emil Pepke, Claimant,* vs. *United States.* To recover goods brought from Manila to Chicago, seized for unpaid duties under the Dingley act.

4 (61d). *Crossman* vs. *United States.* To recover duties exacted on goods brought from Hawaiian Islands after passage and approval of the resolution of annexation.

5 (61e). *Dooley, Smith & Co.* vs. *United States, No. 1.* To recover duties paid in Porto Rico on goods brought from New York after the making of the treaty and prior to the Foraker act.

6 (61e). *Armstrong* vs. *United States.* Same.

7 (61f). *Downes* vs. *Bidwell.* To recover duties exacted on goods brought from Porto Rico to New York under the Foraker act.

8 (61g). *Dooley, Smith & Co.* vs. *United States, No. 2.* To recover duties paid in Porto Rico on goods brought from New York to Porto Rico under the Foraker act.

9 (61h). *Huus* vs. *N. Y. and Porto Rico S. S. Co.* To recover pilotage from an American steamship on the ground that the vessel was subject to pilotage laws because engaged in foreign trade.

After these cases had been argued in the Supreme Court a resolution was passed by the House of Representatives on February 9, 1901, (the Senate concurred on February 15, 1901,) providing for printing twelve thousand copies of the records, briefs and arguments in all of the nine cases above referred to.

The volume consists of 1075 pages of records, briefs, arguments and exhibits, besides an analytical index of 39 pages; for title in full of this volume see INSULAR CASES APPENDIX at end of this volume.

[2] The cases which were not decided on May 27, 1901, were decided on December 2, 1901. The opinions of the court and the dissenting opinions are included in full in the INSULAR CASES APPENDIX (Supplement), pp. 563, *et seq.*, of this volume. They will be officially reported in 183 or 184 U. S. Rep.

§ 61b.

[1] *DeLima* vs. *Bidwell,* and *Goetze* vs. *United States,* 182 U. S. 1.

[2] The treaty was signed in Paris December 10, 1898; was ratified by

Foraker act.[3]   The duties were imposed and collected under
the act of July, 1897,[4] known as the Dingley act; the consignees claimed that the merchandise was free because Porto
Rico was part of the United States; the collector claimed
that for tariff purposes Porto Rico remained a foreign country until Congress legislated in regard to it.   The duties were
paid under protest.   Some of the consignees proceeded under the Customs Administrative Act[5] before the Board of
General Appraisers, which upheld the Collector,[6] and then
appealed from the appraisers to the United States Circuit
Court, which affirmed the appraisers;[7] others brought com-
mon-law actions against the collector personally on the
ground that the exaction was illegal and a mere trespass.[8]
In this case the United States Circuit Court sustained the

the President and Senate of the United States February 6, 1899, and
by the Queen Regent of Spain
March 19, 1899 (30 U. S. Stat. at L.
1754); the ratifications were exchanged and the treaty proclaimed
at Washington April 11, 1899.

[8] The Foraker act was passed
April 12, 1900; it took effect May 1,
1900, 31 U. S. Stat. at L. p. 77,
ch. 191.

[4] The present tariff law under
which duties are collected on merchandise, commonly known as the
Dingley act, was passed July 24,
1897, 30 Stat. at L. p. 151, ch. 11.
The first section is as follows:

Be it enacted, &c.: That on and
after the passage of this Act, unless otherwise specially provided
for in this Act, there shall be
levied, collected, and paid upon all
articles imported from foreign
countries, and mentioned in the
schedules herein contained, the
following rates of duty which are,
by the schedules and paragraphs,
respectively presented, namely:
(then follow the schedules).

[5] The Customs Administrative

Law approved June 10, 1890, 26 U. S.
Stat. at L. p. 131, provides for the
method of recovering duties illegally exacted on *imported* merchandise by collectors.   In the *Insular
Cases* it was held that this law does
not apply to duties illegally exacted
on goods which are not *imported*
in the sense that that word is used
in the tariff laws; that is that only
such goods as are brought from *foreign* ports are imported.   See cases
collated in INSULAR CASES APPEN-
DIX on this point, especially *Woodruff* vs. *Parham*, U. S. Sup. Ct. 1868,
8 Wall. 123, MILLER, J.

[6] Protests of *Mosle Brothers* and
John H. Goetze & Co., before the
U. S. General Appraisers at New
York, February 14, 1900; Opinion
by SOMERVILLE, General Ap-
praiser, 22018, G. A. 4658—Synopsis of Treasury Decisions.

[7] *Goetze* vs. *United States*, U. S.
Cir. Ct. S. D. N. Y. 1900, 103 Fed.
Rep. 72, TOWNSEND, J.

[8] *DeLima* vs. *George R. Bidwell*,
(collector of the Port of New York)
originally brought in New York
State Supreme Court and removed

Collector's demurrer.[9] A suit was also brought in the United States Circuit Court to enjoin the Collector from continuing to exact duties under the Dingley Act after Porto Rico had become a part of the United States. The motion was denied and no.appeal was taken from the decision of the circuit judge.[10] Appeals were taken to the Supreme Court in many of these cases. That court reversed the Circuit Court and the Board of Appraisers, and decided that territory could not be domestic and foreign at the same time; that after the exchange of ratification of the treaty of Paris, Porto Rico ceased to be foreign, and therefore the Dingley Act did not apply to merchandise brought from Porto Rico to New York, and that the duties collected under protest must be

by defendant to United States Circuit Court for Southern District of New York, 1900.

[9] *Pro forma*, see record of *Insular Cases*.

[10] *Lascelles* vs. *Bidwell*, U. S. Cir. Ct. S. D. N. Y. 1900, 102 Fed. Rep. 1004, LACOMBE, J. In this case the author of this volume appeared as attorney and counsel for the plaintiffs who were dealers in Porto Rico sugar. The injunction was asked on the ground that Porto Rico was no longer foreign, but had become a part of the territory of the United States, if not upon the signing of the treaty, not later than the exchange of ratifications. On the argument the District Attorney asked the Court to decide preliminarily whether an injunction would be granted under any circumstances, in view of the provisions of the Customs Administrative Law. The Court consented to consider that point before requiring the District Attorney to argue the question of Porto Rico's status. This case was therefore decided exactly as though the goods had been brought from Boston or Savannah. The entire decision as reported is as follows:

"March 19, 1900.—Motion denied on authority of *Crunkshank* vs. *Bidwell*, 176 U. S. 73. Complainant has an adequate, summary, and expeditious remedy at law under the Customs Administrative Act." No appeal was taken in this case. Under the decision in *DeLima* vs. *Bidwell*, the ruling of the Circuit Judge was error as the Supreme Court decided that the Customs Administrative Act does not apply to duties illegally exacted on goods which are not *imported*, *i. e.*, not brought from a foreign country. The chief ground urged by the plaintiffs in *Lascelles* vs. *Bidwell* was that the continued exaction of duties by the collector on goods from Porto Rico had *broken up* the business of bringing sugar therefrom, and that for such continued loss of business there was no remedy at law, as no opportunity was given of paying the duties on goods coming from Porto Rico during the period of illegal exaction and it was impossible to measure the pecuniary loss sustained by the loss of business. This point does not appear to have been considered.

refunded.[11]   Mr. Justice Brown delivered the opinion of the
court, Chief Justice Fuller and Justices Harlan, Brewer
and Peckham concurred with him; [12] Mr. Justice McKenna
wrote a dissenting opinion in which Justices Shiras and
White concurred; Mr. Justice Gray also delivered a brief
dissenting opinion.

§ 61*c*. **The status of the Philippines; The Diamond
Ring Case.**—Although the Supreme Court decided that
Porto Rico, on the exchange of ratifications of the treaty
of Paris, became domestic territory, and duties on merchandise could not be collected under the Dingley Tariff act as
though it were a foreign country, the Court withheld the
decision in a similar case involving the dutiability of goods
brought from the Philippine Islands for over six months.[1]
Fourteen diamond rings brought from Manila were seized in
Chicago for nonpayment of duties.   The owner filed a claim
denying that the rings were dutiable, as they were brought
from one part of the United States to another.   The United
States demurred to the claim and the demurrer was sustained.[2]   A writ of error was granted by the Supreme Court.
In the *DeLima* case, which involved the status of Porto
Rico, reference was made to the fact that not only had that
island been ceded to the United States, but that the United
States was in possession [3] of the Island.   In the *Diamond
Ring* case the effect of the McEnery Resolution,[4] passed by
the Senate the day after the treaty of peace was ratified,
was considered at length and the Court held that it did not
affect the construction of the treaty.

§ 61*d*. **The Status of the Hawaiian Islands.**—No sepa-

[11] *DeLima* vs. *Bidwell*, U. S. Sup.
Ct. 1901, 182 U. S. 1, Brown, J.

Goetze vs. *United States*, U. S.
Sup. Ct. 1901, 182 U. S. 221, Brown,
J. (No opinion; reference simply
being made to the opinion just delivered in *DeLima* vs. *Bidwell.*)

[12] For abstracts of the opinions in
this case see Appendix at end of
this volume.   The cases have been
reported in some of the Lawyers'
Coöperative Reports, and will appear in 182 U. S. Reports.

§ 61*c*.

[1] *Fourteen Diamond Rings, Pepke,
Claimant,* vs. *United States,* U. S.
Ct. 1901, (decided December 2,
1901).

[2] U. S. District Court, Northern
Dist. of Ill., July, 1900, Kohlsaat,
J. (*pro forma*).

[3] See Insular Cases Appendix
at end of this volume; consult index, thereto, for page references.

[4] See McEnery Resolution on p.
565, *post*.

rate opinion was rendered in the Hawaiian Islands cases.[1] Duties paid under protest on goods brought from Honolulu to New York were ordered to be refunded on the grounds which were stated in the opinion in *DeLima* vs. *Bidwell.*[2]

§ 61e. The Foraker Act.—The cases referred to in the preceding sections involved the payment of duties imposed and collected on merchandise brought to New York and Chicago from Porto Rico, Manila and Honolulu, under the provisions of the Dingley Act, the respective collectors claiming that the places last named remained foreign, so far as the revenue laws of the United States were concerned, until Congress by appropriate legislation determined otherwise. After May 1, 1900, however, duties were collected on goods brought from Porto Rico to New York under the Foraker act,[1] so-called because the senior senator from Ohio introduced it; this act provided that duties should be levied on merchandise brought from Porto Rico to other ports of the United States at the rate of fifteen per cent of the duties collected on similar articles from foreign ports under the existing tariff act.[2] Duties were paid under protest, and the owners brought suits[3] against the collector for the amounts paid, claiming that the act in this respect was in violation of the provisions of the Constitution of the United States in regard to uniformity of duties and imposts throughout the United States. The United States Circuit Court sustained a demurrer to the complaint,[4] and the Supreme Court affirmed this decision on the

§ 61d.

[1] *Crossman* vs. *United States,* U. S. Sup. Ct., 1901, 182 U. S. 221.

[2] The entire opinion is as follows (also entitled in *Geotze* vs. *United States,* BROWN, J.): "As the sole question presented by the record in these cases was whether Porto Rico and the Hawaiian Islands were foreign countries within the meaning of the tariff laws, we must hold, for the reasons stated in *DeLima* vs. *Bidwell,* just decided, that the board of general appraisers had no jurisdiction of the cases. The judgments of the Circuit Court are therefore reversed, and the cases remanded to that court with instructions to reverse the action of the board of general appraisers."

§ 61e.

[1] "An act temporarily to provide revenue and a civil government for Porto Rico and for other purposes;" approved April 12, 1900, 31 U. S. St. at L. 77, ch. 191. Extracts containing the tariff provisions of this act are quoted in the opinion of FULLER, Ch. J., in *Downes* vs. *Bidwell,* 182 U. S. 244, see p. 349.

[2] The Dingley Act, approved July, 1897, 30 St. at L. p. 151, see note 4, p. 120, *ante.*

[3] *Downes* vs. *Bidwell,* U. S. Sup. Ct. 1901, 182 U. S. 244.

[4] U. S. Cir. Ct. S. D. N. Y. Novem-

ground that Congress has power to levy duties on goods brought from a territory of the nature of Porto Rico to other ports of the United States.

This is the most important of the decisions rendered in the *Insular Cases*. There was no majority opinion. Mr. Justice Brown announced the " conclusion and judgment of the Court." Mr. Justice White delivered an opinion reaching the same result but by a different process of reasoning. Justices Shiras and McKenna concurred with Mr. Justice White; Mr. Justice Gray also concurred with him, but filed a brief separate opinion. Chief Justice Fuller wrote a dissenting opinion in which Justices Harlan, Brewer, and Peckham concurred; Mr. Justice Harlan also wrote a separate opinion. The opinions are so lengthy that it is impossible even to give an abstract of them in this section or in the notes.[5]

§ 61*f*. **Duties paid in Porto Rico.**—The cases referred to in the preceding sections involved duties which were paid in New York and Chicago on merchandise brought *from* the new possessions. There were other cases which involved the right of the United States to impose duties or merchandise brought from ports of the States *to* Porto Rico.[1] Duties were imposed and collected under the old Spanish tariff laws for a brief period, then under military orders given by the President, and subsequently under the Foraker act. Two suits were brought, one for duties paid prior to May 1, 1900, under the Spanish tariff laws and the military government, and the other for duties paid after that date under the Foraker act. In the case involving duties paid prior to May 1, 1900, the Court sustained the right to collect duties under any laws or orders in force prior to the exchange of the ratifications of the treaty on April 11, 1899, when Porto Rico became domestic territory.[2] It also decided that all

ber, 1890, LACOMBE, J., (*pro forma*). See *Insular Cases* Record.

[5] The opinions in this case, over one hundred pages in length, are reported in 182 U. S. Rep.; for a synopsis see INSULAR CASES APPENDIX at end of this volume.

§ 61*f*.

[1] *Dooley, Smith & Co.* vs. *United States, No. 1; Same* vs. *Same, No. 2,* U. S. Sup. Ct. 1901, No. 1, 182 U. S. 222; No. 2 not yet decided. Argued January, 1901; *Armstrong* vs. *United States,* U. S. Sup. Ct. 1901. 182 U. S. 243.

[2] " In their legal aspect, the duties exacted in this case were of three classes: (1) The duties prescribed

duties paid after the exchange of ratifications and until the Foraker act took effect were illegally imposed and must be refunded. The case involving the duties paid after the Foraker act took effect has not yet been decided. The counsel who argued that case laid great stress on the point that the imposition by Congress of duties on merchandise taken from a State to any other territory of the United States is equivalent to laying an export tax and, therefore, directly prohibited by the Constitution.[3] There were no cases corresponding to these Porto Rico cases, and affecting duties paid in the Philippines and Hawaiian Islands on merchandise from other ports of the United States.

by General Miles under order of July 26, 1898, which merely extended the existing regulations; (2) the tariffs of August 19, 1898, and February 1, 1899, prescribed by the President as Commander-in-Chief, which continued in effect until April 11, 1899, the date of the ratification of the treaty and the cession of the island to the United States; (3) from the ratification of the treaty to May 1, 1900, when the Foraker act took effect.

"DUTIES PRIOR TO RATIFICATION.

"There can be no doubt with respect to the first two of these classes, namely, the exaction of duties under the war power, prior to the ratification of the treaty of peace. While it is true the treaty of peace was signed December 10, 1898, it did not take effect upon individual rights until there was an exchange of ratification. *Haver* vs. *Yaker*, 9 Wall. 32, *sub nom. Jecker* vs. *Magee*, 19 L. Ed. 571. Upon the occupation of the country by the military forces of the United States, the authority of the Spanish government was superseded but the necessity for a revenue did not cease." The opinion then sustains the right to impose and collect customs as a war measure on all goods, citing numerous cases. "The right to exact duties on goods imported into Porto Rico from New York arises from the fact that New York was still a foreign country with respect to Porto Rico, and from the correlative right to exact at New York duties upon merchandise imported from that island."

"DUTIES AFTER RATIFICATION.

"Different considerations apply with respect to duties levied after the ratification of the treaty and the cession of the island to the United States. Porto Rico then ceased to be a foreign country, and, as we have just held in *DeLima* vs. *Bidwell*, the right of the collector of New York to exact duties upon imports from that island ceased with the exchange of ratifications." The opinion then holds that while there is no doubt as to the right to administer the government under the war power until Congress acted, there is no right to exact duties upon merchandise brought from the United States.

[3] Clause 5, section 9, Article I, of the Constitution is as follows: "No tax or duty shall be laid on articles exported from any State." For the most recent utterances of the

§ 61*g*. **The Porto Rico pilotage case.**—Another case which was decided on May 27, 1901, involving the status of Porto Rico and its relations to other ports of the United States, was the *Pilotage* case.[1]   Under the pilotage laws of the State of New York, American vessels engaged in the coastwise trade are not required to take pilots on entering the harbor of New York; vessels not engaged in the coastwise trade are required to take pilots or to pay half pilotage fees in case of refusal.   An American vessel from Porto Rico having refused to take a pilot, the vessel was libelled for half the amount of the regular fees.   The United States District Court dismissed the libel.[2]   The Circuit Court of Appeals certified to the Supreme Court certain questions as to whether Porto Rico remained a foreign port in the sense in which those words are used in the New York pilotage laws after the exchange of ratifications of the treaty of Paris.[3]   The Supreme Court decided that the ports of Porto Rico are domestic ports and that vessels engaged in trade between those ports and other ports of the United States are engaged in the coastwise trade and not obliged to take pilots under the New York laws as though they came from foreign ports.

§ 61*h*. **Summary of decisions in Insular Cases.**—The principal points decided in the *Insular Cases*, therefore, can be very briefly summarized as follows:

1st. Territory, when ceded to the United States by a foreign power, and actual possession thereof has been delivered to and received by the United States, ceases to be foreign territory, as that expression is used in the tariff laws of the United States, and duties cannot be exacted under tariff laws providing for duties on imports from *foreign* countries.[1]   This also applies to territory annexed by congressional resolution, as were the Hawaiian Islands.[2]

Supreme Court in regard to export taxes, see *Fairbank* vs. *United States*, U. S. Sup. Ct. 1901.   181 U. S. 283, BREWER, J.

§61*g*.

[1] *Huus* vs. *N. Y and Porto Rico S. S. Co.*, U. S. Sup. Ct. 1901, 182 U. S. 392, BROWN, J.

[2] See Record of *Insular Cases*.

[3] For these questions, and cases on definition of foreign and coastwise trade, see INSULAR CASES APPENDIX at end of this volume.

§ 61*h*.

[1] *DeLima* vs. *Bidwell, Goetze* vs. *United States;* see § 61*b*, p. 119, *ante*.

[2] *Crossman* vs. *United States;* see § 61 *d*, p. 122, *ante*.

2d. Congress has power to make rules and regulations regarding such territory, including the right to impose duties on merchandise brought there from other ports of the United States, and in so doing, Congress is not bound by the constitutional limitations in regard to uniformity of imposts and duties throughout the United States.[3]

3d. After the United States has acquired and obtained possession of territory, as in the case of Porto Rico, American vessels trading between ports therein and other ports of the United States are engaged in coastwise, and not in foreign, trade so far as pilotage laws are concerned.[4]

4th. After the United States has acquired territory by conquest and by military occupation and subsequently by cession, the former laws, as modified by the military government established under the war power, remain in force until the exchange of ratification of the treaty of cession, and until that time the territory does not become "domestic" so as to prevent, the collection of duties on merchandise brought from other parts of the United States.[5]

All of the above points were decided by a divided court, dissenting opinions being delivered in all the cases, in one instance the majority of the court being divided on the method of reasoning although the same conclusion was reached.[6]

None of the *Insular Cases* involved right to collect duties on merchandise brought from other ports of the United States *to* the Philippine Islands under the Dingley tariff or under the various tariffs established under executive orders;[7] nor did any of the decisions determine the status of the Philippine Islands,[8] the personal rights, liberties or citizenship of the inhabitants of any of the recently acquired territory.

---

[3] *Downes* vs. *Bidwell;* see § 61e, p. 123, *ante.*

[4] *Huus* vs. *N. Y. & Porto Rico S. S. Co.;* see § 61*g*, p. 126, *ante.*

[5] *Dooley, Smith & Co.* vs. *United States, No. 1; Armstrong* vs. *United States;* see § 61*f*, p. 124, *ante.*

[6] See abstracts of opinion in INSULAR CASES APPENDIX at end of the volume; consult special index thereto.

[7] See note 4 to § 308, p. 441, *post,* as to Spooner Amendment for government of the Philippine Islands.

[8] Several attempts have been made to raise questions before the courts involving the personal rights and liberties of inhabitants of the recently acquired territories. Some of those cases are referred to in § 385 of chap. XII, *post.*

§ 62. **The Mormon Church Case ; Justice Bradley's opinion.**—Many of the cases referred to in the preceding notes,
including Chief Justice Marshall's decision in the *Canter*
case, in regard to the extensive powers possessed by Congress
over the territories had been decided prior to 1889, but some
points still remained to be cleared up when the confiscation
acts passed by Congress in regard to the Mormon Church
were brought before the Supreme Court for adjudication.[1]

The acts were of such a nature that, had they affected
property within the limits of any State, they would unquestionably have been declared unconstitutional. They affected, however, property in territory which had been acquired by the United States from Mexico, and which had
never possessed statehood. The question of the extent of
Congressional power over the territories thus being involved,
Mr. Justice Bradley availed himself of the opportunity to
express the opinion of the court as to the status of such territories in upholding the acts, as follows:

" The power of Congress over the Territories of the United
States is general and plenary, arising from and incidental to
the right to acquire the Territory itself, and from the power
given by the Constitution to make all needful rules and regulations respecting the Territory or other property belonging to the United States. It would be absurd to hold that the
United States has power to acquire territory and no power
to govern it when acquired. . . . Doubtless Congress in

---

§ 62.

[1] The acts of Congress referred to
in the *Mormon Church* case are as
follows :

Organic act organizing a territorial government of Utah, September 9, 1850, (9 U. S. Statutes at
Large, 453), and other acts supplemental thereto. " An act to punish
and prevent the Practice of Polygamy in the Territories of the
United States and other Places and
disapproving and annulling Certain
Acts of the Legislative Assembly
of the Territory of Utah" passed
July 1, 1862, (12 U. S. Statutes at

Large, 501), U. S. Revised Statutes,
§ 5352 in regard to polygamy. The
Edmunds act amending § 5352 of the
Revised Statutes passed March 22,
1882, (22 U. S. Statutes at Large, 30).
Act of February 19, 1887, making
additional provisions as to the prosecutions of polygamy and by
§§ 13, 17 and 26, which are quoted
at length on pp. 7–9, 136 U. S.
Rep., confiscating the property of
the Mormon Church which was
known as the Church of Jesus
Christ of Latter-Day Saints. (24
U. S. Statutes at Large, 637—641.)

legislating for the Territories would be subject to those fundamental limitations in favor of personal rights which are formulated in the Constitution and its amendments; but these limitations would exist, rather by inference and the general spirit of the Constitution from which Congress derives all its powers, than by any express and direct application of its provisions."[2]

§ 63. **Subsequent cases involving same point.**—The doctrine laid down in *Murphy* vs. *Ramsey*[1] and the *Mormon Church* case,[2] that the power of the United States to govern the territories is plenary has been constantly affirmed and followed by the Supreme Court. Chief Justice Waite, and Justices Matthews, Bradley, Gray and Harlan, as well as others, have delivered, and concurred in, opinions sustaining this plenary power. There is not room to quote all of these decisions and opinions, but most of them will be found in the notes to section 61. It is proper, however, to refer to the opinion of Mr. Justice Gray in *Shively* vs. *Bowlby*, in which he says: "By the Constitution, as is now well settled, the United States, having rightfully acquired the Territories, and being the only government which can impose laws upon them, have the entire dominion and sovereignty, national and municipal, Federal and state, over all the Territories, so long as they remain in the territorial condition."[3]

There seems to be no doubt therefore that Congress can legislate for the territories in a different manner, and with far greater power than it can legislate in regard to matters affecting states.

§ 64. **Constitutional limitations, or limitations by fundamental principles.**—In the closing sections of the last chapter, the theory of limitations by fundamental principles was discussed[1]; the basis of that theory can be found in the decisions of the Supreme Court which have been cited in the notes to the last two sections.

---

[2] *Mormon Church* vs. *United States*, U. S. Sup. Ct. 1890, 136 U. S. 1, pp. 42–44, BRADLEY, J.

§ 63.

[1] 114 U. S. 15.

[2] 136 U. S. 1, p. 42, and see § 62, *ante*.

[3] *Shively* vs. *Bowlby*, U. S. Sup. Ct. 1894, 152 U. S. 1, p. 48, GRAY, J., and see numerous cases cited in the opinion on this point.

§ 64.

[1] See §§ 36–41, chap I., *ante*.

After citing Mr. Justice Matthews in *Murphy* vs. *Ramsey*,[2] Mr. Justice Bradley said, in the *Mormon Church* case already cited[3]: "Doubtless Congress in legislating for the Territories would be subject to those fundamental limitations in favor of personal rights which are formulated in the Constitution and its amendments; but these limitations would exist, rather by inference and the general spirit of the Constitution from which Congress derives all its powers, than by any express and direct application of its provisions." Chief Justice Chase declared in *Clinton* vs. *Englebrecht*: "The theory upon which the various governments for portions of the territory of the United States have been organized, has ever been that of leaving to the inhabitants all the powers of self-government consistent with the supremacy and supervision of National authority, and with certain fundamental principles established by Congress."[4]

§ 65. **Justice Harlan's opinion.**—In *McAllister* vs. *United States*,[1] Mr. Justice Harlan, in declaring that territorial courts were not subject to the limitations in the Constitution said that "The whole subject of the organization of territorial courts, the tenure by which the judges of such courts shall hold their offices, the salary they receive and the manner in which they may be removed or suspended from office, was left, by the Constitution, with Congress under its plenary power over the Territories of the United States. How far the exercise of that power is restrained by the essential principles upon which our system of government rests, and which are embodied in the Constitution, we need not stop to inquire; though we may repeat what was said in *Mormon Church* vs. *United States*." He also followed the opinion of Mr. Justice Bradley as expressed in the *Mormon Church* case and quoted in section 62 of this volume.

§ 66. **General summary of views.**—To-day, while many of our most distinguished counsel are engaged in arguing these

---

[2] *Murphy* vs. *Ramsey*, U. S. Sup. Ct. 1885, 114 U. S. 15, 42, MATTHEWS, J.

[3] 136 U. S. 1, p. 42, and see § 62 ante.

[4] *Clinton* vs. *Englebrecht*, U. S.

Sup. Ct. 1871, 13 Wallace 434, p. 441, CHASE, Ch. J.

§ **65.**

[1] *McAllister* vs. *United States*, U. S. Sup. Ct. 1891, 141 U. S. 174, p. 188, HARLAN, J

questions before the Supreme Court, which tribunal may decide them by divided opinions, as has happened in many cases involving political questions, it is impossible for the author of a text-book to predict in advance what the decision of that court will be, and it would be highly presumptuous on his part to declare what it should be; all that the author can do under such circumstances, therefore, is to call the attention of his readers, and those examining this subject, to the cases which have already been decided, and those which are now under consideration bearing upon this question.[1]

§ 67. **Government of territories as affected by treaties of cession.**—So far we have only referred to the right of the United States Government to govern territory under provisions of the Constitution, and by virtue of its inherent power to do so as an attribute of sovereignty and nationality. There are times, however, when the right to govern is affected by clauses or stipulations in a treaty by which the territory is ceded to the United States.

Questions arising under those stipulations do not form a part of the subject-matter of this volume; they will be considered in their proper place as a part of the effect of cessions of territory and change of sovereignty upon personal rights and liberties and upon laws and customs of the ceded territories. There are, however, a few specific instances which will be noted in this volume.

§ 68. **Special clauses in treaty with Spain of 1898.**—The right of the United States to govern the territories recently acquired from Spain will be complicated, so far as decisions of the pending cases already referred to are concerned, by the final clause in the ninth Article of the Treaty of Paris, which provides that the civil and political rights of the native inhabitants of the ceded territory shall be determined by the Congress of the United States.[1]

Undoubtedly when the United States is obliged to accept

§ 66.

[1] See cases collated in notes under §§ 61a–h, ante, since decided.

§ 68.

[1] "The civil rights and political status of the native inhabitants of the territories hereby ceded to the United States shall be determined by Congress." Article IX. Treaty with Spain, December 10, 1898, 30 U. S. Stat. at Large, p. 1759, and see treaty for other special clauses as to rights of inhabitants to renounce or retain allegiance.

territory as a part of an indemnity, or to definitely establish the title of the United States to territory conquered in war, the United States has the right to decline to accept the territory except under such conditions as it is willing to receive it; when a treaty, therefore, contains a stipulation that Congress shall determine the civil and political status of the inhabitants of territory so accepted, it must be admitted that the power of Congress to regulate, fix and determine that status shall not be limited by the same rules as limit Congressional action in regard to matters within the domain of the original States, or those which have been admitted to the Union on an equal basis.   Unless the United States has the right to so qualify its acceptance of territory it might be placed in the position of being obliged to give full political rights to a population entirely diverse in nature, in some respects undesirable, and in any event unaccustomed to our methods of government.

§ 69. **States' Rights and anti-expansion.**—The States' Rights School and the anti-expansionists have certain elements in common, although they by no means constitute the same class.   The States' Rights principles which were developed to the highest degree in the Southern States were by no means antagonistic to the acquisition of territory, for it was largely due to the Southern influence that our greatest acquisitions were made.

In so far, however, as limitations are placed upon the general government, the States' Right school and the anti-expansion school are almost identical; ever since the organization of our government there has been a faction, not necessarily limited to any particular part of the country, but always appearing whenever any acquisition was under consideration, which has opposed the extension of the boundaries of the United States.   Under the leadership of Senator Pickering, it tried to prevent the purchase of Louisiana;[1] the arguments,

---

§ 69.

[1] The Louisiana Purchase, by Binger Hermann, Washington, Government Printing Office, 1898. See page 37 for views of Senator Pickering of Massachusetts, Macy of Connecticut, Plumer of New Hampshire and White of Delaware, Representatives Griswold of Connecticut and Griffin of Virginia, all of whom expressed as their opinion that the annexation of Louisiana and its subsequent incorporation into the Union as

though specious, for a moment frightened Jefferson to the extent of considering the necessity of a constitutional amendment specifically conferring the power to purchase territory and to govern it; he rose above his momentary fears, however, and declared that, as to such matters, the government had, and in fact, that it must have, the power to act for the sake of the existence and the safety of the Union.[2] It again asserted itself when it tried to convince the Supreme Court that the government had no power to acquire Florida, or to govern it after its acquisition, but Chief Justice Marshall suppressed it with one of those opinions which left no uncertainty as to the rulings of the judicial side of the government.[3] It protested against the annexation of Texas, although it must be said, the opposition in this case was mainly due to the fear of extension of slavery, and there are even some of the members of that party to-day who contend that the Lone Star State has no right to membership in the Union, although they admit that it may be too late to raise the question now, and that it might even be impolitic to raise it in some parts of the far Southwest. It raised a great shout of opposition to the purchase of Alaska, and Secretary Seward was derided for his successful negotiations with Russia resulting in the acquisition of what was then called "a garden of snow and ice," but which since then has proved of such inestimable value that a single group of islands has repaid the entire cost of the whole territory.[4]

States were unconstitutional and could only be accomplished by the consent of every State or by a constitutional amendment.

[2] In his brief in the Porto Rico Tariff cases (*Goetze* vs. *United States*) submitted to the Supreme Court in December, 1900, Attorney General Griggs devotes pages 31-40 to "Jefferson's doubts as to the constitutionality of the Louisiana Treaty." He declares that it is "a common error, long disseminated and many times repeated, to assert that Jefferson was under the belief that the United States had no

constitutional power to acquire foreign territory."

[3] "The constitution confers absolutely on the government of the Union the power of making wars and making treaties, consequently the government possesses the power of acquiring territory either by conquest or treaty." *American Ins. Co.* vs. *Canter*, U. S. Sup. Ct. 1828, 1 Peters, 511, p. 542, MARSHALL, Ch. J.

[4] See the adverse opinions as to the value of Alaska expressed in Congress, July 1, 1868, by Mr. Orange Ferriss of New York, Mr.

§ **70. Policy of expansion and acquisition sustained by courts and people.**—This voice of opposition, as loud and as futile as ever, has been heard again within the last three years; ante-bellum doctrines of narrow construction have been revived by those who have called themselves at one time anti-expansionists, and at another, anti-imperialists. It is not the intention of the author to discuss the political issues raised by the recent transactions of the National government; but he alludes to the manner in which the people have sustained the administration as ample evidence of the fact that it has been generally acknowledged, that as to all matters not exclusively within the jurisdiction of any State, the Central Government possesses every attribute of nationality and sovereignty necessary to enable it to act for the general benefit of the people at large; and also that probably during the past three years the element of nationality has had a greater development in the minds of our people, in their capacity as "Americans," than it has had since the pre-revolutionary days when the national spirit found expression in Patrick Henry's famous utterance : "Am I less a Virginian because I am an American?"

Again disavowing any intention to enter upon political discussion, the author feels that it must also be acknowledged that it has been owing to the wide scope of the treaty-making power, and the manner in which it has been exercised, by the United States from 1782, when our first treaty with France gave evidence of the great diplomatic ability of Franklin and his colleagues, to the present time when the treaty concluded at Paris with another power under the administration of Mr. McKinley, also gave evidence of the skill and ability of American diplomats and established the fact, that this country has reached a preëminent position among the nations of the earth ; and that it must also be acknowledged that through the treaty-making power, and its proper and prudent exercise great advantages have been gained, which have inured to every State, and to citizens of every State and Territory.

Washburne of Wisconsin, Messrs. Price of Iowa, Benjamin F. Butler of Massachusetts and others col-lated on page 52 of Binger Hermann's Louisiana Purchase, referred to *supra*, note 1, § 69.

Surely it is not only a selfish position, but one also unfounded in fact or reason, to contend that as the number of States and the area and power of the Union increases, each State diminishes in relative importance. Which one of the thirteen original States would to-day exchange its position as one of the great integral factors of the United States with its present proportions and power, for its relative position of a century ago? The greater the Union—the greater the whole—the greater each one of its component parts; the United States never has increased, and never will increase, either in area, power or in any other manner, except for the common benefit of every State and of every citizen in his dual capacity as a citizen of his own State and of the Union.

If to-day we hold a position in the world of greater strength and influence than we have ever held before—and who can doubt that such is the case—it is because we have overcome at last all petty prejudices and local jealousies, and have fully recognized and realized the great power and ability which is vested in our Central and National Government.

§ 71. **Territorial Expansion the Cornerstone of American prosperity.**—The broad views of such men as Marshall and Story during the great constructive period, and of the men who have followed them in the later post-bellum period, through which we have been, and are now, passing, including such eminent jurists as Justices Field, Bradley, Harlan and Gray, have sustained and strengthened the hands of the National Government, and have made the enlargement of our territory not only possible, but have caused it to result in practical benefits for every State and also for the citizens of the States and of the territory acquired.

In fact, the history of the United States has demonstrated that the policy of expansion and acquisition of territory, based as it is upon the foundation of sovereignty and nationality of the Central Government, is the cornerstone of the great structure of the American Union which has been reared thereon.

The cornerstone must rest upon a sure foundation or the structure based upon it will collapse, but no structure built upon the cornerstone of our policy of expansion will ever meet that fate, for the stone itself is securely supported upon the broadest and strongest foundation of thorough nationality and complete sovereignty, indissolubly cemented with the highest degree of fearless and independent loyalty and patriotism, both national and federal.

136

CHAPTER III.

137

§ 72. Subject, so far, viewed from internal standpoints.

The nationality and sovereignty of the United States has, up to this point been discussed from the standpoints of inhabitants of the United States, and of the States or territories thereof. Under such conditions, the extent thereof must be determined according to municipal and constitutional law, as the same is administered in this country; the sovereignty and reserved powers of the various States, as well as the constitutional limitations upon the Federal Government, must also be taken into consideration.

§ 73. Subject now to be viewed from external standpoints.

—When, however, the nationality and sovereignty of the United States is considered from external standpoints, all of those internal shades of difference are entirely eliminated; no matter how extensive the powers of the States may be as to internal matters they have but little, if any, bearing on foreign complications as viewed from external standpoints.

§ 74. Same distinctions exist as to all federated powers.

—We shall see in the succeeding chapter on the treaty-making power as exercised by the central governments of other confederations, that this distinction always exists as to the internal and external relations of federated governments, although the extent of the power lodged in the central governments, or reserved in the constituent states, may be a matter requiring judicial determination as to internal affairs.[1] The general rule is that when a confederation deals with foreign powers it necessarily does so as a single national unit. This rule is practically universal, as in almost all federations the central government has absorbed all treaty-making power;

§ 74.

[1] See §§ 111 et seq., chapter IV., post.

in fact all the functions of sovereignty, so far as they affect the relations of the confederation or the constituent states with foreign powers, must be exercised by the central government, in order to avoid the complications which would result from their exercise by the individual states, each necessarily establishing different and therefore conflicting relations.[2]

§ 75. **Recent Insular cases decisions only involve these questions from internal standpoints.**—As has been already stated, the recent decisions of the Supreme Court[1] involve all the internal shades of difference between the States of this union, organized territories, such as Arizona and New Mexico, unorganized territories such as Alaska was until recently, and those territories which have been recently acquired, as well as that of the Island of Cuba which, while it has not been acquired by the United States is now occupied by its military forces, and is therefore under its jurisdiction.[2] While the Supreme Court has to some extent avoided deciding all the points which were raised on the arguments, the various degrees of sovereignty possessed by the Central Government, and exercised over the different territories above enumerated, have been discussed as well as the difference in the status of the various territories composing the United States and which are under its jurisdiction. Those decisions, however, do not affect the external relations of the United States with foreign powers, because as to them there is practically very little, if any, difference as to any territory which comes under the jurisdiction of the United States.[3]

§ 76. **Rule from external standpoints, based on international law.**—This condition necessarily results from the

[2] That this position has been taken by the United States as other confederations is demonstrated by the claim in the *Montijo* case. See references at length to the proceedings in §§ 96–100 of this chapter and footnotes thereto.

§ 75.

[1] See the cases collated under § 61, *ante*, and references to pending cases. See also § 101, *post.*

[2] See reference to *Neely* case involving the status of Cuba and statutes affecting Cuba in §§ 106–107, *post,* and notes thereunder.

[3] See extract cited in § 78, note 1 *post, Fong Yue Ting* vs. *United States,* U. S. Sup. Ct. 1893, 149 U. S. 698, GRAY, J.

admitted rule of international law that all the known territory on the face of the earth must be under the jurisdiction of some government, which not only acknowledges that it has jurisdiction thereover, but which is also recognized by the other powers as having, and exercising, such jurisdiction; this rule extends not only to the main territory, but to all territory which is in any way directly or remotely under the jurisdiction of any recognized sovereignty.

§ 77. **Undivided sovereignty of governments exercising jurisdiction recognized by other powers.**—It is a well settled principle of international law that where jurisdiction is exercised *de jure* or *de facto* by any sovereign power, the right of such power to negotiate, and enforce, treaties affecting such territory is recognized by, and binding upon, all other powers treating with it, or having any relations with such territory.

The Supreme Court has decided that wherever the political side of the United States Government recognizes the existence of a government and negotiates with it, the courts must uphold and enforce the treaty so made, whether it be with a foreign power or an Indian tribe; and that it is not within the province of the court to go behind the execution of the treaty and to determine whether it is or is not made by the proper authorities.[1]

§ 78. **Central government of federations the only one recognized by foreign powers.**—This recognition of the United States as a national unit by all other powers is further strengthened by the fact that the States themselves are prohibited by the Constitution from exercising any treaty-

§ 77.
[1] " An objection was taken, on the argument, to the validity of the treaty, on the ground that the Tonawanda band of the Seneca Indians were not represented by the chiefs and head men of the band in the negotiations and execution of it. But the answer to this is, that the treaty, after being executed and ratified by the proper authorities of the Government, becomes the supreme law of the land, and the courts can no more go behind it for the purpose of annulling its effect and operation, than they can behind an act of Congress. (1 Cranch, 103; 6 Pet. 735; 10 How. 442; 2 Pet. 307, 309, 314; 3 Story Const. Law, p. 695.)" *Fellows* vs. *Blacksmith*, U. S. Sup. Ct. 1856, 19 Howard, 366, p. 372, NELSON, J. See also *Jones* vs. *United States*, U. S. Sup. Ct. 1890, 137 U. S. 202, GRAY, J.

making power, or from entering into any negotiations or contracts of any kind with any other power, either State or foreign, as every element of negotiation, as well as of treaty-making, is absolutely confined to the General Government.[1]

§ 79. **Responsibilities as well as benefits result from this rule.**—The proposition above stated carries with it responsibilities as well as benefits. The author does not intend in this volume to go into a lengthy discussion as to the responsibility of the United States government for acts committed in violation of treaty stipulations by States, or by any force which could, or should, be controlled by State authorities. The subject is not only intricate and complicated, but is also exceedingly delicate, and far-reaching in its application; furthermore as the Supreme Court has never authoritatively passed upon the question and definitely determined either the extent of the responsibility of the Central Government for acts of the constituent governments, or the power of the Federal Government to enforce compliance with such stipulations, it would be an academic, rather than a practical discussion, at the present time.

§ 80. **Author's views briefly expressed.**—To the author, however, it seems as though the question of responsibility on the part of the Federal Government for violations of treaties by the action or neglect of the States, is not only a very serious one, but one which sooner or later will give rise to controversies between this government and foreign powers which will eventually be the subject of international arbitration. So long as the States are prohibited from negotiating with foreign powers, those powers will naturally insist that the United States shall itself assume all obligations which may arise from treaty violations, as it is the only power that can deal directly or indirectly with the foreign powers whose interests are affected; while, however, it is a matter of complete indifference to any foreign power having a grievance against the United States, whether the National Government has or

---

§ 78.

[1] "The only Government of this country, which other nations recognize or treat with, is the Government of the Union; and the only American flag known throughout the world is the flag of the United States." *Fong Yue Ting* vs. *United States*, U. S. Sup. Ct. 1893, 149 U. S. 698, p. 711, GRAY, J.

has not the internal power of enforcing compliance with the
treaty stipulation by the separate States, or of compelling
those States to reimburse it for loss resulting from such violation, it is a matter of great importance to the United States,
individually and collectively, that our foreign relations and
the settlement of all disputes arising under treaties, no matter what may be the occasion thereof, should be entirely
controlled by the National Government, in order that no
single State may involve the entire country in international
complications.

§ 81. **Instances in which question has arisen.**—The question of federal responsibility for State violations of treaties
has arisen on several occasions.   A definite determination
of the point, however, has generally been avoided by diplomatic settlements.   The following occurrences, therefore,
are to be considered more as historical episodes, than as legal
precedents.   Four instances will be referred to : The *McLeod*
case in New York in 1841, the Spanish riots of 1851 in New
Orleans, the Mafia riots in Louisiana in 1893, the claim of
the United States against the Republic of Colombia in the
Montijo case in 1871.

§ 82. **The case of the "Caroline"; Great Britain's position.**—In 1837 the steamboat *Caroline* owned by an American citizen was said to be engaged in transporting recruits
and supplies to a rendezvous in Naval Island in Niagara
River for coöperation with some Canadian insurgents.   It
was presumed by Canadian authorities that the boat would
be the means of transferring an expedition to the Canadian
shore ; accordingly a force was dispatched which followed
the boat to the moorings on the American shore, and there
attacked the crew, killing some of them and letting the boat
drift into the river, the current of which carried it over
Niagara Falls resulting in its complete destruction.

This attack was made the subject of diplomatic correspondence, the United States claiming that its territory had
been violated, and the Government of Great Britain maintaining that it was justified on the ground of necessity and
self-preservation.

Later, in 1842, an explanation being made by the British

government, the United States accepted it as satisfactory and allowed the matter to drop.[1]

§ 83. **McLeod's connection with the "Caroline"; his arrest by New York State.**—Some time after the destruction of the *Caroline*, Alexander McLeod, a subject of Great Britain, was arrested by the State of New York on the charge that he had been engaged in the *Caroline* transaction and had committed murder within the jurisdiction of the State of New York. He was indicted, tried and ultimately acquitted. Pending his trial, a writ of *habeas corpus* was applied for on the ground that he was engaged in a governmental act and was not therefore amenable to the local jurisdiction of the State Courts of New York or even those of the United States, as the matter was in course of adjustment by diplomatic departments of the two governments. The State court dismissed the writ and remanded McLeod for trial. Judge Cowen rendered an opinion, in which he asserted that the State of New York had jurisdiction, notwithstanding the matter was the subject of diplomatic discussion between the two countries. In that respect he said :[1]

"But it is said of the case at bar, here is more than a mere approval by the adverse government, that an explanation has been demanded by the secretary of state; and the British ambassador has insisted on McLeod's release, and counsel claim for the *joint* diplomacy of the United States and Eng-

§ 82.

[1] The most complete account of the Caroline and McLeod affairs will be found in Wharton's International Digest, § 21, vol. I., and § 350, vol. III. Citations were there given of all public documents, correspondence and decisions.

§ 83.

[1] Judge Cowen's decision including the extract here quoted from his opinion has been severely criticised. Wharton's Digest in section 350 says: "As to *McLeod's* case, Mr. Webster, in his speech in the Senate on the treaty of Washington (April 6, 1846) said: ' McLeod's case went on in the court of New York, and I was utterly surprised at the decision of that Court on the *habeas corpus*. On the peril and risk of my professional reputation, I now say that the opinion of the court of New York in that case is not a respectable opinion, either on account of the result at which it arrives, or the reasoning on which it proceeds.' In a note it is added that the opinion had been reviewed by Judge Tallmadge, of New York City, and that of this review Chief Justice Spencer said that ' it refutes and overthrows the opinion most amply,' and that Chancellor Kent said, ' It is conclusive at every point. '"

land some such effect upon the power of this court as a cer-
tiorari from us would have upon a county court of general
sessions.   It was spoken of as incompatible with a judicial
proceeding against McLeod in this state; as a suit actually
pending between two nations, wherein the action of the general government comes in collision with, and supersedes
our own.

"To such an objection the answer is quite obvious.   Diplomacy is not a judicial, but executive function; and the
objection would come with the same force whether it were
urged against proceeding in a court of this state, or the
United States.   Whether an actual exertion of the treaty-
making power, by the President and Senate, or any power
delegated to congress by the federal constitution, could work
the consequences contended for, we are not called upon to
inquire: whether the executive of the nation, (supposing
the case to belong to the national court,) or the executive of
this state might not pardon the prisoner, or direct a nolle
prosequi to be entered, are considerations with which we
have nothing to do.

"The executive power is a constitutional department in
this, as in every well organized government, entirely distinct
from the judicial.   And that would be so, were the national
government blotted out, and the state of New York left to
take its place as an independent nation.

"Not only are our constitutions entirely explicit in leaving
the trial of crimes exclusively in the hands of the judiciary:
but neither in the nature of things, nor in sound policy, can
it be confided to the executive power.   That can never act
upon the individual offender; but only by requisition on the
foreign government; and in the instance before us, it has no
power even to enquire whether it be true that McLeod has
personally violated the criminal laws of this state.   It has
charge of the question in its national aspect only.   It must
rely on accidental information, and may place the whole
question on diplomatic considerations.   These may be entirely wide either of the fact or the law as it stands between
this state and the accused.   The whole may turn on questions of national honor, national strength, the comparative
value of national intercourse, or even a point of etiquette.

144

" Upon the principle contended for, every accusation which has been drawn in question by the executive power of two nations, can be adjusted by negotiation or war only. The individual accused must go free, no matter to what extent his case may have been misapprehended by either power. No matter how criminal he may have been, if his country, though acting on false representations of the case, may have been led to approve of the transaction and negotiate concerning it, the demands of criminal justice are at an end.[2]"

§ 84. **Great Britain's position expressed by Mr. Fox.**— While the trial of McLeod was pending the British government made a demand upon the State Department for his release. To this Mr. Forsyth, who was then Secretary of State, replied that the matter was within the jurisdiction of the State of New York, and that the judicial action of that State, under all the circumstances, was proper.

Mr. Fox, the then accredited minister of Great Britain to Washington, was not contented with this, and on March 12, 1841, before the trial of McLeod and after Mr. Webster had become Secretary of State, he delivered a further protest against the continuance of the trial in which he expressed the views of his government in regard to the national responsibility for all acts in violation of treaty or national rights committed by any of the State governments. In the course of his letter he said:

" Her Majesty's government cannot believe that the government of the United States, can really intend to set an example so fraught with evil to the community of nations, and the direct tendency of which must be to bring back into the practice of modern war, atrocities which civilization and Christianity have long since banished.

" Neither can her Majesty's government admit for a moment the validity of the doctrine advanced by Mr. Forsyth, that the federal government of the United States has no power to interfere in the matter in question, and that the decision thereof must rest solely and entirely with the state of New York.

" With the particulars of the internal compact, which may

---

[2] *People* vs. *McLeod*, N. Y. Supreme Ct. 1841, 25 Wendell, 483, pp. 598, 599, COWEN, J.

exist between the several states that compose the Union, foreign powers have nothing to do: the relations of foreign powers are with the aggregate union; that union is to them represented by the federal government; and of that union the federal government is to them the only organ. Therefore, when a foreign power has redress to demand for a wrong done to it by any state of the union, it is to the federal government, and not to the separate state, that such power must look for redress for that wrong. And such foreign power cannot admit the plea that the separate state is an independent body, over which the federal government has no control. It is obvious that such a doctrine, if admitted, would at once go to a dissolution of the union, as far as its relations with foreign powers are concerned; and that foreign powers in such case, instead of accrediting diplomatic agents to the federal government, would send such agents not to that government, but to the government of each separate state; and would make their relations of peace and war with each state, depend upon the result of their separate intercourse with each state, without reference to the relations they might have with the rest.

"Her Majesty's government apprehend, that the above is not the conclusion at which the government of the United States intend to arrive; yet such is the conclusion to which the arguments that have been advanced by Mr. Forsyth necessarily lead.

"But, be that as it may, her Majesty's government formally demand, upon the grounds already stated, the immediate release of Mr. McLeod; and her Majesty's government entreat the President of the United States, to take into his most deliberate consideration the serious nature of the consequences which must ensue from a rejection of this demand."[1]

§ 85. **Mr. Webster's Reply.**—Mr. Webster's reply rather evades the subject of federal responsibility for acts of states; in the course of it, however, he says:

"Soon after the date of Mr. Fox's note, an instruction was

§ 84.
[1] Wharton's Digest, § 21, for citations. See also 25 Wendell, 491, p. 508, where correspondence in full is printed as a note.

given to the attorney general of the United States, from this department, by direction of the President, which fully sets forth the opinions of this government on the subject of McLeod's imprisonment, a copy of which instruction the undersigned has the honor herewith to enclose.

"The indictment against McLeod is pending in a state court; but his rights, whatever they may be, are no less safe, it is to be presumed, than if he were holden to answer in one of the courts of this government.

"He demands immunity from personal responsibility by virtue of the law of nations, and that law in civilized states is to be respected in all courts. None is either so high or so low as to escape from its authority, in cases to which its rules and principles apply.

"This department has been regularly informed by his excellency the Governor of the state of New York, that the chief justice of that state was assigned to preside at the hearing and trial of McLeod's case, but that, owing to some error or mistake in the process of summoning the jury, the hearing was necessarily deferred. The President regrets this occurrence, as he has a desire for a speedy disposition of the subject. The counsel for McLeod have requested authentic evidence of the avowal by the British government, of the attack on and destruction of the 'Caroline,' as acts done under its authority, and such evidence will be furnished to them by this department.

"It is understood that the indictment has been removed into the supreme court of the state, by the proper proceedings for that purpose, and that it is now competent for McLeod, by the ordinary process of *habeas corpus*, to bring his case for hearing before that tribunal.

"The undersigned hardly needs to assure Mr. Fox, that a tribunal so eminently distinguished for ability and learning as the supreme court of the state of New York, may be safely relied upon for the just and impartial administration of the law in this as well as in other cases; and the undersigned repeats the expression of the desire of this government that no delay may be suffered to take place in these proceedings which can be avoided. Of this desire, Mr.

147

Fox will see evidence in the instructions above referred to." [1]

§ 86. **Final disposition of the case ; McLeod's acquittal.**
—After McLeod had been remanded the trial proceeded and resulted in a verdict of acquittal, after which he was released. While this prevented all further complications, it left unde-cided the important questions as to whether or not the Fed-eral Government could have interfered and taken McLeod from the jurisdiction of the State courts, and either tried him under some federal statute, or released him in accordance with diplomatic arrangements made between the two coun-tries.

§ 87. **Federal statutes passed to meet similar cases.**—At that time there were no federal statutes under which the United States could prevent the trial, in State courts, of McLeod or other persons similarly indicted ; in order that the recurrence of such controversies might be prevented there-after, and that the action of a single State might not jeop-ardize the foreign relations of the entire country, the act of August 29, 1842, [1] was passed by Congress under which fed-

---

§ 85.
[1] 1 Wharton's Digest, § 21, for ci-tation. See also, 25 Wendell, 491, 512, 513, where correspondence is printed in full as a note.

§ 87.
[1] "Sec. 752. The several justices and judges of the said [Federal] Courts, within their respective ju-risdictions, shall have power to grant writs of *habeas corpus* for the purpose of an inquiry into the cause of restraint of liberty.

"Sec. 753. The writ of *habeas corpus* shall in no case extend to a prisoner in jail, unless when he is in custody under or by color of the authority of the United States, or is committed for trial before some court thereof; or is in custody for an act done or omitted in pursu-ance of a law of the United States, or of an order, process, or decree of a court or judge thereof; or is

in custody in violation of the Con-stitution or of a law or treaty of the United States; or, being a sub-ject or citizen of a foreign state, and domiciled therein, is in custody for an act done or omitted under any alleged right, title, authority, privilege, protection, or exemp-tion claimed under the commission, or order, or sanction of any foreign state, or under color thereof, the validity and effect whereof depend upon the law of nations; or unless it is necessary to bring the prisoner into court to testify.

"Sec. 754. Application for writ of *habeas corpus* shall be made to the court, or justice, or judge au-thorized to issue the same, by com-plaint in writing, signed by the person for whose relief it is in-tended, setting forth the facts con-cerning the detention of the party restrained, in whose custody he is

eral courts have jurisdiction of such matters. That statute has since been incorporated in sections 752–4 of the Revised Statutes of the United States. The United States courts are thus enabled to investigate the cause of detention of any person held under a State indictment for offences similar to those with which McLeod was charged, and which are really not so much violations of the sovereignty of any particular State as they are of the sovereignty of the United States. The right of the United States to intervene in such cases is apparent when it is considered that if any international complications had arisen owing to the McLeod incident, they would have affected not only the State of New York, but the entire country. Had Great Britain seen fit to resort to arms to redress the injuries which she claimed her citizen has sustained, she would not necessarily have limited her attacks to the northern frontier of New York State, but could have commenced hostilities wherever she saw fit, at any point on land or sea; nor would the State of New York have been able, nor would she have been permitted, to meet these attacks solely with her own State militia. The entire naval and military forces of the United States, as a nation, would necessarily have been called into action in order to repel the invasion by, or the hostile attacks of, a foreign State, on any part of the domain of the United States, State or national.

§ 88. **Anti-Spanish Riots in New Orleans of 1851.**—In August, 1851, a mob in New Orleans demolished the building in which the office of the Spanish consul was located. At the same time attacks were made upon coffee houses and cigar shops kept by Spanish subjects. American citizens were involved in the loss which, in the aggregate, was large. The supposed cause of the mob was the intelligence of the execution of 50 young Americans in Havana and the banishment to Spanish mines of nearly 200 citizens of the United States. The victims were all members of the abortive Lopez expedition against Cuba. In consequence of these depre-

detained, and by virtue of what claim or authority, if known. The facts set forth in the complaint shall be verified by the oath of the person making the application."

5 U. S. Stat. at Large, p. 539; 29 Aug. 1842, c. 257, s. 1; see also Wharton's Int. Law Dig. vol. 1, section 21.

dations of the mob upon the property of the Spanish consul, as well as against Spanish subjects, the Minister of Spain demanded indemnification for all the losses, both official and personal. Mr. Webster admitted that the Spanish consul was entitled to indemnity, and made a proposition as to how the indignity offered to the representative of the Spanish government should be accorded; but when pressed by the Spanish Minister to afford an indemnity to Spanish subjects who were injured by the mob, in common with American citizens, Mr. Webster declined to accede to the demand, and gave as his reasons that as many American citizens had suffered equal loss, the private individuals, Spanish subjects, coming voluntarily to reside in the United States had no cause of complaint, for they were protected by the same laws and the same administration of law as native born citizens of this country.[1]

§ 88.

[1] The history of the anti-Spanish riots in New Orleans will be found in the Foreign Relations Reports for 1851–2, and rehearsed in the Reports for 1891, during the Mafia Riot correspondence. The following is an extract from a note sent by Daniel Webster, Secretary of State, to Mr. Calderon, the Spanish Minister, November 13, 1851:

"The assembling of mobs happens in all countries; popular violences occasionally break out everywhere, setting law at defiance, trampling on the rights of citizens and private men; and sometimes on those of public officers, and the agents of foreign governments, especially entitled to protection. In these cases the public faith and national honor require, not only that such outrages should be disavowed, but also that the perpetrators of them should be punished, whenever it is possible to bring them to justice; and further, that full satisfaction should be made in cases in which a duty to that effect rests with the government, according to the general principles of law, public faith, and the obligation of treaties.

"Mr. Calderon thinks that the enormity of this act of popular violence is heightened by its insult to the flag of Spain. The Government of the United States would earnestly deprecate any indignity offered in this country, in time of peace, to the flag of a nation so ancient, so respectable, so renowned as Spain. No wonder that Mr. Calderon should be proud, and that all patriotic Spaniards of this generation should be proud of the Castilian ensign which in times past has been reared so high and waved so often over fields of acknowledged and distinguished valor; and which has floated, also, without stain, on all seas, and especially, in early days, on those seas which washed the shores of all the Indies.

"Mr. Calderon may be assured that the government of the United States does not and cannot desire

§ 89. Mr. Webster's position.—The above section is quoted almost *verbatim* from a résumé of the occurrences of 1851,

to witness the desecration or degredation of the national banner of his country. It appears, however, that in point of fact no flag was actually flying or publicly exhibited when the outrage took place; but this can make no difference in regard to the real nature of the offence or its enormity. The persons composing the mob knew that they were offering insult and injury to an officer of Her Catholic Majesty, residing in the United States under the sanction of laws and treaties; and, therefore, their conduct admits of no justification. Nevertheless, Mr. Calderon and his government are aware that recent intelligence had been received from Havana, not a little calculated to excite popular feeling in a great city, and to lead to popular excesses. If this be no justification, as it certainly is none, it may still be taken into view, and regarded as showing that the outrage, however flagrant, was committed in the heat of blood, and not in pursuance of any predetermined plan or purpose of injury or insult.

"The people of the United States are accustomed, in all cases of alleged crime, to slow and cautious investigation and deliberate trial before sentence of condemnation is passed, however apparent or however enormous the imputed offence may be. No wonder, therefore, that the information of the execution, so soon after their arrest, of the persons above referred to—most of whom were known in New Orleans, and who were taken not in Cuba, but at sea, endeavoring to escape from the island—should have produced a belief, however erroneous, that they had been executed without any trial whatever, caused an excitement in the city, the outbreak of which the public authorities were unable for the moment to prevent or control.

"Mr. Calderon expresses the opinion that not only ought indemnification to be made to Mr. Laborde, her Catholic Majesty's consul, for injury and loss of property, but that reparation is due also from the government of the United States to those Spaniards residing in New Orleans whose property was injured or destroyed by the mob; and intimates that such reparation had been verbally promised to him. The undersigned sincerely regrets that any misapprehension should have grown out of any conversation between Mr. Calderon and officers of this government on this unfortunate and unpleasant affair; but while this government has manifested a willingness and determination to perform every duty which one friendly nation has a right to expect from another, in cases of this kind, it supposes that the rights of the Spanish consul, a public officer residing here under the protection of the United States Government, are quite different from those of the Spanish subjects who have come into the country to mingle with our own citizens, and here to pursue their private business and objects. The former may claim special indemnity; the latter are entitled to such protection as is afforded to our own citizens.

"While, therefore, the losses of individuals, private Spanish subjects, are greatly to be regretted, yet it is understood that many

151

contained in a note written in 1891 by Mr. Blaine to the
Marquis Imperiali, in regard to the Malia riots, which will be
referred to at a subsequent point in this chapter.[1]

Mr. Webster in 1851 took the position that the widows
and children of the United States citizens who had lost their
lives by mob violence could sue the leaders and members of
the mob only in the courts of the State of Louisiana, while
the widows and children of Spanish subjects had the right to
sue each member of the mob, not only in the State courts,
but also before the federal tribunals for the District of Louisiana ; there was an attempt made to disclaim all responsibility

American citizens suffered equal
losses from the same cause. And
these private individuals, subjects
of her Catholic Majesty, coming
voluntarily to reside in the United
States, have certainly no cause of
complaint, if they are protected by
the same law and the same administration of law as native-born citizens of this country. They have,
in fact, some advantages over citizens of the State in which they
happen to be, inasmuch as they
are enabled, until they become citizens themselves, to prosecute for
any injuries done to their persons
or property in the courts of the
United States, or the State courts,
at their election. The President is
of opinion, as already stated, that
for obvious reasons the case of the
consul is different, and that the
government of the United States
should provide for Mr. Laborde a
just indemnity; and a recommendation to that effect will be laid before Congress at an early period of
its approaching session. This is
all which it is in his power to do.
The case may be a new one; but
the President, being of opinion
that Mr. Laborde ought to be indemnified, has not thought it
necessary to search for precedents.

"In conclusion, the undersigned
has to say, that if Mr. Laborde
shall return to his post, or any
other consul for New Orleans shall
be appointed by her Catholic Majesty's Government, the officers of
this government, resident in that
city, will be instructed to receive
and treat him with courtesy, and
with a national salute to the flag
of his ship, if he shall arrive in a
Spanish vessel, as a demonstration
of respect, such as may signify to
him, and to his government, the
sense entertained by the government of the United States of the
gross injustice done his predecessor
by a lawless mob, as well as the
indignity and insult offered by it to
a foreign State, with which the
United States are, and wish ever
to remain, on terms of the most
respectful and pacific intercourse.
"The undersigned avails himself
of this occasion to offer to Mr. Calderon renewed assurances of his
most distinguished consideration."
(Foreign Relations of the U. S.,
1851–52, pp. 63–65.) See also 2
Wharton's Digest, § 226.

§ 89.

[1] See § 94, *post*, and extracts from
Secretary Blaine's note in the footnote to that section.

on the part of the federal government for the violence done to Spanish citizens.[2]

§ 90. **Indemnity ultimately paid to sufferers.**—Two years later, however, in recognition of the magnanimous conduct of the Queen of Spain in pardoning American citizens who had unjustifiably invaded the Island of Cuba, a joint resolution was adopted by Congress and approved by President Fillmore March 3, 1853, indemnifying the Spanish Consul and other Spanish subjects for the losses sustained in the New Orleans mob of 1851. The State department, however, are on record as stating in the letter above referred to that the considerations upon which this resolution was passed were held not to contravene the original position of Mr. Webster, which was shared also by President Fillmore.[1]

§ 91. **The Mafia Riots in New Orleans of 1891.**—On March 14, 1891, a number of Italians then confined in the jail in New Orleans, were forcibly taken from the jail and hanged, by the action of a large number of citizens.

The episode has passed into history under the title of the Mafia Riots. Many of the respectable citizens of New Orleans, however, claim that it was not in the nature of a riotous outbreak, but a mere enforcement of justice in a summary manner after the local courts had failed to administer it in pursuance of law upon criminals who had, under a regular organization, committed many atrocious crimes, and that the method adopted was the only practical way of putting a complete stop to the outrages which they claimed had been committed through the "Mafia."

The Marquis Rudini immediataly cabled from Rome to Baron Fava, the Italian Minister to the United States, "to denounce immediately to the United States government the atrocious deed of New Orleans, requesting immediate and energetic steps to repress the riot, to protect the Italian colony endangered thereby, and also to severely punish the guilty."

Baron Fava made a formal demand at once upon Mr. Blaine, who was then Secretary of State. A lengthy correspondence ensued between Governor Nicholls of Louisiana

[2] See § 88 *ante.*
§ **90.**

[1] U. S. Foreign Relations Reports 1891, p. 684.

and Mr. Blaine in regard to the occurrences, and between Mr. Blaine and Baron Fava as to the liability of the United States.

§ 92. **Complications arising from the Mafia Riots.**—This correspondence is very lengthy, comprising over fifty pages of the Foreign Relations Reports of 1891.   On April 2, 1891, the Italian government repeated its demand for prompt settlement of its claims, and demanded indemnity for the families of the men who had been killed.

The correspondence shows that, at times, the situation became quite acute and various questions other than the liability of the Federal Government were involved, such as the conduct of the Italians, and whether or not they had retained their citizenship of Italy and were entitled to the protection of the Italian government.   So strained did the relations between the Governments of the United States and Italy become that the Italian Minister withdrew from Washington and diplomatic relations were for a time practically suspended.

We are, however, interested only in the single point as to the position taken in the correspondence by the two governments as to the liability of the Government of the United States, for the failure of the State government of Louisiana, to afford to Italian citizens the protection to life and property which is reciprocally assured to the citizens of the two countries under the then existing treaty stipulations.

§ 93. **Action of the State courts of Louisiana.**—A grand jury, consisting of many prominent citizens of New Orleans, found that the acquittals of the Italians by trial juries were improper, and that the uprising of citizens and the resulting summary executions, or lynchings, were the result of the dangerous form which the " Mafia " had assumed ; and that the respectable element of New Orleans feared that unless some such prompt and energetic action was taken it would be impossible to suppress the Italian secret societies and prevent the recurrence of similar atrocities, which had increased to a tremendous extent owing to the practical immunity afforded by the constant acquittal of persons brought to trial.[1]

§ 93.
[1] The report of the Grand Jury appears at length at page 714 et seq. of the Foreign Relations Reports for 1891.

None of the participants in the "summary execution" of the Italians were indicted or tried. The Italian government protested against the non-punishment of the parties whom it claimed had participated in the killing of Italian citizens and the gross violations of treaty stipulations. In the Circuit Court of the United States it was held that the heirs of the Italians who had been killed could not recover.[2]

[2] This was an action arising out of what are known as the Mafia Riots in New Orleans in 1891. The plaintiff recovered a judgment for five thousand dollars for the death of her son, who was killed during the course of the riots. He was an Italian citizen. The liability of the municipal governments arising out of the treaty relations of the treaty with Italy of 1871, involved this case. The Circuit Court of Appeals reversed the decision with instructions to maintain the exception of non-liability of the city and to dismiss the plaintiff's petition as stated in the opinion (pp. 541–42):

"The City of New Orleans by her pleadings admits the gross negligence charged in the petition in the performance of the duties devolving upon the municipality under the constitution and laws of the state above referred to, whereby Abbagnato lost his life at the hands of a mob while in the custody of the law; and the question presented in this case is whether on such admission of facts the city can be held liable in damages.

"It is well settled that at common law no civil action lies for an injury to a person which results in his death. *Insurance Company* vs. *Brame*, 95 U. S. 754, 756; *Dennick* vs. *Railroad Company*, 103 U. S. 11, 21; *The Harrisburg*, 119 U. S. 199, 214. The rule is the same under the civil law, according to the decisions of the Louisiana Supreme Court. *Hubgh* vs. *The New Orleans and Carrollton Railroad Company*, 6 La. Ann. 495; *Hermann* vs. *The New Orleans and Carollton Railroad Company*, 11 La. Ann. 5. In the absence of a statute giving a remedy, public or municipal corporations are under no liability to pay for the property of individuals destroyed by mobs or riotous assemblages. Addison on Torts (notes by Dudley & Baylies, 1880), sec. 1530; 2 Dillon's Municipal Corporations, sec. 959."

The effect of a treaty upon the question involved was discussed and disposed of at the opening of the opinion as follows:

"The treaty between the Kingdom of Italy and the United States, proclaimed on November 23, 1871, guarantees to the citizens of either nation in the territory of the other 'the most constant protection and security for their persons and property,' and further provides that 'they shall enjoy in this respect the same rights and privileges as are or shall be granted to the natives, on their submitting themselves to the conditions imposed upon the natives.' Treaty of November 23, 1871, 17 Stat. (Treaties) 49, 50, art. 3. This treaty applies to this case only so far as to require that the rights of the plaintiff shall be adjudicated and determined exactly the same as if she were, and her deceased son had been, a native citizen of the United States."

§ 94. **Mr. Blaine's position.**—On April 14, 1891, Secretary Blaine sent a lengthy note to the Marquis Imperiali containing a résumé of the positions taken by the United States on such subjects, and in which he recited the incident of the Spanish Mob of 1851, already referred to in this chapter,[1] and also declared, that "if it shall be found, as seems probable, that criminal proceedings can only be taken in the courts of Louisiana the President can, in this direction, do no more than to urge upon the State officers the duty of promptly bringing the offenders to trial."

A statement at the end of his letter, however, contained a qualified admission as to the liability of the United States, if the facts were as claimed by the Italian government.

Mr. Blaine's letter is exceedingly guarded as to all possible liability of the United States and the extract in the notes appended to this section shows that he took the position that the citizens of foreign countries residing in our States must seek their redress from the courts of those States, and that the United States government does not become the insurer of lives of the citizens of foreign countries, even though it may enter into treaty stipulations with them, but that all it can do or is called upon to do is to afford to citizens of those countries the same rights which citizens of the United States are accorded under similar circumstances.[2]

New Orleans vs. *Abbagnato*, U. S. Cir. Ct. App., 5 Cir., 23 U. S. App. 533, PARDEE, J.

§ 94.
[1] See § 88 *ante.*

[2] The correspondence between this country and Italy in regard to the Mafia Riots appears in the Foreign Relations Reports for 1891. The following is an extract from a note sent on April 14, 1891, by James G. Blaine, then Secretary of State, to the Marquis Imperiali, the Italian minister to the United States:

"If it shall result that the case can be prosecuted only in the State courts of Louisiana, and the usual judicial investigation and procedure under the criminal law is not resorted to, it will then be the duty of the United States to consider whether some other form of redress may be asked. It is understood that the State grand jury is now investigating the affair, and, while it is possible that the jury may fail to present the indictments, the United States cannot assume that such will be the case.

"The United States did not by the treaty with Italy become the insurer of the lives or property of Italian subjects resident within our territory. No Government is able, however high its civilization, however vigilant its police supervision, however severe its criminal code,

§ 95. **Final result of the Mafia cases.**—A year after the Mafia Riots, Secretary Blaine tendered to the Italian government 125,000 francs to be distributed by that government

and however prompt and inflexible its criminal administration, to secure its own citizens against violence promoted by individual malice or by sudden popular tumult. The foreign resident must be content in such cases to share the same redress that is offered by the law to the citizen, and has no just cause of complaint or right to ask the interposition of his country if the courts are equally open to him for the redress of his injuries. The treaty, in the first, second, third, and, notably, in the twenty-third articles, clearly limits the rights guaranteed to the citizens of the contracting powers in the territory of each to equal treatment and to free access to the courts of justice. Foreign residents are not made a favored class. It is not believed that Italy would desire a more stringent construction of her duty under the treaty. Where the injury inflicted upon a foreign resident is not the act of the Government or of its officers, but of an individual or of a mob, it is believed that no claim for indemnity can justly be made, unless it shall be made to appear that the public authorities charged with the peace of the community have connived at the unlawful act, or, having timely notice of the threatened danger, have been guilty of such gross negligence in taking the necessary precautions as to amount to connivance.

"If, therefore, it should appear that among those killed by the mob at New Orleans there were some Italian subjects who were resident or domiciled in that city, agreeably to our treaty with Italy, and not in violation of our immigration laws, and who were abiding in the peace of the United States and obeying the laws thereof and of the State of Louisiana, and that the public officers charged with the duty of protecting life and property in that city connived at the work of the mob, or, upon proper notice or information of the threatened danger, failed to take any steps for the preservation of the public peace and afterwards to bring the guilty to trial, the President would, under such circumstances, feel that a case was established that should be submitted to the consideration of Congress with a view to the relief of the families of the Italian subjects who had lost their lives by lawless violence." (Foreign Relations of the United States, 1891, p. 685.)

Mr. Blaine's note being transmitted to his government called forth the following cable reply from the Marquis Rudini to the Marquis Imperiali which was received at the State Department May 4, 1891:

"I have now before me a note addressed to you by Secretary Blaine, April 14. Its perusal produces a most painful impression upon me. I will not stop to lay stress upon the lack of conformity with diplomatic usages displayed in making use, as Mr. Blaine did not hesitate to do, of a portion of a telegram of mine communicated to him in strict confidence, in order to get rid of a question clearly defined in our official documents, which alone possess a diplomatic value. Nor will I stop to point out the reference in this telegram of mine of March 24, that the words 'punishment of the guilty' in the brevity of telegraphic language

amongst the families of the victims; the letter offering this indemnity disclaimed any liability on the part of the United States government, as appears by the following extract:

" While the injury was not inflicted directly by the United States, the President, nevertheless, feels that it is the solemn duty, as well as the great pleasure, of the national government to pay a satisfactory indemnity.   Moreover the President's instructions carry with them the hope that the transaction of to-day may efface all memory of the unhappy tragedy; that the old and friendly relations of the United States and Italy may be restored; and that nothing un-

signified only that prosecution ought to be commenced, in order that the individuals recognized as guilty should not escape punishment.

" Far above all astute arguments remains the fact that henceforth the Federal Government declares itself conscious of what we have constantly asked, and yet it does not grant our legitimate demands.

"Mr. Blaine is right when he makes the payment of indemnity to the families of the victims dependent upon proof of the violation of the treaty; but we shrink from thinking that he considers that the fact of such violation still needs proof.   Italian subjects acquitted by American juries were massacred in prisons of the State without measures being taken to defend them.

" What other proof does the Federal Government expect of a violation of a treaty wherein constant protection and security of subjects of the contracting parties is expressly stipulated?

" We have placed on evidence that we have never asked anything else but the opening of regular proceedings.   In regard to this, Baron Fava's first note, dated March 15, contained even the formula of the telegram addressed on the same day by Mr. Blaine, under the order of President Harrison, to the governor of Louisiana.   Now, however, in the note of April 14, Mr. Blaine is silent on the subject which is, for us, the main point of controversy.

" We are under the sad necessity of concluding that what to every other government would be the accomplishment of simple duty is impossible to the Federal Government.   It is time to break off the bootless controversy.   Public opinion, the sovereign judge, will know how to indicate an equitable solution of this grave problem.

" We have affirmed, and we again affirm, our right.   Let the Federal Government reflect upon its side if it is expedient to leave to the mercy of each State of the Union, irresponsible to foreign countries, the efficiency of treaties pledging its faith and honor to entire nations.

" The present dispatch is addressed to you exclusively, not to the Federal Government.

" Your duties henceforth are solely restricted to dealing with current business."   (Foreign Relations of the United States, 1891, p. 712.)

toward may ever again occur to disturb their harmonious friendship."

The Marquis Imperiali replied, accepting the indemnity and declaring that the diplomatic relations between Italy and the United States were, from that moment, fully re-established. Thus ended one of those unfortunate occurrences which are possible even in the most civilized countries and which, unless they are settled diplomatically by both sides making concessions, may result in strained relations between governments, which oftentimes are, unhappily, only terminated by war.[1]

§ 95.

[1] The correspondence was as follows:

From Mr. Blaine to the Marquis Imperiali, April 12, 1892:

"Sir: I congratulate you that the difficulty existing between the United States and Italy growing out of the lamentable massacre at New Orleans in March of last year is about to be terminated. The President, feeling that for such an injury there should be ample indemnity, instructs me to tender to you 125,000 francs. The Italian Government will distribute this sum among the families of the victims.

"While the injury was not inflicted directly by the United States, the President nevertheless feels that it is the solemn duty, as well as the great pleasure, of the National Government to pay a satisfactory indemnity. Moreover, the President's instructions carry with them the hope that the transaction of today may efface all memory of the unhappy tragedy; that the old and friendly relations of the United States and Italy may be restored; and that nothing untoward may ever again occur to disturb their harmonious friendship.

"I avail myself of this occasion to assure you that your prolonged service at this capital as chargé des affaires has been marked by every quality that renders you grateful and acceptable to the Government of the United States, and to renew to you the assurance of my high consideration." (Foreign Relations of the United States, 1891, pp. 727, 728.)

The Marquis Imperiali to Mr. Blaine April 12, 1892:

"Mr. Secretary of State: You were pleased to inform me, by your note of today, that the Federal Government has decided to pay to Italy, by way of indemnity, the sum of 125,000 francs, which will be distributed by the Italian Government among the families of the royal subjects who were victims of the massacre which took place March 14, 1891, in the city of New Orleans. Your excellency also expresses the hope that the decision reached by the President will put an end to the unfortunate incident to which that deplorable occurrence gave rise, and that the relations between the two countries will be firmly re-established.

"After having taken note, with much pleasure, of the language used by the President in his message of December last, and after

159

§ 96. **The " Montijo " case; claims by the United States against other confederations; federal responsibility for acts of State.**—In April, 1871, the steamer *Montijo* belonging to citizens of the United States was seized by revolutionists while on a voyage to Panama, being at the time within the jurisdiction of the United States of Colombia.

The claim was duly presented and after an extended diplomatic correspondence an agreement of arbitration was entered into between the United States and the Colombian government in August, 1874.[1] During the course of the correspondence the question of the liability of the central government of Colombia for the acts of the State of Panama which was one of the constituent States forming that confederation was raised. The United States claimed that under the peculiar circumstances the acts constituted a breach of treaty stipulations for which the federal government was liable. On the other hand the Colombian government disclaimed all lia-

having fully appreciated the words of regret and censure uttered with so much authority by the Chief Magistrate of the Republic, and likewise the recommendations that were suggested by the lamentable incident to his lofty wisdom, His Majesty's Government is now happy to learn that the United States acknowledge that it is their solemn duty, and at the same time a great pleasure, to pay an indemnity to Italy.

"The King's Government does not hesitate to accept this indemnity without prejudice to the judicial steps which it may be proper for the parties to take, and, considering the redress obtained sufficient, it sees no reason why the relations between the two Governments, which relations should faithfully reflect the sentiments of reciprocal esteem and sympathy that animate the two nations, should not again become intimate and cordial, as they have traditionally been in the past and as it is to be hoped they will ever be in the future.

"In bringing the foregoing to your knowledge, in virtue of the authorization given me by his excellency the Marquis di Rudini, president of the council, minister of foreign affairs, in the name of the Government of his Majesty, the King of Italy, my August Sovereign, I have the honor to declare to your excellency that the diplomatic relations between Italy and the United States are from this moment fully re-established.

"I hasten, moreover, in obedience to instructions received, to inform you that, pending the minister's return to this capital, I have taken charge of the royal legation in the capacity of chargé d'affaires.

"Be pleased to accept, etc." (Foreign Relations of the United States, 1891, p. 728.)

§ **96.**

[1] Moore's International Arbitrations History, vol. II, p. 1425.

bility, alleging that the improper acts, if any, were committed within the jurisdiction of Panama and were beyond the control of the federal government.

§ 97. **Result of the Arbitration.**—In April, 1875, the Colombian arbitrator filed an opinion holding that the federal government of Colombia had not incurred any liability to the American claimants. The United States arbitrator at the same time filed an opinion maintaining the opposite view. The matter was subsequently referred to an umpire who, in July, 1875, rendered an award in favor of the United States for $33,000, which was considerably less than the demand made by the owners of the steamer.

§ 98. **Decision of the Umpire.**—There were many points in the decision of the umpire, who was Mr. Robert Bunch the British Minister at Bogota, which did not involve the question of responsibility of a federal government for the acts of one of the constituent States, but we refer to the opinion only in that respect. In discussing this question he says: "The reason advanced by the Colombian arbitrator is that the government of that Union cannot be held answerable for the failure of that of Panama to compensate the owners of the Montijo, because the former has no connection with it and private debts, especially with those which have in the case a vicious origin. To this the undersigned (the Umpire) replies, First: That in his opinion the government of the Union has a very clear and decided connection with the debts incurred by the States of the Union towards foreigners whose treaty rights have been invaded or attacked; and Secondly : That the debts so incurred by the separate States are in no way private, but on the contrary, are entirely public in their character."

The Umpire then proceeds to discuss the question; he reviewed the *McLeod* case at length and in referring to it said that undoubtedly the liability of federal powers for acts of the constituent States may produce to the nation at large the gravest complications : he also held that debts contracted by duly authorized officers of a given State are essentially public and can be the subject of an international arbitration of this nature.[1]

A full account of this controversy and the award of the umpire can be found in Chapter XXIX of the second volume of Moore's History of International Arbitration.

§ 98.

[1] "NATIONAL RESPONSIBILITY FOR STATE ACTS.

" 'There remains to be considered the concluding portion of the sixth reason advanced by the Colombian arbitrator, which is that the government of the Union cannot be held answerable for the failure of that of Panama to compensate the owners of the *Montijo* because the former has no connection (*solidaridad*) with private debts, especially with those which have, as in the present case, a vicious origin.

" 'To this the undersigned replies, first, that in his opinion the government of the Union has a very clear and decided connection with the debts incurred by the States of the Union toward foreigners whose treaty rights have been invaded or attacked; and, secondly, that the debts so incurred by the separate States are in no way private, but, on the contrary, entirely public in their character.

" 'As regards the first point, it cannot be denied that the treaties under which the residence of foreigners in Colombia is authorized, and their rights during such residence defined and assured, are made with the general government, and not with the separate States of which the Union is composed. The same practice obtains in the United States, in Switzerland, and in all countries in which the federal system is adopted. In the event, then, of the violation of a treaty stipulation, it is evident that a recourse must be had to the entity with which the international engagements were made. There is no one else to whom application can be directed. For treaty purposes the separate States are nonexistent; they have parted with a certain defined portion of their inherent sovereignty, and can only be dealt with through their accredited representative or delegate, the federal or general government.

" 'But if it be admitted that such is the theory and the practice of the federal system, it is equally clear that the duty of addressing the general government carries with it the right to claim from that government, and from it alone, the fulfillment of the international pact. If a manifest wrong be committed by a separate State, no diplomatic remonstrance can be addressed to it. It is true that in such a case the resident consular officer of a foreign power may call the attention of the transgressing State to the consequences of its action, and may endeavor by timely and friendly intervention on the spot to avoid the necessity of an ultimate application to the general government through the customary diplomatic channel; but should this overture fail, there remains no remedy but the interference of the federal power, which is bound to redress the wrong, and, if necessary, compensate the injured foreigner.

" 'If this rule which the undersigned believes to be beyond dispute, be correctly laid down, it follows that in every case of international wrong the general government of this republic has a very close connection with the proceedings of the separate States of the Union. As it,

§ 99. Moore's History of International Arbitration.—
The author wishes to take this opportunity of expressing the

and it alone, is responsible to foreign nations, it is bound to show in every case that it has done its best to obtain satisfaction from the aggressor.

"'But it will probably be said that by the constitution of Colombia the federal power is prohibited from interfering in the domestic disturbances of the States, and that it cannot in justice be made accountable for acts which it has not the power, under the fundamental charter of the republic to prevent or to punish. To this the undersigned will remark that in such a case a treaty is superior to the constitution, which latter must give way. The legislation of the republic must be adapted to the treaty, not the treaty to the laws. This constantly happens in engagements between separate and independent nations. For the purposes of carrying out the stipulations of a treaty, special laws are required. They are made *ad hoc*, even though they may extend to foreigners' privileges and immunities which the subjects or citizens of one or both of the treaty-making powers do not enjoy at home.

"'That under such a rule apparent injustice may occasionally be committed is probably true. But it is more apparent then real. It may seem at first sight unfair to make the federal power, and through it the taxpayers of the country, responsible, morally and pecuniarily, for events over which they have no control, and which they probably disapprove or disavow, but the injustice disappears when this inconvenience is found to be inseparable from the federal system. If a nation deliberately adopts that form of administering its public affairs, it does so with the full knowledge of the consequences it entails. It calculates the advantages and the drawbacks, and cannot complain if the latter now and then make themselves felt.

"'That this liability of the federal power for the acts of the States may produce to the nation at large the gravest complications is matter of history. Probably the most serious case of this inconvenience on record is that of a British subject named McLeod, whose arrest and trial by the State of New York nearly involved Great Britain and the United States in a war. During the Canadian rebellion, an American steamer called the *Caroline*, which had been engaged in carrying arms to the rebels, was boarded in the night by a party of loyalists, set on fire, and driven over the Falls of Niagara. In this affray an American citizen lost his life. In January, 1841, Alexander McLeod, a British subject, was arrested while engaged in some business in New York State, and imprisoned on a charge of murder because as was alleged, he was concerned in the attack on the vessel. The British Government demanded his release on the ground that he was acting under orders, and that the responsibility rested with Great Britain and not with the individual. The Secretary of State of the United States replied that his government was powerless in the matter, as it could not interfere with the tribunals of the State of New York. Great Britain then caused it to be distinctly understood that the condemnation and execution of

163

great obligation that all students of international law are
under to the Honorable John Bassett Moore for his great

Mr. McLeod would be immediately followed by a declaration of war.
Lord Palmerston, then secretary for foreign affairs, told Mr. Stevenson,
United States minister in London, that such would be the case. Great
efforts were made by the friends of peace, and as much pressure as
could properly be applied to the State of New York was brought to
bear, and McLeod was acquitted. But two great and powerful nations
were on the verge of a disastrous war because the federal power was
held liable for the acts of a separate State.

" 'As regards the second point made by the Colombian arbitrator that
the debts incurred to foreigners by the separate States of the Union are
private in their character, the undersigned can only express his dissent
from the doctrine. If an engagement, pecuniary or other, made by the
constitutional head of a State, acting, as in the present case, 'in virtue
of powers conferred by law,' is to be considered in the same light as
an ordinary mercantile debt and only to be recoverable in the same
manner, the possibility of a State contracting with either native or
foreigners would soon be reduced to very narrow limits. The chances
of repayment would depend on the stability of the contracting government, and this of itself would introduce an element of considerable
uncertainty into such transactions.

" ' The undersigned holds that all debts contracted by duly authorized
officers of a given State are essentially public in their character, and
that their nonpayment can be made the subject of remonstrance by a
foreign nation should the engagements be contracted with its subjects
or citizens. It is quite true that Great Britain, the greatest lender of
money in existence does not feel herself bound to interfere on behalf
of her subjects in every case where they may have lent money to foreign
countries, as she holds, as a general rule, that they may be left to find
their own remedy for their imprudence; but she explicitly declares
that this absentation on her part is a mere matter of discretion, and that
she has the undoubted right to interfere whenever she may see fit to
do so.

" ' 'As regards the 'vicious origin,' of the present debt, the undersigned does not view it in that light; he cannot, therefore, agree with
any deductions from that assumption.

" ' 'For these reasons the undersigned holds, as a general principle,
that the government of the Union is responsible in certain cases for the
wrongs inflicted on foreigners by the separate States, and that debts
contracted by the constituted authorities of those States are not private
in their character. He is compelled, therefore, to dissent from the
sixth reason of the Colombian arbitrator.

" ' 'The undersigned has now reviewed to the best of his ability the
able and elaborate arguments of the honorable, the arbitrator of Colombia on this question. He wishes he could have brought to the task the
same brilliant qualities which Senor Tanco has so liberally displayed,
and it would have been agreeable to him to have concurred in the views

and valuable work on International Arbitration and the position of the United States in regard thereto.

To write a history of the fifty-two arbitrations to which the United States has been a party, with references to all the other arbitrations which have settled international disputes between other countries, amounting in all to over one hundred and fifteen separate cases, is an undertaking which any man may well shrink from, no matter how well qualified he may be for the task; the complete and admirable manner, however, in which Mr. Moore has performed and accomplished his work will always remain a monument not only to his great ability, but also to his untiring perseverance.

No one interested in subjects involving arbitrations, treaty rights, rights of citizenship or other matters connected with the foreign relations of the United States should fail either to read the history or to examine the digest volume, as the scope of the work is so wide that almost every conceivable subject involved in international relations which has been the subject of adjudication by international arbitration can be found at its proper place in Mr. Moore's history.[1]

§ 100. **Importance of the "Montijo" decision on the position of the United States.**—The claim of the owners of the *Montijo* was presented through, and prosecuted by, the State Department of the United States, and the arbitrator appointed by the United States was a government official, being the minister resident to the Colombian government. This decision may at some future time be used as a precedent

of a gentleman whom he so highly esteems.' " Moore, International Arbitrations' History, vol. 2, pages 1439–1442.

§ 99.

[1] Moore John Bassett; International Arbitrations—History.

History and Digest of the International Arbitrations to which the United States has been a Party, together with Appendices containing the Treaties relating to such Arbitrations and Historical and Legal Notes on other International Arbitrations, Ancient and Modern, and on the Domestic Commissions of the United States for the Adjustment of International Claims, By John Bassett Moore, Hamilton Fish Professor of International Law and Diplomacy, Columbia University, New York; Associate of the Institute of International Law; some time Assistant Secretary of State of the United States; author of a work on Extradition and Interstate Rendition, of American Notes on the Conflict of Laws, etc. In six volumes, Washington Government Printing Office, 1898.

against the contention of the United States that it is not responsible for violations of treaty stipulations resulting from the acts, or negligence, of the States composing the Union. There may, however, be some points of difference between the cases which arise hereafter, which will enable the United States Government to distinguish them from this case which involved revolutions, and hostilities in which the armed forces of both State and Federal powers were engaged.

§ 101. **Different meanings of the term " United States "** **when considered from external and internal standpoints** **again referred to.**—The difference between the internal relations of one part of the United States to another, and the relations of the entire country to foreign powers has been the subject of judicial consideration by the courts of the United States on more than one occasion. The cases now pending before the Supreme Court which have already been referred to in this volume involve similar questions and distinctions;[1] a brief reference will be made to some of the decisions of the courts.[2]

§ 102. **Official definition of the word " country."**—The word "country" has been officially defined by Regulation

§ 101.

[1] The status of territories of the United States has already been referred to in the author's note to section 11, on meaning of the term United States. (See pp. 24–28, *ante*.) It was also referred to at the close of chapter I., under sections 36, *et seq.*, pp. 62, *et seq.*; and in chapter III., sections 61, *et seq.*, and notes in regard to the tariff cases now pending in the Supreme Court. See all cases cited under those notes, and see also collation of cases in briefs of Attorney General and opposing counsel in, *Goetze* vs. *United States*, and other Porto Rico cases argued before the Supreme Court, December, 1900, and January, 1901; and opinion, TOWNSEND, J., in U. S. Circuit Court, S. D. N. Y. 1900, 103 Fed. Rep. 72. See also Senate Document No. 234, LVI. Congress, first session, being report on legal status of the territory and inhabitants of the islands acquired by the United States during the war with Spain, considered with reference to territorial boundaries, the Constitution and laws of the United States, by Charles E. Magoon, Law Office, Division of Insular Affairs, War Department, submitted to Secretary of War, Elihu Root, February 12, 1900, presented to the Senate by Cushman K. Davis, Chairman of the Committee on Foreign Relations, March 20, 1900.

[2] See also cases collated in INSULAR CASES APPENDIX at end of this volume on this point.

835 of the Treasury Department of the United States[1] as " embracing all the possessions of any power, however widely separated, which are subject to the same supreme Executive or Legislative authority and control;" this definition was sustained by the Supreme Court in *Stairs* vs. *Peaslee* in 1855, as appears by the following extract from the opinion: "The word country in the revenue laws of the United States has always been construed to embrace all the possessions of a foreign State however widely separated, which are subject to the same supreme Executive and Legislative control. The question was brought before the Treasury Department in 1817; and, on the 29th of September in that year, instructions were issued by the department in a circular addressed to the different collectors, in which the construction above stated is given to the word. The practice of the government has ever since conformed to this construction; and it must be presumed that Congress, in its subsequent legislation on the subject, used the word according to its known and established interpretation. Apart, however, from this consideration, we regard the construction of the Treasury Department as the true one. Congress certainly could not have intended to refer to mere localities or geographical divisions, without regard to the States or nations to which they belonged." [2]

§ 103. **Status of territory conquered by military forces of the United States.**—The unity of all territory under the jurisdiction of the United States, so far as foreign powers are concerned, was the subject of judicial determination by the Supreme Court in 1850 in the case of *Fleming* vs. *Page*, which involved the right of the Federal Government to collect duties on merchandise brought from Tampico, Mexico, while that port was occupied by the American forces during the Mexican War. The case differs materially from those now pending before the Supreme Court in regard to the imposition of duties on goods brought from the Philippines and Porto Rico, in that Tampico was not included in the cession made by Mexico in 1848, but was restored to Mexico by the withdrawal

§ 102.
[1] U. S. Customs Regulations, p. 364, edition 1892.

[2] *Stairs* vs. *Peaslee*, U. S. Sup. Ct. 1855, 18 Howard, 521; page 526, TANEY, Ch. J.

of the American forces after the Treaty of Peace had been ratified.

§ 104. **Fleming vs. Page ; The Tampico Duty case ; Chief Justice Taney's opinion.**—The Supreme Court in this case sustained the right of the United States to collect duties on goods brought from Tampico on the ground that the mere conquest and occupation of territory by the military forces of the United States did not extend the boundaries of the Union in such manner as to make the conquered territory an actual part of the Union ; in regard to the effect of such conquest as between the United States and any foreign powers the opinion says :[1]

" It is true, that, when Tampico had been captured, and the State of Tamaulipas subjugated, other nations were bound to regard the country, while our possession continued, as the territory of the United States, and to respect it as such.   For, by the laws and usages of nations, conquest is a valid title,

---

§ 104.

[1] *Fleming* vs. P*age*, U. S. Sup. Ct., 1850, 9 Howard, 603, p. 615, TANEY, Ch. J.

Secretary of State Buchanan, on October 7, 1848, prior to any congressional action, as to the Mexican territory, or the establishment of collection districts therein, wrote as follows in regard to the *de facto* government still existing in California: " This government *de facto* will of course, exercise no power inconsistent with the provisions of the Constitution of the United States, which is the supreme law of the land. For this reason no import duties can be levied in California on articles the growth, produce, or manufacture of the United States, as no such duties can be imposed in any other part of our Union on the products of California. Nor can new duties be charged in California upon such foreign productions as have already paid duties in any of our ports of entry, for the obvi-

ous reason that California is within the territory of the United States. I shall not enlarge upon this subject, however, as the Secretary of the Treasury will perform that duty."

Quoted in *Cross* vs. *Harrison*, U. S. Sup. Ct. 1853, WAYNE, J., 16 Howard, 164, p. 185.

The same rule was followed with regard to Alaska, as appears by various circulars from the Treasury Department to Collectors, abstracts of which appear on pages 10 and 20 of the Synopsis of Decisions for 1868, from the latter of which it appears that on April 6, 1868, the Collector at New York was notified that merchandise shipped from Alaska after June 20, 1867, the date of the ratification of the Treaty with Russia, was entitled to entry free of duty; the act extending the laws of the United States to Alaska was not passed until July 27, 1868, 15 U. S. Stat. at Large, p. 240.

while the victor maintains the exclusive possession of the conquered country. The citizens of no other nation, therefore, had a right to enter it without the permission of the American authorities, nor to hold intercourse with its inhabitants, nor to trade with them. As regarded all other nations, it was a part of the United States, and belonged to them as exclusively as the territory included in our established boundaries." The opinion then continues to draw a distinction between the effect of conquest as to foreign powers and as to citizens of the Union, and in that respect, it says: "But yet it was not a part of this Union. For every nation which acquires territory by treaty or conquest holds it according to its own institutions and laws. And the relation in which the port of Tampico stood to the United States while it was occupied by their arms did not depend upon the laws of nations, but upon our own Constitution and acts of Congress. The power of the President under which Tampico and the State of Tamaulipas were conquered and held in subjection was simply that of a military commander prosecuting a war waged against a public enemy by the authority of his government. And the country from which these goods were imported was invaded and subdued, and occupied as the territory of a foreign, hostile nation, as a portion of Mexico, and was held in possession in order to distress and harass the enemy. While it was occupied by our troops, they were in an enemy's country, and not in their own; the inhabitants were still foreigners and enemies, and owed to the United States nothing more than the submission and obedience, sometimes called temporary allegiance, which is due from a conquered enemy, when he surrenders to a force which he is unable to resist. But the boundaries of the United States, as they existed when war was declared against Mexico, were not extended by the conquest; nor could they be regulated by the varying incidents of war, and be enlarged or diminished as the armies on either side advanced or retreated. They remained unchanged. And every place which was out of the limits of the United States, as previously established by the political authorities of the government, was still foreign; nor did our laws extend over it. Tampico was, therefore, a foreign port when this shipment was made.

" Again, there was no act of Congress establishing a custom house at Tampico, nor authorizing the appointment of a collector; and, consequently, there was no officer of the United States authorized by law to grant the clearance and authenticate the coasting manifest of the cargo, in the manner directed by law, where the voyage is from one port of the United States to another. The person who acted in the character of collector in this instance, acted as such under the authority of the military commander, and in obedience to his orders; and the duties he exacted, and the regulations he adopted, were not those prescribed by law, but by the President in his character of commander-in-chief. The custom house was established in an enemy's country, as one of the weapons of war. It was established, not for the purpose of giving to the people of Tamaulipas the benefits of commerce with the United States, or with other countries, but as a measure of hostility, and as a part of the military operations in Mexico; it was a mode of exacting contributions from the enemy to support our army, and intended also to cripple the resources of Mexico, and make it feel the evils and burdens of the war. The duties required to be paid were regulated with this view, and were nothing more than contributions levied upon the enemy, which the usages of war justify when an army is operating in the enemy's country. The permit and coasting manifest granted by an officer thus appointed, and thus controlled by military authority, could not be recognized in any port of the United States, as the documents required by the act of Congress when the vessel is engaged in the coasting trade, nor could they exempt the cargo from the payment of duties.

" This construction of the revenue laws has been uniformly given by the administrative department of the government in every case that has come before it. And it has, indeed, been given in cases where there appears to have been stronger ground for regarding the place of shipment as a domestic port. For after Florida had been ceded to the United States, and the forces of the United States had taken possession of Pensacola, it was decided by the Treasury Department, that goods imported from Pensacola before an act of Congress was passed erecting it into a collection district, and author-

170

izing the appointment of a collector, were liable to duty. That is, that although Florida had, by cession, actually become a part of the United States, and was in our possession, yet, under our revenue laws, its ports must be regarded as foreign until they were established as domestic, by act of Congress; and it appears that this decision was sanctioned at the time by the Attorney-General of the United States, the law officer of the government. And although not so directly applicable to the case before us, yet the decisions of the Treasury Department in relation to Amelia Island, and certain ports in Louisiana, after that province had been ceded to the United States, were both made upon the same grounds. And in the latter case, after a custom-house had been established by law at New Orleans, the collector at that place was instructed to regard as foreign ports Baton Rouge and other settlements still in the possession of Spain, whether on the Mississippi, Iberville, or the sea-coast. The Department in no instance that we are aware of, since the establishment of the government, has ever recognized a place in a newly acquired country as a domestic port, from which the coasting trade might be carried on, unless it had been previously made so by act of Congress."

§ 105. **The position reversed; the "Castine" Case; War of 1812; Justice Story's opinion.**—In deciding the *Tampico* case the Supreme Court adopted the reverse position, although under the reversed conditions it was consistent, to that which it had taken as to the status of American territory, conquered and occupied, by British forces, during the War of 1812, and subsequently surrendered pursuant to the Treaty of Peace executed at Ghent on the conclusion of that War. The port of Castine, Maine, was captured by the British forces; during the period of conquest goods were imported into the port; owing, however, to the occupation by the British troops no duties were collected thereon by the United States custom authorities; after the war actions were commenced by the United States for the unpaid duties; the Supreme Court held that so far as the execution of the laws of the United States were concerned, the territory ceased, for the time being, to be under the jurisdiction of the United States, and merchants, therefore, were not obligated to pay

171

duties during the period of occupation.   Mr. Justice Story says in his opinion : [1]

" Under these circumstances, we are all of opinion, that the claim for duties cannot be sustained.   By the conquest and military occupation of Castine, the enemy acquired that firm possession which enabled him to exercise the fullest rights of sovereignty over that place.   The sovereignty of the United States over the territory was, of course, suspended, and the laws of the United States could no longer be rightfully enforced there, or be obligatory upon the inhabitants who remained and submitted to the conquerors.   By the surrender the inhabitants passed under a temporary allegiance to the British government, and were bound by such laws, and such only, as it chose to recognize and impose.   From the nature of the case, no other laws could be obligatory upon them, for where there is no protection or allegiance or sovereignty, there can be no claim to obedience.   Castine was, therefore, during this period, so far as respected our revenue laws, to be deemed a foreign port; and goods imported into it by the inhabitants, were subject to such duties only as the British government chose to require.   Such goods were in no correct sense imported into the United States.   The subsequent evacuation by the enemy, and resumption of authority by the United States, did not, and could not, change the character of the previous transactions.   The doctrines respecting the *jus postliminii* are wholly inapplicable to the case.   The goods were liable to American duties, when imported, or not at all.   That they are so liable at the time of importation is clear from what has been already stated; and when, upon the return of peace, the jurisdiction of the United States was re-assumed, they were in the same predicament as they would have been if Castine had been a foreign territory ceded by treaty to the United States, and the goods had been previously imported there.   In the latter case, there would be no pretence to say that American duties could be demanded; and, upon principles of public or municipal law, the cases are not distinguishable.

§ 105.
[1] *United States* vs. *Rice*, U. S. | Sup. Ct. 1819, 4 Wheaton, 246, p. 254, STORY, J.

172

The authorities cited at the bar would, if there were any doubt, be decisive of the question. But we think it too clear to require any aid from authority."

§ 106. **Status of Cuba.**—The same questions that arose after the War of 1812, and the Mexican War, have arisen not only in regard to the territory which was actually ceded by Spain to the United States, but also in regard to Cuba, which was not ceded to the United States, although Spain relinquished her sovereignty thereover, the United States assuming by the terms of the treaty the obligations arising under international law by reason of the occupation of the Island by the military forces of this country.

What the internal relations of the United States and Cuba may be is beyond the province of this volume : but undoubtedly, so far as foreign relations are concerned, the decision of the Supreme Court in *Fleming* vs. *Page* is directly in point. At the present time there is no local government of Cuba, and if any question should arise involving foreign powers, it would have to be settled through the medium of the United States Government, as the military forces of the United States are in occupation of the Island.[1]

§ 106.
[1]NOTE AS TO STATUS OF CUBA.

The principal executive, congressional and judicial precedents relating to Cuba and the status thereof, so far as its relations with the United States are concerned are: (1) The Teller resolution of April 20, 1898; (2) the stipulations in regard to Cuba in the treaty with Spain of December 10, 1898; (3) The Foraker Amendment as to franchises in Cuba; (4) the executive orders relating to the government of Cuba and the regulation of its commerce, as promulgated by the President through the War Department; (5) the decision of the United States Supreme Court in the case of *Neely* vs. *Henkel*, in regard to the extradition of Neely under the statute passed in regard to the extradition of prisoners charged with crime from the United States to any place under the occupation of the military forces thereof; (6) the Platt amendment in regard to the relations of the United States to Cuba, and the establishment thereof, and the Cuban constitution.

The documents referred to will be given in order below with the exception of the decision in *Neely* vs. *Henkel*, which appears as a footnote to section 107, *post*.

1. THE TELLER RESOLUTION.

"(No. 24.) Joint resolution for the recognition of the independence of the people of Cuba, demanding that the Government of Spain relin-

§ 107. **Status of Cuba involved in the Neely case; extradition.**—The status of Cuba was involved and determined

quish its authority and government in the Island of Cuba, and to withdraw its land and naval forces from Cuba and Cuban waters, and directing the President of the United States to use the land and naval forces of the United States to carry these resolutions into effect.

"Whereas the abhorrent conditions which have existed for more than three years in the Island of Cuba, so near our own borders, have shocked the moral sense of the people of the United States, have been a disgrace to Christian civilization, culminating, as they have, in the destruction of a United States battleship, with two hundred and sixty-six of its officers and crew, while on a friendly visit in the harbor of Havana, and cannot longer be endured, as has been set forth by the President of the United States in his message to Congress, of April eleventh, eighteen hundred and ninety-eight, upon which the action of Congress was invited: Therefore,

"*Resolved by the Senate and House of Representatives of the United States of America in Congress assembled,* First. That the people of the Island of Cuba are, and of right ought to be, free and independent.

"Second. That it is the duty of the United States to demand, and the Government of the United States does hereby demand, that the Government of Spain at once relinquish its authority and government in the Island of Cuba and withdraw its land and naval forces from Cuba and Cuban waters.

"Third. That the President of the United States be, and he hereby is, directed and empowered to use the entire land and naval forces of the United States, and to call into the actual service of the United States the militia of the several States, to such extent as may be necessary to carry these resolutions into effect.

"Fourth. That the United States hereby disclaims any disposition or intention to exercise sovereignty, jurisdiction, or control over said Island except for the pacification thereof, and asserts its determination, when that is accomplished, to leave the government and control of the Island to its people."

"Approved, April 20, 1898." (U. S. Stat. at Large, Vol. 30, pp. 738–739.)

2. STIPULATIONS AS TO CUBA IN TREATY WITH SPAIN, 1898.

"ARTICLE I. Spain relinquishes all claim of sovereignty over and title to Cuba.

"And as the Island is, upon its evacuation by Spain, to be occupied by the United States, the United States will, so long as such occupation shall last, assume and discharge the obligations that may under international law result from the fact of its occupation, for the protection of life and property."

"ARTICLE XVI. It is understood that any obligations assumed in this treaty by the United States with respect to Cuba are limited to the time of its occupancy thereof; but it will, upon the termination of such oc-

in decisions already made by the Circuit Courts of the United States, and is also involved in questions which have been sub- mitted to the Supreme Court.

cupancy, advise any Government established in the island to assume the same obligations." 30 U. S. Stat. at Large, 1754–1761.

3. THE FORAKER AMENDMENT AS TO FRANCHISES IN CUBA.

Chap. 423 (army appropriation bill), 55th Congress, Sess. III, approved March 3, 1899: " § 2, That no property, franchises, or concessions of any kind whatever shall be granted by the United States, or by any military or other authority whatever, in the Island of Cuba during the occupation thereof by the United States." 30 U. S. Stat. at Large, 1064, p. 1074.

4. EXECUTIVE ORDERS RELATING TO CUBA.

Immediately after the exchange of the treaty of peace and even prior to its ratification, Spain withdrew from Cuba and relinquished all sovereignty thereover. The formal act took place on January 1, 1899, and on that day the Military Governor, Major General John R. Brooke, U. S. A., appointed by the President of the United States, assumed control of the Island.

The best synopsis of the orders issued by the Military Governor, and the method of administering the affairs of the Island of Cuba will be found in the civil report of Major General John R. Brooke, October 1, 1899, published by the War Department, Washington, 1900; special attention is called to the report of Major Edgar S. Dudley, Judge-Advocate, U. S. V.,—Judge-Advocate for the Division of Cuba, September 30, 1899,—pages 163 et seq. of Major General Brooke's report, and to the lists and synopses of military orders at pages 167, et seq., and 429, et seq. of the same volume.

These orders show that up to this time Cuba is under a strictly military government, and that both as to military and civil jurisdiction the authority of the commander in the field is practically supreme. The orders are promulgated by the Military Governor and are as a general rule formulated as to all matters of importance at Washington by the War Department. The rules of international law as to military occupancy control the relation of the United States with Cuba, and the President as Commander in Chief is supreme in power, acting, as must necessarily be the case, through the War Department and the Military Governor.

5. DECISION IN NEELY VS. HENKEL.

See note A to § 107, p. 178, *post*.

6. THE PLATT AMENDMENT AS TO RELATIONS WITH CUBA.

During the fall of 1900, General Leonard Wood, Military Governor of Cuba, promulgated an order permitting the people of Cuba to hold a constitutional convention: That convention met at Havana and prepared

Persons charged with committing crimes in Cuba, and who have come to the United States, have been arrested, and in

a proposed constitution for Cuba. It ignored the relations of the United States with Cuba and accordingly, prior to March 4, 1901, when Congress adjourned, questions arose as to the course to be pursued by the President in regard to withdrawing the United States troops from Cuba if a constitution satisfactory to the United States should be adopted. The terms upon which Congress authorized the President to withdraw the troops were formulated in a series of resolutions prepared by the HONORABLE ORVILLE H. PLATT, senator from Connecticut, and offered by him in the Senate on February 27, 1901, as an amendment to the then pending army appropriation bill. They were adopted and incorporated in the bill and subsequently were accepted by the House, and the bill thus amended became a law by approval of the President on March 2, 1901.

The amendment as adopted is as follows:

" That in fulfillment of the declaration contained in the joint resolution approved April 20, 1898, entitled, ' For the recognition of the independence of the people of Cuba, demanding that the Government of Spain relinquish its authority and government in the Island of Cuba, and to withdraw its land and naval forces from Cuba and Cuban waters, and directing the President of the United States to use the land and naval forces of the United States to carry these resolutions into effect,' the President is hereby authorized to ' leave the government and control of the Island of Cuba to its people ' so soon as a government shall have been established in said island under a constitution which, either as a part thereof or in any ordinance appended thereto, shall define the future relations of the United States with Cuba, substantially as follows:

" I. That the government of Cuba shall never enter into any treaty or other compact with any foreign power or powers which will impair or tend to impair the independence of Cuba, nor in any manner authorize or permit any foreign power or powers to obtain by colonization or for military or naval purposes or otherwise, lodgment in, or control over any portion of said island.

" II. That said government shall not assume or contract any public debt, to pay the interest upon which, and to make reasonable sinking fund provision for the ultimate discharge of which, the ordinary revenues of the islands, after defraying the current expenses of Government, shall be inadequate.

" III. That the government of Cuba consents that the United States may exercise the right to intervene for the preservation of Cuban independence, the maintenance of a government adequate for the protection of life, property, and individual liberty, and for discharging the obligations with respect to Cuba imposed by the treaty of Paris on the United States, now to be assumed and undertaken by the government of Cuba.

" IV. That all Acts of the United States in Cuba during its military occupancy thereof are ratified and validated, and all lawful rights acquired thereunder shall be maintained and protected.

some cases transferred to Cuba, while in others (notably in the case of one Neely) the right of the government to transfer or extradite them from places in the United States to Cuba was challenged and submitted to the Supreme Court.

In the case of Neely, who was about to be transferred to Cuba under an act of Congress specially passed for that purpose, Justice Lacombe refused to release him on *habeas cor-*

" V. That the government of Cuba will execute, and as far as necessary extend, the plans already devised or other plans to be mutually agreed upon, for the sanitation of the cities of the island, to the end that a recurrence of epidemic and infectious diseases may be prevented, thereby assuring protection to the people and commerce of Cuba, as well as to the commerce of the southern ports of the United States and the people residing therein.

" VI. That the Isle of Pines shall be omitted from the proposed constitutional boundaries of Cuba, the title thereto being left to future adjustment by treaty.

" VII. That to enable the United States to maintain the independence of Cuba, and to protect the people thereof, as well as for its own defense, the government of Cuba will sell or lease to the United States lands necessary for coaling or naval stations at certain specified points, to be agreed upon with the President of the United States.

"VIII. That by way of further assurance, the government of Cuba will embody the foregoing provisions in a permanent treaty with the United States."

As to many of the points therein contained the Platt amendment, as it is called, is really nothing more than a very broad construction of the Monroe Doctrine as it could be enunciated in regard to Cuba even if the terms of the Amendment were not incorporated in the Cuban Constitution or in any treaty. The United States having expended several hundred million dollars in relieving both Cuba and ourselves from the intolerable condition caused by the misgovernment of Spain, should certainly have the right before withdrawing from Cuba and leaving the inhabitants of that island to govern themselves, to properly protect the interests of the United States, so that no European complications can ever again arise in regard to that Island, which, while it should be self-governed, should not be left in such a position that it could again menace our own peace and safety, or require our intervention, as would undoubtedly be the case if it were permitted to make treaties with, or borrow money from, European governments. To the author it seems as though Senator Platt had, with his usual good sense and thorough mastery of international and constitutional law, formulated in the amendment which will always be associated with his name, a practical and complete solution of the whole question. Cuba will obtain her self-government, and the United States will be relieved from fear of foreign complications, and at the same time the pledge contained in the **Teller** resolution of April 20, 1898, will be fully complied with.

12

pus proceedings holding that the United States had power to deal with the extradition questions involved as Congress had done in passing the act. This case will be discussed at greater length in the subsequent sections devoted to extradition cases; it is referred to here simply as the status of Cuba.[1]

Judge Lacombe evaded the direct question, holding the statute which Congress had passed provided for exactly such cases and was within the constitutional power of Congress.[2] In the *Cox* case in Louisiana, Judge Duggan held in September, 1899, before the passage of the act, that for purposes such as extradition, a requisition of the military governor of Cuba on the governor of a state, for the extradition or rendition of a person charged with crime, should be treated in the same manner as though the requisition came from the governor of a territory.[3] A

§ 107.
[1] See §§ 432 *et seq.* chap. XV, Vol. II.
[2] 103 Fed. Rep. 626 and 631.

[3] See opinion in full in brief of Assistant Attorney General Beck in Neely case.

A. OPINION OF SUPREME COURT IN CASE OF NEELY VS. HENKEL.

Since this section was written and while this volume was in press, the Supreme Court has decided the *Neely* case. The opinion was delivered by Mr. Justice Harlan and is as follows: (180 U. S. Rep. 109)

By § 5270 of the Revised Statutes of the United States it is provided:

"Whenever there is *a treaty or convention for extradition* between the Government of the United States and any *foreign* government, any justice of the Supreme Court, circuit judge, district judge, commissioner, authorized so to do by any of the courts of the United States, or judge of a court of record of general jurisdiction of any State, may, upon complaint made under oath, charging any person found within the limits of any State, District, or Territory with having committed within the jurisdiction of any such foreign government any of the crimes provided for by such treaty or convention, issue his warrant for the apprehension of the person so charged, that he may be brought before such justice, judge or commissioner, to the end that the evidence of criminality may be heard and considered. If, on such hearing, he deems the evidence sufficient to sustain the charge under the provisions of the proper treaty or convention, he shall certify the same, together with a copy of all the testimony taken before him, to the Secretary of State, that a warrant may issue upon the requisition of the proper authorities of such foreign government, for the surrender of such person according to the stipulations of the treaty or convention; and he shall issue his

§ 108. Uncertainty as to Status of Cuba from internal standpoint.—It will thus be seen that the present status of

warrant for the commitment of the person so charged to the proper jail, there to remain until such surrender shall be made."

This section was amended by Congress June 6th, 1900, by adding thereto the following proviso:

" *Provided,* That whenever any *foreign* country *or territory,* or any part thereof, *is occupied by or under the control of the United States,* any person who shall violate, or who has violated, the criminal laws *in force therein,* by the commission of any of the following offenses, namely: Murder, and assault with intent to commit murder; counterfeiting or altering money, or uttering or bringing into circulation counterfeit or altered money; counterfeiting certificates or coupons of public indebtedness, bank notes, or other instruments of public credit, and the utterance or circulation of the same; forgery or altering, and uttering what is forged or altered; *embezzlement or criminal malversation of the public funds, committed by public officers, employés, or depositaries;* larceny or embezzlement of an amount not less than one hundred dollars in value, robbery; burglary, defined to be the breaking and entering by night-time into the house of another person with intent to commit a felony therein; and the act of breaking and entering the house or building of another, whether in the day or night-time, with the intent to commit a felony therein; the act of entering or of breaking and entering the offices of the government and public authorities, or the offices of banks, banking houses, savings banks, trust companies, insurance, or other companies, with the intent to commit a felony therein; perjury or the subornation of perjury; rape; arson; piracy by the law of nations; murder, assault with intent to kill, and manslaughter, committed on the high seas, on board a ship owned by or in control of citizens or residents of such foreign country or territory and not under the flag of the United States, or of some other government; malicious destruction of or attempt to destroy railways, trams, vessels, bridges, dwellings, public edifices or other buildings, when the act endangers human life, *and who shall depart or flee, or who has departed or fled, from justice therein to the United States, or to any Territory thereof, or to the District of Columbia,* shall, when found therein, be liable to arrest and detention by the authorities of the United States, and *on the written request or requisition of the military governor* or *other chief executive officer in control of such foreign country or territory shall be returned and surrendered* as hereinafter provided to such authorities for trial under the laws in force *in the place where such offense was committed.* All the provisions of sections fifty-two hundred and seventy to fifty-two hundred and seventy-seven of this title, so far as applicable, shall govern proceedings authorized by this proviso: *Provided further,* That such proceedings shall be had *before a judge of the courts of the United States only, who shall hold such person on evidence establishing probable cause that he is guilty of the offense charged; And provided further,* That no return or surrender shall be made of any person charged with the commission of

Cuba is involved in many legal complications and that no succinct statement as to its exact relations to the United

any offense of a political nature. If so held such person shall be returned and surrendered to the authorities in control of such foreign country or territory on the order of the Secretary of State of the United States, and such authorities shall secure to such person a fair and impartial trial." 31 Stat. at L. 656, chap. 793.

On the 28th day of June, 1900, a warrant was issued by Judge Lacombe of the Circuit Court of the United States for the Southern District of New York commanding the arrest of Charles F. W. Neely, who, "being then and there a public employé, to wit, Finance Agent of the Department of Posts in the city of Havana, Island of Cuba, on the 6th day of May in the year of our Lord one thousand nine hundred, or about that time, having then and there charge of the collection and deposit of moneys of the Department of Posts of the said city of Havana, did unlawfully and feloniously take and embezzle from the public funds of the said Island of Cuba, the sum of $10,000 and more, being then and there moneys and funds which had come into his charge and under his control in his capacity as such public employé and finance agent, as aforesaid, and by reason of his said office and employment, thereby violating chapter 10, article 401, of the Penal Code of the said Island of Cuba —that is to say, a crime within the meaning of the said act of Congress, approved June 6th, 1900, as aforesaid, relating to the 'embezzlement or criminal malversation of the public funds committed by public officers, employés, or depositaries.'" The warrant directed the accused to be brought before the judge in order that the evidence of probable cause as to his guilt could be heard and considered, and, if deemed sufficient, that the same might be certified with a copy of all the proceedings to the Secretary of State, that an order might issue for his return and surrender pursuant to the authority of the above act of Congress.

The warrant of arrest was based on a verified written complaint of an Assistant United States Attorney for the Southern District of New York.

On the same day and upon a like complaint a warrant was issued against Neely by the same judge, commanding his arrest for the crime of having unlawfully and fraudulently—while employed in and connected with the business and operations of a branch of the service of the Department of Posts in Havana, Cuba, between July 1st, 1899, and May 1st, 1900—embezzled and converted to his own use postage stamps, moneys, funds, and property belonging to and in the custody of that department, which had come into his custody and under his authority as such employé, to the amount of $57,000, in violation of §§ 37 and 55 of the Postal Code of Cuba.

Neely having been arrested under these warrants, application was made by the United States for his extradition to Cuba. The accused moved to dismiss the complaints upon various grounds. That motion having been denied, the case was heard upon evidence. In disposing of the application for extradition, Judge Lacombe said: "In the opin-

States or as to its own status, considered in connection with the legal rights of its inhabitants can be formulated at the

ion of this court, the Government has abundantly shown that there is probable cause to believe that Neely is guilty of the offence of 'embezzlement or criminal malversation of the public funds,' he being at that time a 'public officer,' or 'employé,' or 'depositary.' Such an offense is obnoxious to the Penal Code in force in Cuba, Article 401 of which provides that 'the public employé who, by reason of his office, has in his charge public funds or property, and who should take (or consent that others should take) any part therefrom, shall be punished,' etc. There is no merit in the contention that this article applies only to persons in the public employ of Spain. Spain having withdrawn from the island, its successor has become the 'public' to which the Code, remaining unrepealed, now refers. The suggestion that under this Penal Code no public employé could be prosecuted or punished until his superior had heard the case and turned the offender over to the criminal law for trial is matter of defense, and need not be considered here. The evidence shows probable cause to believe that the prisoner is guilty of an offense defined in the act of June 6th, 1900, and which is also a violation of the criminal laws in Cuba, and upon such evidence he will be held for extradition." But, it was further said: "Two obstacles now exist. He [the accused] has been held to bail in this court upon a criminal charge of bringing into this district government funds embezzled in another district. He has also been arrested in a civil action brought in this court to recover $45,000, which, it is alleged, he has converted. When both of these proceedings have been discontinued, the order in extradition will be signed. This may be done on August 13th at 11 A. M."

Subsequently, August 9th, 1900, Neely presented in the court below his written application for a writ of *habeas corpus*, and prayed that he be discharged from restraint in the extradition proceedings. He claimed on various grounds that the act of June 6th, 1900, under which he was arrested, detained and imprisoned was in violation of the Constitution of the United States.

The application for the writ of *habeas corpus* having been denied, and an appeal having been duly taken, the petitioner was remanded to the custody of the marshal to await the determination of such appeal in this court.

I. That at the date of the act of June 6th, 1900, the Island of Cuba was "occupied by" and was "under the control of the United States," and that it is still so occupied and controlled, cannot be disputed. This court will take judicial notice that such were, at the date named and are now, the relations between this country and Cuba. So that the applicability of the above act to the present case—and this is the first question to be examined—depends upon the inquiry whether, within its meaning, Cuba is to be deemed a *foreign* country or territory.

We do not think this question at all difficult of solution if regard be had to the avowed objects intended to be accomplished by the war with Spain and by the military occupation of that Island. Let us see what

present time.   The counsel in the *Neely* case have argued
before the Supreme Court that Cuba is really a friendly power

were those objects as they are disclosed by official documents and by the
public acts of the representatives of the United States.

On the 20th day of April, 1868, Congress passed a joint resolution.
(For this resolution in full see note 1 on Status of Cuba § 106, p. 173, *ante.*)

The adoption of this joint resolution was followed by the act of April
25th, 1898, by which Congress declared: " 1. That war be, and the same
is, hereby declared to exist, and that war has existed since the 21st day
of April, 1898, including said day, between the United States of America and the Kingdon of Spain.   2. That the President of the United
States be, and he hereby is, directed and empowered to use the entire land
and naval forces of the United States, and to call into the actual service of the United States the militia of the several states to such extent
as may be necessary to carry this act into effect."   30 Stat. at L. 364,
chap. 189.

The war lasted but a few months.   The success of the American
Arms was so complete and overwhelming that a Protocol of Agreement between the United States and Spain embodying the terms of a
basis for the establishment of peace between the two countries was
signed at Washington on the 12th of August, 1898.   By that agreement
it was provided that "Spain will relinquish all claim of sovereignty over
and title to Cuba," and that the respective countries would each appoint commissioners to meet at Paris and there proceed to the negotiation and conclusion of a treaty of peace.   30 Stat. at L. 1742.

Commissioners possessing full authority from their respective Governments for that purpose having met in Paris, a treaty of peace was
signed on December 10th, 1898, and, ratifications having been duly exchanged, it was proclaimed April 11th, 1899.   30 Stat. at L. 1754.

That treaty contained, among other provisions, the following:

(Articles I and XVI quoted *verbatim* as in note 1 on Status of Cuba
to § 106, p. 174, *ante.*)

On the 13th of December, 1898, an order was issued by the Secretary
of War stating that, by direction of the President, a division to be
known as the division of Cuba, consisting of the geographical departments and provinces of the Island of Cuba, with headquarters at Havana, was created and placed under the command of Major General John
R. Brooke, United States Army, who was required, in addition to his
command of the troops in the Division, to "exercise the authority of
Military Governor of the Island."   And on December 28th, 1898, General Brooke, by a formal order, in accordance with the order of the President, assumed command of that division, and announced that he would
exercise the authority of Military Governor of the Island.

On the 1st day of January, 1899, at the palace of the Spanish Governor-
General in Havana, the sovereignty of Spain was formally relinquished
and General Brooke immediately entered upon the full exercise of his
duties as Military Governor of Cuba.

Upon assuming the positions of Military Governor and Major General

and that the occupation of the United States is improper, illegal and unwarranted by the Constitution ; inasmuch, how-

commanding the Division of Cuba, General Brooke issued to the People of Cuba the following proclamation:

" Coming among you as the representative of the President, in furtherance and in continuation of the humane purpose with which my country interfered to put an end to the distressing condition in this island, I deem it proper to say that the object of the present Government is to give protection to the people, security to persons and property, to restore confidence, to encourage the people to resume the pursuits of peace, to build up waste plantations, to resume commercial traffic, and to afford full protection in the exercise of all civil and religious rights. To this end, the protection of the United States government will be directed, and every possible provision made to carry out these objects through the channels of *civil administration, although under military control*, in the interest and for the benefit of all the people of Cuba, and those possessed of rights and property in the island. The civil and criminal code which prevailed prior to the relinquishment of Spanish sovereignty will remain in force, with such modifications and changes as may from time to time be found necessary in the interest of good government. The people of Cuba, without regard to previous affiliations, are invited and urged to co-operate in these objects by the exercise of moderation, conciliation, and good-will one toward another and a hearty accord in our humanitarian purposes will insure kind and beneficent government. The Military Governor of the island will always be pleased to confer with those who may desire to consult him on matters of public interest."

On the 11th day of January, 1899, the Military Governor, " in pursuance of the authority vested in him by the President of the United States, and in order to secure a better organization of the civil service in the Island of Cuba," ordered that thereafter "the civil government shall be administered by four.Departments, each under the charge of its appropriate Secretary," to be known, respectively, as the Departments of State and Government, of Finance, of Justice and Public Instruction, and of Agriculture, Commerce, Industries and Public Works, each under the charge of a Secretary. To these Secretaries "were transferred, by the officers in charge of them, the various bureaus of the Spanish civil government." Subsequently, by order of the Military Governor, a Supreme Court for the island was created, with jurisdiction throughout Cuban territory, composed of a President or Chief Justice, six Associate Justices, one Fiscal, two Assistant Fiscals, one Secretary or Chief Clerk, two Deputy Clerks, and other subordinate employés, with administrative functions, as well as those of a court of justice in civil and criminal matters. By order of a later date, issued by the Military Governor, the jurisdiction of the ordinary courts of criminal jurisdiction was defined.

Under date of July 21st, 1899, by direction of the Military Governor, a code known as the Postal Code was promulgated and declared to be

ever, as there is a *de facto* occupation it is exceedingly doubtful whether the Supreme Court will investigate the legal

the law relating to postal affairs in Cuba. That Code abrogated all laws then existing in Cuba inconsistent with its provisions. It provided that the director general of Posts of the Island should have the control and management of the Department of Posts, and prescribed numerous criminal offenses, affixing the punishments for each. It is not disputed that one of the offenses charged against Neely is included in those defined in the Postal Code established by the Military Governor of Cuba, and that the other is embraced by the Penal Code of that Island which was in force when the war ensued with Spain, and which by order of the Military Governor remained in force, subject to such modifications as might be found necessary in the interest of good government.

On the 13th day of June, 1900, the present Military Governor of Cuba, General Leonard Wood, made his requisition upon the President for the extradition of Neely under the act of Congress.

The facts above detailed make it clear that within the meaning of the act of June 6th, 1900, Cuba is foreign territory. It cannot be regarded, in any constitutional, legal or international sense, a part of the territory of the United States.

While by the act of April 25th, 1898, declaring war between this country and Spain, the President was directed and empowered to use our entire land and naval forces, as well as the militia of the several States to such extent as was necessary, to carry such act into effect, that authorization was not for the purpose of making Cuba an integral part of the United States but only for the purpose of compelling the relinquishment by Spain of its authority and government in that Island and the withdrawal of its forces from Cuba and Cuban waters. The legislative and executive branches of the government, by the joint resolution of April 20th, 1898, expressly disclaimed any purpose to exercise sovereignty, jurisdiction or control over Cuba "except for the pacification thereof," and asserted the determination of the United States, that object being accomplished, to leave the government and control of Cuba to its own people. All that has been done in relation to Cuba has had that end in view and, so far as the court is informed by the public history of the relations of this country with that Island, nothing has been done inconsistent with the declared object of the war with Spain.

Cuba is none the less foreign territory, within the meaning of the act of Congress, because it is under a Military Governor appointed by and representing the President in the work of assisting the inhabitants of that island to establish a government of their own, under which, as a free and independent people, they may control their own affairs without interference by other nations. The occupancy of the Island by troops of the United States was the necessary result of the war. That result could not have been avoided by the United States consistently

status of such occupation; it is the author's view, although it may be prematurely expressed, that the Supreme Court

with the principles of international law or with its obligations to the people of Cuba.

It is true that as between Spain and the United States—indeed, as between the United States and all foreign nations—Cuba, upon the cessation of hostilities with Spain and after the treaty of Paris, was to be treated as if it were conquered territory. But as between the United States and Cuba that Island is territory held in trust for the inhabitants of Cuba, to whom it rightfully belongs, and to whose exclusive control it will be surrendered when a stable government shall have been established by their voluntary action.

In his message to Congress, of December 6th, 1898, the President said that "as soon as we are in possession of Cuba and have pacified the Island, it will be necessary to give aid and direction to its people to form a government for themselves," and that, " until there is complete tranquillity in the Island and a stable government inaugurated, military occupation will be continued." Nothing in the treaty of Paris stands in the way of this declared object, and nothing existed, at the date of the passage of the act of June 6th, 1900, indicating any change in the policy of our Government as defined in the joint resolution of April 20th, 1898. In reference to the declaration in that resolution, of the purposes of the United States in relation to Cuba, the President in his annual message of December 5th, 1899, said that the pledge contained in it "is of the highest honorable obligation, and must be sacredly kept." Indeed, the treaty of Paris contemplated only a temporary occupancy and control of Cuba by the United States. While it was taken for granted by the treaty that, upon the evacuation by Spain, the island would be occupied by the United States, the treaty provided that, "so long as such occupation shall last " the United States should "assume and discharge the obligations that may, under international law, result from the fact of its occupation for the protection of life and property." It further provided that any obligations assumed by the United States, under the treaty, with respect to Cuba, were "limited to the time of its occupancy thereof," but that the United States, upon the termination of such occupancy, should "advise any government established in the Island to assume the same obligations."

It cannot be doubted that when the United States enforced the relinquishment by Spain of her sovereignty in Cuba and determined to occupy and control that Island until there was complete tranquillity in all its borders and until the people of Cuba had created for themselves a stable government, it succeeded to the authority of the displaced government so far at least that it became its duty under international law and pending the pacification of the Island, to protect in all appropriate legal modes the lives, the liberty, and the property of all those who submitted to the authority of the representatives of this country. That duty was recognized in the Treaty of Paris; and the act of June 6th, 1900, so far as it applied to cases arising in Cuba, was in aid or execu-

will hold that the mere fact certified on the record of a *de
facto* occupation will be taken as evidence of the fact, and

tion of that treaty and in discharge of the obligations imposed by its
provisions upon the United States. The power of Congress to make all
laws necessary and proper for carrying into execution as well the powers enumerated in § 8 of article I. of the Constitution, as all others vested
in the Government of the United States, or in any Department or the officers thereof, includes the power to enact such legislation as is appropriate to give efficacy to any stipulations which it is competent for the
President by and with the advice and consent of the Senate to insert in
a treaty with a foreign power. What legislation by Congress could be
more appropriate for the protection of life and property in Cuba, while
occupied and controlled by the United States, than legislation securing
the return to that island, to be tried by its constituted authorities, of
those who, having committed crimes there, fled to this country to escape arrest, trial and punishment? No crime is mentioned in the extradition act of June 6th, 1900, that does not have some relation to the
safety of life and property. And the provisions of that act requiring
the surrender of any public officer, employé, or depositary fleeing to
the United States after having committed in a foreign country or territory occupied by or under the control of the United States the crime
of "embezzlement or criminal malversation of the public funds" have
special application to Cuba in its present relations to this country.

We must not be understood, however, as saying that, but for the obligation imposed by the Treaty of Paris upon the United States to protect life and property in Cuba pending its occupancy and control of
that island, Congress would have been without power to enact such a
statute as that of June 6th, 1900, so far as it embraced citizens of the
United States or persons found in the United States who had committed crimes in the foreign territory so occupied and controlled by the
United States for temporary purposes. That question is not open on
this record for examination, and upon it we express no opinion. It is
quite sufficient in this case to adjudge, as we now do, that it was competent for Congress, by legislation, to enforce or give efficacy to the
provisions of the treaty made by the United States and Spain with respect to the Island of Cuba and its people.

II. It is contended that the act of June 6th, 1900, is unconstitutional
and void in that it does not secure to the accused, when surrendered to
a foreign country for trial in its tribunals, all of the rights, privileges,
and immunities that are guaranteed by the Constitution to persons
charged with the commission in this country of crime against the
United States. Allusion is here made to the provisions of the Federal
Constitution relating to the writ of *habeas corpus*, bills of attainder,
ex post facto laws, trial by jury for crimes, and generally to the fundamental guaranties of life, liberty and property embodied in that instrument. The answer to this suggestion is that those provisions have
no relation to crimes committed without the jurisdiction of the United
States against the laws of a foreign country.

that the right of the forces to occupy the territory is a matter
entirely within the executive and political departments of

In connection with the above proposition, we are reminded of the
fact that the appellant is a citizen of the United States. But such citizenship does not give him an immunity to commit crime in other countries, nor entitle him to demand, of right, a trial in any other mode
than that allowed to its own people by the country whose laws he has
violated and from whose justice he has fled. When an American citizen commits a crime in a foreign country he cannot complain if required to submit to such modes of trial and to such punishment as the
laws of that country may prescribe for its own people, unless a different mode be provided for by treaty stipulations between that country
and the United States. By the act in question the appellant cannot be
extradited except upon the order of a judge of a court of the United
States, and then only upon evidence establishing probable cause to believe him guilty of the offense charged; and when tried in the country
to which he is sent, he is secured by the same act "a fair and impartial trial,"—not necessarily a trial according to the mode prescribed by
this country for crimes committed against its laws, but a trial according to the modes established in the country where the crime was committed, provided such trial be had without discrimination against the
accused because of his American citizenship. In the judgment of Congress these provisions were deemed adequate to the ends of justice in
cases of persons committing crimes in a foreign country or territory
"occupied by or under the control of the United States," and subsequently fleeing to this country. We cannot adjudge that Congress in
this matter has abused its discretion, nor decline to enforce obedience
to its will as expressed in the act of June 6th, 1900.

III. Another contention of the appellant is that as Congress, by the
joint resolution of April 20th, 1898, declared that "the people of Cuba
are, and of right ought to be, free and independent," and as peace has
existed since, at least, the military forces of Spain evacuated Cuba on
or about January, 1899, the occupancy and control of that island under
the military authority of the United States is without warrant in the
Constitution and an unauthorized interference with the internal affairs
of a friendly power; consequently it is argued the appellant should
not be extradited for trial in the courts established under the orders issued by the Military Governor of the island. In support of this proposition it is said that the United States recognized the existence of the
Republic of Cuba, and that the war with Spain was carried on jointly
by the allied forces of the United States and of that Republic.

Apart from the view that it is not competent for the judiciary to
make any declaration upon the question of the length of time during
which Cuba may be rightfully occupied and controlled by the United
States in order to effect its pacification—it being the function of the
political branch of the government to determine when such occupation
and control shall cease, and therefore when the troops of the United
States shall be withdrawn from Cuba—the contention that the United

the government, with which the judicial department will not
interfere.

States recognized the existence of an established government known as
the Republic of Cuba, but is now using its military or executive power
to displace or overthrow it, is without merit. The declaration by Congress that the people of Cuba were and of right ought to be free and
independent was not intended as a recognition of the existence of an
organized government instituted by the people of that Island in hostility
to the government maintained by Spain. Nothing more was intended
than to express the thought that the Cubans were entitled to enjoy—
to use the language of the President in his message of December 5th,
1897—that "measure of self-control which is the inalienable right of
man, protected in their right to reap the benefit of the exhaustless
treasure of their country." In the same message the President said:
"It is to be seriously considered whether the Cuban insurrection possesses beyond dispute the attributes of statehood, which alone can demand the recognition of belligerency in its favor. The same requirement must certainly be no less seriously considered when the graver issue
of recognizing independence is in question." Again, in his message of
April 11th, 1898, referring to the suggestion that the independence of
the Republic of Cuba should be recognized before this country entered
upon war with Spain, he said: "Such recognition is not necessary in
order to enable the United States to intervene and pacify the island.
To commit this country now to the recognition of any particular government in Cuba might subject us to embarrassing conditions of international obligation toward the organization to be recognized. In case
of intervention our conduct would be subject to the approval or disapproval of such government. We should be obliged to submit to its direction and to assume to it the mere relation of a friendly ally." To
this may be added the significant fact that the first part of the joint
resolution as originally reported from the senate committee read as
follows: "That the people of the island of Cuba are and of right ought
to be free and independent, *and that the government of the United States
hereby recognizes the Republic of Cuba as the true and lawful government
of the Island.*" But upon full consideration the views of the President
received the sanction of Congress, and the words in italics were stricken
out. It thus appears that both the legislative and executive branches
of the government concurred in not recognizing the existence of any
such government as the Republic of Cuba. It is true that the co-operation of troops commanded by Cuban officers was accepted by the military authorities of the United States in its efforts to overthrow Spanish
authority in Cuba. Yet from the beginning to the end of the war the
supreme authority in all military operations in Cuba and in Cuban waters against Spain was with the United States, and those operations
were not in any sense under the control or direction of the troops commanded by Cuban officers.

We are of opinion, for the reasons stated, that the act of June 6th,
1900, is not in violation of the Constitution of the United States, and

Whatever the status of Cuba may be as to the United States, therefore, its status as to other powers is that, so long as the occupation of the military forces of the United States continues, it must necessarily be considered as much under the jurisdiction of the United States government as though it were an integral part of the territory thereof.

§ 109. **National unity as to all foreign powers, a principle enunciated by the Congress of the Confederation, and continued until the present time.**—One of the earliest acts of the Continental Congress was to pass a resolution that in our dealings with foreign powers the United States and colonies should be considered as one nation.[1] This resolution was passed at a time when the people of the States had by no means surrendered the same extent of power to the Central Government as was subsequently vested in it and is therefore a clear indication that from the earliest times unity, so far as foreign powers were concerned, became, and it ever since has remained, one

---

that this case comes within the provisions of that act. The court below having found that there was probable cause to believe the appellant guilty of the offences charged, the order for his extradition was proper, and no ground existed for his discharge on *habeas corpus*.

The judgment of the Circuit Court is, therefore,

Affirmed.

§ 109.

[1] 3 Secret Journals of Congress, 452. "March 26, 1784: Congress took into consideration the report of a committee, consisting of Mr. Jefferson, Mr. Gerry and Mr. Williamson to whom were referred sundry letters from the ministers of the United States in Europe. And sundry instructions to the ministers relative to the formation of commercial treaties with sundry European nations being under debate, and the third article or instruction being amended to read as follows: 'That these United States be considered in all such treaties, and in every case arising under them, as one nation, upon the principles of the Federal constitution.'

"A motion was made by Mr. Ellery, seconded by Mr. Howell, to strike out that instruction; and on the question, Shall it stand, the yeas and nays being required by Mr. Reed. New Hampshire, Mr. Foster, Mr. Blanchard; Massachusetts, Mr. Gerry, Mr. Partridge; New York, Mr. Paine; New Jersey, Mr. Beatty, Mr. Dick; Pennsylvania, Mr. Mifflin, Mr. Montgomery; Maryland, Mr. Stone, Mr. Chase; Virginia, Mr. Jefferson, Mr. Hardy, Mr. Mercer, (Mr. Lee, no), Mr. Monroe; North Carolina, Mr. Williamson, Mr. Spaight; South Carolina, Mr. Read, Mr. Beresford, (eight states besides New York not counted, only one delegate voting) AYE; Rhode Island, Mr. Ellery, Mr. Howell; Connecticut, Mr. Sherman, Mr. Wadsworth; two states, NO. 'So

of the fundamental principles upon which the United States was based.[2]

The principle then enunciated of unity as to foreign powers has been so continuously and consistently adhered to by the United States, and adopted by all foreign powers, that it never can be receded from, but must be accepted as a part of the organic law of this country, carrying with it all the benefits derivable therefrom as well as all the responsibilities which can be based thereon.

it was resolved in the affirmative.' " See comments of J. C. Bancroft Davis' notes to Miller's Lectures on the Constitution of the United States, pp. 53-54.

[2] Since the completion of this chapter the Supreme Court has decided several of the *Insular Cases* in which the *status* of some of the recently acquired possessions of the United States has been determined. Those cases are discussed in another part of this volume (§ 61, pp. 117, *et seq.*, and other sections there referred to *post*, and appendix at end of volume), and there is not room for any extended reference to those decisions at this point. The question of national unity and the complete control of foreign relations by the Central Government was raised and numerous cases cited in regard thereto. See collation of cases in INSULAR

CASES APPENDIX at end of this volume. Amongst those cases will be found the following:

Barron vs. *Baltimore*, U. S. Sup. Ct. 1833, 7 Peters, 243, MARSHALL, Ch. J.;

Briscoe vs. *Bank*, U. S. Sup. Ct. 1837, 11 Peters, 257, McLEAN, J.;

Chinese Exclusion Cases, U. S. Sup. Ct. 1889, 130 U. S. 581, FIELD, J.; also 1893, 149 U. S. 698, GRAY, J.;

Cross vs. *Harrison*, U. S. Sup. Ct. 1853, 16 How. 164, WAYNE, J.;

Ekiu v. *United States*, U. S. Sup. Ct. 1891, 142 U. S. 651, GRAY, J.;

Fleming vs. *Page*, U. S. Sup. Ct. 1850, 9 How. 603, TANEY, Ch. J.;

Geofroy vs. *Riggs*, U. S. Sup. Ct. 1890, 133 U. S. 258, FIELD, J.;

Neagle, In re, U. S. Sup. Ct. 1890, 135 U. S. 1, MILLER, J.;

United States vs. *Rice*, U. S. Sup. Ct. 1819, 4 Wheat. 246, STORY, J.

PART II.

HISTORICAL REVIEW OF THE TREATY–MAKING POWER OF THE UNITED STATES.

CHAPTER IV.

THE TREATY-MAKING POWER AS AN ATTRIBUTE OF SOVEREIGNTY AND AS EXERCISED BY CENTRAL GOVERNMENTS OF CONFEDERATED POWERS.

§ 110. **Ancient origin of treaties.**—Treaties, leagues and compacts have been made from time immemorial between different powers, states, tribes, peoples and princes. The Bible records many instances of treaties and leagues; one

191

very notable case was the compact made by the Children of
Isreal with the Gibeonites when they were entering the Promised Land, and which is especially analogous to the question
under consideration, as it was made between the chiefs of the
two nations; notwithstanding the fraud by which the Gibeonites procured exemption from the general slaughter to
which all the other tribes of Canaan had been doomed, the
compact was suffered to remain inviolate, although the Children of Isreal themselves resented it, because the tribal chiefs
in whom the power was vested had exercised it, and thus
had plighted the faith of the nation, thereby binding all the
tribes and members thereof, making it impossible for them
to recede from the compact, although they meted out a prolonged punishment on the Gibeonites for the fraud and deceit
which had been practiced.[1]   We are also told at a later period
of the terrible retribution which resulted from Saul's violation of that treaty.[2]   The histories of Rome and Greece are
replete with instances in which their relations with other
peoples were established and maintained by treaties.[3]

§ 111. **Treaty-making always vested in highest powers;
Professor Woolsey's views.**—There are recorded instances
of treaty-making during the entire known history of the
world; in almost every case it will be found that the right
has been vested in the highest governmental power; in fact,
the right of negotiation with foreign powers has not only
always been considered as a badge, or attribute, of complete
nationality and sovereignty, but, as a general rule, the power
of negotiation does not exist in those political bodies which
lack any of the elements of complete nationality and sovereignty; nor can the right be exercised by any person or power
other than the highest sovereign power or the duly qualified
representatives thereof.   That the right of making treaties
is an essential attribute of sovereignty to be exercised only
by the highest power, and that States which have parted
with their sovereignty or any part thereof, have no treaty-
making power, is a rule which has practically been admitted

§ 110.
[1] Joshua, chap. IX, 3–27.
[2] 2 Samuel, chap. XXI, 1–12.
[3] See Walker's History of the

Law of Nations, vol. 1, Cambridge,
Engl. 1899, p. 34, for Jewish Treaties; pp. 47–61, for Roman Treaties;
p. 78 for Saracen Treaties.

by all writers on international law,[1] and which has also been incorporated into the organic law of nearly all constitutionally governed countries.[2] Professor Theodore S. Woolsey's views on this subject are expressed in his book on international law in the extract quoted in the note to this section.[3]

§ 111.
[1] See the provisions in constitutions as to treaty-making power collated in note to § 130 of this chapter, *post*.

[2] For the serious consequences of departing from this rule in regard to treaties between the Indian tribes and the United States, see §§ 401–406, chap. XIV, Vol. II.

[3] PROFESSOR WOOLSEY'S VIEWS.

"Sec. 101. *Of the right of contract and especially of treaties*. A contract is one of the highest acts of human free will: it is the will binding itself in regard to the future, and surrendering its right to change a certain expressed intention, so that it becomes morally and jurally a wrong to act otherwise; it is the act of two parties in which each or one of the two conveys power over himself to the other in consideration of something done or to be done by the other. The binding force of contracts is to be deduced from the freedom and foresight of man, which would have almost no sphere in society or power of co-operation, unless trust could be excited. Trust lies at the basis of society; society is essential for the development of the individual; the individual could not develop his free forethought, unless an acknowledged obligation made him sure in regard to the actions of others. That nations, as well as individuals, are bound by contract, will not be doubted when we remember that they have the same properties of free will and forecast; that they could have no safe intercourse otherwise, and could scarcely be sure of any settled relations towards one another except a state of war, and that thus a state of society, to which the different needs and aptitudes of the parts of the world invite men would be impossible. We have already seen, that without this power a positive law of nations could not exist, which needs for its establishment the consent of all who are bound by its provisions. National contracts are even more solemn and sacred than private ones, on account of the great interests involved of the deliberateness with which the obligations are assumed, of the permanence and generality of the obligations,—measured by the national life, and including thousands of particular cases,—and of each nation's calling, under God, to be a teacher of right to all within and without its borders.

"Contracts can be made by states with individuals or bodies of individuals, or with other states. Contracts between states may be called conventions or treaties. Among the species of treaties those which put an end to a war and introduce a new state of intercourse, or treaties of peace, will be considered here, only so far as they partake of the general character of treaties: their relations to war will be considered in the chapter devoted to that subject.

"Sec. 102. Treaties allowed under the law of nations are uncon-

13

§ 112. **Views of Professor Lawrence.**—"We begin with *Sovereign States.* In order clearly to understand their nature and the nature of their subjection to International Law, it will be necessary to pass through an ascending series of conceptions, beginning with the comparatively rudimentary one of a state. A state may be defined as *A political community, the members of which are bound together by the tie of common subjection to some central authority, whose commands the bulk of them habitually obey.* This central authority may be vested in an individual or a body of individuals; and, though it may be patriarchal, it must be something more than parental; for a family as such is not a political community and therefore not a state. The methods by which the central authority is created are outside our present subject. Whether a political community is governed by a line of hereditary monarchs, or by persons elected from time to time by the votes of a greater or less number

strained acts of independent powers, placing them under an obligation to do something which is not wrong, or,—

"1. Treaties can be made only by the constituted authorities of nations, or by persons specially deputed by them for that purpose. An unauthorized agreement, or a *sponsio*, like that of the consul Postumius at the Caudine Forks, does not bind the sovereign,—it is held,—for the engager had no power to convey rights belonging to another. And yet it may be morally wrong in a high degree for the sovereign to violate such an engagement of a subordinate; for it might be an act of extreme necessity, to which the usual forms of governmental proceedings would not apply. Moreover the actions of military or naval commanders must be to a certain extent left without positive restrictions, and usage might be pleaded for many transactions of this nature. Again, from the nature of the case a faction, a province, or an integral part of a *close* confederation has no treaty-making power; although a *loose* confederation, like the Germanic, might exist, while conceding such a prerogative to its members. Individuals, or other dependent bodies, can make commercial arrangements with a foreign power, unless their laws forbid; but the arrangements apply to a particular case, and obligate none else; they are like any other private contracts; nor has a government over such a contracting party anything to do in the premises, save to protect and, if expedient, to afford its redress against injustice. *Political* engagements, or such as affect a body politic, can be made only by political powers. And the actual sovereign alone, or a power possessing the attributes of sovereignty at the time, can bind a nation by its engagements." Woolsey's Introduction to the study of International Law, § 101 –102, pp. 158–159, 6th ed. New York, 1891

of its members, it is a state provided that the obedience of the bulk of the people is rendered to the authorities. If there is no such obedience, there is anarchy; and in proportion as obedience is lacking the community runs the risk of losing its statehood. A mere administrative division of a greater whole, such as a French Department or an English County, would not be called a state; but we should not refuse the title to a community like Canada which is not entirely free from political subjection, though we should probably indicate the absence of complete self-government by speaking of it as a Dependent State.

"We have seen what is meant by a state. If we add to the marks already given in our definition of it, the further mark that the body or individual who receives the habitual obedience of the community does not render the like obedience to any earthly superior, we arrive at the conception of a *Sovereign or Independent State,* which possesses not only internal sovereignty, or the power of dealing with domestic affairs, but external sovereignty also, or the power of dealing with foreign affairs. The commonwealths which compose the American Union possess all the features we have enumerated as the distinguishing marks of states. They are, therefore, rightly so called; but historical and political reasons have sometimes caused them to be alluded to as Sovereign States. Strictly speaking, this is a mistake. By the Constitution of the United States all dealings with foreign powers are left to the central government. The Executive and Legislature of any and every state in the Union are devoid of the slightest power to act in these matters, and have to submit to what is done by the authorities at Washington. They have none of the attributes of external sovereignty. They cannot make war or peace, nor can they send agents to foreign powers or receive agents from them. In other words, they are states, but they are not Sovereign States."[1]

§ 113. **Views of Henry Wheaton.**—"The power of nego-

§ 112.
[1] Lawrence's Principles of International Law, § 43, pp. 56–57, Boston, 1895. See also same volume, § 144, pp. 263–264, for Professor Lawrence's views as to treaty-making power of confederations. See also note to § 114, *post.*

tiating and contracting public treaties between nation and nation exists in full vigor in every sovereign state which has not parted with this portion of its sovereignty, or agreed to modify its exercise by compact with other states. . . . Thus the several States of the North American Union are expressly prohibited from entering into any treaty with foreign powers; . . . whilst the sovereign members of the Germanic Confederation retain the power of concluding treaties of alliance and commerce, not inconsistent with the fundamental laws of the Confederation. The Constitution, or fundamental law, of every particular State must determine in whom is vested power of negotiating and contracting treaties with foreign powers.[1] "

The power referred to by Wheaton as retained by the constituent sovereignties of the Germanic Confederation to continue to exercise foreign relations proved so embarrassing that when the present German Empire was organized the several States and sovereignties composing it were compelled to surrender the treaty-making power absolutely to, and vest it in, the Central Government, by which it is exclusively exercised with as far-reaching powers as though the Empire were a single unit.[2]

§ 114. **In confederations the treaty-making power is in the Central Government.**—As the treaty-making power is lodged in the highest governmental authority in each state, it follows that in confederated states the power must be lodged in the central government of the federation, as under no other circumstances could it be properly exercised. The impracticability of allowing constituent states to exercise any treaty-making power was demonstrated in the case of the North German Confederation, and as just stated, that method was abandoned on the formation of the Empire.[1]

§ 113.

[1] Wheaton's Elements of International Law, part 3, chap. II, § 1, p. 185, Philadelphia, 1836; part 3, chap. II, § 1, p. 441, of Lawrence's Wheaton, 2d edition, Boston. 1863; chap. II, § 252, p. 356, of Boyd's Third English edition, London, 1889; chap. II, § 252, p. 328 of Dana's Wheaton, Eighth edition, Boston, 1866.

[2] For constitutional provisions as to the exercise of the treaty-making power in Germany, see §§ 128 and 130 and foot-notes thereunder, *post.*

§ 114.

[1] See § 113, *ante,* and foot-note.

It may be too broad an assertion to state that the treaty-making power never exists in constituent States, but as a general principle it may be said that the central government of federations is the only government which other powers will recognize in dealing with any matter affecting the entire federation or any of the constituent states, and that this rule has not only been generally adopted as a principle of international law but also of the constitutional law of nearly all existing confederations.[2]   The views of some authorities on international law are collated in the footnote hereto.[3]

[2] See collation of constitutional provisions as to treaty making in note to § 130, *post.*

[3] PROFESSOR LAWRENCE'S VIEWS.

" The Sovereign States which are Subjects of International Law are regarded as units in their dealings with other states.   They are corporate bodies, acting through their governments.   Each state is bound by the engagements entered into by its rulers on its behalf, as long as they have been made in accordance with its own law and constitution. Other states have no right to dictate what individual or body in a state shall conduct its external affairs.   As long as there is such an individual or body of individuals, they must transact their business with him or them.   If no such authority exists, they can decline to transact business at all; and if a state remains for any length of time in such a condition of revolution or anarchy that no one has authority to speak on its behalf, it will soon cease to be a Subject of International Law in its existing form, though in all probability its territory and people will enter into new combinations and still retain under changed conditions some place in the ranks of civilized states.   The continuity of a state, and consequently its liability to be called upon to fulfill the international obligations it has contracted, is not affected by change of government or loss of outlying territory.   But if it splits up into several states, or is obliterated altogether like Poland, or enters with others, like each of the American colonies whose independence was recognized by Great Britain in 1783, into a union for the formation of a new state, it loses its corporate existence as a Subject of International Law.   When this happens, the circumstances of each case decide what is to become of the debts and other obligations with which the lost state was burdened.   In some instances they disappear with the body corporate to which they belonged; in others an equitable division of them is made. The law of nations lays down no clear rules with regard to these matters; but it does clearly say that if a state desires to have intercourse with other states, there must be some authority within it capable of pledging it to a given course of conduct.

" This is true of Confederations no less than of States which are organic wholes in their internal organization.   Confederations are generally

197

§ 115. **Views of Professor Hall.**—William E. Hall, whose works to-day rank among the leading English authorities on

divided into two kinds, for neither of which is there a good term in the English language. The first, called in German a *Bundesstaat*, comprises those unions in which the central authority alone can deal with foreign powers and settle external affairs, the various members of the Confederation having control over their internal affairs only. In the second, called a *Staatenbund*, are included all Confederations where the States which have agreed to unite have retained for themselves the power of dealing directly with others in some matters, the remaining external affairs being reserved by the federal bond to the central authority. Unions of the first kind have been called Supreme Federal Governments, unions of the second kind Systems of Confederated States. The best examples of the former now in existence are the United States of America and the Swiss Confederation. No good example of the latter remains to the present time; but the German Bund from 1815 to 1866 exhibited to the world in full perfection the disadvantages of this kind of union. From the point of view of International Law, a *Bundesstaat* does not differ from an ordinary Sovereign State. It forms but one state in relation to foreign powers, though internally it may consist of many states. But as these states have no right of sending and receiving diplomatic missions, or making peace or war, foreign powers have as little to do with them as they have with the administrative divisions of an ordinary state. The case of a *Staatenbund* is different. It is a bundle of separate states, each of which retains some of the rights of external sovereignty while it is deprived of the remainder. Accordingly the states which compose it must be placed by International Law among those part-sovereign communities which we have to consider as the second class among its subjects. They are something more than administrative divisions of a larger whole. They are something less than Sovereign States.

" It is sometimes exceedingly difficult to refer a given Confederation to either of the types depicted above. The Swiss Confederation, for instance, was at its inception a union of the looser kind. It is now a Supreme Federal Government, or *Bundesstaat*. But at certain periods of its history it could hardly have been called one or the other with any regard to accuracy. At the present time the new German Empire, which was constituted in 1871 in consequence of the successful war with France, is in much the same predicament. The central authority makes war and peace, sends and receives ambassadors, and negotiates treaties for political and commercial objects. But the governments of some of the states which form the empire have the right of accrediting diplomatic representatives to foreign powers and receiving representatives from them to deal with matters not reserved to the Imperial Government. Moreover, Bavaria and Saxony have ministers for foreign affairs. Probably the diplomatists in question are not overwhelmed with work; for it is difficult to discover in the Constitution of the Empire any matters left for them to deal with. But since a right of sepa-

international law, referred to the treaty-making power in the following words: "It follows from the position of a State

rate diplomatic intercourse with foreign powers is vested in the more important of the federated states, we are unable to say that the Confederation is a true *Bundesstaat*, however insignificant the deflections from that type may be. At the same time it is equally impossible to call it a *Staatenbund*, in view of the fact that for all practical purposes the central authority alone transacts the external business of the Union. There can, however, be no doubt that, if the Confederation lasts, the subordinate states will rapidly lose whatever control over their relations with foreign powers they may still possess." Lawrence's Principles of International Law, Boston, 1895, section 45, pp. 60-63.

DR. PHILLIMORE'S VIEWS.

"C. We now arrive at the second branch of this part of our subject— namely, the consideration of several States under a Federal Union. The examples in modern times of this description of States are the following:—

"1. The Germanic Confederation (*Der Deutsche Bund*) (*a*), the North German Confederation from 1866 to 1871, the German Empire since 1871.

"2. The Confederated Cantons of Switzerland.

"3. The United Republics of North America.

"4. The United Republics of Central and South America:—namely, first, The United Provinces of Guatemala, or the Republic of Central America; secondly, The United Provinces of Rio de la Plata, or the Argentine Republic.

"CI. States under a Federal Union may be classed under two principal heads:—First. Those which have retained their Independent and Individual Sovereignty, especially as to the adjustment of their *external* relations with other Nations, and belong to a system of Confederated States only for purposes of domestic and *internal* policy, and of mutual assistance and defence. (*Staatenbund*) (*b*).

"But the Laws of this Federal Body have only effect and force in the separate members of the system through the agency and application of the particular laws and jurisdiction of each individual Government; therefore, as far as Foreign Power is concerned, these Confederated States must be considered as individually responsible for their conduct, and as separate Independent States. In this class must be ranked the existing Germanic Confederation.

"Secondly. The Federal Union may be so adjusted that the management of the external relations of the respective members of the Union be absolutely vested in a Supreme Federal Power." Phillimore's International Law, 3d edition, London, 1899, vol. 1, pp. 156-157.

GARDNER'S INSTITUTES.

"Nations, by their fundamental laws, may respectively limit the authority of the treaty-making power; but if there be no limitation,

as a moral being, at liberty to be guided by its own will, that
it has the power of contracting with another State to do any
acts which are not forbidden, or to refrain from any acts
which are not enjoined by the law which governs its international relations, and this power being recognized by international law, contracts made in virtue of it, when duly concluded, become legally obligatory. . . .

" The antecedent conditions of a treaty may be stated as
follows: The parties to it must be capable of contracting;
the agents employed must be duly empowered to contract on
their behalf; the parties must be so situated that the consent
of both may be regarded as freely given; and the objects of
the agreement must be in conformity with law.

" All States which are subject to international law are capable of contracting, but they are not all capable of contracting for whatever object they may wish.   The possession of
full independence is accompanied by full contracting power;
but the nature of the bond uniting members of a confederation, or joining protected or subordinate States to a superior,
implies either that a part of the power of contract normally
belonging to a State has been surrendered, or else that it
has never been acquired.   All contracts, therefore, are void
which are entered into by such States in excess of the powers
retained by, or conceded to, them under their existing relations with associated or superior States." [1]

§ 116. **Views of Professor Pomeroy.**—John Norton Pomeroy, whose opinion upon the general subject is strengthened
by the fact that he is one of the leading authorities upon con-

treaties of peace as well as others, may, by virtue of the nation's right
of eminent domain, and of a general treaty-making power, alien any
part of the public domain or property, and abandon for the public advantage, all private claims and property of the citizens of either contracting party upon the other, or its citizens. (Wheat. Int. L. p. 4, c. 4,
Sec. 1, 2, 3).

"In the United States, if private property and private claims are
abandoned by a treaty of peace, as was done by our treaty of peace of
1848 with Mexico, the Constitution requires Congress to pay our citizens for the private property so abandoned; and it has been done."
Gardner's Institutes of American International Law, New York, 1860,
p. 584.

§ 115. | X, §§ 107–108, pp. 339–340, 4th edi-
[1] Hall's International Law, chap. | tion, Oxford and London, 1895.

stitutional law of the United States, says: "The right to enter into treaties at will is certainly one of the most important that belong to States. As all States are equal, they all have the same capacity to contract with other bodies politic. Deprive a nation of any portion of this capacity, and we would reduce it from its position of equality, and at the same time would restrict its complete independence and sovereignty. The want of complete power, therefore, to enter into treaties is a sure badge of inferiority and dependence. . . . The very definition indicates that all sovereign independent States have full capacity to enter into whatever treaties they please. The right of negotiating and contracting treaties is one of the rights most essential to sovereignty and equality. A protected State may, if it has retained its sovereignty, enter into treaties and alliances, unless the power has been expressly renounced or cannot be exercised consistently with the conditions of its protection. But so far as the capacity had been surrendered or restricted, just so far would the State have limited its attributes of sovereignty and equality."[1]

§ 117. **Constitutional limitations on treaty-making.**— While the power to make treaties is vested in the highest power, its exercise may, of course, be subject to certain constitutional limitations. This is the case with the United States, the Constitution of which requires the ratification of treaties made by the Executive by a two-thirds vote of the Senate.[1] The element of sovereignty in the Central Government, and the power of negotiation in the Executive thereof, however, are not affected by such limitations, as they do not detract from the completeness of the power, when it is properly and constitutionally exercised. This point was thoroughly appreciated as an elementary principle of international law prior to the adoption of the Constitution and even of the Articles of Confederation.

§ 116.

[1] Pomeroy's International Law, Woolsey's Edition, chap. IX, §§ 258-260, pp. 323-324, Boston and New York, 1886; See also views of Professor Pomeroy as to extent of treaty-making power of the United States, §§ 268-271 of this volume, post.

§ 117.

[1] U. S. Constitution, article II, § 2, clause 2.

Vattel who, at the middle of the eighteenth century was one of the leading authorities on international law, says: "Public treaties can only be made by the superior powers, by sovereigns, who contract in the name of the State. . . . The sovereign who possesses the full and absolute authority has, doubtless, a right to treat in the name of the State he represents; and his engagements are binding on the whole nation. But all rulers of States have not a power to make public treaties by their own authority alone: some are obliged to take the advice of a senate, or of the representatives of the nation. It is from the fundamental laws of each State that we must learn where resides the authority that is capable of contracting with validity in the name of the State." [2] According to Halleck, "the treaty-making power of the State is determined by its own Constitution and fundamental law." [3] The views of Professor Glenn and Professor Lawrence on this point are quoted in the note to this section. [4]

[2] Vattel on the Law of Nations, Chitty and Ingraham, Philadelphia 1870, p. 192.

[3] Halleck's International Law, Sir Sherstone Baker's 3d English edition, London, 1893, vol. 1, p. 276.

GLENN.

[4] "100. Treaties Defined. Treaties are agreements made and entered into by one independent state with another, or others, in conformity to law, by which it places itself under an obligation. The following agreements are not considered treaties:

"(a) Agreements entered into by a state with private individuals.

"(b) Agreements concluded between a state and the church upon religious or political matters, and especially concordats of different states with the pope.

"(c) Agreements concluded by sovereigns or sovereign dynasties, whether among themselves or with foreign states, relative to their personal or dynastic pretensions to the government of a country.

"The three classes of agreements mentioned above are all of such a nature as to form no part of public international law, as they are either made between a state and private individuals or by agents of the state in their individual character.

"Essentials of valid Treaty.

"101. The essentials of a valid treaty or contract between two or more independent states are:

"(a) Capacity of the parties to contract.

"(b) Duly-empowered agents to act on behalf of the states.

"(c) Freedom of consent.

"(d) The object of the contract must be in conformity to law.

"Every independent state is capable of entering into treaties with another state or states, but the fundamental law of a state may impose certain restrictions upon

§ 118. **Commencement of modern period of international law.**—Although treaties and leagues existed in ancient and medieval times, they did not begin to assume the prominent part in the political history of the world which they have since attained, and now occupy, until the middle of the seventeenth century and shortly after Hugo Grotius, whose memory was so fitly celebrated by the American delegates to the Peace Conference at The Hague, had surprised all thinking men with his great book *De Jure Belli ac Pacis*, published in 1625. According to Dr. Wheaton, whose views in this respect have been generally adopted, the peace of Westphalia of 1648, which was evidenced by the treaty made at that time and place between the principal nations of Europe, may be chosen as the epoch from which the history of modern international law commences; this great transaction marks a most important era, not only in the history of international law, but also in the progress of European civilization.[1]

§ 119. **Disregard of colonies in treaties made by European powers as to American affairs.**—From that time it became the settled custom of the great powers of Europe to

the method of entering into such agreements, which must be taken into consideration by the parties to the contract. In the United States and other confederations the executive or treaty-making power cannot finally conclude treaties without the consent of the legislative bodies. The latter have to concur, and up to the time that this final consent of the concurring body has been obtained the other parties to the contract can withdraw their assent, unless this right has been waived." Glenn's International Law, St. Paul, 1895, pp. 139–142.

LAWRENCE.

"We will now pass on to consider the treaty-making power and its methods of action, in so far as they are dealt with by International Law. In each state the right of making treaties rests with those authorities to whom it is confided by the political constitution. As long as there is some power in a country whose word can bind the whole body politic, other states must do their international business with it, and have no right to inquire into its nature and the circumstances of its creation. But other important matters connected with treaties are of international concern. The first of these to be discussed is *The nature and necessity of ratification*." Lawrence's Principles of International Law, sec. 152, Boston, 1895, p. 284.

§ **118.**
[1] Wheaton's History of the Law of Nations, p. 69, New York, 1845; Walker's History of the Law of Nations, Cambridge, 1899, p. 147–148.

adjust all matters of dispute at the conclusion of every war by treaties. During the seventeenth and eighteenth centuries the American possessions of the European powers were in the early stages of development, their value was uncertain, and they were frequently used as make-weights in the adjustment of European disputes. The vast tracts of sparsely settled territory on the western side of the Atlantic were parceled out, sold, exchanged or otherwise disposed of, or affected in some manner, either as to the ownership thereof, or the sovereignty thereover, without any regard whatever to the wishes of the inhabitants, but simply according to the relative strength of the European nations, which were constantly engaged in warfare with each other, and which often found these possessions available in forcing settlements, or obtaining concessions, in their European controversies. Thus the treaty of Utrecht in 1713, and the treaty terminating the French and English war in 1763, as well as other treaties, greatly altered the relations of the American colonies to their European motherlands, notwithstanding the fact that the colonists had no voice whatever in framing or ratifying them.[1] During this period the frequent transfers from one nation to another of colonial possessions, and sovereignty thereover, as well as the frequent similar transfers of European possessions

§ 119.

[1] Some of the principal treaties made by European powers prior to 1783 and which affected American colonies were as follows:

(1) The Treaty of Ryswick, between England and France concluded September 10–20, 1697, being "Articles of Peace between the most Serene and Mighty Prince William the Third, King of Great Britain, and the most Serene and Mighty Prince Lewis the Fourteenth, the most Christian King, concluded in the Royal Palace at Ryswick, the 10–20 day of September, 1697." This treaty was the conclusion of the war of the Palatinate, known as King William's, or Frontenac's War, which was one of the contests finally resulting in the overthrow of the French power in America. By Section 7 it is provided as follows:

"The most Christian King shall restore to the said King of Great Britain, all countries, islands, forts, and colonies, wheresoever situated, which the English did possess before the declaration of this present war. And in like manner the King of Great Britain shall restore to the most Christian King all countries, islands, forts, and colonies, wheresoever situated, which the French did possess before the said declaration of war; and this restitution shall be made, on both sides, within the space of six months, or sooner if it can be done. . . ."

firmly established, as a principle of international law, the right of sovereign powers to negotiate and conclude treaties affecting territory, and the transfer thereof, by and through the highest sovereign power having jurisdiction over the transferred territory, without regard to the wishes of the people, or, as it has been lately expressed, "the consent of

Section 8 provided for the formalities in connection with the transfer. For a summary of this treaty and references to the authorities relating thereto see Macdonald's Select Charters of American History, pp. 222, 223. See also Chalmers' Collection of Treaties, vol. I, pp. 332–340.

(2) The Treaty of Utrecht, between England and France, March 31–April 11, 1713, being "The Treaty of Peace and Friendship between the most Serene and most Potent Princess Anne, by the grace of God, Queen of Great Britain, France, and Ireland, and the most Serene and most Potent Prince Lewis the XIVth, the most Christian King, concluded at Utrecht, the 31–11 day of March–April, 1713." This treaty was concluded between France and Great Britain on the termination of the war of the Spanish succession, which in America was known as Queen Anne's War. Arts. X–XV (quoted at length in Macdonald's Select Charters) relate to the restoration by France to Great Britain of Hudson Bay and Newfoundland, France retaining Canada. It appears in Chalmers' Collection of Treaties, vol. I, pp. 340–390. See also Macdonald's Select Charters of American History, pp. 229–232.

(3) The Treaty of Aix-la-Chapelle, October 18, 1748, between England, France, The Netherlands, and other powers, being "The Definitive Treaty of Peace and Friendship between his Britannic Majesty, the most Christian King, and the States General of the United Provinces; concluded at Aix-la-Chapelle, the 18th day of October, N. S. 1748; to which the Empress, Queen of Hungary, the Kings of Spain and Sardinia, the Duke of Modena, and the Republic of Genoa, have acceded." By this treaty, at the conclusion of the War of the Austrian Succession, known in America as King George's War, Art. V provided:

"V. All the conquests that have been made since the commencement of the war, or which, since the conclusion of the preliminary articles, signed the 30th of April last may have been or shall be made, either in Europe, or the East or West Indies, or in any other part of the world whatsoever, being to be restored without exception, in conformity to what was stipulated by the said preliminary articles, and by the declarations since signed; the high contracting parties engage to give orders immediately for proceeding to that restitution. . . . "

Art. IX provided for the details for the restoration of the conquered territory. An abstract of this treaty, together with memorandum of authorities in regard thereto, will be found in Macdonald's Select Charters of American History, pp. 251–253. See also Chalmers' Collection of Treaties, vol. I, pp. 424–442.

the governed," which was discussed at length in the preceding chapter.[2]

§ 120. **Treaty-making power of Great Britain vested in the Crown.**—This treaty-making power, as it was exercised prior to the Confederation and has ever since been exercised by European powers, is probably the most far-reaching power and the highest prerogative that still remains vested in the Crown in those countries in which constitutional government has been combined with monarchical institutions.

Notwithstanding the great constitutional liberties of England, the treaty-making power still remains in the British crown, and, according to Halleck, "In Great Britain the treaty-making power is a branch of the prerogative of the Crown, has in theory no limits." He however qualifies this by the statement that Parliament, by its power of legislation, may render a treaty ineffectual by refusing either to appropriate the money or to enact the legislation necessary to carry it into effect.[1] The views of one of the leading author-

(4) The Treaty of Paris, February 10, 1763, between England, France, Spain and Portugal, being "The Definitive Treaty of Peace and Friendship, between his Britannic Majesty, the most Christian King, and the King of Spain; concluded at Paris, the 10th day of February, 1763. To which the King of Portugal acceded on the Same Day." This treaty was made on the termination of the Seven Years' War, known in America as the French and Indian War. The articles relating to America, by which Great Britain practically acquired all of the French possessions, with the exception of some islands, and by which Great Britain restored Cuba to Spain, and Spain transferred Florida to Great Britain, are Arts. IV-IX XVII-XX. An abstract of this treaty and the articles relating to America and references to the authorities will be found in Macdonald's Select Charters of American History, pp. 261–266. See also Chalmers' Collection of Treaties, vol. 1, pp. 467–483.

(5) There was a treaty of offensive and defensive alliance between France and Spain signed August 15, 1761, and a secret treaty between France and Spain concluded November 3, 1762, ceding Louisiana and New Orleans to Spain, the cession being to compensate Spain for the loss of Florida which Spain ceded to Great Britain.

(6) See also the treaties between Great Britain and France and Great Britain and Spain made September 3, 1783, at the same time as the treaty with the United States. Snow's American Diplomacy, pp. 1–11.

[2] See chap. II, §§ 46-49, *ante*.

§ 120.

[1] Halleck's International Law. See Sherstone Baker's 3d English edition, London, 1893, vol. 1, p. 308.

ities on Crown prerogatives are quoted in the notes to this section.[2]

[2] ANSON ON THE CROWN.

"Sec. 3. *War, Peace and Treaties.* The Queen, acting on the advice of her Ministers, makes war and peace. The House of Commons may refuse supplies for a war, or either House may express its disapproval by resolutions condemnatory of the ministerial policy, or by address to the Crown, or by making the position of the ministry in other ways untenable: but Parliament has no direct means either of bringing about a war or of bringing a war to an end.

"Nor does a decided expression of opinion by the House of Commons always overbear the policy of a ministry. In 1782 a resolution of the House of Commons, followed by an address to the Crown, caused Lord North to take steps to end the war with the American Colonies; but in 1857 a resolution of the House, condemnatory of the war with China, caused Lord Palmerston to appeal to the country, with the result that a majority of his supporters were returned at a general election.

"The prerogative of the Crown in making peace is so much involved in questions as to the prerogative in making treaties that the two must be dealt with together. Parliament has only indirect means of bringing a war to a close, but it is hard to conceive of a peace concluded simply by a cessation of hostilities and mutual assurances of amity. Some engagements must be entered into or territory ceded, and a question arises in this form: No one but the Crown can bind the community by treaty, but can the Crown invariably do so without the co-operation of Parliament?

"This much appears to be certain; that where a treaty involves either a charge on the people or a change in the law of the land it may be made, but cannot be carried into effect, without the sanction of Parliament. Such treaties are therefore made subject to the approval of Parliament and are submitted for its approval before ratification, or ratified under condition.

"Such are treaties of commerce which might require a change in the character or the amount of duties charged on exported or imported goods: or extradition treaties which confer on the executive a power to seize, take up and hand over to a foreign state, persons who have committed crime there and taken refuge here.

"The question whether the Crown can, by treaty merely, extend to foreigners immunities from the law of the land, which would affect the private rights of citizens, was raised in the case of the *Parlement Belge.*

"It was alleged in that case that the Queen had by convention with the King of the Belgians, conferred upon a ship, assumed by the Court to be a private ship engaged in trade, the immunities of a public ship, or ship of war, so as to disentitle a British subject from proceeding against her for injuries sustained in a collision. Sir Robert Phillimore held that the treaty-making prerogative did not extend this length and gave judgment against the ship. His decision was reversed by the

§ 121. Colonies have no treaty-making power except through the Crown.—The principle, however, that the

Court of Appeal, but on a different ground, namely, that the *Parlement Belge was* a public ship, although not a ship of war, being used for a national purpose, the transmission of mails. The Court carefully abstained from expressing any opinion on the point on which Sir Robert Phillimore mainly rested his judgement.

"The same question was raised, and evaded, in *Walker* vs. *Baird.* The working of a lobster factory on the coast of Newfoundland was stopped by an officer intrusted with the enforcement of an agreement made between the Queen and the Government of France. The owner of the factory brought an action, and it was held to be no defence to allege that the conduct of the officer was 'an act of state.' Whether or no it could be justified by the treaty-making power of the Crown was discussed but not settled, inasmuch as the statement of defense assumed that the mere allegation that the acts were done in pursuance of a treaty took the matter out of the cognizance of the Court. This was not the view of the Judicial Committee.

"It was admitted that the Crown 'could not sanction an invasion by its officers of the rights of private individuals whenever it was necessary in order to compel obedience to the terms of a treaty.'

"'Whether the power contended for does exist in the case of treaties of peace, and whether if so it exists equally in the case of treaties akin to a treaty of peace, or whether in both or either of these cases interference with private rights can be authorized otherwise than by the legislature, are grave questions upon which their Lordships do not find it necessary to express an opinion.'

"The extent of the royal prerogative as regards the cession of territory has been discussed with vehemence of late, and left unsettled. Various limitations have been alleged. It is said that the Queen may cede territories acquired by conquest, or Crown colonies, but not other territory, that she may not cede territory in respect of which Parliament has legislated, that her powers of cession at the end of a war are different from and larger than her powers in time of peace. But this much is clear, that there is no authority beyond *dicta* of lawyers, expressed in Parliamentary debate or otherwise, for any such limitation on the powers of the Crown as has been alleged.

"In 1876 a case came before the Judicial Committee of the Privy Council in which the High Court of Bombay had held, for the purposes of its judgment, that territory had been ceded and that the Crown had no power to make such cession in time of peace without consent of Parliament. The Judicial Committee reversed the judgment of the Indian Court, holding that what had taken place did not amount to a cession, but their Lordships expressly stated that they entertained grave doubts 'as to the soundness of the general abstract doctrine laid down.'

"In 1890 the Queen in concluding a treaty with the Emperor of Germany, which provided among other things for the cession of Heligoland to the Emperor, was advised by her Ministers to make the cession con-

treaty-making power is vested in the Crown, and does not
reside in any other department of Government, executive or

ditional on the approval of Parliament. This invitation to Parliament
to share in the exercise of the prerogative rights of the Crown, and
therewith to assume the responsibilities of the Executive, was much
criticised in debate. The state of the question was most fully and
clearly put by Mr. Gladstone:—

"'There is one thing which I think is still higher than the *dicta* of
legal authorities, in this important question, and it is our long, uniform and unbroken course of practice. It is one thing to stand upon
the opinion of an ingenious or even a learned man: it is another thing
to cite the authority of an entire State, signified in practical conclusions, after debate and discussion in every possible form, all bearing in
one direction, and stamped with one and the same character. It is
hardly possible, I believe, to conceive any kind of territory—colonies
acquired by conquest, colonies acquired by settlement, with representative institutions or without representative institutions—it is not possible to point out any class of territory where you cannot show cases of
cession by the Crown without the authority of Parliament.'

"The precedent is an unfortunate one. Either House of Parliament
can always signify its disapprobation of a treaty, and a ministry can always, if strong enough, procure a vote expressive of approval. But to
make the ratification of a treaty depend upon the goodwill of a popular
assembly seems to be an abnegation on the part of the Executive of a
responsibility which Ministers ought to be ready to assume on behalf of
the Crown.

"Sec. 4. *Foreign Jurisdiction.*

"The Queen has power 'by treaty, capitulation, grant, usage, sufferance, and other lawful means,' to exercise jurisdiction within divers
foreign countries.

"The history of foreign jurisdiction of this nature begins with the
Levant Company, which obtained a charter in 1581, renewed in 1606
and 1662, conferring power to appoint consuls who should administer
justice between merchants 'in all places in the dominion of the Grand
Seignior, and in other places in the Levant Seas.' By capitulations
made with the Ottoman Porte suits between subjects of the Crown
were, throughout the territories specified in the charter, to be decided
by the judges therein described, and not by the local Courts.

"Usage appears to have extended this jurisdiction from cases in which
both parties were British subjects, to cases in which the defendant only
was a British subject, and to cases of crimes committed by British subjects.

"When the Levant Company ceased to exist it became necessary to
provide for the exercise of this jurisdiction otherwise than by the Company's charter, and perhaps also some doubts had arisen as to the power
of the Crown to create such jurisdiction by mere exercise of the prerogative. In 1843 began the series of Foreign Jurisdiction Acts, which
are now consolidated in the Act of 1890 (53 & 54 Vict. c. 37). The pur-

14

legislative, central or colonial, continues to-day as a recognized rule in the government of Great Britain and its colonies.[1] Notwithstanding the apparent independence of the

port of these Acts has been to give to the Crown full power to provide by Order in Council for the exercise of such jurisdictions, wherever 'by treaty, capitulation, grant, usage, sufferance, and other lawful means,' they have been acquired or have come into existence.

"Foreign jurisdictions exercised in consular courts exist at the present time (1) in civilized independent states by virtue of express treaty, as in Turkey, Persia, China and Japan; (2) in protected states with a settled form of government, as in the protected African communities, where the relation of suzerain and dependent state involves such a jurisdiction; (3) in countries with no settled form of government, as in the African spheres of influence, or in the Pacific islands.

",Where such a jurisdiction takes its origin from treaty, its extent and the persons over whom it may be exercised must be the matter of express agreement. In the other cases, the exercise of jurisdiction over others than the Queen's subjects must be a question of international law, which I do not propose to discuss.

"It is enough here to call attention to these foreign, or consular jurisdictions, and to point out the three stages by which they come into being:—

"(1) The treaty or rule of international law which renders their existence possible;

"(2) The Statute which gives and defines the power by which the Queen creates them;

"(3) The Order in Council by which they are in fact created, and their extent prescribed as to the law to be administered and the persons who are to be subject to it." Anson's Law of the Constitution, Part II, The Crown, 2d Edition, London, 1896, pp. 296 to 302.

§ 121.

[1] "Sec. 4. As a colony, a possession, or a dependency constitutes only a part of the State, it cannot in itself be regarded, in international law, as a distinct political organization. Hence, any public or private corporation, created by, and deriving its authority from, a State cannot of itself constitute a separate and independent sovereignty. Thus, the East India Company, although exercising the sovereign powers of peace and war, with respect to the native princes and people, acted in subordination to the supreme power of the British Empire, and was represented by the British Government in all its relations with foreign sovereigns and States.

"Sec. 5. The mere fact of dependence, however, does not prevent a State from being regarded in international law as a separate and distinct sovereignty, capable of enjoying the rights and incurring the obligations incident to that condition. Much more importance is attached to the nature and character of its connection with other States, and the degree and extent of its dependence. Thus, many States, regarded as sovereign, do not exercise the right of self-government entirely in-

self-governing colonies of Great Britain, not one of them possesses any treaty-making power. The only difference between that power as it has existed for centuries, and was exercised in regard to the American Colonies prior to the Revolution, and as it is exercised to-day, is that the Crown recognizes the necessity of acceding to the wishes and expressed desires of the colonies, and, therefore, does not attempt to force treaties upon them without the prior assurance that the stipulations entered into with foreign governments will be acceptable to the colonies affected thereby. The adoption of this policy however, cannot be construed as an admission on the part of the Crown that the treaty-making power has been in any way diminished, or that the Crown does not possess the power and the right to exercise it in every possible manner and to its full extent. At the present time all treaties between Great Britain and other powers which affect any of the colonies, even though they may relate exclusively to a single colony, are negotiated through the Foreign Office in London, by the British Ambassador to the other contracting government, or by commissioners specially appointed for the purpose by the Crown, and whose instructions emanate from the Foreign Office; while as a matter of form, practice and policy, due regard is generally, as it always should be, paid to the wishes of the colonies, there is no instance of a treaty being independently negotiated or concluded by any one of them with any sovereign power.[2]

§ 122. **Status of Dominion of Canada as to treaty-making power.**—There is no treaty-making power in the executives, or in the Parliaments, of the Dominion of Canada or of any of the Provinces composing that Dominion; no matter how exclusively the subject of any treaty stipulation may affect Canada and Canadian interests, the treaty in order to have any legal effect whatever must be concluded between the

dependent of other States, but have their sovereignty limited and qualified in various degrees, either by the character of their internal constitution, by stipulations of unequal treaties of alliance, or by treaties of protection or of guarantee made by a third Power." Halleck's International Law, Baker's 3d English edition, London, 1893, vol. 1, pp. 67–68.

[2] See instances referred to in footnotes to § 122, *post.*

other contracting sovereign power and His Britannic Majesty. This is because the Dominion of Canada is not a fully sovereign State. A treaty negotiated by the Secretary of State of the United States and the British Ambassador relating to Canadian matters might be ratified by the Senate and by the Foreign Office in London; if it were unacceptable to the Canadian Parliament the necessary legislation, or appropriations, to carry it into effect might not be passed; in that manner the final effect of an unsatisfactory treaty might be defeated and, therefore, as a matter of practice and policy, the treaty-making power is not now, as a general rule, exercised by the British Crown except through the agency of Commissioners representing the colonies whose interests are to be affected; the final exchange of ratifications of negotiated treaties is also generally withheld until the Parliaments of the colonies affected have expressed their approval.[1] Notwithstanding this practice, however, the principle remains unaffected, that the treaty is concluded by the highest sovereign power, and not through the colonial government. The negotiating commissioners always hold their powers from the Crown, and not from any colonial authority; in fact if negotiations in regard to a treaty affecting only colonial interests were commenced by any nation with persons claiming to represent any colony of Great Britain, the first step would be the examination of the powers of the plenipotentiaries, and only such commissions, or as they are called in diplomatic terms, full powers, as emanated from the Foreign Office at London with the Royal approval, and so certified by the Secretary of Foreign Affairs of the Imperial Government, would be accepted as authority for the continuance of the negotiations.[2]

§ 122.

[1] After the treaties of Washington of 1871, legislation of the Dominion of Canada and of the Provinces was necessary to carry out the provisions therein as to fisheries and the reciprocal custom provisions as to free entry of fish products. See U. S. Foreign Relations under Great Britain for years 1871, 1872 and

1873. After the Bayard-Chamberlain treaty of 1888 had been concluded in Washington, it was discussed in the Dominion Parliament at great length before the consent of the Dominion was transmitted to the Imperial Government.

[2] There have been several instances in which treaties affecting Canadian interests have been concluded be-

§ 123. **Concrete example of above principles.**—To take a concrete example : Suppose that the State of New York and the Province of Ontario desired to enter into some reciprocal

tween the United States and Great Britain. I. The Marcy-Elgin reciprocity treaty of 1854; II. The Treaty of Washington of 1871, which, however, related to matters other than Canadian, notably the Alabama claims; III. The Bayard-Chamberlain fisheries treaty of 1888 which was not ratified by the Senate of the United States and therefore never became effectual; IV. There was also a joint High Commission appointed in 1898 which has not yet concluded any treaty but which was appointed to consider Canadian matters exclusively.

In all cases the plenipotentiaries were appointed by the Crown and held their powers from the secretary of foreign affairs. In every case the British Commissioners included Canadians, but the authority to negotiate was derived from the Imperial and not the Dominion Government.

The "full powers" of the Commissioners are headed: "VICTORIA, REG.-VICTORIA, by the Grace of God, Queen of the United Kingdom of Great Britain and Ireland, Defender of the Faith, &c., &c., &c., To All and Singular to whom these Presents shall come, Greeting:" whether they relate to general or Imperial matters or the affairs of Colonies. See Foreign Relations of U. S. of 1873, p. 495, for a form of "full power."

ANGLO–AMERICAN JOINT HIGH COMMISSION OF 1898.

This Commission is still in existence, although it has held no meeting since February, 1899. It was appointed pursuant to an informal protocol made May 30, 1898. Subsequently Commissioners were appointed to whom "full powers" were issued by their respective Governments. The United States Commissioners were Charles W. Fairbanks, United States Senator from Indiana (chairman of the American Commissions); George Gray, United States Senator from Delaware who resigned to act as Commissioner on the Spanish Treaty of Peace and whose place was filled by Charles J. Faulkner, then United States Senator from West Virginia; Nelson Dingley, Maine, chairman of the Ways and Means Committee of the House of Representatives, who died in December, 1898, and whose place was filled by his successor as such chairman, Sereno F. Payne, New York; John W. Foster, Indiana, former Secretary of State and Special Commissioner to Great Britain and Russia in regard to seal fisheries; John A. Kasson, Iowa, Special Commissioner Plenipotentiary on reciprocity agreements with foreign countries and T. Jefferson Coolidge, of Massachusetts. The British Commissioners were The Right Honorable Lord Herschell, G. C. B., formerly Lord Chancellor of Great Britain (chairman of the British Commission), The Right Honorable Sir Wilfred Laurier, G. C. M. G., The Honorable Sir Richard J. Cartwright, G. C. M. G., The Honorable Sir Louis H. Davies, K. C. M. G., Mr. John Charlton, M. P., The Honorable Sir James S. Winter, K. C. M. G., all of whom held high office in Canada except Lord Herschell and

213

arrangement, as the to preservation of fish in Lake Ontario.
Neither the State nor the Province could conclude any treaty
or arrangement; nor could the State of New York and the
Dominion of Canada do so; nor yet the Province of Ontario
and the United States. The only possible method of obtaining the desired result would be for the representatives of His
Majesty and the authorized Commissioners of the United
States, either through the Foreign Office and the State Department, or by special appointees *ad hoc* to meet and negotiate a treaty between the United States and His Britan-

Sir James S. Winter, the latter representing Newfoundland on the
Commission.

Chandler P. Anderson, New York,
was Secretary of the American Commission, Henri Burassa, Quebec,
member of Dominion Parliament,
and W. Chauncey Cartwright of the
British Foreign Office were Secretaries for the British Commission.
The author of this volume was attached to the Commission as legal
expert (see § 445, chap. XIV, *post*).
The Commission met in Quebec during August and September, 1898,
and in Washington during October,
1898–February, 1899; it adjourned
indefinitely in February, 1899, the
commissioners not being able to
agree upon any practical method
of adjusting the Alaska boundary,
and it not being deemed advisable
to continue negotiations in regard
to other matters until some satisfactory solution of the boundary
question was arrived at. The proceedings of this Commission have
not yet been published.

Amongst the subjects considered by the Commission were provisions in respect to the following
matters: fur seals in Bering Sea
and waters of the North Pacific
Ocean; fisheries off the Atlantic
and Pacific coasts and in the inland
waters of their common frontier;

the delimitation and establishment
of the Alaska-Canadian boundary;
the transit of merchandise in transportation to or from either country
across intermediate territory of the
other; the transit of merchandise
from one country to be delivered at
points in the other beyond the frontier; the alien-labor laws as applicable to the subjects or citizens of the
United States and of Canada; mining rights of the citizens or subjects of each country within the
territory of the other; such read-
justment and concessions as may be
deemed mutually advantageous, of
customs duties applicable in each
country to the products of the soil
or industry of the other, upon the
basis of reciprocal equivalents; a
revision of the agreement of 1817
respecting naval vessels on the
Lakes; the more complete definition and marking of any part of the
frontier line, by land or water,
where the same is now so insufficiently defined or marked as to be
liable to dispute; the conveyance
for trial or punishment of persons
in the lawful custody of the officers
of one country through the territory of the other; also any other
unsettled difference referred to it
by mutual consent of both governments.

nic Majesty. This treaty would have to be ratified by the Senate, and the ratifications thereof exchanged either in Washington or in London, or elsewhere, by express permission of the Foreign Office and the State Department, before it would become operative. After these formalities had been completed, however, it would be binding, as an international compact, upon the United States, and every State of the Union, and also upon Great Britain, the Dominion of Canada and every Province thereof; and, under the treaty-making power, and its effect upon subordinate governments, the Parliament of Great Britain or of the Dominion of Canada and the Congress of the United States could carry out the provisions of the treaty by appropriate legislation, regardless of whether such provisions were acceptable either to the State of New York or the Province of Ontario.

§ 124. **Actual practice to appoint Commissioners from locality affected.**—The fact that it has been the actual practice in such cases to appoint Commissioners from the territory affected, so that a treaty can be framed which will meet the requirements of the case and will be satisfactory to local interests, has given rise on some occasions to the idea that the Commissioners were the appointees of the local governments and not of the Central Government; such, however, has never been, and never can be the case so long as the written Constitution of the United States, the unwritten Constitution of the English people, and the principles of international law remain unchanged. It will be seen by examining the precedents referred to in the notes to this and the preceding sections that the relations between the United States and the Dominion of Canada, as well as of the several States forming the United States, and the several Provinces forming the Dominion, have always been negotiated, adjusted and determined by treaties concluded and ratified in this manner.[1]

§ 125. **Territorial origin of States of the Union.**—The States of the Union, other than the thirteen original States, and Texas, have all been carved out of territory which originally belonged either to some of the States individually, as was the case with Vermont, Maine, and Kentucky; from the

§ 124.

[1] See footnote to § 122, p. 213, *ante.*

Northwest and other territory ceded by some of the States
to the Central Government, as was the case with Michigan,
Indiana and other States in the Northwest, and with Tennessee, Mississippi and other States in the South ; from territory acquired by the United States by purchase from governments holding it as a colonial possession, as was the case
with Louisiana, Missouri and Florida and other States carved
out of the Louisiana and Florida purchases ; from territory
which was a part of the ceding country itself, as was the
case with the States carved from the Mexican cession, such
as California and Nevada ; it might be said that Oregon and
Washington stand on a different basis, but they never possessed any other government than that accorded to them by
the United States which added them to its territory by virtue of the discovery, and occupation, of the Columbia River
watershed.   As the thirteen original States never had any
local government which possessed, or exercised, treaty-making power,[1] and as all of the other States were carved out of
territory which never had any local self-government whatever, it is a self-evident proposition that the treaty-making
power never existed in, or was exercised by the individual
States of the Union, or for that matter by any power other
than in Central or National government.   This statement
applies to every State and Territory of the Union, with the
exception of Texas and Hawaii both of which actually were
sovereign States prior to their being merged into the Union,
and each of which, as a sovereign State, had exercised the
treaty-making power prior to its territory becoming a part
of the United States.[2]

§ 125.
[1] See § 179, post.

[2] " That a union of the colonies
into one general government, for
any purpose, could not take place
without the sanction of Parliament
was always assumed in both countries.   The sole instance in which
a plan of union was publicly proposed and acted upon, before the
Revolution, was in 1753–4, when
the Board of Trade sent instructions to the Governor of New York
to make a treaty with the Six Nations of Indians ; and the other
colonies were also instructed to
send commissioners to be present
at the meeting, so that all the provinces might be comprised in one
general treaty, to be made in the
King's name.   It was also recommended by the home government,
that the commissioners at this
meeting should form a plan of
union among the colonies for their
mutual protection and defence

§ 126. No State or Territory ever possessed treaty-making power except Texas and Hawaii.—None of the States or Territories composing the United States, therefore, have ever actually possessed, or exercised, any treating-making power with the exception of Texas and Hawaii.[1] Prior to the Declaration of Independence the thirteen original States were still Colonies of Great Britain and as such did not possess any treaty-making power or even the right to negotiate with any foreign power, or with each other.

against the French. Twenty-five commissioners assembled at Albany in May, 1754, from New Hampshire, Massachusetts, Rhode Island, Connecticut, New York, Pennsylvania, and Maryland. In this body a plan of union was digested and adopted, which was chiefly the work of Dr. Franklin. It was agreed that an act of Parliament was necessary to authorize it to be carried into effect. It was rejected by all the colonial assemblies before which it was brought, and in England it was not thought proper by the Board of Trade to recommend it to the King. In America it was considered to have too much of *prerogative* in it, and in England to be too *democratic*. It was a comprehensive scheme of government, to consist of a governor-general, or president-general, who was to be appointed and supported by the crown, and a grand council, which was to consist of one member chosen by each of the smaller colonies, and two or more by each of the larger. Its duties and powers related chiefly to defence against external attacks. It was to have a general treasury, to be supplied by an excise on certain articles of consumption. See the history and details of the scheme, in Sparks's Life and Works of Franklin, I. 176, III. 22–55; Hutchinson's History of Mas-

sachusetts, III. 23; Trumbull's History of Connecticut, II. 355; Pitkin's History of the United States, I. 140–146. In 1788, Franklin said of it: 'The different and contradictory reasons of dislike to my plan make me suspect that it was really the true medium; and I am still of opinion it would have been happy for both sides, if it had been adopted. The colonies so united would have been sufficiently strong to have defended themselves; there would have been no need of troops from England; of course the subsequent pretext for taxing America, and the bloody contest it occasioned, would have been avoided. But such mistakes are not new; history is full of the errors of states and princes.' (Life of Franklin, by Sparks, I. 178.) We may not join in his regrets now.'' Constitutional History of the United States, by George Ticknor Curtis, vol. 1, p. 4, *note*. For an abstract of the Albany Plan of Union, see McDonald's Select Charters, p. 253, *et seq.*

§ 126.

[1] Both of these powers had entered into treaties with the United States and with other powers. For treaties with Hawaii see U. S. Treaty Volumes, editions 1889 and 1899, under appropriate headings; for treaties with Texas see 8 U. S. Stat. at L., pp. 510–511.

The ideas of united action and of independence were so interwoven that no individual treaty-making power was ever exercised by any of the States prior to, or after, the Declaration of Independence. Under the Articles of Confederation the States forbade the exercise of the treaty-making power by themselves and vested it exclusively in the Congress,[2] where it remained until it was turned over to the Federal Government under the Constitution. During the War of the Revolution the treaty-making power was exercised by the Congress, not only as a power delegated by the Articles of Confederation, but also as a high act of sovereignty, under the revolutionary government. In fact the power was construed as extending to the control, so far as foreign relations were concerned, of matters otherwise exclusively within State jurisdiction, as was evidenced by some of the provisions of the French treaty of 1778.[3]

§ 127. **That of Texas and Hawaii ceased on their becoming part of the United States.**—In both of these instances the treaty-making power, which existed in its full strength and power prior to the respective annexations to the United States, terminated the moment that the annexations were completed.

[2] Article VI of the Confederation was as follows:

"No State without the consent of the United States in Congress assembled, shall send any embassy to, or receive any embassy from, or enter into any conference, agreement, alliance or treaty with any king, prince or state; nor shall any person holding any office of profit or trust under the United States, or any of them, accept any present, emolument, office or title of any kind whatever from any king, prince or foreign state; nor shall the United States in Congress assembled, or any of them, grant any title of nobility.

No two or more States shall enter into any treaty, confederation or alliance whatever between them, without the consent of the United States in Congress assembled, specifying accurately the purposes for which the same is to be entered into, and how long it shall continue. . . ."

§ Article IX of the Confederation is as follows:

"The United States in Congress assembled, shall have the sole and exclusive right and power . . . of sending and receiving ambassadors;—entering into treaties and alliances, provided that no treaty of commerce shall be made whereby the legislative power of the respective States shall be restrained from imposing such imposts and duties on foreigners, as their own people are subjected to, or from prohibiting the exportation or importation of any species of goods or commodities whatsoever—. . . ."

[3] See § 151, pp. 261, *et seq. post.*

From the date of the admission of Texas as a State of the Union and of the annexation of Hawaii as a territory, all treaty-making power absolutely ceased, except as it has since been exercised through the Executive Department of the Federal Government subject to the ratification of the Senate as required by the Constitution. The United States was bound in good faith to recognize the obligations in treaties existing at the times of the annexations and to make proper provision for their fulfilment. All adjustments, however, have necessarily been made through the Central Government, and not through local authorities, and all commercial regulations have necessarily been put under the control of the National Government.[1]

§ 127.

[1] Texas was admitted by Joint Resolution No. 8 of Congress approved March 1, 1845, 5 U. S. Stat. at Large, p. 797. This resolution expressly provided that all questions of boundary that might arise with other governments should be subject to adjustment by the government of the United States.

The Hawaiian Islands were annexed by Joint Resolution No. 55, approved July 7, 1898, 30 U. S. Stat. at Large, p. 797, and which provided that "The existing treaties of the Hawaiian Islands with foreign nations shall forthwith cease and determine, being replaced by such treaties as may exist, or as may be hereafter concluded, between the United States and such foreign nations. The municipal legislation of the Hawaiian Islands, not enacted for the fulfillment of the treaties so extinguished, and not inconsistent with this joint resolution nor contrary to the Constitution of the United States nor to any existing treaty of the United States, shall remain in force until the Congress of the United States shall otherwise determine.

"Until legislation shall be enacted extending the United States customs laws and regulations to the Hawaiian Islands the existing customs relations of the Hawaiian Islands with the United States and other countries shall remain unchanged.

"The public debt of the Republic of Hawaii, lawfully existing at the date of the passage of this joint resolution, including the amounts due to depositors in the Hawaiian Postal Savings Bank, is hereby assumed by the Government of the United States; but the liability of the United States in this regard shall in no case exceed four million dollars. So long, however, as the existing government and the present commercial relations of the Hawaiian Islands are continued as hereinbefore provided, said government shall continue to pay the interest on said debt.

"There shall be no further immigration of Chinese into the Hawaiian Islands, except upon such conditions as are now or may hereafter be allowed by the laws of the United States; and no Chinese, by reason of anything herein con-

§ 128. Treaty-making power of Germany.—The Empire of Germany is composed of a number of principalities which possessed, or claimed to possess, full sovereignty prior to the formation of the Confederation and of the Empire. Under the old North German Confederation they were to some extent permitted to exercise the treaty-making power and other sovereign States, until a recent period, were accustomed to enter into direct relations with these constituent States. All foreign relations are carried on now, however, as they have been since 1871, exclusively through the proper officers of the Empire, who act in this respect as personal representatives of the Emperor of Germany. All the obligations existing under treaties which had been made prior to the formation of the Empire in 1871 were assumed by it, so far as they relate to the territory of the constituent States, which originally negotiated them. Since 1871 no new treaties have been made by any of the constituent governments, and the treaty-making power of the entire Empire, and all of the constituent States, is exercised exclusively by the Emperor and his representatives.[1] The views of Professor Burgess as to the nature of the German constitution and the prerogatives of the Emperor are quoted in the note to this section.[2]

---

tained, shall be allowed to enter the United States from the Hawaiian Islands." See also as to effect of annexation upon revenue and other laws, the following cases, the first two affecting Texas and the third Hawaii.

Oakley vs. *Bennett*, U. S. Sup. Ct. 1850, 11 Howard 33, McLEAN, J.; *Calkin* vs. *Cocke*, U. S. Sup. Ct. 1852, 14 Howard 227, NELSON, J.; *Peacock, &c.,* vs. *Hawaii; Lewis* vs. *Same,* Supreme Ct. Hawaii, 1899, 12 Hawaii 27, FREAR J.

§ 128.

[1] For the Constitution of Germany and provisions as to treaty-making power, see footnote under § 130, p. 224, *post.*

[2] In Chapter III, pages 109, *et seq.*, Professor Burgess in his Political Science and Constitutional Law, gives a history of the formation of the Constitution of the present German Empire. On pages 119–120, vol. 1, he says:

"The attempt of France to prevent the complete union of all the German states into one national state, precipitated that union. At the moment of the triumph of the German arms over those of France, the King of Bavaria took the initiative. (The diary of the Emperor Frederic seems to show that he did so under considerable pressure from the Prussians.) The President of the North German Union, the King of Prussia, was already empowered, by the second paragraph of the seventy-ninth article of the North German constitution, to lay propo-

§ 129. **Treaty-making power of South American Countries.**—The same rule applies to relations established with

sitions before the legislature of the North German Union for the entrance of the South German states or any of them into the Union; which entrance would be accomplished, so far as the North German Union was concerned, by a legislative act. During the course of the month of November, 1870, the President of the North German Union entered into treaties with the Grand Dukes of Hesse and Baden and with the Kings of Wurtemberg and Bavaria, which contained the articles of union of these states with the North German Union and the pledge to establish the German Empire on the 1st of January, 1871. These treaties were submitted by these respective Princes to the legislatures of their respective states and were ratified in the manner prescribed by the constitutions of these respective states for making constitutional changes. The constitution of the North German Union already specially provided for this case, in Art. 79, authorizing the Federal Council and Diet to ratify such agreements by way of legislation. The constitution of the German Union or the German Empire was thus, at first, contained in several instruments. This was clumsy and confused. The union of the several instruments into one was manifestly necessary. After the representatives from the new states had appeared in both the Federal Council (*Bundesrath*) and Diet (*Reichstag*), the chancellor proposed a revision of the constitution as to form. This was carried by a great majority in both bodies. No new provisions were introduced into the organic law, and no existing provisions were modified, (except a clause providing for the constitution of a committee in the Bundesrath for foreign affairs.) The revision was, we may say, wholly formal. It bears the date April 16, 1871, while the birth moment of the Empire must be placed at January 1, preceding."

And on page 124, vol. 1, he expresses his views as to the unity of the German Empire as follows:

"My view is, therefore, that the German people resident within the twenty-two purely German states had, by 1866, reached a point in their national development where the ethnical unity was bound to pass over into political unity; that the German state had become existent subjectively, as idea in the consciousness of the people, and that the impulse to objectify the idea in institutions and laws was the force which employed the customary forms of legality in the attainment of the result; but the original power was in that force, not in those forms. It was fortunate for the continued existence of these that they proved elastic enough to permit the entrance of that force. It was not compelled, thus, to cast them aside and create its own more natural forms. The task of the commentator, however, is made much more difficult on account of this fact. He, and those who read him, are obliged to preserve a constant tension of mind in distinguishing these forms when filled with the new power, from the same as containing only the old power. Both he and they almost inadvertently glide into the

the Confederated Governments of South America.   Republics composed of constituent states, and similar in many respects to the United States of North America exist in South America.   The treaty-making power is in every instance vested exclusively in the central government.   The Argentine Republic is a confederation composed of several States, all of which exercise local sovereignty in the same manner as the several States of this Union exercise it.   The relations of all other nations, however, are with the central government which possesses exclusively the treaty-making power.   Treaties made, however, are binding upon the constituent States exactly as treaties made by the Executive of the

juristic processes, and, delighted with a show of logical exactness, forget that the juristic theory will not contain the demonstrations of war and violence and the evolutions of power with which the birth moment of the new state was attended." . . .

"The Emperor is vested, by Article 11 of the Imperial constitution, with the power to represent the Empire internationally, and for this purpose to send and receive ambassadors, to make agreements, treaties and alliances with foreign powers, and to declare war and make peace.   But if the treaties touch any subject already regulated by an Imperial law, constitutional or statutory, then the consent of the Federal Council is necessary to their conclusion and of the Diet also to their validity; and to every declaration of offensive war the consent of the Federal council is necessary.   These are most important and thorough going limitations upon the treaty-making and the war powers of the Emperor. They provide, in the first place, against any conflict which might arise between the treaties and the constitution and laws, by requiring the consent of the amending power

to such treaties as may touch upon a provision of the constitution, and of the legislative power to such as may touch upon a provision of the statute law.   A treaty cannot change a law in the Imperial system, without the consent of the law-making power, but a law may change a treaty without the consent of the Emperor.   There is, thus, no chance for arbitrary action on the part of the Emperor in the exercise of this power. . . . The independent prerogative of the Emperor, as international representative of the Empire, consists, thus, only of the powers to appoint and to receive ambassadors, other public ministers and consuls, to negotiate all treaties, to conclude treaties of peace and such other treaties as do not conflict with the constitution and the laws, and to wage defensive war. The president of a republic should not be intrusted with powers less than these."   Burgess' Political Science and Constitutional Law, Vol. 2, pp. 276, 277.   It will be seen that the limitations on the German Emperor are through the medium of the Federal government and not through the medium of any of the States.

United States, and ratified by the Senate in accordance with
the Constitution, become the supreme law of the land—and
binding upon the States of this Union, and the inhabitants
thereof.

§ 130. **Other instances of treaty-making power.**—It is
hardly worth while to collate as a part of the text all of the
instances in which treaty-making power is vested in the
central government or the highest recognized sovereign of
the different countries of the world.

In the notes, appended to this and the preceding sections,
a number of instances are noted in which the treaty-making
power has been lodged, as it is in the United States and in
Great Britain, in the Central Government, or in the Crown.[1]

§ 130.

[1] NOTE ON THE TREATY-MAKING POWER AS EXERCISED BY
THE SOVEREIGN POWER OF NATIONS OTHER THAN THE
UNITED STATES.

The government which does not to some extent exercise jurisdiction
over constituent and confederated powers is the exception rather than
the rule at the present time—Germany, Belgium, most of the South and
Central American Republics, are all confederations, and even China is
to some extent a conglomeration of provinces, which claim to have a
certain degree of local sovereignty. All of these powers are, however,
National as to treaty-making and in their relations with other nations
internal subdivisions are ignored.

The constitutions of several foreign powers and states were collected
for reference and use of the New York State Constitutional Convention
of 1894 under the title of " FOREIGN CONSTITUTIONS " and from that
convenient handbook the author has extracted the following provisions
relating to the treaty-making power as contained in the existing constitutions of Belgium, Germany, Japan, Mexico, Honduras, Venezuela,
and the Argentine Confederation. The treaty-making power as it is exercised by the Crown of Great Britain is the subject of another note.
(See pp. 207, *et seq, ante.*)

BELGIUM.

By the Constitution of Belgium, the King is required to take an
oath to observe the Constitution and laws of the Belgian people, and to
maintain their national independence and the integrity of their country;
the legislative power is vested in the House of Representatives and the
Senate, but the treaty-making power is lodged in the King by Art. 68
as follows:

" Art. 68. The King shall command the land and naval forces, declare
war, make treaties of peace, of alliance and of commerce. He shall
give information in respect to the foregoing matters to the two Houses

The provisions relating to treaties in the Constitution

as soon as the interest and safety of the State permit it, joining there-with the customary communications.

"Treaties of commerce and those which might seriously burden the State, or individually bind the Belgians, shall go into effect only after having received the assent of the houses.

"No cession, no exchange, no addition of territory can take place except by law. In no case shall the secret articles of a treaty be destructive of the published articles."

Belgium is a federal government, the kingdom being divided into numerous provinces, all of which have the right of local government. Compilation of Foreign Constitutions, compiled for the New York State Constitutional Convention, 1894, pp. 33–54; see p. 45.

GERMANY.

The provisions of the Constitution of the German Empire relating to treaty-making are as follows:

"Art. IV (p. 267). The following matters shall be under the supervision and legislative control of the Empire.

"1. Regulations relating to migration within the Empire; matters of domicile and settlement; the right of citizenship; the issuing and examination of passports; surveillance of foreigners; trade and industry, including insurance, so far as these matters are not already provided for by Article 3 of this Constitution (in Bavaria, however, exclusive of matters relating to domicile and settlement), and finally matters relating to colonization and emigration to foreign countries. . . .

"Art. 7 (p. 267). The organization of a general system of protection for German trade in foreign countries; of German navigation, and of the German flag on the high seas; likewise the organization of a general consular representation to be maintained by the Empire. . . .

"Art. 11 (p. 270). To the King of Prussia shall belong the Presidency of the Confederation, and he shall have the title of German Emperor. The Emperor shall represent the Empire among nations, declare war and conclude peace in the name of the same, enter into alliances and other conventions with foreign countries, accredit ambassadors and receive them.

"For a declaration of war in the name of the Empire, the consent of the Federal Council shall be required, except in case of an attack upon the territory of the Confederation or its coasts.

"So far as treaties with foreign countries refer to matters which, according to Article 4, are to be regulated by imperial legislation, the consent of the Federal Council shall be required for their conclusion, and the approval of the Diet shall be necessary to render them valid. . . .

"Art. 53 (p. 279). The navy of the Empire is a united one, under the supreme command of the Emperor. The Emperor is charged with its constitution and organization; he shall appoint the officers and officials of the navy, and in his name these and the seamen shall be sworn in.

adopted by the Southern States which attempted to se-

"The harbor of Kiel and the harbor of the Jade are imperial war harbors.

" The expenditure required for the establishment and maintenance of the navy and the institutions connected therewith, shall be defrayed from the treasury of the Empire.

"All seafaring men of the Empire, including machinists and hands employed in ship-building, are exempt from serving in the army, but are obliged to serve in the imperial navy.

" The distribution of requisitions to supply the ranks of the navy shall be made according to the actual seafaring population, and the number furnished in accordance herewith by each State shall be deducted from the number otherwise required for the army. . . .

" Art. 56 (p. 280). The Emperor shall have the supervision of all consular affairs of the German Empire, and he shall appoint consuls, after hearing the committee of the Federal Council on trade and commerce.

" No new State consulates are to be established within the jurisdiction of the German consuls. German consuls shall perform the functions of State consuls for the States of the union not represented in their district. All the State consulates now existing shall be abolished as soon as the organization of the German consulates shall be completed in such a manner, that the representation of the separate interests of all the federal states shall be recognized by the Federal Council as satisfactorily secured by the German consulates." Compilation of Foreign Constitutions, compiled for New York Constitutional Convention, 1894, pp. 259–286. See also § 128 and notes thereunder, pp. 220, et seq., ante.

JAPAN.

By Article 13 of the Constitution of the Empire of Japan, the Emperor declares war, makes peace and conducts treaties. Compilation of Foreign Constitutions, compiled for the New York Constitutional Convention, 1894. pp. 309–318; see p. 313.

MEXICO.

Mexico is a federation. The constitution of 1857 defines sovereignty in Title II. as follows:

" Art. 39 (p. 234). The national sovereignty resides essentially and originally in the people. All public power emanates from the people, and is instituted for their benefit. The people have at all times the inalienable right to alter or modify the form of their government.

Art. 40. The Mexican people voluntarily constitute themselves a democratic, federal, representative republic, composed of States free and sovereign in all that concerns their internal government, but united in a federation established according to the principles of this fundamental law.

" Art. 41. The people exercise their sovereignty by means of Federal officers in cases belonging to the Federation, and through those of the States in all that relates to the internal affairs of the States within the limits respectively established by this Federal Constitution, and by the

15

cede from the Union in 1861 were similar to those in the

special Constitutions of the States, which latter shall in no case contravene the stipulations of the Federal Compact."

Subdivision *a* of Article 72 B (p. 342) defining the exclusive powers of the Senate includes the right "to approve the treaties and diplomatic Conventions which the Executive may make with foreign powers."

Amongst the powers of the President, (Art. 85, sections X. and XI. p. 349) are: :

"X. To direct diplomatic negotiations and to make treaties with foreign powers, submitting them for the ratification of the Federal Congress.

"XI. To receive ministers and other envoys from foreign powers."

The powers of the judiciary which are determined by Art. 97, sections VI. and VII. (p. 351) include:

"VI. Civil or criminal cases that may arise under treaties with foreign powers.

"VII. Cases concerning diplomatic agents and consuls." Compilation of Foreign Constitutions compiled for New York Constitutional Convention, 1894, pp. 319–356.

HONDURAS.

In the Constitution of the Republic of Honduras adopted November, 1880, Article 73, a part of the President's duties are defined as follows:

"Art. 73 (p. 304). (1) He concludes and signs treaties of peace, of commerce, of navigation, of alliance, of neutrality, and other negotiations necessary for the maintenance and cultivation of good international relations.

"(2) He nominates the diplomatic and consular agents of the Republic, receives the Ministers, and admits the Consuls of foreign nations.

But Congress has the power, as provided in Article 45, (p. 299,) (3) to approve or reject treaties made with foreign powers. Compilation of Foreign Constitutions, compiled for the New York Constitutional Convention, 1894, pp. 287–306.

VENEZUELA.

Venezuela is a federation made up of a number of states each one of which is declared to be free and independent by Article XII. of the Constitution.

The prerogatives of the President are defined by Article 65, (p. 431) subdivision 3, "to receive and welcome public ministers" and subdivision 4, "to sign the official letters to the Sovereigns or Presidents of other countries. . ." Article 66, subdivision 5, (p. 431) "to direct negotiations and celebrate all kinds of treaties with other nations, submitting these to the National Legislature;" and there is a special provision in Article 116 (p. 438) that "the national executive will negotiate with the governments of America over treaties of alliance and confederation."

The Constitution of Venezuela is peculiar in that it requires by Article 109 (p. 438) that "in all international treaties of commerce and

Constitution of the United States and are also included in the notes.[2]

friendship this clause will be inserted, to wit: 'All the disagreements between the contracting parties must be decided without an appeal to war, by the decision of a power or friendly powers.'" Compilation of Foreign Constitutions, compiled for the New York Constitutional Convention, 1894, pp. 409–439.

ARGENTINE REPUBLIC.

The existing Constitution of the Argentine Republic was adopted September 25, 1860.

In its preamble it recites that the representatives in the constituent Congress for the purpose of framing a Constitution made the Constitution for the Argentine Nation; it also recites that the provinces form the Nation; the Federal Government guarantees to protect the Republican form of government and to repel foreign invasion in the provinces.

Many of the provisions of the Constitution of the United States are bodily incorporated into this Constitution.

While every province can have its own Constitution it must be framed upon the basis of a Republican representative system of government and be in harmony with the Federal Constitution.

The provisions in regard to treaties are as follows:

"Art. XXVII (p. 10). The Federal Government shall be bound to strengthen, by means of treaties, consistent with the principles of public law established by this Constitution, the commercial and peaceful relations of the Argentine Nation with foreign countries.

"Art. XXVIII (p. 11). No principle, guaranty, or right recognized in the preceding articles can be altered by the laws which may be enacted to carry it into practice. . . ."

"Art. XXXI (p. 11). The present Constitution, the national laws which in pursuance thereof may be enacted by Congress, and the treaties with foreign nations are the supreme law of the nation; and the provincial authorities shall be bound to abide by them, any provision in their own provincial constitution or laws to the contrary notwithstanding. This rule is not applicable to the Province of Buenos Ayres so far as the treaties ratified after the compact of the 11th of November, 1859, are concerned."

"Art. LXVII (p. 18). The National Congress shall have power. . . . (19), To approve or reject the treaties concluded with any foreign nations, and the concordats entered into with the Holy See, and to make rules for the exercise of patronage in church matters in the whole nation."

"Art. LXXXVI. The President of the nation shall have the following powers:

"1 (p. 22). As the chief magistrate of the nation he has in his charge the general administration of all the executive business of the country.

"2. He can issue such instructions and make such rules as may be

[2] For note 2, see p. 229.

§ 131. Treaty-making power as an attribute of sovereignty evidenced in cases of cession of territory.—The fact

necessary for the execution of the laws of the nation, taking care, however, not to change, by any provision, in the former, the spirit of the latter. . . .

"14 (p. 24). He concludes and signs the treaties of peace, commerce, navigation, alliance, limits, and neutrality, as well as the concordats, and all other arrangements or agreements required for the maintenance of friendly relations with the foreign powers. He also receives the ministers accredited by the latter and admits their consuls.

"Art. C (p. 26). The Supreme Court, as well as the federal inferior tribunals, shall have jurisdiction in all cases and causes, not mentioned in number 2 of article 67, of the present Constitution, involving points to be decided either by the same Constitution, the federal laws, or foreign treaties, and also in all cases and causes concerning ambassadors, public ministers and foreign consuls, admiralty cases, or cases falling under maritime jurisdiction, or cases and causes in which the nation has an interest as a party thereto, or cases between the Provinces with each other, or between a Province and the citizens of another, or between a province or its citizens against a foreign citizen or State. . . ."

"Art. CIV (p. 27). The Provinces retain all the powers not delegated by the present Constitution to the Federal Government, as well as all the powers expressly reserved by them, through special agreements, at the time of their admission into the Union.

"Art. CV. Each Province shall have its own local institutions and laws, and shall be governed by them. They elect their governors, legislators, and provincial functionaries of all classes, without intervention of the Federal Government.

"Art. CVI. Each Province shall enact its own Constitution, subject to the provisions of article V.

"Art. CVII. The Provinces shall have the power to conclude, with the knowledge of the federal Congress, such partial treaties as may be necessary for the purposes of administration of justice, or for regulating financial interests, or undertaking public works; and to promote, by means of protective laws and at their own expense, their own industries, immigration into their territories, the building of railroads and navigable canals, the settlement and colonization of the provincial lands, the introduction and establishment of new industries, the importation of foreign capital and the exploration of their rivers.

"Art. CVIII. The Provinces cannot exercise any power delegated to the nation. They cannot without authority from the Federal Congress, enter into any partial treaties of a political character, or pass laws relating to the domestic or foreign commerce or navigation, or establish provincial custom-houses, coin money, or create banks of emission. Neither can they enact any civil, commercial, criminal or mineral codes, subsequent to the promulgation of the national ones enacted by Congress, or pass laws especially applicable to themselves on the subject of citizenship, naturalization, bankruptcies and counterfeiting of money

that the treaty-making power is an attribute of sovereignty
is further evidenced by the fact that only sovereign powers

or State bonds, or establish tonnage duties, arm war vessels, or raise
armies, except in cases of foreign invasion or of such imminent danger
as to admit of no delay, and on condition that they give full and prompt
account of it to the Federal Government, or appoint or receive foreign
agents, or permit new religious orders to be admitted.

"Art. CIX. No Province can declare or wage war against another.
Their complaints against each other must be submitted for decision to
the Supreme Court of Justice. Actual hostilities on the part of one
Province against another shall be deemed to be acts of civil war, sedi-
tious and riotous, which the Federal Government has the duty to put
down and repress under the laws.

"Art. CX. The Governors of the Provinces shall be the natural agents
of the Federal Government for the enforcement of the Constitution and
the laws of the nation." Compilation of Foreign Constitutions, compiled for the New York State Constitutional Convention, 1894, pp. 1–34.

[2] THE CONFEDERATE STATES.

Prior to the attempted secession of the Southern States, questions had
been raised on many occasions both in Congress and in the courts as
to the extent of the treaty-making power vested in the Federal Government and as to what limitations existed thereon; the secessionists were
always, naturally, the most ardent advocates, for the extension of
States rights, and for the contraction of all power in the Central Government; notwithstanding this, however, when the seceding States attempted to organize a Confederate Government, they adopted a Constitution in which they expressly declared that they were sovereign and
independent States and afterwards substantially followed the Constitution of the United States. The entire Constitution will be found as an
Appendix in the 2d volume of Curtis' Constitutional History of the
United States, pp. 569, et seq. The clauses relating to treaty are as follows: Article II, section 2, in enumerating the President's powers says:
"He shall have power, by and with the advice of the Senate to make
treaties, provided two-thirds of the Senate present concur." Similar
limitations were placed upon the States in regard to the exercise of
foreign relations as appears by section 8, article 1, which is as follows:

"Article 1, § 10. 1. No State shall enter into any treaty, alliance, or
Confederation; grant letters of marque and reprisal; coin money; make
anything but gold and silver coin a tender in payment of debts; pass any
bill of attainder, or ex post facto law, or law impairing the obligation
of contracts; or grant any title of nobility.

"2. No State shall, without the consent of the Congress, lay any imposts or duties on imports or exports, except what may be absolutely
necessary for executing its inspection laws; and the net produce of all
duties and imposts, laid by any State on imports or exports, shall be
for the use of the treasury of the Confederate States, and all such laws
shall be subject to the revision and control of Congress.

can cede territory and transfer sovereignty thereover. Attempts on the part of the inhabitants of any territory belonging to a sovereign State, whether by the act of unorganized
masses or of any organized local government, to separate
themselves from the former sovereign, and to unite with any
other territory are always considered as acts of rebellion
on the part of the inhabitants of the territory itself, and as a
casus belli on the part of the Government accepting their adhesion, or by reason of such adhesion, asserting any sovereignty over the territory involved. The desire of the inhabitants of the seceding territory to separate themselves from
the mother country is, under international law, no palliation
of the act of any government which either actively assists
such separation, or tacitly consents to receive and extend its
sovereignty over the territory. The United States fully
recognized this principle of international law when it ab-

" 3. No State shall, without the consent of Congress, lay any duty of
tonnage, except on sea-going vessels, for the improvement of its rivers
and harbors navigated by the said vessels; but such duties shall not
conflict with any treaties of the Confederate States with foreign nations;
and any surplus revenue thus derived, shall, after making such improvement, be paid into the common treasury. Nor shall any State
keep troops or ships of war in time of peace, enter into any agreement
or compact with another State, or with a foreign power, or engage in
war, unless actually invaded, or in such imminent danger as will not
admit of delay. But when any river divides or flows through two or
more States, they may enter into compacts with each other to improve
the navigation thereof."

The judicial power was, by section 2, Article III, extended to all cases
arising under the Constitution, the laws of the Confederate States and
treaties made, or which should be made, under its authority.

Clause 3 of Article VI was as follows:

"This Constitution, and the laws of the Confederate States made in
pursuance thereof, and all treaties made or which shall be made under
the authority of the Confederate States, shall be the supreme law of
the land; and the Judges in every State shall be bound thereby, anything in the Constitution or laws of any State to the contrary notwithstanding." (This is an exact paraphrase of the corresponding clause
of Article VI of the Constitution of the United States.)

It appears from this that although the ardent advocates of State's rights
and of the strict construction of the Constitution have declared that the
treaty-making power as it is vested in the Executive of the United States
subject only to ratification by two-thirds of the Senate ought to be limited, and that the rights of "Sovereign States" should not be subordi-
nated to the treaty stipulations of the Federal Government, that when

stained from receiving Texas in any capacity until that State had established its independence of Mexico beyond all question;[1] that independence had been fully established as a fact

the most extreme exponents of that school endeavored to form a constitution for themselves, they not only placed no limitations upon the power, to be exercised by the President and Senate, but they also made treaties the supreme law of the land, and binding upon the Judges in every State, exactly as provided in the Constitution of the United States; in the limitations upon the States while permitting them to lay certain tonnage duties, they especially provided that they must not in any way conflict with the treaties made by the Central Government. If the maxim "Imitation is the sincerest flattery" is true, there can be no doubt that the framers of the Constitution of the so-called Confederate States of America paid the highest possible compliment, not only to the framers of the Constitution of the United States but also to those judges of the Supreme Court who had, on repeated occasions, sustained the treaty-making power of the United States as being the supreme law of the land and paramount to the laws of any State of the Union conflicting therewith.

§ 131.

[1] See special message of President Andrew Jackson, to Congress, December 21, 1836, in regard to the then contemplated recognition of Texas as an independent State, which he concludes as follows:

"The title of Texas to the territory she claims is identified with her independence. She asks us to acknowledge that title to the territory, with an avowed design to treat immediately of its transfer to the United States. It becomes us to beware of a too early movement, as it might subject us, however unjustly, to the imputation of seeking to establish the claim of our neighbors to a territory with a view to its subsequent acquisition by ourselves. Prudence, therefore, seems to dictate that we should still stand aloof and maintain our present attitude, if not until Mexico itself or one of the great foreign powers shall recognize the independence of the new Government, at least until the lapse of time or the course of events shall have proved beyond cavil or dispute the ability of the people of that country to maintain their separate sovereignty and to uphold the Government constituted by them. Neither of the contending parties can justly complain of this course. By pursuing it we are but carrying out the long established policy of our Government—a policy which has secured to us respect and influence abroad and inspired confidence at home. Having thus discharged my duty, by presenting with simplicity and directness the views which after much reflection I have been led to take of this important subject, I have only to add the expression of my confidence that if Congress shall differ with me upon it, then judgment will be the result of dispassionate, prudent, and wise deliberation, with the assurance that during the short time I shall continue connected with the Government I shall promptly and cordially unite with you in such measures as may be deemed best fitted to increase the prosperity and

for at least eight or nine years before the resolutions were adopted for the annexation and admission of Texas as a State. When Texas became one of the States of the Union, therefore, it was not the act of a revolting province accomplished with the aid and assistance of a government which should have remained neutral, for the United States had so remained during the Texan war for independence. The war between Texas and Mexico had resulted in Texas establishing its own government based upon the sovereign will of its people, and the government so established was, in 1845, exercising full and uncontrolled sovereignty over the Territory embraced in the boundaries of the Republic of Texas. The annexation of Texas was the result of proper action, properly taken, by two sovereign powers, each of which was fully able to contract with the other, as neither owed any allegiance to, or were under the control of, any other government or power which could place any limitations upon its action.

§ 132. **General application of principles.**—These same principles apply to all States exercising control over other powers by virtue of a confederation in which a central government has been created, or where the central and sovereign power has acquired control, or ownership of colonial possessions, or has assumed the protectorate over territory which has parted with any portion of its sovereignty, although in the last instance the exercise of the treaty-making power by either the protecting or protected state in regard to the relations of the latter with other foreign powers must necessarily be determined to a large extent, if not entirely, by the terms of the protectorate.

§ 133. **Power only to be exercised by governments possessing complete sovereignty.**—The proposition, therefore, which is stated at the outset of this chapter, that the treaty-making power is an attribute of sovereignty, and can only be exercised by a government possessing every element of nationality and sovereignty, is demonstrated by historical and legal precedents and by the opinions of the most eminent writers upon this subject. It can also be stated that

perpetuate the peace of our favored country.   ANDREW JACK- | SON." Richardson's Messages of the Presidents, vol. III, pp. 268–269.

the treaty-making power is a necessary accompaniment to the exercise of complete sovereignty and nationality; furthermore it cannot, without the greatest injury to both the central and constituent governments, ever be exercised by any power which does not possess every element of sovereignty.[1] Treaty stipulations can only be maintained and enforced by a governing power which possesses every such element of sovereignty.[2] This applies not only to the en-

§ 133.

[1] The effect of negotiating treaties with Indian tribes was so disastrous that the United States finally stopped it by act of Congress. This will be referred to at greater length in chapter XIV which is devoted exclusively to Indian treaties (see § 403 *et seq.* Vol. II). The compilation of Indian treaties (U. S. Government Printing Office, 1873), shows that all sorts of contracts, deeds and agreements, not only with dependent Indian nations, but also with subordinate tribes, and even with chiefs of Indians bands, were dignified with the title of treaties, and that an endless amount of confusion and litigation arose from this improper use of the treaty-making power. It must be noted, however, that the United States never permitted any *foreign* nation to make treaties with Indians; the general principle, as stated in this section, therefore, was not violated by the fact that contractual relations were entered into by the United States with dependent Indian nations, tribes and bands, and that the contracts evidencing the same were · called treaties.

[2] Several eminent publicists have expressed themselves on this subject; some of these opinions are referred to at an earlier point in this chapter (pp. 197, *et seq.*); two

additional quotations will be given to close the chapter.

LAWRENCE: "Every independent member of the family of nations possesses to the full the right of sending diplomatic ministers to other states; but it belongs to part-sovereign communities only in a limited form, the exact restrictions upon the diplomatic activity of each being determined by the instrument which defines its international position. Egypt, for instance, under the Sultan's Firmans of 1866 and 1867 may negotiate commercial and postal conventions with foreign powers, provided they do not contain political arrangements; and to this condition the Firman of 1879 added the further obligation of communicating them to the Porte before they are published. In the case of the looser sort of Confederations the treaty-making and negotiating power of the states which comprise them is limited by the federal act. Thus each member of the German Confederation which existed from 1815 to 1866 was bound not to do anything in its alliances with foreign powers against the security of the Confederation or any member of it, and when war was declared by the Confederation no member of it could negotiate separately with the enemy. Permanently neutralized states can

forcement of treaty stipulations as to the other contracting power, but also to the maintenance, in good faith, of those stipulations by every individual and government, local or constituent, under the control, or protection, of the sovereign power which has entered into, and is bound by, the treaties. In the succeeding chapters of this volume the author hopes to demonstrate that the treaty-making power of the Central Government of the United States is not only one of the greatest powers which has been confided to it, but that it is also one which it possesses in its fullest strength, and which it is able to exert over every person and State in the Union; that this power is in conformity with international law, as well as with the constitutional and municipal law of the United States, and of every State composing the Union, and that its existence in, and its exercise by, the Central Government inures alike to the benefit of every State individually, and to the Union as a whole.

make no diplomatic agreements which may lead them into hostilities for any other purpose than the defence of their own frontiers. Belgium, for instance, though she took part in the Conference of London of 1867, which decreed and guaranteed the neutralization of Luxemburg did not sign the Treaty of Guarantee because it bound the signatory powers to defend the Duchy from wanton attack." Lawrence's Principles of International Law, pp. 263-264.

PHILLIMORE.

"XLVIII. The first point to be considered is, who are competent to contract a Treaty? This compe-

tence is possessed by all independent kingdoms.

"A protected State may, if it has retained its sovereignty, make Treaties and Alliances, unless the power has been expressly renounced, or cannot be exercised consistently with the conditions of its protection. We have seen that States under a Federal Union may or may not, according to the terms of their confederation, be competent to enter into Treaties with foreign nations. . . .

"No subordinate corporations in a State can be contracting parties to a Treaty with a Foreign State." Phillimore Int. Law, 3d edition, vol. II, pp. 73-75.

234

CHAPTER V.

TREATIES, AND THE TREATY-MAKING POWER OF THE UNITED STATES AS EXERCISED PRIOR TO AND UNDER THE CONFEDERATION.

§ 134. **Treaty making and sovereignty as to colonies by central governments.**—It has been shown in the preceding chapters that the treaty-making power is necessarily an attribute of complete sovereignty; it has also been shown that the United States government possesses such complete sovereignty and, therefore, possesses every attribute thereof; it is necessary, however, to refer to the period between the time when the original States of the Union were colonies, possessed of no self-government which was capable of exercising the treaty-making power, and the formation and adoption of the Federal Constitution, when, as States they finally prohibited all exercise of that power except through the medium of the Central Government. The thirteen years which elapsed from 1774 to 1787 was, so to speak, a period of transition, during part of which a purely revolutionary government existed, and during the balance of which the Articles of Confederation formed the basis of the Federal Government, except so far as certain broad functions of sovereignty were exercised by Congress, the basis of which was not any written articles, but the necessities of the occasion, and the fact that the colonies had become a unit as to national matters coevally with the first expression of their intention to become independent.

§ 135. **Colonies as the subject of treaties between European powers.**—Prior to the revolution, and the forming and adoption of the Articles of Confederation, or even the first meeting of the Colonial Congress, the American colonies had been, on more than one occasion, the subject-matter of treaties made by and between European nations without any intervention on their part, or even their expression of approval or protest being asked or permitted. Vital interests both as to intercolonial and trans-Atlantic affairs had been seriously affected without allowing the inhabitants of the great colonies in America any voice whatever.[1] Under such a training, the representatives of the colonies who met in Philadelphia, as well as all thinking men in the separate colonies who took any part whatever in the local government, fully understood, and fully appreciated, the extent and

§ 135.
[1] See collation of treaties in note under § 119, p. 204, *ante.*

far-reaching effects of the treaty-making power, and of the treaties concluded between sovereign powers, not only directly upon the contracting governments, but also upon all the people, whatever their local government might be, over whom the sovereignty and jurisdiction of the contracting powers extended. They were also fully aware of the fact that, as colonies, they were powerless to enter into any treaties or negotiations with each other, or with foreign powers, in regard to any matter whatever, even though their own interests might be vitally and individually affected thereby. They were obliged, therefore, to understand that if, as constituent states of a confederation, they either delegated to a central government, or conceded that a central government possessed, the treaty-making power, such power could be exercised by that central or federal government in the same far-reaching manner as it had always been exercised by the previously dominant power of Great Britain, until its jurisdiction was completely thrown off by the colonies, when they made their first move to resist the royal orders, which was equivalent to an unwritten declaration of independence.

§ 136. **Nature of allegiance of American colonies to mother country.**—By the expression "prior to the confederation" in the caption of this chapter, the only period that can be comprehended is the brief space of time that elapsed between the throwing off of the allegiance of the colonies and the adoption of the Articles of Confederation.

There is, of course, no doubt whatever as to the fact that, prior to the Revolution, the people of the colonies owed allegiance to the Crown of Great Britain. Exactly what that allegiance was, *i. e.*, whether it was in any way connected with the colonies as separate entities, or with them as a whole, is still a matter of discussion, as is also the exact time when the colonies and colonists became free from all allegiance to the mother country. These points will always be difficult to determine, as the people of the colonies were, for a long period, prior to July 4, 1776, engaged in actual rebellion, which finally resulted in the recognition of their independence. The Continental Congress in fact had been, and was, exercising the functions of a revolutionary government, for and on behalf of all the colonies, for many months prior to the promulgation of the Declaration of Independence.[1]

§ 137. **Birth of United States ; Declaration of Independence.**—It is generally considered that the birth of the United States was on the 4th day of July, 1776, and that it was evidenced by the promulgation of the Declaration of Independence. If, however, as the Supreme Court has declared, the United States was born as a nation with the Declaration,[1] it was certainly conceived, as such, not later than the assembling of the first Congress, or, at the very latest, at the battle of Lexington.[2] The colonies had, prior thereto, practically acted as independent States. They had always done so, however, as an entity and not in their separate capacities. When they issued that memorable document, they did so as a whole and not separately. They did, indeed, declare that they already existed as free and independent States, and not that they intended to become so at a future time; but they did this as the United States through the medium of delegates to a Congress which exercised functions of national sovereignty

---

§ 136.

"[1] The continental government, which commissioned and sent Washington to take the command of the army which it had adopted, consisted solely of a body of delegates, chosen to represent the people of the several colonies or states, for certain purposes of national defence, safety, redress, and finally, revolution." Constitutional History of the United States by George Ticknor Curtis, vol. I, chapter 3, entitled, "The Revolutionary Government." p. 38; and see also *Penhallow* vs. *Doane,* U. S. Sup. Ct. 1795, 3 Dallas 54, PATERSON, J.; *Ware* vs. *Hylton,* U. S. Sup. Ct. 1796, 3 Dallas 199, CHASE, J.; extracts from these opinions as quoted in Story's Commentaries will be found in note 1, under § 143, p. 246, *post* of this volume; also *Chisholm* vs. *Georgia,* U. S. Sup. Ct. 1793, 2 Dallas 419, and see § 138, p. 242, *post.*

§ 137.

[1] *Harcourt* vs. *Gaillard,* U. S. Sup. Ct. 1827, 12 Wheaton, 523, JOHNSON, J., in which it was held, as stated in the syllabus, that "A grant made by the British governor of Florida, after the declaration of independence within the territory lying between the Mississippi and the Chatahouchee rivers, and between the 31st degree of north latitude, and a line drawn from the mouth of the Yazoo river due east to the Chatahouchee, is invalid as the foundation of title in the Courts of the United States." *Chisholm* vs. *Georgia,* U. S. Sup. Ct. 1793, 2 Dallas 419, and see further reference to this case in § 138, p. 242, *post,* and extract from opinion of JAY, Ch. J., in note under § 143, p. 246, *post.*

[2] The Battle of Lexington was fought April 19, 1775. See note on national unity prior to Declaration

for the joint benefit of all the people of the good colonies of North America.[3] This demonstrated the co-ordinate births of the principles of unity and independence in our national

of Independence under § 147, p. 254, *post.*

[3] The Declaration of Independence did not have the usual preamble and recital as to the names of the States or colonies; in fact the names of the colonies do not appear in the document; throughout the document the word "we" is used without any declarative words whatsoever, leaving it simply to the persons signing it to specify in what capacity it was executed. The concluding sentence is as follows:

"We, therefore, the Representatives of the United States of America In General Congress, assembled, appealing to the Supreme Judge of the World for the rectitude of our intentions, do, in the Name, and by Authority of the good People of these Colonies solemnly Publish and Declare, That these United Colonies are, and of Right ought to be Free and Independent States; that they are Absolved from all Allegiance to the British Crown, and that all political connection between them and the State of Great Britain, is and ought to be totally dissolved; and that as Free and Independent States, they have full Power to levy War, conclude Peace, contract Alliances, establish Commerce, and to do all other Acts and Things which Independent States may of right do. And for the support of this Declaration, with a firm reliance on the Protection of Divine Providence, We mutually pledge to each other our Lives, our Fortunes and our sacred Honor."

BURGESS.

"Complete geographical separation and a partial ethnical separation from the motherland, together with complete geographical unity, substantial ethnical unity, and almost complete identity of interests among themselves were the forces which conspired, at last, to awaken the consciousness of the people of these thirteen colonies to the fact that they had attained the natural conditions of a sovereignty,—a State. The impulse to objectify this consciousness in institutions became irresistible. Its first enduring form was the Continental Congress. This was the first organization of the American state. From the first moment of its existence there was something more upon this side of the Atlantic than thirteen local governments. There was a sovereignty, a state; not in idea simply or upon paper, but in fact and in organization. The revolution was an accomplished fact before the declaration of 1776, and so was independence. The act of the 4th of July was a notification to the world of *faits accomplis.* A nation and a state did not spring into existence through that declaration, as dramatic publicists are wont to express it. Nations and states do not spring into existence. The significance of the proclamation was this: a people testified thereby the consciousness of the fact that they had become, in the progressive development of history, one whole, separate, and adult nation, and a national state, and that they were determined to defend this natural status against the now

political history.   It has been so decided by the Supreme
Court.[4]   Story, in his Commentaries, says " that the colonies

no longer natural supremacy of a
foreign state.   French statesmen
had foreseen and predicted this development and result a decade before the stamp act.   The American
state, organized in the Continental
Congress, proclaimed to the world
its sovereign existence, and proceeded, through this same organization, to govern itself generally,
for the time being and to authorize
the people resident within the separate colonies to make temporary
arrangement for their local government, upon the basis of the widest
possible suffrage."   Burgess' Political Science and Constitutional
Law, vol. I, p. 100.

CURTIS.

" This celebrated instrument, regarded as a legislative proceeding,
was the solemn enactment, by the
representatives of all the colonies,
of a complete dissolution of their
allegiance to the British crown.
It severed the political connection
between the people of this country
and the people of England, and at
once erected the different colonies
into free and independent states.
The body by which this step was
taken constituted the actual government of the nation, at the time,
and its members had been directly
invested with competent legislative
power to take it, and had also been
specially instructed to do so.   The
consequences flowing from its adoption were, that the local allegiance
of the inhabitants of each colony
became transferred and due to the
colony itself, or as it was expressed
by the Congress, became due to
the laws of the colony, from which
they derived protection; that the

people of the country became
thenceforth the rightful sovereign
of the country; that they became
united in a national capacity, as
one people; that they could thereafter enter into treaties and contract alliances with foreign nations,
could levy war and conclude peace,
and do all other acts pertaining to
the exercise of a national sovereignty; and finally, that, in their
national capacity, they became
known and designated as the United States of America.   This Declaration was the first national
state paper in which these words
were used as the style and title of
the nation.   In the enacting part
of the instrument, the Congress
styled themselves 'the representatives of the United States of America in general Congress assembled;'
and from that period the previously
' United Colonies' have been known
as a political community, both
within their own borders and by
the other nations of the world, by
the title which they then assumed.
" The title of ' The United States
of America' was formally assumed
in the Articles of Confederation,
when they came to be adopted.
But it was in use, without formal
enactment, from the date of the
adoption of the Declaration of Independence.   On the 9th of September, 1776, it was ordered that
in all continental commissions and
other instruments, where the words
' United Colonies' had been used,
the style should be altered to the
' United States. '   Journals of Congress, vol II, p. 349."   Curtis's Constitutional History of the United
States, pp. 35–36, vol. 1.
[4] For note 4, see p. 241.

did not severally act for themselves, and proclaim their own independence." Continuing, he says: "It is true that some of the States had previously formed incipient governments for themselves; but it was done in compliance with the recommendations of Congress. . . . But the declaration of independence of all the colonies was the united act of all. It was 'a declaration by the representatives of the United States of America in Congress assembled'; 'by the delegates appointed by the good people of the colonies,' as in a prior declaration of rights they were called. It was not an act done by the State governments then organized, nor by persons chosen by them. It was emphatically the act of the whole *people* of the united colonies, by the instrumentality of their representatives, chosen for that among other purposes. It was not an act competent to the State governments, or any of them, as organized under their charters, to adopt. Those charters neither contemplated the case nor provided for it. It was an act of original, inherent sovereignty by the people themselves, resulting from their right to change the form of government, and to institute a new one, whenever necessary for their safety and happiness. So the Declaration of Independence treats it. No State had presumed of itself to form a new government, or to provide for the exigencies of the times, without consulting Congress on the subject; and when any acted, it was in pursuance of the recommendation of Congress. It was, therefore, the achievement of the whole for the benefit of the whole. The people of the united colonies made the united colonies free and independent States, and absolved them from all allegiance to the British Crown. The Declaration of Independence has accordingly always been treated as an act of paramount and sovereign authority, complete and perfect, *per se*, and *ipso facto* working an entire dissolution of all political connection with, and allegiance to, Great Britain. And this, not merely as a practical fact, but in a legal and constitutional view of the matter by courts of justice."[5]

---

[4] See § 143, pp. 246, *et seq. post*, and extracts from Story, Curtis, Miller, Davis and Cooley, and cases cited on this point.

[5] Commentaries on the Constitution of the United States by Joseph Story, LL. D., 5th ed., Boston, 1891, vol. I, sec. 211, pp. 153-155.

§ 138. **Chisholm vs. Georgia; views of Chief Justice Jay.**
—This was also the decision in the case of *Chisholm* vs. *Georgia*,[1] in which it was held that the " Revolution, or rather, the Declaration of Independence, found the people *already* united for general purposes, and at the same time providing for their more domestic concerns by State conventions, and other temporary arrangements. From the Crown of *Great Britain*, the sovereignty of their country passed to the people of it; and it was then not an uncommon opinion, that the unappropriated lands, which belonged to that Crown, passed not to the people of the Colony or State within whose limits they were situated, but to the whole people; on whatever principles this opinion rested, it did not give way to the other, and thirteen sovereignties were considered as emerged from the principles of the Revolution, combined with local convenience and considerations; the people nevertheless continued to consider themselves, in a national point of view, as one people; and they continued without interruption to manage their national concerns accordingly; afterwards, in the hurry of the war, and in the warmth of mutual confidence, they made a confederation of the States, the basis of a general government."

§ 139. **Extent of Sovereignty in the Continental Congress.**—From the time the first Continental Congress assembled at Philadelphia, September 5, 1774, until the present time there has been an active and unending discussion as to the extent of sovereignty which was vested in that Congress, either in its capacity as a revolutionary government prior to, or in its capacity as a Congress of delegates from various States subsequent to, the adoption of the Articles of Confederation. In many respects this has become a purely academic question; it is, however, of vital importance, as a demonstration of the truth of the statement already made, that at the very moment the colonies decided to throw off their allegiance to Great Britain, if not prior thereto, it was a recognized fact, and one which was acted upon from the moment that resolu-

---

§ **138.**

[1] *Chisholm* vs. *Georgia*, U. S. Sup. Ct. 1793, 2 Dallas, 419, p. 462, JAY, Ch. J., IREDELL, BLAIR, WILSON and CUSHING, JJ., and see extract from opinion of JAY, Ch. J., in note to § 143, p. 246, *post.*

tion was framed until the Constitution was adopted, that the colonies in so doing acted, not in their separate and individual capacities, but unitedly as one people, and as one nation, and that no steps were taken to achieve independence until it had been ascertained that unity of action had already been achieved. In fact, a long and interesting investigation of historical facts and documents, connected with these elements of the origin of our national life and of the opinions of many of our ablest historians and jurists, who have closely studied the subject in all of its varied aspects, has necessarily led to but one conclusion: that the duality of the Government of the United States, as hereinbefore expressed, to wit: as a federation only in regard to internal affairs, and as a nation in regard to all matters of common interest or external relations, with every element of complete sovereignty and nationality vesting in the Central Government as to national matters, was coeval, and ever has been, co-existent, with the idea of independence and self-government of the colonies, and of the States; and that as a principle of political science, or political history, the United States existed as an independent nation prior to the transformation of many of the colonies into States.

§ 140. **States' Rights School contention.**—The quotations already given from Story's Commentaries and from Chief Justice Jay's opinion in *Chisholm* vs. *Georgia*, show that the views expressed in the preceding section have been adopted by many great thinkers; notwithstanding these expressions, however, as well as many others of a similar nature, there has been a constant effort on the part of the strict States' Rights School to divest the Continental Congress, in any and all of its capacities, of every right and power to exercise the functions of a national government, and also to divest the government under the Confederation of every attribute of sovereignty, even including those powers which were absolutely essential for the prosecution of the revolutionary war, the preservation of the Union, the assertion and maintenance of independence and the establishment and proper conduct of the relations of the nation, or community, with other countries, and all of which powers were so necessary for the preservation of the whole and of each individual

part, that Congress actually exercised them whether it did
so under an improper assumption of power or from the actual possession thereof; certainly the doctrine of *omnia præ-
sumuntur rite esse acta* ought to apply in a case of this
nature.

§ 141. **Broader views of Marshall and others.**—The
theory of the nationality and sovereignty of the Central
Government, as it appears from decisions made by Chief Justices Jay and Marshall, and as enunciated by Story, Curtis
and Miller, is that a Government was constituted which not
only possessed the powers which were delegated to it by the
Articles of Confederation, and by the instructions of the delegates, but which also possessed inherently or, as Mr. Davis
has expressed it in his notes to Justice Miller's Lectures, *unconsciously*, national and sovereign powers. Mr. Davis discusses this view of the subject and shows by the actual work
performed by the Continental Congress, as well as by the
Congress under the Confederation, that elements of nationality and sovereignty must have existed, because the acts
done could only have been accomplished by the exercise of
sovereignty by a fully sovereign power, and not by one of
limited or delegated powers; in fact, he says: "That the
Statesmen in the Continental Congress felt that they formed
part of a National Government, ruling, in its proper sphere,
over a Federation of United States, and exercising powers to
which each of those States must of necessity be subordinate.
. . . The simple truth is, that the United States, under
the Articles of Confederation, like the United Colonies after
the battle of Lexington, existed as a Sovereign Power from
the necessities of the emergency. The Colonies were com-
pacted together by the blows of a common enemy." [1]

§ 142. **Views of Calhoun and Tucker.**—John C. Calhoun
and John Randolph Tucker have adopted what they called
the separate or State unit system, and by elaborate arguments have endeavored to show that the earlier Congresses
could not exercise any authority whatever prior to the adoption of the Articles of Confederation, except in pursuance of
the instructions of delegates, and subsequently thereto only

§ 141.
[1] Miller's Lectures on the Consti-   tution; J. C. Bancroft Davis' notes
on Lecture I, p. 57.

in pursuance of the strictly delegated authority contained in the instrument itself; in his Discourse on the Constitution and Government of the United States, Mr. Calhoun has elaborately stated this proposition as his theory of State sovereignty,[1] and Mr. Tucker in the treatise already referred to has elaborated upon, and endeavored to support, it by including as a part of his work all of the instructions of the States to their respective delegates,[2] with the evident intention of proving thereby the limited bound, within which the powers of members individually, and of the Congress as a whole, were confined; also for the purpose of drawing a general deduction therefrom that beyond these limits no power or sovereignty existed whatever. This view is only sustainable by eliminating every power which is granted, by the rules of international law and by the elementary principles of political science, to all revolutionary governments and to all central governments of confederations, and also by asserting that the exercise of those powers by the Continental Congress was wholly illegal.

§ 142.

[1] Works of John C. Calhoun; edited by Richard K. Cralle, New York, April, 1888, Vol. 1, p. 110 et seq.

[2] John Randolph Tucker declares "The Journal of the second session of Congress opens thus: 'A number of delegates from the colonies of New Hampshire, Massachusetts Bay, down to South Carolina, agreeable to their *appointment and orders* received from their *respective colonies.*' This statement settles adversely the assumption of Judge Story that the members of Congress were not the delegated agents of the governments of the colonies, but represented the original powers of the people. This record states that they sat under the 'appointment and orders received from their respective colonies.' The authority given to the deputies to this Congress differs in terms from that given for the members of the prior Congress. A summary of each of these will be given in a note." Tucker on the Constitution, vol. 1, p. 215, Chicago, 1899. Then follows in a note a summary of the instructions of all of the thirteen colonies with the exception of Rhode Island and Georgia, which, Mr. Tucker states, did not appear.

The conclusion reached by Mr. Tucker is stated on page 217 as follows: "One thing is settled beyond question; that the dogmatic statement of Judge Story that the Congress thus assembled exercised *de facto* and *de jure* a sovereign authority; not as the delegated agents of the governments *de facto* of the colonies, but in virtue of original power derived from the people,' is wholly unsustained and is completely refuted by the facts."

§ 143. **Views of Calhoun and Tucker refuted by Justice Story and others.**—Both Mr. Calhoun and Mr. Tucker, however, seem to have entirely lost sight of the propositions maintained by Story,[1] Curtis,[2] Cooley[3] Miller, Bancroft Davis,

§ 143.

[1] JUDGE STORY'S VIEWS.

"In confirmation of these views, it may not be without use to refer to the opinions of some of our most eminent judges, delivered on occasions which required an exact examination of the subject. In *Chisholm's Executors* vs. *The State of Georgia*, Mr. Chief Justice Jay, who was equally distinguished as a Revolutionary statesman and a general jurist, expressed himself to the following effect: 'The Revolution, or rather the Declaration of Independence, found the *people* already united for general purposes, and at the same time providing for their more domestic concerns by State conventions and other temporary arrangements. From the crown of Great Britain the sovereignty of their country passed to the *people* of it; and it was then not an uncommon opinion that the unappropriated lands which belonged to that crown passed, not to the people of the colony or States within whose limits they were situated, but to the *whole people*. On whatever principle this opinion rested, it did not give way to the other; and *thirteen sovereignties* were considered as emerging from the principles of the Revolution, combined by local convenience and considerations. The people, nevertheless, continued to consider themselves, in a national point of view, as *one people;* and they continued without interruption to manage their national concerns accordingly.' In *Penhallow* vs. *Doane*, Mr. Justice Paterson, who was also a revolutionary statesman, said, speaking of the period before the ratification of the confederation: 'The powers of Congress were revolutionary in their nature, arising, out of events adequate to every national emergency, and coextensive with the object to be attained. Congress was the general, supreme, and controlling council of the nation, the centre of force, and the sun of the political system. Congress raised armies, fitted out a navy, and prescribed rules for their government, etc. These high acts of sovereignty were submitted to, acquiesced in, and approved of by the *people* of America, etc. The danger being imminent and common, it became necessary for the people or colonies to coalesce and act in concert, in order to divert or break the violence of the gathering storm. They accordingly grew into union, and formed one great political body, of which Congress was the directing principle and soul, etc. The truth is, that the States, individually, were not known nor recognized as sovereign by foreign nations, nor are they now. The States collectively under Congress, as their connecting point or head, were acknowledged by foreign powers as sovereign, particularly in that acceptation of the term which is applicable to all great national concerns, and in the exercise of which

[2] For note 2, see p. 247.

[3] For note 3, see p. 248.

and others, who support the broader doctrine that the ideas
of independence and unity were of twin birth and co-ordinate

other sovereigns would be more immediately interested.' In *Ware* vs.
Hylton, Mr. Justice Chase, himself also a Revolutionary statesman, said:
'It has been inquired, what powers Congress possessed from the first
meeting in September, 1774, until the ratification of the confederation
on the 1st of March, 1781. It appears to me that the powers of Congress
during that whole period were derived from the *people* they represented,
expressly given through the medium of their State conventions or State
legislatures; or that after they were exercised, they were impliedly ratified by the acquiescence and obedience of the *people*, etc. The powers
of Congress originated from necessity, and arose out of it, and were
only limited by events; or, in other words, they were revolutionary in
their nature. Their extent depended on the exigencies and necessities
of public affairs. I entertain this general idea, that the several States
retained all internal sovereignty; and that Congress properly possessed
the rights of external sovereignty. In deciding on the powers of Congress, and of the several States before the confederation, I see but one
safe rule, namely, that all the powers actually exercised by Congress
before that period were rightfully exercised on the presumption, not to
be controverted, that they were so authorized by the people they represented, by an express or implied grant; and that all the powers exercised by the State conventions or State legislatures were also rightfully
exercised on the same presumption of authority from the people.' "
Commentaries on the Constitution of the United States by Joseph Story,
L. L. D. 5th edition, Boston, 1891, vol. I, § 216, pp. 159–160.

[2] MR. CURTIS' VIEWS.

The instructions to delegates also appear in a condensed form as a
foot-note to pages 11 and 12 of volume 1, Curtis' Constitutional History of the United States. Mr. Curtis has followed the views of Mr.
Justice Story; his views are expressed as follows, pages 25 and 26:
" It is apparent, therefore, that, previously to the Declaration of Independence, the people of the several colonies had established a national government of a revolutionary character, which undertook to
act, and did act, in the name and with the general consent of the inhabitants of the country. This government was established by the
union, in one body, of delegates representing the people of each colony;
who, after they had thus united for national purposes, proceeded, in
their respective jurisdictions, by means of conventions and other temporary arrangements, to provide for their domestic concerns by the establishment of local governments, which should be the successors of
that authority of the British crown which they had 'everywhere suppressed.' The fact that these local or state governments were not
formed until a union of the people of the different colonies for national purposes had already taken place, and until the Congress had
authorized and recommended their establishment, is of great importance in the constitutional history of this country; for it shows that no

growth, and that it is only through the central body
that those great powers which none of the States possess

colony, acting separately for itself, dissolved its own allegiance to the
British crown, but that this allegiance was dissolved by the supreme
authority of the people of all the colonies, acting through their general
agent, the Congress, and not only declaring that the authority of Great
Britain ought to be suppressed, but recommending that each colony
should supplant that authority by a local government, to be framed by
and for the people of the colony itself.

" The powers exercised by the Congress, before the Declaration of
Independence, show, therefore, that its functions were those of a revolutionary government. It is a maxim of political science, that, when
such a government has been instituted for the accomplishment of great
purposes of public safety, its powers are limited only by the necessities
of the case out of which they have arisen, and of the objects for which
they were to be exercised. When the acts of such a government are
acquiesced in by the people, they are presumed to have been ratified by
the people. To the case of our Revolution these principles are strictly
applicable throughout. The Congress assumed at once the exercise of
all the powers demanded by the public exigency, and their exercise of
those powers was fully acquiesced in and confirmed by the people. It
does not at all detract from the authoritative character of their acts,
nor diminish the real powers of the Revolutionary Congress, that it
was obliged to rely on local bodies for the execution of most of its orders, or that it couched many of those orders in the form of recommendations. They were complied with and executed, in point of fact,
by the provincial congresses, conventions, and local committees to such
an extent as fully to confirm the revolutionary powers of the Congress,
as the guardians of the rights and liberties of the country. But we
shall see, in the further progress of the history of the Congress, that
while its powers remained entirely revolutionary, and were consequently
coextensive with the great national objects to be accomplished, the
want of the proper machinery of civil government and of independent
agents of its own rendered it wholly incapable of wielding those powers
successfully."

³ JUDGE COOLEY'S VIEWS.

" The government of the United States is the existing representative
of the national government which has always in some form existed over
the American states. Before the Revolution, the powers of government,
which were exercised over all the colonies in common, were so exercised
as pertaining either to the Crown of Great Britain or to the Parliament;
but the extent of those powers, and how far vested in the Crown and
how far in the Parliament, were questions never definitely settled, and
which constituted subjects of dispute between the mother country
and the people of the colonies, finally resulting in hostilities. That the
power over peace and war, the general direction of commercial intercourse with other nations, and the general control of such subjects as
fall within the province of international law, were vested in the home

in their individual, or, as the disciples of the States' Rights School call it, their sovereign, capacity, can be exercised in any manner whatever, either in theory or in practice.

government, and that the colonies were not, therefore, sovereign States, in the full and proper sense of that term, were propositions never seriously disputed in America, and indeed were often formally conceded; and the disputes related to questions as to what were or were not matters of internal regulation, the control of which the colonists insisted should be left exclusively to themselves.

"Besides the tie uniting the several colonies through the Crown of Great Britain, there had always been a strong tendency to a more intimate and voluntary union, whenever circumstances of danger threatened them; and this tendency led to the New England Confederacy of 1643, to the temporary Congress of 1690, to the plan of union agreed upon in Convention of 1754, but rejected by the colonies as well as the Crown, to the Stamp Act Congress of 1765, and finally to the Continental Congress of 1774. When the difficulties with Great Britain culminated in actual war, the Congress of 1775 assumed to itself those powers of external control which before had been conceded to the Crown or to the Parliament, together with such other powers of sovereignty as it seemed essential a general government should exercise, and thus became the national government of the United Colonies. By this body, war was conducted, independence declared, treaties formed, and admiralty jurisdiction exercised. It is evident, therefore, that the States, though declared to be ' sovereign and independent,' were never strictly so in their individual character, but were always, in respect to the higher powers of sovereignty, subject to the control of a central authority, and were never separately known as members of the family of nations. The Declaration of Independence made them sovereign and independent States, by altogether abolishing the foreign jurisdiction, and substituting a national government of their own creation.

" But while national powers were assumed by and conceded to the Congress of 1775–76, that body was nevertheless strictly revolutionary in its character, and, like all revolutionary bodies, its authority was undefined, and could be limited only, *first*, by instructions to individual delegates by the States choosing them; *second*, by the will of the Congress; and *third*, by the power to enforce that will. As in the latter particular it was essentially feeble, the necessity for a clear specification of powers which should be exercised by the national government became speedily apparent, and led to the adoption of the Articles of Confederation. But those articles did not concede the full measure of power essential to the efficiency of a national government at home, the enforcement of respect abroad, or the preservation of the public faith or public credit; and the difficulties experienced induced the election of delegates to the Constitutional Convention held in 1787, by which a constitution was formed which was put into operation in 1789. As much larger powers were vested by this instrument in the general government than had ever been exercised in this country by either the

Mr. Davis has rendered an inestimable service in collating the incidents in which, prior to the Constitution, Congress exercised the functions of a national government, notably

Crown, the Parliament, or the Revolutionary Congress, and, larger than those conceded to the Congress under the Articles of Confederation, the assent of the people of the several States was essential to its acceptance, and a provision was inserted in the Constitution that the ratification of the conventions of nine States should be sufficient for the establishment of the Constitution between the States so ratifying the same. In fact, the Constitution was ratified by conventions of delegates chosen by the people in eleven of the States, before the new government was organized under it; and the remaining two, North Carolina and Rhode Island, by their refusal to accept, and by the action of the others in proceeding separately, were excluded altogether from that national jurisdiction which before had embraced them. This exclusion was not warranted by anything contained in the Articles of Confederation, which purported to be articles of ' perpetual union;' and the action of the eleven States in making radical revision of the Constitution, and excluding their associates for refusal to assent, was really revolutionary in character, and only to be defended on the same ground of necessity on which all revolutionary action is justified, and which in this case was the absolute need, fully demonstrated by experience, of a more efficient general government.

" Left at liberty now to assume complete powers of sovereignty as independent governments, these two States saw fit soon to resume their place in the American family, under a permission contained in the Constitution; and new States have since been added from time to time, all of them, with a single exception, organized by the consent of the general government, and embracing territory previously under its control. The exception was Texas, which had previously been an independent sovereign State, but which, by the conjoint action of its government and that of the United States, was received into the Union on an equal footing with the other States.

" Without, therefore, discussing, or even designing to allude to any abstract theories as to the precise position and actual power of the several States at the time of forming the present Constitution, it may be said of them generally that they have at all times been subject to some common national government, which has exercised control over the subjects of war and peace, and other matters pertaining to external sovereignty; and that when the only three States which ever exercised complete sovereignty accepted the Constitution and came into the Union, on an equal footing with all the other States, they thereby accepted the same relative position to the general government, and divested themselves permanently of those national powers which the others had never exercised. And the assent once given to the Union was irrevocable. ' The Constitution in all its provisions looks to an indestructible Union composed of indestructible States. (*Texas* vs. *White*, CHASE, Ch. J., 7 Wallace 700, p. 725.) ' " Cooley's Constitutional Lim-

in cases of prize capture, and the acquisition of territory, neither of which functions could have been exercised by a government which did not possess plenary power and complete sovereignty and nationality.[4]

§ 144. **Views of Justice Miller and Mr. Davis.**—The apparent repetition of some of the points elaborated in the preceding chapter, and which will be referred to again at a later point in this volume, is due to the fact that we cannot properly trace the history of the treaty-making power prior to the Constitution, or reconcile the well-known and conceded weakness of the Union under the Confederation, with the strong powers that were vested in it in regard to those national matters, unless we keep them constantly and prominently in view; it is necessary also to appreciate that the weakness of the Confederacy was not due to a lack of power to decree, but of power to compel obedience to decrees when made, in fact, as Mr. Davis says, "in studying the ante-Con-

itations, Chapter II. pp. 7-11, and see numerous cases cited, and also quotations from the Federalist.

STORY.

"The same body, in 1776, took bolder steps, and exerted powers which could in no other manner be justified or accounted for, than upon the supposition that a national union for national purposes already existed, and that the Congress was invested with sovereign power over all the colonies for the purpose of preserving the common rights and liberties of all. They accordingly authorized general hostilities against the persons and property of British subjects; they opened an extensive commerce with foreign countries, regulating the whole subject of imports and exports; they authorized the formation of new governments in the colonies; and finally they exercised the sovereign prerogative of dissolving the allegiance of all colonies to the British crown. The validity of these acts was never doubted or denied by the people. On the contrary, they became the foundation upon which the superstructure of the liberties and independence of the United States has been erected. Whatever, then, may be the theories of ingenious men on the subject, it is historically true that before the Declaration of Independence these colonies were not, in any absolute sense, sovereign states; that that event did not find them or make them such; but that at the moment of their separation they were under the domain of a superior controlling national government whose powers were vested in and exercised by the general Congress with the consent of the people of all the States." Commentaries on the Constitution of the United States, by Joseph Story, L.L. D., 5th Ed., Boston, 1891, vol. 1, § 214, p. 157.

[4] For views of Justice Miller and Mr. Davis see § 144 and notes thereto.

stitutional history of the United States, we may often find Congress weak in action, but never irresolute or weak in asserting its Federal powers. Before the Declaration of Independence it claimed and exercised the National Powers which until then had been wielded by the King of Great Britain. When that Declaration was proclaimed, it pressed this claim with stronger emphasis, if not with better right. This power it handed over to the government of the Confederation, which was in fact the Congress itself ; and that government, in its turn deposited the power in the new Union, as defined by the Constitution." [1]

§ 144.

[1] Miller's Lectures on the Constitution; J. C. Bancroft Davis' notes to Lecture I, pp. 57-8. In the same chapter (pp. 36-37) Mr. Davis says:

" This outbreak of a state of war found in each Colony or Province, an organized government with separate functions, exercising a limited sovereignty under the king of Great Britain. Many of the broader powers and functions of National Sovereignty, which the Constitution now places in the government of the United States, then resided in the British king and Parliament. When British sovereignty fell, such powers were assumed and exercised, without question, by the Congress of the United Colonies, before the United States existed as an independent nation; months before the Articles of Confederation were agreed to; years before they became operative by receiving the assent of all the States. They were never enjoyed or exercised by the states separately; and consequently, as an historic fact, independently of theory, they could not have been retained when the States conferred upon the general Government other enumerated powers in the Articles of Confederation.

" Unconsciously to themselves the people of the United States were absorbed into a new nationality by the very fact of their combined resistance to Great Britain. They carried on war; they officered and maintained armies; they commissioned vessels of war; they borrowed money and issued evidences of debt therefor; they created prize courts; they acquired territory and determined what the nature of its civilization should be; they made treaties with foreign powers; and in many ways, both before and after the adoption of the Articles of Confederation, they exercised the highest powers of sovereignty.

" This Congress was both the Executive and the Legislature of the Nation. It was the body which framed the Articles of Confederation, and many of its members were also in the Convention which framed the Constitution of the United States. Unless that Constitution is to be construed theoretically, and without regard to the incidents of the national history of which it was the outcome, a knowledge of what that Congress did, derived from historical investigation, must help us in comprehending what sort of a government the framers of the Constitution intended to

§ 145. **The Continental Congress a revolutionary government.**—These general statements in regard to the high acts of sovereignty exercised by the earlier Congresses are strengthened by an examination of the history of those organizations. The first Continental Congress assembled at Philadelphia on September 5, 1774, and organized itself as a deliberative body representing the various colonies of North America. It was essentially a revolutionary government, the outgrowth of necessity for immediate and united action of the colonies; it consisted of delegates, or, as they were called in many proceedings, committees of the colonies. Eleven colonies only were represented on the first day. At that time no Articles of Confederation existed, nor in fact were there any written articles which either held the colonies together, or clothed the delegates with any general powers; nor were there any established principles at the outset by which the nature of the Union could be determined; it, therefore, became necessary at once to formulate some system of government which should be binding upon all the different colonies or states, as from that time thereafter they have ever since been called.[1]

§ 146. **Nature of Congress prior to Constitution.**—The Continental Congress acted somewhat in the nature of a general committee, or commission, for the thirteen colonies without any constitutional foundation or written agreement whatever, from 1774 until 1777; the Articles of Confederation were completed and offered to the States for their ratification in November, 1777, but the assent of all of the States was not obtained until March, 1781.[1] During this period of

establish. To cover this whole ground would be to write the legislative history of those eventful fourteen years. I select from all its legislation three subjects: 1. The Appellate Prize Courts; 2. The Treaties negotiated with Foreign Powers; 3. The acquisition of the Territory to the northwest of the Ohio, and the exclusion of slavery from it."

§ 145.
[1] For an extended history of the earlier Congresses of the United States, see Curtis' Constitutional History of the United States, edition of 1889, New York, vol. I, chapters I–IV, and Story's Commentaries,, vol. I, § 198.

§ 146.
[1] For dates of adoption of Articles of Confederation, see note 1 to § 148, p. 257, *post.*

nearly seven years the basis for the existence of the Continental Congress was simply the recognized unity of the States as a matter of necessity and policy; all of the States from time to time sent delegates, the number varying according to the whim or fancy of each State, for as each was allowed to determine the number of its delegates within certain bounds, no undue advantage was obtained by increasing the number of delegates as a single vote was allowed to each State, regardless of the number of delegates representing it.

§ 147. **Independence, preservation of States' rights, National unity—all united in original and subsequent governments of United States.**—At the first meeting of these delegates questions naturally arose in regard to the extent of the national, or federal rights, which were exercisable by the Congress, as distinguished from the rights of the States, whose powers as to local affairs were not to be encroached upon any more than was absolutely necessary; great difficulty was encountered in framing a system of government and vesting the Continental Congress with governmental powers owing to the great jealousy with which the rights of the States were closely guarded; thus at the very outset of our recorded political history we find that the three great ideas, or principles, which have ever since dominated the government of the American people had already sprung into existence, and entered into the formation of the government, to wit: Independence, Preservation of States' rights, and National Unity.[1]

§ 147.

[1] NATIONAL UNITY PRIOR TO DECLARATION OF INDEPENDENCE.

The first page of Bancroft's History of the Constitution of the United States is entitled " A retrospect—Movements towards Union, 1641-1781," see also Elliott's Debates, vol. I, pp. 42-60, " Gradual Approaches towards Independence."

There is an exposition of this national unity, as it existed between the colonies, in the compilation of Select Charters and Other Documents illustrative of American history from 1606 to 1775, edited with notes by William Macdonald, published by the Macmillan Company, New York and London, 1899; this volume contains eighty documents affecting the relations of the American colonies with European countries, especially Great Britain, and with each other. As stated by Mr. Macdonald in his preface, it is a companion volume to his Select Documents Illustrative of the History of the United States, 1776-1861, also published

These principles have consistently and concurrently existed since that first meeting of the Continental Congress in Phila-

by the Macmillan Company, New York and London. Some of these documents are referred to in the following note:

On Thursday, October 20, 1774, the following "Association" was read in the Continental Congress and signed; it begins with the usual preamble:

"We, his Majesty's most loyal subjects, the delegates of the several colonies of New Hampshire, Massachusetts Bay, Rhode Island, Connecticut, New York, New Jersey, Pennsylvania, the three lower counties of New Castle, Kent, and Sussex, on Delaware, Maryland, Virginia, North Carolina, and South Carolina, deputed to represent them in a Continental Congress, held in the city of Philadelphia, on the fifth day of September, 1774, avowing our allegiance to his Majesty; our affection and regard for our fellow-subjects in Great Britain and elsewhere; affected with the deepest anxiety and most alarming apprehensions at those grievances and distresses with which his Majesty's American subjects are oppressed; and having taken under our most serious deliberation the state of the whole Continent, find that the present unhappy situation of our affairs is occasioned by a ruinous system of Colonial Administration, adopted by the British Ministry about the year 1763, evidently calculated for enslaving these Colonies, and, with them, the British Empire."

After recitals of their grievances the non importation agreement of 1774 was made; the association is referred to here because throughout the entire document, which appears at length on pp. 443–447, second volume of Curtis' Constitutional History of the United States, the colonies are referred to as a single territory, America, and, except in the recital, there is no reference to the separate colonies; the tenor of the instrument shows clearly that in this matter they considered themselves a unit.

On Thursday, July 6, 1775, in the Continental Congress a declaration was prepared by the representatives of the United Colonies of North America setting forth the causes for the necessity of taking up arms, in the course of which the following occurs:

"Our cause is just. Our union is perfect. Our internal resources are great, and, if necessary, foreign assistance is undoubtedly attainable. We gratefully acknowledge, as single instances of the Divine favour towards us, that His providence would not permit us to be called into this severe controversy until we were grown up to our present strength, had been previously exercised in warlike operations, and possessed of the means of defending ourselves. With hearts fortified with these animating reflections, we most solemnly, before *God* and the world, *declare*, that, exerting the utmost energy of those powers which our beneficent Creator hath graciously bestowed upon us, the arms we have been compelled by our enemies to assume, we will, in defiance of every hazard, with unabating firmness and perseverance, employ for the preservation of our liberties; being, with one mind, resolved to die freemen rather than live slaves.

delphia in 1774; they have never conflicted with each other except when the advocates of one principle have endeavored to give it undue prominence over the others; when, however, each is given its due and proper sphere, they co-operate like

"Lest this Declaration should disquiet the minds of our friends and fellow-subjects in any part of the Empire, we assure them that we mean not to dissolve that union which has so long and so happily subsisted between us, and which we sincerely wish to see restored. Necessity has not yet driven us into that desperate measure, or induced us to excite any other nation to war against them.   We have not raised armies with ambitious designs of separating from *Great Britain*, and establish-ing independent states.   We fight not for glory or for conquest.   We exhibit to mankind the remarkable spectacle of a people attacked by unprovoked enemies, without any imputation or even suspicion of of-fense.   They boast of their privileges and civilization, and yet proffer no milder conditions than servitude or death.

"In our own native land, in defence of the freedom that is our birth-right, and which we ever enjoyed till the late violation of it; for the protection of our property, acquired solely by the honest industry of our forefathers and ourselves, against violence actually offered, we have taken up arms.   We shall lay them down when hostilities shall cease on the part of the aggressors, and all danger of their being renewed shall be removed, and not before."   1 Journal of Congress, p. 134, *et seq.*, Macdonald's Select Charters, p. 374, Curtis' Constitutional History of the United States, vol. II, p. 453, see p. 457.

"We thus see that from the first dawn of our national existence, through every form which it has yet assumed, a dual character has con-stantly attended our political condition.   A nation has existed because there has all along existed a central authority having the right to pre-scribe the rule of action for the whole people on certain subjects, occa-sions and relations.   In this sense and in no other, to this extent but no further, we have been since 1776, and are now a nation.   At the be-ginning the limits of this central authority, in respect to which we are a nation, were defined by general popular understanding; but more recently they were fixed in written terms and public charters, first by the Articles of Confederation, and ultimately, with a more enlarged scope and a more efficient machinery, by the Constitution.   The latter instrument made this central authority a government proper, but with limited and defined powers, which are supreme within their own appro-priate sphere.   In like manner, from the beginning, there has existed another political body—distinct, sovereign within its own sphere, and independent as to all the powers and objects of government not ceded or restrained under the Federal Constitution.   This body is the state— a political corporation of which each inhabitant is a subject, as he is at the same time a subject of that other political corporation known as the United States."   Curtis' Constitutional History of the United States, vol. II, p. 551.

the parts of a perfect machine, each one performing its own duties without interfering with the others, but all so necessary for the perfect working of the whole machine that if any one of them should drop out or be impaired, the entire structure would fall to pieces and its operations cease at once.

§ 148. **Adoption of Articles of Confederation.**—Prior to the adoption of the Articles of Confederation by any of the States which did so, the delegates met in a somewhat spontaneous, or voluntary, manner for the purpose of protecting the common interests of all the States during the progress of the Revolution by a central government. After the adoption by eight of the States of the Articles of Confederation in July, 1778, and until they were adopted by the State of Maryland in March, 1781, some of the States were represented under the original voluntary system and others under the Articles of Confederation.[1] During the whole period every State was exercising certain powers, which might be called sovereign, in regard to matters within its own jurisdiction, and the Continental Congress was exercising sovereign powers of the highest order for the joint benefit of all the States as a nation.

§ 149. **National unity and State independence.**—Those who believe in the nationality of the United States have

§ 148.

[1] See Curtis' Constitutional History of the United States, vol. I, chap. V, for history of Adoption of Articles of Confederation. On p. 86 the following occurs.

"The last clause of the Articles of Confederation directed that they should be submitted to the legislatures of all the states to be considered; and if approved of by them, they were advised to authorize their delegates to ratify the instrument in Congress; upon which ratification it was to become binding and conclusive. On the 20th of June, 1778, a call was made in Congress for the report of the delegations on the action of their several states, and on the 26th of the same month a form of ratification was adopted for signature. On the 9th of July the ratification was signed by the delegates of eight states: New Hampshire, Massachusetts, Rhode Island, Connecticut, New York, Pennsylvania, Virginia, and South Carolina. North Carolina ratified the Articles on the 21st of July; Georgia on the 24th; New Jersey on the 26th of November; Delaware on the 5th of May, 1779; Maryland on the 1st of March, 1781. On the 2d of March, 1781, Congress met under the Confederation." Curtis' Constitutional History, vol. I, p. 86. See also Elliot's Debates, vol. I, p. 84.

largely based their theory of the nationality and sovereignty
of the Central Government on the fact that regardless of all
paper instruments and delegated authorities, the moment the
colonies threw off their allegiance to Great Britain they became, as to common affairs, a united nation and a single people, and that this national unity was so complete that it was
vested in the Central Government with the same completeness as the sovereignty over local affairs remained vested in
the States.[1]

§ 149.

[1] VON HOLST.

Professor Von Holst, who declares in the last volume of his Constitutional History of the United States that he spent twenty-four years in the
preparation of the work, and who is, therefore, certainly so far as experience is concerned, qualified to express an opinion, says on page 2 of
volume I: "It was long before the ill-will, which the systematic disregard by parliament of the rights of the colonists had excited, triumphed
over this feeling.   Even in August and September, 1775, that is, half a
year after the battle of Lexington, so strong was the Anglo-Saxon spirit
of conservatism and loyalty among the colonists, that the few extremists
who dared to speak of a violent disruption of all bonds entailed chas-
tisement upon themselves and were universally censured.   But the eyes
of the colonists had been for some time so far opened that they hoped to
make an impression on parliament and the king only by the most energetic measures.   They considered the situation serious enough to warrant and demand that they should be prepared for any contingency.
Both of these things could evidently be accomplished in the right way
and with the requisite energy, only on condition that they should act
with their united strength.

"The difficulties in the way of this, however, were not insignificant.
The thirteen colonies had been founded in very different times and
under very different circumstances.   Their whole course of development, their political institutions, their religious views and social relations, were so divergent, the one from the other, that it was easy to
find more points of difference between them than of similarity and
comparison.   Besides, commercial intercourse between the distant colonies, in consequence of the great extent of their territory, the scantiness of the population, and the poor means of transportation at the
time, was so slight that the similarity of thought and feeling, which
can be the result only of a constant and thriving trade, was wanting.

"The solidarity of interests, and what was of greater importance at
the time, the clear perception that a solidarity of interests existed, was
therefore based mainly on the geographical situation of the colonies.
Separated by the ocean, not only from the mother country, but from
the rest of the civilized world, and placed upon a continent of yet
unmeasured bounds, on which nature had lavished every gift, it was impossible that the thought should not come to them, that they were, in-

§ 150. Treaty-making power assumed by Congress as an attribute of sovereignty.—We find, therefore, that, although

deed, called upon to found a 'new world.' They were not at first wholly conscious of this, but a powerful external shock made it soon apparent how widely and deeply this thought had shot its roots. They could not fail to have confidence in their own strength. Circumstances had long been teaching them to act on the principle 'Help thyself.' Besides, experience had shown them, long years before, that—even leaving the repeated attacks on their rights out of the question—the leading-strings by which the mother country sought to guide their steps obstructed rather than helped their development, and this in matters which affected all the colonies alike.

"Hence, from the very beginning, they considered the struggle their common cause. And even if the usurpations of parliament made themselves felt in some parts of the country much more severely than in others, the principle involved interested all to an equal extent.

"Massachusetts recommended, in 1774, the coming together of a general congress, and on September 4th, of the same year, 'the delegates nominated by the good people of these colonies,' met in Philadelphia.

"Thus, long before the colonies thought of separation from the mother country, there was formed a revolutionary body, which virtually exercised sovereign power. How far the authority of this first congress extended, according to the instructions of the delegates, it is impossible to determine with certainty at this distance of time. But it is probable that the original intention was that it should consult as to the ways and means best calculated to remove the grievances and to guaranty the rights and liberties of the colonies, and should propose to the latter a series of resolutions, furthering these objects. But the force of circumstances at the time compelled it to act and order immediately, and the people, by a consistent following of its orders, approved this transcending of their written instructions. The congress was therefore not only a revolutionary body from its origin, but its acts assumed a thoroughly revolutionary character. The people, also, by recognizing its authority, placed themselves on a revolutionary footing, and did so not as belonging to the several colonies, but as a moral person; for to the extent that congress assumed power to itself and made bold to adopt measures national in their nature, to that extent the colonists declared themselves prepared henceforth to constitute one people, inasmuch as the measures taken by congress could be translated from words into deeds only with the consent of the people. . . . Each individual colony became a state only in so far as it belonged to the United States and in so far as its population constituted a part of the people. The thirteen colonies did not, as thirteen separate and mutually independent commonwealths, enter into a compact to sever the bonds which connected them with their common mother country, and at the same time to proclaim the act in a common manifesto to the world; but the 'one people' of the united colonies dissolved that political connection with the English nation, and proclaimed themselves

Congress did not meet under the Articles of Confederation until March 2, 1781, nearly seven years after it was first organized, and up to that time possessed no treaty-making power *delegated* to it by *all* the States, it had already concluded treaties with other sovereign powers on behalf of the States, and in doing so had exercised one of the highest attributes of sovereignty in a manner, and with results, which would have been wholly illegal and inoperative if it had not possessed the highest degree of sovereignty as to matters in which all of the thirteen States had a common and national interest.[1] On February 6, 1778, Benjamin Franklin, Silas Deane and Arthur Lee, as commissioners representing the thirteen United States of North America, concluded two treaties with France, one of amity and commerce[2] and the

resolved, henceforth, to constitute the one perfectly independent people of the United States. The Declaration of Independence did not create thirteen sovereign states, but the representatives of the people declared that the former English colonies, under the name which they had assumed of the United States of America, became, from the fourth day of July, 1776, a sovereign state and a member of the family of nations, recognized by the law of nations; and further, that the people would support their representatives with their blood and treasure, in their endeavor to make this declaration a universally recognized fact. Neither congress nor the people relied in this upon any positive right belonging either to the individual colonies or to the colonies as a whole. Rather did the Declaration of Independence and the war destroy all existing political jural relations, and seek their moral justification in the right of revolution inherent in every people in extreme emergencies." Von Holst's Constitutional History of the United States, vol. 1, pp. 2–5, 6–7. In the note to pages 2–5 he refers to Story's Commentaries, decisions of the Supreme Court in *Ware* vs. *Hylton*, and in *Chisholm* vs. *Georgia*, Ramsey's History of the United States and other authorities cited in this volume. See also quotations from J. C. Bancroft Davis' notes to Miller's Lectures on the Constitution already quoted in §§ 141 and 144 and notes, pp. 244 and 252, *ante*.

§ 150.

[1] That this point was raised at the time appears by the statement in Rives' Life and Times of James Madison quoted in note under § 153, p. 264, *post*.

[2] Treaty of Amity and Commerce between the most Christian King and the thirteen United States of North America, to wit: New Hampshire, Massachusetts Bay, Rhode Island, Connecticut, New York, New Jersey, Pennsylvania, Delaware, Maryland, Virginia, North Carolina, South Carolina, and Georgia, concluded at Paris February 6, 1778; ratified by the Continental Congress May 4, 1778; ratifications exchanged at Paris July 17, 1778. U. S. Treaties and Conventions, edition 1889, p. 296; 8 U. S. St. at L. p. 12 (French and English text).

other of alliance,[3] both of which were ratified by the Continental Congress, May 4, 1778, and thereupon became binding upon all the States of the Union represented by the Continental Congress and, although the treaty of amity and commerce related in some respects to matters wholly within the jurisdiction of the separate States, the Continental Congress assumed to act for and on behalf of the State separately and collectively, and no question ever seems to have been raised as to its authority to do so.

§ 151. **Treaties with France made with States by name.** —In making these treaties the direct power of the Commissioners appointed by the Continental Congress to represent the States in their individual capacity, was evidenced by the fact that the treaties themselves recited that they were made between " the most Christian King" and the *thirteen United States of North America*, enumerating the original States by name,[1] and the treaty itself, therefore, is indisputable proof, as well as an admission of the fact, that the Continental Congress possessed the treaty-making power even prior to the adoption of the Articles of Confederation by all of the States, thus further demonstrating the proposition that in all confederations the power of negotiating and establishing relations with foreign powers necessarily rests in its fullest extent with the central government, as a matter of international law and political science resting upon general principles, and not upon the terms of any express delegation.

§ 152. **Principles established by treaties with France.** — The principle established by the negotiation and ratification of the treaties with France is very important; it cannot be brushed lightly aside as an unauthorized act or on the theory that in the turmoil and confusion of revolutionary times an assumption of power by the Continental Congress was overlooked; for, although as Justice Story says in the quotation

[3] Treaty of Alliance between the Most Christian King and the United States of North America, to wit: etc. (same as above) concluded at Paris February 6, 1778; ratified by the Continental Congress May 4, 1778; ratifica- tions exchanged at Paris July 17, 1778. U. S. Treaties and Conventions, edition 1889, p. 307; 8 U. S. St. at L. p. 6 (French and English text).

§ 151.
[1] See footnote to § 150, *ante*.

hereafter included in this chapter, *inter arma silent leges*,[1] the question of maintaining the rights of every State was foremost in the minds of all who were interested in the local governments of the States as well as in the federal or national government.   Vattel, Montesquieu, Rousseau and many other authorities were well known, and had been diligently studied by the framers of American Constitutions, both State and Federal.   Thomas Jefferson and James Madison had enriched their libraries in Virginia by the importation of books from Paris; Samuel Adams, the father of the Revolution, and John Adams, as well as James Otis, were thoroughly versed in political science, and all the proceedings of the Continental Congress were watched and discussed in every town from Boston to Georgia, so that no act could be passed, or measure enacted, which would · deprive the States of any of those rights of local self-government which they held as sacred as the great principle of independence itself.[2]

§ 153. **Advantages derived by all States under treaties with France.**—The treaty of commerce with France also clearly demonstrates the practical side of the question under discussion.   Article XI contained a provision which inured to the benefit of all the citizens of the American States by exempting them from the *droit d'aubaine*, a tax which was a burden upon all foreigners holding property in France;[1] it

§ **152.**

[1] See § 162, p. 282, *post.*

[2] It was the discussion of these points that resulted in the action of Virginia in regard to the French treaties referred to in note 2, to § 153, p. 264, *post.*

§ **153.**

[1] The full text of Article XI is as follows:

" ARTICLE XI.

"The subjects and inhabitants of the said United States, or any one of them, shall not be reputed *aubains* in France, and consequently shall be exempted from the *droit d'aubaine*, or other similar duty, under what name soever. They may by testament, donation or otherwise, dispose of their goods, movable and immovable, in favour of such persons as to them shall seem good, and their heirs, subjects of the said United States, residing whether in France or elsewhere, may succeed them *ab intestat*, without being obliged to obtain letters of naturalization, and without having the effect of this concession contested or impeded under pretext of any rights or prerogative of provinces, cities or private persons; and the said heirs, whether such by particular

is a notable fact, therefore, and one always to be remembered especially by those who are jealous of States' rights that one of the first results of the exercise of its treaty-making power, as an attribute of sovereignty by the Central Government of the United States, was to obtain a substantial benefit for the people of every State, and one which they could not have obtained in any other manner; and also that this benefit was obtained by simply giving a corresponding

title, or *ab intestat*, shall be exempt from all duty called *droit detraction*, or other duty of the same kind, saving nevertheless the local rights or duties as much and as long as similar ones are not established by the United States, or any of them. The subjects of the most Christian King shall enjoy on their part, in all the dominions of the said States, an entire and perfect reciprocity relative to the stipulations contained in the present article, but it is at the same time agreed that its contents shall not affect the laws made, or that may be made hereafter in France against emigrations which shall remain in all their force and vigour, and the United States on their part, or any of them, shall be at liberty to enact such laws, relative to that matter as to them shall seem proper." U. S. Treaties and Conventions, edition 1889, p. 299.

"The *droit d'aubaine*, a right claimed by most sovereigns of that time to confiscate to their own use the succession of an unnaturalized foreigner dying within their dominions, and which Montesquieu styled 'an absurd right,' Congress, in its plan for a treaty, asked the king of France to abandon. Article II of the Treaty of Commerce of 1778, as negotiated, complied with this request, but accompanied it with a declaration that French-

men should 'enjoy on their part, in all the dominions of the said States, an entire and perfect reciprocity relative to the stipulations contained in the present article.' The treaty of 1782 with the Netherlands (Art. VI) gave, in the place of this abandonment, the right to the Dutch foreigner residing in the United States, to dispose of his property there by testament, donation or otherwise; the right to receive the succession *ab intestato*, in case there was no will; and the right for a guardian or tutor to a minor, to act in his behalf in receiving, keeping, and alienating his property. This precedent was followed in the Treaty of 1783 with Sweden (Art. VI), and in the Treaty of 1785 with Prussia (Art. X).

"In many other respects these several treaties, made before the adoption of the Constitution, and largely upon the suggestions in the plan of Congress which was promulgated before the Articles of Confederation were adopted, secured the assent of the contracting parties to important principles, some of which were not then universally recognized as constituting part of the public law which could govern the intercourse of nations with each other." Davis' Notes to Lecture 1, Miller on the Constitution, pp. 50–51.

concession in return therefor, and exempting citizens of France from similar burdens, if any existed, in this country; this exemption could not have been given effectually by the States themselves, as they could not exercise the treaty-making power. At the outset, therefore, there was a practical exhibition of the great benefits to be derived from vesting the treaty-making power in the Central Government and admitting it to have as far-reaching an extent as possible.[2]

[2] The State of Virginia took a peculiar but effective method of endorsing the action of Congress in ratifying the Treaties with France. It can best be described by quoting from an eminent Virginian an account of the proceedings. "The day after · Mr. Jefferson's election, a resolution of an unusual and anomalous character was adopted by the legislature of Virginia. It served, however, to evince her earnest attachment to the common cause, and a strong determination to defeat the machinations of its adversaries, whether foreign or domestic. In the insidious efforts made, during the last year, to regain for England her lost American empire, it was frequently insinuated by the royal commissioners that the ratification of the French alliance by Congress was not binding upon the national faith, as the articles of confederation, which gave to that body authority to conclude treaties with foreign powers, had not received the confirmation of *all* the states, which was made necessary to their validity. Maryland had not yet given her signature to them; whereby the compact remained without *full binding* force upon any of the parties.

"It was in this state of things that Virginia, with the view of cutting off pernicious intrigues, whether from within or without, to detach her from the French alliance, or to seduce any portion of her people by the dangerous and delusive project of a separate arrangement with the enemy, which the terms of the alliance expressly forbade, determined to silence at once all cavils as to the obligation of the treaty, so far as she was concerned, by a formal ratification of it by her own act and in her own name. Accordingly, on the 2d day of June, 1779, a resolution was passed by the legislature, *nemine contradicente,* declaring that 'the treaties of alliance and commerce between His Most Christian Majesty of France on the one part, and the Congress of the United States of America on the other part, ought to be ratified and confirmed, so far as in the power of this Commonwealth, and the same are hereby ratified, confirmed, and declared binding on this Commonwealth.' The governor was, at the same time, requested 'to notify the Minister of His Most Christian Majesty, resident at Philadelphia, the above ratification under the Seal of the Commonwealth.' (Journal of House of Delegates, May Session, 1779, p. 32). This proceeding,—doubtless an irregularity in a diplomatic and political sense,—stands redeemed to every ingenuous mind by the loyal motives of national honor and inflexible patriotism which dictated it." History of the

§ 154. **Treaties with France concluded prior to final ratification of Articles of Confederation.**—Although the Articles of Confederation had not been ratified by all the States when the treaties with France were concluded, they had been framed and submitted to all the States for adoption and had been ratified by some of the States; the necessity for vesting the treaty-making power in the Central Government had been recognized by the delegates who had been entrusted with the preparation of that instrument; the Articles were drawn in the full spirit of State sovereignty, the first and second articles expressly providing that each State should retain its sovereignty and continue to exercise every power not expressly delegated to the Congress; the necessity of not only vesting the treaty-making power exclusively in the Central Government, but also of excluding the separate States from any participation therein was evidenced by the provisions of Article VI under which the States surrendered the right to send or receive Ambassadors or to enter into any conferences, agreements or treaties of any kind with any other power or with each other except upon the consent of Congress.[1]

Life and Times of James Madison by William C. Rives, Boston, 1859, vol. 1, pp. 203–205.

§ **154.**

[1] Number VI of the Articles of Confederation was as follows:

"No State, without the consent of the United States in Congress assembled, shall send any embassy to, or receive any embassy from, or enter into any conference, agreement, alliance or treaty with any king, prince, or state; nor shall any person holding any office of profit or trust under the United States, or any of them, accept of any present, emolument, office, or title of any kind whatever from any king, prince, or foreign state; nor shall the United States in Congress assembled, or any of them, grant any title of nobility.

"No two or more states shall enter into any treaty, confederation, or alliance whatever between them, without the consent of the United States in Congress assembled, specifying accurately the purposes for which the same is to be entered into, and how long it shall continue. No state shall lay any imposts or duties which may interfere with any stipulations in treaties entered into by the United States in Congress assembled, with any king, prince, or state, in pursuance of any treaties already proposed by Congress to the courts of France and Spain.   . . ." (The remainder of this section restricts the states from engaging in warfare, except in case of attack, invasion, or imminent danger not admitting of delay.)

The first clause of Number IX

§ 155. **Great extent of treaty-making power of Congress fully appreciated by States.**—Congress was also clothed with the sole and exclusive power of sending and receiving ambassadors, and of entering into treaties and alliances, with the exception of such commercial treaties as restrained the States from imposing similar imposts and duties on foreigners as were imposed on their own people, or from prohibiting exports and imports;[1] this reservation of customs regulations to the States was one of the chief causes for the ultimate abandonment of the Articles of Confederation and the adoption of the Constitution in which broader powers were vested in the Central Government, as to the regulation of commerce, and no limitations were expressly placed on the treaty-making power. The Articles of Confederation, and the powers therein contained as to treaty-making, were ratified by some of the States, after full notice that Congress had determined that its rights under the treaty-making power extended to internal affairs of the different States whenever the general good of the Union depended upon the establishment of mutual and reciprocal agreements with foreign powers; although the regulation of their domestic affairs had been reserved to the States by the Articles of Confederation, the treaties with France and the treaties which were negotiated with other powers by Congress under the Confederation, uniformly asserted the nationality of the Government of the United States not only as to its dealings with foreign powers, but as to its relations with the several States.[2]

§ 156. **Other treaties made by Congress.**—Speaking of other treaties made by Congress under the general powers

of the Articles of Confederation contained the following provision: "The United States in Congress assembled shall have the sole and exclusive right and power . . . of sending and receiving ambassadors; entering into treaties and alliances, provided that no treaty of commerce shall be made whereby the legislative power of the respective States shall be restrained from imposing such imposts and duties on foreigners as their own people are subjected to, or from prohibiting the exportation or importation of any species of goods or commodities whatsoever. . . ."

§ 155.

[1] See notes to § 154, p. 265, *ante*.

[2] See extracts from Miller's Lectures on the Constitution, already cited, and to be cited under the next and other sections of this chapter.

possessed and delegated to it, Mr. Davis says, in the same notes from which we have previously cited:

"The favored nation clause put Prussia on the best footing in the ports of Charleston, Boston, Philadelphia and New York, no matter what the Legislatures of South Carolina, Massachusetts, Pennsylvania, or New York might say. Aliens were permitted to hold personal property and dispose of it by testament, donation, or otherwise, and the exaction of State dues in excess of those exacted from citizens of the State in like cases were forbidden. The right was secured to aliens to frequent the coasts of each and all the States, and to reside and trade there. Resident aliens were assured against State legislation to prevent the exercise of liberty of conscience and the performance of religious worship; and when dying, they were guaranteed the right of decent burial and undisturbed rest for their bodies." [1]

From 1782 until the government was re-organized under the Constitution in 1789, the Articles of Confederation were the sole written authority for congressional action; during that period treaties were made by plenipotentiaries appointed by Congress with France, Great Britain, The Netherlands, Sweden and Morocco, by all of which matters otherwise wholly within State jurisdiction were seriously affected; [2] these treaties were ratified in Congress by the requisite number of States, and, as was afterwards held by the Supreme Court, modified the State laws wherever they conflicted therewith, without any further action by the States themselves, and were paramount to the adverse legislation by which some of the States endeavored to defeat the object of the treaties. [3] During the last years of the Confederation the question of the paramountcy of treaties was discussed in the Congress, and John Jay, then Secretary of Foreign Affairs, submitted an elaborate report in regard thereto,

§ 156.

[1] Miller's Lectures on the Constitution; J. C. Bancroft Davis' Notes to Lecture I, p. 53. See also quotation from Curtis' Constitutional History of United States under § 160, p. 280, *post*.

[2] See list of these treaties in notes under § 160, p. 278, *post*.

[3] See decisions cited in chap. XI, §§ 324 *et seq.*, Vol. II, pp. 6, *et seq.*

some extracts from which are quoted in the notes to this section.[4]

§ 157. Names of States recited in preambles of treaties.

—In some of the treaties above enumerated the recital clauses contain the names of the separate States, with the statement that the Commissioners represented them; in all instances, however, the Commissioners were appointed solely by the Continental Congress, and in no instance did they hold their commissions from any of the States;[1] the principle was thus

§ 157.
[1] See captions of treaties in notes under § 150, p. 261, *ante*, and § 160, p. 278, *post*.

[4] SECRETARY JOHN JAY'S REPORT.

The report of John Jay, Secretary of Foreign Affairs of the Confederation, is dated October 13, 1786. It occupies pages 185 to 287 of volume IV of the Secret Journals of Congress (edition of 1821, published under resolutions of Congress, March, 1818, and February, 1820).

It commences: "The secretary of the United States for the department of foreign affairs, to whom was referred a letter of the 4th March last, from the honourable John Adams, esquire, together with the papers that accompanied it, reports,

"That as the subject of these papers and of this report appears to your secretary in a very important point of light, he thinks they should be so incorporated as that the record of the latter in this office may always exhibit an entire and complete view of the whole business. He therefore reports, ..."

Then follows a Memorial which John Adams, who was then Minister from the United States to England, had presented to the British Ministry, asking for the evacuation by British troops of the western forts of the United States, pursuant to the treaty of peace, and the answer received by Mr. Adams, in which exception was taken to the failure of the United States to comply with Article IV of the same treaty, which "stipulates, that creditors on either side shall meet with no lawful impediment to the recovery of the full value in sterling money, of all *bona fide* debts heretofore contracted."

The Minister of Foreign Affairs (Lord Carmarthen) concluded his note as follows (pp. 188–189):

"The little attention paid to the fulfilling this engagement on the part of the subjects of the United States in general, and the direct breach of it in many particular instances, have already reduced many of the king's subjects to the utmost degree of difficulty and distress; nor have their applications for redress, to those whose situations in America naturally pointed them out as the guardians of publick faith, been as yet successful in obtaining them that justice to which, on every principle of law as well as of humanity, they were clearly and indisputably entitled.

established that the Central Government acted as the agent

"The engagements entered into by treaty ought to be mutual and equally binding on the respective contracting parties. It would therefore be the height of folly as well as injustice, to suppose one party alone obliged to a strict observance of the publick faith, while the other might remain free to deviate from its own engagements, as often as convenience might render such deviation necessary, though at the expense of its own national credit and importance.

"I flatter myself, however, sir, that justice will speedily be done to British creditors; and I can assure you, sir, that whenever America shall manifest a real determination to fulfil her part of the treaty, Great Britain will not hesitate to prove her sincerity to co-operate in whatever points depend upon her for carrying every article of it into real and complete effect.

"The enclosed paper contains a state of the grievances complained of by merchants and other British subjects having estates, property and debts due to them in the several states of America.   I am, sir, your most obedient, humble servant,   CARMARTHEN.

"John Adams, Esq., etc."

The "state of grievances" contained in Lord Carmarthen's note was a detailed enumeration of acts passed by the legislatures of the several States interfering with, or creating impediments to, the recovery of debts; laws passed by Massachusetts, New York, Pennsylvania, Virginia, Maryland, North Carolina, South Carolina, Georgia, were set forth in the order named and the points in them which "impeded" the collection of debts were specified in detail (pages 189–203).

Continuing his report the secretary says (pages 203–205):

"On considering the before recited papers, these important questions present themselves:

"1. Whether any individual state has a right, by acts of their own internal legislature, to explain and decide the sense and meaning in which any particular article of a national treaty shall be received and understood within the limits of that state ?

"2. Whether any and which of the acts enumerated in the list of grievances do violate the treaty of peace between the United States and Great Britain ?

"3. In case they or any of them should be found to violate it, what measures should be adopted in relation to Great Britain ?   And

"4. What measures should be adopted in relation to the state or states which passed the exceptionable acts ?

"Of these in their order; and

"1. Of the right of an individual state to enact in what sense a national treaty shall be understood within its particular limits.

"Your secretary considers the thirteen independent sovereign states as having, by express delegation of power, formed and vested in Congress a perfect though limited sovereignty for the general and national purposes specified in the confederation.   In this sovereignty they cannot severally participate (except by their delegates) or have concurrent

of the separate States, so far as foreign relations were con-

jurisdiction; for the ninth article of the confederation most expressly conveys to Congress the sole and *exclusive* right and power of determining on war and p*eace*, and of entering into treaties and alliances, etc.

" When therefore a treaty is constitutionally made, ratified and published by Congress, it immediately becomes binding on the whole nation, and superadded to the laws of the land, without the intervention, consent or fiat of state legislatures. It derives its obligation from its being a compact between the sovereign of this, and the sovereign of another nation; but laws or statutes derive their force from being acts of a legislature competent to the passing of them. Hence it is clear, that treaties must be implicitly received and observed by every member of the nation; for as state legislatures are not competent to the making of such compacts or treaties, so neither are they competent, in that capacity, authoritatively to decide on or ascertain the construction and sense of them. When doubts arise respecting the construction of state laws, it is common and proper for the state legislatures by explanatory or declaratory acts to remove those doubts; but when doubts arise respecting the construction of a treaty, they are so far from being cognizable by a state legislature, that Congress itself has no authority to settle and determine them. For as the legislature only, which constitutionally passes a law, has power to revise and amend it, so the sovereigns only, who are parties to the treaty, have power by posterior articles and mutual consent to correct or explain it.

" All doubts, in cases between private individuals, respecting the meaning of a treaty, like all doubts respecting the meaning of a law, are in the first instance mere judicial questions; and are to be heard and decided in the courts of justice having cognizance of the causes in which they arise, and whose duty it is to determine them according to the rules and maxims established by the laws of nations for the interpretation of treaties.

" If this reasoning and these principles be right, as your secretary thinks they are, it follows of consequence that no individual state has a right by legislative acts to decide and point out the sense in which their particular citizens and courts shall understand this or that article of a treaty. A contrary doctrine would not only militate against the common and received principles and ideas relative to this subject, but would prove as ridiculous in practice, as it appears irrational in theory; for in that case, the same article of the same treaty may by law mean one thing in New Hampshire, another in New York, and neither the one nor the other in Georgia.

" It would be foreign to the object of this report to inquire how far such legislative acts are valid and obligatory even within the limits of the state passing them. Much might be said on that head; certain, however, it is, that they cannot bind either of the contracting sovereigns, and consequently cannot bind their respective nations.

" 2. Whether any and which of the acts mentioned in the list of grievances do violate the treaty with Great Britain? "

cerned, thus demonstrating that, wherever sovereignty does

The report then proceeds to discuss the effect of Articles IV, V and VI of the treaty. The relative rights of the Central Government and the States are referred to on pages 208–210 as follows:

"But admitting that the United States had a right to extinguish, remit or confiscate debts due from their citizens to British subjects, it still remains to be *required* whether, and in what manner, and by what acts they exercised that right? For if they did not exercise this right at all, then it will follow that these debts were neither extinguished, remitted nor confiscated, and consequently, that the article cannot be considered as *restoratory;* nothing being more clear than that restoration always implies previous deprivation.

"Here a very important question presents itself, viz. Whether the state legislatures can derive a right, from the existence of war between their sovereign and a foreign one, to extinguish, remit or confiscate, by their acts, debts due from their citizens to the subjects of that foreign sovereign?

"The rights to make war, to make peace, and to make treaties, appertaining *exclusively* to the national sovereign, that is, to Congress, your secretary is of opinion that the thirteen state legislatures have no more authority to exercise the powers, or pass acts of sovereignty on those points, than any thirteen individual citizens. To execute the laws, or exercise the rights of war against a national enemy, belongs only to the national sovereign, or to those to whom the national sovereign may constitutionally delegate such authority. So that whatever right each state, individually considered, may have to sequester or confiscate the property of their own proper citizens, yet with respect to the common enemy of the nation, they can separately do no act of national sovereignty; for surely a thirteenth part of a nation can with no propriety assume a power of doing national acts proper only to the national sovereign. However recent may be the date of the confederation, yet a union founded in compact, and vesting the rights of war and peace in Congress, preceded it; and your secretary is exceedingly mistaken if there ever was a period since the year 1775, to this day, when either of the then colonies, now states, were in capacity to pass state laws for sequestering or confiscating the debts or property of a national enemy. It was then, and afterwards, by virtue of national commissions, that the enemy's property on the sea was liable to be captured and confiscated; and equal authority was necessary to justify the confiscation of their property found on the land. Whatever state acts therefore may have been passed during the war, exercising rights accruing to the sovereign from the laws of nations respecting war, they cannot, in the opinion of your secretary, be obligatory on either of the belligerent sovereigns, and consequently not on any of their respective citizens or subjects.

"Your secretary would not have it inferred from these remarks, that the states have passed *general* laws for confiscating British debts due from their citizens. His design in these remarks is to obviate any argu-

reside, the National Government exercises it for all the

ments that might be drawn from certain other acts less general and direct, but in his opinion equally improper, such for instance as those whereby certain British subjects were declared traitors, and whereby, as a consequence of treason, the debts due to them became payable to the state to which those British subjects were declared to be traitors; for such laws, however absurd, do exist.   There are also certain other laws authorizing the payment of debts due to certain individuals to be made at the state treasury in paper money," etc.,

The report then takes up the acts of the state legislatures referred to in Lord Carmarthen's note; pages 213–274 are devoted to an examination of many acts and resolutions with the opinion of the Secretary expressed separately as to each, in some cases to the effect that the act is not a violation of the treaty, and in other cases that it is; on pages 274–275, referring to an exceedingly drastic act of the New York legislature, he says:

" This intemperate act was passed after the treaty had been ratified by both nations, and most clearly violates the sixth article in various respects too obvious and decided to require enumeration or discussion.

" Your secretary has reason to believe that there are some other acts not particularized in the list of grievances, which, on being compared with the treaty, would appear in some respects inconsistent with it; but as the principles applied by this report to the other acts, will also apply to all of the like kind, he thinks the investigation may here be concluded with propriety.

" From the aforegoing review of the several acts complained of, it is manifest, that the fourth and sixth articles of the treaty have been violated by certain of them.

" The next inquiry in order seems to be, Whether these violations can be justified or excused by any prior ones on the part of Britain ?

" There is no doubt but that Britain has violated the seventh article, which provides 'that his Britannick majesty shall with all convenient speed, and without causing any destruction, or carrying away any negroes, or other property of the American inhabitants, withdraw all his armies, garrisons and fleets from the said United States, and from every post, place and harbour within the same.'

" The violations of this article alluded to, are these, viz.

" 1. That on the evacuation of New York, negroes belonging to American inhabitants were carried away.

" 2. That his Britannick majesty's garrisons have not been withdrawn from, but still keep possession of certain posts and places within the United States.

" With respect to the negroes, it may be proper to distinguish them into *three* classes.

" 1. Such as in the course of the war were captured and disposed of as booty by the enemy.

" 2. Such as remained with and belonged to American inhabitants within the British lines.

States as a national unit, either in its own right, or as agent

"3. Such as, confiding in proclamations and promises of freedom and protection, fled from their masters without, and were received and protected within, the British camps and lines.

"The stipulation, 'not to carry away any negroes or other property of the American inhabitants,' cannot in the opinion of your secretary be construed to extend to, and comprehend the *first* class. By the laws of war all goods and chattels captured and made booty *flagrante bello*, become the property of the captors. Whether men can be so degraded as under any circumstances to be with propriety denominated goods and chattels, and under that idea capable of becoming booty, is a question on which opinions are unfortunately various, even in countries professing christianity and respect for the rights of mankind. Certain it is that our laws assert, and Britain by this article as well as by her practice admits, that man may have property in man. If so, it is fair reasoning to conclude that this like other movable property is capable of changing owners by capture in war. The article places 'negroes and other property of the American inhabitants' on the same footing; so that if it means that captured negroes shall not be carried away, it must also mean that no other captured property shall be carried away, which would in other words amount to an agreement that the British fleet and army should leave behind all the booty then in this country, which they had taken from American inhabitants at any period of the war. It would be a task beyond the abilities of your secretary to raise such a construction of the article on any principles capable of supporting it."

The Secretary then shows that although the violations of Great Britain were continuous, the enforcement of the state laws were also continuous and after saying that there had been violations of the treaty justly chargeable to both parties he refers to the legislative acts and says (pages 280 -283):

"All these acts were in force on and long after the day of the date of the treaty, viz. 3d September, 1783.

"In whatever light, therefore, deviations from the treaty prior to its final conclusion and ratification may be viewed, it is certain that deviations on our part preceded any on the part of Britain; and therefore instead of being justified *by* them, afforded excuse *to* them.

"As to the detention of our posts, your secretary thinks that Britain was not bound to surrender them until we had ratified the treaty. Congress ratified it 14th January, 1784, and Britain on the 9th April following. From that time to this, the fourth and fifth articles of the treaty have been constantly violated on our part by legislative acts then and still existing and operating.

"Under such circumstances, it is not a matter of surprise to your secretary that the posts are detained; nor in his opinion would Britain be to blame in continuing to hold them until America shall cease to impede her enjoying every essential right secured to her, and her people and adherents, by the treaty.

"Your secretary has heard another reason or excuse assigned to jus-

18

for all the States collectively, if not in their individual capacities.

tify deviating from the fourth article, and restraining British creditors in the recovery of their debts, viz. that by giving time to the debtor, he became more able to pay the debt; and as that additional ability was a benefit to the creditor, the latter ought not to complain of the restraint which produced it.

"Although this argument may be somewhat ingenious, it unfortunately proves too much. By the treaty a British creditor has a right to sue when he pleases; and by the common law a farmer has a right to plough when he pleases, a merchant to send out his vessels when he pleases, and every man to eat and drink when he pleases.

"Admit that a British creditor would do better to delay his suits, that a farmer was about to plough in an improper manner or season, that a merchant had ordered his vessels to sea when a hurricane was expected, or that a certain gentleman injured his health by intemperance; admit these facts; would it thence follow that every or any good natured officious man, who might think himself more judicious and prudent, has a right to hinder the creditor from suing, the farmer from ploughing, the merchant from despatching his vessels, or the *bonvivant* from indulging his appetite ? Surely not.

"In short, as your secretary is uninformed of any facts or matters that can justify the violations on our part, the only question which seems to remain to be considered is, What is to be done ?

"The United States in Congress assembled have neither committed, nor approved, of any violation of the treaty. To their conduct no exceptions are taken; but to their justice an appeal is made relative to the conduct of particular states. The United States must, however, eventually answer for the conduct of their respective members; and for that, and other reasons suggested by the nature of their sovereignty and the articles of confederation, your secretary thinks they have good right to insist and require that national faith and national treaties be kept and observed throughout the union; for otherwise it would be in the power of a particular state, by injuries and infractions of treaties, to involve the whole confederacy in difficulties and war.

"In his opinion it would highly become the dignity of the United States to act on such occasions with the most scrupulous regard to justice and candour towards the injured nation, and with equal moderation and decision towards the delinquent state or states.

"In the present case he thinks it would be proper to resolve,

"1. That the legislatures of the several states cannot of right pass any act or acts for interpreting, explaining or construing a national treaty, or any part or clause of it; nor for restraining, limiting or in any manner impeding, retarding or counteracting the operation or execution of the same; for that on being constitutionally made, ratified and published, they become, in virtue of the confederation, part of the law of the land, and are not only independent of the will and power of such legislatures, but also binding and obligatory on them.

274

§ 158. **Treaty of peace with Great Britain.**—The preliminary Articles of Peace[1] concluded between the United States

"2. That all *such* acts or parts of acts as may be now existing in either of the states, repugnant to the treaty of peace, ought to be forthwith repealed; as well to prevent their continuing to operate as violations of that treaty, as to avoid the disagreeable necessity there might otherwise be of raising and discussing questions touching their validity and obligation.

"3. That it be recommended to the several states, to make such repeal rather by describing than reciting the said acts; and for that purpose to pass an act, declaring in general terms, that all such acts and parts of acts repugnant to the treaty of peace between the United States and his Britannick majesty, or any article thereof, shall be and thereby are repealed; and that the courts of law and equity in all causes and questions cognizable by them respectively, and arising from or touching the said treaty, shall decide and adjudge according to the true intent and meaning of the same, anything in the said acts or parts of acts to the contrary thereof in any wise notwithstanding."

The Secretary concludes his report as follows (page 286-287):

"Although strict justice requires that they who have wrongfully suffered should as far as possible receive retribution and compensation, yet as it would be very difficult, if practicable, to prevail on the states to adopt such a measure, he thinks it best to be silent about it, especially as the United States have neither the power nor the means of doing it without their concurrence.

"Besides, as the detention of the posts has been and continues injurious to the United States, the consequences of their respective violations may be set against each other; and although the account may not be exactly balanced, yet it cannot be well expected that in affairs of such magnitude, the same regard can be had to minutiæ as in transactions between individuals.

"This report is on a subject no less new and singular than important. Your secretary is not conscious of any errors in it; and yet there may be some. He hopes the facts are not mistaken or misstated. He believes his reasoning on them to be just; and he flatters himself whatever mistakes relative to either may be discovered, that they will be treated with candour, and ascribed neither to want of attention, nor of care, but to that fallibility, from which few, if any, even of the wisest and most able, are wholly exempt."

§ 158.

[1] Provisional Articles agreed upon, by and between Richard Oswald, Esquire, the Commissioner of his Britannic Majesty, for Treating of Peace with the Commissioners of the United States of America, in behalf of his said Majesty on the one part, and John Adams, Benjamin Franklin, John Jay and Henry Laurens, four of the Commissioners of the said States for Treating of Peace with the Commissioner of His said Majesty, on their behalf, on the other part. To be inserted in, and to constitute the Treaty of Peace proposed to be concluded between the Crown of Great Britain and the said United States; but which Treaty is not to be concluded

and Great Britain, September 3, 1783, which afterwards became the Definitive Treaty of Peace,[2] was the first treaty which was made directly in the name of the United States, although Article I, in which the independence of the States is recognized, enumerates them by name.[3] This treaty although made under the Confederation was subsequently assumed (as were all other then existing treaties) by the Constitution and thus became the supreme law of the land. As such it was the basis for the declaration by the Supreme Court, that State statutes which were repugnant to treaty stipulations were absolutely void, pursuant to Article VI of the Constitution, that all treaties made, or which should be made, under the authority of the United States should be binding upon the judges of all the courts, anything in the laws or Constitution of any of the States to the contrary notwithstanding. Article IV of both treaties provided that cred-

until terms of a Peace shall be agreed upon between Great Britain and France and His Britannic Majesty shall be ready to conclude such Treaty accordingly. Concluded at Paris, November 30, 1782. Proclamation ordered by the Continental Congress, April 11, 1783, U. S. Treaties and Conventions edition, 1889, p. 370; 8 U. S. St. at L. p. 54.

[2] Definitive Treaty of Peace; concluded September 3, 1783; ratified by the Continental Congress January 14, 1784; proclaimed January 14, 1784; U. S. Treaties and Convention edition, 1889, p. 375; 8 U. S. St. at L. p. 80; Compilation of Treaties in Force, 1899, p. 200.

[3] Articles I and II of the Provisional Articles and of the Definitive Treaty, are as follows: "His Britannic Majesty acknowledges the said United States, viz. New Hampshire, Massachusetts Bay, Rhode Island, and Providence Plantations, Connecticut, New York, New Jersey, Pennsylvania, Delaware, Maryland, Virginia, North Carolina, South Carolina, and Georgia, to be

free, sovereign and independent States; that he treats with them as such, and for himself, his heirs and successors, relinquishes all claims to the Government, propriety and territorial rights of the same, and every part thereof.

"Article II. And that all disputes which might arise in future, on the subject of the boundaries of the said United States may be prevented, it is hereby agreed and declared, that the following are, and shall be the boundaries, viz:" (The boundaries then follow of the entire country and not of each state separately; the outside boundaries include territory in what was then the northwestern corner of the country, which was outside of the boundaries of any of the States under the most extensive claims which any one of them could put forward.) U. S. Treaties and Conventions, edition, 1889, pp. 375, 376; 8 U. S. Stat. at L. pp. 54-55 and pp. 80-81; Compilation of Treaties in Force 1899, p. 200.

itors on either side should meet with no lawful impediment to the recovery of full value in sterling money of all *bona fide* debts theretofore contracted;[4] in the great case of *Ware* v. *Hylton*, which will be referred to hereafter, this clause, although in conflict with confiscation acts of various States was held to be binding upon the State courts, and was to be considered as paramount to all conflicting State laws which were pleaded in bar by American debtors in actions brought by British creditors to recover confiscated debts.[5]

§ 159. **Special provisions of Article V.**—Article V.[1] stipulated that Congress should earnestly recommend to the Legislatures of the several States to provide for the restitution of all confiscated estates belonging to British subjects and also of estates and property of persons resident in the dis-

---

[4] Article IV, as quoted in footnote, is identical in both treaties, so that articles referred to may be of either treaty, but the Definitive Treaty is generally referred to as that became the final basis of the relations between the United States and Great Britain after January 14, 1784. Article IV is quoted at length as a note to § 159.

[5] *Ware* vs. *Hylton*, U. S. Supreme Ct. 1796, 3 Dallas, 199, and see full reference to this and other cases involving same point in §§ 324 *et seq.* and notes Vol. II, pp. 6, *et seq.*

§ 159.

[1] Articles IV. and V. of the Provisional Articles, and of the Definitive Treaty of Peace were as follows:

" Article IV.—It is agreed that creditors on either side shall meet with no lawful impediment to the recovery of the full value in sterling money of all *bona fide* debts heretofore contracted.

"Article V.—It is agreed that the Congress shall earnestly recommend it to the legislatures of the respective States to provide for the restitution of all estates, rights and properties which have been confiscated, belonging to real British subjects, and also of the estates, rights and properties of persons resident in districts in the possession of His Majesty's arms, and who have not borne arms against the said United States: And that persons of any other description shall have free liberty to go to any part or parts of any of the thirteen United States, and therein to remain twelve months, unmolested in their endeavours to obtain the restitution of such of their estates, rights and properties as may have been confiscated: And that Congress shall also earnestly recommend to the several States a reconsideration and revision of all acts or laws regarding the premises, so as to render the said laws or acts perfectly consistent, not only with justice and equity, but with that spirit of conciliation which, on the return of the blessings of peace, should universally prevail: And that Congress shall also earnestly recommend to the several States that the estates, rights and properties of such last-mentioned persons,

tricts in possession of His Majesty's arms who had not borne arms against the United States. It was also agreed that other legislation consistent with justice and equity and the spirit of conciliation, which should universally prevail on the return of the blessings of peace, should be recommended earnestly to the several States. This clause was inserted because at that time some of the States which had confiscated property were in actual possession and ownership of the same; as a matter of fact, however, the laws regarding confiscation of property referred to in Article V are no more within the exclusive province of State legislation than were the laws affecting the rights of creditors for the recovery of money, which were provided for by the absolute stipulations in Article IV. It would have been equally within the scope of the treaty-making power to have made the stipulations as absolute in those respects as in the others had the commissioners plenipotentiary seen fit to do so.[2]

§ 160. **Other treaties made by Congress under confederation again referred to.**—In 1782 John Adams, on behalf of the United States, concluded a treaty of amity and commerce with the States-General of the United Netherlands, which was ratified by the Continental Congress, January 23, 1783, and which contained a clause regulating testamentary provisions, which are always under State control, so far as they affect property within the State.[1] He also negotiated another treaty relating to captured vessels.[2]

shall be restored to them, they refunding to any persons who may be now in possession the *bona fide* price (where any has been given) which such persons may have paid on purchasing any of the said lands, rights or properties since the confiscation. And it is agreed, that all persons who have any interests in confiscated lands, either by debts, marriage settlements or otherwise, shall meet with no lawful impediment in the prosecution of their just rights." For the broad construction placed on this

recommendation see **Mr.** Justice Washington's charge in *Gordon* vs. *Kerr*, 1 Wash. C. C. 322, and referred to in § 354, Vol. II, p. 46.

[2] Note 266 *et seq. post*, and especially Professor Pomeroy's views as stated in § 270 *post*.

§ 160.

[1] Treaty of Amity and Commerce between the United States and the States-General of the United Netherlands, concluded at The Hague, October 8, 1782; ratified by the Continental Congress, and proclaimed January 23, 1783. United

[2] For note 2, see p. 279.

In April, 1783, Benjamin Franklin concluded a treaty of amity and commerce with the King of Sweden, containing provisions in regard to the disposition of property similar to those in the treaty with France.[3]

In 1785 Benjamin Franklin, John Adams and Thomas Jefferson concluded a treaty of amity and commerce with the King of Prussia, which contained provisions for the disposition of personal property;[4] this treaty is remarkable as containing the first enunciation of the policy of the United States that private and unoffending property on the sea should be free from capture during war.[5]

States Treaties (ed. 1889), p. 749; 8 U. S. Stat. at L. p. 32 (English and Dutch text).

[2] This convention was concluded, ratified and proclaimed at the same time. United States Treaties (ed. 1889), p. 759; 8 U. S. Stat. at L. p. 50 (English and Dutch text).

[3] Treaty of Amity and Commerce, concluded at Paris, April 3, 1783, between the King of Sweden and the thirteen United States of America; ratified by the Continental Congress July 29, 1783, proclaimed September 25, 1783, United States Treaties (ed. 1889), p. 1042; 8 U. S. Stat. at L. p. 60 (English and French text).

[4] Treaty of Amity and Commerce between His Majesty the King of Prussia and the United States of America; (the plenipotentiaries signed separately at different places and at different dates during July, August, September, 1785) ratified by the Continental Congress, May 17, 1786; exchanged at The Hague, October, 1786, U. S. Treaties and Conventions (ed. 1889), p. 899; 8 U. S. Stat. at L. p. 84 (English and French text).

[5] " ARTICLE XXIII.

" If war should arise between the two contracting parties, the mer-chants of either country then residing in the other shall be allowed to remain nine months to collect their debts and settle their affairs, and may depart freely, carrying off all their effects without molestation or hindrance. And all women and children, scholars of every faculty, cultivators of the earth, artizans, manufacturers, and fishermen, unarmed and inhabiting unfortified towns, villages, or places, and in general all others whose occupations are for the common subsistence and benefit of mankind, shall be allowed to continue their respective employments, and shall not be molested in their persons, nor shall their houses or goods be burnt or otherwise destroyed, nor their fields wasted by the armed force of the enemy, into whose power by the events of war they may happen to fall; but if anything is necessary to be taken from them for the use of such armed force, the same shall be paid for at a reasonable price. And all merchant and trading vessels employed in exchanging the products of different places, and thereby rendering the necessaries, conveniences, and comforts of human life more easy to be obtained, and more general, shall be allowed to pass free

In 1787 John Adams and Thomas Jefferson concluded a treaty of peace and friendship with the Emperor of Morocco.[6]

The commercial relations of the United States in 1783 are summarized by Mr. Curtis in the quotation in the notes to this section.[7] It does not appear that any other treaties than

and unmolested; and neither of the contracting Powers shall grant or issue any commission to any private armed vessels, empowering them to take or destroy such trading vessels or interrupt such commerce."

For the author's views on this subject and history of the American position in regard thereto, see document on Freedom of Private Property on the Sea from Capture During War, prepared for the State Department by Charles Henry Butler, and transmitted to the Peace Conference at The Hague, during its sessions in June, 1899.

[6] Treaty of Peace and Friendship between the United States and the Emperor of Morocco, concluded January, 1787; ratified by the Continental Congress July 18, 1787. United States Treaties (ed. 1889), p. 724; 8 U. S. Stat. at L. 100.

[7] "The actual commercial relations of the United States with other countries, when the peace took place, were confined to treaties of amity and commerce with France, Sweden, and the Netherlands; the two latter transcending, in some degree, the powers of the Confederation. In 1776 the Revolutionary Congress had adopted a plan of treaties to be proposed to France and Spain, which contemplated that the subjects of each country should pay no duties in the other except such as were paid by natives, and should have the same rights and privileges as natives in respect to navigation and com-

merce. When a treaty of amity and commerce came to be concluded with France, in 1778, the footing on which the subjects of the two countries were placed, in the dominions of each other, was that of the most favored nations, instead of that of natives. The Articles of Confederation, proposed in 1777, and finally ratified in March, 1781, reserved to the states the right of levying duties and imposts, excepting only such as would interfere with any treaties that might be made 'pursuant to the treaties proposed to France and Spain.' The United States could, therefore, constitutionally complete these two treaties, and such as were dependent upon them, but no others which should have the effect of restraining the legislatures of the states from prohibiting the exportation or importation of any species of goods or merchandise, or laying whatever duties or imposts they thought proper.

"In 1782, negotiations were entered into for a similar treaty with the States-General of the Netherlands. When the instructions to Mr. Adams to negotiate this treaty were under consideration in Congress, it was recollected that the French treaty contained a stipulation the effect of which would enable the heirs of the subjects of either party, dying in the territories of the other, to inherit real property, without obtaining letters of naturalization. The doubt suggested itself—as it well might—

those above enumerated were concluded prior to the adoption of the Constitution, with the possible exception of a consular convention with France and some agreements with Indian tribes. In regard to this class of treaties, it is proper to note, at this point, although it will be the subject of more extended reference in a subsequent chapter, that treaties made by the Central Government with Indians frequently affected property situated wholly within a *single* State, and in the decisions hereafter quoted it will be found that the courts, both State and Federal, have sustained the treaty-making power (apart from the constitutional power to regulate commerce with Indians) as paramount in that respect.

§ 161. **Other sovereign and national powers exercised by earlier Congresses.**—While discussion in this volume is confined to the treaty-making power, it is proper to note that from 1774 to 1788 Continental Congresses exercised other powers which are analogous to the treaty-making power, in that they are inherent attributes of sovereignty and can be only exercised by sovereign and national powers. These are especially referred to in Mr. Davis' Notes as prize

whether such an indefinite license to aliens to possess real property within the United States was not an encroachment upon the rights of the states. It seems to have been expected, when the French treaty was entered into, that the states would acquiesce in this provision, on account of the peculiar relations of this country to France, and because of the saving clause in the Articles of Confederation in favor of the treaties to be made with that power and with Spain. But such a stipulation as this was clearly not within the meaning of that clause; and it was received with great repugnance by many of the states. In the treaty with the Netherlands it was proposed to insert a similar provision; but it was found to be extremely improbable that the states would comply with a similar engagement with another power. The language was therefore varied, so as to give the privilege of inheritance only as to the 'effects' of persons dying in the country—an expression which would probably exclude real property, but which might possibly be construed to include it.

"With regard to duties and imposts, the Dutch treaty contained the same stipulation as the French, putting the subjects of either power on the footing of the most favored nations, and thereby holding out to the subjects of the United Provinces the promise of an equality, under the laws of the United States, with the subjects of France. The same stipulation was inserted in a treaty subsequently made at Paris with the King of Sweden.

"If these stipulations were supposed or intended to be binding upon the states, so as to restrain

jurisdiction[1] and the acquisition of territory[2] — his remarks on these points are worthy of careful consideration.

The history of the Confederation, as it has been told by Mr. Justice Story in his Commentaries and by George Ticknor Curtis and Professor Von Holst in their histories of the Constitution, also demonstrates the existence and exercise of all of the attributes of nationality and sovereignty which have already been referred to.[3]

§ 162. **Views of Justice Story.**—In this respect, Justice Story bases his views largely upon the utterances of Chief Justice Jay and of Justices Paterson and Chase in *Chisholm* vs. *Georgia*,[1] all of whom were revolutionary heroes, and whose knowledge of the legal status of the Confederation was based upon their actual experience and association with public affairs during its existence; the author of this volume feels that he cannot better conclude this chapter upon the nature of the treaty-making power under the Confederation than by quoting at length the concluding sentences of Judge Story's chapter upon the general status and powers of that government.

" In respect to the powers of the Continental Congress exercised before the adoption of the Articles of Confederation, few questions were judicially discussed during the Revolutionary contest; for men had not leisure in the heat of war nicely to scrutinize or weigh such subjects; *inter arma silent leges.* The people, relying on the wisdom and patriotism of Congress, silently acquiesced in whatever authority they assumed. But soon after the organization of the present government, the question was most elaborately discussed

them from adopting, within their respective jurisdictions, any other rule than that fixed by the French treaty, for the subjects of the United Provinces and the King of Sweden, it is quite clear that the Articles of Confederation gave no authority to Congress to make them. They could have no effect, therefore, in producing a uniformity of regulation throughout the United States with regard to the trade with Sweden and the Netherlands." Curtis' Constitutional History of the United States, vol. 1, pp. 188-190.

§ 161.
[1] Miller's Lectures on the Constitution; J. C. Bancroft Davis' Notes to Lecture I, p. 37 *et seq.*

[2] *Idem*, p. 57 *et seq.*

[3] See notes to § 142, p. 245, § 149, pp. 258, *et seq., ante.*

§ 162.
[1] See note to § 143, p. 246, *ante,*

before the Supreme Court of the United States, in a case calling for an exposition of the appellate jurisdiction of Congress in prize causes before the ratification of the confederation. The result of that examination was, as the opinions already cited indicate, that Congress, before the confederation, possessed, by the consent of the people of the United States, sovereign and supreme powers for national purposes; and among others the supreme powers of peace and war, and, as an incident, the right of entertaining appeals in the last resort in prize causes, even in opposition to State legislation. And that the actual powers exercised by Congress, in respect to national objects, furnished the best exposition of its constitutional authority, since they emanated from the representatives of the people, and were acquiesced in by the people." [2] While this volume has been in press a work has been published by an eminent authority [3] on the diplomatic history of our country in which extended references are made to the treaties under the Confederation. [4]

which also contains quotations from Story's Commentaries. [2] Commentaries on the Constitution of the United States, by	Joseph Story, LL. D., 5th Edition, Boston, 1891, vol. I., § 217, pp. 160–161.

[3] JOHN W. FOSTER ON TREATIES OF THE CONFEDERATION.

In " A Century of American Diplomacy " by former Secretary of State John W. Foster (New York and Boston, 1901), the author devotes several chapters of that interesting volume to the diplomatic results achieved by the representatives of this country prior to the adoption of the Constitution. Chapter I (pp. 1–40), "The Revolutionary Period," treats of the condition of international law in 1776, and the negotiations with the French court resulting in the treaties of commerce and alliance of 1778; chapter II (pp. 41–72), is devoted to the negotiations with Spain and Holland, and the inception of the peace negotiations with Great Britain; chapter III (pp. 73–102), " Peace under the Confederation," gives the history of the Provisional Articles of 1782 and the Definitive Treaty of Peace of 1783, the treaties with Prussia and other countries, and concludes with an account of the diplomatic representatives of our country during the Revolutionary period (for Mr. Foster's opinion of Benjamin Franklin, see note on p. 298 of this volume, *post*); chapter IV (pp. 104–135), contains a history of the organization of the Department of State.

[4] In speaking of the treaties which were concluded between the United States and foreign powers during the ante-Constitutional period, and of the high attainments of the American statesmen of that period in

international law and diplomacy, Mr. Foster says (pp. 92-94): "The year following the peace with England, John Adams, Franklin, and Thomas Jefferson were appointed commissioners to negotiate treaties of commerce with various European governments, and the convention with Prussia of 1785 was the outcome of this appointment. It was mainly the work of Dr. Franklin, and in it were inserted the principles for which he had so long contended as to neutrality, privateering, and the exemption of private property on the sea from confiscation in war. It was called 'a beautiful abstraction;' a dream of the philosopher who vainly sought to mitigate the cruelties of war; and when the treaty came to be renewed in 1799 these provisions were omitted. Franklin's efforts, however, have not been entirely in vain. In the Declaration of Paris of 1856, adopted by the great powers of Europe, privateering was abolished; and when the adhesion of the United States to the declaration was asked, Secretary Marcy proposed as an amendment that private property of belligerents at sea be exempt from capture; and because of the refusal of the powers to admit that principle, the adhesion of the United States was withheld. Our country, through the recent action of President McKinley in asking its adoption by the Hague conference, is on record as still advocating Franklin's liberal principle. The treaty with Prussia has the unique feature of having been signed by the four signatory parties thereto at four different dates and at three different places; the instrument being signed by Mr. Adams in London, by the Prussian minister at the Hague, by Dr. Franklin in Paris, July 9, and by Mr. Jefferson, July 28, he having arrived in the interim in that city from America.

"Other treaties of the ante-Constitutional period were those with Morocco in 1787 and the Consular Convention of 1788 with France. It is of interest to note the part which the Continental Congress played in the negotiation of all the treaties, from that with France of 1788 up to the adoption of the Constitution. There being no distinct head of the government, Congress took the part of the Executive in initiating and directing the negotiations. The terms of all treaties to be made were discussed in their details; and in almost all cases the draft or plan was first adopted by Congress, before being sent to our ministers abroad for negotiation with the other contracting party. Mention has already been made of the advanced state of international law assumed by American statesmen as indicated in the French treaty of commerce of 1778, and the same characteristic marks all the other commercial treaties— greater guarantees and privileges to commerce, the recognition of a genuine neutrality, an effort to alleviate the horrors of war, and a restraint upon its distinctive propensities. That the old nations of Europe were willing at the instance of this infant republic to consecrate these advanced principles in treaties was high praise for the statesmen of our Revolutionary period. Nor is all the credit to be given to our representatives abroad,—Franklin, Adams, Jay, and Jefferson. A share of the praise is due likewise to the controlling members of the Continental Congress."

284

CHAPTER VI.

PROCEEDINGS OF THE CONSTITUTIONAL CONVENTION OF 1787
RELATING TO TREATIES AND THE TREATY-MAKING POWER OF
THE FEDERAL GOVERNMENT.

285

§ 163. **Critical period of American history.**—The six years intervening between the conclusion in 1782, of the Provisional Articles which were afterwards incorporated into the Definitive Treaty of Peace by which the war of the Revolution was terminated and Great Britain recognized the independence of the United States,[1] and the adoption of the Constitution in 1788, has been fitly described by one of our greatest historians as the critical period of American history.[2]

§ 164. **Retrograde from unity.**—There can be no question that after the independence which the colonies had asserted by the Declaration of Independence in 1776 had become an accomplished fact in 1783, and the *States*, as they were described in the Definitive Treaty of Peace, had felt their "sovereignty" in a practical manner, there was an apparent diminution in the desire for unity which had played such an important part in the assertion of independence. This was the natural result of the removal of the chief cause which had led to their united action; for, after they had achieved their independence, the States did not feel the pressing need of united protection against a common foe; local feelings, therefore, revived, and the great powers which had been exercised by the Continental Congress during the war period

§ 163.
[1] For dates and titles of these treaties see § 158, note, p. 275, *ante*.

[2] Professor John Fiske, see note under next section.

were not only more closely scrutinized, but each State desired to extend its own sovereignty as far as possible, and also to limit the supervising or central powers of the Federal Government to the narrowest possible limits.[1]

One of the evidences of the lack of power in the Central Government of the Confederation was its inability to enforce treaty stipulations which it had entered into with foreign powers, especially those relating to the collection of debts due to British subjects.[2] The defiant attitude of the States in disregarding these national obligations was one of the prime causes which led to strengthening the Central Government and placing it in the position not only of making, but also of carrying out treaty obligations. The unfortunate results of this attitude of the States are shown by the extracts from the records of Congress which are quoted in the notes to this section.[3]

§ 164.

[1] Critical Period of American History, by Professor John Fiske; History of the People of the United States, by Professor John Bach McMaster, vol. I, chaps. III and IV.

[2] See § 156, pp. 268, *et seq.*, *ante.*

[3] CONGRESS OF THE CONFEDERATION AND VIOLATIONS BY STATES OF TREATY STIPULATIONS.

" Resolved, that the legislatures of the several states cannot *of right* pass any act or acts, for interpreting, explaining, or construing a national treaty or any part or clause of it; nor for restraining, omitting or in any manner impeding, retarding or counteracting the operation and execution of the same, for that, on being *constitutionally made, ratified and published*, they become in virtue of the confederation, p*art of the law of the land*, and are not only independent of the will and power of such legislatures, but also binding and obligatory upon them." Journals of Congress, ed. 1801, vol. 12, p. 24, March 21, 1787.

On the previous April 13th, the United States, in Congress assembled, unanimously recommended the several States to enact identical laws of the following frame: " Whereas certain laws or statutes made and passed in some of the United States, are regarded and complained of as repugnant to the treaty of peace with Great Britain, by reason whereof not only the good faith of the United States pledged by that treaty, has been drawn into question, but their essential interests under that treaty greatly affected. And whereas justice to Great Britain, as well as regard to the honor and interests of the United States, require that the said treaty be faithfully executed, and that all obstacles thereto, and particularly such as do or may be construed to proceed from the laws of this state, be effectually removed.

" Therefore,

§ 165. Inability of Central Government to enforce its decrees.—During this period it was demonstrated that the Central Government under the Articles of Confederation was not strong enough to enforce the powers which had been delegated to it, and which it possessed; it also became very evident that unless it were clothed with greater executive power the United States, as a Nation, would become disintegrated, and instead of remaining a single strong nation, would be separated into thirteen insignificant States; theoretically it possessed every element of sovereignty, but practically it was unable to exert any of them.[1]

"Be it enacted by . . . and it is hereby enacted by the authority of the same, that such of the acts or part of acts of the legislature of this state, as are *repugnant to the treaty of* peace between the United States and his Britannic Majesty, or any article thereof, shall be, and hereby are, repealed. And further, that *the courts of law and equity* within this state be, and they hereby *are directed and required* in all causes and questions cognizable by them respectively, and arising from or touching the said treaty, to *decide and adjudge* according to the tenor, true intent and meaning of the same, *anything in the said acts, or parts of acts, to the contrary thereof in any wise notwithstanding.*" Journals of Congress, ed. 1801, vol. 12, p. 35, April 13, 1787. . . .

" Such a general law would, we think, be preferable to one that should minutely enumerate the acts and clauses intended to be repealed: because omissions might accidentally be made in the enumeration, or questions might arise, and perhaps not be satisfactorily determined, respecting particular acts or clauses, about which contrary opinions may be entertained. *By repealing in general terms all acts and clauses repugnant to the treaty, the business will be turned over to its proper department, viz., the judicial; and the courts of law will find no difficulty in deciding whether any particular act or clause is or is not contrary to the treaty.*" Journals of Congress, ed. 1801, vol. 12, p. 36, April 13, 1787.

" When the framers met in convention the violation of the treaty of peace by certain of the states was one of the most pressing anxieties of the political situation of the Union. It was also an anxiety most fruitful of results in developing the frame of the constitution. The treaty of peace was intimately connected with the origin and form of paragraph 2, article VI." Judicial Power and Unconstitutional Legislation, by Brinton Coxe, pp. 274–276.

An interesting history of the condition of affairs of the United States as they were affected by the violations of treaties and the unfortunate condition of foreign relations of this country will be found in the first chapter, pp. 40–50, of vol. 1 of Von Holst's Constitutional History of the United States.

[1] For note 1 see p. 289.

The prospects were discouraging even to the most sanguine, and were bitterly disappointing to those who having done the most to procure the independence of the colonies, were most anxious to preserve the integrity of the Union.[2]

The salvation of the Republic, and the continuance of the national life which had its inception at the first meeting of the Constitutional Congress, which was born with the Declaration of Independence, and which had struggled through its infantile period under the protection of the Articles of Confederation, was, however, now to be assured by the patriotic efforts of the far-seeing statesmen who had thoroughly mastered the situation and, therefore, were able to diagnose the conditions and to prescribe the proper remedies.

The fact was recognized that, although *national life* existed, there was not sufficient *national power* deposited in,

§ 165.

[1] As to the extent of power of the Congress of the Confederation, but inability to enforce its resolves, see Davis' notes to Miller's Lectures on the Constitution, p. 57, and quoted in § 144, p. 252, *ante.*

[2] "Another and a severer trial awaited them. They were not only to be taught once more that a mere federative union was a rope of sand, but they were also to be taught that a government instituted upon this principle for the purposes of a war, in which the separate members of the confederacy had a common interest, would not answer the exigencies of a country like this in time of peace. They were to learn, by a trying experience, that the vast concerns of peace are far more complex than the concerns of war; that there were important functions of government to be discharged upon this continent, which only national power and national authority can accomplish, and that those functions are essential, not only to the prosperity and happiness of this nation, but to the continued existence of republican liberty within the states themselves. They were to learn this through a state of things verging upon anarchy; amid the decay of public virtue, the conflict of sectional interests, and the almost total dissolution of the bands by which society is held together. In this state of things was to be at last developed the fundamental idea on which the Constitution of the United States now rests—the political union of the *people* of the United States for certain limited purposes, as distinguished from a union of the *states* of which they are citizens.

" We have, therefore, now reached the first stage in the constitutional history of the country. What has thus far been stated comes to a single point, the earliest great illustration of the radical defects in a purely federative union. The next stage which succeeds presents the second illustration of this important truth." Curtis' Constitutional History of the United States, vol. 1, pp. 84–85.

and confided to, the Central Government, to make it strong
and healthy, and that the only method by which the life
and strength of the Union could be preserved was by a further infusion of blood from the constituent elements into
the main body.

§ 166. **Dangers appreciated by Washington and others.**
—Men like Washington, Franklin, Madison, Hamilton, Randolph, Morris and others were far-seeing enough to appreciate the disasters which would necessarily follow the disin-
tegration of the Union. This was not due to any lack of
loyalty to their native states; they were too sensible, however,
to permit local pride and prejudice to hide from them the
inevitable results of a separation of the States. Each knew
that, no matter how strong he might consider his own State
as compared with other States in North America, it would, by
itself, be no match whatever for any one of the great powers
of Europe; they also saw that the individual life of each State
could only be preserved in the same manner that its independence had been won,—by a continuance of the united
action in which all the States had joined, and by means of
which Great Britain had finally been forced to recognize the
independence of all of the thirteen States at one time by the
Definitive Treaty of Peace.[1]

§ 167. **Unity impossible without greater power in Central Government.**—The necessity of union being admitted,
it necessarily followed that it would be impossible to maintain any central government unless the essential powers of
government were more securely vested in it than those powers were vested in the then existing Central Government
under the Articles of Confederation. As to no departments
of the government was this fact more clearly realized than
it was as to the regulation of interstate and international
relations; when, therefore, the Constitutional Convention
met at Philadelphia in 1787, the great questions before
it were how the powers of the Central, Federal or National
Government should be enlarged and extended, and not
how they should be withdrawn or contracted; how much
more power would the States surrender to the Central Gov-

§ 166.
[1] See Extract from Curtis' Con- stitutional History of the United States, under § 167 p. 291, *post.*

ernment, and not how much power would the Central Government surrender to the States; to what extent should the national powers already exercised by the Central Government under the Articles of Confederation be recognized in regard to matters which are purely national and in which no particular State had any separate interest, and not how should they be disavowed or exterminated; how the Central Government might be able to effectually enforce its inherent and delegated powers, notwithstanding the opposition of the States, and not how the States might be able to prevent the enforcement of those powers.[1]

§ 167.

[1] " We are now approaching the period when the American people began to perceive that something more was necessary to their safety and happiness than the formation of state governments; when they found, or were about to find, that some digested system of national government was essential to the great objects for which they were contending; and that, for the formation of such a government, other arrangements than the varying instructions of different colonies or states to a body of delegates were indispensable. The previous illustrations, drawn from the civil and military history of the country, have been employed to show the character and operation of the revolutionary government, the end of which is drawing near. For we have seen that the great purpose of that government was to secure the independence of each of these separate communities or states from the crown of Great Britain; that it was instituted by political societies having no direct connection with each other except the bond of a common danger and a common object; and that it was formed by no other instrumentality, and possessed no other agency, than a single body of delegates assembled in a congress. For certain great purposes, and in order to accomplish certain objects of common interest, a union of the people of the different states had indeed taken place, bringing them together to act through their representatives; but this union was now failing, from the want of definite powers; from the unwillingness of the people of the country to acquiesce in the exercise of the general revolutionary powers with which it was impliedly clothed; and from the want of suitable civil machinery. In truth, the revolutionary government was breaking down, through its inherent defects, and the peculiar infelicity of its situation. Above all, it was breaking down from the want of a civil executive to take the lead in assuming and exercising the powers implied from the great objects for which it was contending. Its legislative authority, although defined in no written instruments or public charters, was sufficient, under its implied general powers, to have enabled it to issue decrees directing the execution, by its own agents, of all measures essential to the national safety. But this authority was never exercised, partly because the states were un-

§ 168. **Constitutional Convention and its results.**—That these questions were all answered by the Convention in such manner that every improvement and every change was towards the enlargement, and not toward the diminution, of the powers of the National Government is evidenced by the Constitution of the United States, the result of the deliberations of the Convention, and which has stood the test of time for over a century and which, in the words of that great English statesman, William E. Gladstone, was "the greatest work of man ever produced at a given time."[1]

It is beyond the scope of this volume to enter into any complete history of the Constitutional Convention, although the author is tempted to devote more space than can fairly be allotted to it, for no subject furnishes more interesting material for investigation, discussion or historical research than the proceedings of that body of men, all able and distinguished,[2] and who, for five months, sat behind closed doors,

willing to execute it, but chiefly because no executive agency existed to represent the continental power and enforce its decrees.

"It is a singular circumstance that, while the revolutionary government was left to conduct the great affairs of the continent through the mere instrumentality of a congress of delegates, and was thus failing for the want of departments and powers, the states were engaged in applying those great principles in the organization and construction of popular governments, under which they may be formed with rapidity and ease, and which are capable of the most varied adaptation to the circumstances and wants of a free people." Curtis's Constitutional History of the United States, vol. 1, pp. 79–80.

"Congress assembled, under the Confederation, on the 2d of March, 1781, and the Treaty of Peace, which put an end to the war and admitted the independence of the United States, was definitively signed on the 3d of September, 1783, and was ratified and proclaimed by Congress on the 14th of January, 1784." Curtis's Constitutional History of the United States, vol. 1, p. 104.

§ 168.

[1] "As the British Constitution is the most subtile organism which has proceeded from progressive history, so the American Constitution is the most wonderful work ever struck off at a given time by the brain and purpose of man." See title page of Bancroft's History of the Constitution of the United States, vol. 1.

[2] In chapter XVI of the first volume of his Constitutional History, Mr. George Ticknor Curtis names George Washington of Virginia, Alexander Hamilton of New York, James Madison of Virginia, Benjamin Franklin of Pennsylvania, Gouverneur Morris, then of Pennsylva-

and finally produced, as the result of their labors, patience, skill, ability, and, above all, patriotism, the Constitution of the United States.[3] In this volume we can only refer to those proceedings in so far as they relate to the treaty-making power; the object of this chapter is to examine the proceedings and note the gradual evolution of Article VI by which treaties are made the supreme law of the land, from the form in which it first appeared until the perfected form in which it was finally incorporated into the Constitution, and adopted as a part of the fundamental written law of the United States. The method in which the Convention was called and the status of the delegates is the subject of a note to this section.[4]

nia, Rufus King of Massachusetts, Charles Cotesworth Pinckney of South Carolina, and Edmund Randolph of Virginia as the nine persons who were the most important members of the Constitutional Convention, and who exercised the largest influence upon its decision; after giving an account of the life and work of those nine persons in the same order as they are mentioned above, he says on page 313, that all of the fifty-five members of the Convention were able and distinguished men; in regard to certain of them he says as follows: "But the entire list embraced other men of great distinction and ability, celebrated, before and since the Convention, in that period of the political history of America which commenced with the Revolution and closed with the eighteenth century. Such were Roger Sherman of Connecticut, Robert Morris of Pennsylvania, John Dickinson of Delaware, John Rutledge and Charles Pinckney of South Carolina, and George Mason of Virginia. Of the rest, all were men of note and influence in their respective states, possessing the full confi-

dence of the people whom they represented."

[3] Clause 2 of article VI of the Constitution is quoted at length in § 6, p. 7, ante.

[4] Chapter XV of vol. I, of Curtis' Constitutional History of the United States, pp. 221–256, contains a very interesting account of the origin of the Federal Convention.

The best detailed history, however, can be found in Volume I of Elliot's Debates, where the records are collected. Pages 108, et seq., Volume I, contain the report of the States on the Regulations of Commerce; there is also on page 112 a copy of a letter to be sent to the Legislatures of the several States, showing the principles on which the alterations enlarging the powers of Congress had been proposed, and in which the difficulties are pointed out of allowing the different States to legislate in regard to commerce and at the same time of preserving treaty relations with foreign countries. On page 114 is the resolution proposed by Mr. Madison, in the House of Delegates of Virginia, and the proposition of the General Assembly of Virginia,

§ 169. **Convention a unit in lodging treaty-making power in Central Government.**—The proceedings of the Convention, as they have been preserved by Madison, Yates and Elliot,[1] show that the Convention recognized that in some cases

for a meeting of commissioners of the different States in regard to the regulation of commerce by the Central Government. A meeting of commissioners took place September 11, 1876, at Annapolis; New York, New Jersey, Pennsylvania, Delaware, and Virginia were the only States represented. (Elliot, vol. I, p. 116.) The commissioners prepared a report which they submitted to their own legislatures, and also to the Congress of the United States.

On February 21, 1787, a committee in Congress passed a resolution as follows (Elliot, vol. I, p. 120):

" Whereas, there is provision, in the Articles of Confederation and Perpetual Union, for making alterations therein, by the assent of a Congress of the United States, and of the legislatures of the several states; and whereas experience hath evinced that there are defects in the present Confederation; as a mean to remedy which, several of the states, and particularly the state of New York, by express instructions to their delegates in Congress, have suggested a convention for the purposes expressed in the following resolution; and such convention appearing to be the most probable mean of establishing in these states a firm national government,—

" *Resolved*, That, in the opinion of Congress, it is expedient that, on the second Monday of May next, a convention of delegates, who shall have been appointed by the several states, be held at Philadelphia, for the sole and express purpose of revising the Articles of Confederation, and reporting to Congress and the several legislatures such alterations and provisions therein as shall, when agreed to in Congress and confirmed by the states, render the federal Constitution adequate to the exigencies of government and the preservation of the Union."

When the Convention met it was found that sixty-five delegates had been appointed. Of these ten never attended; thirty-nine attended, took part in the debates, and signed the Constitution; sixteen attended, and did not sign.

A complete list of the delegates and the names of those who attended will be found on pages 124–125, Elliot, vol. I. Each State adopted its own form for the credentials of its delegates. They are printed in full, pages 126–139, Elliot, vol. I.

Bancroft, McMaster, Fiske, and the other authorities referred to in note 1, § 169, page 297, *post*, also have interesting accounts of the calling of this Convention.

§ 169.

NOTE ON AUTHORITIES ON FEDERAL AND STATE CONSTITUTIONAL CONVENTIONS.

[1] The authorities on the Federal Convention of 1787, which framed the Constitution of the United States, and the State Conventions to which the Constitution was submitted for ratification are limited in number;

the power of the Central Government must be widely extended
and that of the States narrowly restricted; this was pecu-

for, although much has been written upon the subject nearly all the
commentators and historians base their statements upon the documents
which have been collected and published by direction of Congress. The
principal sources from which all writers on Constitutional history have
drawn are as follows; viz:

ELLIOT'S DEBATES.

"The debates in the several State Conventions, on the adoption of the
Federal Constitution, as recommended by the General Convention at
Philadelphia in 1787. Together with the Journal of the Federal Convention, Luther Martin's Letter, Yates' Minutes, Congressional Opinion,
Virginia and Kentucky Resolutions of 1798–99 and other illustrations of
the Constitution in five volumes. Collected and revised from contemporary publications by Jonathan Elliot," 1st edition, 1830; 2d edition,
1836. Republished under the sanction of Congress, Philadelphia, 1866.

The contents of the five volumes are as follows:

Volume I contains the Constitution, Declaration of Independence,
Articles of Confederation, proceedings prior to, and which led to the
adoption of the Federal Constitution, Proceedings and Journal of the
Federal Convention, Dates and Forms of Ratifications by the States,
Amendments to the Constitution, Luther Martin's Letter, Yates' Minutes
of the Convention, and certain other papers expressive of views of individual members of the Convention.

Volume II contains proceedings of the State Conventions of Massachusetts, Connecticut, New Hampshire, New York, Pennsylvania and
Maryland.

Volume III is devoted exclusively to the proceedings of the State
Convention of Virginia.

Volume IV contains the proceedings of the State Conventions of
North Carolina and South Carolina, and a number of other documents
relating to the construction of the Constitution, including the Virginia
and Kentucky Resolutions, Mr. Madison's letters on Tariff and Banks,
and a digest of decisions of the courts involving Constitutional Principles.

Volume V contains the Diary kept by Mr. Madison of the debates of
the Congress of the Confederation from November, 1782, to April, 1787,
and which are known as the Madison Papers.

THE JOURNALS OF CONGRESS.

The records of the Congress under the Confederation are not as complete as the records of Congress since the adoption of the Constitution.
There are, however, a number of volumes which contain valuable data as
to the action of Congress in regard to the Constitution and its adoption.
The author has used the edition published in 1821 under the direction
of the President of the United States conformably to the Resolution of
Congress of March 27, 1818, and April 21, 1820, volume IV. of which

liarly the case in regard to the treaty-making power; in fact, the Convention was almost a unit in lodging it absolutely and exclusively in the Central Government without any express

contains some valuable data in regard to the Constitution. Other editions were published in Philadelphia in 1801, and in Washington in 1823.

THE MADISON PAPERS.

" The papers of James Madison, purchased by order of Congress; being his Correspondence and Reports of Debates during the Congress of the Confederation, and his Report of Debates in the Federal Convention, now published from the original manuscripts, deposited in the Department of State, by direction of the Joint Library Committee of Congress, under the superintendence of Henry D. Gilpin;" three volumes, Washington, 1840.

Volume I contains the Debates in 1776 on the Declaration of Independence, and on a few of the Articles of Confederation, preserved by Thomas Jefferson; Letters of Mr. Madison preceding the Debates of 1783.

Volume II contains the Debates of Congress of the Confederation from February 19, 1787, to April 25, 1787, Correspondence of Mr. Madison during and subsequent to the Debates in the Congress of the Confederation, from February 15, 1787, to December 2, 1788; Debates in the Federal Convention from Monday, May 14, 1787, to Monday, August 6, 1787.

. Volume III contains Debates in the Federal Convention from Tuesday August 7, 1787, until its final adjournment Monday September 17, 1789, and notes and references to the Journal of Conventions. The references in the subsequent sections of this chapter are all made to the Madison Papers as they are official; the citations, however, can be found in Elliot's Debates and other editions of Madison's Journal by reference to the dates.

MADISON'S JOURNAL.

" Journal of the Federal Convention kept by James Madison, reprinted from the edition of 1840, which was published under direction of the United States Government from the original manuscripts with a complete index;" edited by E. H. Scott, Chicago, Albert Scott & Co., 1893; although the author refers in the notes only to the Madison Papers the citations can easily be found in this edition of Madison's Journal by reference to the dates, which are given in all cases.

YATES' SECRET PROCEEDINGS.

"Secret Proceedings and Debates of the Convention assembled at Philadelphia in the year 1787, for the purpose of forming the Constitution of the United States of America, from the notes taken by the late Robert Yates, Esq., Chief Justice of New York, and copied by John Lansing, Jun. Esq., late Chancellor of that State, members of that Convention, (and other documents enumerated, relating to the Constitution)." Albany, N. Y., 1821.

limitation whatever; it is apparent on the record that the delegates unanimously appreciated the important hearing which our foreign relations had upon the welfare of the country even at that early period in American history.

§ 170. **Organization of Convention ; Washington chosen President.**—The first business of the Convention was to organize and to elect a President. No better choice could have been made than the one who had already received the title of " Father of his Country," and to whom the sentence, " First in war, first in peace, first in the hearts of his countrymen," was to be not only a perpetual but an appropriate tribute of affection.[1] It was fitting, indeed, that the man who had led the armies of the united Colonies, through a war which had resulted in their independence, against a common foe, should

---

§ 170.
[1] In the resolution presented to the House of Representatives on December 26, 1799, on the death of Washington, Henry Lee of Virginia thus described him.   Madison's Papers, vol. II, p. 722,

BANCROFT, CURTIS, MCMASTER, FISKE, MEIGS.

History of the Formation of the Constitution of the United States of America, by George Bancroft. In two volumes. 6th edition, New York, 1893.

Constitutional History of the United States, by George Ticknor Curtis, two volumes, 2d edition; volume I, History of the Convention; volume II, Subsequent History of the United States as to constitutional points.

History of the People of the United States from the Revolution to the Civil War, by John Bach McMaster. In five volumes, New York, 1893, volume 1, chapters II to V, inclusive, relate to the "breaking up" of the Confederation and the adoption of the Constitution.

The Critical Period of American History, 1783–1789, by John Fiske, Boston and New York, 1888, 1899.

" The Growth of the Constitution in the Federal Convention of 1787, an effort to trace the origin and development of each separate clause from its first suggestion in that body to the form finally approved; containing also a *fac-simile* of a heretofore unpublished manuscript of the first draft of the tribunal made for use in the Committee of Details," by William M. Meigs. Second edition, Philadelphia and London, 1900.

There are numerous other able and interesting histories of, and commentaries on, the Constitution which give detailed accounts of the Federal and State Conventions, but the author considers that in consulting, and referring to those enumerated in this note, the student of Constitutional history will obtain a thorough knowledge of all the known history of the formation and adoption of the Constitution.

now preside over their peaceful councils in the Convention which was to perpetuate the national independence, the achievement of which had been to such a great extent, the result of his efforts and ability. It was fitting, also, that the nomination of George Washington for the Presidency of the Convention should come from Pennsylvania, as Benjamin Franklin could have been the only possible competitor. It appears from Mr. Madison's notes that the Doctor himself was to have made the nomination, but was prevented from attending the first meeting by the state of the weather and the condition of his health.[2] Throughout the whole course of the Convention we can see the effects of the great strength, and, at the same time, the moderation and the complete self-control of those two men, Washington and Franklin, one of them, the greatest soldier, and the other, the greatest diplomat, that their country has ever produced.[3]

[2] Madison's Journal of the Constitutional Convention, Edition 1893, p. 54, note.

[3] SECRETARY FOSTER'S OPINION OF BENJAMIN FRANKLIN AS A DIPLOMAT.

"In closing the review of the Revolutionary period, I desire to add a word as to the men who represented our country abroad from the Declaration of Independence to the adoption of the Constitution. In the list are the illustrious names of Franklin, Adams, Jay, and Jefferson, men whose career abroad compares favorably with that of the best trained diplomats of Europe. But there were many others, although near a score of agents and diplomatic representatives, some associated with Franklin, and others on independent missions. The record they made was not altogether a creditable one. While most of them were inspired by patriotic motives, some were guilty of treachery; bickering, faultfinding, and jealousy prevailed; and drunk-enness and dishonesty marked the career of more than one of them. It constitutes a record which I am pleased to say could hardly be repeated in our day. In the midst of this mixture of good and evil, the calm and upright character of Franklin stands out in bold relief. He did not escape criticism and scandal, but in his long service he never failed in his duty as a diplomat and patriot. As we have seen, his acts were not above criticism, his temper was not always under control, and we could wish, for its influence on the generations after him, that his private life had been more pure. But when we review the history of our Revolutionary period, the place in the public esteem and in value of service to the country, next to Washington, must be given, not to that stern patriot John Adams, not to Patrick Henry, Thomas Jefferson, nor to any military hero, but to Benjamin Franklin, our first and greatest diplomat."

The deep-seated conviction in Washington's mind that there must be, not only a union, but a thoroughly *national* union, is evidenced by his own writings prior to the Constitutional Convention; in this respect Mr. Curtis says in his Constitutional History, which has already been quoted from to such an extent that the author feels that he must express his great appreciation of the ability of Mr. Curtis, and the assistance which he has rendered to all students of constitutional history, both as to historical facts and legal precedents: " It had become evident to him that we never should establish a national character, nor be justly considered and respected by the nations of Europe, without enlarging the powers of the federal government for the regulation of commerce. The objection which had been hitherto urged, that some states might be more benefited than others by a commercial regulation, seemed to him to apply to every matter of general utility. ' We are,' said he, writing in the summer of 1785, ' either a united people under one head, and for federal purposes, or we are thirteen independent sovereignties eternally counteracting each other. If the former, whatever such a majority of the States as the Constitution points out conceivēs to be for the benefit of the whole, should, in my humble opinion, be submitted to by the minority. Let the Southern States always be represented ; let them act more in union ; let them declare freely and boldly what is for the interest of, and what is prejudicial to, their constituents; and there will, there must be, an accommodating spirit. In

And in a footnote Mr. Foster adds the following:

" There is a curious letter of Mr. Jefferson, in which, some years after the event, he refers to the death of Dr. Franklin in connection with an incident of Washington's cabinet. The King and Convention of France, and the House of Representatives of the United States, had decreed mourning, and Jefferson proposed that the executive department also should wear mourning. To this Washington objected, because he should not know where to draw the line. He writes: ' I told him the world had drawn so broad a line between himself and Dr. Franklin, on the one side, and the residue of mankind, on the other, that we might wear mourning for them, and the question remain new and undecided as to all others.' (8 Writings of Jefferson, 264.) " A Century of American Diplomacy, by John W. Foster, chapter III, Peace under the Confederation, pp. 101–102, Boston and New York, 1900.

the establishment of a navigation act, this, in a particular manner, ought and will doubtless be attended to. If the assent of nine states, or, as some propose, of eleven, is necessary to give validity to a commercial system, it insures this measure, or it cannot be obtained.' " [4]

§ 171. **Opening business of Convention, May 25th; Randolph's resolutions, May 29th.**—The original date for which convention had been called was May 14th, but on that day only a small number of delegates assembled. Seven states were not represented until the 25th, when the President was elected; on May 28th the Convention again met, but only for the adoption of rules; [1] on May 29th, Mr. Edmund Randolph, of Virginia, opened the main business and stated to the Convention that a closer federal union was necessary, as the Confederation possessed no security for the States on account of the lack of authority in the Central Government, of which he cited many examples, laying particular stress upon the fact that Congress had no power to punish the infractions of treaties which had become so notorious as to prejudice us in the eyes of other nations. "He commented on the difficulty of the crisis and the necessity of preventing the fufilment of the prophecies of the American downfall." He submitted a series of resolutions, embracing changes that ought to be made in the construction of the federal system; he then proceeded to enumerate the defects of the present system, and first and foremost he placed the fact that "the Confederation produced no security against foreign invasion; Congress not being permitted to prevent a war, nor to support it by their own authority. Of this he cited many examples, most of which tended to show that they could not cause infractions of treaties or of the law of nations to be punished; that particular States might by their conduct provoke war without control." [2] The sixth resolution of this series provided that " the National Legislature ought to be empowered to enjoy the legislative rights vested in Con-

---

[4] Curtis' Constitutional History of the United States, New York, 1899, vol. 1, chap. XVI, p. 266, quoting from IX Washington's Writings, 166.

§ 171.
[1] Madison Papers, vol. II, p. 722.
[2] *Idem*, p. 730.

gress by the Confederation, and, moreover to legislate in all cases to which the separate States are incompetent, or in which the harmony of the United States may be interrupted by the exercise of individual legislation; to negative all laws passed by the several States contravening, in the opinion of the National Legislature, the Articles of Union, or any treaty subsisting under the authority of the Union; and to call forth the force of the Union against any member of the Union failing to fulfill its duty under the Articles thereof." [3] Mr. Randolph concluded with an exhortation not to suffer the present opportunity of establishing general peace, harmony, happiness and liberty in the United States to pass away unimproved. [4]

§ 172. **Pinckney's plan; treaties to be made by Senate; May 29th.**—Mr. Charles Pinckney, of South Carolina, also submitted a plan of government, in which he proposed that the source of authority should be changed from the States, as it was described in the Articles of Confederation, to *We, The People of the States of* (enumerating them by name), as well as many other changes which were afterwards incorporated in the Constitution. [1] This draft contained a proposition for a Senate, some of whose exclusive powers were, "to declare war; and to make treaties; and to appoint ambassadors and other ministers to foreign nations, and judges of the Supreme Court." [2] It also contained prohibitions against any state entering into any treaty or alliance, or confederation, or compact with other States. [3] Article VI, as proposed in his draft, contained a clause which is almost identical in wording with the corresponding clause which was finally incorporated in the Constitution: "All acts made by the Legislature of the United States pursuant to this Constitution, and all treaties made under the authority of the United States, shall be the supreme law of the land; and all judges shall be bound to consider them as such in their decisions." [4] It is well to note that, although nearly every paragraph of this plan, including the one just quoted, were subsequently changed as to some of

---

[3] Madison Papers, vol. II, p. 732.
[4] *Idem*, p. 735.
§ 172.
[1] *Idem*, p. 735, *et seq.*

[2] *Idem*, p. 742.
[3] *Idem*, p. 744.
[4] *Idem*, p. 741.

their details, and many of the great principles at first proposed were altered or modified, the expression that treaties made by the United States should be the supreme law of the land, and that all judges should be bound to so consider them, remained intact, until it was finally adopted in the finished instrument, with the exception of a few words inserted to make the principle established somewhat stronger and broader.   Mr. Pinckney's plan was referred to the Committee of the Whole, together with Governor Randolph's resolutions,[5] and they were afterwards discussed in that committee, article by article; not, however, until after there had been a discussion as to the nature of the proposed government, the details of which appear in the notes to this section.[6]

[5] Madison Papers, vol. II, p. 746.
[6] Wednesday May 30 *In Committee of Whole.*

"The propositions of Mr. Randolph which had been referred to the Committee being taken up, he moved, on the suggestion of Mr. G. Morris, that the first of his propositions,—to wit: '*Resolved that the Article of Confederation ought to be so corrected and enlarged, as to accomplish the objects proposed by their institution; namely, common defence, security of liberty, and general welfare,*—should mutually be postponed, in order to consider the three following:

· "' 1. That a union of the States merely federal will not accomplish the objects proposed by the Articles of Confederation, namely, common defence, security of liberty, and general welfare.

"' 2. That no treaty or treaties among the whole or part of the States, as individual sovereignties, would be sufficient.

"' 3. That a *national* government ought to be established, consisting of a *supreme* Legislative, Executive and Judiciary.'

"The motion for postponing was seconded by Mr. G. Morris, and unanimously agreed to.

"Some verbal criticisms were raised against the first proposition, and it was agreed, on motion of Mr. Butler, seconded by Mr. Randolph, to pass on to the third, which underwent a discussion, less, however, on its general merits than on the force and extent of the particular terms *national* and *supreme.*

"Mr. Charles Pinckney wished to know of Mr. Randolph, whether he meant to abolish the State governments altogether. Mr. Randolph replied, that he meant by these general propositions merely to introduce the particular ones which explained the outlines of the system he had in view.

"Mr. Butler said, he had not made up his mind on the subject, and was open to the light which discussion might throw on it. After some general observations, he concluded with saying, that he had opposed the grant of powers to Congress heretofore, because the whole power was vested in one body. The proposed distribution of the powers

§ 173. Pinckney's plan to negative State laws; Madison's views; June 8th.

§ 173. **Pinckney's plan to negative State laws; Madison's views; June 8th.**—In discussing the policy of giving the national legislature authority to negative State laws, Mr. Pinckney said, on June 8th, that unless such power were given, however extensive the national prerogatives might be on paper, it would be impossible to defend them; that already acts of Congress had been defeated by this means, and that foreign treaties had frequently been violated. He contended that "this universal negative was, in fact, the corner-stone of an efficient National Government; and that, as it had existed under the British Government, the negative of the Crown had been found beneficial;" and he added, "the States are more one nation now, than the colonies were then." [1]

with different bodies changed the case, and would induce him to go great lengths.

"General Pinckney expressed a doubt whether the act of Congress recommending the Convention, or the commissions of the Deputies to it, would authorize a discussion of a system founded on different principles from the Federal Constitution.

"Mr. Gerry seemed to entertain the same doubt.

"Mr. Gouverneur Morris explained the distinction between a *federal* and a *national, supreme* government; the former being a mere compact resting on the good faith of the parties; the latter having a complete and *compulsive* operation. He contended that in all communities there must be one supreme power, and one only." Madison Papers, vol. II, pp. 746–748.

§ 173.

[1] Friday, June 8th, *In Committee of the Whole.*

"On a reconsideration of the clause giving the National Legislature a negative on such laws of the States as might be contrary to the Articles of Union, or treaties with foreign nations:

"Mr. Pinckney moved, 'that the National Legislature should have authority to negative all laws which they should judge to be improper.' He urged that such a universality of the power was indispensably necessary to render it effectual; that the States must be kept in due subordination to the nation; that if the States were left to act of themselves in any case, it would be impossible to defend the national prerogatives, however extensive they might be, on paper; that the acts of Congress had been defeated by this means; nor had foreign treaties escaped repeated violations; that this universal negative was in fact the cornerstone of an efficient national Government; that under the British Government the negative of the Crown had been found beneficial; and the *States* are more one nation now, than the *colonies* were then.

"Mr. Madison seconded the motion. He could not but regard an indefinite power to negative legislative acts of the States as absolutely necessary to a perfect system.

The power of negativing state legislation was not vested in the National Government in so many words, for eventually Mr. Pinckney's motion was lost, although it was supported by some of the strongest men in the Convention, including Mr. Madison; in fact, at one time it was adopted in Committee of the Whole. So far as treaties are concerned, however, the object of his motion was practically, although indirectly, attained by the clause which he, himself, had framed and which, when it was subsequently incorporated in Article VI of the Constitution, made treaties the supreme law of the land, and under which the Supreme Court of the United States has held that the stipulations in a treaty, as well as the appropriate legislation enforcing it, override all

Experience had evinced a constant tendency in the States to encroach on the Federal authority; to violate national treaties; to infringe the rights and interests of each other; to oppress the weaker party within their respective jurisdictions. A negative was the mildest expedient that could be devised for preventing these mischiefs. The existence of such a check would prevent attempts to commit them. Should no such precaution be engrafted, the only remedy would be in an appeal to coercion. Was such a remedy eligible? Was it practicable? Could the national resources, if exerted to the utmost, enforce a national decree against Massachusetts, abetted, perhaps, by several of her neighbors? It would not be possible. A small proportion of the community, in a compact situation, acting on the defensive, and at one of its extremities, might at any time bid defiance to the national authority. Any government for the United States, formed on the supposed practicability of using force against the unconstitutional proceedings of the States, would prove as visionary and fallacious as the government of Congress. The negative would render the use of force unnecessary. The States could of themselves pass no operative act, any more than one branch of a legislature, where there are two branches, can proceed without the other. But in order to give the negative this efficacy, it must extend to all cases. A discrimination would only be a fresh source of contention between the two authorities. In a word, to recur to the illustrations borrowed from the planetary system, this prerogative of the General Government is the great pervading principle that must control the centrifugal tendency of the States; which, without it, will continually fly out of their proper orbits, and destroy the order and harmony of the political system.

"Mr. Williamson was against giving a power that might restrain the States from regulating their internal police.

"Mr. Gerry could not see the extent of such a power, and was against every power that was not necessary." Madison Papers, vol. II, pp. 821–823.

State legislation, thus practically negativing any that may be in conflict therewith.[2]

§ 174. Consideration of treaty-making power; June 13th.—The method of exercising the treaty-making power appears to have been considered for the first time on June 13th, on which day the Committee rose, after making a report, the sixth paragraph of which was as follows:

"*Resolved*, That the National Legislature ought to be empowered to enjoy the legislative rights vested in Congress by the Confederation; and moreover to legislate in all cases to which the separate States are incompetent, *or in which the harmony of the United States may be interrupted by the exercise of individual legislation ;* to negative all laws passed by the several States contravening, in the opinion of the National Legislature the Articles of Union, or any treaties subsisting under the authority of the Union."[1]

§ 175. Mr. Paterson's "New Jersey" plan submitted; June 14th and 15th.—On June 14th, Mr. Paterson of New Jersey, on behalf of an element of the Convention from Connecticut, New Jersey, New York, Delaware, and which possibly included Mr. Martin of Maryland, and which was to some extent dissatisfied with the report of the Committee of the Whole,[1] asked leave to submit a form of government

---

[2] See chap. XI, §§ 324, *et seq.* Vol. II, and cases there collated, on relative effect of State laws and treaty stipulations.

§ 174.

[1] Madison Papers, vol. II, p. 859; (italics in quotation are the author's.)

§ 175.

[1] "This plan had been concerted among the Deputation, or members thereof, from Connecticut, New York, New Jersey, Delaware, and perhaps Mr. Martin, from Maryland, who made with them a common cause, though on different principles. Connecticut and New York were against a departure from the principle of the Confederation, wishing rather to add a few new powers to Congress than to substitute a National Government. The States of New Jersey and Delaware were opposed to a National Government, because its patrons considered a proportional representation of the States as the basis of it. The eagerness displayed by the members opposed to a National Government, from these different motives, began now to produce serious anxiety for the result of the Convention. Mr. Dickinson said to Mr. Madison, 'You see the consequence of pushing things too far. Some of the members from the small States wish for two branches in the General Legislature, and are friends to a good National Government;

known as the New Jersey Plan; in presenting it, he described it as being "more purely federal" than the one suggested by the Committee.[2]

The proposition consisted of a series of resolutions which were presented on the following day, June 15th; the first resolution was to the effect "that the Articles of Confederation ought to be so revised, corrected and enlarged, as to render the Federal Constitution adequate to the exigencies of government, and the preservation of the Union;"[3] he proposed to give the Federal judiciary jurisdiction in all cases involving the construction of treaties.[4] The sixth resolution was as follows:

"6. *Resolved*, that all acts of the United States in Congress, made by virtue and in pursuance of the powers hereby, and by the Articles of Confederation, vested in them, and all treaties made and ratified under the authority of the United States, shall be the supreme law of the respective States, so far forth as those acts or treaties shall relate to the said States or their citizens; and that the Judiciary of the several States shall be bound thereby in their decisions, anything in the respective laws of the individual States to the contrary notwithstanding: and that if any State, or any body of men in any State, shall oppose or prevent the carrying into execution such acts or treaties, the Federal Executive shall be authorized to call forth the power of the confederated States, or so much thereof as may be necessary, to enforce and compel an obedience to such acts or an observance of such treaties."[5]

It will be seen that, so far as the treaty-making power was concerned, the only change suggested by Mr. Paterson was to enlarge the authority of the United States and to make treaties, not as Mr. Pinckney had suggested, "the supreme law of the land," but the "supreme law of the respective States;" in fact, so important did he consider this treaty-making power that he considered it to be necessary not only

but we would sooner submit to foreign power, than submit to be deprived in both branches of the legislature, of an equality of suffrage, and thereby be thrown under the domination of the larger States.'" Madison Papers, vol. II, p. 862, note.

[2] *Idem*, p. 862.
[3] *Idem*, p. 863.
[4] *Idem*, p. 866.
[5] *Idem*, p. 866.

to clothe the United States with power to enforce, and compel, obedience to the acts of Congress, but also to enforce the observance of all treaties made by the United States.

§ 176. **Power to make and enforce treaties a practical matter in 1787.**—In this respect it must be remembered that the discussion in the Constitutional Convention in regard to the supervisory powers of the Federal Government over the States in regard to the enforcement, and the prevention of violations, of treaty stipulations, was by no means either academic, or confined to mere future possibilities; at that time the country was in a great state of excitement over the proper enforcement of the provisions of the treaty of peace regarding the collection of debts owing by Americans to citizens of Great Britain,[1] and also in regard to the navigation of the Mississippi River as it would be affected by the then proposed treaty with Spain, which, as the owner of Louisiana and New Orleans country, controlled the mouth of that river.[2] It was therefore, in view of actually existing circumstances that the Constitutional Convention not only declined to place any limitations upon the treaty-making power, but also expressly provided that all treaties made, or which should be made, under the authority of the United States were paramount to the laws and the constitutions of the several States; in fact, some of the burning questions of the day and hour were the treatment to be accorded to British creditors and American debtors, and the relative effect of treaty provisions providing for the payment of the debts to British citizens, and of the laws which had been passed by some of the States confiscating the identical debts for State use.[3]

Professor McMaster, in the Third Chapter of the First Volume of his able and interesting "History of the People of the United States," has given a detailed account of the conditions of the mercantile relations between this country and Great Britain as they were affected by the treaty stipu-

---

§ 176.
[1] See pp. 268, et seq., ante.
[2] For the effect of this particular element upon the ratification of the Constitution see § 222, post, relating to the Convention in Virginia.

[3] See *Ware* vs. *Hylton*, U. S. Supreme Ct., 1796, 2 Dallas, 199, and other cases collated in §§ 324 et seq., Vol. II, pp. 6, et seq.

lations, and the construction and misconstruction thereof,
and the confusion which had resulted from the efforts made
by some of the legislatures and courts to evade the provisions
of the treaties in regard thereto.[4]

§ 177. **Work of Convention continued ; Alexander
Hamilton's views, June 18th. Mr. Madison's views,
June 19th.**—The Convention again resolved itself into a Committee of the Whole to consider jointly the plans proposed
by Governor Randolph, Mr. Pinckney and Mr. Paterson.

We cannot refer to all the differences between these various plans, or the discussions in the Convention in regard
thereto, as we must necessarily confine ourselves exclusively
to the proceedings relating to the treaty-making power.

On June 18th, Alexander Hamilton is reported as having
taken part in the debate of the Convention for the first time
on this subject. Before offering his resolution he made some
remarks, prefacing them with the statement that he had
hitherto kept silent " partly from respect to others whose superior abilities, age and experience, rendered him unwilling
to bring forward ideas dissimilar to theirs, and partly from
his delicate situation with respect to his own State, to whose
sentiments, as expressed by his colleagues, he could by no
means accede." [1]   After this modest disclaimer, the man who
above all others was to aid and assist in the final ratification
of the Constitution, when framed and submitted to the people, and to the State conventions, gave his reasons for dissenting to some extent from the plans before the Convention, and urged that the strongest power possible be given
to the Central Government. He then offered a series of
resolutions in regard to the legislative and executive powers,
one of which provided that the Executive should " with the
advice and approbation of the Senate, have the power of
making all treaties." [2]   During the debate which followed
and extended through several succeeding sessions, Mr. Madison stated, on June 19th, that he did not think Mr. Pater-

---

[4] Chapter III, The Low State of
Trade and Commerce, John Bach
McMaster's History of the People
of the United States, New York,
1893, vol. I, p. 221.

§ 177.
[1] Madison Papers, vol. II, p. 878.
[2] *Idem*, p. 891.

son's plan went far enough in the general surrender of power to the Confederation; in the course of his remarks, he said :[3]

" Will it prevent the violations of the law of nations and of treaties which, if not prevented, must involve us in the calamities of foreign wars? The tendency of the States to these violations has been manifested in sundry instances. The files of Congress contain complaints already, from almost every nation with which treaties have been formed.[4] Hitherto indulgence has been shown us. This cannot be the permanent disposition of foreign nations. A rupture with other powers is the greatest of calamities. *It ought, therefore, to be effectually provided, that no part of a nation shall have it in its power to bring them on the whole.* The existing Confederacy does not sufficiently provide against this evil. The proposed amendment to it does not supply the omission. It leaves the will of the States as uncontrolled as ever." The views of some of the other members of the Convention as they were expressed in this debate are included in the notes to this section.[5]

[3] Madison Papers, vol. II, p. 896; (the italics are the author's.)

[4] For the complaints to which Mr. Madison alluded see §§ 157, 164, *ante.*

[5] Tuesday, June 19th, *In Committee of the Whole.*

"The first Resolution, 'that a national Government ought to be established, consisting, etc.,' being taken up,

" Mr. Wilson observed that, by a national Government, he did not mean one that would swallow up the State Governments, as seemed to be wished by some gentlemen. He was tenacious of the idea of preserving the latter. He thought, contrary to the opinion of Colonel Hamilton, that they might not only subsist, but subsist on friendly terms with the former. They were absolutely necessary for certain purposes, which the former could not reach. All large governments must be subdivided into lesser ju-

risdictions. As examples, he mentioned Persia, Rome, and particularly the divisions and subdivisions of England by Alfred.

"Colonel Hamilton coincided with the proposition as it stood in the Report. He had not been understood yesterday. By an abolition of the States, he meant that no boundary could be drawn between the National and State Legislatures; that the former must therefore have indefinite authority. If it were limited at all, the rivalship of the States would gradually subvert it. Even as corporations, the extent of some of them, as Virginia, Massachusetts, etc., would be formidable. As *States*, he thought they ought to be abolished. But he admitted the necessity of leaving them in subordinate jurisdictions. The examples of Persia and the Roman Empire, cited by Mr. Wilson, were, he thought, in

§ 178. Mr. Paterson's views contrasted with those of Mr. Madison and Mr. Hamilton.—The great difference be-

favor of his doctrine, the great powers delegated to the Satraps and Proconsuls having frequently produced revolts and schemes of independence.

"Mr. King wished, as everything depended on this proposition, that no objection might be improperly indulged against the phraseology of it. He conceived that the import of the term 'States,' 'sovereignty,' '*national*,' 'federal,' had often been used and implied in the discussions inaccurately and delusively. The States were not 'sovereigns' in the sense contended for by some. They did not possess the peculiar features of sovereignty,—they could not make war, nor peace, nor alliances, nor treaties. Considering them as political beings, they were dumb, for they could not speak to any foreign sovereign whatever. They were deaf, for they could not hear any propositions from such sovereign. They had not even the organs or faculties of defence or offence, for they could not of themselves raise troops or equip vessels, for war. On the other side, if the union of the States comprises the idea of a confederation, it comprises that also of consolidation. A union of the States is a union of the men composing them, from whence a *national* character results to the whole. Congress can act alone without the States; they can act, and their acts will be binding, against the instructions of the States. If they declare war, war is *de jure* declared; captures made in pursuance of it are lawful; no acts of the States can vary the situation, or prevent the judicial consequences. If the States, therefore,

retained some portion of their sovereignty, they had certainly divested themselves of essential portions of it. If they formed a confederacy in some respects, they formed a nation in others. The Convention could clearly deliberate on and propose any alterations that Congress could have done under the Federal Articles. And could not Congress propose, by virtue of the last Article, a change in any article whatever,—and as well that relating to the equality of suffrage, as any other? He made these remarks to obviate some scruples which had been expressed. He doubted much the practicability of annihilating the States; but thought that much of their power ought to be taken from them.

"Mr. Martin said, he considered that the separation from Great Britain placed the thirteen States in a state of nature towards each other; that they would have remained in that state till this time, but for the Confederation; that they entered into the Confederation on the footing of equality; that they met now to amend it, on the same footing; and that he could never accede to a plan that would introduce an inequality, and lay ten States at the mercy of Virginia, Massachusetts and Pennsylvania.

"Mr. Wilson could not admit the doctrine that when the colonies became independent of Great Britain, they became independent also of each other. He read the Declaration of Independence, observing thereon, that the *United Colonies* were declared to be free and independent States; and **inferring,**

310

tween Mr. Paterson and Mr. Madison was that the former was essentially a Federalist, while the latter was more of a Nationalist; in his later years, however, Mr. Madison became somewhat narrower in his views in regard to Constitutional construction, even to the extent of limiting the very powers which he, himself, had done so much to vest in the Central Government.[1]

On June 21st Mr. Madison clearly expressed his views in that respect as follows : " Were it practicable for the General Government to extend its care to every requisite object without the co-operation of the State Governments, the people would not be less free as members of one great Republic, than as members of thirteen small ones. A citizen of Delaware was not more free than a citizen of Virginia ; nor would either be more free than a citizen of America. Supposing, therefore, a tendency in the General Government to absorb the State

that they were independent, not *individually* but *unitedly*, and that they were confederated, as they were independent States.

"Colonel Hamilton assented to the doctrine of Mr. Wilson. He denied the doctrine that the States were thrown into a state of nature.. He was not yet prepared to admit the doctrine that the Confederacy could be dissolved by partial infractions of it. He admitted that the States met now on an equal footing, but could see no inference from that against concerting a change of the system in this particular. He took this occasion of observing, for the purpose of appeasing the fear of the small States, that two circumstances would render them secure under a national Government in which they might lose the equality of rank which they now held: one was the local situation of the three largest States, Virginia, Massachusetts and Pennsylvania. They were separated from each other by distance of place, and equally so, by all the peculiarities which distinguish the interests of one State from those of another. No combination, therefore, could be dreaded. In the second place, as there was a gradation in the States, from Virginia, the largest, down to Delaware, the smallest, it would always happen that ambitious combinations among a few States might and would be counteracted by defensive combinations of greater extent among the rest. No combination has been seen among the large counties, merely as such, against lesser counties. The more close the union of the States, and the more complete the authority of the whole, the less opportunity will be allowed to the stronger States to injure the weaker." Madison Papers, pp. 904 –908.

§ 178.

[1] A notable case in which Mr. Madison's views in regard to the limitations on the Federal Government was his veto of the Cumber-

Governments, no *fatal* consequence could result. Taking the reverse as the supposition, that a tendency should be left in the State Governments towards an independence of the General Government, and the gloomy consequences need not be pointed out." [2]

Notwithstanding the divergence of their opinions in some respects, both Mr. Madison and Mr. Hamilton were thoroughly agreed that the treaty power should be exclusively and effectually lodged in the Central Government. Their subsequent relations in the preparation and publication of the Federalist is conclusive evidence that, on the great fundamental principles of establishing a strong national, or central government, they were in thorough accord with each other. [3]

§ 179. **Mr. King's views on Sovereignty of States.**— During the course of the same debate Mr. King, referring to the phraseology which had been used, said that some expressions had been improperly used during the discussion; he conceived that the import of the terms, " States," "sovereignty," "*national*," and " federal," had been often used inaccurately and delusively. The report of the Convention shows that some of the ablest minds composing it recognized the extreme importance of the nationality and sovereignty of the Central Government and its superiority, so far as matters within its scope are concerned, to the State Governments, especially in regard to the foreign relations of the Union; Mr. King is reported as saying that so far from the States being " sovereigns " in a political sense, they were deaf and dumb as they did not possess some of the peculiar features of sovereignty, amongst them that of making treaties with foreign powers.[1] Mr. Gerry and Mr. Martin also made some remarks, on a subsequent day, on the subject of State sovereignty which are quoted in the notes.[2]

---

land Road bill on March 3, 1887, the last day of his second term as President of the United States. See Richardson's Messages of the Presidents, vol. I, p. 584.

[2] Madison Papers, vol. II, pp. 924 –925.

[3] See Extracts from Federalist, in chap. VIII, *post.*

§ 179.

[1] See Extract from Madison Papers, quoted in note 4 under § 177, p. 310, *ante.*

[2] Friday, June 29th, *In Convention.*

§ 180. **Dangerous differences in Convention on other subjects; Compromises reached.**—For nearly a month after this the Convention was engaged in discussing questions relating to the powers of the Executive, the length of his term of office, the nature of State representation and apportionment, the methods of election of the two houses of Congress, and of estimating the population of the States; these discussions at times became so heated that on more than one occasion an adjournment *sine die*, without accomplishing any result seemed inevitable; it was only by the earnest efforts of such men as Franklin, Madison, Hamilton and Sherman in compelling compromises as to those details that the Convention was held together and thus enabled to complete the work which finally crowned its efforts.[1]

§ 181. **Luther Martin's motion in regard to treaties; July 17th.**—On July 17th, on motion of Mr. Luther Martin, the following resolution was agreed to *nem. con.* :

"That the Legislative acts of the United States made by virtue and in pursuance of the Articles of Union, and all treaties made and ratified under the authority of the United States, shall be the supreme law of the respective States, as far as those acts or treaties shall relate to the said States, or

"Mr. Gerry urged, that we never were independent States, were not such now, and never could be, even on the principles of the Confederation. The States, and the advocates for them, were intoxicated with the idea of their *sovereignty*. He was a member of Congress at the time the Federal Articles were formed. The injustice of allowing each State an equal vote was long insisted on. He voted for it, but it was against his judgment, and under the pressure of public danger, and the obstinacy of the lesser States. The present Confederation he considered as dissolving. The fate of the Union will be decided by the Convention. If they do not agree on something, few delegates will probably be appointed to Congress. If **they** do Congress will probably be kept up till the new system should be adopted. He lamented that, instead of coming here like a band of brothers, belonging to the same family, we seem to have brought with us the spirit of political negotiators.

"Mr. L. Martin remarked, that the language of the States being *sovereign and independent*, was once familiar and understood; though it seemed now so strange and obscure. He read those passages in the Articles of Confederation which describe them in that language." Madison Papers, pp. 995–996.

§ 180.
[1] See especially in regard to proposed adjournment *sine die*, Madison Papers, vol. II, pp. 1107–1113, Session of July 16th.

their citizens and inhabitants; and that the Judiciaries of the several States shall be bound thereby in their decisions, anything in the respective laws of the individual States to the contrary notwithstanding." [1]

It is significant that this resolution was adopted immediately after the rejection of the resolution to the effect that the Federal Congress should have the right to negative laws passed by the Legislatures of the respective States, which had previously been adopted by the Convention in Committee of the Whole; as stated above, the practical effect of the negative of State legislation so far as the relations affected by treaties with foreign powers is concerned, has been preserved by the paramount provisions of Article VI of the Constitution. [2]

§ 182. **Mr. James Wilson's views on Treaties.**—During the debate in regard to the powers of the Senate which had preceded this, Mr. Wilson of Pennsylvania, while urging a nine year term for Senators in order to give stability to the Senate as a body, made some observations, on June 26th, which he believed had not been suggested up to that time, as follows: "Every nation may be regarded in two relations, first, to its own citizens; secondly, to foreign nations. It is, therefore, not only liable to anarchy and tyranny within, but has wars to avoid and treaties to obtain from abroad. The Senate will probably be the depositary of the powers concerning the latter objects. It ought therefore to be made respectable in the eyes of foreign nations. The true reason why Great Britain has not yet listened to a commercial treaty with us has been, because she had no confidence in the stability or efficacy of our Government." [1]

§ 183. **Committee of Detail; resolutions as to Treaties; July 26th.**—Mr. Madison's Journal does not again refer to the treaty power until July 26th, when the Convention adjourned until August 6th, after appointing a Committee of Detail to draft a form of Constitution embodying the principles which had been agreed upon, and having also adopted for the guidance of the Committee a series of twenty-three resolutions, numbers 6 and 7 thereof being as follows:

§ 181.
[1] Madison Papers, vol. II, p. 1119.
[2] See § 173, p. 303, *ante*.

§ 182.
[1] Madison Papers, vol. II, p. 968.

"6. *Resolved,* That the National Legislature ought to possess the legislative rights vested in Congress by the Confederation; and, moreover, to legislate in all cases for the general interests of the Union, *and also in those to which the States are separately incompetent, or in which the harmony of the United States may be interrupted by the exercise of individual legislation.*

"7. *Resolved,* That the legislative acts of the United States, made by virtue and in pursuance of the Articles of Union, and all treaties made and ratified under the authority of the United States, shall be the supreme law of the respective States, as far as those acts or treaties shall relate to the said States, or their citizens and inhabitants; and that the Judiciaries of the several States shall be bound thereby in their decisions, anything in the respective laws of the individual States to the contrary notwithstanding." [1]

The sixth resolution was apparently a mere expression of the reason for the adoption of the seventh resolution which subsequently became Article VIII of the draft and Article VI of the Constitution. The question, therefore, of the possible interruption of harmony of the Union in its relations with foreign powers must be regarded as a powerful factor in construing Article VI as it was finally adopted.

§ 184. **First draft submitted; treaties to be supreme law; August 6th.**—On August 6th the Committee of Detail reported the first draft of the Constitution, in which the sixth and seventh resolutions of July 26th were embodied as: Article VIII: "The acts of the Legislature of the United States made in pursuance of this Constitution, and all treaties made under the authority of the United States, shall be the supreme law of the several States, and of their citizens and inhabitants; and the Judges in the several States shall be bound thereby in their decisions, anything in the Constitutions or laws of the several States to the contrary notwithstanding."

Section 1, Article IX of the first draft of the Committee of Detail was as follows: "The Senate of the United States

§ 183.
[1] Madison Papers, vol. II, pp. 1221 -1222. (The italics in Resolution No. 6 are the author's.)

315

shall have power to make treaties, and to appoint ambassadors, and judges of the Supreme Court."

Article X which provided for the powers and duties of the Executive, did not clothe him with any power or duties as to making treaties, except that he should receive Ambassadors, and might correspond with the supreme executives of the several States; nor was any direct provision made in Article XI, which related to the judiciary, by which any special jurisdiction in regard to treaties was given to the Supreme Court or national judiciary.

Article XIII of the draft was as follows: "No State, without the consent of the Legislature of the United States, . . . shall keep troops or ships of war in time of peace; nor enter into any agreement or compact with another State, or with any foreign power; nor engage in any war, unless it shall be actually invaded by enemies, or the danger of invasion be so imminent as not to admit of a delay until the Legislature of the United States can be consulted." Article XII also contained a prohibition against any State entering into any treaty, alliance or confederation, or granting any title of nobility.[1]

§ 185. **Discussion of draft; Colonel Mason's views; August 15th.**—The draft was submitted to the Convention and was discussed section by section; the treaty clause was not reached until August 23d; but on the 15th in a discussion regarding the various relative powers of the Senate and the House of Representatives, Colonel Mason declared that he was extremely anxious to take away as much power as he could from the Senate, which in his opinion, "could already sell the whole country by means of treaties;" Mr. Mercer also contended that the Senate ought not to have the power of making treaties, as this power belonged to the Ex-

§ 184.

[1] The draft appears at pp. 1234–1242, Madison Papers, vol. II; Articles VIII and IX at p. 1234; Article X at p. 1236; Article XI at p. 1238; Articles XII and XIII at p. 1239.

For the development and changes of this and other articles of the Constitution, see The Growth of the Federal Constitution in the Federal Convention of 1787; an effort to trace the origin and development of each separate clause from its first suggestion in that body to the form finally adopted, by William M. Meigs, 2d edition, Philadelphia and London, 1901.

316

ecutive; he added that treaties should not be final so as to have the effect of altering the laws of the land until ratified by the legislative authority, as was the case in Great Britain, and he called attention to the fact at this time, so that his friends might fully appreciate the importance of the clause.[1]

§ 185.

[1] Wednesday, August 15th, *In Convention.* . . .

"Article 6, section 12, was then taken up.

"Mr. Strong moved to amend the article so as to read, 'Each House shall possess the right of originating all bills, except bills for raising money for the purposes of revenue, or for appropriating the same, and for fixing the salaries of the officers of the Government, which shall originate in the House of Representatives; but the Senate may propose or concur with amendments as in other cases.'

"Colonel Mason seconds the motion. He was extremely earnest to take this power from the Senate, who he said could already sell the whole country by means of treaties.

"Mr. Gorham urged the amendment as of great importance. The Senate will first acquire the habit of preparing money-bills, and then the practice will grow into an exclusive right of preparing them.

"Mr. Gouverneur Morris opposed it, as unnecessary and inconvenient.

"Mr. Williamson. Some think this restriction on the Senate essential to liberty; others think it of no importance. Why should not the former be indulged? He was for an efficient and stable government; but many would not strengthen the Senate, if not restricted in the case of money-bills. The friends of the Senate, would therefore, lose more than they would gain, by refusing to gratify the other side. He moved to postpone the subject, till the powers of the Senate should be gone over.

"Mr. Rutledge seconds the motion.

"Mr. Mercer should hereafter be against returning to a reconsideration of this section. He contended (alluding to Mr. Mason's observations) that the Senate ought not to have the power of treaties. This power belonged to the Executive department; adding, that treaties would not be final, so as to alter the laws of the land, till ratified by legislative authority. This was the case of treaties in Great Britain; particularly the late treaty of commerce with France.

"Colonel Mason did not say that a treaty would repeal a law; but that the Senate, by means of treaties, might alienate territory, etc., without legislative sanction. The cessions of the British Islands in the West Indies, by treaty alone, were an example. If Spain should possess herself of Georgia, therefore, the Senate might by treaty dismember the Union. He wished the motion to be decided now, that the friends of it might know how to conduct themselves.

"On the question for postponing section 12, it passed in the affirmative,—

"New Hampshire, Massachusetts, Virginia, North Carolina, South Carolina, Georgia, aye—6; Connecticut, New Jersey, Pennsyl-

§ 186. Treaties the supreme law; resolutions regarding same; August 23d.—When Article VIII of the draft was reached on August 23d there does not appear to have been any discussion in regard to it; a resolution offered by Mr. Rutledge was adopted *nem. con.* amending it but practically without any change so as to read as follows:

"This Constitution, and the laws of the United States made in pursuance thereof, and all the treaties made under the authority of the United States, shall be the supreme law of the several States and of their citizens and inhabitants; and the Judges of the several States shall be bound thereby in their decisions, anything in the Constitutions or laws of the several States to the contrary notwithstanding."[1]

Mr. Morris then offered a resolution which was also agreed to *nem. con.*, to strike out of the eighteenth clause of Section 1 of Article VII of the draft, the power of the United States "to enforce treaties," as being superfluous, for since the treaties were to be laws, the power to enforce them already existed.[2]

A motion was also similarly adopted to alter that part of the same clause of Section 1, Article VII, which authorized Congress to call forth the aid of the militia to enforce treaties after the words "laws of the Union," on the ground that by the adoption of Article VIII the words treaties were superfluous, inasmuch as they were to be the laws of the Union.[3]

In the second draft some of the provisions were so transposed that Article VIII subsequently became and remained Article VI.

Mr. Pinckney also moved to amend Section 1 of Article VII, by adding that Congress should not only have the right to make all laws necessary and proper for carrying into execution the foregoing powers, as well as all other powers vested by the Constitution in the government of the United States, or in any department or office thereof, but that Congress should also have the additional power to "negative all laws passed by the several States interfering, in the

vania, Delaware, Maryland, no—5."
Madison Papers, vol. III, pp. 1330–1332.

§ 186.
[1] Madison Papers, vol. III, p. 1408.
[2] *Idem,* p. 1409.
[3] *Idem,* p. 1409.

opinion of the Legislature, with the general interests and harmony of the Union."[4] Mr. Roger Sherman expressed his opinion that this was unnecessary, because the laws (which, as we have already seen, include treaties) of the Central Government were supreme and paramount to the State laws according to the plan as it then stood; a motion to commit was lost, and Mr. Pinckney's resolution was voted down.[5]

Article IX giving the Senate power to make treaties and appoint ambassadors and Judges of the Supreme Court was then taken up; the convention disagreed in several respects, and after an equally divided vote its consideration was postponed; subsequently it was referred to the Committee of Eleven.[6]

§ 187. **Debate as to ratification of treaties; August 23d.**—The debate of August 23d as to the ratification of treaties continued, Messrs. Madison, Morris, Gorham, Wilson, Dickinson, Randolph and Dr. Johnson taking part therein; Mr. Morris wished a saving clause inserted to the effect that "no treaty should be binding on the United States which is not ratified by law."[1] It became apparent

[4] *Idem*, p. 1409.
[5] *Idem*, p. 1410.
[6] *Idem*, pp. 1412 *et seq*., and see quotation at length under § 187, *post*.

§ 187.
[1] Thursday, August 23d, *In Convention.*

"Article 9, Sec. 1, being resumed, to wit: 'The Senate of the United States shall have power to make treaties, and to appoint Ambassadors, and Judges of the Supreme Court'—

"Mr. Madison observed, that the Senate represented the States alone; and that for this as well as other obvious reasons, it was proper that the President should be an agent in treaties.

"Mr. Gouverneur Morris did not know that he should agree to refer the making of treaties to the Senate

at all, but for the present would move to add, as an amendment to the section, after 'treaties,' the following: 'but no treaty shall be binding on the United States which is not ratified by law.'

"Mr. Madison suggested the inconvenience of requiring a legal *ratification* of treaties of alliance, for the purposes of war, etc., etc.

"Mr. Gorham. Many other disadvantages must be experienced, if treaties of peace and all negotiations are to be previously ratified; and if not previously, the ministers would be at a loss how to proceed. What would be the case in Great Britain, if the King were to proceed in this manner? American ministers must go abroad not instructed by the same authority (as will be the case with other ministers) which is to ratify their proceedings.

that the Convention was not satisfied that the Senate should make treaties; it was, therefore, referred back to a Com-

"Mr. Gouverneur Morris. As to treaties of alliance, they will oblige foreign powers to send their ministers here, the very thing we should wish for. Such treaties could not be otherwise made, if his amendment should succeed. In general he was not solicitous to multiply and facilitate treaties. He wished none to be made with Great Britain, till she should be at war. Then a good bargain might be made with her. So with other foreign powers. The more difficulty in making treaties, the more value will be set on them.

"Mr. Wilson. In the most important treaties, the King of Great Britain, being obliged to resort to Parliament for the execution of them, is under the same fetters as the amendment of Mr. Morris's will impose on the Senate. It was refused yesterday to permit even the Legislature to lay duties on exports. Under the clause without the amendment, the Senate alone can make a treaty requiring all the rice of South Carolina to be sent to some one particular port.

"Mr. Dickinson concurred in the amendment, as most safe and proper, though he was sensible it was unfavorable to the little States, which would otherwise have an *equal* share in making treaties.

"Doctor Johnson thought there was something of solecism in saying, that the acts of a minister with plenipotentiary powers from one body should depend for ratification on another body. The example of the King of Great Britain was not parallel. Full and complete power was vested in him. If the Parliament should fail to provide the

necessary means of execution, the treaty would be violated.

"Mr. Gorham, in answer to Mr. Gouverneur Morris, said, that negotiations on the spot were not to be desired by us; especially if the whole Legislature is to have anything to do with treaties. It will be generally influenced by two or three men, who will be corrupted by the ambassadors here. In such a government as ours, it is necessary to guard against the Government itself being seduced.

"Mr. Randolph, observing that almost every speaker had made objections to the clause as it stood, moved, in order to a further consideration of the subject, that the motion of Mr. Gouverneur Morris should be postponed; and on this question, it was lost, the States being equally divided,

"New Jersey, Pennsylvania, Delaware, Maryland, Virginia, aye—5; Massachusetts, Connecticut, North Carolina, South Carolina, Georgia, no—5.

"On Mr. Gouverneur Morris's motion,—

"Pennsylvania, aye—1; Massachusetts, Connecticut, New Jersey, Delaware, Maryland, Virginia, South Carolina, Georgia, no—8; North Carolina, divided.

"The several clauses of Article 9, Sec. 1, were then separately postponed, after inserting, 'and other public ministers,' next after 'ambassadors.'

"Mr. Madison hinted for consideration whether a distinction might not be made between different sorts of treaties; allowing the President and Senate to make treaties eventual, and of alliance for

320

mittee of Five; it was, however, apparently finally intrusted to the Committee of Eleven, which included certain modifications as to this subject in its report on September 4th, which will be hereafter alluded to.[2]

§ 188. Amendments to draft as to treaties; August 25th. —On August 25th, several days after Article VIII of the draft, afterwards Article VI of the Constitution, had been unanimously adopted, Mr. Madison, seconded by Mr. Morris, offered a resolution, which was adopted *nem. con.*, that the article should be reconsidered by the insertion of the words, "or which shall be made;" this was done so as to obviate all doubt concerning pre-existing treaties, by making the words "all treaties made" to refer to them, as the words inserted would refer to future treaties.[1] The attention of the Convention was thus again especially called to the power which Mr. Mason had already said was great enough "to sell the Union,"[2] and the delegates were fully advised that no matter how great the power might be, it related not only to the treaties already made by the Congress of the Confederation, but to every one that might thereafter be made and ratified.

§ 189. Jurisdiction of Supreme Court over treaty cases; Senate to ratify treaties; September 4th–10th.—When the articles relating to the power of the Supreme Court were discussed, on motion of Mr. Rutledge, an amendment was unanimously adopted giving that Court jurisdiction in regard to all treaties made by the United States, that branch of its jurisdiction having apparently been overlooked by the Committee of Detail.[1]

On September 4th the Committee of Eleven, consisting of one member for every State then represented, made a report in which a number of matters on which the Convention had disagreed were disposed of by modified clauses to be inserted at their proper place in the Constitution as already framed.

---

limited terms, and requiring the concurrence of the whole Legislature in other treaties.

"The first Section of Article 9, was finally referred, *nem. con.*, to the Committee of five, and the House then adjourned." Madison Papers, vol. III, pp. 1412–1415.

[2] See § 189, note 2 on p. 322, *post.*
§ 188.
[1] Madison Papers, vol. III, p. 1430.
[2] See § 185, p. 317, *ante.*
§ 189.
[1] Madison Papers, Vol. III., p. 1439.

The seventh recommendation provided, that the President, by and with the advice and consent of the Senate, should make treaties, thus returning to Mr. Hamilton's original suggestion, with the limitation, however, that no treaty should be made without the consent of two thirds of the members present.[2] Some of the members thought that the negotiation of treaties should be intrusted to the executive alone.[3] After some discussion, on September 6th,[4] as to the

[2] Tuesday, September 4th, *In Convention.* "Mr. Brearly, from the Committee of eleven, made a further partial Report as follows: "The Committee of eleven, to whom sundry resolutions, etc., were referred on the thirty-first of August, report, that in their opinion the following additions and alterations should be made to the Report before the Convention, viz: "1. The first clause of Article 7, Section 1, to read as follows: 'The Legislature shall have power to lay and collect taxes, duties, imposts and excises, to pay the debts and provide for the common defence and general welfare of the United States.' . . . 7. Section 4. 'The President, by and with the advice and consent of the Senate, shall have power to make treaties; and he shall nominate, and, by and with the advice and consent of the Senate, shall appoint ambassadors, and other public ministers, Judges of the Supreme Court, and all other officers of the United States whose appointments are not otherwise herein provided for. But no treaty shall be made without the consent of two-thirds of the members present.'" Madison Papers, Vol. III, pp. 1485-1488.

[3] "The negotiation of treaties was obviously a function that should be committed to the executive alone. But a treaty might undertake to dismember a state of part of its territory, or might otherwise affect its individual interests; and even where it concerned only the general interests of all the states, there was a great unwillingness to intrust the treaty-making power exclusively to the president. Here the states, as equal political sovereignties, were unwilling to relax their hold upon the general government; and the result was that provision of the Constitution which makes the consent of two-thirds of the Senators present necessary to the ratification of a treaty." Curtis' Constitutional History of the United States, vol. I, p. 468.

[4] Thursday, September 6th, *In Convention.*

"Mr. Wilson said, that he had weighed carefully, the Report of the Committee for remodelling the constitution of the Executive; and on combining it with other parts of the plan, he was obliged to consider the whole as having a dangerous tendency to aristocracy; as throwing a dangerous power into the hands of the Senate. They will have, in fact, the appointment of the President, and through his dependence on them, the virtual appointment to offices; among others, the officers of the Judiciary department. They are to make treaties; and they are

required majority, this recommendation was adopted on September 7th;[5] but on the following day the matter was reconsidered; there was an active debate during which

to try all impeachments. In allowing them thus to make the Executive and Judiciary appointments, to be the court of impeachments, and to make treaties which are to be laws of the land, the Legislative, Executive and Judiciary powers are all blended in one branch of the Government. The power of making treaties involves the case of subsidies, and here, as an additional evil, foreign influence is to be dreaded. According to the plan as it now stands, the President will not be the man of the people, as he ought to be; but the minion of the Senate. He cannot even appoint a tide-waiter without the Senate. He had always thought the Senate too numerous a body for making appointments to office. The Senate will, moreover, in all probability, be in constant session. They will have high salaries. And with all those powers, and the President in their interest, they will depress the other branch of the Legislature, and aggrandize themselves in proportion. Add to all this, that the Senate, sitting in conclave, can by holding up to their respective States various and improbable candidates, contrive so to scatter their votes, as to bring the appointment of the President ultimately before themselves. Upon the whole, he thought the new mode of appointing the President, with some amendments, a valuable improvement; but he could never agree to purchase it at the price of the ensuing parts of the Report, nor befriend a system of which they made a part.

"Mr. Gouverneur Morris expressed his wonder at the observations of Mr. Wilson, so far as they preferred the plan in the printed Report, to the new modification of it before the House; and entered into a comparative view of the two, with an eye to the nature of Mr. Wilson's objections to the last." Madison Papers, Vol. III, pp. 1504-1506.

[5] Friday, September 7th, *In Convention.*

"The fourth section, to wit.: 'The President, by and with the advice and consent of the Senate, shall have power to make treaties,' etc., was then taken up.

"Mr. Wilson moved to add, after the word 'Senate,' the words, 'and House of Representatives.' As treaties, he said, are to have the operation of laws, they ought to have the sanction of laws also. The circumstance of secrecy in the business of treaties formed the only objection; but this, he thought, so far as it was inconsistent with obtaining the legislative sanction, was outweighed by the necessity of the latter.

"Mr. Sherman thought the only question that could be made was, whether the power could be safely trusted to the Senate. He thought it could; and that the necessity of secrecy in the case of treaties forbade a reference of them to the whole legislature.

"Mr. Fitzimmons seconded the motion of Mr. Wilson; and on the question,—Pennsylvania, aye— 1; New Hampshire, Massachusetts, Connecticut, New Jersey, Delaware, Maryland, Virginia, North Carolina, South Carolina, Georgia, no—10.

various amendments were offered and the danger of the treaty-making power being vested in too small a coterie was referred to as a probable source of danger by several mem-

"The first sentence, as to making treaties, was then agreed to, *nem. con.* . . .

"The fourth section. 'The President by and with the advice and consent of the Senate shall have power to make treaties. *But no treaty shall be made without the consent of two-thirds of the members present,*' — being considered, and the last clause being before the House, —

"Mr. Wilson thought it objectionable to require the concurrence of two-thirds, which puts it into the power of a minority to control the will of a majority.

"Mr. King concurred in the objection; remarking that as the Executive was here joined in the business, there was a check which did not exist in Congress, where the concurrence of two-thirds was required.

"Mr. Madison moved to insert, after the word 'treaty,' the words 'except treaties of peace;' allowing these to be made with less difficulty than other treaties. It was agreed to, *nem. con.*

"Mr. Madison then moved to authorize a concurrence of two-thirds of the Senate to make treaties of peace, without the concurrence of the President. The President, he said, would necessarily derive so much power and importance from a state of war, that he might be tempted, if authorized, to impede a treaty of peace.

"Mr. Butler seconded the motion.

"Mr. Gorham thought the se-

curity unnecessary, as the means of carrying on the war would not be in the hands of the President, but of the Legislature.

"Mr. Gouverneur Morris thought the power of the President in this case harmless; and that no peace ought to be made without the concurrence of the President, who was the general guardian of the national interests.

"Mr. Butler was strenuous for the motion, as a necessary security against ambitious and corrupt Presidents. He mentioned the late perfidious policy of the Stadtholder in Holland; and the artifices of the Duke of Marlborough to prolong the war of which he had the management.

"Mr. Gerry was of opinion that in treaties of peace a greater rather than a less proportion of votes was necessary, than in other treaties. In treaties of peace the dearest interests will be at stake, as the fisheries, territories, etc. In treaties of peace also, there is more danger to the extremities of the continent, of being sacrificed, than on any other occasion.

"Mr. Williamson thought that treaties of peace should be guarded at least by requiring the same concurrence as in other treaties.

"On the motion of Mr. Madison and Mr. Butler, — Maryland, South Carolina, Georgia, aye — 3; New Hampshire, Massachusetts, Connecticut, New Jersey, Pennsylvania, Delaware, Virginia, North Carolina, no — 8.

"On the part of the clause concerning treaties, amended by the

bers; the report of the committee was finally readopted as it stood on September 7th.[6]

exception as to treaties of peace,— New Hampshire, Massachusetts, Connecticut, Delaware, Maryland, Virginia, North Carolina, South Carolina, aye—8; New Jersey, Pennsylvania, Georgia, no—3.'' Madison Papers, Vol. III, pp. 1518-1522.

[6] Saturday, September 8th, *In Convention.*

"The last Report of the Committee of Eleven (see the fourth of September) was resumed.

"Mr. King moved to strike out the exception of treaties of peace, from the general clause requiring two-thirds of the Senate for making treaties.

"Mr. Wilson wished the requisition of two-thirds to be struck out altogether. If the majority cannot be trusted, it was a proof, as observed by Mr. Gorham, that we were not fit for one society.

"A reconsideration of the whole clause was agreed to.

"Mr. Gouverneur Morris was against striking out the exception of treaties of peace. If two-thirds of the Senate should be required for peace, the Legislature will be unwilling to make war for that reason, on account of the fisheries, or the Mississippi, the two great objects of the Union. Besides, if a majority of the Senate be for peace, and are not allowed to make it, they will be apt to effect their purpose in the more disagreeable mode of negativing the supplies for the war.

"Mr. Williamson remarked, that treaties are to be made in the branch of the Government where there may be a majority of the States, without a majority of the people. Eight men may be a majority of a quorum, and should not have the power to decide the conditions of peace. There would be no danger, that the exposed States, as South Carolina or Georgia, would urge an improper war for the Western territory.

"Mr. Wilson. If two-thirds are necessary to make peace, the minority may perpetuate war, against the sense of the majority.

"Mr. Gerry enlarged on the danger of putting the essential rights of the Union in the hands of so small a number as a majority of the Senate, representing, perhaps, not one-fifth of the people. The Senate will be corrupted by foreign influence.

"Mr. Sherman was against leaving the rights established by the treaty of peace, to the Senate; and moved to annex a proviso, that no such rights should be ceded without the sanction of the Legislature.

"Mr. Gouverneur Morris seconded the ideas of Mr. Sherman.

. "Mr. Madison observed that it had been too easy, in the present Congress, to make treaties, although nine States were required for the purpose.

"On the question for striking out 'except treaties of peace,'—

"New Hampshire, Massachusetts, Connecticut, Pennsylvania, Virginia, North Carolina, South Carolina, Georgia, aye—8; New Jersey, Delaware, Maryland, no—3.

"Mr. Wilson and Mr. Dayton moved to strike out the clause, requiring two-thirds of the Senate, for making treaties; on which, Delaware, aye—1; New Hampshire,

§ 190. Committee to make final draft ; President to make treaties ; September 10th and 12th.—On September 10th, all of the disputed questions having been discussed and settled, a " Committee of Style and Arrangement "[1] was appointed to

Massachusetts, New Jersey, Pennsylvania, Maryland, Virginia, North Carolina, South Carolina, Georgia, no—9; Connecticut, divided.

" Mr. Rutledge and Mr. Gerry moved that ' no treaty shall be made without the consent of two-thirds of all the members of the Senate,'—according to the example in the present Congress.

" Mr. Gorham. There is a difference in the case, as the President's consent will also be necessary in the new government.

" On the question,—

" North Carolina, South Carolina, Georgia, aye—3; New Hampshire, Massachusetts, (Mr. Gerry, aye), Connecticut, New Jersey, Pennsylvania, Delaware, Maryland, Virginia, no—8.

" Mr. Sherman moved that ' no treaty shall be made without a majority of the whole number of the Senate.'

" Mr. Gerry seconded him.

" Mr. Williamson. This will be less security than two-thirds, as now required.

" Mr. Sherman. It will be less embarrassing.

" On the question, it passed in the negative,—

" Massachusetts, Connecticut, Delaware, South Carolina, Georgia, aye—5; New Hampshire, New Jersey, Pennsylvania, Maryland, Virginia, North Carolina, no—6.

" Mr. Madison moved that a quorum of the Senate consist of two-thirds of all the members.

" Mr. Gouverneur Morris. This will put it in the power of one man to break up a quorum.

" Mr. Madison. This may happen to any quorum.

" On the question, it passed in the negative,—

" Maryland, Virginia, North Carolina, South Carolina, Georgia, aye—5; New Hampshire, Massachusetts, Connecticut, New Jersey, Pennsylvania, Delaware, no—6.

" Mr. Williamson and Mr. Gerry, moved that ' no treaty should be made without previous notice to the members, and a reasonable time for their attending.'

" On the question,—all the States, no; except North Carolina, South Carolina, and Georgia, aye.

" On a question on the clause of the Report of the Committee of eleven, relating to treaties by two-thirds of the Senate,—all the States were, aye; except Pennsylvania, New Jersey, and Georgia, no.

" Mr. Gerry moved, that ' no officer shall be appointed but to offices created by the Constitution or by law.' This was rejected as unnecessary,—

" Massachusetts, Connecticut, New Jersey, North Carolina, Georgia, aye—5; New Hampshire, Pennsylvania, Delaware, Maryland, Virginia, South Carolina, no—6."
Madison Papers, Vol. III, pp. 1524–1528.

§ 190.
[1] In chapter XI of the second volume of the History of the Constitution of the United States entitled " The Last Days of the Convention," Mr. Bancroft says, in regard to this committee, pp. 207–209:

" The committee to whom the constitution was referred for the

make the final draft.[2]   That Committee reported on September 12th;[3] in regard to treaties, Section 2, Article II, provided that the President should have the "power, by and with the advice and consent of the Senate, to make treaties, provided two thirds of the Senators present concur."[4]   Section 2, Article III, provided that the judicial power of the United

arrangement of its articles and the revision of its style were Johnson, Hamilton, Gouverneur Morris, Madison, and King. The final draft of the instrument was written by Gouverneur Morris, who knew how to reject redundant and equivocal expressions, and to use language with clearness and vigor; but the convention itself had given so minute, long-continued, and oft-renewed attention to every phrase in every section, that there scarcely remained room for improvement except in the distribution of its parts.

"Its first words are: 'We the people of the United States, in order to form a more perfect union, to establish justice, ensure domestic tranquillity, provide for the common defence, promote the general welfare, and secure the blessings of liberty to ourselves and our posterity, do ordain and establish this constitution for the United States of America.' Here is no transient compact between parties: it is the institution of government by an act of the highest sovereignty; the decree of many who are yet one; their law of laws, inviolably supreme, and not to be changed except in the way which their forecast has provided.

"The names of the thirteen States, so carefully enumerated in the articles of confederation and in the treaty of peace, were omitted, because the constitution was to go into effect on its acceptance by nine of them, and the states by which it would be ratified could not be foreknown. The deputies in the convention, representing but eleven states, did not pretend to be 'the people'; and could not institute a general government in its name. The instrument which they framed was like the report of a bill beginning with the words 'it is enacted,' though the binding enactment awaits the will of the legislature; or like a deed drawn up by an attorney for several parties, and awaiting its execution by the principals themselves. Only by its acceptance could the words 'we the people of the United States' become words of truth and power.

"The phrase 'general welfare,' adopted from the articles of confederation, though seemingly vague, was employed in a rigidly restrictive sense to signify 'the concerns of the union at large, not the particular policy of any state.' The word 'national' was excluded from the constitution, because it might seem to present the idea of the union of the people without at the same time bringing into view, that the one republic was formed out of many states. Toward foreign powers the country presented itself as one nation. The arrangement of the articles and sections is faultless; the style of the whole is nearly so."

[2] Madison Papers, vol. III, p. 1542.
[3] Idem, p. 1543.
[4] Idem, p. 1555.

States should extend to "all cases, both in law and equity, arising under this Constitution, the laws of the United States, and treaties made, or which shall be made, under their authority."[5]   Article VI composed of a single section, was divided into three clauses, the second of which related to treaties and was as follows: "This Constitution, and the laws of the United States which shall be made in pursuance thereof; and all treaties made, or which shall be made, under the authority of the United States, shall be the supreme law of the land; and the judges in every State shall be bound thereby, anything in the Constitution or laws of any State to the contrary notwithstanding."[6]

The power of Congress, by Section 8 of Article I, included the right "to make all laws which shall be necessary and proper for carrying into execution the foregoing powers, and all other powers vested by this Constitution in the Government of the United States, or in any department or officer thereof."[7]   Section 10 of the same Article provided that without the consent of Congress no State should "enter into any agreement or compact with another State, or with any foreign power."[8]

In his Constitutional History, Mr. George Ticknor Curtis has summarized the reasons for vesting the treaty-making power in the President, with the limitations thereover involved in the necessary two thirds ratification; they are quoted in the notes to this section.[9]

[5] *Idem*, p. 1556.
[6] *Idem*, p. 1559.
[7] *Idem*, p. 1551.
[8] *Idem*, p. 1552.
[9] "The power to make treaties, which had been given to the Senate by the committee of detail, and which was afterwards transferred to the president, to be exercised with the advice and consent of two thirds of the senators present, was thus modified on account of the changes which the plan of government had undergone, and which have been previously explained. The power to declare war having been vested in the whole legislature, it was necessary to provide the mode in which a war was to be terminated. As the president was to be the organ of communication with other governments, and as he would be the general guardian of the national interests, the negotiation of a treaty of peace, and of all other treaties, was necessarily confided to him. But as treaties would not only involve the general interests of the nation, but might touch the particular interests of individual states, and, whatever their effect, were to be part of the supreme law of the land, it was necessary to give to the senators, as the direct representatives of the states, a concurrent authority with

§ 191. **Letter to Congress, accompanying Constitution as to ratification by the people, instead of by legislatures of the States.**—This draft of the Committee on Style and Arrangement was accompanied by a letter submitting the Constitution to the consideration of the people of the United

the president over the relations to be affected by them. The rule of ratification suggested by the committee to whom this subject was last confided was, that a treaty might be sanctioned by two thirds of the senators present, but not by a smaller number. A question was made, however, and much considered, whether treaties of peace ought not to be subjected to a different rule. One suggestion was, that the Senate ought to have power to make treaties of peace without the concurrence of the president, on account of his possible interest in the continuance of a war from which he might derive power and importance. But an objection, strenuously urged, was that, if the power to make a treaty of peace were confided to the Senate alone, and a majority of two thirds of the whole Senate were to be required to make such a treaty, the difficulty of obtaining peace would be so great that the legislature would be unwilling to make war on account of the fisheries, the navigation of the Mississippi, and other important objects of the Union. On the other hand, it was said that a majority of the states might be a minority of the people of the United States, and that the representatives of a minority of the nation ought not to have power to decide the conditions of peace.

"The result of these various objections was a determination on the part of a large majority of the states not to make treaties of peace an exception to the rule, but to provide a uniform rule for the ratification of all treaties. The rule of the Confederation, which had required the assent of nine states in Congress to every treaty or alliance, had been found to work great inconvenience; as any rule must do which should give to a minority of states power to control the foreign relations of the country. The rule established by the Constitution, while it gives to every state an opportunity to be present and to vote, requires no positive quorum of the Senate for the ratification of a treaty; it simply demands that the treaty shall receive the assent of two thirds of all the members who may be present. The theory of the Constitution undoubtedly is, that the president represents the people of the United States generally, and the senators represent their respective states; so that, by the concurrence which the rule thus requires, the necessity for a fixed quorum of the states is avoided, and the operations of this function of the government are greatly facilitated and simplified. The adoption, also, of that part of the rule which provides that the Senate may either 'advise or consent,' enables that body so far to initiate a treaty as to propose one for the consideration of the president—although such is not the general practice." Curtis' Constitutional History of the United States, vol. I, pp. 579–581.

States, and stating, in the following words, that the question of the governmental powers which the States should surrender to, and vest in, the General Government had been the object of great consideration :

" The friends of our country have long seen and desired, that the power of making war, peace, and treaties ; that of levying money, and regulating commerce, and the correspondent executive and judicial authorities, should be fully and effectually vested in the general government of the Union. . . . It is obviously impracticable, in the federal government of these States, to secure all rights of independent sovereignty to each, and yet provide for the interest and safety of all. Individuals entering into society must give up a share of liberty, to preserve the rest. . . . In all our deliberations on this subject, we kept steadily in our view that which appeared to us the greatest interest of every true American, the consolidation of our union, in which is involved our prosperity, felicity, safety, perhaps our national existence." [1]

§ 192. **Constitution adopted ; September 15th.**—Even after the Committee on Style and Arrangement had submitted what was supposed to be the final draft, there were several meetings, in which the report was discussed. It does not appear, however, that any of the alterations suggested related to the treaty-making power ; on September 15th the Constitution, as amended, was adopted by all the State delegations, although some of the individual members, including Mr. Gerry, Colonel Mason and Mr. Randolph,[1] stated that they would withhold their names, their objections as stated did not relate to the fact that the treaty-making power was vested in the Central Government.[2] In fact, Mr. Randolph in his opening remarks had referred to the centralization of the treaty-making power, and the enforcement of treaty stipulations, as some of the chief grounds for lodging more extensive powers in the Central Government.[3]

§ 191.
[1] Madison Papers, vol. III, pp. 1560–1561.
§ 192.
[1] Mr. Randolph, however, afterwards supported the Constitution in the State Convention of Virginia. See § 213, *post*.
[2] Madison Papers, vol. III, pp. 1600–1603.
[3] See § 171, p. 300, *ante*.

§ 193. **Constitution signed ; Convention adjourns ; September 17th.**—The Constitution was ordered to be engrossed, the Convention adjourned to meet again on September 17th, when the engrossed copy was presented for signature by Dr. Franklin, but was read by Mr. Wilson.[1] At the last moment there was one change made, and the only occasion occurred on which the President of the Convention is reported as taking actual part in the debates, although there is abundant evidence that the part taken by him in controlling the feelings of the members, and thus preventing any final rupture, was an all important element in the success of the Convention. This change simply made thirty thousand, instead of forty thousand, the minimum basis of Congressional representation.[2] The members then proceeded to sign the Constitution as engrossed,[3] and containing all the provisions as to the treaty-making power above referred to, after which the Convention was dissolved by an adjournment *sine die.*[4]

§ 194. **What the Records of the Convention demonstrate.**—The records of the Constitutional Convention, and the provisions adopted, and incorporated in the Constitution, conclusively demonstrate, as to the treaty-making power:

First: That the unfortunate condition of the Union when the convention convened was largely due to the fact, that, although the Central Government possessed power to make treaties, it did not possess sufficient power to enforce them, and that the Convention unanimously agreed that it would only be by giving to, or vesting in, the Central Government the most exclusive powers, both as to the making and enforcing of treaties, and also by entirely debarring the States from any participation therein, that the foreign relations of the Union could be preserved, and the nation strengthened in its commercial relations which were then assuming larger proportions every year.

Second: That the treaty-making power was lodged in the Central Government, as a matter of course, and that as to that element there was unanimity in the Convention.

§ 193.
[1] Madison Papers, vol. III, p. 1596.
[2] *Idem,* p. 1599.
[3] *Idem,* p. 1605. (Their names appear at p. 1623.) For Constitution in full see pp. 519, *et seq., post.*
[4] *Idem,* p. 1624.

Third: That the States were absolutely prohibited from exercising any treaty-making power or entering into foreign relations of any kind, and that the Convention was also a unit on this point.

Fourth: That the treaty-making power was vested in the Central Government without any limitation whatever, and not only were no limitations suggested, but the wide scope of the power was fully appreciated even to the extent of "selling the Union."[1]

Fifth: That the only restraints placed upon the treaty-making power were as to the method in which treaties must be made and ratified, and that those restrictions related only to the method of exercising the power, and not to its scope or its supremacy.

Sixth: That the Convention was unanimous on the point that all provisions of treaties must be enforced for the sake of the national honor, and that the Central Government must have the power to enforce them, and to such end all treaties, as well as the appropriate legislation to make them effectual, must be superior to the constitutions and laws of the several States, and binding upon all the judges, as was expressed in Article VI of the Constitution.

§ 195. **Ratification of the Constitution by the people; Madison's views.**—During the debates the question of the method of ratification of the Constitution—whether by the State Legislatures or by the people—had been several times discussed. Mr. Madison declared as early as July 23d that the State Legislatures were incompetent to ratify the proposed changes in the Articles of Confederation as they would make essential inroads on the State Constitutions; and that although the Constitutions of some of the States might have given the power to concur in confederations, certainly some of the States had not done so, and in those cases the ratification must necessarily be obtained from the people themselves. He considered the difference between a system founded on Legislatures only, and one founded on the consent of the people, to be the true difference between a league, or treaty, and a Constitution; he urged, by all means, that the States

§ 194.
[1] See § 185, p. 317, *ante.*

by Conventions, and not by their Legislatures, should ratify the Constitution in order to make it binding upon all the people.[1]

Mr. Madison's wise and prudent counsel prevailed; the

§ 195.

[1] Monday, July 23d, *In Convention.* . . .

The nineteenth Resolution (of the Committee of the Whole) referring the new Constitution to Assemblies to be chosen by the people, for the express purpose of ratifying it, was next taken into consideration.

"Mr. Ellsworth moved that it be referred to the Legislatures of the States for ratification. Mr. Paterson seconded the motion.

"Colonel Mason considered a reference of the plan to the authority of the people, as one of the most important and essential of the Resolutions. . . . Mr. Randolph; . . . It is of great importance, therefore, that the consideration of this subject should be transferred from the Legislatures, where this class of men (local demagogues) have their full influence, to a field in which their efforts can be less mischievous. It is moreover worthy of consideration, that some of the States are averse to any change in their Constitution, and will not take the requisite steps, unless expressly called upon, to refer the question to the people.

"Mr. Gerry . . . considered the Confederation to be paramount to any State Constitution. The last Article of it, authorizing alterations, must consequently be so as well as the others; and every thing done in pursuance of the article, must have the same high authority with the article.

"Mr. Gorham was against referring the plan to the Legislatures. . . .

"Mr. Ellsworth . . . thought more was to be expected from the Legislatures than the people. . . . The Legislatures were considered as competent. . . .

"Mr. Williamson thought the Resolution (the nineteenth) so expressed, as that it might be submitted either to the Legislatures or to Conventions recommended by the Legislatures. He observed that some Legislatures were evidently unauthorized to ratify the system. He thought, too, that Conventions were to be preferred, as more likely to be composed of the ablest men in the States.

"Mr. Gouverneur Morris considered the inference of Mr. Ellsworth from the plea of necessity, as applied to the establishment of a new system, on the consent of the people of a part of the States, in favor of a like establishment, on the consent of a part of the Legislatures, as a *non sequitur.* If the Confederation is to be pursued, no alteration can be made without the unanimous consent of the Legislatures. Legislative alterations not conformable to the Federal compact would clearly not be valid. The Judges would consider them as null and void. Whereas, in case of an appeal to the people of the United States, the supreme authority, the Federal compact may be altered by a *majority of them,* in like manner as the Constitution of a particular State may be altered by a majority of the people of the State. The amendment moved by Mr. Ells-

Constitution was sent to the Federal Congress with the request to have it ratified by Conventions of delegates chosen by the people of each State, but to be called by the respec-

worth erroneously supposes, that we are proceeding on the basis of the Confederation. This Convention is unknown to the Confederation.

" Mr. King thought with Mr. Ellsworth that the Legislatures had a competent authority, the acquiescence of the people of America in the Confederation being equivalent to a formal ratification by the people. He thought with Mr. Ellsworth, also, that the plea of necessity was as valid in the one case, as the other. At the same time, he preferred a reference to the authority of the people expressly delegated to Conventions, as the most certain means of obviating all disputes and doubts concerning the legitimacy of the new Constitution, as well as the most likely means of drawing forth the best men in the States to decide on it. He remarked that among other objections, made in the State of New York to granting powers to Congress, one had been, that such powers as would operate within the States could not be reconciled to the Constitution, and therefore were not grantable by the Legislative authority. He considered it as of some consequence, also, to get rid of the scruples which some members of the State Legislatures might derive from their oaths to support and maintain the existing Constitutions.

" Mr. Madison thought it clear that the Legislatures were incompetent to the proposed changes. These changes would make essential inroads on the State Constitutions; and it would be a novel and dangerous doctrine, that a Legislature could change the Constitution under which it held its existence. There might indeed be some Constitutions within the Union, which had given a power to the Legislature to concur in alterations of the Federal compact. But there were certainly some which had not; and in the case of these, a ratification must of necessity be obtained from the people. He considered the difference between a system founded on the Legislatures only, and one founded on the people, to be the true difference between a *league* or *treaty*, and a *Constitution*. The former, in point of *moral obligation*, might be as inviolable as the latter. In point of *political operation*, there were two important distinctions in favor of the latter. First, a law violating a treaty ratified by a pre-existing law might be respected by the Judges as a law, though an unwise or perfidious one. A law violating a Constitution established by the people themselves, would be considered by the Judges as null and void. Secondly, the doctrine laid down by the law of nations in the case of treaties is, that a breach of any one article by any of the parties frees the other parties from their engagements. In the case of a union of people under one constitution, the nature of the pact has always been understood to exclude such an interpretation. Comparing the two modes, in point of expediency, he thought all the considerations which recommended this Convention, in preference to Congress, for proposing the reform, were in favor of State Con-

tive State Legislatures.[2]   The ratification, therefore, of the perfected work of the Constitutional Convention not only

ventions, in preference to the Legislatures for examining and adopting it.

"On the question on Mr. Ellsworth's motion to refer the plan to the Legislatures of the States,—Connecticut, Delaware, Maryland, aye—3; New Hampshire, Massachusetts, Pennsylvania, Virginia, North Carolina, South Carolina, Georgia, no—7.

"Mr. Gouverneur Morris moved, that the reference of the plan be made to one General Convention, chosen and authorized by the people, to consider, *amend*, and establish the same. Not seconded.

"On the question for agreeing to the nineteenth Resolution, touching the mode of ratification as reported from the Committee of the Whole, viz., to refer the Constitution, after the approbation of Congress, to assemblies chosen by the people,—New Hampshire, Massachusetts, Connecticut, Pennsylvania, Maryland, Virginia, North Carolina, South Carolina, Georgia, aye—9; Delaware, no—1." Madison Papers, Vol. II, pp. 1177–1185.

[2] In his American Constitutional Law, already referred to, Mr. Hare says, vol. I, pp. 89–91: "When the Convention met at Philadelphia, the people of the United States, not less than the people of the States, came through their agents, and being present in both capacities, might determine in which they would act in framing the Constitution. Whether it should be made by the people of the United States and sanctioned by the States, or made by the States and sanctioned by the people, might seem immaterial, because it would in either

way be the deed of both. The former method, that the people of the United States should ordain, and the States ratify, was adopted. For if it should be alleged at any future period that the American people had no national or organic existence, and that the States were the sole authors of the Constitution, and might undo what they had done, it would still be obvious that the States mutually agreed that such a people should be regarded as existing, and that the government should be treated as its handiwork, they would, on a well-known and familiar principle which the law has derived from ethics, be precluded for all the purposes of that government, from denying what they had solemnly admitted. I refer to the doctrine of estoppel, that what is held forth as an inducement to others, shall not be retracted after they have acted on the faith of the assurance. The effect was to place the sovereignty of the new government on a basis which was as unalterable as if the Conventions of the various States had publicly proclaimed and crowned a king.   There are, as Mr. Madison contended in the remarks already cited, and as Jackson insisted in his proclamation against nullification, grants which must be irrevocable in order to attain their object; and the establishment of a government is one of them. Whether the newly created sovereignty was vested in a commonwealth or in a monarchy, it would on every principle of national and public law have a claim to the allegiance of its subjects which it might enforce by arms.

assured its permanency but also its nationality and absolutely verified the preamble, " We, the people," thus forever obviating all questions as to the increased authority of the Federal Government, as well as the additional limitations

(Citing in a note *United States* vs. *Maurice*, MARSHALL, Ch. J., 2 Brock, 96, p. 109, and *Van Brocklin* vs. *Temple*, 117 U. S. 151, p. 154.)

"Established not by one, by two, or by three of the States, but by the people of all the States, speaking in their collective capacity as the people of the United States, the union could not be dissolved consistently with that well known maxim that the power which bound is the only one that can unloose, unless all concurred, and then only because the concurrence of the citizens of all the States in such an act would, on a principle already stated, be in effect a renunciation or abdication by the people of the United States."

Mr. Curtis says in his Constitutional History of the United States, 2d Vol, pp. 115–116:

"The reader who has followed me through the preceding volume has seen that at a very early period in the deliberations of the convention it was settled that the new government must be divided into the three departments of the legislature, the executive, and the judicial, and that it must be a *national* government. It may here be useful to condense into one statement what has already been given in greater detail in regard to the early distinction between a 'national' and a 'federal' government. It has appeared that many important members of the convention admitted at once the necessity for a more efficient government than that of the first Confederacy of the states, but they believed that the existing system of the Union could be made to answer all requirements by distributing its powers into the three departments of a legislative, an executive, and a judiciary, without altering the principle which made the Union a close league between sovereign states for certain purposes common to them all. But under this principle there had been no mode by which the legislative, the executive, or the judicial powers could be made to act directly upon individuals, whether those powers were vested in one body of men or in several bodies. Nor had such a mode of action upon individuals been devised in any of the confederacies between different states, either in ancient or in modern times. It was found that in order to reach and introduce the principle of direct action upon the individual citizen, some means must be discovered by which the powers of the central government, whatever they were to be, could be made supreme over the separate powers of the states, in case of any conflict. To abolish the states, or to fuse all the elements of political sovereignty into one mass, was out of the question. The convention was not assembled and had not been instituted with any design or expectation that the people of the states would merge themselves in one national democracy, or deposit the whole of their respective sovereignties in the hands of a central government of **any form or** description."

upon State Sovereignty, and making the Constitution, the laws of the United States, and all treaties made under their authority, the supreme law of the land and absolutely binding not only on the judges, as expressed in the Constitution, but also upon all the inhabitants of all the States.[3]

§ 196. **Results of the Convention; Washington's meditation.**—But whether the members of that Convention themselves knew what they had accomplished will never be known. Perhaps some of them thoroughly appreciated that they had laid the foundations of a Nation, perhaps others felt that the State life had been preserved to the exclusion of all centralization. Bancroft declares the members were awe-struck at the result of their councils; the Constitution was a nobler work than any one of them had believed it possible to devise, and he adds that they all dined together, and took a cordial leave of each other; a single line in that summary of the day's work contains a wondrous world of thought. "Washington," he says "retired at an early hour of the evening to meditate on the momentous work which had been executed."[1] That great man well knew that the sun carved upon the back of the chair which he had occupied during those long sessions, and which had been so effectively used as a simile by Doctor Franklin at the close of the final session, not only was a rising and not a setting sun,[2] but that it was rising upon a nation that, through the efforts of men who, like himself, had buried all local selfishness in the noble efforts they had made during the past months, was fully endowed with every attribute of nationality and sovereignty which would enable it ere the close of

[3] See opinions of Supreme Court as to the nature of the ratification of the Constitution cited, and quoted from, in § 27, pp. 47 *et seq. ante.*

§ 196.

[1] Bancroft's History of the Constitution of the United States, 6th Edition, New York, 1893, vol. 2, p. 222.

[2] "The Constitution being signed by all the members, except Mr. Randolph, Mr. Mason and Mr. Gerry, who declined giving it the sanction of their names, the Convention dissolved itself by an adjournment sine die.

"Whilst the last members were signing, Doctor Franklin, looking towards the President's chair, at the back of which a rising sun happened to be painted, observed to a few members near him, that painters had found it difficult to

the then approaching century to take its proper place as one of the greatest powers of the earth.

distinguish in their art, a rising, from a setting sun. I have, said he, often and often, in the course of the session, and the vicissitudes of my hopes and fears as to its issue, looked at that behind the President, without being able to tell whether it was rising or setting: but now at length, I have the happiness to know, that it is a rising, and not a setting sun." Madison Papers, Vol. III, p. 1624.

"The story is told that at the last session of the convention which framed the Constitution of the United States, and after the final draft had been adopted and the delegates were about to disperse, the venerable Franklin rose, and, pointing to the quaint back of the chair which Washington had occupied while presiding, and on which there was carved a half sun with rays radiating from it, said: ' As I have been sitting here all these weeks, I have often wondered whether yon sun is rising or setting. But now I know that it is a rising sun.'

"The old man's prophecy has been fulfilled. Cannot we make it applicable to the present crisis, and as by the sword of Washington the sun of liberty rose o'er our country, and by the pen of Lincoln the single cloud of slavery that darkened it was swept away, so under the guidance of our noble President and Commander-in-Chief who can doubt but that the same sun that sheds its rays of happiness and peace over our own land, will also shed them alike on the land of our neighbor, and that beneath their heat tyranny and oppression will forever melt away from the Western Hemisphere over which nature and our honor have made us the natural guardians of peace and liberty." Voice of the Nation, by Charles Henry Butler, April, 1898, quoting above incident and applying it to Message of President McKinley of April 11, 1898, in regard to Cuba.

CHAPTER VII.

PROCEEDINGS OF THE CONSTITUTIONAL CONVENTIONS OF THE SEVERAL STATES, IN SO FAR AS THEY RELATE TO THE TREATY-MAKING POWER OF THE NATIONAL GOVERNMENT.

339

§ 197. **Constitution to be ratified by States.**—A great victory had been achieved in the Federal Constitutional Convention; a harder battle was, however, to be fought before the Constitution of the United States, as the sovereign act of the *People*, was to take the place of the Articles of Confederation of the *States*, and to effectually unite into one great nation the various Commonwealths which were fast drifting apart owing to the inefficacy of those Articles.

It was necessary to submit the Constitution to the people of the thirteen different States, and to obtain the ratification of at least nine,[1] and eventually of them all, before the Union could be considered as absolutely safe.[2]

It was by no means an easy task to obtain this result when the theory of States' rights had such able vindicators as Patrick Henry, Luther Martin, Elbridge Gerry, Samuel Adams, and Colonel Mason.

The Federal Convention had, as we have seen, recommended that the ratification should be by State conventions and not by State legislatures;[3] this course was adopted by Congress and the report of the Federal Convention was transmitted to the legislatures of the respective States in order that the State conventions might be called at once.[4]

§ 197.

[1] Constitution of United States, Article VII.

[2] See note under § 169, pp. 294 *et seq.*, *ante*, for authorities on proceedings of State conventions to which the Constitution was, referred. The references in the notes to the subsequent sections of this chapter will principally be to volumes II, III and IV of Elliot's Debates; references will also be made to Curtis' Constitutional History of the United States, and to certain special histories written in regard to the State conventions of Pennsylvania, Maryland, Virginia and Massachusetts.

[3] See § 195, p. 332 *et seq.*, *ante*.

[4] *The United States in Congress assembled*, Friday, September 28th, 1787.

" *Present,* —New Hampshire, Massachusetts, Connecticut, New York, New Jersey, Pennsylvania, Delaware, Virginia, North Caro-

§ 198. **Delaware the first State to ratify.**—On September 14, 1787, the Constitutional Convention adjourned; the States were notified by Congress on September 28th, and on December 7, Delaware headed the list of ratifying States by a unanimous ratification.[1]

§ 199. **Convention meets in Pennsylvania; prominent members.**—On November 20th, however, the first State convention had convened in Philadelphia, to discuss the fate of the Constitution in Pennsylvania where its ratification was neither prompt nor unanimous. The convention included Frederick Augustus Muhlenberg, afterwards Speaker of the first House of Representatives, Timothy Pickering, afterwards Secretary of State, Benjamin Rush, James Wilson, afterwards a Judge of the United States Supreme Court, Thomas McKean, Chief Justice of the State, and many others of great ability.[1] After a protracted discussion in which the Constitutional party was led by James Wilson, and their opponents by William Findlay, the Constitution was ratified on December 12th.

§ 200. **Views of minority opposing ratification.**—When

lina, South Carolina, and Georgia; and for Maryland, Mr. Ross.

"Congress having received the report of the Convention, lately assembled in Philadelphia,

"*Resolved, unanimously,* That the said report, with the resolutions and letter accompanying the same, be transmitted to the several legislatures, in order to submit to a convention of delegates, chosen in each state by the people thereof, in conformity to the resolves of the Convention made and provided in that case." Elliot's Debates, vol. I, p. 18.

§ 198.

[1] The ratifications by the several States appear to have been put into authoritative form for transmission to Congress on the following dates (taken from the formal ratifications as collected in Elliot's Debates, vol. I, pp. 319–343):

(1) Delaware, December 7, 1787; (2) Pennsylvania, December 12, 1787; (3) New Jersey, December 18, 1787; (4) Connecticut, January 9, 1788; (5) Massachusetts, February 7, 1788; (6) Georgia, January 2, 1788; (7) Maryland, April 28, 1788; (8) South Carolina, May 23, 1788; (9) New Hampshire, June 21, 1788; (10) Virginia, June 26, 1788; (11) New York, July 26, 1788; (12) North Carolina, November 21, 1789; (13) Rhode Island, May 29, 1790.

§ 199.

[1] Elliot's Debates, vol. II, pp. 415–546; Curtis' Constitutional History of the United States, vol. I, pp. 641–646; Pennsylvania and the Federal Constitution, 1787–1788, edited by John Bach McMaster and Frederick D. Stone, published by the Historical Society of Pennsylvania, 1888.

the ratification of the Constitution by the Pennsylvania
convention became inevitable, the minority submitted a
written statement of their reasons for dissent; they laid
great stress upon the vast extent of the treaty-making power,
lodged in the Central Government, in which respect they declared that no treaty which should be directly opposed to
the existing laws of the United States in Congress assembled,
should be valid until such laws should have been repealed,
or made conformable to such treaty; neither should any
treaties be valid which were in contradiction to the Constitution of the United States, or the constitution of the several
States.[1] They gave as the foundation of their objections to
the Senate and its powers, various reasons, some of which
are quoted in the notes to this section.[2]

§ 201. **Subsequent protest of minority to force the adoption of amendments.**—The non-participation in treaty-mak-

§ 200.

[1] McMaster and Stone, p. 463.

[2] "The Senate has, moreover, various and great executive powers, viz. in concurrence with the president-general, they form treaties with foreign nations, that may control and abrogate the constitutions and laws of the several States. Indeed, there is no power, privilege or liberty of the State governments, or of the people, but what may be affected by virtue of this power. For all treaties, made by them, are to be the 'supreme law of the land; anything in the constitution or laws of any State, to the contrary notwithstanding.'

"And this great power may be exercised by the President and ten senators (being two-thirds of four-teen, which is a quorum of that body). What an inducement would this offer to the ministers of for-eign powers to compass by brib-ery such *concessions* as could not otherwise be obtained. It is the unvaried usage of all free States, whenever treaties interfere with the positive laws of the land, to make the intervention of the leg-islature necessary to give them operation. This became necessary, and was afforded by the parliament of Great Britain, in consequence of the late commercial treaty be-tween that kingdom and France. As the Senate judges on impeach-ments, who is to try the members of the Senate for the abuse of this power! And none of the great appointments to office can be made without the consent of the Senate.

"Such various, extensive, and im-portant powers combined in one body of men, are inconsistent with all freedom; the celebrated Mon-tesquieu tells us, that 'when the legislative and executive powers are united in the same person, or in the same body of magistrates, there can be no liberty, because apprehensions may arise, lest the same monarch *or senate* should en-act tyrannical laws, to execute them in a tyrannical manner.' " Mc-Master and Stone, p. 476.

ing, of the House of Representatives, the popular, or national, branch of Congress, was one of the particular grounds taken by the minority in this convention for opposing the ratification of the Constitution. Subsequently another effort was made to induce Pennsylvania to take an adverse stand to the Constitution as ratified; on September 3, 1788, nine months after the ratification, a number of Pennsylvanians met at Harrisburg, and, after organizing with Blair McClenahan as Chairman and John A. Hanna as Secretary, presented an address to the General Assembly of the State urging it to take measures to procure the adoption of certain amendments to the Constitution as ratified, one of which was that "to Article VI, Clause 2, be added the following proviso, viz: Provided, always, That no treaty, which shall hereafter be made, shall be deemed or construed to alter or affect any law of the United States, or of any particular State, until such treaty shall have been laid before and assented to by the House of Representatives in Congress."[1] From this it appears that the wide extent of power lodged in the President and two-thirds of the Senate was not only fully appreciated, but was also greatly feared, by the signers of this petition, and that the great publicity given to these proceedings at the time put the people, not only of Pennsylvania, but also of the other States, thoroughly on notice.

§ 202. **Ratification by New Jersey.**—New Jersey followed shortly after this, the convention of that State unanimously ratifying the Constitution on December 12, 1787, although the Anti-Federalists of New York and Pennsylvania used every effort to persuade their intermediate neighbors to reject it.[1]

§ 203. **Georgia and Connecticut ratify; conditions in other States.**—Georgia was the first of the Southern States to fall into line,[1] while Connecticut, under the leadership of

§ 201.
[1] Elliot's Debates, vol. II, pp. 542–546; McMaster and Stone, p. 564.
§ 202.
[1] Curtis' Constitutional History

of the United States, vol. I, p. 645–646; Elliot's Debates, vol. I, p. 320:
§ 203.
[1] Elliot's Debates, vol. I, p. 323; Curtis' Constitutional History of the United States, vol. I, p. 646.

Oliver Ellsworth, occupied the corresponding position in New England.[2]

By January 9, 1788, five States had ratified the Constitution, and all had done so unconditionally; the ratifications by four more were necessary before it could become operative. But, as Mr. Curtis says in his Constitutional History, " a new act in the drama was to open with the New Year."[3] Massachusetts, New York and Virginia were, indeed, to ratify the Constitution, but subject to conditions, either in form or in spirit; amendments were to be proposed and insisted upon, and for a long time the fate of the Constitution hung in the balance; from January 9, 1788, when the sessions of the Massachusetts convention commenced until June 25th, when the ratification by the Virginia convention made the plan an assured success, in fact, even until July 26th, when the Constitution was ratified by the New York convention, the all absorbing thought and the single universal topic of the country was the Constitution, and its adoption or rejection.

§ 204. **Massachusetts Convention meets; members composing it.**—On January 9, 1788, the special convention called for consideration of the Constitution and composed of 355 delegates met at Boston, Massachusetts.[1]

It included many remarkable men, some of whom were foremost citizens of the State; there were others, however, who had actually participated in Shay's Rebellion and who were opposed to the adoption of the Constitution or, probably, to the establishment of any strong central government which could, and would, enforce law and order.

Among some of the ablest members were Fisher Ames, John Winthrop, James Bowdoin, John Hancock, William Cushing, Francis Dana, Rufus King, and Judge Sumner.[2]

John Hancock was chosen President, and William Cushing, Vice President, of the convention. On February 2d,

[2] Elliot's Debates, vol. II, pp. 185–202; Curtis' Constitutional History of the United States, vol. 1, p. 647.
[3] Idem p. 648.
§ 204.
[1] Elliot's Debates, vol. II, pp. 1–183. Curtis' Constitutional History of the United States, vol. I, p. 649; Massachusetts and the Federal Convention by Samuel Bannister Harding, New York and London, 1896.
[2] Elliot's Debates, vol. II, pp. 178–181.

the Constitution was ratified by a vote of 187 to 168;[8] the narrow majority of 19 was undoubtedly secured by the adoption of a resolution that certain amendments should be recommended to Congress as the wish of the State in regard to the Constitution. Some of these suggestions were incorporated in the amendments which were passed by the first Congress and immediately ratified by the States, and thus became incorporated in the Constitution almost at the outset of the Government. None of the amendments suggested by the Massachusetts convention related to the treaty-making power.[4]

§ 205. **Position of Samuel Adams; Constitution ratified.** —During the proceedings of this convention the Constitution was discussed in all of its varied phases and aspects. It was ably supported; it was vigorously condemned. It was well known at the outset that Samuel Adams, "Father of the Revolution," or, as he is also called "The American Cato,"[1] was to a certain extent opposed to the Constitution; for a long time many of his followers withheld any expression of their views, while they waited for him to announce the course which he intended to take. Not until the last days of the convention did he finally declare that he would vote for ratification; in doing so he admitted that he had his doubts, and that he could not digest every part of it as readily as some of the other gentlemen had done; he felt, however, that it was the best that could be obtained, and on the whole that ratification would be better than rejection. The following extract from his remarks shows that he fully appreciated the importance of lodging the treaty-making power in the Central Government. "But, sir," he declared, "there are many parts of it I esteem as highly valuable, particularly the article which empowers Congress to regulate commerce, to form treaties, &c. For want of this power in our national head, our friends are grieved, and our enemies insult us. Our ambassador at the Court of London is considered as a mere cipher, instead of the representative of the United

---

[8] Elliott's Debates, vol. II, p. 181.

[4] A list of the suggested amendments will be found at p. 177 of Elliot's Debates, vol. II.

§ 205.

[1] Curtis' Constitutional History of the United States, vol. I, p. 651.

States.   Therefore, it appears to me, that a power to remedy this evil should be given to Congress, and the remedy applied as soon as possible."[2]

Mr. Adams's scruples were no doubt removed by the adoption of the resolution suggesting the proposed amendments; he is recorded in the yeas and nays as having voted for the ratification; undoubtedly the great weight of his influence largely aided in the ratification of the Constitution by the State of Massachusetts.

§ 206. **Ratification by Maryland; Luther Martin's protest.**—On April 28, 1778, Maryland ratified the Constitution; this however, was not done without a struggle, nor until after Luther Martin had thrown his powerful influence in opposition to it, and had presented to the Legislature a lengthy address embodying his reasons for refusing to sign the Constitution and for urging his own State to withhold its ratification.   Some of the grounds of his views are quoted in the note to this section.[1]

---

[2] Elliot's Debates, vol. II, p. 123–124.

§ **206.**

[1] " It was urged, that the government we were forming was not in reality a *federal* but a *national* government, not founded on the principles of the *preservation*, but the *abolition* or *consolidation* of all *state governments*—That we appeared *totally to have forgotten* the business for which we were sent, and the situation of the country for which we were preparing our system—That we had not been sent to form a government over the *inhabitants* of America, considered as *individuals*, that as individuals they were all subject to their respective state governments, which governments would still remain, tho' the federal government should be dissolved—That the *system of government* we were *entrusted* to prepare, was a government over *these thirteen states*; but that in our proceedings, we adopted principles which would be right and proper, *only* on the supposition that there were *no state governments at all*, but that *all the inhabitants* of this *extensive continent* were in their *individual capacity, without government*, and in a *state of nature*—That accordingly the system proposes the legislature to consist of *two branches*, the *one* to be drawn from the *people at large*, immediately in their *individual capacity*; the *other* to be chosen in a *more select manner*, as a *check* upon the *first*—It is in its very *introduction* declared to be a compact between the *people* of the United States as *individuals*; and it is to be *ratified* by the *people* at large in their capacity as *individuals*; all which it was said, would be quite right and proper, if there were *no state governments*, if *all the people* of this continent were in a *state of nature*, and we were forming one *national* government *for*

§ 207. **The Constitution in South Carolina; Mr. Pinckney's views.**—A majority of the States had now ratified the Constitution, but under the terms of the instrument the ratifications of two more were required; six were still to be heard from.

A fierce battle was fought in the South Carolina Legislature over the question of calling a constitutional convention,[1] with the result of calling one for the 12th of May, on which day it met at Charleston.[2] Governor Thomas Pinckney was elected President. Charles Cotesworth Pinckney, Rawlins Lowndes and David Ramsay took prominent parts in the discussion.

One of the subjects of debate in the legislature was the treaty-making power; Charles Cotesworth Pinckney, who had been a delegate to the Federal Convention, explained the reasons for vesting the treaty-making power in the Executive and Senate. During his remarks he said that the subject had appeared to be of such magnitude that a committee of one member from each State had been appointed to consider and report upon it;[3] some of the members of that committee were in favor of vesting the treaty-making power in the legislature, but the elements of secrecy and despatch, which are so frequently necessary in negotiations, evinced the impropriety of that course; the same reason showed the impropriety in placing it solely in the House of Representatives. A few of the members were desirous that the President, alone, might possess it. At last, however, it was agreed to give the President the power of proposing treaties as he was ostensibly the head of the nation, and of vesting in the Senate, where each State had an equal voice, the power of agreeing or disagreeing with the terms proposed. "On the whole," he said, "a large majority of the Convention thought

them as *individuals*, and is nearly the same as was done in most of the *states*, when they formed their governments *over the people* who compose them." (The italics are so in the original as published by Yates.) Elliot's Debates, vol. I, p. 344; see pp. 359–360; vol. II, pp. 547–556; Yates' Secret Journal of the Federal Convention, pp. 38–39; Curtis' Constitutional History of United States, vol. I, p. 656–657.

§ **207.**

[1] Elliot's Debates, vol. IV, pp. 253–342; Curtis' Constitutional History, vol. I, p. 658.

[2] Elliot's Debates, vol. IV, p. 316.

[3] *Idem* p. 264.

this power would be more safely lodged where they had finally vested it, than anywhere else. It was a power that must necessarily be lodged somewhere : political caution and republican jealousy rendered it improper for us to vest it in the President alone ; the nature of negotiation, and the frequent recess of the House of Representatives, rendered that body an improper depository of this prerogative. The President and Senate joined were, therefore, after much deliberation, deemed the most eligible corps in whom we could with safety vest the diplomatic authority of the Union." [4]

General Pinckney spoke frequently during the debate and on more than one occasion gave particular attention to the treaty-making power and the propriety of vesting it in the President and Senate. [5]

[4] Elliot's Debates, vol. IV, p. 265.

[5] On Thursday, January 17th, Charles Cotesworth Pinckney made his strongest address in the Legislature on the subject of the treaty-making power in the course of which he "observed that the honorable gentleman (Mr. Lowndes) who opposed the new Constitution had asserted that treaties made under the old Confederation were not deemed paramount to the laws of the land, and that treaties made by the king of Great Britain required the ratification of Parliament to render them valid. The honorable gentleman is surely mistaken in his assertion. His honorable friend (Chancellor Rutledge) had clearly shown that, by the 6th, 9th, and 13th Articles of the old Confederation, Congress have a power to make treaties, and each state is pledged to observe them; and it appears, from the debates of the English Parliament, that the House of Commons did not ratify, but actually censure, the peace made by the king of Great Britain with America; yet the very members who censured it acknowledged it was binding on the nation. (Here the general read extracts from the parliamentary debates of the 17th and 21st of February, 1784.) Indeed, the doctrine that the king of Great Britain may make a treaty with a foreign state, which shall irrevocably bind his subjects, is asserted by the best writers on the laws and constitution of England—particularly by Judge Blackstone, who, in the first book of his Commentaries, (ch. 7, p. 257), declares 'that it is the king's prerogative to make treaties, leagues, and alliances, with foreign states and princes, and that no other power in the kingdom can legally delay, resist, or annul them.' If treaties entered into by Congress are not to be held in the same sacred light in America, what foreign nation will have any confidence in us? Shall we not be stigmatized as a faithless, unworthy people, if each member of the Union may, with impunity, violate the engagements entered into by the federal government? Who will confide in us? Who will treat with us if our practice should be conformable to

§ 208. **Rawlin, Lowndes' opposition; Mr. Pringle's views.**
—Replying to Mr. Pinckney, Rawlin, Lowndes declared

this doctrine? Have we not been deceiving all nations, by holding forth to the world, in the 9th Article of the old Confederation, that Congress may make treaties, if we, at the same time, entertain this improper tenet, that each state may violate them? I contend that the article in the new Constitution, which says that treaties shall be paramount to the laws of the land, is only declaratory of what treaties were, in fact, under the old compact. They were as much the law of the land under that Confederation, as they are under this Constitution; and we shall be unworthy to be ranked among civilized nations if we do not consider treaties in this view. Vattel, one of the best writers on the law of nations, says, 'There would be no more security, no longer any commerce between mankind, did they not believe themselves obliged to preserve their faith, and to keep their word. Nations, and their conductors, ought, then, to keep their promises and their treaties inviolable. This great truth is acknowledged by all nations. Nothing adds so great a glory to a prince and the nation he governs, as the reputation of an inviolable fidelity to his engagements. By this, and their bravery, the Swiss have rendered themselves respectable throughout Europe. This national greatness of soul is the source of immortal glory; upon it is founded the confidence of nations, and it thus becomes a certain instrument of power and splendor.' Surely this doctrine is right; it speaks to the heart, it impresses itself on the feelings of mankind, and convinces us that the tranquil-

lity, happiness, and prosperity, of the human race, depend on inviolably preserving the faith of treaties.

"Burlamaqui, another writer of great reputation on political law, says 'that treaties are obligatory on the subjects of the powers who enter into treaties; they are obligatory as conventions between the contracting powers; but they have the force of law with respect to their subjects.' These are his very words: 'Ils ont force de loi a l'égard des sujets, considérés comme tels; and it is very manifest,' continues he, 'that two sovereigns, who enter into a treaty, impose, by such treaty, an obligation on their subjects to conform to it, and in no manner to contravene it.' It is remarkable that the words made use of by Burlamaqui establish the doctrine, recognized by the Constitution, that treaties shall be considered as the law of the land; and happy will it be for America if they shall be always so considered: we shall then avoid the disputes, the tumults, the frequent wars, we must inevitably be engaged in, if we violate treaties. By our treaty with France, we declare she shall have all the privileges, in matters of commerce, with the most favored nation. Suppose a particular state should think proper to grant a particular privilege to Holland, which she refuses to France; would not this be a violation of the treaty with France? It certainly would; and we in this state would be answerable for the consequences attending such violation by another State; for we do not enter into treaties as separate states, but as united states; and all the members of the Union are an-

that in no case in the history of the known world was there an instance of the rulers of a republic being allowed to go swerable for the breach of a treaty by any one of them. South Carolina, therefore, considering its situation, and the valuable produce it has to export, is particularly interested in maintaining the sacredness of treaties, and the good faith with which they should be observed by every member of the Union. But the honorable gentleman complains that the power of making treaties is vested in the President and Senate, and thinks it is not placed so safely with them as with the Congress under the old Confederation. Let us examine this objection. By the old Confederation, each state had an equal vote in Congress, and no treaty could be made without the assent of the delegates from nine states. By the present Constitution, each state sends two members to the Senate, who vote *per capita;* and the President has power, with advice and consent of the Senate, to make treaties, provided two-thirds of the Senate present concur. This inconvenience attended the old method: it was frequently difficult to obtain a representation from nine states; and if only nine states were present, they must all concur in making a treaty. A single member would frequently prevent the business from being concluded; and if he absented himself, Congress had no power to compel his attendance. This actually happened when a treaty of importance was about to be concluded with the Indians; and several states, being satisfied, at particular junctures, that the nine states present would not concur in sentiments on the subject of a treaty, were indifferent whether their members attended or not. But now that the senators vote individually, and not by states, each state will be anxious to keep a full representation in the Senate; and the Senate has now power to compel the attendance of its own members. We shall thus have no delay, and business will be conducted in a fuller representation of the states than it hitherto has been. All the members of the Convention, who had served in Congress, were so sensible of the advantage attending this mode of voting, that the measure was adopted unanimously. For my own part, I think it infinitely preferable to the old method. So much for the manner of voting.

"Now let us consider whether the power of making treaties is not as securely placed as it was before. It was formerly vested in Congress, who were a body constituted by the legislatures of the different states in equal proportions. At present, it is vested in a President, who is chosen by the people of America, and in a Senate, whose members are chosen by the state legislatures, each legislature choosing two members. Surely there is greater security in vesting this power as the present Constitution has vested it, than in any other body. Would the gentleman vest it in the President alone? If he would, his assertion that the power we have granted was as dangerous as the power vested by Parliament in the proclamations of Henry VIII, might have been, perhaps, warranted. Would he vest it in the House of Representatives? Can secrecy be expected in sixty-five members? The idea is absurd.

so far and that even the most arbitrary kings possessed nothing like the treaty-making power vested in the Executive and Senate.[1] The records of the South Carolina discussions, as they have been preserved in Elliot's debates, show that the treaty-making power was one of the principal causes of objection to calling a State constitutional convention. Mr. Pringle (the Speaker) spoke of the great power that the President and Senate might have, declaring that it gave scope to a great deal of declamation upon the danger, but he conceived that there must be mistakes and stated that the making of treaties is justly a part of the prerogative of the Executive as they must be conducted with despatch and secrecy, nor did he think that the apprehended dangers could ensue from vesting the treaty-making power with the President and the Senate.

He took a different view from the other gentlemen in regard to the effect of treaties upon laws; in regard to this he said: "Although the treaties they make may have the force of laws when made, they have not, therefore, legislative power. It would be dangerous, indeed, to trust them with the power of making laws to affect the rights of individuals; for this might tend to the oppression of individuals, who could not obtain redress. All the evils would, in that case, flow from blending the legislative, executive, and judicial powers. This would violate the soundest principles of policy and government. It is not with regard to the power of making treaties as of legislation in general. The treaties will affect all the individuals equally of all the states. If the President and Senate make such as violate the fundamental laws, and subvert the Constitution, or tend to the destruction of the

Besides, their sessions will probably last only two or three months in the year; therefore, on that account, they would be a very unfit body for negotiation whereas the Senate, from the smallness of its numbers, from the equality of power which each state has in it, from the length of time for which its members are elected, from the long sessions they may have without any great inconvenience to themselves or constituents, joined with the president, who is the federal head of the United States, form together a body in whom can be best and most safely vested the diplomatic power of the Union." Elliot's Debates, vol. IV, pp. 277–281.

§ 208.

[1] Elliot's Debates, vol. IV, p. 266; this was in reply to General Pinckney's first speech.

happiness and liberty of the states, the evils, equally oppressing all, will be removed as soon as felt, as those who are oppressed have the power and means of redress.   Such treaties,
not being made with good faith, and on the broad basis of
reciprocal interest and convenience, but by treachery and a
betraying of trust, and by exceeding the powers with which
the makers were intrusted, ought to be annulled.   No nations
would keep treaties thus made.   Indeed, it is too much the
practice for them to make mutual interest and convenience
the rule of observation, or period of duration.   As for the
danger of repealing the instalment law, the gentleman has
forgot that one article ordains that there shall be no retrospective law.   The President and Senate will, therefore,
hardly ever make a treaty that would be of this kind." [2]

§ 209. **Other views expressed on treaty-making power.**
—Dr. David Ramsay asked during the discussion some very
pertinent questions and inquired, whether " the gentleman
meant us ever to have any treaties at all.   If not superior
to local laws, who will trust them ?   Would not the question
naturally be, ' Did you mean, when you made treaties, to
fulfill them ?'   Establish once such a doctrine, and where
will you find ambassadors ?   If gentlemen had been in the
situation of receiving similar information with himself, they
would have heard letters read from our ambassadors abroad,
in which loud complaints were made that America had become faithless and dishonest.   Was it not full time that such
conduct as this should be amended ?" [1]

There were many other views expressed during the addresses in this debate, on both sides of the question, some
of the members taking very extreme views.   The result of
the debate in the Legislature foreshadowed the result in the
convention.

§ 210. **Constitution ratified by South Carolina.**—The
convention which met at Charleston on May 12th, 1788,[1]
on May 21st, ratified the Constitution by a vote of 149 to
73.[2]   The records of the debate in the Legislature are much
fuller than those of the proceedings of the constitutional

[2] Elliot's Debates, vol. IV, p. 269.
§ 209.
[1] *Idem*, p. 270.

§ 210.
[1] Elliot's Debates, vol. IV, p. 317.
[2] *Idem*, p. 340.

convention; the records of the convention show, however, that the questions relating to the treaty-making power assumed great importance in the consideration of the Constitution, and that the people of South Carolina were fully aware of the far-reaching effect which that power might have upon the local affairs of States, and individuals.

§ 211. **Constitutional convention meets in Virginia.**— In Virginia the constitutional convention met at Richmond June 2, 1788; the Honorable Edmund Pendleton was elected President.[1] The convention continued in session for over three weeks, the Constitution being finally ratified, on June 25th, after great opposition, by a vote of 89 to 79; although the ratification of the Constitution as proposed was unconditional, numerous amendments were suggested and recommended, and many of them were subsequently incorporated in the amendments approved by the first Congress.[2] The ratification of Virginia, however, contained certain reservations as to the right of Virginia to resume the delegated powers whenever the same should be perverted to their injury or oppression.[3]

The proceedings of the constitutional convention of Virginia are the most elaborately reported of all of the State conventions, the record comprising an entire volume of Elliot's Debates of over 650 pages. It will, therefore, be impossible in a summary of this nature to refer at length to all the references which were made to the treaty-making power; extracts of sufficient length and number will be given from, and references made to, the speeches on both sides of the question, however, to show that the extent of the treaty-making power as vested in the Central Government was one of the principal topics of discussion, and that the Convention ratified the Constitution with full knowledge of the great power that was given by it in this respect.

§ 212. **Opposition led by Patrick Henry.**—The opposition to the ratification was led by Patrick Henry, then 52 years of age and in the height of his unbounded popularity, which

§ 211.
[1] Elliot's Debates, vol. III, p. 1.

[2] Elliot's Debates, vol. III, pp. 659, et seq.
[3] Idem, p. 656.

he used to the utmost to defeat the Constitution.[1]   He, who, when the independence of the Union was in jeopardy, had

§ 212.

[1] "They were led, as I have already said they were to be, by Patrick Henry, whose reputation had suffered no abatement since the period when he blazed into the darkened skies of the Revolution—when his untutored eloquence electrified the heart of Virginia, and became, as has been well said, even 'a cause of the national independence.' He had held the highest honors of the state, but had retired, poor, and worn down by twenty years of public service, to rescue his private affairs by the practice of a profession which, in some of its duties, he did not love, and for which he had, perhaps, a single qualification in his amazing oratorical powers. His popularity in Virginia was unbounded. It was the popularity that attends genius, when thrown with heart and soul, and with every impulse of its being, into the cause of popular freedom; and it was a popularity in which reverence for the stern independence and the self-sacrificing spirit of the patriot was mingled with admiration for the splendid gifts of oratory which Nature, and Nature alone, had bestowed upon him. But Mr. Henry was rightly appreciated by his contemporaries. They knew that, though a wise man, his wisdom lacked comprehensiveness, and that the mere intensity with which he regarded the ends of public liberty was likely to mislead his judgment as to the means by which it was to be secured and upheld. The chief apprehension of his opponents, on this important occasion, was lest the power of his eloquence over the feelings or prejudices of his auditory might lead the sober reflections of men astray.

"He was at this time fifty-two years of age. Although feeling or affecting to feel himself an old and broken man, he was yet undoubtedly master of all his natural powers. Those powers he exerted to the utmost to defeat the Constitution in the convention of Virginia. He employed every art of his peculiar rhetoric, every resource of invective, of sarcasm, of appeal to the fears of his audience for liberty; every dictate of local prejudice and state pride. But he employed them all with the most sincere conviction that the adoption of the proposed Constitution would be a wrong and dangerous step. Nor is it surprising that he should have so regarded it. He had formed to himself an ideal image which he was fond of describing as the American spirit. This national spirit of liberty, erring perhaps at times, but in the main true to right and justice as well as to freedom, was with him a kind of guardian angel of the republic. He seems to have considered it able to correct its own errors without the aid of any powerful system of general government—capable of accomplishing in peace all that it had unquestionably effected for the country in war. As he passed out of the troubles and triumphs of the Revolution into the calmer atmosphere of the Confederation, his reliance on this American spirit, and his jealousy for the maxims of public liberty, led him to regard that system as perfect, because it had no direct legislative authority." Curtis' Constitutional

354

declared that he was not the less a Virginian because he was an American, now took the leadership of the State's rights side of the controversy and became one of the most ardent advocates which that doctrine has ever had; he declared that he could not endure the thought of a government external to that of Virginia, and yet possessing the power of direct taxation over the people of his State; he regarded with utter abhorrence the idea of laws binding upon the people of Virginia made by other people of the United States.

Opposing every element of nationality, he objected to the preamble and asked by what authority the delegates to the Constitutional Convention had used the expression, " We, the People," instead of " We, the States." [2] He charged and predicted that eventually the government would become a monarchy, and as expressed by Elliott, " strongly and pathetically expatiated on the probability of the President's enslaving America and the horrible consequences that must result." [3]

§ 213. **Governor Randolph's position.**—He was answered by Governor Randolph, who had declined to sign the Constitution, as a member of the Federal Convention, but having realized that the Constitution, as submitted to the States, must either be ratified, or the Union would be dissolved, patriotically waived his personal feelings and made every exertion for its ratification, and in so doing greatly aided the cause in the Virginia convention.[1]

§ 214. **Opposing forces in Virginia convention.**—The debate thus opened by Patrick Henry and Edmund Randolph was continued by them throughout the session, Rawlins Lowndes, Colonel Mason, Mr. Grayson and Mr. Nicholas opposing the Constitution on various grounds, while James Madison, James Monroe, John Rutledge, John Marshall and Edmund Pendleton, with the able assistance of the friends of ratification, finally overcame the tremendous tide of opposition which had been raised by these opponents to the Union, and thus achieved one of the greatest victories for rati-

History of the United States, vol. 1, pp. 663–664.

[2] Elliot's Debates, vol. III, p. 22.

[3] *Idem*, p. 60.

§ **213.**

[1] Elliot's Debates, vol. III, p. 652, and see also § 192, chap. VI, p. 330, *ante.*

fication of the Constitution. Undoubtedly the great weight of Virginia's adoption of the Constitution turned the scale in the few remaining States in which the question was under consideration and insured beyond all peradventure the ratification, not only by the requisite number of States to put the instrument into force, but also to make it a practical measure; for even with the co-operation of nine States it would have been impossible to have carried out the plan of Union, without the acquiescence of Virginia and New York.[1]

§ 215. **Mr. Madison's views.**—Mr. Madison spoke of the necessity of a strong government, especially in regard to our foreign relations, referring to the weakness of the Confederation in this respect, he said : " The Confederation is so notoriously feeble, that foreign nations are unwilling to form any treaties with us; they are apprized that our general government cannot perform any of its engagements, but that they may be violated at pleasure by any of the states. Our violation of treaties already entered into proves this truth unequivocally. No nation will, therefore, make any stipulations with Congress, conceding any advantages of importance to us : they will be the more averse to entering into engagements with us, as the imbecility of our government enables them to derive many advantages from our trade, without granting us any return. But were this country united by proper bands, in addition to other great advantages, we could form very beneficial treaties with foreign states. But this can never happen without a change in our system. Were we not laughed at by that minister of that nation, from which we may be able yet to extort some of the most salutary measures for this country ? Were we not told that it was necessary to temporize till our government acquired consistency. Will any nation relinquish national advantages to us? You will be greatly disappointed, if you expect any such good effects from this contemptible system. Let us recollect our conduct to that country from which we have received the most friendly aid. How have we dealt with that benevolent ally ? Have we complied with our most sacred obligations to that

§ 214.
[1] For the effect of the ratification by Virginia on the convention then in session in New York, see Curtis' Constitutional History of the United States, vol. I, p. 680.

nation? Have we paid the interest punctually from year to year? Is not the interest accumulating, while not a shilling is discharged of the principal? The magnanimity and forbearance of that ally are so great that she has not called upon us for her claims, even in her own distress and necessity. This, sir, is an additional motive to increase our exertions. At this moment of time a very considerable amount is due from us to that country and others." [1]

§ 216. **Mr. Henry again expresses his views.**—During the debates Colonel Mason reiterated the fear which he had expressed in the Federal Convention [1] of the great danger contained in the treaty-making clause; he declared that a very small number of Senators, in collusion with the President, could practically dismember the Union.

Mr. Henry agreed with Mr. Mason and " begged the gentiemen to consider the condition this country would be in if two thirds of a quorum should be empowered to make a treaty: they might relinquish and alienate territorial rights, and our most valuable commercial advantages. In short, if anything should be left us, it would be because the President and senators were pleased to admit it. The power of making treaties, by this Constitution, ill-guarded as it is, extended farther than it did in any country in the world. Treaties were to have more force here than in any part of Christendom; for he defied any gentleman to show anything so extensive in any strong, energetic government in Europe. Treaties rest, says he, on the laws and usages of nations. To say that they are municipal, is, to me, a doctrine totally novel. To make them paramount to the Constitution and laws of the states, is unprecedented. I would give them the same force and obligation they have in Great Britain, or any other country in Europe. Gentlemen are going on in a fatal career; but I hope they will stop before they concede this power unguarded and unaltered." [2]

---

§ 215.

[1] Elliot's Debates, vol. III, p. 135. A parenthetical clause follows stating that Mr. Madison here mentioned the amount due to different foreign nations. The amounts are not specified in the report.

§ 216.

[1] Elliot's Debates, vol. III, p. 499, and see also § 185, p. 317, *ante.*

[2] Elliot's Debates, vol. III, p. 500.

§ 217. Mr. Madison's reply to Mr. Henry.—Mr. Madison at this point denied that the treaty-making power involved the right of dismembering the Union;[1] in reading these debates, it must be remembered that it was the object of the opponents of the Constitution to exaggerate the extent of the powers lodged in the Central Government; and also that its supporters endeavored to minimize the effects and extent of those powers in order that the instrument might not be rejected on the ground that too extensive powers had been reposed in the various branches of the Central Government.

§ 218. Treaty-making power as it affected Virginia; the navigation of the Mississippi.—It must also be remembered that the effect of treaties upon the condition of the Union was more of a real issue in the Virginia convention than it was in any of the other State conventions; the right of the navigation of the Mississippi at that time was the burning question of the day; negotiations which were then pending with Great Britain and Spain in regard to this important subject were more fully appreciated in Virginia than in any other State because they had a practical, in fact a vital, bearing upon local affairs and interests; Kentucky, at that time, formed the Western part of Virginia, and extending, as it did, to the Mississippi, the right of the navigation of that river to the Gulf was an absolute essential to its existence.[1]

The right, therefore, of the Federal Government to make treaties with foreign powers which would affect the great highways of commerce was one which was a personal matter with every delegate in the convention;[2] Mr. Grayson, who

§ 217.
[1] Elliot's Debates, vol. III, p. 501.
§ 218.
[1] McMaster's History of the People of the United States, vol. I, chapter IV.
[2] " Among the topics on which they expended a great deal of force was that of the navigation of the Mississippi. They employed this subject for the purpose of influencing the votes of members who represented the interests of that part of Virginia which is now Kentucky.

They first extorted from Madison and other gentlemen, who had been in the Congress of the Confederation, a statement of the negotiations which had nearly resulted in a temporary surrender of the right in the Mississippi to Spain. They then made use of the following argument. It had appeared, they said, from those transactions, that the Northern and Middle States, seven in number, were in favor of bartering away this great interest for commercial privileges and ad-

took the lead on this point, feared the power vested in the Central Government and that it might use such power in some manner that would impair the right of navigation of the Mississippi; he declared that the Constitution, if

vantages; that those states, particularly the Eastern ones, would be influenced further by a desire to suppress the growth of new states in the western country, and to prevent the emigration of their own people thither, as a means of retaining the power of governing the Union; and that the surrender of the Mississippi could be made by treaty, under the Constitution, by the will of the president and the votes of ten senators, whereas, under the Confederation, it never could be done without the votes of nine states in Congress." Curtis' Constitutional History of the United States, vol. I, pp. 671–672.

"The Treaty of Peace with Great Britain recognized, as the southern boundary of the United States, a line drawn from a point where the thirty-first degree of north latitude intersected the river Mississippi, along that parallel due east to the middle of the river Appalachicola; thence along the middle of that river to its junction with the Flint River; thence in a straight line to the head of St. Mary's River; and thence down the middle of that river to the Atlantic Ocean. At the time of the negotiation of this treaty West Florida was in the possession of Spain; and a secret article was executed by the British and American plenipotentiaries, which stipulated that in case Great Britain, at the conclusion of a peace with Spain, should recover or be put in possession of West Florida, the north boundary between that province and the United States should be a line drawn from the mouth of the river Yassous, where it unites with the river Mississippi, due east to the river Appalachicola. The treaty also stipulated that the navigation of the Mississippi, from its source to the ocean, should forever remain free and open to the subjects of Great Britain and the citizens of the United States.

"When the treaty came to be ratified and published, in 1784, the Spanish government was already acquainted with this secret article. Justly assuming that no treaty between Great Britain and the United States could settle the boundaries between the territories of the latter power and those of Spain, or give of itself a right to navigate a river passing wholly through their dominions, they immediately caused it to be signified to Congress that, until the limits of Louisiana and the two Floridas should be settled and determined, by an admission on the part of Spain that they had been rightfully described in the treaty with England, they must assert their territorial claims to the exclusive control of the river; and also that the navigation would under no circumstances be conceded, while Spain held the right to its control. To accommodate these difficulties, Congress resolved to send Mr. Jay, their secretary of foreign affairs, to Spain; but his departure was prevented by the arrival in the United States of Don Diego Guardoqui, as minister from Spain, charged with the negotiation of a treaty." Curtis' Constitutional History of the United States, vol. I, pp. 210–211.

adopted, would be the great charter of America paramount to everything, and that once having been consented to, it could not be receded from. "Such is my repugnance," he said, " to the alienation of the right which I esteem so important to the happiness of my country, that I would object to this Constitution if it contained no other defect." [3]

§ 219. **Patrick Henry on the prerogatives of the King of Great Britain ; other views.**—Questions as to the extent of the power of the King of Great Britain having been raised, and the statement made that he had as much power to make treaties as was given to the President, and two thirds of the Senate, Patrick Henry declared that " he would have had no objections to that plan if the Constitution had made the President a king." He declared, however, that under the treaty section, " the Constitution of the States might be most flagrantly violated without remedy." [1]

Governor Randolph claimed that the Constitution controlled the exercise of the functions granted under it, and marked out the powers to be exercised, and that therefore the fourth article secured the Union against any dismemberment by means of treaties. [2]

The debate was continued at the next session, Mr. Grayson again maintaining that the treaty-making clause invested the Federal Government with sufficient power to give up the Mississippi River. [3]

George Nicholas, citing Blackstone as to the prerogatives of the King of Great Britain, said that treaties made here, if valid, would probably be the supreme law of the land; he maintained, however, no treaty could be made that was " repugnant to the spirit of the Constitution, or inconsistent with the delegated powers. The treaties they make must be under the authority of the United States, to be within their province. It is sufficiently secured, because it only declares that, in pursuance of the powers given, they shall be the supreme law of the land, notwithstanding anything in the Constitution or laws of the particular States." [4]

[3] Elliot's Debates, vol. III, p. 502.
§ 219.
[1] Elliot's Debates, vol. III, p. 502.

[2] *Idem*, p. 504.
[3] *Idem*, p. 505.
[4] *Idem*, p. 507.

§ 220. **Views of Mr. Corbin on necessity of treaty-making powers in Central Government.**—Mr. Corbin "largely expatiated on the propriety of vesting this power in the General Government, in the manner proposed by the plan of the Convention. He also contended that the empire could not be dismembered without the consent of the part dismembered.[1] . . . He insisted that no part of the Constitution was less exceptionable than this; and that if there were any sound part in the Constitution, it was in this clause. He declared that the representatives were properly excluded from the treaty-making power on account of the impossibility of a large house acting in regard thereto. It would be dangerous to give this power to the President alone;" continuing he said: "It is therefore given to the President and the Senate (who represent the states in their individual capacities) conjointly. In this it differs from every government we know. It steers with admirable dexterity between the two extremes, neither leaving it to the executive, as in most other governments, nor to the legislative, which would too much retard such negotiation."[2]

The object of avoiding the separate legislation by the different States was the keynote of his following remarks: "But, say gentlemen, all treaties made under this Constitution are to be the supreme law of nations; that is, in their way of construction, paramount to the Constitution itself, and the laws of Congress. It is as clear as that two and two make four, that the treaties made are to be binding on the states only. Is it not necessary that they should be binding on the states? Fatal experience has proved that treaties would never be complied with, if their observance depended on the will of the states; and the consequences would be constant war. For if any one state could counteract any treaty, how could the United States avoid hostility with foreign nations? Do not gentlemen see the infinite dangers that would result from it, if a small part of the community could drag the whole confederacy into war?"[3]

§ 221. **Patrick Henry's views as to effect of treaties on States.**—Mr. Henry again laid particular stress on the effect

<hr>

§ 220.
[1] Elliot's Debates, vol. III, p. 509.

[2] *Idem*, pp. 509–510.
[3] *Idem*, p. 510.

of this treaty power upon the States, and the superiority
that treaty law would have over them, in many respects.
He said : " We are told that the state rights are preserved.
Suppose the state right to territory be preserved; I ask and
demand, How do the rights of persons stand, when they
have power to make any treaty, and that treaty is paramount to constitutions, laws, and everything ?   When a person shall be treated in the most horrid manner, and most
cruelly and inhumanly tortured, will the security of territorial rights grant him redress ?   Suppose an unusual punishment in consequence of an arrest similar to that of the
Russian ambassador; can it be said to be contrary to the
state rights ? . . .   We are so used to speak of enormity of powers, that we are familiarized with it.   To me
this power appears still destructive; for they can make any
treaty.   If Congress forbears to exercise it, you may thank
them ; but they may exercise it if they please, and as they
please.   They have a right, from the paramount power given
them, to do so.   Will the gentleman say that this power is
paramount to the state laws only ?   Is it not paramount to
the Constitution and everything ?   Can anything be paramount to what is paramount ?   Will not the laws of Congress be binding on Congress, as well as on any particular
state ?   Will they not be bound by their own acts ? " [1]

§ 222. **Mr. Madison's support of Constitutional provisions as to treaties ; final debate.**—Mr. Madison again expressed his approval of the power, and declared that it
already existed in the Confederation, as Congress was authorized to make treaties, and said: "Many of the states
have recognized the treaties of Congress to be the supreme
law of the land.   Acts have passed, within a year, declaring
this to be the case.   I have seen many of them.   Does it
follow, because this power is given to Congress, that it is
absolute and unlimited ?   I do not conceive that power is
given to the President and Senate to dismember the empire,
or to alienate any great, essential right.   I do not think the
whole legislative authority have this power.   The exercise

§ 221.

[1] Elliot's Debates, vol. III, pp. 512-514.

of the power must be consistent with the object of the delegation."[1]

Later, Mr. Dawson declared that the treaty power was
insufficiently guarded.[2] Mr. Grayson reiterated his prior
contention that under that power the Union could be dismembered; treaties should be in the hands of three-fourths
of both houses of Congress.[3] At the close of the debate Mr.
Henry, in making a final stand against ratification, said:
" Another thing which they have not mentioned, is the power
of *treaties*. Two thirds of the senators present can make
treaties; and they are, when made, to be the supreme law of
the land, and are to be paramount to the state constitutions.
We wish to guard against the temporary suspension of our
great national rights. We wish some qualification of this
dangerous power. We wish to modify it. One amendment
which has been wished for, in this respect is, that no treaty
should be made without the consent of a considerable majority of both houses."[4] Mr. Henry, however, was a patriot,
and after the Constitution was adopted as the law of the
land became one of its loyal supporters.[5]

§ 223. **Constitution finally ratified by Virginia; amendments suggested.**—The Constitution was finally ratified in
the manner above stated; an additional resolution was also

§ 222.

[1] Elliot's Debates, vol. III, pp.
514, *et seq.*

[2] *Idem*, p. 610.

[3] *Idem*, p. 613.

[4] *Idem*, p. 650.

[5] " The conduct of Mr. Henry,
when he saw that the adoption of
the Constitution was inevitable,
was all that might have been expected from his patriotic and un-
selfish character. ' If I shall be in
the minority,' he said, ' I shall have
those painful sensations which
arise from a conviction of being
overpowered in a good cause. Yet
I will be a peaceable citizen. My
head, my hand, and my heart shall
be free to retrieve the loss of liberty, and remove the defects of this
system in a constitutional way. I
wish not to go to violence, but will
wait with hopes that the spirit
which predominated in the Revolution is not yet gone, nor the cause
of those who are attached to the
Revolution yet lost. I shall, therefore, patiently wait in expectation
of seeing this government so
changed as to be compatible with
the safety, liberty, and happiness
of the people.' This noble and dis-
interested patriot lived to find the
Constitution all that he wished it
to be, and to enroll himself, in the
day of its first serious trial, among
its most vigorous and earnest defenders." Curtis' Constitutional
History of the United States, p. 682.

adopted recommending certain amendments, which were to be transmitted by the President of the convention with the ratification to the United States in Congress assembled.[1]

Number Seven of the proposed amendments was: "That no commercial treaty shall be ratified without the concurrence of two thirds of the whole number of the members of the Senate; and no treaty, ceding, contracting, restraining, or suspending, the territorial rights or claims of the United States, or any of them, or their, or any of their rights or claims to fishing in the American seas, or navigating the American rivers, shall be made, but in cases of the most urgent and extreme necessity; nor shall any such treaty be ratified without the concurrence of three fourths of the whole number of the members of both houses respectively."[2]

Certainly no one will contend for a moment that the full extent of the treaty-making power, as vested in the Central Government of the United States, was not thoroughly understood in the State of Virginia before the Constitution was ratified.

§ 224. **Ratification by New Hampshire; action of Rhode Island; Convention in New York.**—While the convention in Virginia was in progress, the convention in New York commenced; the delegates assembled at Poughkeepsie on the 17th of June.[1] During the sessions of this convention the Constitution was ratified in Virginia on June 25th, and in New Hampshire on June 21st;[2] on the 26th of July, 1788, the ratification of the Constitution by the State of New York made it binding upon all the States except North Carolina and Rhode Island. The former did not ratify the Constitution in its first Convention as we shall see, and the other rejected it by an alleged popular vote but one which could hardly be considered as binding upon the State, as the Federalists practically refused

§ 223.
[1] Elliot's Debates, vol. III, p. 659.
[2] *Idem*, p. 660.
§ 224.
[1] Elliot's Debates, vol. II, p. 205; Curtis' Constitutional History of the United States, vol. I, p. 674.
[2] *Idem*, p. 677; see also " A brief view of the influences that moved the adoption of the Federal Constitution by the State of New Hampshire; " an address delivered before the Grafton and Coös Counties (N. H.) Bar Association, by Albert Stillman Batchellor, at the meeting held at Berlin, N. H., January 27, 1899 (N. H. Bar Association Pamphlets, vol. 141).

to participate therein; subsequently, however, better counsel prevailed and both States recognizing the impossibility of remaining outside of the Union united with their sister States, North Carolina on November 21, 1789, and Rhode Island on May 29, 1790.[3]

§ 225. **Personnel of New York Convention.**—The list of 65 delegates composing the New York convention contains the names of John Jay, Alexander Hamilton, Robert R. Livingston, Governor George Clinton, Lewis Morris, Peter Van Ness, as well as those of many other prominent men who met and discussed the Constitution in its every aspect.

The report in Elliot's Debates shows that the laboring oar in this convention was handled by Alexander Hamilton, who had to meet the weight of all the opposing forces which were marshaled by Governor Clinton, who was violently opposed to the Constitution, and who having been elected President of the convention, did everything within his power to defeat the ratification.[1]

§ 226. **Treaty-making power referred to.**—The same practical fear in regard to the navigation of the Mississippi which to so great an extent had animated the opposition in Virginia did not exist in the State of New York, and, therefore, there was less discussion in regard to the treaty-making power in that convention than there had been in Virginia. Mr. G. Livingston, however, expressed his fear that the Senate might become a dangerous body as the Senators possessed

---

[3] See U. S. Statutes at Large, vol. I, pp. 99 and 126, for the statutes declaring North Carolina and Rhode Island to be States of the Union. As to North Carolina see §§ 227–230, pp. 366 et seq., post.

RATIFICATION OF RHODE ISLAND.

On pp. 334–336, vol. I, of Elliot's Debates will be found a lengthy ratification of the Constitution by Rhode Island which contains the Constitution at length, a declaration of rights, a long list of proposed amendments, the ratification of which the senators and repre-sentatives are urged to procure; the ratification itself, however, was absolute in form and appears to have been "Done in Convention," at Newport, May 29, 1790; none of the amendments referred to the treaty-making power. Curtis' Constitutional History of the United States, vol. 1, pp. 692–697.

§ 225.

[1] Elliot's Debates, vol. II, pp. 205–414; Curtis' Constitutional History of the United States, vol. 1, p. 674 et seq., and see p. 691 for "Honors paid to Hamilton."

too much power in their capacity as counsel to the President and in the formation of treaties,[1] and urged an amendment against reëlections.   Mr. Lansing took the same view,[2] and Mr. R. R. Livingston spoke against the proposed change.[3] On the 7th of July, while the Convention was in Committee of the Whole, Mr. Lansing, who had been one of the delegates to the Federal Convention, but who had withdrawn therefrom, proposed the following amendments: " Resolved, as the opinion of this Committee that no treaty ought to operate so as to alter the constitution of any state; nor ought any commercial treaty to operate so as to abrogate any law of the United States."[4]

It does not appear what action was taken on this particular recommendation as the reports are very brief; subsequently the Constitution was unconditionally ratified, but a circular letter was written to the Governors of all the other States urging the adoption of certain amendments although it does not appear exactly what the amendments were.[5]   To a great extent, however, they were the same as those submitted by some of the other States and in the list thereof Mr. Lansing's amendment as to the effect of treaties does not appear; the fact that it was offered shows that the effect of treaties upon State laws was one of the points considered by the convention.

§ 227. **North Carolina rejects the Constitution; Judge Iredell's views on treaty-making.**—On July 21, 1788, the constitutional convention met in North Carolina, and on August 2d, after a protracted debate, refused to ratify the Constitution.[1]   One of the principal subjects of discussion at this convention was the treaty-making power vested in Federal Government; amongst the delegates was James Iredell, afterwards an Associate Justice of the Supreme Court, and who delivered an opinion in regard to the treaty-making power in the case of *Ware* vs. *Hylton,* hereafter referred to.[2]

---

§ 226.
[1] Elliot's Debates, vol. II, p. 287.
[2] *Idem*, p. 289.
[3] *Idem*, p. 291.
[4] *Idem*, p. 409.
[5] *Idem*, pp. 413–414.

§ 227.
[1] Elliot's Debates, vol. IV, pp. 1–252; Curtis' Constitutional History of the United States, pp. 692, *et seq.*
[2] *Ware* vs. *Hylton,* U. S. Sup. Ct.

It is said that President Washington derived his conviction of Iredell's fitness for the Supreme Court bench from a perusal of the debates in the North Carolina convention and of his reply to George Mason's "Objection to the Constitution," which will also be referred to hereafter.[3] Mr. Iredell threw some light on the discussion as to the treaty-making power in the Federal Convention during his remarks, when he said: "Suppose there had been such a council as was proposed (evidently referring to some such suggestion made at the Federal Convention), consisting of thirteen, one from each state, to assist the President in making of treaties, etc.; more general alarm would have been excited, and stronger opposition made to this Constitution, than even at present.[4]

§ 228. **Views of other delegates.**—In the course of the debates it was urged that as "treaties were the supreme law of the land the House of Representatives ought to have a vote in making them as well as in passing them." Mr. J. M'Dowall dwelt at great length upon the small number of legislators, who, acting with the President, might make a treaty. He declared; "These ten men who constitute a quorum may make treaties and alliances. They may involve us in any difficulties, and dispose of us in any manner, they please. Nay," he continued, "eight is a majority of a quorum, and can do everything but make treaties. How unsafe are we, when we have no power of bringing those to an account! it is absurd to try them before their own body. Our lives and property are in the hands of eight or nine men. Will these gentlemen entrust their rights in this manner?"[1] Mr. Davie replied that "although treaties are mere conventional acts between the contracting parties, yet, by the law of nations, they are the supreme law of the land to their respective citizens or subjects. All civilized nations have concurred in considering them as paramount to an ordinary act of legislation. A due observance of treaties makes nations more friendly to each other, and is the only means of rendering less frequent those mutual hostilities which tend to depopulate and ruin contending nations. It extends and facilitates

1796, 3 Dallas, 199; see also § 324, Vol. II, pp. 6, *et seq.*
[3] See §§ 252–253, *post.*

[4] Elliot's Debates, vol. IV, p. 128.
§ 228.
[1] Elliot's Debates, vol. IV, p. 119.

that commercial intercourse, which, founded on the universal protection of private property, has in a measure, made the world one nation." [2] The remarks which followed this clearly indicated that it was understood that the method adopted in the treaty with Great Britain of urging State legislation in regard to matters within the domain of State jurisdiction, which the Federal Government might affect by negotiations and treaties with foreign nations was considered a failure and should be forever avoided thereafter.

§ 229. **Mr. Davie's views continued.**—This condition was plainly expressed in the following remarks of Mr. Davie: "The power of making treaties has, in all countries and governments, been placed in the executive departments. This has not only been grounded on the necessity and reason arising from that degree of secrecy, design, and despatch, which is always necessary in negotiations between nations, but to prevent their being impeded, or carried into effect, by the violence, animosity, and heat of parties, which too often infect numerous bodies. Both of these reasons preponderated in the foundation of this part of the system. It is true, sir, that the late treaty between the United States and Great Britain has not, in some of the states, been held as the supreme law of the land. Even in this state, an act of Assembly passed to declare its validity. But no doubt that treaty was the supreme law of the land without the sanction of the Assembly; because, by the Confederation, Congress has power to make treaties. It was one of those original rights of sovereignty which were invested in them; and it was not the deficiency of constitutional authority in Congress to make treaties that produced the necessity of a law to declare their validity; but it was owing to the entire imbecility of the Confederation." [1]

§ 230. **Resolutions of North Carolina as to position of that State on Constitution, and relations to other states.**— Towards its close, the convention went into Committee of the Whole and adopted resolutions to the effect that a declaration

---

[2] Elliot's Debates, vol. IV, p. 119.
§ 229.
[1] Elliot's Debates, vol. IV, pp. 119–120.

of rights should be added to the Constitution and also certain other amendments before North Carolina could adopt it.[1]

One of the proposed amendments was identical with the corresponding amendment proposed by the Virginia convention in regard to treaties.[2] Another was as follows: "23. That no treaties which shall be directly opposed to the existing laws of the United States in Congress assembled shall be valid until such laws shall be repealed, or made conformable to such treaty; nor shall any treaty be valid which is contradictory to the Constitution of the United States."[3]

As the Committee of the Whole had recommended that the Constitution should not be ratified until the amendments proposed had been made to the Constitution, the convention, after passing a resolution that the legislature be recommended to provide for levying imposts on goods imported into North Carolina from the United States, in case the United States should levy any imposts on goods brought into any of the States from North Carolina, adjourned *sine die.*[4]

§ 230.
[1] Elliot's Debates, vol. IV, p. 243.
[2] *Idem*, p. 245, and see § 223, p. 364, *ante.*
[3] *Idem*, p. 246.
[4] In Elliot's Debates, vol. IV, p. 251, the following record occurs:
"August 2, 1788.
"*Whereas* this Convention has thought proper neither to ratify nor reject the Constitution proposed for the government of the United States, and as Congress will proceed to act under the said Constitution, ten States having ratified the same, and probably lay an impost on goods imported into the said ratifying states,—
"*Resolved*, That it be recommended to the legislature of this state, that whenever Congress shall pass a law for collecting an impost in the states aforesaid, this state enact a law for collecting a similar impost on goods imported into this state, and appropriate the money arising therefrom to the use of Congress.

"*Resolved, unanimously,* That it be recommended to the General Assembly to take effectual measures for the redemption of the paper currency, as speedily as may be, consistent with the situation and circumstances of the people of this state.

"*Resolved, unanimously,* That the honorable the president be requested to transmit to Congress, and to the executives of all the States by name, a copy of the resolution of the Committee of the whole Convention on the subject of the Constitution proposed for the government of the United States, concurred with by this Convention, together with a copy of the resolutions on the subject of impost and paper money."

Another Convention, or a later

§ 231. **Ratification by eleven States makes Constitution effective.**—Thus the Constitution by the ratification of two more than the requisite number of States became the foundation of the great governmental superstructure which has since been erected upon it and which has successfully defied all attacks, practical and theoretical, from both internal and external forces.[1]

meeting of the same Convention appears to have been held. In Elliot's Debates, vol. I, p. 333, the following occurs:

"*State of North Carolina in Convention.*

"Whereas the General Convention which met in Philadelphia, in pursuance of a recommendation of Congress, did recommend to the citizens of the United States a Constitution or form of government in the following words, namely,— 'We, the people,' &c. (Here follows the Constitution of the United States, *verbatim.*) *Resolved,* That this Convention, in behalf of the freemen, citizens and inhabitants of the state of North Carolina, do adopt and ratify the said Constitution and form of government.

"Done in Convention this 21st day of November, 1789.

SAMUEL JOHNSON,
President of the Convention.

J. HUNT,
JAMES TAYLOR,
Secretaries.

On February 8, 1790 an act of Congress was passed giving effect to the Laws of the United States in North Carolina, 1 U. S. Stat. at Large, p. 99. Other acts were necessary, but after that date North Carolina was on an equal footing with the other states.

§ 231.
[1] *Ratifications of the Constitution.*

The Constitution was adopted by a Convention of the States September 17, 1787, and was subsequently ratified by the several States, in the following order, viz: Delaware, December 7, 1787; Pennsylvania, December 12, 1787; New Jersey, December 18, 1787; Georgia, January 2, 1788; Connecticut, January 9, 1788; Massachusetts, February 6, 1788; Maryland, April 28, 1788; South Carolina, May 23, 1788; New Hampshire, June 21, 1788; Virginia, June 26, 1788; New York, July 26, 1788; North Carolina, November 21, 1789; Rhode Island, May 29, 1790. The State of Vermont, by convention, ratified the Constitution on the 10th of January, 1791, and was, by an act of Congress of the 18th of February, 1791, "received and admitted into this Union as a new and entire member of the United States of America."

Ratifications of the Amendments to the Constitution.

The first ten amendments (with two others which were not ratified by the requisite number of States) were submitted to the several State Legislatures by a resolution of Congress which passed on the 25th of September, 1789, at the first session of the First Congress and were subsequently ratified by the Legislatures of the requisite number of States.

CHAPTER VIII.

THE TREATY-MAKING POWER AS A FACTOR IN THE GREAT NATIONAL DEBATE OF 1787-8.

§ 232. **Graudeur of the Constitution as a subject for study.**—There is no grander subject for study, no nobler theme for literature, than the Constitution of the United States, not only from historical, but also from ethical and ethnical points of observation; it is no wonder, therefore, that it has been the object of thought, study and expression of opinion, by many of the ablest legal scholars, in our own country, and also in those other countries, where the practical operation of the Constitution was watched, at first with doubt, and afterwards in wonder and with admiration.[1]

From the day of its promulgation as the finished work of the Constitutional Convention until the present time, essays, pamphlets, brochures, and commentaries upon, and analyses, and histories of, the Constitution have constantly appeared, until the published literature upon this single subject would, if it were all collected, constitute a library of no mean size.

§ 233. **Difficulty of selecting extracts from prominent writers.**—From this great mass of learning it is difficult to select the limited number of extracts for which space can be afforded in this volume; while, however, only a few will be quoted, an attempt will be made in culling these extracts from a vast amount of corroborative expressions, to select examples which will show the general tendency of opinion of the leading publicists upon the particular element of the subject which is under discussion.

§ 234. **Constitutional literature divided into two classes.**—Constitutional literature can be divided into two classes: first, that which appeared during the progress of the State conventions, and prior to the ratification of the Constitution, and which was published for the purpose of urging, or opposing, its adoption, and which, as was natural under the circumstances, was extremely partisan in its nature, either extolling the merits, or denouncing the demerits, of the Constitution,

§ 232.
[1] See Gladstone's statement quoted in § 168, p. 292, *ante*.

"The Federal Constitution has survived the mockery of itself in France and in Spanish America. Its success has been so great and striking, that men have almost forgotten that, if the whole of the known experiments of mankind in government be looked at together, there has been no form of government so unsuccessful as the Republican." *Popular Government*, Henry Sumner Maine, London, 1885, p. 292.

according to the views of the respective authors; second, that which has been written and published since the Constitution has become the greatest factor in our organic law, and which includes all that has been written for the purpose of expounding, interpreting and construing its various provisions, or reviewing them from historical and legal standpoints.

§ 235. **Pre-ratification literature a large element in procuring adoption of the Constitution.**—To the first class of literature the adoption of the Constitution was largely due. The able work of its sponsors and defenders in the State constitutional conventions was, of course, the prime factor in procuring its ratification in eleven of the thirteen States; at the same time, however, that the State conventions were in progress a great national debate was conducted in the newspapers, and also by the publicists of the time. It was an age of pamphleteering; many of the most prominent Federalists and Anti-Federalists published their views on the subject under assumed names—generally classic, but sometimes provincial—according to the then prevalent custom.[1] The records of this great debate form a valuable part of our National literature, and in collecting, collating and publishing them in a convenient and lasting form Paul Leicester

§ 235.

[1] The following names appear in Ford's Collection of Essays and Pamphlets: "Cassius," supposed to be written by James Sullivan; "Agrippa," credited, though not definitely, to James Winthrop; "A Landholder," generally credited to Oliver Ellsworth; "A Countryman" and "A Citizen of New Haven," both credited to Roger Sherman; "Cato," credited to George Clinton; "Cæsar," credited to Alexander Hamilton; "Sydney," credited to Robert Yates; "Caution," credited to Samuel Chase; "A Friend of the Constitution," credited to Daniel Carroll; "A Plaindealer," credited to Roane Spencer; "A Letter of a Steady and Open Republican," credited to Charles Pinckney; "A Federal Farmer," credited to Richard Henry Lee; "Marcus," credited to James Iredell; "Civis," credited to David Ramsay; "A Columbian Patriot," credited to Elbridge Gerry; "A Citizen of America," credited to Noah Webster; "A Citizen of New York," credited to John Jay; "A Plebeian," credited to Melancthon Smith; "A Citizen of Philadelphia," credited to Peletiah Webster; "Fabius," credited to John Dickinson; "Aristides," credited to Alexander Contee Hanson; "An American Citizen," credited to Tench Coxe; letters of Edmund Randolph, James Wilson, Luther Martin, Hugh Williamson, and others appeared over their own names.

Ford has rendered an important service to his country, and one which is, and always will be, appreciated by students of constitutional history.[2]

§ 236. This chapter devoted to pre-ratification literature. —This chapter will be exclusively devoted to the literature of the pre-ratification period, and the succeeding chapter to that which has been produced since the Constitution became the law of the land.

§ 237. The Federalist; its appearance and its effect.— The foremost position in the list of pre-ratification literature must be given to the eighty-five numbers of the Federalist,[1] which, appearing under the single assumed, and at that

---

[2] The best collection of these pamphlets can be found in two volumes:

Pamphlets on the Constitution of the United States, published during its Discussion by the People, 1787-1788, edited with notes and a Bibliography, by Paul Leicester Ford, Brooklyn, N. Y. 1888.

Essays on the Constitution of the United States, published during its Discussion by the People, 1787-1788, edited by Paul Leicester Ford, Brooklyn, N. Y., Historical Printing Club, 1892.

§ 237.

An extensive bibliography of this class of Constitutional literature will be found at pp. 385–441 of the "Pamphlets," which will also be found as an appendix to the second volume of Curtis' Constitutional History of the United States.

Some of the pamphlets and essays published in Pennsylvania will be found at the end of McMaster and Stone's Pennsylvania and the Federal Constitution.

See also § 250 and note thereunder, p. 387, *post*.

NOTES ON THE FEDERALIST.

[1] EDITIONS.

There are over twenty-four different editions of the Federalist enumerated in Paul Leicester Ford's bibliography of the Constitution, compiled in 1888 and included as an appendix to his Pamphlets on the Constitution. Ford's bibliography is also found at pp. 709, *et seq.* of volume II of Curtis' Constitutional History of the United States; a list of 24 editions will also be found in Lodge's Federalist, pp. xxxv, *et seq.* The author of this volume has consulted four editions of the Federalist, compiled and annotated respectively, by Henry B. Dawson, Henry Cabot Lodge, Paul Leicester Ford and J. C. Hamilton. References will not be given in notes to the extracts from the Federalist in this, and the succeeding sections, as editions vary as to paging, but the numbers are practically the same in all; the only change being that the insertion of No. XXX in modern editions makes a difference of one in subsequent numbers (see Dawson's edition, p. lv). The author has followed the text in the edition edited by Henry Cabot Lodge and published by G. P. Putnam's Sons, New York and London, 1894.

time unrecognized, name of Publius, stand as a monument to the joint and co-operating genius of Hamilton, Madison and Jay, whose efforts as delegates to the Federal and State conventions, and as authors of the Federalist, undoubtedly accomplished more practical results than those of any other three men in originally framing the Constitution in the Federal Convention, and finally procuring its ratification by the States. It not only served its purpose in America, in advocating the adoption of the Constitution, but it has also taken its place in Europe as a text book of high authority on popular government.[2] The Supreme Court of the United States

---

[2] AN ENGLISH VIEW OF THE FEDERALIST.

" The antecedents of a body of institutions like this, and its mode of growth, manifestly deserve attentive study; and fortunately the materials for the inquiry are full and good. The papers called the 'Federalist,' which were published in 1787 and 1788 by Hamilton, Madison, and Jay, but which were chiefly from the pen of Hamilton, were originally written to explain the new Constitution of the United States, then awaiting ratification, and to dispel misconstructions of it which had got abroad. They are thus, undoubtedly, an *ex post facto* defence of the new institutions, but they show us with much clearness either the route by which the strongest minds among the American statesmen of that period had traveled to the conclusions embodied in the Constitution, or the arguments by which they had become reconciled to them. The 'Federalist' has generally excited something like enthusiasm in those who have studied it, and among these there have been some not at all given to excessive eulogy. Talleyrand strongly recommended it; and Guizot said of it that, in the application of the elementary principles of government to practical administration, it was the greatest work known to him. An early number of the 'Edinburgh Review' (No. 24), described it as a 'work little known in Europe, but which exhibits a profundity of research and an acuteness of understanding which would have done honour to the most illustrious statesmen of modern times.' The American commendations of the 'Federalist' are naturally even less qualified. ' I know not,' wrote Chancellor Kent, ' of any work on the principles of free government that is to be compared in instruction and in intrinsic value to this small and unpretending volume of the 'Federalist;' not even if we resort to Aristotle, Cicero, Machiavel, Montesquieu, Milton, Locke, or Burke. It is equally admirable in the depth of its wisdom, the comprehensiveness of its views, the sagacity of its reflections, and the freshness, patriotism, candour, simplicity, and eloquence, with which its truths are uttered and recommended.' Those who have attentively read these papers will not think such praise pitched, on the whole, too high. Perhaps the part of it least thoroughly deserved is that given to their supposed profundity of research.

has on more than one occasion referred to it in deciding con-

There are few traces in the 'Federalist' of familiarity with previous speculations on politics, except those of Montesquieu in the 'Esprit des Lois,' the popular book of that day. The writers attach the greatest importance to all Montesquieu's opinions. They are much discomposed by his assertion, that Republican government is necessarily associated with a small territory, and they are again comforted by his admission, that this difficulty might be overcome by a confederate Republic. Madison indeed had the acuteness to see that Montesquieu's doctrine is as often polemical as philosophical, and that it is constantly founded on a tacit contrast between the institutions of his own country, which he disliked, with those of England, which he admired. But still his analysis, as we shall hereafter point out, had much influence upon the founders and defenders of the American Constitution. On the whole, Guizot's criticism of the 'Federalist' is the most judicious. It is an invaluable work on the application of the elementary principles of government to practical administration. Nothing can be more sagacious than its anticipation of the way in which the new institutions would actually work, or more conclusive than its exposure of the fallacies which underlay the popular objections to some of them.

" It is not to be supposed that Hamilton, Jay, and Madison were careless of historical experience. They had made a careful study of many forms of government, ancient and modern. Their observations on the ancient Republics, which were shortly afterwards to prove so terrible a snare to French political theorists, are extremely just. The cluster of commonwealths woven together in the 'United Netherlands' is fully examined, and the weaknesses of this anomalous confederacy are shrewdly noted. The remarkable structure of the Romano-German Empire is depicted, and there is reason to suspect that these institutions, now almost forgotten, influenced the framers of the American Constitution, both by attraction and by repulsion. But 'far the most important experience to which they appealed was that of their own country, at a very recent date. The earliest link had been supplied to the revolted colonies by the first or American 'Continental' Congress, which issued the Declaration of Independence. There had subsequently been the 'Articles of Confederation,' ratified in 1781. These earlier experiments, their demonstrable miscarriage in many particulars, and the disappointments to which they gave rise, are a storehouse of instances and a plentiful source of warning and reflection to the writers who have undertaken to show that their vices are removed in the Constitution of 1787–89.

"Nevertheless, there is one fund of political experience upon which the 'Federalist' seldom draws, and that is the political experience of Great Britain. The scantiness of these references is at first sight inexplicable. The writers must have understood Great Britain better than any other country, except their own. They had been British subjects during most of their lives. They had scarcely yet ceased to breathe the atmosphere of the British Parliament and to draw strength from

stitutional questions, always with respect, although on some
points it has not agreed with the authors, notably in regard

> its characteristic disturbances. Next to their own stubborn valour, the
> chief secret of the colonists' success was the incapacity of the English
> generals, trained in the stiff Prussian system soon to perish at Jena, to
> adapt themselves to new conditions of warfare, an incapacity which
> newer generals, full of admiration for a newer German system, were
> again to manifest at Majuba Hill against a meaner foe. But the colo-
> nists had also reaped signal advantage from the encouragements of the
> British Parliamentary Opposition. If the King of France gave 'aid,'
> the English Opposition gave perpetual ' comfort' to the enemies of the
> King of England. It was a fruit of the English party system which
> was to reappear, amid much greater public dangers, in the Peninsular
> War; and the revelation of domestic facts, the assertion of domestic
> weakness, were to assist the arms of a military tyrant, as they had as-
> sisted the colonists fighting for independence. Various observations in
> the 'Federalist' on the truculence of party spirit may be suspected of
> having been prompted by the recollection of what an Opposition can do.
> But there could be no open reference to this in its pages; and, on the
> whole, it cannot but be suspected that the fewness of the appeals to
> British historical examples had its cause in their unpopularity. The
> object of Madison, Hamilton, and Jay was to persuade their country-
> men; and the appeal to British experience would only have provoked
> prejudice and repulsion. I hope, however, to show that the Constitu-
> tion of the United States is coloured throughout by political ideas of
> British origin, and that it is in reality a version of the British Consti-
> tution, as it must have presented itself to an observer in the second
> half of the last century." (Citing especially Numbers 5, 14, 19, 20, 69 and
> 70, and referring to Bancroft's History of the Constitution of the Uni-
> ted States, vol. II, p. 336.) Popular Government, Sir Henry Sumner
> Maine, John Murray, London, 1885, Essay IV, pp. 202-207.

A FRENCH VIEW OF THE FEDERALIST.

In Hamilton's edition of the Federalist the following occurs (page
lxxxviii), after referring to some of the earliest American editions: " No
other edition was published in the United States until the year 1802,
three or more translations—the first in 1792—having, in the meantime,
appeared in Paris, during the exciting discussions which then occupied
the people of France. Talleyrand appreciating it, said to the Duc
D'Aranda, envoy at the French Court from Spain—' Vouz avez lu Le
Fédéraliste ?'—' Non,' replied D'Aranda,—' Lisez donc lisez,' was the
significant answer. Guizot, another distinguished statesman of France,
observed, ' In the application of elementary principles of government to
practical administration, it was the greatest work known to him.' " See
also the opinions of Chancellor KENT and Mr. Justice STORY referred to
in Hamilton's Edition of the Federalist immediately following the above
quotation.

to the effects of treaties with foreign powers, as contracts and as laws.[3]

§ 238. **Treaty-making power referred to in the Federalist and in other publications.**—The treaty-making power vested by the Constitution in the Central Government was equally prominent as a factor in this National discussion as it had been in the several State conventions to which reference has been made in the preceding chapter. It would require too much space to quote all that appears in the Federalist and other pamphlets, published at that time, on the subject of treaties, and the treaty-making power; the few selections quoted in the text and the notes show that the people at large, as well as the delegates to the conventions, thoroughly understood what a far-reaching power it was, how exclusively it was lodged in the Central Government, and how necessary this was to the future peace and happiness of the Union. The authors of the Federalist seem to have considered these propositions elementary principles for the government of confederated Republics.

§ 239. **The Federalist, No. XXII, reference to treaties.**—Referring to treaties the author of No. XXII,[1] says: "A circumstance which crowns the defects of the Confederation remains yet to be mentioned,—the want of a judiciary power. Laws are a dead letter without courts to expound and define their true meaning and operation. The treaties of the United States, to have any force at all, must be considered as part of the law of the land. Their true import, as far as respects individuals, must, like all other laws, be ascertained by judicial determinations. To produce uniformity in these determinations, they ought to be submitted, in the last resort, to one SUPREME TRIBUNAL. And this tribunal ought to be instituted under the same authority which forms the treaties themselves. These ingredients are both indispensable. If there is in each State a court of final

§ 237.

[3] See § 320, p. 460, *post.* For views of Chief Justice MARSHALL as to the Federalist and Alexander Hamilton, see *Cohens* vs. *Virginia*, U. S. Sup. Ct., 6 Wheaton, 264, MARSHALL, Ch. J.

§ 239.

[1] Published in the New York Packet, Friday, December 14, 1787; credited by Lodge to Hamilton.

jurisdiction, there may be as many different final determinations on the same point as there are courts. There are endless diversities in the opinions of men. We often see not only different courts but the judges of the same court differing from each other. To avoid the confusion which would unavoidably result from the contradictory decisions of a number of independent judicatories, all nations have found it necessary to establish one court paramount to the rest, possessing a general superintendence, and authorized to settle and declare in the last resort a uniform rule of civil justice. . . . The treaties of the United States, under the present Constitution,[2] are liable to the infractions of thirteen different legislatures, and as many different courts of final jurisdiction, acting under the authority of those legislatures. The faith, the reputation, the peace of the whole Union, are thus continually at the mercy of the prejudices, the passions, and the interests of every member of which it is composed. Is it possible that foreign nations can either respect or confide in such a government? Is it possible that the people of America will longer consent to trust their honor, their happiness, their safety, on so precarious a foundation ? "

§ 240. **The Federalist, No. XXIII, the treaty-making power should have no constitutional shackles.**—The author of No. XXIII,[1] gives his reasons for believing that the powers entrusted to the federal government, in which that of treaty-making is included, " ought to exist without limitation, *because it is impossible to foresee or define the extent and variety of national exigencies, or the correspondent extent and variety of the means which may be necessary to satisfy them.*[2] The circumstances that endanger the safety of nations are infinite, and for this reason no constitutional shackles can wisely be imposed on the power to which the care of it is committed. This power ought to be co-extensive with all the possible combinations of such circumstances ; and ought to be under the direction of the same councils which are appointed to preside over the common defence."

[2] Refers to Articles of Confederation.

§ 240.

[1] Published in the New York Packet, Tuesday, December 18, 1787; credited by Lodge to Hamilton.

[2] The italics are so in Lodge's edition.

§ 241. **The Federalist, No. XXXIX ; duality of the Central Government.**—A strong exposition of the duality of the Federal-National Government will be found in No. XXXIX,[1] in which the author declares, in the final sentence, in support of his point that the proposed Constitution is not, strictly speaking, either National or Federal, but is a composition of both, that : "In its foundation it is federal, not national; in the sources from which the ordinary powers of the government are drawn, it is partly federal, and partly national; in the operation of these powers, it is national, not federal; in the extent of them, again, it is federal, not national; and, finally, in the authoritative mode of introducing amendments, it is neither wholly federal nor wholly national."

§ 242. **The Federalist, No. XLII ; treaties with foreign nations.**—In No. XLII[1] the power to make treaties with foreign nations is again referred to, and the author of that number makes these concise remarks made in regard thereto : "This class of powers forms an obvious and essential branch of the federal administration.   If we are to be one nation in any respect, it clearly ought to be in respect to other nations.

"The powers to make treaties and to send and receive ambassadors, speak their own propriety.   Both of them are comprised in the articles of Confederation, with this difference only, that the former is disembarrassed, by the plan of the convention, of an exception, under which treaties might be substantially frustrated by regulations of the States."

§ 243. **The Federalist, No. XLV ; enlargement of congressional powers.**—In No. XLV[1] it is stated that the change from the articles of Confederation to the Constitution consisted much less in the addition of new powers to the Union than invigoration of its original powers.   Continuing, the Federalist says : "The regulation of commerce, it is true, is a new power ; but that seems to be an addition which few

§ 241.
[1] Published in the Independent Journal (date not given); credited by Lodge to Madison.
§ 242.
[1] Published in the New York

Packet, Tuesday, January 22, 1788; credited by Lodge to Madison.
§ 243.
[1] Published in the Independent Journal (date not given); credited by Lodge to Madison.

oppose, and from which no apprehensions are entertained. The powers relating to war and peace, armies and fleets, treaties and finance, with the other more considerable powers, are all vested in the existing Congress by the articles of Confederation. The proposed change does not enlarge these powers; it only substitutes a more effectual mode of administering them."

§ 244. **The Federalist, No. LXIV; importance of treaty-making power.**—In No. LXIV,[1] after quoting the section giving power to the President to make treaties by and with the consent of the Senate, provided that the requisite number concur, the author says: " The power of making treaties is an important one, especially as it relates to war, peace, and commerce ; and it should not be delegated but in such a mode, and with such precautions, as will afford the highest security that it will be exercised by men the best qualified for the purpose, and in the manner most conducive to the public good. The convention appears to have been attentive to both these points: they have directed the President to be chosen by select bodies of electors, to be deputed by the people for that express purpose ; and they have committed the appointment of senators to the State legislatures. This mode has, in such cases, vastly the advantage of elections by the people in their collective capacity, where the activity of party zeal, taking advantage of the supineness, the ignorance, and the hopes and fears of the unwary and interested, often places men in office by the votes of a small proportion of the electors."

§ 245. **The Federalist, No. LXIV; same subject continued.**—The author again says, in the same number: " It was wise, therefore, in the convention to provide, not only that the power of making treaties should be committed to able and honest men, but also that they should continue in place a sufficient time to become perfectly acquainted with our national concerns, and to form and introduce a system for the management of them." Continuing, he says:

" It seldom happens in the negotiation of treaties, of whatever nature, but that perfect *secrecy* and immediate *despatch*

§ 244.
[1] Published in the New York | Packet, Friday, March 7, 1788; credited by Lodge to Jay.

are sometimes requisite. There are cases where the most useful intelligence may be obtained, if the persons possessing it can be relieved from apprehensions of discovery. Those apprehensions will operate on those persons whether they are actuated by mercenary or friendly motives; and there doubtless are many of both descriptions, who would rely on the secrecy of the President, but who would not confide in that of the Senate, and still less in that of a large popular Assembly. The convention have done well, therefore, in so disposing of the power of making treaties, that although the President must, in forming them, act by the advice and consent of the Senate, yet he will be able to manage the business of intelligence in such a manner as prudence may suggest."

After showing the wisdom of confiding the treaty-making power to the Executive, and to the Senate, that being the smaller body of Congress and therefore better fitted for the purpose on account of the secrecy and despatch requisite in the negotiation of treaties, the Federalist answers those who had objected to the provision making treaties the supreme law of the land by saying, in the same number:[1]

"Others, though content that treaties should be made in the mode proposed, are averse to their being the *supreme* laws of the land. They insist, and profess to believe, that treaties like acts of assembly, should be repealable at pleasure. This idea seems to be new and peculiar to this country, but new errors, as well as new truths, often appear. These gentlemen would do well to reflect that a treaty is only another name for a bargain, and that it would be impossible to find a nation who would make any bargain with us, which should be binding on them *absolutely*, but on us only so long and so far as we may think proper to be bound by it. They who make laws may, without doubt, amend or repeal them; and it will not be disputed that they who make treaties may alter or cancel them; but still let us not forget that treaties are made, not by only one of the contracting parties, but by both; and consequently, that as the consent of both was essential to their formation at first, so must it ever after-

§ 245.
[1] No. LXIV.

wards be to alter or cancel them. The proposed Constitution, therefore, has not in the least extended the obligation of treaties. They are just as binding, and just as far beyond the lawful reach of legislative acts now, as they will be at any future period, or under any form of government."[2] It must be noted, however, that the views expressed by the Federalist in this number have not always been acquiesced in, or followed by, the Supreme Court. This will be referred to at length in a subsequent chapter on the relative effects of treaty stipulations and United States statutes.[3]

§ 246. The Federalist, No. LXIX : the treaty-making power of the United States compared with that of Great Britain.—In No. LXIX[1] the treaty-making power as vested in the President and Senate is compared to the treaty-making power as exercised by the king of Great Britain and the reasons for the vesting the treaty-making power, in its widest scope in the Executive, are given as follows: "The President is to have power, with the advice and consent of the Senate, to make treaties, provided two thirds of the senators present concur. The king of Great Britain is the sole and absolute representative of the nation in all foreign transactions. He can of his own accord make treaties of peace, commerce, alliance, and of every other description. It has been insinuated, that his authority in this respect is not conclusive, and that his conventions with foreign powers are subject to the revision, and stand in need of the ratification, of Parliament. But I believe this doctrine was never heard of, until it was broached upon the present occasion. Every jurist[2] of that kingdom, and every other man acquainted with its Constitution, knows, as an established fact, that the prerogative of making treaties exists in the crown in utmost plenitude; and that the compacts entered into by the royal authority have the most complete legal validity and perfection, independent of any other sanction.

[2] For views of John Jay on the treaty-making power of the confederation, see his letter to Congress referred to at length in note 4 under § 157, p. 268, *et seq.*, *ante*.

[3] See note 3 under § 237, p. 378, *ante*, and § 313, p. 449, *post.*

§ 246.

[1] Published in the New York Packet, Friday, March 14, 1788, credited by Lodge to Hamilton.

[2] The Federalist here cites Blackstone's Commentaries, vol. I, p. 257.

The Parliament, it is true, is sometimes seen employing itself in altering the existing laws to conform them to the stipulations in a new treaty; and this may have possibly given birth to the imagination, that its coöperation was necessary to the obligatory efficacy of the treaty. But this parliamentary interposition proceeds from a different cause: from the necessity of adjusting a most artificial and intricate system of revenue and commercial laws, to the changes made in them by the operation of the treaty; and of adapting new provisions and precautions to the new state of things, to keep the machine from running into disorder. In this respect, therefore, there is no comparison between the intended power of the President and the actual power of the British sovereign. The one can perform alone what the other can only do with the concurrence of a branch of the legislature. It must be admitted, that, in this instance, the power of the federal Executive would exceed that of any State Executive. But this arises naturally from (the exclusive possession by the Union of that part of)[3] the sovereign power which relates to treaties. If the Confederacy were to be dissolved, it would become a question, whether the Executives of the several States were not solely invested with that delicate and important prerogative."

§ 247. **The Federalist, No. LXXV; advantages of the United States plan; treaties as contracts.**—In Number LXXV[1] the Federalist again reverts to the provision that the President "is to have power, ' by and with the advice and consent of the Senate to make treaties, provided two thirds of the Senators present concur.' " In support of this provision he says that although it has been assailed on different grounds with no small degree of vehemency, he does not scruple to declare his firm persuasion that it is one of the best digested and most unexceptionable parts of the plan. He discusses and shows the advantages of the system as compared with the alternative methods of placing the power in the hands of the President alone, or of the Senate alone, or of allowing the House of

---

[3] The words in parenthesis appear in Dawson's edition of the Federalist, but are omitted in Lodge's edition.

§ 247.

[1] Published in the Independent Journal (date not given); credited by Lodge to Hamilton.

Representatives to participate therein. He demonstrates that requiring the concurrence of two thirds of the whole Senate instead of those present, would have proved an embarrassment rather than a benefit.

In speaking of treaties in this number, the Federalist takes the ground that treaty-making is not either strictly executive or legislative; in this respect he says: "The power of making treaties is, plainly, neither the one nor the other. It relates neither to the execution of the subsisting laws, nor to the enaction of new ones, and still less to an exertion of the common strength. Its objects are CONTRACTS with foreign nations, which have the force of law, but derive it from the obligations of good faith. They are not rules prescribed by the sovereign to the subject, but agreements between sovereign and sovereign. The power in question seems therefore to form a distinct department, and to belong, properly, neither to the legislative nor to the executive."

As stated in a previous section, we shall have occasion to refer again to these views of the Federalist in a subsequent chapter.[2]

§ 248. The Federalist, No. LXXX ; treaty-making power of National Government necessary for peace of Union.— In Number LXXX[1] the necessity of submitting the matters involving the peace of the Union to the national judiciary is stated as follows: "The fourth point rests on this plain proposition, that the peace of the WHOLE ought not to be left at the disposal of a PART. The Union will undoubtedly be answerable to foreign powers for the conduct of its members. And the responsibility for an injury ought ever to be accompanied with the faculty of preventing it. As the denial or perversion of justice by the sentences of courts, as well as in any other manner, is with reason classed among the just causes of war, it will follow that the federal judiciary ought to have cognizance of all causes in which the citizens of other countries are concerned. This is not less essential to the preservation of the public faith, than to the security of the

---

[2]See § 245, p. 381, *ante*, and § 313, p. 449, *post*

§ 248.

[1]In Lodge's edition this is stated as being taken from McLean's edition of 1788 and credited to Hamilton.

public tranquillity. A distinction may perhaps be imagined between cases arising upon treaties and the laws of nations and those which may stand merely on the footing of the municipal law. The former kind may be supposed proper for the federal jurisdiction, the latter for that of the States. But it is at least problematical, whether an unjust sentence against a foreigner, where the subject of controversy was wholly relative to the *lex loci*, would not, if unredressed, be an aggression upon his sovereign, as well as one which violated the stipulations of a treaty or the general law of nations. And a still greater objection to the distinction would result from the immense difficulty, if not impossibility, of a practical discrimination between the cases of one complexion and those of the other. So great a proportion of the cases in which foreigners are parties, involve national questions, that it is by far most safe and most expedient to refer all those in which they are concerned to the national tribunals."

§ 249. **Authorship of the Federalist.**—The author of this volume does not intend to enter into any discussion as to the authorship of the various numbers of the Federalist;[1] there can be no doubt that in the various extracts given the views expressed on the treaty-making power represented the opinions of Madison, Hamilton and Jay, all of whom were thoroughly conversant with the history of confederated governments, and the general rules of political science connected therewith; the most casual examination of the records of the Federal and State Constitutional Conventions, and of the Federalist, will show that no men were better qualified to

---

§ **249.**

[1] Mr. Lodge devotes Part I of his Introduction to the authorship of the "Federalist" (pp. xxiii–xxxv). On page xxiii he says: "The discussion about the 'Federalist' began nearly seventy years ago has continued at intervals down to the present day (1894), and culminated some twenty years since in two most elaborate essays, one by Mr. Henry B. Dawson, the other by Mr. John C. Hamilton, which were prefixed to the editions of the 'Federalist,' published by those two gentlemen respectively. It is of course idle to suppose that anything cannot be written which will convince or satisfy everybody as the true answer to this long mooted question." The reader of this book is referred to the three editions of the "Federalist" above referred to, all of which have tables in the introductions giving the various claims as to the authorship of the "Federalist."

express opinions upon the subjects than the three authors of the Federalist. No. LXIV [2] which was devoted entirely to a discussion of treaty-making power, was undoubtedly the work of John Jay, who had been Secretary of Foreign Relations under the Confederation, and had represented the United States in foreign countries, and who subsequently performed the duties of Secretary of State for a brief period under President Washington, was Minister to England, and negotiated the treaty with that country, which has always borne his name, and who was also the first Chief Justice of the United States. Surely no one could be better qualified to speak upon the subject of treaty-making than that eminent jurist who had devoted so much of his life thereto and whose utterances in that regard have always been rightly considered as entitled to the greatest weight and respect.[3]

§ 250. **Other publications prior to ratification.**—Even at the risk of devoting too much space to this class of literature, a few other extracts from pamphlets published during the ratification contest will be given, and in order to show that it was by no means a one-sided affair some will be selected from pamphlets published with the hope, and for the purpose—fortunately unsuccessful—of defeating the ratification of the Constitution.[1]

§ 251. **Richard Henry Lee's opposition; the "Federal Farmer."**—Richard Henry Lee of Virginia, a bitter opponent

---

[2] See §§ 244–5, pp. 381, *et seq.,* ante.

[3] See note 4, § 156, pp. 268, *et seq.,* ante.

§ 250.

[1] A number of letters which will be found in Ford's Essays and Pamphlets were written in opposition to the adoption of the Constitution in Massachusetts; of these, Mr. Ford states (p. 51, Essays) that the letters of "Agrippa" were the ablest anti-federal publications printed in Massachusetts, and showed especial ability in arguing the dangers and defects of a plan of government which was

both so peculiarly needed, and so especially advantageous to the State of Massachusetts, that its adoption was only endangered by certain questions of local politics, which could not even enter into the discussion. They were noticed, or replied to, in the Massachusetts Gazette, December 21, 1787, by "Charles James Fox;" December 27, 1787, and January 4, 1788, by "Kempis O'Flannigan," January 22 and January 25, 1788, by "Junius," and in the letters of "Cassius," printed in the same volume.

of the Constitution, expressed his views under the title of "The Federal Farmer" in regard to treaties as follows: "4th. There are certain rights which we have always held sacred in the United States, and recognized in all our constitutions, and which, by the adoption of the new constitution in its present form, will be left unsecured. By article 6, the proposed constitution, and the laws of the United States, which shall be made in pursuance thereof; and all treaties made, or which shall be made under the authority of the United States, shall be the supreme law of the land; and the judges in every state shall be bound thereby; anything in the constitution or laws of any state to the contrary notwithstanding.

" It is to be observed that when the people shall adopt the proposed constitution it will be their last and supreme act; it will be adopted not by the people of New Hampshire, Massachusetts, etc., but by the people of the United States; and wherever this constitution, or any part of it, shall be incompatible with the ancient customs, rights, the laws or the constitutions heretofore established in the United States, it will entirely abolish them and do them away: And not only this, but the laws of the United States which shall be made in pursuance of the federal constitution will be also supreme laws, and wherever they shall be incompatible with those customs, rights, laws or constitutions heretofore established, they will also entirely abolish them and do them away.

" By the article before recited, treaties also made under the authority of the United States, shall be the supreme law: It is not said that these treaties shall be made in pursuance of the constitution—nor are there any constitutional bounds set to those who shall make them: The president and two thirds of the senate will be empowered to make treaties indefinitely, and when these treaties shall be made, they will also abolish all laws and state constitutions incompatible with them. This power in the president and senate is absolute, and the judges will be bound to allow full force to whatever rule, article or thing the president and senate shall establish by treaty, whether it is practicable to set any bounds to those who make treaties, I am not able to say; if not, it proves that this power ought to be more safely lodged."[1]

§ 252. **George Mason's protest.**—George Mason, who was also a bitter opponent of the Constitution published a violent pamphlet attacking it in many respects; he considered that by declaring all treaties supreme laws of the land the Executive and the Senate had in many instances an exclusive power of legislation which might have been avoided by proper distinction with respect to treaties, by requiring the assent of the House of Representatives.[1]

§ 253. **Judge Iredell's answer; " Marcus."**—Judge Iredell of North Carolina to whose able work in the convention of that State we have already alluded[1] and to whom we shall allude in a later chapter, in regard to his opinion in the great case of *Ware* vs. *Hylton* in which the treaty-making power under the Constitution was discussed and construed,[2] answered Colonel Mason under the name of " Marcus," in one of the best pamphlets published during the period. In regard to the treaty-making power Judge Iredell argued that it was already the law of the land and had been so determined by Congress in unanimously resolving to adopt the very sensible letter of Mr. Jay's[3] to the effect " that a treaty when once made pursuant to the sovereign authority, *ex vi termini* became immediately the law of the land." Continuing, Judge Iredell said: "It seems to result unavoidably from the nature of the thing, that when the constitutional right to make treaties is exercised, the treaty so made should be binding upon those who delegated authority for that purpose. If it was not, what foreign power would trust us? And if this right was restricted by any such fine checks as Mr. Mason has in his imagination, but has not thought proper to disclose, a critical occasion might arise, when for want of a little rational confidence in our own government, we might be obliged to submit to a master in an enemy. Mr. Mason wishes

§ 251.

[1] Ford's Pamphlets on the Constitution, p. 311. The punctuation is so in the original.

§ 252.

[1] Ford's Pamphlets on the Constitution, pp. 327, *et seq.*, see p. 331.

§ 253.

[1] See § 227, p. 366, *ante.*

[2] See § 328, Vol. II, p. 9.

[3] For an extended reference to Jay's report, or letter, see note under § 156, pp. 268, *et seq., ante.*

the House of Representatives to have some share in this business, but he is immediately sensible of the impropriety of it, and adds 'where it can be done with safety.' And how is it to be known whether it can be done with safety or not, but during the pendency of a negotiation? Must not the President and Senate judge whether it can be done with safety or not? If they are of opinion it is unsafe, and the House of Representatives of course not consulted, what becomes of this boasted check, since, if it amounts to no more than the President and Senate may consult the House of Representatives if they please, they may do this as well without such a provision as with it. Nothing would be more easy than to assign plausible reasons, after the negotiation was over, to show that a communication was unsafe, and therefore surely a precaution that could be so easily eluded, if it was not impolitic to the greatest degree, must be thought trifling indeed. It is also to be observed, that this authority, so obnoxious in the new Constitution (which is unfortunate in having little power to please some persons, either as containing new things or old), is vested indefinitely and without restriction in our present Congress, who are a body constituted in the same manner as the Senate is to be, but there is this material difference in the two cases, that we shall have an additional check, under the new system of a President of high personal character chosen by the immediate body of the people." [4]

§ 254. **David Ramsay's letters; " Civis."**—David Ramsay of South Carolina, who had also been a delegate to his own State convention, issued an address to his friends, countrymen, and fellow citizens under the title of " Civis " in which he disposed of the objections as to the treaty-making power as follows: "It has been objected, that the president, and two-thirds of the senate, though not of your election, may make treaties binding on the state. Ask these objectors—do you wish to have any treaties? They will say yes. Ask then who can be more properly trusted with the power of making them, than they to whom the convention have referred it? Can the state legislatures? They would consult their local

<hr/>

[4] Ford's Pamphlets on the Constitution, pp. 333, *et seq.*, see p. 355.

interests.—Can the Continental House of Representatives? When sixty-five men can keep a secret, they may.—Observe the cautious guards which are placed round your interests. Neither the senate nor president can make treaties by their separate authority.—They must both concur.—This is more in your favour than the footing on which you now stand. The delegates in Congress of nine states, without your consent, can now bind you; by the new constitution there must be two-thirds of the members present, and also the president, in whose election you have a vote. Two-thirds are to the whole, nearly as nine to thirteen. If you are not wanting to yourselves by neglecting to keep up the state's compliment of senators, your situation with regard to preventing the controul of your local interests by the Northern States, will be better under the proposed constitution than it is now under the existing confederation." [1]

§ 255. **Public knowledge as to the treaty-making power and its effects.**—Any one, therefore, who examines the records of the great contests over the adoption of the Constitution in the State conventions, and in the country at large, must inevitably reach the conclusion, that Article VI, making treaties the supreme law of the land and paramount to all State legislation, was based upon the acknowledged weakness of the Confederation, not only as to the making of treaties, but also as to enforcement and fulfilment of treaty obligations. It is also apparent that a majority of the people, including many who were opposed to the Constitution on other grounds, considered that in our relations with foreign powers, whether the subject-matter related to national affairs, or those within the control of the States, or even of individuals, the Central Government must be clothed with the absolute and exclusive power to negotiate and conclude treaties of every class; that it had been effectually demonstrated that the policy adopted by the Confederation, in regard to the treaty of peace with Great Britain, of urging legislation upon the various States to carry treaty stipulations into effect was an impracticable and unsatisfactory method of dealing with foreign powers; that the unwillingness or failure of many of the States

§ 254.
[1] Fords' Pamphlets on the Constitution, p. 376.

to act in accordance with the suggestions of Congress, or their subsequent unwillingness or inability to conform to the conditions of the treaty, had placed us in an unenviable position with all the foreign powers, many of whom had lost confidence in us, and to whom the United States were[1] fast becoming objects of ridicule, rather than of the great respect to which, as a nation, they were entitled; that under the new Constitution, and in a large measure owing to the additional powers with which Article VI clothed the Central Government, this confidence and respect were immediately regained, and have ever since been retained, as they undoubtedly always will be if we continue to recognize that those powers rightfully exist and that they should be exercised on every proper occasion.   Nor can the position ever be taken that the various clauses in regard to treaties and the treaty-making power in the Constitution were not appreciated, or were in any way disregarded, by the people in the discussions upon the ratification of that instrument; the reverse of this proposition was indeed the fact.

§ 256. **Importance of treaty-making power appreciated by the people, and by the delegates to State conventions.** —The records of the State conventions show that the delegates were fully alive to the importance, and the far-reaching extent, of the power; and that the possibility of its being used to the detriment of the States formed an important factor in the discussions in the conventions; the extracts quoted from the pamphlets of the day show that it was not only discussed in the State conventions, but that it was also discussed and considered by the people themselves.

In the next chapter we will refer to the opinions expressed by some writers since the Constitution became the supreme law of the land, and which will show what they thought in regard to the extent of, and limitations upon, the treaty-making power of the United States.

§ 255.

[1] The use of *were* instead of *was* in this instance is intentional as under the Confederation, after the close of the war, the States were drifting so far from union that they were regarded as separate entities by foreign powers rather than as the component parts of a single entity, as they should have been, and have been since the adoption of the Constitution.

CHAPTER IX.

§ 257. Pre-ratification literature necessarily academic. —The extracts in the preceding chapter are all taken from pamphlets published for or against the Constitution before it was ratified, and when the effect and extent of its provisions could only be treated in a prophetic manner and from an academic standpoint.

Written in the abstract, and based upon hypothetical conditions, they were, therefore, necessarily largely theoretical

393

and did not relate to the application of the provisions of the Constitution to any concrete conditions; with the exception of the Federalist, few of them, if any, have ever been regarded by the courts as affording any basis for the construction of any of the clauses of the Constitution; in this volume they have been referred to, as evidence of the fact that the treaty-making power was thoroughly understood by the people before the constitution was adopted, rather than as legal authority for the extent of the power.[1]

§ 258. **Different status of post-ratification literature.**— The moment, however, that the Constitution became the fundamental basis of the Government of the United States, practical questions, as to the interpretation and application of its provisions, arose, and from that time the literature regarding the Constitution can be divided into two classes: First, views of expounders who have discussed it in commentaries and text-books from legal and political standpoints in connection with the adjudicated law of this and other countries; second, decisions of the courts upon constitutional points which have arisen in actions at law and required the judicial construction and interpretation of the instrument itself, and in which the judges, delivering their opinions in regard thereto, have expressed their views as to the nature, scope and extent of the provisions of the Constitution involved in the actions, as well as to the general nature and powers of the Government of the United States.

§ 259. **Treaty-making power furnishes many questions for discussion.**—It will readily be seen that the nature and extent of the treaty-making power vested in the General Government by the Constitution, and of the effects of treaties upon the laws of the United States, and of the various States, have continuously afforded opportunities, both for the expounders of the Constitution in treatises, and for the judges in decisions, to express their views on constitutional questions; in fact, as will be seen in the next chapter, one of the first great constitutional controversies in which the power of the Union was asserted, and was upheld by the Supreme Court as superior to the law of any of the States, related to

§ 257.
[1] See § 255, p. 391, *ante.*

the treaty-making power. In the case of *Ware* vs. *Hylton*[1] this question was discussed in an action submitted to, and decided by, the Supreme Court, and the provisions of the Constitution in regard to treaties were judicially construed and determined.

§ 260. **Opinions of publicists—not judicial decisions—discussed in this chapter.**—The judicial decisions will be reserved for subsequent chapters,[1] and the balance of this chapter will be devoted to referring briefly to the opinions of some of the ablest writers upon the Constitution, and giving a summary of their views in regard to the nature and extent of the treaty-making power as it is vested in the Central Government of the United States. It will only be possible to give extracts from a few of the many eminent writers upon constitutional law and treaties.[2]

§ 261. **Views of William Rawle; 1825.**—One of the earliest expounders of the Constitution was William Rawle, whose book, published in 1825, was immediately recognized, and has ever since retained its position, as an able exposition of the subject, notwithstanding some of the extreme views of the author.[1]

Mr. Rawle was an ardent exponent of the States' rights school: in fact, he believed in the right of secession; he gave, however, the widest possible scope to the treaty-making power. The following extract shows that he realized how fully the framers and ratifiers of the Constitution appreciated the nature and extent of this power when they vested it in the Central Government of the United States.

" The nature and extent of this constitutional power underwent full examination, in the state conventions. The most general terms are used in the Constitution. The powers of

---

§ 259.

[1] See § 324, Vol. II, pp. 6 *et seq.*

§ 260.

[1] Chaps. XI–XIV, *post.*

[2] The student who desires to further investigate this subject will find two very complete bibliographies of the subject. One, as the Appendix to the second volume of Curtis' Constitutional History of

the United States, and the other in Paul Leicester Ford's collections of Pamphlets on the Constitution. See also list of authorities referred to, at commencement of this Volume.

§ 261.

[1] A view of the Constitution of the United States by William Rawle, 1st edition, Philadelphia, 1825, 2d edition, 1829.

congress in respect to making laws we shall find are laid under several restrictions. There are none in respect to treaties. Although the acts of public ministers, less immediately delegated by the people than the house of representatives; the president constitutionally and the senate, both constitutionally and practically, two removes from the people, are by the treaty making power, invested with the high and sole control over all those subjects which properly arise from intercourse with foreign nations, and may eventually effect important interests at home. To define them in the Constitution would have been impossible, and therefore a general term could alone be made use of, which is, however, to be scrupulously confined to its legitimate interpretation. Whatever is wanting in an authority expressed, must be sought for in principle, and to ascertain whether the execution of the treaty making power can be supported, we must carefully apply to it the principles of the Constitution from which alone the power proceeds.

" In its general sense, we can be at no loss to understand the meaning of the word treaty. It is a compact entered into with a foreign power, and it extends to all those matters which are generally the subjects of compact between independent nations. Such subjects are peace, alliance, commerce, neutrality, and others of a similar nature. To make treaties is an essential attribute of a nation. One which disabled itself from the power of making, and the capacity of observing and enforcing them when made, would exclude itself from the international equality which its own interests require it to preserve, and thus in many respects commit an injury on itself. In modern times and among civilized nations, we have no instances of such absurdity. The power must then reside somewhere. Under the articles of confederation it was given with some restrictions, proceeding from the nature of that imperfect compact, to congress, which then nominally exercised both the legislative and executive powers of general government. In our present Constitution no limitations were held necessary. The only question was where to deposit it. Now this must be either in congress generally, in the two houses exclusive of the president, in the president conjunctly with them or one of them, or in the president alone. . . .

" There is a variance in the words descriptive of laws and those of treaties—in the former it is said those which shall be made *in pursuance of the Constitution*, but treaties are described as having been made, or which shall be made *under the authority of the United States.*

" The explanation is, that at the time of adopting the Constitution, certain treaties existed, which had been made by congress under the confederation, the continuing obligations of which it was proper to declare. The words ' *under the authority of the United States,*' were considered as extending equally to those previously made, and to those which should subsequently. be effected. But although the former could not be considered as made pursuant to a Constitution which was not then in existence, the latter would not be unless they are conformable to its Constitution. . . .

" Having felt the necessity of the treaty-making power, and having fixed on the department in which it shall be vested, the people of course excluded from all interference with it, those parts of the government which are not described as partaking of it. The representation held out by our Constitution to foreign powers, was, that the president with the advice and consent of the senate, could bind the nation in all legitimate compacts: but if pre-existent acts, contrary to the treaty, could only be removed by Congress, this representation would be fallacious; it would be a just subject of reproach, and would destroy all future confidence in our public stipulations. The immediate operation of the treaty must therefore be to overrule all existing legislative acts inconsistent with its provisions." [2]

§ 262. **Mr. Rawle's acquaintance with members of Constitutional Convention.**—Mr. Rawle had the advantage of personal acquaintance with members of the Constitutional Convention, and with the Judges of the Supreme Court who had been called upon to construe it, and he was well able to write upon the subject, having full knowledge of the circumstances under which the instrument itself was framed and ratified. In another part of his work, in which he discussed

[2] *Idem*, p. 57–61, 1st edition; pp. 64–67, 2d edition.

the effect of Article VI upon the State constitutions and legislation, he recognized the necessity of central action without any reference whatever to the States; in this respect he says: "The effect of a treaty on state constitutions and state laws cannot be questioned. Without considering whether it operates directly as a repeal of them, we are warranted in saying that an act done under a state law, in opposition to a treaty, cannot be set up as a legal bar to a proceeding founded on a treaty.

"The inability of the Confederation to enforce the treaties made by them was severely felt. Many state laws which had been passed, during, or shortly after the war of the revolution, were inconsistent with some of the articles of the treaty of peace with Great Britain, and that power, complaining of injuries sustained in consequence thereof, postponed the fulfillment of the treaty in some points on their part. The inadequacy of the powers of congress to enforce it were then sensibly felt, and a serious declaration that a treaty, in virtue of the confederation, was part of the law of the land and obligatory on the several legislatures, was transmitted to all the states, with an urgent recommendation that the states themselves would repeal all those acts and parts of acts that were repugnant to the treaty. In this respect the want of a judicial power was strongly perceived.

"After the adoption of the Constitution, its retrospective effect upon the opposing laws of a state, passed even before the treaty, was speedily and fully established by the Supreme Court of the United States."[1]

§ 263. **Views of William A. Duer; 1833.**—Another of the early commentators of the Constitution was William A. Duer who as early as 1833, published his first text book on the Constitution,[1] which was afterwards followed by his Constitutional Jurisprudence[2] in which he declared that "*the powers*

---

§ 262.

[1] A view of the Constitution of the United States, by William Rawle, Philadephia, 1825 and 1829, 1st edition p. 68; 2d edition, p. 74.

§ 263.

[1] Outlines of the Constitutional Jurisprudence of the United States,

by William Alexander Duer, LL. D. New York, 1833.

[2] A course of Lectures on the Constitutional Jurisprudence of the United States by William Alexander Duer, 2d edition, Boston, 1856.

to make treaties, and to send and receive ambassadors and other public ministers and consuls, are essential attributes of national sovereignty, and of that international equality which the interests of every sovereignty require it to preserve."³

The opening pages of his seventh Lecture, which are quoted at length in the notes show how thoroughly he had examined this point and how consistent it is with the nationality and sovereignty of the United States.⁴

³ *Idem*, p. 227.

⁴ Lecture VIII, p. 227, *idem*, continues:

"The powers vested in the General Government for regulating foreign intercourse, consist,

"*First.* Of the powers to make treaties, and to send and receive Ambassadors, and other public Ministers, and Consuls.

"*Secondly.* Of the power to define and punish piracies and felonies committed on the high seas, and other offences against the law of nations; and,

"*Thirdly.* Of the power of regulating foreign commerce; including a power to prohibit, after a certain period, now elapsed, the importation of slaves.

"This class of powers forms an obvious and essential branch of Federal administration; for if the United States are one nation in any respect, they are most clearly so in respect to other nations.

"1. *The powers to make treaties, and to send and receive Ambassadors and other public Ministers, and Consuls*, are essential attributes of national sovereignty, and of that international equality which the interests of every sovereignty require it to preserve. Both powers were possessed by Congress under the Confederation, but not to the extent to which they are now en-

joyed; for then the former power was embarrassed by an exception, under which treaties might be substantially frustrated by regulations of the States, and the latter did not comprehend 'other public ministers and consuls.'

"As treaties with France and Holland, and especially the treaty of peace with Great Britain, existed when the Constitution was adopted, it became necessary to vary its terms in regard to treaties, from those relative to the laws of the United States; the declaration it contains in respect to the supremacy of the latter operating only in future, while in reference to the former the terms are, ' All treaties made, *or which shall be made*, under the authority of the United States, shall be the supreme law of the land.' These terms were intended to apply equally to previously existing treaties, as well as to those made subsequently to the Constitution; and it has, accordingly, been adjudged, by the Supreme Court, that they effectually repeal so much of the State laws and Constitutions as are repugnant to them.

"More general and extensive terms, also, are used in vesting the power with respect to treaties, than in conferring that relative to laws; and, while the latter is laid

§ 264. George Ticknor Curtis' Constitutional History of the United States.—The Constitutional History of the Uni-

under several restrictions, there are none imposed on the exercise of the former, notwithstanding it is committed to the President and Senate, in exclusion of the House of Representatives, and is executed through the instrumentality of agents delegated for the purpose. And although the President and Senate are thus invested with this high and exclusive control over all those subjects of negotiation with foreign powers, which, in their consequences, may affect important domestic interests, yet it would have been impossible to have defined a power of this nature, and, therefore, general terms only were used. These general expressions, however, ought strictly to be confined to their legitimate signification; and in order to ascertain whether the execution of the treaty-making power can be supported in any given case, those principles of the Constitution, from which the power proceeds, should carefully be applied to it. The power must, indeed, be construed in subordination to the Constitution; and however, in its operation, it may qualify, it cannot supersede or interfere with, any other of its fundamental provisions, nor can it ever be so interpreted as to destroy other powers granted by that instrument. A treaty to change the organization of the Government, or annihilate its sovereignty, or overturn its Republican form, or to deprive it of any of its constitutional powers, would be void; because it would defeat the will of the people, which it was designed to fulfill.

" A treaty, in its general sense, is a compact entered into with a foreign power, and extends to all matters which are usually the subject of compact between independent nations. It is, in its nature, a *contract*, and not a Legislative act; and does not, according to general usage, effect of itself the objects intended to be accomplished by it, but requires to be carried into execution by some subsequent act of sovereign power by the contracting parties, especially in cases where it is meant to operate within the territories of either of them. With us, however, a different principle is established, in certain cases. It has been settled by the Supreme Court, that, inasmuch as the Constitution declares a treaty to be the law of the land, it is to be regarded in Courts of Justice as equivalent to an act of Legislature, whenever it operates of itself without requiring the aid of any legislative provision. But when the terms of any treaty stipulation import an *executory* contract, it addresses itself to the political, and not to the Judicial department for execution, and Congress must pass a law in execution of the compact, before it becomes a rule for the Courts. The Constitution does not expressly declare whether treaties are to be held superior to the Acts of Congress, or whether the laws are to be deemed coequal with, or superior to treaties; but the representation it holds forth to foreign powers, is that the President, by and with the advice and consent of the Senate, may bind the nation in all legitimate contracts; and if pre-existing laws, contrary to a treaty, could only be abrogated by Congress, this repre-

ted States by George Ticknor Curtis will perpetuate the name of that author as long as the Constitution shall remain the

sentation would be fallacious. It would subject the public faith to just imputation and reproach, and destroy all confidence in the national engagements. The immediate operation of a treaty must, therefore, be to overrule all existing laws incompatible with its stipulations.

"Nor is this inconsistent with the power of Congress to pass subsequent laws, qualifying, altering or wholly annulling, a treaty; for such an authority, in certain cases, is supported on grounds wholly independent of the treaty-making power. For, as Congress possesses the sole right of declaring war, and as the alteration or abrogation of a treaty tends to produce it, the power in question may be regarded as an incident to that of declaring war. The exercise of such a right may be rendered necessary to the public welfare and safety, by measures of the party with whom the treaty was made, contrary to its spirit, or in open violation of its letter; and on such grounds alone can this right be reconciled either with the provisions of the Constitution, or the principles of public law. A memorable instance has occurred in our history of the annulment of a treaty by the act of the injured party. In the year 1798, Congress declared that the treaties with France were no longer obligatory on the United States, as they had been repeatedly violated by the French Government, and our just claims for reparation disregarded. Nevertheless, all treaties, as soon as ratified by competent authority, become of absolute efficacy, and, as long as they continue in

force, are binding upon the whole nation. If a treaty require the payment of money to carry it into effect, and the money can only be raised or appropriated by an Act of the Legislature, it is morally obligatory upon the legislative power to pass the requisite law; and its refusal to do so would amount to a breach of the public faith, and afford just cause of war. That department of the Government which is intrusted with the power of making treaties may bind the national faith at its discretion; for the treaty-making power must be coextensive with the national exigencies, and necessarily involves in it every branch of the national sovereignty, of which the operation may be necessary to give effect to negotiations and compacts with foreign nations. If a nation have conferred on its Executive department, without reserve the right of treating and contracting with other sovereignties, it is considered as having invested it with all the power necessary to make a valid contract, because that department is the organ of the Government for the purpose, and its contracts are made by the deputed will of the nation. The fundamental laws of the State may withhold from it the power of alienating the public domain, or other property belonging to it; but if there be no express provision of that kind, the inference is that it has confided to the department, charged with the duty and the power of making treaties, a discretion commensurate with all the great interests of the nation. (Citing Vattel's Law of Nations, b. 1, ch. 21, sec. 2; 3 Dall. 199;

26

foundation of our Government. He states the reason for the adoption of Article VI, in clear and concise terms as follows:

Grotius' Law of War and Peace, b. 3, ch. 20, sec. 7; *ibid.* b. 4, ch. 2, secs. 11, 12; 1 Cranch, 103.)

" The concurrence of each branch of the Legislative power, we have seen, is necessary to a declaration of war, while the President with the advice and consent of the Senate alone, may conclude a treaty of peace. Now a power to make treaties necessarily implies a power to settle the terms on which they shall be concluded; and foreign States could not deal safely with the Government on any other presumption. That branch of the Government which is intrusted thus largely and generally with authority to make valid treaties of peace, can, of course, bind the nation by the alienation of part of its territory; and this, according to an approved writer on the law of nations, (Grotius, b. 4, ch. 2, secs. 11, 12) is equally the case, whether that territory be already in the occupation of the enemy, or remain in possession of the nation, or whether the property be public or private. In a case decided in the Supreme Court of the United States, it was admitted that individual rights acquired by war, and vested rights of the citizen, might be sacrificed by treaty for national purposes. (1 Cranch, 103.)

"And in another case, it was held to be a clear principle of national law, that private rights might be surrendered by treaty to secure the public safety, but the Government would be bound to make compensation and indemnity to the individual whose rights had thus been sacrificed.

"The conclusion of a treaty of commerce and navigation with Great Britain, in 1794, gave rise to much public discussion as to the nature and extent of the treaty-making power. A resolution was passed by the House of Representatives, requiring the President to lay before them a copy of his instructions to the Minister who conducted the negotiation, with the correspondence and other documents, relative to the treaty, excepting such papers as any existing negotiations might render it improper to disclose."

Mr. Duer then quotes largely from the reply of President Washington to this resolution which is quoted in full as a note to § 292 *post* of this volume, and in which he refused to comply with the request.

"The principles thus laid down by General Washington, were so far acquiesced in by the House, that they passed a resolution, disclaiming the power to interfere in making treaties; but asserting the right of the House of Representatives, whenever stipulations are made on subjects committed by the Constitution to Congress, to deliberate on the expediency of carrying them into effect; and subsequently it was declared, by a small majority, to be expedient to pass the laws necessary for carrying the treaty into effect. From that time the question remained undisturbed until the conclusion of a convention with Great Britain, in 1815, when the House of Representatives, after much debate, passed a bill specifically enacting, on a particular subject, the same provisions which were contained

"The articles specially designed to assert and carry out the supremacy of the National Government, as they came from the Committee, embodied the resolutions on the same subject which had passed the Convention. The only material addition consisted in the qualification that the legislative acts of the United States, which were to be the supreme law, were such as should be made in pursuance of the Constitution. Subsequently the article was so amended as to make the Constitution, the laws passed in pursuance of it, and the treaties of the United States the supreme law of the land, binding upon all judicial officers.

"It is a remarkable circumstance that this provision was originally proposed by a very earnest advocate of the rights of the States—Luther Martin. His design, however, was to supply a substitute for a power over State legislation, which had been embraced in the Virginia plan, and which was to be exercised through a negative by the national legislature upon all laws of the States contravening, in their opinion, the Articles of Union or the treaties subsisting under the authority of the Union. The purpose of the substitute was to change a legislative into a judicial power, by transferring from the national legislature to the judiciary the right of determining whether a state law supposed to be in conflict with the Constitution, laws, or treaties of the Union should be inoperative or valid. By extending the obligation to regard the requirements of the national Constitution and laws to the judges of the state tribunals, their supremacy in all the judicatures of the country was secured. This obligation

as stipulations in the treaty. This dangerous innovation on the treaty-making power was warmly opposed by a minority in the House, and disagreed to by the Senate; but, after several conferences between them, the affair terminated in a compromise which it is difficult to reconcile with a sound construction of the Constitution. The law passed on the occasion briefly declares that so much of any Act as imposes a duty on tonnage, contrary to the provisions of the con-vention with Great Britain, should, *from the date of that instrument,* and during its continuance, be of no force or effect; thus setting a precedent which may produce future difficulty in our national legislation, though the Judicial tribunals would probably regard such a law as a work of supererogation, or a mere nullity, and, from its retroactive operation, at variance with the spirit of the Constitution." (For citation see head of this note.)

was enforced by the oath or affirmation to support the Constitution of the United States ; and, as we shall see hereafter, lest this security should fail, the final determination of questions of this kind was drawn to the national judiciary, even when they might have originated in a state tribunal."[1]

§ 265. **Joseph Story, the commentator of the Constitution.**—Joseph Story was but nine years of age when the Constitution was finally ratified, but he had the double advantage of acquaintance with many of those who had participated in framing it, and of being called upon to construe it as one of the Justices of the Supreme Court of the United States at the very early age of thirty-two, being the youngest man who ever sat upon that bench.[1]

While the palm for Constitutional exposition must necessarily be given to the great Chief Justice, the centennial of whose appointment[2] has this year been celebrated throughout the United States in a manner appropriate to the occasion, and to the memory of one of the greatest jurists and most distinguished statesmen of this, or any other country, we must not overlook the debt of gratitude we owe to Joseph Story, for many years Marshall's associate upon the Supreme Court of the United States, and who not only displayed great ability in his opinions, on constitutional and other ques-

§ 264.
[1] Constitutional History of the United States from the Declaration of Independence to the close of the Civil War, by George Ticknor Curtis, in two volumes, 2d edition, New York, 1889, p. 554.

§ 265.
[1] Joseph Story, born Sept. 18, 1779, appointed Associate Justice of the Supreme Court 1811, by President Madison, died Sept. 10, 1845.

His decisions extend through thirty-five volumes of the Reports of the Supreme Court; many of them relate to constitutional construction, and several of them to the question under discussion.

[2] John Marshall of Virginia was born September 24, 1755, he was appointed Chief Justice of the United States by President John Adams early in 1801. He assumed his place as Chief Justice on February 4, 1801, and occupied that position until his death, July 6, 1835. On February 4, 1901, centennial anniversary exercises were held under the auspices of the American Bar Association in Washington, D. C.; the New York State and New York City Bar associations jointly in Albany, N. Y., and under various local associations in many other cities of the United States, Chief Justice Fuller, Associate Justice Gray, John M. Dillon, Wayne McVeagh, Wm. Wirt Howe, W. Bourke Cochran and others delivering addresses at various places.

tions of law, but who, on some occasions, forced the entire Court into uniting with him in expounding the limitations upon, and at the same time expanding the powers of, the Federal Government.

§ 266. **Story's views on Article VI of the Constitution.** —His "Commentaries" on the Constitution published in 1833, at once became, as they have ever since remained, a standard authority on the construction of the Constitution from legal and historical standpoints. In speaking of Article VI, he says:[1] "The propriety of this clause would seem to result from the very nature of the Constitution. If it was to establish a national government that government ought, to the extent of its powers and rights, to be supreme. It would be a perfect solecism to affirm that a national government should exist with certain powers, and yet that in the exercise of those powers it should not be supreme. . . . In regard to treaties, there is equal reason why they should be held, when made, to be the supreme law of the land. It is to be considered that treaties constitute solemn compacts of binding obligation among nations; and unless they are scrupulously obeyed and enforced, no foreign nation would consent to negotiate with us; or if it did, any want of strict fidelity on our part in the discharge of treaty obligations would be visited by reprisals or war.[2] It is, therefore, indispensable that they should have the obligation and force of a law, that they may be executed by the judicial power, and be obeyed like other laws. This will not prevent them from being canceled or abrogated by the nation upon grave and suitable occasions; for it will not be disputed that they are subject to the legislative power, and may be repealed, like other laws, at its pleasure, or they may be varied by new treaties.[3] Still, while they do subsist they ought to have a positive binding efficacy as laws upon all the States and all

§ 266.

[1] Commentaries on the Constitution of the United States, with a Preliminary Review of the Constitutional History of the Colonies and States before the adoption of the Constitution, by Joseph Story, LL. D., in two volumes, 5th edition, by Melville M. Bigelow, Ph. D., Boston, 1891, vol. II, § 1837–1840, pp. 603–607.

[2] Citing the Federalist, No. 64. (See §§ 244–245, pp. 381 *et seq. ante.*)

[3] See numerous cases cited in notes on p. 605, 2 Story's Com.

the citizens of the States. The peace of the nation, and its good faith, and moral dignity indispensably require that all State laws should be subjected to their supremacy. . . It is notorious that treaty stipulations (especially those of the treaty of peace of 1783) were grossly disregarded by the States under the confederation. They were deemed by the States not as laws, but like requisitions of mere moral obligation and dependent upon the good-will of the States for their execution. Congress, indeed, remonstrated upon this construction as unfounded in principle and justice. But their voice was not heard.

" Power and right were separated; the argument was all on one side, but the power was on the other. *It was probably to obviate this very difficulty* [4] that this clause was inserted in the Constitution; and it would redound to the immortal honor of its authors if it had done no more than to bring treaties within the sanctuary of Justice as laws of supreme obligation. . . . It is melancholy to reflect that conclusive as this view of the subject is in favor of the supremacy clause, it was assailed with great vehemence and zeal by the adversaries of the Constitution. . . . The very circumstance that an objection was made demonstrated the utility, nay, the necessity of the clause, since it removed every pretence under which ingenuity could, by its miserable subterfuges, escape from the controlling power of the Constitution.

" To be fully sensible of the value of the whole clause, we need only suppose for a moment that the supremacy of the State constitutions had been left complete by a saving clause in their favor. . . . The new Congress would have been reduced to the same impotent condition with their predecessors. . . . As the Constitutions of the States differ much from each other, it might happen that a treaty or national law, of great and equal importance to the States, would interfere with some and not with other constitutions, and would consequently be valid in some of the States, at the same time that it would have no effect in others." [5]

[4] The italics are the author's.

[5] Justice Story follows this with a discussion of the question as to how far the treaty-making power embraces commercial regulations; this subject will be referred to in the next chapter.

§ 267. **Judge Cooley's "Constitutional Limitations;"**
1873.—Forty years after Justice Story's Commentaries had
appeared, Mr. Justice Cooley of Michigan issued the first edition of his "Treatise on Constitutional Limitations," which
has since then run through numerous editions, and holds high
rank as an authority, especially as to the constitutional limitations resting upon the legislative powers reserved to the
States.   He, also, recognized the absolute necessity of empowering the Central Government of the United States to
make treaties in such manner that there could be no collision
between State and National authorities, as would certainly
be the result if the adjustment of international matters were
regulated by legislation in over forty-five different States.
Nothing more hopeless can be imagined than the prospect of
uniformity in such cases; he gives to treaties the highest
authority allowed by almost any writer on the subject, either
in text-books, or in decisions, and in the following paragraph,
after quoting Article VI, at length, he shows how essential
this power is to the protection of the National jurisdiction:

"It is essential to the protection of the national jurisdiction, and to prevent collision between State and national
authority, that the final decision upon all questions arising
in regard thereto should rest with the courts of the Union;
and as such questions must frequently arise first in the State
courts, provision is made by the Judiciary Act for removing
to the Supreme Court of the United States the final judgment or decree in any suit, rendered in the highest court of
law or equity of a State in which a decision could be had, in
which is drawn in question the validity of a treaty, or statute of, or authority exercised under the United States, and
the decision is against its validity; or where is drawn in
question the validity of a statute of, or an authority exercised
under any State, on the ground of its being repugnant to
the Constitution, treaties, or laws of the United States, and
the decision is in favor of its validity; or where any title,
right, privilege, or immunity is claimed under the Constitution or any treaty or statute of or commission held or authority exercised under the United States, and the decision is
against the title, right, privilege, or immunity specially set

407

up or claimed by either party under such Constitution, treaty, statute, commission or authority." [1]

In his "General Principles of Constitutional Law," in which he also discusses the same subject, he says:

"A State law must yield to the supreme law, whether expressed in the Constitution of the United States or in any of its laws or treaties, so far as they come in collision, and whether it be a law in existence when the 'supreme law' was adopted, or enacted afterwards. The same is true of any provision in the constitution of any State which is found to be repugnant to the Constitution of the Union. And not only must the judges in every State, be bound by such supreme law, but so must the State itself, and every official in all its departments, and every citizen." [2]

§ 268. **Professor Pomeroy's Views.** — Another recent writer on the Constitution whose books have great weight in regard to its construction is Professor John Norton Pomeroy, whose "Introduction to the Constitutional Law of the United States" has already reached its ninth edition. He has, perhaps, more than any other writer, examined the subject of the treaty-making power, and his opinion, amply sustained by citations and extracts from other authorities, is unequivocally expressed as follows:

"Of the unlimited extent and transcendent importance of this (treaty-making) function thus confided to the Executive, either alone or in connection with the Senate, there can be no doubt.[1] . . . The Constitution places no express limits whatever upon the subjects, conditions, or contents of treaties. The President shall have power to make treaties. Now, the subjects to which these international compacts

§ 267.

[1] A Treatise on the Constitutional Limitations which rest upon the Legislative Power of the States of the American Union, by Thomas M. Cooley, LL. D., 6th edition, edited by Alexis C. Angell, Boston, 1890, pp. 18–19.

[2] The General Principles of Constitutional Law in the United States of America, by Thomas M. Cooley, LL.D., 3d edition, by An-

drew C. McLaughlin, A.M., LL.B., Boston, 1898, pp. 32–33. And see numerous authorities cited in notes thereto.

§ 268.

[1] An Introduction to the Constitutional Law of the United States, by John Norton Pomeroy, 9th edition, revised and enlarged by Edmund H. Bennett, Boston and New York, 1886, § 670, p. 563.

may legitimately refer, are innumerable; the stipulations they may legitimately contain, are equally various, dependent on numberless changes of circumstances and relations. They may affect most vitally the interest of the nation as a whole, or the private and personal interests of individuals. . . . The genus, treaties, includes all the usual kinds and sorts." [2]

He expresses, however, an opinion that there are some implied limitations, as for instance the deprivation of Congress or the Judiciary, or the President, of any general powers which are granted by the Constitution, or any general change in the form of government of this country, but, with this exception, he does not consider that there are any limitations, and draws particular attention to the fact that all "treaties made by the authority of the United States are, equally with the Constitution and the laws of Congress passed under it, the supreme law of the land, and are binding upon, and superior to, state authority, whether that be expressed in state constitutions or state laws." [3]

§ 269. **Professor Pomeroy's broad views in regard to the Executive and foreign relations.**—The most pertinent part of his conclusions upon this subject are found in the following remarks, "upon the scope and extent of this executive function of regulating foreign relations, and its influence and effect upon the general powers of the national government." Continuing he says: "There is here, as I believe, a mine of power which has been almost unworked, a mine rich in beneficent and most efficacious results. The President may, and must, manage the foreign relations; he may, in the manner prescribed, enter into treaties. . . . Where the act is legislative in its nature, the Congress may legislate; where the act is executive in its nature, the President may execute. . . . But Congress may, in aid of this function of the President, pass laws which are addressed directly to the separate states, and which control the acts of their governments. The states have no international *status*; but they may, through their governments, do such acts as endanger the foreign relations of the nations; for these acts

[2] *Idem*, § 674, p. 566.   [3] *Idem*, § 675, p. 567.

the Government is responsible to the foreign power, and cannot evade the responsibility by asserting its want of control over the state. As the responsibility rests upon it, the power must belong to it. . . . I am of opinion that the general government, under its function of controlling international relations, has the power by proper legislation, to prevent a state from repudiating its public debt, so far as that debt may be held by foreign citizens. I repeat, that in this Executive attribute, and in the capacity of Congress to pass laws in aid thereof, there is a source of power which has, as yet, been little resorted to, which has even been little thought of, but which is fruitful in most important and salutary results.

"When we reflect upon the great variety of treaties which may be made, and the compulsive character which the Constitution stamps upon them, the power of the general government, through their means to control state legislation is even more plainly apparent." [1]

§ 270. **Professor Pomeroy on State statutes and treaty stipulations.**—Referring to the provisions in one of the treaties with France, in which the United States agreed to urge the various States to make laws permitting aliens to acquire real estate, which provisions he considers useless, he says: "If the treaty had expressly declared that French subjects may have full powers and rights to acquire and hold lands in any part of the United States, such compact would have overridden, in favor of Frenchmen, any state law forbidding aliens to acquire and hold real property. And such compact would have executed itself; it would have become part of the supreme law of the land; it would have required no congressional sanction; state courts would have been bound to give it force. In fact, the treaty of 1794, between Great Britain and the United States, contained a provision identical in principle with the one supposed; for the citizens of each country were allowed to hold and inherit lands held by them or their ancestors in the other country prior to the Revolution. It is, therefore, possible at the present day for a British subject to inherit lands in the United States, notwithstanding the laws of the particular state in which they are situated may deny to an alien this capacity. The validity of the stipulation has been repeatedly recognized and affirmed by the national and state courts, and many existing titles are based upon it."[1]

§ 271. **Views of Story, Iredell and Pomeroy identical as to State statutes and treaty stipulations.**—Thus we have the evidence of Story,[1] Iredell[2] and Pomeroy, three eminent authorities on constitutional law, that the very object of Article VI was to do away forever with the policy of urging legislation upon the States, which had been adopted with such mortifying results by the framers of the Treaty of 1783, and that it was undoubtedly the intention of the framers of the Constitution to obviate such difficulties, and for that purpose the clause making treaties binding upon the States and superior to their laws and constitutions was incorporated in the instrument.[3]

§ 272. **Chancellor Kent's opinion.**—To any question, regarding the fundamental law of this country answer can almost always, if not always, be found in the Commentaries of Chancellor Kent; his views on the treaty-making power of the United States leave little room for doubt either as to the existence of that power, or as to its extent. In Lect. XIII he says: "The President has also the power, by and with the advice and consent of the Senate, to make treaties, provided two thirds of the senators present concur.

"Writers on government have differed in opinion as to the nature of this power, and whether it be properly, in the natural distribution of power, of legislative or executive cognizance. As treaties are declared by the Constitution to be a part of the supreme law of the land, and as by means of them new relations are formed and obligations contracted, it might seem to be more consonant to the principles of republican government to consider the right of concluding specific terms of peace as of legislative jurisdiction. This has generally been the case in free governments. The de-

§ 270.
[1] Pomeroy's   Introduction   to Constitutional Law, § 681, pp. 571–572.

§ 271.
[1] See § 266, p. 405, *ante.*
[2] See § 253, p. 389, *ante.*
[3] See also § 277, p. 415, *post.*

terminations respecting peace, as well as war, were made in the public assemblies of the nation at Athens and Rome, and in all the Gothic governments of Europe, when they first arose out of the rude institutions of the ancient Germans. On the other hand, the preliminary negotiations which may be required, the secrecy and despatch proper to take advantage of the sudden and favorable turn of public affairs, seem to render it expedient to place this power in the hands of the executive department. The Constitution of the United States has been influenced by the latter more than by the former considerations, for it has placed this power with the President, under the advice and control of the Senate, who are to be considered, for this purpose, in the light of an executive council. The President is the constitutional organ of communication with foreign powers, and the efficient agent in the conclusion of treaties; but the consent of two thirds of the senators present is essential to give validity to his negotiations. To have required the acquiescence of a more numerous body would have been productive of delay, disorder, imbecility, and probably, in the end, a direct breach of the Constitution. The history of Holland shows the danger and folly of placing too much limitation on the exercise of the treaty-making power. By the fundamental charter of the United Provinces peace could not be made without the unanimous consent of the provinces; and yet, without multiplying instances, it is sufficient to observe, that the immensely important and fundamental treaty of Munster, in 1648, was made when Zealand was opposed to it; and the peace of 1661, when Utrecht was opposed. So feeble are mere limitations upon paper,—mere parchment barriers, when standing in opposition to the strong force of public exigency." [1]

In referring to Chancellor Kent's views in regard to the extent of the treaty-making power of the United States, Professor Woolsey in his " International Law " says:

" An interesting inquiry here arises, whether the treaty-

§ 272.

[1] Commentaries on American Law, by James Kent, vol. I, 12th edition edited by O. W. Holmes, Jr.

and 14th edition edited by John M. Gould, Boston, 1896, p. 346 (*284) and see also the notes to that page.

making power in a federative union, like the United States, can alienate the domain of one of the States without its consent. Our government, when the northeastern boundary was in dispute, declared that it had no power to dispose of territory claimed by the State of Maine. 'The better opinion would seem to be,' says Chancellor Kent, 'that such a power of cession does reside exclusively in the treaty-making power under the Constitution of the United States, although a sound discretion would forbid the exercise of it without the consent, of the interested State."[2]

§ 273. **Numerous other opinions in support of broadest powers.**—These quotations could be multiplied until reiterations of principle became wearisome, and extracts could be added from many other eminent writers who have contributed the results of their thought and experience to constitutional literature, including Mr. Calhoun,[1] who imposes more limitations on the Federal Government than almost any other writer on the subject, but who acknowledges the wide scope of the treaty-making power, although he also imposes some limitations upon it. It would, however, simply be in the nature of cumulative evidence, to add additional excerpts, and therefore no further quotations will be made; but the reader is referred to the opinions of the judges of our highest Courts, both Federal and State, which are collated in the subsequent chapters.

§ 274. **Narrower views of some authorities on the Constitution.**—All of the expounders of the Constitution, however, do not take such broad views of the extent and scope of the treaty-making power as it has been vested in the Central Government by the provisions of the Constitution, and while the author does not agree with them, as must be apparent to any reader of this volume, he desires to present the views of both schools of Constitutional construction.

§ 275. **John Randolph Tucker's views.**—Some of them contend that the treaty-making power is limited in many ways and probably John Randolph Tucker is the best representative of the school which would enforce limitations upon

[2] Woolsey's International Law, § 103, p. 160, in regard to this subject; see also § 426, Vol. II.

§ 273.
[1] See § 276, *post*, and §§ 482, and 483, Vol. II.

this power.   His views as expressed in his work on the Constitution are very largely a condensation of his views expressed in a report from the Committee of Judiciary in 1887
in regard to the reciprocity treaty with the Hawaiian Islands
to which reference will be made in a subsequent chapter.[1]

Mr. Tucker's views as to limitations, however, are here
quoted at length in regard to the effect of treaties upon the
essential liberties of the people.   In that respect he says

"A treaty, therefore, cannot take away essential liberties
secured by the Constitution to the people.   A treaty cannot
bind the United States to do what their Constitution forbids them to do.   We may suggest a further limitation: a
treaty cannot compel any department of the government
to do what the Constitution submits to its exclusive and
absolute will.   On these questions the true canon of construction, that the treaty-making power, in its seeming absolute-
ness and unconditional extent, is confronted with equally
absolute and unconditional authority vested in the judiciary.
Therefore, neither must be construed as absolute and uncon-
ditioned, but each must be construed and conditioned upon
the equally clear power vested in the others.   For example,
Congress has power to lay and collect duties; the President
and Senate have power to make and contract with a foreign
nation in respect to such duties.   Can any other construction be given to these two apparently contradictory powers
than that the general power to make treaties must yield to
the specific power of Congress to lay and collect all duties;
and while the treaty may propose a contract as to duties on
articles coming from a foreign nation, such an executory
contract cannot be valid and binding unless Congress, which
has supreme authority to lay and collect duties, consents to
it.   If it is then asked, how are you to reconcile these two
powers which appear to be antagonistic, the answer is clear.
Congress has no capacity to negotiate a treaty with a foreign
power.   The extent of its membership makes this impracticable.   The Constitution, therefore, left the House of Representatives out of all consideration in negotiating treaties.
The executory contract between the United States and a for-

§ 275.
[1] See § 307, *post*.   For other ex- | pressions of Mr. Tucker's views,
see § 10, *ante* and § 480, Vol. II.

eign nation is therefore confided to the one man who can conduct the negotiations, and to a select body who can advise and consent to the treaty he has negotiated. But this executory contract must depend for its execution upon the supreme power vested in Congress 'to lay and collect duties.' It is therefore a contract not completed, but inchoate, and can only be completed and binding when Congress shall by legislation consent thereto, and lay duties in accordance with the executory contract or treaty. The same reasoning may apply to all of the great powers vested in Congress, such as to 'borrow money, regulate commerce, coin money, raise armies and provide a navy, make laws as to naturalization, bankruptcies, and exercise exclusive legislation' in the District of Columbia and territories of the country. If these are sought by treaty to be regulated by the President and Senate, it can only be done when the Congress vested with these great powers shall give its unconditional consent."[2]

§ 276. **John C. Calhoun's views.**—The views of Mr. Calhoun are so fully stated in a later section of this book in regard to limitations of the treaty-making power, that they will not be referred to at length at this point. In some respects, however, he is inconsistent with his general theories as to lack of all nationality in the Central Government, as he admits the necessity of placing the treaty-making power exclusively in its hands.[1]

§ 277. **Improper use of treaty stipulations as to urging State legislation.**—In view of the great preponderance of the weight of authority on the side of the broad construction of the powers of the Central Government, it is strange, that notwithstanding the opinions of the eminent jurists and commentators whose views have been given above, Commissioners who have been intrusted with the high and honorable duty of concluding treaties between the United States and foreign powers, have, on more than one occasion, reverted to,

[2] The Constitution of the United States. A Critical Discussion of its Genesis, Development and Interpretation by John Randolph Tucker; edited by Henry St. George Tucker. In two volumes, Chicago, 1899, vol. II, §§ 353–356. For quotation see pp. 725–726.
§ **276.**
[1] See §§ 482–483, chap. XV, Vol. II.

and used, the antiquated system of 1783, and have agreed to
" urge legislation upon the various States," [1] to carry out
treaty stipulations, instead of making the stipulations absolutely, as the United States has the right to do, as well as to
enforce them when made, and in regard to which the States
have no power or voice whatever. It remains to be seen
whether that policy will be continued, or whether, resting
on its complete nationality, as well as upon its delegated
power under the Constitution, the Central Government of
the United States shall finally and forever relegate that policy to the past, where it belongs, and shall exercise those
powers which necessarily and properly belong to it, and which
cannot be called in question by any foreign State with which
it contracts, or be disputed by any of the States for whom
the Central Government is the only medium of communication with foreign powers, with full power in this respect, to
bind them, jointly and separately, federally and nationally.

§ 278. **This chapter confined to extent of treaty-making
power.**—The opinions quoted in this chapter refer only to
the *extent* of the treaty-making power, and not in any way
to the construction of treaties, the relative effect of treaties
and legislation, or the right of the House of Representatives
to participate in the treaty-making power. Some opinions
which have been expressed in those respects will be referred
to, and to some extent quoted from, in subsequent chapters
which will be devoted to the consideration of those branches
of the subject-matter.

§ 277.

[1] See Article XXVII, Treaty of
1871 (Washington) with Great Britain, in which this Government
"engages to urge upon the State
Governments to secure to the subjects of Her Britannic Majesty the
use of the several State canals connected with the navigation of the
lakes or rivers traversed by or contiguous to the boundary line between the possessions of the high
contracting parties, on terms of
equality with the inhabitants of
the United States." U. S. Treaties,
edition, 1889, p. 489; Compilation
of Treaties in Force, edition, 1899,
p. 253. "Urging" compliance
upon the States apparently consisted of the Secretary of State
writing to the respective Governors
of New York, Indiana, Illinois,
Michigan, Ohio, Pennsylvania and
Wisconsin an identic letter advising
them of the treaty, inclosing a copy,
with special reference to Article XXVII, and requesting compliance therewith. See Foreign Relations of U. S. for 1871, p. 531.

CHAPTER X.

THE TREATY-MAKING POWER AND THE RELATIONS OF BOTH HOUSES
OF CONGRESS THERETO, AS THE SAME HAS BEEN THE SUBJECT
OF CONGRESSIONAL DEBATE AND ACTION.

27   417

§ 279. **First Congress under Constitution meets ; earliest tariff statutes.**—The first Congress, under the new Constitution, met in the City of New York on March 4, 1789. No act was passed until June 1st, when the first statute of the United States Government was enacted, regulating the time and manner of administering oaths of office;[1] on July 4, 1789, Congress exercised its power to protect by tariff the manufactures of the United States, by the second statute placed upon the statute books of the United States, the first section of which is as follows : " Whereas, it is necessary for the support of government, for the discharge of debts of the United States, and the encouragement and protection of manufactures that duties be laid on goods, wares and merchandise imported : *Be it enacted by the Senate and House of Representatives in Congress assembled,* That from and after the first day of August next ensuing, the several duties hereinafter mentioned shall be laid on the following goods, wares and merchandise imported into the United States from any foreign power or place, that is to say : " and then follow the schedules.[2]

§ 280. **Power of United States to protect manufactures discussed.**—In the debate on this statute many questions were raised as to the power of the United States to "protect" manufactures : while it was conceded that the right existed to raise revenue, "protection" to many seemed beyond the power of the Central Government, because it was not specifically named or enumerated in the Constitution as having been delegated by the States. Under the leadership of James Madison, however, the bills became statutes, and the Central Government, at the first opportunity, thus exerted on behalf of the industries of the States, the protecting power which the States themselves could not have done under any circumstances or conditions.[1]

§ 280.

[1] For interesting accounts of the debate on the first tariff acts see McMaster's History of the People of the United States, vol. I, pp. 545, et seq.; see also History of the Protective Tariff Laws by R. W. Thompson, ex-Secretary of the Navy of the United States, 3d edition, Chicago, 1888, from which the following extract is taken (from chap. IV, p. 47-54):

" The first important law passed by the first Congress indicated its character so plainly as to leave no room for any doubt whatsoever. Its title was, 'An act for laying a duty on goods, wares and merchandise imported into the United States;' and its first section, or that part which properly stands as its preamble, is in these expressive words:

" 'Whereas, it is necessary for the support of the Government, the discharge of the debts of the United States, and the *encouragement and protection of manufactures*, that duties be laid on goods, wares and merchandise imported.'

" Plainer, simpler, or more expressive language could not be found. It is not equivocal in the least, and every common-sense man, with ordinary intelligence, can understand its meaning. It asserts three distinct propositions: *first*, that duties should be laid for the support of the Government; *second*, that they should be laid for the payment of the public debt; and *third*, that they should be also laid for the encouragement and protection of manufactures. Each of these propositions was distinct from the other two. Yet, whether considered singly or combined, they involved the exercise by Congress of clearly granted constitutional power—about which, at that time, there was no difference of opinion.

" It has been said that this preamble was written by Mr. Madison. This is probably true, as the sentiments conveyed by its language were precisely such as he was known to entertain, and, more than once, expressed. His authorship of it, however, is not material, inasmuch as—being a member of Congress at the time—he supported and voted for the bill, which passed the House of Representatives by a vote nearly unanimous, there having been only eight votes against it. The duties discriminated in favor of manufactures, and were therefore protective as the language above quoted expressly imports. The preamble was manifestly intended to convey this idea, for, although not absolutely necessary to the law, it furnishes a rule of interpretation by which its true

§ 281. **Department of Foreign Affairs established; the State Department.**—The third statute imposed a duty on tonnage, and the fourth was "An Act for establishing an Executive Department to be denominated the Department of Foreign Affairs," passed July 27, 1789,[1] which is the foundation of the present State Department of the United States through which all negotiations of treaties, and all relations with foreign powers ever since that date have been, and at present are, conducted. The Department of State as it now exists was organized under subsequent acts of Congress, and is now conducted under the provisions of the Revised Statutes in relation thereto.

§ 282. **No treaties negotiated until 1794.**—Although immediately after the adoption of the Constitution, the courts were called upon to construe the effects of the treaties which had been negotiated under the Confederation,[1] and to determine the rights, duties and liabilities which had been created thereby, no new treaty was concluded by the United States, under the power vested in the Executive and Senate, until more than five years after the adoption of the Constitution; in fact, it was not until Washington's second term of office

meaning is to be ascertained—it is, in other words, an index to point out the legislative intention. The history of this law is, consequently most instructive, not only on account of its great general importance, but because it identifies Mr. Madison, by his direct agency in the House of Representatives, and Washington, by his approval of it as President, and nearly all the members of the first Congress. with the first distinctive measure of protection which the exigencies of the public service and the common interests of the country demanded at the very beginning of the Government. . . .

"In supporting the measure, Mr. Madison said: ' There may be some manufactures which, being once formed, can advance toward perfec-

tion without any adventitious aid, while others, for want of the *fostering hand of the Government*, will be unable to go on at all.' In this apt language Mr. Madison embraced the whole question of constitutional power. Although it had not been insisted that the protection of manufactures would violate the Constitution, yet, with the motive already indicated, he probably desired to place the question of constitutionality beyond all cavil, by asserting, at once and unqualifiedly, that the power existed as a necessary part of the machinery of the new Government."

§ 281.
[1] 1 U. S. Stat. at L. p. 28.

§ 282.
[1] *Ware* vs. *Hylton*, U. S. Sup. Ct. 1796, 3 Dallas, 199 and see § 324, *et*

that the powers vested in him as President to make treaties by and with the consent of two-thirds of the Senate, was exercised.

§ 283. **Jay's treaty; excitement and opposition.**—In 1794, however, the famous Jay treaty[1] was concluded between Great Britain and the United States; at once excited discussion arose; questions involving the extent of the treaty-making power, as to the right of the President and the Senate to make treaties, the extent to which treaties could alter existing legislation, and also the right or duty of the House of Representatives to participate in the ratification of the treaty, or, if not in the ratification itself, in the legislation necessary to make the treaty effectual, were debated, not only in Philadelphia where Congress then met, but throughout the entire fifteen States, for by that time Vermont and Kentucky had been admitted to the Union.[2]

§ 284. **Strained relations between United States and Great Britain; Washington's message.**—Grave causes of difference existed at the time of the negotiation of this treaty between the United States and Great Britain;[1] in fact, the

seq., Vol. II, for this and other cases affecting treaty of peace with Great Britain.

§ 283.

[1] See note to § 285, p. 422, *post.*

[2] Vermont was admitted as the fourteenth State of the Union on March 4, 1791 (1 U. S. St. at L. p. 191; act passed February 18, 1791). Kentucky was admitted as the fifteenth State on June 1, 1792 (1 U. S. St. at L. p. 189; act passed February 4, 1791).

§ 284.

[1] In speaking of this treaty, J. C. Bancroft Davis makes the following remarks, and gives the following references in his notes on Great Britain, p. 1321, in the 1889 edition of the "Compilation of Treaties between the United States and Foreign Powers:"

"The treaty concluded by Jay on the 19th of November, 1794, re-moved or suspended these grave causes of difference. It named a day for the withdrawal of British troops from the territories of the United States. The United States undertook to make compensation to British creditors who had been prevented by 'lawful impediments,' in violation of the treaty of 1783, from the recovery of their debts. Great Britain agreed to make compensation to the merchants and citizens of the United States whose vessels had been illegally captured or condemned. The United States undertook to make compensation to certain British subjects whose vessels or merchandise had been captured within the jurisdiction of the United States and brought into the same; or had been captured by vessels originally armed in the ports of the United States. It was agreed that provisions and other

relations between the two countries had become so strained that President Washington informed both Houses of Congress by a special message in regard to the occupation by the British of forts in the Western Territory that "this new state of things suggests the propriety of placing the United States in a posture of effectual preparation for an event which, notwithstanding the endeavors making to avert it, may, by circumstances beyond our control, be forced upon us."[2]

§ 285. **Rights of the people; necessity of legislation to enforce the treaty.**—The Jay treaty[1] was the first one negotiated under the constitutional power, and it gave rise to many important points affecting the people in their relations, both as to those matters which were admittedly under Federal control, and as to those which were admittedly, in the absence of foreign relations, exclusively under State jurisdiction; not only national and commercial relations were affected, but the relations of individual debtors to British cred-

articles not generally contraband of war should not be confiscated if seized, but that the owners should be fully indemnified; and that vessels approaching a blockaded port, in ignorance of the blockade, should not be detained, nor the cargo confiscated unless contraband.

"The instructions to Jay embraced many other subjects. How far they were executed, and why he failed to comply with some of them, will appear by reference to the instructions and correspondence which accompanied the President's message of June 8, transmitting the Treaty to the Senate. The reasons which induced the President and his advisers to assent to it are detailed in a letter from Pickering to Monroe of September 12, 1795. This treaty was the cause of the long and able debates in Congress, which have been referred to in the Introductory

Note. On the 5th of May, 1796, President Washington submitted to the Senate an explanatory article with the reasons which had made it necessary, and another explanatory article was added in March, 1798.

"The appropriations for carrying into effect the Treaty of 1794 were made by Congress on the 6th of May, 1796, and by Parliament on the 4th of July, 1797." See § 295, p. 429, post.

[2] The message was a very brief one dated May 21, 1794, and will be found in Richardson's Messages of the Presidents, vol. I, p. 155.

§ 285.

[1] Treaty of Amity, Commerce and Navigation; concluded November 19, 1794; ratifications exchanged at London, October 28, 1795, proclaimed, February 29, 1796; U. S. Treaties and Conventions, edition, 1889, p. 379, 8 U. S. St. at L. p. 116.

itors were adjusted and settled. As existing legislation conflicted to some extent with the provisions of the treaty, the question was at once raised whether Article VI of the Constitution, which makes treaties the supreme law of the land, obviated the necessity of new legislation to carry those provisions into effect, or whether the treaty was a simple contract which required congressional action to carry it out and render its stipulations effective and binding upon the people.

§ 286. **General discussion of these questions.**—All of these points were debated not only in Congress and in State Legislatures, but also by the people through the medium of the press and pamphlets, and at mass meetings.[1] It is necessary, therefore, to briefly review the historical facts connected with the negotiation and ratification of this treaty, as well as the proceedings in Congress relating thereto; this is the more important as questions which were almost identical, arose, and were debated on the same lines, in regard to treaties concluded at a later period, and which will be hereafter referred to.[2]

§ 287. **John Jay's mission to England; negotiation of treaty.**—John Jay was appointed Envoy Extraordinary to His Britannic Majesty, April 16, 1794.[1] He was confirmed on the 19th, and went at once to London, where he entered into negotiations with the Foreign Office, then under the control of Lord Grenville; on the 19th of November, 1794, he concluded the treaty which ever since has been known by his name, and which was the basis of our commercial relations with Great Britain from its ratification until the war of 1812. The instrument reached the Secretary of State at Philadelphia on March 7, 1795, just after Congress had adjourned. The president called a special session of the Senate for June 8, 1795; when it convened Washington transmitted the treaty with a brief message, stating that it was "for you in your

§ 286.

[1] See McMaster's History, vol. 2, chap. IX.

[2] See § 299, p. 432, *post*, for reference to subsequent occasions on which this question was discussed in Congress.

§ 287.

[1] The documents relating to John Jay's mission to England will be found in vol. I, Foreign Relations of the United States (Folio). They are condensed in Mr. J. C. Bancroft Davis' U. S. Treaties and Conventions, edition, 1889, pp. 1321-1322.

wisdom to decide whether you will advise and consent that said treaty be made between the United States and His Britannic Majesty." [2]

§ 288. **Ratification of treaty with amendment.**—The Senate finally agreed to ratify the treaty provided Article XII, which related to the West India Treaty, would be suspended by an additional article. This concession was made by Great Britain, and the additional article was incorporated in the treaty; it was ratified, as thus amended, by the close vote of 20 to 10, exactly two thirds, the required constitutional majority.[1] The ratifications were signed by the President, transmitted to London and exchanged October 28, 1795.[2]

§ 289. **Popular excitement; French and English parties.** —From the time that the treaty was published until long after Congress had convened in December, meetings were held throughout the whole country, most of them for the purpose of denouncing the treaty, but some of them to urge its ratification. By reason of the great friendly feeling for France, and the unfriendly feeling against Great Britain, which naturally existed as the outcome of the war for Independence which had terminated less than a dozen years earlier, great party feeling was stirred up against the treaty, and to a great extent the people of the United States were divided into what might be called British and French parties; it was indeed a strange sight to see the people of this Republic divided on issues affecting two foreign European nations.[1]

§ 290. **Meeting of Congress; message of the President.** —While the treaty had a large majority in the Senate, such was not the case in the House of Representatives. Congress met on the 7th of December, 1795, and was opened, accord-

---

[2] Richardson's Messages of the Presidents vol. 1, p. 170.

§ 288.

[1] For reference to other treaties similarly ratified with amendments see § 465, chap. XVI, Vol. II.

[2] U. S. Treaties and Conventions, edition, 1889; pp. 379, 1321; see also McMaster's History of the People of the United States, vol. 2, chap. IX.

§ 289.

[1] A graphic account of this national debate will be found in the 9th chapter of the 2d. volume of McMaster's History of the People of the United States, to which students of this incident of American political history are referred, as in detail it would require more space than can be devoted to it in this volume.

ing to the custom of those days, by the President, in person. No direct reference was made, however, to the treaty either in his opening address, or in the reply which it was then customary for the Houses to make to the President's address, except as the general hope was expressed in the House reply, that, by treaty and amicable negotiation, all causes of external discord might be "extinguished on terms compatible with our national rights and honor and with our Constitution and great commercial interests."[1]

Not until March 1, 1796, were the ratifications returned; the treaty together with the fact that the ratifications had been exchanged being transmitted in a message of less than six lines by the President to both Houses of Congress. Debate at once began in Congress as to the extent of the binding force of those stipulations in the treaty which either conflicted with existing legislation, or which required new legislation, or appropriations of money, to carry them into effect.

§ 291. **Request of House of Representatives for papers relating to treaty.**—On March 2d, Mr. Livingston offered a resolution requesting the President to lay before the House copies of the instructions to the Minister of the United States who had negotiated the treaty with Great Britain, together with the correspondence and other documents relating thereto, with the exception of such papers as any existing negotiations might render improper to be disclosed; debate then followed which lasted for more than two weeks, in which many leading members participated, and the treaty-making power was discussed in every phase and aspect, both as to its extent, and as to the effect of treaties upon legislation, both State and Federal.[1] On March 24th, the resolution was carried by sixty-two to thirty-seven. Messrs. Livingston and Gallatin were sent as a committee to present the resolution to the President, who replied, as they reported to the House on their return, "that he would take it into consideration."

§ 290.
[1] Richardson's Messages of the Presidents, vol. 1, p. 182–189.

§ 291.
[1] Reference is again made to Mc-Master's History, vol. 2, chap. IX.

§ 292. **President Washington's reply to the House.**—The reply returned by the President to the House of Represen-tatives, March 30, 1796, showed that he thoroughly appreci-ated the effect of acceding to the request, as well as the ef-fect that the precedent, if established, might have in altering the entire plan of the Constitution, as to the powers and func-tions of the Executive. He, therefore, declined to furnish the papers. This reply is one of those documents that will endure in the constitutional history of this country as long as the Constitution stands, a monument alike to Washington's astute diplomacy as well as to his great ability. It is of sufficient importance to be quoted at length, and it will be found in its entirety in the notes to this section.[1]

§ 292.

[1] " United States, March 30, 1796.

' To the House of Representatives of the United States:

" With the utmost attention I have considered your resolution of the 24th instant, requesting me to lay before your House a copy of the instructions to the minister of the United States who negotiated the treaty with the King of Great Brit-ain, together with the correspond-ence and other documents relative to that treaty, excepting such of the said papers as any existing ne-gotiation may render improper to be disclosed.

"In deliberating upon this subject it was impossible for me to lose sight of the principle which some have avowed in its discussion, or to avoid extending my views to the consequences which must flow from the admission of that principle.

"I trust that no part of my con-duct has ever indicated a disposi-tion to withhold any information which the Constitution has en-joined upon the President as a duty to give, or which could be required of him by either House of Con-gress as a right; and with truth I affirm that it has been, as it will continue to be while I have the honor to preside in the Government, my constant endeavor to harmon-ize with the other branches thereof so far as the trust delegated to me by the people of the United States and my sense of the obligation it imposes to 'preserve, protect, and defend the Constitution' will per-mit.

"The nature of foreign negotia-tions requires caution, and their success must often depend on se-crecy; and even when brought to a conclusion a full disclosure of all the measures, demands, or eventual concessions which may have been proposed or contemplated would be extremely impolitic; for this might have a pernicious influence on future negotiations, or produce immediate inconveniences, perhaps danger and mischief, in relation to other powers. The necessity of such caution and secrecy was one cogent reason for vesting the power of making treaties in the President, with the advice and consent of the Senate, the principle on which that body was formed confining it to a

§ 293. Effect of Washington's reply; action by the House.—By this move Washington forced the House of Rep-

small number of members. To admit, then, a right in the House of Representatives to demand and to have as a matter of course all the papers respecting a negotiation with a foreign power would be to establish a dangerous precedent.

"It does not occur that the inspection of the papers asked for can be relative to any purpose under the cognizance of the House of Representatives, except that of an impeachment, which the resolution has not expressed. I repeat that I have no disposition to withhold any information which the duty of my station will permit or the public good shall require to be disclosed; and, in fact, all the papers affecting the negotiation with Great Britain were laid before the Senate when the treaty itself was communicated for their consideration and advice.

"The course which the debate has taken on the resolution of the House leads to some observations on the mode of making treaties under the Constitution of the United States.

"Having been a member of the General Convention, and knowing the principles on which the Constitution was formed, I have ever entertained but one opinion on this subject; and from the first establishment of the Government to this moment my conduct has exemplified that opinion—that the power of making treaties is exclusively vested in the President, by and with the advice and consent of the Senate, provided two-thirds of the Senators present concur; and that every treaty so made and promulgated thenceforward be-

came the law of the land. It is thus that the treaty-making power has been understood by foreign nations, and in all the treaties made with them *we* have declared and *they* have believed that, when ratified by the President, with the advice and consent of the Senate, they became obligatory. In this construction of the Constitution every House of Representatives has heretofore acquiesced, and until the present time not a doubt or suspicion has appeared, to my knowledge, that this construction was not the true one. Nay, they have more than acquiesced; for till now, without controverting the obligation of such treaties, they have made all the requisite provisions for carrying them into effect.

"There is also reason to believe that this construction agrees with the opinions entertained by the State conventions when they were deliberating on the Constitution, especially by those who objected to it because there was not required in *commercial treaties* the consent of two-thirds of the whole number of the members of the Senate instead of two thirds of the Senators present, and because in treaties respecting territorial and certain other rights and claims the concurrence of three-fourths of the whole number of the members of both Houses, respectively, was not made necessary.

"It is a fact declared by the General Convention and universally understood that the Constitution of the United States was the result of a spirit of amity and mutual concession; and it is well known

resentatives to recognize the fact that the treaty-making
power of the Constitution was lodged in the Executive, subject only to the ratification of two-thirds of the Senate, and
that the House could not participate therein as a matter of
right, to any extent whatever; a resolution was at once
passed by the House of Representatives, which recognized
the sound basis on which the President's reply was based,
and in which that body distinctly disclaimed any agency in
making treaties, but asserted the principle that when a call
was made on the President for information it was not necessary to state why the information was wanted; the object
of this resolution was evidently to convey the idea that the
House did not wish to investigate as to *how* the Executive had
made the treaty, but to ascertain what legislation was necessary to carry it into effect, and what the duty of the House
was in this respect.   It was, however, a distinct victory for
the Executive.[1]

§ 294. **Other treaties ratified by the Senate, and before
the House.**—Meanwhile other treaties had been negotiated
with Spain, Algiers, and some of the Indian tribes, all

that under this influence the
smaller States were admitted to an
equal representation in the Senate
with the larger States, and that
this branch of the Government was
invested with great powers, for on
the equal participation of those
powers the sovereignty and political safety of the smaller States
were deemed essentially to depend.

"If other proofs than these and
the plain letter of the Constitution
itself be necessary to ascertain
the point under consideration,
they may be found in the journals
of the General Convention, which
I have deposited in the office of
the Department of State. In those
journals it will appear, that a
proposition was made 'that no
treaty should be binding on the
United States which was not ratified by law,' and that the proposition was explicitly rejected.

"As, therefore, it is perfectly
clear to my understanding that
the assent of the House of Representatives is not necessary to the
validity of a treaty; as the treaty
with Great Britain exhibits in itself all the objects requiring legislative provision, and on these the
papers called for can throw no
light, and as it is essential to the
due administration of the Government that the boundaries fixed by
the Constitution between the different departments should be
preserved, a just regard to the
Constitution and to the duty of my
office, under all the circumstances
of this case, forbids a compliance
with your request. Go. WASHING-
TON." Richardson's Messages of
the Presidents, vol. 1, p. 194–196.

§ 293.

[1] See McMaster's History, vol. II,
chap. IX, p. 276.

of which had been ratified by the Senate; the House, therefore, had before it at this time no less than four treaties,
every one of which had, according to the Constitution, become the supreme law of the land, but all requiring more or
less Congressional legislation to make them operative in certain respects, such as tariff, tonnage dues, establishment of
commissions and appropriations; the chief questions which
had been raised in regard to the treaty with Great Britain
were equally applicable to all of the treaties, and they necessarily assumed even greater proportions than before, so that the
position became more and more complicated as the debate
continued.

§ 295. **Fisher Ames's address and argument; treaty
legislation enacted.**—The leading speech of this debate was
made by Fisher Ames,[1] in Committee of the Whole in support of a resolution for the enactment of legislation to carry
the treaties into effect; under the influence of a great burst
of oratory from that eminent Bostonian, the resolution was
adopted by a tie vote of the Committee, which was made
affirmative by the casting vote of the chairman; the Committee at once rose, the session of the House was resumed,
and the resolution carried by a vote of fifty-one to forty-
eight.   On May 6, 1796, the legislation was enacted and approved, giving effect to all provisions of the above mentioned
treaties which required legislative assistance.[2]

§ 296. **Position of House of Representatives in treaty
matters defined.**—Thus ended the first of the great parliamentary battles fought by the House of Representatives to
gain control of the treaty-making power of the United
States; while one point was definitely settled, other points
still remain unsettled, as several of them do to-day.   It was
definitely decided that the House of Representatives had no
voice whatever in the negotiation or ratification of a treaty;
that the treaty-making power is vested exclusively in the
Executive, subject only to the prescribed ratification by two-

---

§ 295.

[1] For an account of Mr. Ames, and
this address, see McMaster's History, vol. 2, chap. IX, pp. 277, *et
seq.*

[2] Fourth Congress, Sess. I, chapters XVII, XVIII, XIX and XX;
1 U. S. Stat. at L. 459, 460.   The
acts are very brief, the four together
occupying only a page and a half.

thirds of the Senate; that when the Executive makes a treaty and the Senate ratifies it in a constitutional manner, the treaty becomes the supreme law of the land; on the other hand, as was subsequently stated by Chief Justice Marshall in one of the opinions which will be referred to at greater length in a subsequent chapter,[1] it was practically decided that although a treaty becomes the supreme law of the land as soon as it is ratified as to every provision which can be enforced without legislation, it remains ineffectual as to those matters which do require legislation, or the appropriation of money, and can only be enforced after *both* Houses of Congress enact appropriate legislation, in the shape of entirely new laws, or those which modify or repeal such existing statutes as conflict with the treaty, or which appropriate money to carry out such provisions as entail expenditures and payments.

§ 297. **Practical results of this method.**—During the ninety-five years which have elapsed since the debate over the Jay treaty in the House of Representatives many statutes have been passed to carry out treaty stipulations,[1] both as to appropriations and other measures necessary to make treaties negotiated by the Executive and ratified by the Senate effective. Many of these statutes have been modifications of tariff and tonnage laws, some of them general in their nature and scope, and therefore applicable to all treaties of the class referred to in the statutes, and others specific and applicable only to the treaty specified. It would hardly be worth while to enumerate all of them; a few examples are given in the notes appended to this section, which indicate the vari-

§ 296.

[1] *Foster & Elam* vs. *Neilson*, U. S. Sup. Ct. 1829; 2 Peters, 253. MARSHALL, Ch. J., and see § 314, *post*, and § 364, Vol. II.

§ 297.

[1] Reference has already been made to the statutes carrying out the treaties with Great Britain and other powers in May, 1796 (see note 2, § 295, *ante*).

Many of the statutes enacted by Congress carrying out the provi-sions of claims conventions will be found either in full, or fully referred to, in Moore's History of Arbitration under the history of the various arbitrations, or adjustments by commissions between the United States and foreign governments.

After the treaties with Great Britain in regard to Canadian matters, fisheries, reciprocal tariff arrangements, etc., statutes have always been passed to make the

ous methods which have been adopted by Congress to carry out the contract elements of treaties with foreign powers.[2]

§ 298. **Good faith in this respect always shown by Congress.**—It is a remarkable fact that while the great moral question still remains undecided as to how far the House of Representatives is bound, as a matter of good faith, to carry out, by legislative enactments and appropriations, provisions of treaties, which, without its participation or approval, and possibly against its own judgment, have been made by the President and ratified by the Senate, it has remained so in theory only and not in practice; as a matter of fact, no treaty has ever been made and ratified, by which the faith of the Union has been pledged, that the House has not fully carried out by enacting the necessary legislation so far as appropriations and modifications of existing laws are concerned; indeed, instances might be cited in which members of the House of Representatives have waived party and personal feelings so that there could be no question as to the good faith of the United States in carrying out treaty stipulations.[1]

treaty stipulations effectual. In regard to extradition cases there was much question as to the necessity of legislation, but that is now obviated by the statute of 1848 (9 U. S. Stat. at L. p. 302), the provisions of the Revised Statutes, (§§ 5270, et seq.) and the amendments thereto which cover not only all existing treaties but all treaties hereafter made, so far as extradition provisions are concerned. See §§ 432, et seq., post.

[2] Consult Index of U. S. Rev. Stat. under TREATIES. See also for various general provisions as to carrying out treaty stipulations.

§ 298.

[1] A notable instance was after the commission appointed under the Treaty of Washington of 1871, to adjust the difference to be paid by the United States for the excess of value of fishery privileges off the British coast, granted to American fishermen, over those granted to Canadian fishermen along the coasts of the United States rendered its decision awarding $5,500,000 to Great Britain. This award, known as the Halifax award, was made in 1877. It was considered as unjust and excessive, and grave questions were raised as to the appointment of the third arbitrator. Many members of Congress thought that the award was so unjust that it should not be paid, the feeling, however, that the United States was bound to pay it as the result of a treaty obligation prevailed, and on June 20, 1878, the amount was included in the final clause of the Sundry Civil Expense act; the act, however, placed the amount of the award under the direction of the President to be paid by him, "if after correspondence with the British Government, on the subject of the conformity of the awards to the re-

§ 299. **Subsequent debates in Congress on same subject.**
—Congressional debate similar to that over the Jay treaty,
as to the extent of the rights and the duty of the House of
Representatives in regard to legislation necessary and proper
to make treaties effectual, has often been renewed; but it will
only be possible in a volume of this size to refer briefly to
the most important occasions; which were in 1816, in regard
to the Commercial Treaty with Great Britain;[1] in 1834 in
regard to the treaty with France;[2] in 1867 after the treaty
with Russia ceding Alaska;[3] in 1887 while the Hawaiian
treaty was pending;[4] and in 1899 after the treaty with Spain
terminating the Spanish war and ceding Porto Rico, Guam
and the Philippines.[5] [a]

§ 300. **After commercial treaty of 1815 with Great
Britain.**—After the ratification of the Treaty of Commerce
of 1815 with Great Britain, an extended debate took place
in the House on this subject; one element of Congress took
the position that the treaty itself so altered existing laws
that no further legislation was necessary, while the other
led by Mr. Tucker,[1] (progenitor of John Randolph Tucker,
whose report seventy years later followed the same views
of his ancestor,[2]) contended that no commercial regulation
could be made by a treaty, or that any laws could be modified to comply therewith without the action of both Houses.
Mr. Randolph, another progenitor of John Randolph Tucker,
took the same view.[3]   The debate was lengthy and can be
found in full in the Annals of Congress for the First Session

quirements of the treaty and to the
terms of the question thereby submitted to the Commission, the President shall deem it his duty to make
the payment without further communication with Congress," and if
he deemed it necessary for the honor
of the Nation so to do. See Resolution, 20 U. S. Stat. at L. p. 240.
For a full account of this affair and
the protest of the United States
against the award, prepared by Mr.
Wm. M. Evarts, Secretary of State,
and the circumstances under which
the $5,500,000 was paid on Novem-

ber 21, 1878, see Foreign Relations
Reports of the United States for
1878, pp. 290, *et seq.*, and volume 2,
Moore's Hist. of Arbitration.
  § 299.
  [1] See § 300, *post.*
  [2] See § 304, p. 437, *post.*
  [3] See § 305, p. 438, *post.*
  [4] See § 307, p. 439, *post.*
  [5] See § 308, p. 440, *post.*
  [a] See note on p. 458, *post.*
  § 300.
  [1] Annals of Cong., 1815–16, p. 463.
  [2] See § 307, p. 439, *post.*
  [3] Annals of Cong., 1815–16, p. 533.

of the Fourteenth Congress, 1815–1816; the necessary acts were finally passed by which the tariff was regulated and the treaty carried into effect.[4]

§ 301. **Views of Mr. King of Massachusetts.**—In the course of the debate Mr. Cyrus King of Massachusetts stated that he had made an investigation of the question with the following result:

"The result of my investigation on this subject is: that whenever a treaty or convention does, by any of its provisions, encroach upon any of the enumerated powers vested by the Constitution in the Congress of the United States, or any of the laws by them enacted in execution of those powers, such treaty or convention, after being ratified, must be laid before Congress, and such provisions cannot be carried into effect without an act of Congress. For instance, whenever a treaty affected duties on imposts, enlarging or diminishing them, as the present one did to diminish; whenever a treaty went to regulate commerce with foreign nations, as that expressly did with one, as the power to lay duties and the power to regulate commerce are expressly given to Congress, such provisions of such treaty must receive the sanction of Congress before they can be considered as obligatory and as part of the municipal law of this country. And this construction is strengthened by a part of the general power given to Congress, following the enumerated powers, 'to make all laws which shall be necessary and proper, for carrying into execution the foregoing powers, and all other powers vested by the Constitution in the Government of the United States, or in any department or office thereof.' In other words, for carrying into execution the treaty-making power (that being among the other powers) in all cases where it has been exercised on subjects, placed by the Constitution within the control of the legislative department. This construction is further strengthened by the concession of honorable gentlemen, in one case, that where appropriations of money are necessary for carrying the provisions of any treaty into effect, there legislative provision is necessary. Now, sir, to concede that the sanction of Congress is necessary in one case of

4 3 U. S. Stat. at L. p. 255.

enumerated and specified power, is to concede it in all such cases. Nor, sir, can any serious inconvenience arise from this construction. As to negotiations with foreign Powers, our Ministers will always know the peculiar structure of our Government; nor can foreign Ministers, who may ever be sent to treat with us, be ignorant thereof. Besides, the distinction, as to the several kinds of treaties, is well known; some, respecting solely our external relations, or the intercourse between our Government and that of a foreign Power, will execute themselves, or are perfect without any legislative aid; and it can instantly be determined, from the nature of the provisions, when legislative aid is necessary. Further, sir, your Government has well understood this distinction. Some treaties they, by their proclamations, merely ratify and confirm, where legislative aid is necessary, as in the present case; others, they not only ratify and confirm, but enjoin an observance thereof upon all our citizens, as will be seen by turning to the ratification, by Mr. Jefferson, of several treaties published in the seventh volume United States laws. The fear that the President and Senate (they must both, or two-thirds of the latter, concur) will agree with the House in passing an improper law on the subject of a treaty which they had before ratified, cannot be well founded. There is much more reason to fear that they may be induced to ratify a treaty requiring legislative provision, which the House ought to refuse. Should a case of that kind occur, while I have the honor to be one of the Representatives of the people, I shall have no hesitation, with my brethren, to interpose ourselves between the Executive and the people, in the defence of their rights, or the freedom of our country. Far, then, from shrinking from what my honorable friend is pleased to call an awful responsibility, I should think it a sacred duty to meet the crisis, resist the encroachment, and leave the consequences with God. I never will consent that the House of Representatives of the people shall become a mere Parliament of Paris, to register the edicts of the President. I shall vote for the bill."[1]

§ 302. **Presentation of other side by Mr. Hardin.**—The

§ 301.

[1] Annals of Congress, 1815–1816, pp. 538–539.

other side of the question was presented by Mr. Hardin as follows:

"Gentlemen had said, that, on a commercial subject, no treaty could be obligatory, because the Constitution had assigned to Congress the regulation of commerce. Where, then, said he, will gentlemen stop? To Congress, they say, is delegated the exclusive jurisdiction over everything. According to their construction, therefore, the treaty-making power was impotent, a nullity, it could do nothing; it could not make peace, because peace repeals war, the right of making which is delegated to Congress: and it could not form alliances, for the same reason. But gentlemen, he observed, seemed not to recollect the old logical maxim, that he who proves too much, proves nothing. The President, say they, cannot repeal the excise!—no; but the President can make a peace without the concurrence of that House, and fortunate it was, that he could do so. We now, said Mr. H., feel the happy effects of that power, and conceive that a treaty of peace has been accomplished without any encroachments, or pretended encroachments on our Congressional acts. The power to treat generally, he said, was vested in the President by the Constitution—but to the law of nations it was left, to determine the limitations of that power. If it be true, said Mr. H., that by the terms of the Constitution of the United States, this treaty is already the law of the land, then is the treaty guaranteed by that Constitution; and yet gentlemen insist that it is not valid, and that this House ought to be consulted. By the Constitution we are forbidden to be heard in the subject, yet they will have it otherwise, and by this species of indirection, this left-handed course, bring the treaty under our legislative cognizance. Sir, I say we cannot do indirectly that which we are forbidden to do directly. Treaties might be made, no doubt, he said, for the execution of which it might be necessary to call upon the House to make laws; offensive and defensive treaties for instance, which could not otherwise be carried into effect; but when, as in the present case, the treaty was complete, and capable of executing itself, nothing of the kind was necessary.

"As to the instance which had been adduced of Congress

435

being called upon to enact laws for carrying treaties into
effect, he believed that there was not one of them similar to
this. The case of Jay's Treaty was not. The Federalists
supported that on two grounds: one that it was a good
treaty; the other that, whether good or bad, it would not
be consistent with the honor of the country to reject it; but
it never was brought forward as this is, a re-echo of itself in
the shape of a bill. And as to the cases taken from the proceedings of the British records, the organization of that government was in all respects so different from that of ours,
that it was impossible to argue fairly or conclusively from
the one, to the other." [1]

§ 303. **Result of conference; extract from report.**—The
Conference Committee between the House and the Senate
made a report in which this point was discussed at length,
and should be examined by any one studying this subject;
it contains the following statement of principles:

" Without entering upon an extensive inquiry in relation
to the treaty-making power, the committee will venture to
define, as accurately as they can, the real line which at present divides the contending parties. It is of less importance
to ascertain how far they have heretofore disagreed, or may
hereafter differ, than to discover what it is precisely that now
divides them.

" In the performance of this duty the committee of the
House of Representatives are inclined to hope that it will
sufficiently appear, that there is no irreconcilable difference
between the two branches of the Legislature.

" They are persuaded that the House of Representatives
does not assert the pretension that no treaty can be made without their assent; nor do they contend that in all cases legislative aid is indispensably necessary, either to give validity
to a treaty, or to carry it into execution. On the contrary,
they are believed to admit, that to some, nay many treaties,
no legislative sanction is required, no legislative aid is necessary.

" On the other hand the committee are not less satisfied that
it is by no means the intention of the Senate to assert the

§ 302.
[1] Annals of Congress, 1815–1816, pp. 544–545.

treaty-making power to be in all cases independent of the legislative authority. So far from it, that they are believed to acknowledge the necessity of legislative enactment to carry into execution all treaties which contain stipulations requiring appropriations, or which might bind the nation to lay taxes, raise armies, to support navies, to grant subsidies, to create States, or to cede territory; if indeed this power exists in the Government at all. In some or all of these cases, and probably in many others, it is conceived to be admitted, that the legislative body must act, in order to give effect and operation to a treaty; and if in any case it be necessary, it may confidently be asserted that there is no difference in principle between the Houses; the difference is only in the application of the principle. For if, as has been stated, the House of Representatives contend that their aid is only in some cases necessary, and if the Senate admit that in some cases it is necessary, the inference is irresistible, that the only question in each case that presents itself is, whether it be one of the cases in which legislative provision is requisite for preserving the national faith, or not." [1]

§ 304. **President Jackson's views in 1834 in regard to French treaty of 1831.**—In 1834 the question was again raised in connection with the refusal of France to carry out the reciprocal provisions contained in the treaty of 1831. President Jackson took the position that a treaty involving commercial regulations had to be submitted to Congress in order to be carried into full execution.[1]

§ 303.

[1] Annals of Congress, 1815–1816, pp. 1018–1023, see p. 1019.

§ 304.

[1] Annual Register, 1834, Public Documents, p. 352, and cited by Mr. Tucker in his Report on Treaty with Hawaiian Islands, referred to in § 307, p. 439, post. Mr. Tucker states that the propositions asserted by President Jackson were (page 16 of the Report): "1. That the treaty involved commercial regulations and rates of duties, which had to be submitted to Congress

to be carried into full execution. 2. That France, having by the treaty (1831) recognized a *precedent* obligation for depredations on our commerce, though her legislative department refused to comply with its provisions, should be forced to comply by acts of retaliation." In commenting on these propositions Mr. Tucker says: "This is assumed to be a concession by the President in respect to the effect of the treaty on the national faith of France, without the concurrence of her legislative de-

In 1844, Mr. Rufus Choate submitted a report from the Committee on Foreign Relations to the Senate,[2] and which Mr. Tucker quotes in the report of 1837, which will be referred to later at greater length,[3] in which it was declared that the legislature is the department of Government by which commerce should be regulated, and that notwithstanding the provisions in the Constitution as to the treaty-making power, the legislative will is paramount to that of the Executive in regard to all matters relating to commerce and revenue.

§ 305. **Question again raised regarding Alaska purchase in 1867.**—Probably the occasion upon which this question was most extensively debated in Congress,[1] and with more definite results, was after the treaty with Russia of 1867, ceding Alaska to the United States, had been ratified by the Senate, and the question of appropriating $7,200,000 to make the stipulated payment therefor was before the House of Representatives.

partment, that a like construction should prevail as to our Constitution. It is obvious that had the obligation of France been created by the treaty, instead of being only recognized as a pre-existing obligation, the conclusion would have been just. But President Jackson insisted that it had pre-existed for a long time, and had been too long disregarded, and that the refusal of the French Chambers to carry out the pre-existing obligation, so recognized by the treaty, authorized the United States to enforce the prior claim, and not to punish the violation of the treaty. And the President further insisted that Congress had carried out the treaty of 1831 by enacting commercial and duty regulations favorable to France, and which she was receiving, and yet refused compliance with her just duty to our people (see 4 U. S. Stat. at Large, pp. 574–576)."

See also Richardson's Messages of the Presidents, vol. III, p. 97; see p. 101-3, Andrew Jackson's Sixth Annual Message, December, 1834. For French Treaty of 1831, see U. S. Treaties and Conventions, edition, 1889, p. 345; 8 U. S. Stat. L. p. 430 (French and English text).

[2] The report of this committee will be found according to Mr. Tucker in Senate Journal, 28th Congress, 1st Session, 1843–1844, pp. 445, *et seq.;* a long quotation therefrom will be found in Mr. Tucker's Report referred to in § 307, p. 439, *post.*

[3] See § 307, p. 439, *post.*

§ 305.

[1] Convention for the Cession of Russian Possessions in North America to the United States (Seward-Stoeckl) concluded March 30, 1867; ratified by the Senate April 9, 1867; ratifications exchanged and proclaimed June 20, 1867; U. S. Treaties and Conventions, ed. 1889, p. 937; U. S. Treaties in Force 1899, p. 537; 15 U. S. Stat. at L., p. 539 (French & English text).

A faction of the House, decidedly in the minority, but sufficiently strong to make itself heard, appears to have taken great umbrage at the action of the Senate, in ratifying a treaty by which the United States acquired territory, and for which a specified payment was to be made, without first obtaining the consent of the House of Representatives, or some expression of approval from that body; every effort was made to defeat the act appropriating the money for the payment until the Senate would first recognize the right of the House of Representatives to participate in the treaty-making power. Many of the Representatives who were in favor of the acquisition of Alaska opposed the appropriation because they desired to have the power of the House in regard to treaties recognized.

§ 306. **Position of House on Alaska purchase ; the Senate makes concessions.**—A concise history of this matter appears in Wharton's International Law, where the details can be found at length.[1] The record shows that the House asserted its position to some advantage at this time, as the Act of Congress[2] which was finally passed contained a concession by which the Senate admitted that under some circumstances treaty stipulations "cannot be carried into full force and effect except by legislation to which the consent of both houses of Congress is necessary."

§ 307. **Question raised in 1887 on Hawaiian reciprocity treaty ; Mr. Tucker's report.**—In 1887 the question was before the House of Representatives on a resolution directing the Judiciary Committee to inquire into the facts relating to the treaty of 1884,[1] extending the reciprocity treaty of 1875 with the Hawaiian Islands, and to report "whether a treaty

§ 306.
[1] Wharton's International Law Digest, vol. 2, § 131a, pp. 15, et seq. See also Binger Hermann's Louisiana Purchase, 1898, pp. 52–55.
[2] 15 U. S. St. at L., p. 198.
§ 307.
[1] Treaty of Reciprocity with Hawaiian Islands, concluded January 30, 1875; ratification advised by the Senate March 18, 1875; exchanged and proclaimed June 3, 1875. U.

S. Treaties and Conventions, edition 1889, p. 546. By this treaty certain articles specified in Article I, including "Sandwich Island sugar," were admitted free of duty into the United States and a number of articles were similarly admitted into the Hawaiian Islands from the United States. See *Netherclift* vs. *Robertson*, U. S. Circ. Ct. S. D. N. Y. 1886, 23 Blatchford, 546, COXE, J.

which involves the rate of duty to be imposed on any article, or the admission of any article free of duty,[2] can be valid and binding without the concurrence of the House of Representatives, and how far the power conferred on the House by the Constitution of the United States to originate measures to lay and collect duties can be controlled by the treaty-making power under said Constitution."

It was on this resolution that Mr. Tucker prepared and submitted the report which has already been alluded to and which contains many interesting points as to the history of congressional debate on this subject.[3] The report contains from fifteen to twenty thousand words and is a lengthy review of the history of treaty stipulations and subsequent legislation, citing many congressional precedents, judicial decisions, and opinions of publicists. The conclusions reached were stated in the report as follows:

"(1) That the President, by and with the advice and consent of the Senate, cannot negotiate a treaty which shall be binding on the United States, whereby duties on imports are to be regulated, either by imposing or remitting, increasing or decreasing them, without the sanction of an act of Congress; and that the extension of the term for the operation of the original treaty or convention with the Government of the Hawaiian Islands, proposed by the supplementary convention of December 6, 1884, will not be binding on the United States without like sanction, which was provided for in the original treaty and convention, and was given by act of Congress.

"(2) That the President is respectfully requested to withhold final action upon the proposed convention, and to condition its final ratification upon the sanction of an act of

---

[2] Treaty of Reciprocity with Hawaiian Islands, concluded December 6, 1884; ratification advised by Senate, with Amendments, January 20, 1887; proclaimed November 9, 1887. U. S. Treaties and Conventions, edition 1889, p. 1187. By this treaty the reciprocity provisions were extended for seven years, and there was granted to the United States the exclusive right to establish a coaling station at Pearl River Harbor.

[3] House of Representatives, Report No. 4177, 49th Congress, 2d Session, March 3, 1887. From Mr. Tucker of the Committee on the Judiciary, on Treaty with the Hawaiian Islands.

Congress, in respect of the duties upon articles to be imported from the Hawaiian Islands." [4]

§ 308. **Treaty of Paris with Spain, 1898 ; what legislation necessary.**—The treaty of peace with Spain was concluded in Paris on December 10, 1898; it was ratified by the Senate on February 6, 1899, and the ratifications were exchanged April 11, 1899; questions have already been raised as to how far that treaty has become effectual without legislation; so far, however, as the necessary appropriations were concerned the House of Representatives lost no time in passing the bill providing the $20,000,000 for the payment to Spain ; [1] legislation has also been enacted in regard to the status of the inhabitants in Porto Rico ; [2] and the act in some particulars has been sustained as constitutional by the Supreme Court of the United States ; [3] but up to the present time there has been no legislation in regard to the Philippine Islands, except to place the Government thereof in the hands of the President ; [4] an act has also been passed appoint-

[4] See page 23 of Mr. Tucker's Report.

§ 308.

[1] An act making an appropriation to carry out the obligations of the treaty between the United States and Spain concluded December 10, 1898. " *Be it enacted,* etc. . . . There is hereby appropriated, out of any money in the treasury not otherwise appropriated, the sum of $20,000,000. Approved March 2, 1899." 30 U. S. Stat. at Large, p. 993. The entire act consists of only seven lines.

[2] An Act temporarily to provide revenues and a civil government for Porto Rico, and for other purposes. Approved April 12, 1900. U. S. Stat. 1899–1900, p. 77.

[3] See note 6 to this section on next page.

[4] THE SPOONER AMENDMENT.

" All military, civil, and judicial powers necessary to govern the Philippine Islands, acquired from Spain by the treaties concluded at Paris on the tenth day of December, 1898, and at Washington on the seventh day of November, 1900, shall, until otherwise provided by Congress, be vested in such person or persons and shall be exercised in such manner as the President of the United States shall direct, for the establishment of civil government and for maintaining and protecting the inhabitants of said islands in the free enjoyment of their liberty, property, and religion: *Provided,* That all franchises granted under the authority hereof shall contain a reservation of the right to alter, amend, or repeal the same.

" Until a permanent government shall have been established in said archipelago full reports shall be made to Congress on or before the first day of each regular session of all legislative acts and proceedings

ing a commission to adjust the claims of citizens of the United States assumed by the treaty.[5] The question whether the

of the temporary government instituted under the provisions hereof; and full reports of the acts and doings of said government, and as to the condition of the archipelago and of its people, shall be made to the President, including all information which may be useful to the Congress in providing for a more permanent government: P*rovided*, That no sale or lease or other disposition of the public lands or the timber thereon or the mining rights therein shall be made: *And provided further*, That no franchise shall be granted which is not approved by the President of the United States, and is not in his judgment clearly necessary for the immediate government of the islands and indispensable for the interest of the people thereof, and which cannot, without great public mischief, be postponed until the establishment of permanent civil government; and all such franchises shall terminate one year after the establishment of such permanent civil government.

"All laws or part of laws inconsistent with the provisions of this Act are hereby repealed. Approved March 2, 1901." The foregoing was offered as an amendment to the Army Appropriation Bill by Senator John C. Spooner of Wisconsin, and was incorporated as a part of the Act when passed. It constitutes the last sentences of the Act. 31 U. S. Stat. L., p. 895, *et seq.* See p. 910.

[5] An Act to carry into effect the stipulations of article seven of the treaty between the United States and Spain concluded on the tenth day of December, 1898. Approved

March 2, 1901. Public Act, No. 115. 31 U. S. Stat. at Large, pp. 877–880.

Article VII is as follows:

"The United States and Spain mutually relinquish all claims for indemnity, national and individual, of every kind, of either Government, or of its citizens or subjects, against the other Government, that may have arisen since the beginning of the late insurrection in Cuba and prior to the exchange of ratifications of the present treaty, including all claims for indemnity for the cost of the war.

"The United States will adjudicate and settle the claims of its citizens against Spain relinquished in this article." 30 U. S. Stat. at Large p. 1757.

By an act of Congress, approved March 2, 1901, a commission of five was constituted to receive, examine and adjudicate all claims of citizens of the United States against Spain. The commission "shall adjudicate said claims according to the merit of the several cases, the principles of equity and of international law." The commission shall make rules of precedure but the act provides generally for the form and manner of presentation of claims which must be presented and filed within six months after the first meeting of the commission (April 8, 1901). Awards shall only be made for actual and direct damages proved; remote or prospective damages and interest are not to be allowed. Awards are final but "when the commission is in doubt as to any question of law arising upon the facts in any case before them, they may state the facts and

442

clause ceding the territory was an absolute stipulation which immediately made the Philippine Islands, as well as Porto Rico and Guam, a part of the territory of the United States, so that the laws and Constitution of the United States extended thereover, is at this time (May, 1901) still pending before the Supreme Court of the United States, and undoubtedly the opinions which will be rendered in the cases now under consideration by that court will definitely settle many important points as to how far treaty stipulations become operative *ex proprio vigore*, and without legislative assistance.[6]

the question of law so arising and certify the same to the Supreme Court of the United States for its decision, and said Court shall have jurisdiction to consider and decide the same." The commission is to continue in force for two years, but the President has discretionary power to extend this period six months at a time when in his judgment such extension is necessary. A large number of claims have already been filed, including many for destruction of property in Cuba, and for loss of life, damages for illegal imprisonment; many members of the families of seamen and marines who were killed, and some of those who were injured, by the explosion of the U. S. Battleship Maine in Havana Harbor on February 15, 1898, have filed claims on the ground that the explosion was the result of negligence or actual connivance of the Spanish authorities and that the United States has assumed these as well as other claims. The author of this volume is of counsel for a number of these claimants. At this time (Dec'r, 1901) the United States Government has not filed any answer or demurrer but has made a motion to dismiss the claims on the ground that the commission has no jurisdiction of this class of

claims. That motion will probably be argued in October, 1901. The members of the Commission are William E. Chandler, President; Gerritt E. Diekema, James Perry Wood, William A. Maury and William L. Chambers; William E. Spear, clerk; William E. Fuller, assistant attorney general, in charge of the claims on behalf of the Government of the United States. In regard to the status of claims of individual citizens of the United States against foreign governments and the right of the United States to release foreign governments by treaty therefrom, and the rights of the claimants against the United States in such cases, see §§ 442, *et seq.*, chap. XV, Vol. II.

[6] Since the above was written opinions have been delivered (May 27–28, 1901) in several of the cases referred to. They are discussed at length in §§ 61a–61h, pp. 117–127, *ante*, under other sections there referred to and abstracts of some of the opinions appear in the INSULAR CASES APPENDIX at the end of this volume. The right of Congress to impose duties on goods brought from ports in territory acquired by the United States by treaties of cession from foreign powers to other ports of the United States was sustained in the case of *Downes*

§ 309. **Opinions of publicists on this subject.**—Some further opinions on this subject, as they have been expressed by Kent,[1] Duer, Calhoun, Webster, Wheaton and others, may

vs. *Bidwell*, 182 U. S. 244. See § 61e, p. 122, *ante*, or INSULAR CASES APPENDIX for details. The Spooner Amendment and the right to vest the President and his appointees with all military, civil and judicial power necessary to govern territory belonging to the United States were not involved in any of the cases decided.

§ 309.

[1] Chancellor Kent in Lecture XIII, p. 286, says:

" The question whether a treaty, constitutionally made, was obligatory upon Congress, equally as any other national engagement would be, if fairly made by the competent authority, or whether Congress had any discretionary power to carry into effect a treaty requiring the appropriation of money, or other act to be done on their part, or to refuse it their sanction, was greatly discussed in Congress in the year 1796, and again in 1816. The House of Representatives, at the former period, declared by resolution, that when a treaty depended for the execution of any of its stipulations on an act of Congress, it was the right and duty of the House to deliberate on the expediency or inexpediency of carrying such treaty into effect. It cannot be mentioned at this day, without equal regret and astonishment, that such a resolution passed the House of Representatives on the 7th of April, 1796. But it was a naked abstract claim of right, never acted upon; and Congress shortly after-

wards passed a law to carry into effect the very treaty with Great Britain which gave rise to that resolution. President Washington, in his message to the House of Representatives of the 30th of March, 1796, explicitly denied the existence of any such power in Congress; and he insisted that every treaty duly made by the President and Senate, and promulgated, thenceforward became the law of the land.

" If a treaty be the law of the land, it is as much obligatory upon Congress as upon any other branch of the government, or upon the people at large, so long as it continues in force and unrepealed. The House of Representatives are not above the law, and they have no dispensing power. They have a right to make and repeal laws, provided the Senate and President concur; but without such concurrence, a law in the shape of a treaty is as binding upon them as if it were in the shape of an act of Congress, or of an article of the Constitution, or of a contract made by authority of law. The argument in favor of the binding and conclusive efficacy of every treaty made by the President and Senate is so clear and palpable, that it has probably carried very general conviction throughout the community; and this may now be considered as the decided sense of public opinion. This was the sense of the House of Representatives, in 1816, and the resolution of 1796 would not now be repeated."

444

be found in Wharton's Digest following the Alaska[2] case, and in Mr. Tucker's report of 1887.[3]

Kent's Commentaries, Lect. XIII, pp. 286–287.

Chancellor Kent then quoted the following from Story's Commentaries: "(a) The treaty-making power is necessarily and obviously subordinate to the fundamental laws and constitution of the state, and it cannot change the form of the government, or annihilate its constitutional powers." Story's Comm. on the Constitution, ii, sec. 1502.

[3] See § 307, and note 3, p. 440, *ante*.

[2] EXTRACTS FROM WHARTON'S DIGEST.
(§ 131a, pp. 23–27.)

KENT.

" Treaties of peace, when made by the competent power, are obligatory upon the whole nation. If the treaty requires the payment of money to carry it into effect, and the money cannot be raised but by an act of the legislature, the treaty is morally obligatory upon the legislature to pass the law, and to refuse it would be a breach of the public faith. The department of the Government that is intrusted by the Constitution with the treaty-making power is competent to bind the national faith in its discretion, for the power to make treaties of peace must be co-extensive with all the exigencies of the nation, and necessarily involves in it that portion of the national sovereignty which has the exclusive direction of diplomatic negotiations and contracts with foreign powers. All treaties made by that power become of absolute efficacy, because they are the supreme law of the land. There can be no doubt that the power competent to bind the nation by treaty may alienate the public domain and property by treaty. If a nation has conferred upon its executive department, without reserve, the right of treating and contracting with other states, it is considered as having invested it with all the power necessary to make a valid treaty. That department is the organ of the nation, and the alienations by it are valid, because they are done by the reputed will of the nation. The fundamental laws of a State may withhold from the executive department the power of transferring what belongs to the States, but if there be no express provision of that kind the inference is that it has confided to the department charged with the power of making treaties a discretion commensurate with all the great interests and wants and necessities of the nation. 1 Kent's Com. 162."

DUER.

" If a treaty be the law of the land, it is as much obligatory upon Congress as upon any other branch of the Government, or upon the people at large, so long as it continues in force and unrepealed. The House of Representatives are not above the law, and they have no dispensing power. They have a right to make and to repeal laws, provided the Senate and President concur, but without such concurrence a law in the shape of a treaty is as binding upon them as if it were in the shape of an act of Congress, or of an article of the Constitution, or of a contract

445

At the end of the notes in Wharton's Digest on this subject, the following conclusion is reached and stated:

made by authority of law.   The argument in favor of the binding and conclusive efficacy of every treaty made by the President and Senate is so clear and palpable, that it has probably carried very general conviction throughout the community; and this may now be considered as the decided sense of public opinion.

"If a treaty require the payment of money to carry it into effect, and the money can only be raised or appropriated by an act of the legislature, the existence of the treaty renders it morally obligatory on Congress to pass the requisite law, and its refusal to do so would amount to a breach of the public faith, and afford just cause of war.   That department of the Government which is intrusted by the Constitution with the power of making treaties is competent to bind the national faith at its discretion; for the power to make treaties must be co-extensive with the national exigencies, and necessarily involves in it every portion of the national sovereignty, of which the co-operation may be necessary to give effect to negotiations and contracts with foreign nations.   If a nation confer on its executive department without reserve the right of treating and contracting with other sovereignties, it is considered as having invested it with all the power necessary to make a valid contract, and that it is the organ in making its contracts; and such alienations are valid, because they are made by the reputed assent of the nation.   Duer's Outlines of Constitutional Jurisprudence of the United States, 138."

CALHOUN.

"The treaty-making power is limited by all the provisions of the Constitution which inhibit certain acts from being done by the Government. It is also limited by such provisions of the Constitution as direct certain acts to be done in a particular way, and which prohibit the contrary, of which a striking example is to be found in that which declares that no money shall be drawn from the Treasury but in consequence of appropriations to be made by law.   This not only imposes an important restriction on the power, but gives to Congress as the law-making power, and to the House of Representatives, as a portion of Congress, the right to withhold appropriations, and thereby an important control over the treaty-making power, whenever money is required to carry a treaty into effect, which is usually the case, especially in reference to those of the most importance.   There still remains another and more important limitation, but of a more general and indefinite character.   It can enter into no stipulation calculated to change the character of the Government, or to do that which can only be done by the constitution-making power, or which is inconsistent with the nature and structure of the Government.   Calhoun's Discourse on Government, 1 Works, 201."

WHEATON.

"Mr. Wheaton's letter to Mr. Butler, Attorney General, on the refusal of the French Chamber to appropriate the sum necessary for the pay-

"The question, therefore, which was agitated in 1796, whether Congress can, under the Constitution, refuse, in its

ment of the fund agreed on by the French indemnity treaty, has been already cited. (*Supra*, § 9; *infra*, § 318. See also Halleck's Int. Law (Baker's ed.) 232, citing Wheaton's Life of Pinkney, 517-'49; 1 Kent's Com., 285; President's Mess. Dec. 1834; Ann. Reg., 1834, 361.) This is another form of stating the position elsewhere mentioned, that a treaty may bind internationally when it would not bind municipally. (*Supra*, § 9.) The United States, for instance, may by statute impose on its own citizens less stringent rules of neutrality than it imposes on itself by treaty; but such municipal laxity on its part will not relieve it from its obligations by treaty or by international law. (See *infra*, § 402, Wharton.) A Government also is liable for violations of international duty by its judiciary. (*Infra*, § 329a, Wharton.)

"It is not inconsistent with this position that the United States is not liable for a treaty which the Senate refuses to ratify, since no Government is internationally liable on a treaty not agreed to by the treaty-making power. (See Wharton, §§ 9 and 318.)"

A GERMAN'S VIEW OF THE QUESTION.

"That a treaty cannot invade the constitutional prerogatives of the legislature is thus illustrated by a German author, who has given to the subject a degree of elaborate and extended exposition which it has received from no writer in our own tongue. Congress has under the Constitution the right to lay taxes and imposts, as well as to regulate foreign trade, but the President and Senate, if the 'treaty-making power' be regarded as absolute, would be able to evade this limitation by adopting treaties which would compel Congress to destroy its whole tariff system. According to the Constitution, Congress has the right to determine questions of naturalization, of patents, and of copyright. Yet, according to the view here contested, the President and Senate, by a treaty, could on these important questions utterly destroy the legislative capacity of the House of Representatives. The Constitution gives Congress the control of the Army. Participation in this control would be snatched from the House of Representatives by a treaty with a foreign power by which the United States would bind itself to keep in the field an army of a particular size. The Constitution gives Congress the right of declaring war; this right would be illusory if the President and Senate could by a treaty launch the country into a foreign war. The power of borrowing money on the credit of the United States resides in Congress; this power would cease to exist if the President and Senate could by treaty bind the country to the borrowing of foreign funds. By the Constitution 'no money shall be drawn from the Treasury, but in consequence of appropriations made by law;' but this limitation would cease to exist if by a treaty the United States could be bound to pay money to a foreign power. . . . Congress would cease to be the law-making power as is prescribed by the Constitution; the law-making power would be the President and the Senate. Such a con-

447

legislative capacity, to pass acts for the execution of treaties duly ratified, remains still open. Yet two positions may be regarded as accepted in the practical working of our Government. One is that without a congressional vote there can be no appropriation of money which a treaty requires to be paid. The other is that it should require a very strong case to justify Congress in refusing to pass an appropriation which is called for by a treaty duly ratified." [4]

§ 310. **Supreme Court decisions on this subject.**—The decisions of the Supreme Court as to necessity of legislation to carry into effect treaty stipulations which in any way change existing tariff laws, or other statutory provisions of the United States, will be referred to in a subsequent chapter, but the doctrine laid down by Mr. Justice Curtis in the case of *Taylor* vs. *Morton*, which will be hereafter quoted at length, to the effect that such legislation is necessary, has been accepted as the law in regard to that class of treaty stipulations, and followed in judicial and congressional action. [1]

§ 311. **General conclusions : power of Congress to frustrate and abrogate treaties.**—It must be recognized, therefore, that, while the treaty-making power of the United States is undoubtedly vested in the Executive subject to ratification by two-thirds of the Senate, it is still within the power of Congress—that is, a majority of both Houses of that body—to control the ultimate effect of all treaty stipulations which in any way conflict with any existing laws of the United States, or which require legislation to make them effectual, or which require the appropriation of money to

dition would become the more dangerous from the fact that treaties so adopted, being on this particular hypothesis superior to legislation, would continue in force until superseded by other treaties. Not only, therefore, would a Congress consisting of two houses be made to give way to an oligarchy of President and Senate, but the decrees of this oligarchy, when once made, could only be changed by concurrence of President and of Senatorial majority of two thirds. Ueber den Abschluss von Staatsverträgen, von Dr. Ernest Meier, Professor der Rechte an der Universität Halle, Leipzig, 1874."

[4] Wharton's International Law Digest, vol. 2, § 131a, pp. 23–27.

§ 310.

[1] *Taylor* vs. *Morton*, U. S. Cir. Ct. Mass. 1855; 2 Curtis, 454; CURTIS, Associate Justice of Supreme Court, sitting as Circuit Judge; affirmed U. S. Sup. Ct. 1862; 2 Black.

fulfil them. This can be done either by enacting legislation contrary to the terms and spirit of the provisions of the treaty, or by refusing to enact the legislation necessary to carry them out.

Furthermore, Congress, by act or by resolution, can abrogate a treaty, and thereby render futile the treaty-making power as exercised by the constitutional authorities.[1]

§ 312. **Moral and ethical questions arising.**—Upon this point many moral, ethical and speculative questions might be raised; it is fortunate, however, that the mere existence of power does not mean that such power has been or will be misused; undoubtedly, although opportunities may exist for raising the questions as to the effect of this power to annul, or to render treaty stipulations void, Congress will continue to adhere to its established custom of enacting all proper legislation necessary to carry out treaties made by the government, when they are in the nature of contracts and legislation is required to make them operative, and to carry out the obligations assumed by the government to other nations, the failure to comply with which would involve national repudiation and bad faith.[1]

§ 313. **Alexander Hamilton's views in Federalist not followed by the Supreme Court.**—In this respect the construction of the treaty-making power by the Courts and Congress, and the relative effect of treaties and legislation has been different from that which some of the framers of the Constitution placed upon it. Alexander Hamilton considered that treaties of the United States made with foreign powers would not only have the force of law, but would derive that force from the obligations of good faith, and that neither Congress nor the Executive could violate provisions of treaties by enacting laws in conflict therewith.[1]

481, CLIFFORD, J. And see §§ 367 et seq., Vol. II, for extracts from opinion in the Circuit Court which was followed by the Supreme Court.

§ 311.

[1] See § 365, Vol. II, and notes thereunder.

§ 312.

[1] See § 298, p. 413, *ante.*

§ 313.

[1] " NO. LXXV OF THE FEDERALIST.

" With regard to the intermixture of powers, I shall rely upon the explanations already given in other places, of the true sense of the rule upon which that objection is founded; and shall take it for granted, as an inference from

We shall see, however, that the Supreme Court has taken a different view, and, although the Executive, with the ratification of two-thirds of the Senate, can make a treaty—that is to say, a contract—with a foreign nation, such contract can be violated by an act of Congress passed after the treaty has been ratified, and that if the treaty provides for the modification of existing legislation, as for instance, a different tariff rate, the treaty will not go into effect in that respect unless Congress enacts new legislation, or modifies existing legislation, in accordance with the treaty provisions.[2]

them, that the union of the Executive with the Senate, in the article of treaties, is no infringement of that rule. I venture to add, that the particular nature of the power of making treaties indicates a peculiar propriety in that union. Though several writers on the subject of government place that power in the class of executive authorities, yet this is evidently an arbitrary disposition; for if we attend carefully to its operation, it will be found to partake more of the legislative than of the executive character, though it does not seem strictly to fall within the definition of either of them. The essence of the legislative authority is to enact laws, or in other words, to prescribe rules for the regulation of the society; while the execution of the laws, and the employment of the common strength, either for this purpose or for the common defence, seem to comprise all the functions of the executive magistrate. The power of making treaties is, plainly, neither the one nor the other. It relates neither to the execution of the subsisting laws, nor to the enaction of new ones; and still less to an exertion of the common strength. Its objects are CONTRACTS with foreign nations, which have the

force of law, but derive it from the obligations of good faith. They are not rules prescribed by the sovereign to the subject, but agreements between sovereign and sovereign. The power in question seems therefore to form a distinct department, and to belong, properly, neither to the legislative nor to the executive. The qualities elsewhere detailed as indispensable in the management of foreign negotiations, point out the Executive as the most fit agent in those transactions; while the vast importance of the trust, and the operation of treaties as laws, plead strongly for the participation of the whole or a portion of the legislative body in the office of making them." The author then proceeds to demonstrate the superior fitness of the Senate for this participation of the two-thirds majority—making a sufficiently strong check upon it to protect the interests of the people.

For comment on this utterance of The Federalist, see Tucker on the Constitution, vol. 2, p. 729.

[2] See §§ 314, et seq., post, of this chapter, and see also chap. XII, post, which is devoted entirely to the relative effects of treaty stipulations and Federal statutes.

§ 314. **Position of Supreme Court as to treaty violations; burden thrown on Congress.**—This apparently puts the Supreme Court in the position of declaring that the United States has a right to violate its contracts, and is not bound in the same manner as individuals are. The records of that Court, however, show that no decision of the Supreme Court has ever relieved the United States from its liability to another nation for violating treaty stipulations; that Court, speaking through its most eminent members, has often said, and undoubtedly will continue to say, that treaties or contracts made with foreign nations and which require legislation to make them effective, cannot become effective without legislation, and also that they can be violated, by legislation inconsistent therewith; it has always sounded to Congress the warning note that, although the courts cannot enforce treaty stipulations, except so far as they are self-operative and require no legislative assistance, Congress must beware of the reclamations, which can, and may, be made by foreign nations upon this Government for its failure to fulfil treaty stipulations, or for its violations thereof, as those stipulations not only have all the attributes of contracts between individuals, but are also clothed with the sanctity of national good faith which never should be violated, and which never can be violated without far-reaching and unfortunate results.

§ 315. **Difference between municipal and international law in this respect.**—In discussing this proposition we must remember that two classes of law are involved and that the decisions of the Supreme Court in regard to the apparent violation of treaty stipulations have, as a general rule, been made in cases involving the interests of citizens of the United States, or which have related to the conduct of officers of the United States within its own territory, and which have not related to claims, arising directly under the treaty, and made by one of the national contracting parties against the other; that is, under the municipal law of the United States, as administered by our Federal and State Courts, the statutes of the United States must be followed. If, therefore, Congress does not choose to carry out a treaty, or if it prefers to violate one, citizens of the United States, or even subjects of foreign powers, seeking relief in our courts, may not, in that manner, be able to obtain redress for grievances arising from the failure of the Government of the United States to comply with treaty stipulations. The courts are bound by the laws enacted by Congress, and cannot declare them either unconstitutional or inoperative because they violate national contracts or national good faith and honor. If, through congressional failure, or neglect, to carry out treaty stipulations for the benefit of citizens of a foreign country, citizens of the United States suffer damage, they have no redress whatever, as the contract was not made for their benefit, and they cannot complain if Congress by its negative or positive action renders those stipulations valueless; if citizens of the foreign country suffer damage by such legislation, their remedy is not through the courts, which are necessarily bound by the statute law, but they must apply for redress through their own government, with whom the treaty is made, and their claims can then be settled according to the rules of international law, either diplomatically through the various State and Foreign Offices, by international arbitration, or if that, unfortunately, shall fail, by the Court of last resort for nations—war.[1]

§ 316. **Treaty with Denmark considered in this respect ; tariff legislation.**—To take a concrete example ; the treaties with Denmark provided that there should be no higher duties charged on goods brought from Denmark or Danish possessions, than were charged on similar goods brought from other countries.[1] After the Hawaiian treaty

§ 315.

[1] For international claims arising from legislation which violates treaty stipulation, see Wharton's Digest of International Law, vol. 2, § 138, p. 65, and see p. 70.

§ 316.

[1] Treaty of Friendship, Commerce and Navigation; concluded April 26, 1826, ratification exchanged at Copenhagen August 10, 1826, U. S. Treaties and Conventions, edition, 1887, p. 231, U. S. Treaties in Force, edition, 1899, p. 152.

This treaty was abrogated in 1856, but was revived by the convention exempting American vessels from the Sound and Belts dues concluded April 11, 1857; ratifications exchanged at Washington January 12, 1858, which contained the following:

ARTICLE IV.

No higher or other duties shall be imposed on the importation into the United States of any article, the produce or manufacture of the

of 1875 [2] which provided for admitting sugar from those Islands free, it was claimed by importers of sugar from the Danish West Indies that under the treaties of 1826 and 1857 they were entitled to similarly import their sugar free of duty. The Supreme Court, however, decided that as Congress had not seen fit after the ratification of the Hawaiian treaty, to enact legislation for the free admission of such sugar, the courts could not relieve the importers from duties under the provisions of the general tariff law. On the argument of this case counsel having suggested that the National good faith and honor were involved, the Court asked the pertinent question whether the government of Denmark had made any claim under the treaty, which could be considered by the Court as it did not appear that any such claim had been made, and the Court decided that even if there had been a breach of the treaty it was not in the power of the court in the absence of Congressional legislation to rectify it, but that it would be a matter of reclamation by the gov-

dominions of His Majesty the King of Denmark; and no higher or other duties shall be imposed on the importation into the said dominions of any article, the produce or manufacture of the United States, than are or shall be payable on the like articles, being the produce or manufacture of any other foreign country. Nor shall any higher or other duties or charges be imposed in either of the two countries on the exportation of any articles to the United States, or to the dominions of His Majesty the King of Denmark, respectively, than such as are or may be payable on the exportation of the like articles to any other foreign country. Nor shall any prohibition be imposed on the exportation or importation of any articles, the produce or manufacture of the United States, or of the dominions of His Majesty the King of Denmark, to or from the territories of the United States, or to or from the said dominions, which shall not equally extend to all other nations.

ARTICLE V

The general convention of friendship, commerce and navigation, concluded between the United States and His Majesty the King of Denmark, on the 26th of April, 1826, and which was abrogated on the 15th of April, 1856, and the provisions contained in each and all of its articles, the 5th article alone excepted, shall, after the ratification of this present convention, again become binding upon the United States and Denmark; it being, however, understood, that a year's notice shall suffice for the abrogation of the stipulations of the said convention hereby renewed.

[2] Convention respecting commercial reciprocity, concluded January 30, 1875, ratification exchanged June 3, 1875, U. S. Treaties and Conventions, edition, 1887, p. 546.

ernment of Denmark upon the Government of the United States, and that the question before the court must be decided strictly by the municipal law of the United States as it had been established by Congress.[3]

§ 317. **Chinese exclusion; conflict of statutes and treaties ; opinion of Justice Field.**—Another, and perhaps the most notable example of the apparent violation of treaties by the United States, through Congressional action, was the exclusion of the Chinese from our ports notwithstanding treaty stipulations as to reciprocal rights of subjects of the Chinese Empire and citizens of the United States to freely come and go, each in the territory of the other. The Chinese Exclusion Acts were claimed by many to be in direct violation of these treaty stipulations and the various Acts were tested in the courts and numerous decisions were rendered as to their validity and constitutionality. The courts uniformly sustained the Acts as constitutional. In 1889 Judge Field delivered a leading opinion of the Supreme Court on this subject in one of the Chinese cases from which the following extract is taken :[1]

" The validity of this act, as already mentioned, is assailed as being in effect an expulsion from the country of Chinese laborers in violation of existing treaties between the United States and the government of China, and of rights vested in them under the laws of Congress. The objection that the act is in conflict with the treaties was earnestly pressed in the court below, and the answer to it constitutes the principal part of its opinion.[2] Here the objection made is, that the act of 1888 impairs a right vested under the treaty of 1880, as a law of the United States, and the statutes of 1882 and of 1884 passed in execution of it. It must be conceded that the act of 1888 is in contravention of express stipulations of the treaty of 1868 and of the supplemental treaty

[3] *Bartram* vs. *Robertson*, U. S. Sup. Ct. 1887, 122 U. S. 116, FIELD, J., and see extract from opinion in note on treaty and tariff cases under § 371, Vol. II, pp. 71, *et seq.*

§ 317.

[1] *Chae Chan Ping* vs. *United States*, (Chinese exclusion case)

U. S. Sup. Ct. 1889, 130 U. S. 581, FIELD, J., affirming *In re Chae Chan Ping*, U. S. Cir. Ct. California, 1888, 36 Fed. Rep. 431, SAWYER, J.

[2] Citing *In re Chae Chan Ping*, U. S. Cir. Ct. Cal., 1888, 36 Fed. Rep. 431, SAWYER, J.

of 1880, but it is not on that account invalid or to be restricted in its enforcement. The treaties were of no greater legal obligation than the act of Congress. By the Constitution, laws made in pursuance thereof and treaties made under the authority of the United States are both declared to be the supreme law of the land, and no paramount authority is given to one over the other. A treaty, it is true, is in its nature a contract between nations and is often merely promissory in its character, requiring legislation to carry its stipulations into effect. Such legislation will be open to future repeal or amendment. If the treaty operates by its own force, and relates to a subject within the power of Congress, it can be deemed in that particular only the equivalent of a legislative act, to be repealed or modified at the pleasure of Congress. In either case the last expression of the sovereign will must control.

"The effect of legislation upon conflicting treaty stipulations was elaborately considered in the Head Money Cases, and it was there adjudged ' that so far as a treaty made by the United States with any foreign nation can become the subject of judicial cognizance in the courts of this country, it is subject to such acts as Congress may pass for its enforcement, modification, or repeal.' [3] This doctrine was affirmed and followed in *Whitney* vs. *Robertson*, 124 U. S. 190, 195. It will not be presumed that the legislative department of the government will lightly pass laws which are in conflict with the treaties of the country; but that circumstances may arise which would not only justify the government in disregarding their stipulations, but demand in the interests of the country that it should do so, there can be no question. Unexpected events may call for a change in the policy of the country. Neglect or violation of stipulations on the part of the other contracting party may require corresponding action on our part. When a reciprocal engagement is not carried out by one of the contracting parties, the other may also decline to keep the corresponding engage-

[3] *Edye* vs. *Robertson*, U. S. Cir. Ct. S. D. N. Y. 1883, 21 Blatchf. 460, BLATCHFORD, J., affirmed U. S. Sup. Ct. 1884, 112 U. S. 580, MIL-LER, J. Head Money Cases. And see extract from opinion in sec. 376, Vol. II, p. 82.

ment.   In 1798 the conduct towards this country of the government of France was of such a character that Congress declared that the United States were freed and exonerated from the stipulations of previous treaties with that country."[4]

§ 318. **This same subject treated at length in a subsequent chapter.**—It is, however, rather anticipating the regular order to refer to decisions of the courts, at this point; the legal principles established in the Chinese exclusion cases will be discussed as to the relative effects of treaty stipulations, and State laws in the next chapter,[1] and as to United States statutes in the next chapter but one.[2]

The specific instances in which treaties have been held to operate without legislation, whereby they have annulled State legislation or prior congressional legislation and where they have been affected or abrogated by subsequent legislation of Congress, also form the subject of a subsequent chapter,[3] and no further reference will be made now to them in this chapter which should have been confined to the Congressional debates and action in regard thereto; in concluding this chapter on the participation of both houses in the treaty-making power, however, attention is called to the fact that while congressional action,—that is action by a majority of both houses,—may, contrary to the expectations of the framers of the Constitution, seriously affect treaty stipulations made with foreign powers, there is nothing in any of the cases decided, or in any congressional action already taken, which places any limitations upon the treaty-making power as it exists in the Central Government.   The possibility of a majority of both houses of Congress being able, with the President's consent, to override, or of a majority of one branch being able to frustrate, the Executive and two-thirds of the Senate, is not to be regarded a limitation upon the power, proceeding from any external or superior force, but only a difficulty in exercising it, owing to disagreement between themselves of the various elements of the Central

[4] The quotation is on pages 599–601, 130 U. S. Rep.

§ 318.

[1] Chapter XI, and see especially §§ 336, *et seq.*, Vol. II, pp. 24, *et seq.*

[2] Chapter XII, and see especially §§ 379, *et seq.*, Vol. II, pp. 87, *et seq.*

[3] Chapter XII, and see especially §§ 379, *et seq.*, Vol. II, pp. 87, *et seq.*

Government itself.   The power, as lodged in the Central
Government in all of its breadth and scope, in all of its far-
reaching effects over the Union and all of the constituent
parts thereof, in all of its varied phases and aspects, has never
been diminished by any of the decisions of the court or positions taken in Congress, and which relate only to the method
of exercising the power, or of modifying the effects thereof,
by the National Government itself, or of the various Departments of the National Government.[2]

[2] CONGRESSIONAL DISCUSSION OF 1902 AS TO CONTROL OF HOUSE OF
REPRESENTATIVES OVER TARIFF LAWS AND TREATY STIPULATIONS
AFFECTING TARIFF.

The discussion as to the power of the House of Representatives to
control tariff legislation and the necessity of Congressional action to
make treaty stipulations affecting tariff provisions effectual, has been
renewed in the 57th Congress just as this volume is going to press.

On January 29th, 1902, Senator Cullom of Illinois, Chairman of the
Committee on Foreign Relations, delivered an address in the Senate of
the United States on the extent of the treaty-making power (Cong.
Rec. January 29, 1902, pp. 1104–1111), in which he declared (p. 1111)
that the "authority of the House of Representatives in reference to
treaties has been argued and discussed for more than a century, and
has never been settled in Congress, and perhaps never will be. The
House, each time the question was considered, insisted upon its powers, but nevertheless has never declined to make an appropriation to
carry out the stipulations of a treaty, and I contend that it was bound
to do this, at least as much as Congress can be bound to do anything
when the faith of the nation had been pledged. And this appears to
me to be the only case in which any action by the House is necessary,
unless the treaty itself stipulates, expressly or by implication, for such
Congressional action."

Senator Cullom cited the instances on which this subject has been
discussed in Congress. He referred to the Hawaiian, Canadian and
Mexican reciprocity treaties, and declared that they did not go into
effect without legislation because the treaty expressly provided that
legislation must first be enacted; he said (p. 1110): "In the reciprocity
treaty with Mexico, negotiated by General Grant, Congress failed to
enact the necessary laws and the treaty never went into practical effect.

"Had the provision for Congressional action been omitted in the
Hawaiian, Canadian and Mexican reciprocity treaties, they would have
become effective at once upon the exchange of ratifications."

The House of Representatives took up the gage thrown down by
Senator Cullom, and on January 31st, 1902 (Cong. Rec., p. 1193), the
following Resolution (House No. 114), was offered by Mr. Dalzell of
Pennsylvania, from the Committee on Rules, and was agreed to:

" *Whereas*, it is seriously claimed that under the treaty-making power of the Government, and without any action whatever on the part of the House of Representatives, or by Congress, reciprocal trade agreements may be negotiated with foreign governments that will of their own force operate to supplant, change, increase, or entirely abrogate duties on imports collected under laws enacted by Congress and approved by the Executive for the purpose of raising revenue to maintain the Government: Now, therefore, be it

" *Resolved by the House of Representatives*, that the Committee on Ways and Means be directed to fully investigate the question of whether or not the President, by and with the advice and consent of the Senate, and independent of any action on the part of the House of Representatives, can negotiate treaties with foreign governments by which duties levied under an act of Congress for the purpose of raising revenue are modified or repealed, and report the result of such investigation to the House."

The resolution was adopted without debate, but Mr. Moody (Massachusetts) asked " if there is any instance in our history where there has been a change in the tariff laws through the operation of a treaty without the concurrence of the House of Representatives ? " To which Mr. Dalzell replied: " I will say to the gentleman from Massachusetts that I know of none. "

RIGHT TO MAKE TREATY STIPULATIONS EFFECTUAL BY EXECUTIVE PROCLAMATION.

The real question involved in the present Congressional debate is whether treaty stipulations as to tariff can be made effectual by Executive proclamation instead of by legislation. This involves the same question that was raised, but never finally decided, in regard to extradition treaties. See *British Prisoners* and other cases cited in § 374, pp. 79, *et seq., ante.*

The general extradition statute relates to all treaties then or thereafter made regardless of time and extent of privileges. No such provisions exist in the tariff laws. The act of 1897 (30 U. S. St. at L., p. 151, see pp. 203–205) provides that certain specified treaty stipulations made as to reciprocal trade relations may, within a specified time, be enforced by proclamation, but no general law exists giving the Executive general power outside of those limitations. The positions maintained by the two Houses of Congress must stand or fall according to such construction of the provisions of the Constitution as to treaty-making, as the Supreme Court shall finally determine. See the cases cited in §§ 365, *et seq.*, of chap. XII, pp. 67, *et seq.*, of Vol. II.

B. Note 1 to § 298, p. 431, *ante.* The treaties made with Mexico in 1883 (U. S. Tr. and Con., ed. 1889, 714), contained reciprocal trade provisions as to duties. They were not to go into effect until Congress passed the necessary legislation. It does not appear that this legislation was ever enacted.

INSULAR CASES APPENDIX.

459

INSULAR CASES APPENDIX.

TABLE OF CONTENTS TO APPENDIX.

461

SUPPLEMENT.

OPINIONS OF DECEMBER 2, 1901.

THE INSULAR CASES.

QUESTIONS INVOLVED.

The *Insular Cases*, so-called because they involved the status of the possessions ceded to the United States by Spain, by the Treaty of 1898 (for this treaty in full see p. 508, *post*, of this APPENDIX), were nine in number and were argued before the Supreme Court of the United States during the October term of 1900. They are briefly discussed in chapter II, §§ 61–61*h*, pages 118, *et seq.*, *ante*. They are also referred to, and cited at other points in both volumes as the decisions have a direct bearing upon, and application to, many of the subdivisions of this book, both in regard to the nationality and sovereignty of the United States and the extent and effect of the treaty-making power.

THE INSULAR CASES RECORDS.

As stated in note 1 to § 61*a*, page 118, *ante*, after the arguments of these cases before the Supreme Court and pursuant to a joint Resolution of Congress (passed by the House of Representatives February 9, 1901, and concurred in by the Senate February 15, 1901), 12,000 copies of the "records, briefs and arguments of counsel," were printed for the use of Congress and the several departments of the Government with the following official title:

"*The Insular Cases*, Comprising the Records, Briefs, and Arguments of Counsel in the *Insular Cases* of the October Term, 1900, in the Supreme Court of the United States, including the appendices thereto. Compiled and Published Pursuant to H. R. Con. Res. No. 72, Fifty-Sixth Congress, Second Session. By Albert H. Howe, Clerk of Printing Records, 1901. Washington, Government Printing Office, 1901."

This combined record consists of 1,075 pages besides an analytical table of contents of 39 pages. The following summaries have been compiled from this volume, to which reference is constantly made.

The nine cases which were argued, the points involved in each, and the time when, and counsel by whom, they were respectively argued, and the citations of the decisions in the official reports of the Supreme Court of the United States, are as follows:

I.

JOHN H. GOETZE DOING BUSINESS UNDER THE FIRM NAME AND STYLE OF JOHN H. GOETZ & CO., APPELLANT, vs. THE UNITED STATES.

Appeal from the Circuit Court of the United States for the Southern District of New York. No. 340. October Term, 1900. Record filed July 9, 1900.

30 465

For John H. Goetze:

COMSTOCK & BROWN (56 Pine St., N. Y.) Attorneys, and EDWARD C. PERKINS (115 Broadway, N. Y.) and EVERIT BROWN (56 Pine St., N. Y.) of counsel, and J. B. HENDERSON, Washington (in the Supreme Court).

For the United States:

Before the General Appraisers, WILLIAM J. GIBSON, New York. In the Circuit Court, HENRY L. BURNETT, United States District Attorney.

In the Supreme Court, JOHN W. GRIGGS, Attorney General of the United States.

The petition was originally filed under the Customs Administrative Act for a refund of duties paid under protest on goods from Porto Rico entered in the Port of New York in April and June, 1899, after the ratification of the treaty of 1898 with Spain and prior to the Foraker Act. The proceedings before the appraisers were entitled, "In the Matter of Protest, Nos. 54053 F and 54168 F of John H. Goetze & Co." The Board of General Appraisers, before whom the proceedings were brought, decided on February 14, 1900, that Porto Rico was a foreign country for tariff purposes. For the decision in full see Exhibit D, pp. 8, et seq. Ins. Cas. Rec. and Treasury Decisions, volume 3, 1900, 22018 G A. 4658. Opinion by H. M. SOMERVILLE, Gen'l Appr., concurred in by GEO. C. TICHENOR and I. F. FISCHER, Gen'l Apprs. Subsequently Goetze & Co. appealed from the decision of the Board of General Appraisers to the Circuit Court of the United States for the Southern District of New York. The case was tried before WILLIAM K. TOWNSEND, District Judge sitting at Circuit, and on June 14, 1900 he filed an opinion affirming the Board of General Appraisers. (For opinion in full see pp. 21, et seq. Ins. Cas. Rec., and 103 Fed. Rep. 72.) Thereafter Goetze & Co. appealed to the Supreme Court of the United States on assignment of error (Ins. Cas. Rec. p. 35). The writ was allowed by E. H. LACOMBE, U. S. Circuit Judge (Ins. Cas. Rec. p. 37).

On October 8, 1900, a motion was made by the appellant to advance the cause upon the docket of the Supreme Court (Ins. Cas. Rec., pp. 41, et seq.) in which the Attorney General joined. The application was granted in this and other cases involving similar questions. These cases were argued simultaneously on December 18 and 19, 1900.

Briefs were filed on behalf of the appellant by EDWARD C. PERKINS, ALBERT COMSTOCK, EVERIT BROWN and JOHN B. HENDERSON of counsel (pp. 45-136, Ins. Cas. Rec., and see analysis and list of cases cited in Table of Contents, Ins. Cas. Rec, pp. i-v.)

A brief was filed in this case and in the case of *Fourteen Diamond Rings* referred to at a later point in this Appendix by JOHN W. GRIGGS, Attorney General, on behalf of the United States (Ins. Cas. Rec. pp. 137-237,) and containing as appendices (on pp. 226-236) the Protocol of August 12, the treaty of 1898 with Spain, extracts from other treaties and the record in *Loughborough* vs. *Blake*, (U. S. Sup. Ct. 1821, 5 Wheaton, 317, MARSHALL, Ch. J.) A brief was also filed with leave of the court on behalf of "Industrial Interests in the States," by E. HAM and ALEX-

ANDER PORTER MORSE, Attorneys, and CHARLES F. MANDERSON of counsel, which sustained the position of the United States (pp. 239-273, Ins. Cas. Rec.). For analysis of these briefs and list of cases cited, see Table of Contents, Ins. Cas. Rec. pp. v–xiv. Subsequently a brief was also filed in support of the position of the Government of the United States by Charles A. Gardiner of New York City (195 Broadway). It was not included in the Insular Cases Record. The argument of the counsel for appellant is included in the briefs already referred to. At the same time argument was heard in the *Fourteen Diamond Rings* case referred to at another point in this Appendix and which involved the status of the Philippine Islands.

The argument of the Attorney General appears in Ins. Cas. Rec. at pp. 275-337, and an analysis and list of authorities cited in the Table of Contents, Ins. Cas. Rec. pp. xiv–xvii.

This case was decided May 27, 1901, in favor of the importers; no opinion was delivered as the court, BROWN, J., held that as the sole question was whether Porto Rico was a foreign country within the meaning of tariff laws, the reasons stated in *De Lima* vs. *Bidwell*, decided the same day applied, (182 U. S. 221; see opinion in full p. 506, *post*, of this Appendix.)

II.

FOURTEEN DIAMOND RINGS, EMIL J. PEPKE, CLAIMANT, *vs.* THE UNITED STATES.

In error to the District Court of the United States for the Northern District of Illinois. No. 419, October, 1900, transcript filed September 17, 1900. Ins. Cas. Rec. 369.

For the claimant, LAWRENCE HARMON and CHARLES H. ALDRICH, Chicago, Ill., Attorneys in both the District and the Supreme Court.

For the United States:
In the District Court, S. H. BETHEA, United States District Attorney for the Northern District of Illinois.
In the Supreme Court, JOHN W. GRIGGS, Attorney General, and JOHN K. RICHARDS, Solicitor General of the United States.

This case involves the right of the United States to collect duties under the Dingley Act on goods brought from the Philippine Islands after the ratification of the treaty of peace; it corresponds with the *De Lima* case in all respects except in so far as there may be any difference between the status of Porto Rico and that of the Philippine Archipelago as possessions or territories of the United States. If there were no difference as to the status of the different territories which were ceded by the treaty of December, 1898, the decision would naturally have followed that of the *De Lima* case; the fact that the court decided the *De Lima* case and did not decide an apparently similar case affecting the Philippines naturally affords a basis for the inference that at least one member of the court considers that there is a difference between the status of the Philippines and that of Porto Rico.

The rings were seized on an information by the United States filed June 11, 1900 (Ins. Cas. Rec. p. 369). The claimant interposed a plea that the goods were non-dutiable having been brought from another part of the United States (Ins. Cas. Rec. 373). The United States demurred and on July 10, 1900, a *pro forma* judgment sustaining the demurrer was entered, C. C. KOHLSAAT, J., Ins. Cas. Rec. p. 376.

A writ of error was allowed. A motion was made before the Supreme Court to advance the cause, which was granted and the case set down with the *Goetze* case for argument in December, 1900, (Ins. Cas. Rec. p. 385). The case was reached and argued December 18 and 19.

Two brief were filed for the plaintiff in error (claimant below) by CHARLES H. ALDRICH and LAWRENCE HARMON, Attorneys. The cause was argued for the claimant, plaintiff in error, by CHARLES H. ALDRICH. Ins. Cas. Rec. pp. 387-491 (including appendix), and for analysis and list of authorities cited, see Table of Contents, Ins. Cas. Rec. pp. xvii–xx.

The briefs and arguments of the United States in this case were the same as those filed in the *Goetze* case. See p. 466, *ante*, of this Appendix.

This case has not yet been decided, November, 30, 1901.

III.

ELIAS S. A. DE LIMA, ELIAS A. DE LIMA AND EDWARD DE LIMA, COM-POSING THE FIRM OF D. A. DE LIMA & CO., PLAINTIFFS IN ERROR, VS. GEORGE R. BIDWELL.

In error to the Circuit Court of the United States for the Southern District of New York. No. 456, October Term, 1900. Transcript filed October 23, 1900. (Ins. Cas. Rec. p. 493.)

For De Lima & Co.
COUDERT BROS., 71 Broadway; New York City, Attorneys. FREDERICK R. COUDERT, JR., CHARLES FREDERICK ADAMS and PAUL FULLER, New York, of counsel.

For George R. Bidwell (collector), etc:
In the Circuit Court HENRY L. BURNETT, United States District Attorney, for the Southern District of New York.
In the Supreme Court JOHN W. GRIGGS, Attorney-General of the United States, and JOHN K. RICHARDS, Solicitor General.

This action was commenced in September, 1899, in the Supreme Court of the state of New York (First Judicial Department) to recover certain duties paid to the defendant, the United States collector of customs at the port of New York, on sugars brought from Porto Rico after the exchange of ratifications of the treaty of 1898 with Spain, and prior to the Foraker Act taking effect. The plaintiff claimed that the duties, which were paid under protest, had been wrongfully exacted by the defendant under color of his office as such collector. (For complaint, see Ins. Cas. Rec. p. 495). The cause was removed by the defendant to the United

States Circuit Court (Ins. Cas. Rec. p. 497), in which court the defendant demurred; on October 16, 1900, the demurrer was sustained (*pro forma*) ALFRED C. COXE, J., and judgment to that effect entered in favor of the defendant (Ins. Cas. Rec. p. 499), following the decision of TOWNSEND, J., in the *Goetze* case referred to on p. 466, *ante*, of this Appendix (103 Fed. Rep. 72). A writ of error was allowed (Ins. Cas. Rec. p. 503). A motion to advance was made before the Supreme Court and granted, (Ins. Cas. Rec. p. 505).

This case was reached on January 8, 1901, and argued simultaneously with other cases, involving similar questions.

A brief was filed for the plaintiffs in error by Messrs. COUDERT, ADAMS and FULLER, and a separate brief in reply by Mr. FULLER (Ins. Cas. Rec. pp. 509-582); FREDERICK R. COUDERT, JR., argued the case for the appellants (Ins. Cas. Rec. pp. 583-608; and for analysis and list of authorities cited in briefs and arguments, see Table of Contents, Ins. Cas. Rec. pp. xx-xxiii.)

Two briefs were filed for the United States by JOHN K. RICHARDS, Solicitor General, which was entitled not only in this case but in *Downes* vs. *Bidwell, Dooley* vs. *United States,* (2 cases), *Armstrong* vs. *United States* and *Crossman* vs. *United States,* all of which were argued together. (Ins. Cas. Rec. pp. 609-662.) A supplemental argument was made by the Attorney General (Ins. Cas. Rec. pp. 663-684). The cases were orally argued by the Solicitor General on July 9, 1901 (Ins. Cas. Rec. pp. 685-720, and for analysis and list of authorities cited, see Table of Contents, Ins. Cas. Rec. pp. xxiii-xxvii).

The Supreme Court reversed, May 27, 1901, (182 U. S. Rep. 1), the judgment of the Circuit Court, holding that the duties were illegally exacted because Porto Rico was not "foreign" country within the meaning of the tariff laws, after the ratification of the treaty, but was territory of the United States.

JUSTICE BROWN'S OPINIONS IN DE LIMA CASE.

The opinion was delivered by Justice BROWN with whom Chief Justice FULLER and Justices HARLAN, BREWER and PECKHAM concurred; a dissenting opinion was delivered by Justice MCKENNA in which Justices SHIRAS and WHITE concurred; Mr. Justice GRAY also delivered a dissenting opinion (see p. 474 of this appendix, *post*).

Justice BROWN in his opinion declared that by the "ratification of the Treaty of Paris, Porto Rico became territory of the United States although not an organized territory in the technical sense of the word;" and that it did not continue in its status of foreign territory so as to permit of collection of duties on merchandise brought therefrom under the existing tariff laws providing for the imposing of duties on goods brought from foreign countries. (30 U. S. Stat. at L., p. 151, Chap. 11, First Session, Fifty-fifth Congress, approved July 24, 1897, known as the Dingley Act.) The first section of this act is as follows:

Be it enacted, etc., "That on and after the passage of this Act, unless otherwise specially provided for in this Act, there shall be levied, collected, and paid upon all articles imported from foreign countries, and mentioned in the schedules herein contained, the rates of duty which are, by the schedules and paragraphs, respectively prescribed."

He refers to *Fleming* vs. *Page* (see § 104, p. 168, *ante*), and *United States* vs. *Rice* (see § 105, p. 171, *ante*), declaring that the former was properly decided, but that the views expressed by Chief Justice TANEY to the effect that territory when acquired by treaty did not become subject to the custom laws of the United States prior to the establishment of a collection district by Congress, were mere *dicta* and not binding upon the conscience of the Court.

The opinion reviews the tariff history of the acquired possessions of Louisiana, Florida, Texas, California and Alaska; reference to the subjects discussed in this opinion will be found under the appropriate sections in regard to the government of territories (see § 101, p. 166, *ante*); when treaties take effect (see § 383, p. 127, Vol. II); legislation and treaties (see § 365, p. 67, Vol. II).

The opinion concludes as follows (182 U. S. pp 194, *et seq.*):

"From this *résumé* of the decisions of this court, the instructions of the executive departments, and the above act of Congress, it is evident that, from 1803, the date of Mr. Gallatin's letter, to the present time, there is not a shred of authority, except the *dictum* in *Fleming* vs. *Page*, (practically overruled in *Cross* vs. *Harrison*,) for holding that a district ceded to and in possession of the United States remains for any purpose a foreign country. Both these conditions must exist to produce a change of nationality for revenue purposes. Possession is not alone sufficient, as was held in *Fleming* vs. *Page;* nor is a treaty ceding such territory sufficient without a surrender of possessions. (*Keene* vs. *McDonough*, 8 Pet. 308; *Pollard's Heirs* vs. *Kibbe*, 14 Pet. 353, 406; *Hallet* vs. *Hunt*, 7 Ala. 882, 899; *The Fama*, 5 Ch. Rob. 97.) The practice of the executive departments thus continued for more than half a century, is entitled to great weight, and should not be disregarded nor overturned except for cogent reasons, and unless it be clear that such construction be erroneous. (*United States* vs. *Johnston*, 124 U. S. 236, and other cases cited.)

"But were this presented as an original question we should be impelled irresistibly to the same conclusion.

"By article II, section 2, of the Constitution, the President is given power, 'by and with the advice and consent of the Senate, to make treaties, provided that two-thirds of the Senators present concur;' and by Art. 6, 'this Constitution and the laws of the United States, which shall be made in pursuance thereof; and all treaties made or which shall be made, under the authority of the United States, shall be the supreme law of the land.' It will be observed that no distinction is made as to the question of supremacy between laws and treaties, except that both are controlled by the Constitution. A law requires the assent of both houses of Congress, and, except in certain specified cases, the signature of the President. A treaty is negotiated and made by the President, with the concurrence of two-thirds of the Senators present, but each of them is the supreme law of the land.

"As was said by Chief Justice Marshall in *The Peggy* (1 Cranch, 103, 110): 'Where a treaty is the law of the land, and as such affects the rights of parties litigating in court, that treaty as much binds those rights, and is as much to be regarded by the court as an act of Congress.' And in *Foster* vs. *Neilson*, (2 Pet. 253, 314,) he repeated this in substance: 'Our Constitution declares a treaty to be the law of the land. It is, consequently, to be regarded in courts of justice as equivalent to an act of the legislature, whenever it operates of itself without the aid of any legislative provision.' So in *Whitney* vs. *Robertson*, (124 U. S. 190): 'By the Constitution a treaty is placed on the same footing, and made of like obligation, with an act of legislation. Both are declared by that instrument to be the supreme law of the land, and no superior efficacy is given to either over the other. When the two relate to the same subject, the courts will always endeavor to construe them so as to give effect to both, if that can be done without violating the language of either; but if the two are inconsistent, the one last in date will control the other, provided always that the stipulation of the treaty on the subject is self-executing.' To the same effect are the *Cherokee Tobacco* (11 Wall. 616,), and the *Head Money Cases*, (112 U. S. 580).

"One of the ordinary incidents of a treaty is the cession of territory. It is not too much to say it is the rule, rather than the exception, that a treaty of peace, following upon a war, provides for a cession of territory to the victorious party. It was said by Chief Justice Marshall in *American Ins. Co.* vs. *Canter* (1 Pet. 511, 542): 'The Constitution confers absolutely upon the Government of the Union the powers of making war and of making treaties; consequently that Government possesses the power of acquiring territory, either by conquest or by treaty.' The territory thus acquired is acquired as absolutely as if the annexation were made, as in the case of Texas and Hawaii, by an act of Congress.

"It follows from this that by the ratification of the treaty of Paris the island became territory of the United States—although not an organized territory in the technical sense of the word.

"It is true Mr. Chief Justice Taney held in *Scott* vs. *Sandford*, (19 How. 393,), that the territorial clause of the Constitution was confined, and intended to be confined, to the territory which at that time belonged to or was claimed by the United States, and was within their boundaries, as settled by the treaty with Great Britain; and was not intended to apply to territory subsequently acquired. He seemed to differ in this construction from Chief Justice Marshall in the *American &c. Ins. Co.* vs. *Canter*, (1 Pet. 511, 542,) who, in speaking of Florida before it became a State, remarked that it continued to be a territory of the United States, governed by the territorial clause of the Constitution.

"But whatever be the source of this power, its uninterrupted exercise by Congress for a century, and the repeated declarations of this court, have settled the law that the right to acquire territory involves the right to govern and dispose of it. That was stated by Chief Justice Taney in the *Dred Scott* case. In the more recent case of *National Bank* vs. *County of Yankton*, (101 U. S. 129,) it was said by Mr. Chief Justice Waite that Congress 'has full and complete legislative authority over the people of the territories and all the departments of the territorial government. It may do for the territories what the people, under the

Constitution of the United States, may do for the States.' Indeed, it is scarcely too much to say that there has not been a session of Congress since the Territory of Louisiana was purchased, that that body has not enacted legislation based upon the assumed authority to govern and control the territories. It is an authority which arises, not necessarily from the territorial clause of the Constitution, but from the necessities of the case, and from the inability of the States to act upon the subject. Under this power Congress may deal with territory acquired by treaty; may administer its government as it does that of the District of Columbia; it may organize a local territorial government; it may admit it as a State upon an equality with other States; it may sell its public lands to individual citizens or may donate them as homesteads to actual settlers. In short, when once acquired by treaty, it belongs to the United States, and is subject to the disposition of Congress.

"Territory thus acquired can remain a foreign country under the tariff laws only upon one of two theories: either that the word 'foreign' applies to such countries as were foreign at the time the statute was enacted, notwithstanding any subsequent change in their condition, or that they remain foreign under the tariff laws until Congress has formally embraced them within the customs union of the States.

"The first theory is obviously untenable. While a statute is presumed to speak from the time of its enactment, it embraces all such persons or things as subsequently fall within its scope, and ceases to apply to such as thereafter fall without its scope. Thus, a statute forbidding the sale of liquors to minors applies not only to minors in existence at the time the statute was enacted, but to all who are subsequently born; and ceases to apply to such as thereafter reach their majority. So, when the Constitution of the United States declares in Art. I, sec. 10, that the States shall not do certain things, this declaration operates not only upon the thirteen original States, but upon all which subsequently become such; and when Congress places certain restrictions upon the powers of a territorial legislature, such restrictions cease to operate the moment such territory is admitted as a State.

"By parity of reasoning a country ceases to be foreign the instant it becomes domestic. So, too, if Congress saw fit to cede one of its newly acquired territories (even assuming that it had the right to do so) to a foreign power, there can be no doubt that from the day of such cession and the delivery of possession, such territory would become a foreign country, and be reinstated as such under the tariff laws. Certainly no act of Congress would be necessary in such case to declare that the laws of the United States had ceased to apply to it.

"The theory that a country remains foreign with respect to the tariff laws until Congress has acted by embracing it within the customs union, presupposes that a country may be domestic for one purpose and foreign for another. It may undoubtedly become necessary for the adequate administration of a domestic territory to pass a special act providing the proper machinery and officers, as the President would have no authority, except under the war power, to administer it himself; but no act is necessary to make it domestic territory if once it has been ceded to the United States. We express no opinion as to whether Congress is bound to appropriate the money to pay for it. This has been much discussed by writers on constitutional law, but it is not necessary to consider it in this case, as Congress made prompt appropriation of the money stipulated in the treaty. This theory also presupposes that territory may be held indefinitely by the United States; that it may be treated in every particular, except for tariff purposes, as domestic territory; that laws may be enacted and enforced by officers of the United States sent there for that purpose; that insurrections may be suppressed, wars carried on, revenues collected, taxes imposed; in short that everything may be done which a government can do within its own boundaries, and yet that the territory may still remain a foreign country. That this state of things may continue for years, for a century even, but that until Congress enacts otherwise, it still remains a foreign country. To hold that this can be done as matter of law we deem to be pure judicial legislation. · We find no warrant for it in the Constitution or in the powers conferred upon this court. It is true the nonaction of Congress may occasion a temporary inconvenience ; but it does not follow that courts of justice are authorized to remedy it by inverting the ordinary meaning of words.

" If an act of Congress be necessary to convert a foreign country into domestic territory, the question at once suggests itself what is the character of the legislation demanded for this purpose ? Will an act appropriating money for its purchase be sufficient? Apparently not. Will an act appropriating the duties collected upon imports to and from such country for the benefit of its government be sufficient? Apparently not. Will acts making appropriations for its postal service, for the establishment of lighthouses, for the maintenance of quarantine stations, for erecting public buildings, have that effect? Will an act establishing a complete local government, but with the reservation of a right to collect duties upon commerce, be adequate for that purpose? None of these, nor altogether, will be sufficient, if the contention of the Government be sound, since acts embracing all these provisions have been passed in connection with Porto Rico, and it is insisted that it is still a foreign country within the meaning of the tariff laws. We are unable to acquiesce in this assumption that a territory may be at the same time both foreign and domestic.

" A single further point remains to be considered: It is insisted that an act of Congress, passed March 24, 1900, (31 Stat. 151,) applying for the benefit of Porto Rico the amount of the customs revenue received on importations by the United States from Porto Rico since the evacuation of Porto Rico by the Spanish forces, October 18, 1898, to January 1, 1900, together with any further customs revenues collected on importations from Porto Rico since January 1, 1900, or that shall hereafter be collected under existing law, is a recognition by Congress of the right to collect such duties as upon importations from a foreign country, and a recognition of the fact that Porto Rico continued to be a foreign country until Congress embraced it within the customs union. It may be seriously questioned whether this is anything more than a recognition of the fact that there were moneys in the Treasury not subject to existing appropriation laws.   Perhaps we may go farther and say that, so far as these duties were paid voluntarily and without protest, the legality of the payment was intended to be recognized; but it can clearly have no retroactive effect as to moneys theretofore paid under protest, for which an action to recover back had already been brought.   As the action in this case was brought March 13, 1900, eleven days before the act was passed, the right to recover the money sued for could not be taken away by a subsequent act of Congress.   Plaintiffs sue in assumpsit for money which the collector has in his hand justly and equitably belonging to them.   To say that Congress could by a subsequent act deprive them of the right to prosecute this action, would be beyond this power. In any event, it should not be interpreted so as to make it retroactive. (*Kennett's Petition*, 24 N. H. 139; *Alter's Appeal*, 67 Penn. St. 341; *Norman* vs. *Heist*, 5 W. & S. 171; *Donavan* vs. *Pitcher*, 53 Ala. 411; *Palairet's Appeal*, 67 Penn. St. 479; *State* vs. *Warren*, 28 Md. 338.)

" We are therefore of opinion that at the time these duties were levied Porto Rico was not a foreign country within the meaning of the tariff laws but a territory of the United States, that the duties were illegally exacted and that the plaintiffs are entitled to recover them back.

" The judgment of the Circuit Court for the Southern District of New York is therefore reversed and the case remanded to that court for further proceedings in consonance with this opinion."

OTHER OPINIONS IN DE LIMA CASE.

Chief Justice FULLER and Justices HARLAN, BREWER and PECKHAM concurred; Mr. Justice McKENNA wrote a dissenting opinion in which Justice SHIRAS and WHITE concurred; Mr. Justice GRAY wrote a separate dissenting opinion which was as follows (182 U. S. p. 220): "I am compelled to dissent from the judgment in this case.   It appears to me irreconcilable with the unanimous opinion of this court in *Fleming* vs. *Page*, 9 How. 603, and with the opinions of the majority of the Justices in the case, this day decided, of *Downes* vs. *Bidwell*."

In his dissenting opinion Mr. Justice McKENNA (182 U. S. pp. 200, *et seq.*) also refers at length to the cases of *Fleming* vs. *Page*, *United States* vs. *Rice*, and *Cross* vs. *Harrison*, and reaches a conclusion that Porto Rico did not become territory of the United States by the mere effect of the treaty and its ratification, and that congressional action was necessary before it could become incorporated as a part of the territory of the United States and thereby cease to be foreign so far as the revenue laws of the United States were concerned.

IV.

SAMUEL B. DOWNES, DOING BUSINESS UNDER THE FIRM NAME OF S. B. DOWNES & CO., PLAINTIFFS IN ERROR, VS. GEORGE R. BIDWELL.

In error to the Circuit Court of the United States for the Southern District of New York.

Transcript of Record filed December 11, 1900, No. 507 (Ins. Cas. Rec. p. 721).

For Downes & Co.:
COUDERT BROS., 71 Broadway, New York City. FREDERICK R. COUDEBT, JR., and PAUL FULLER, for counsel.

For the defendant (collector):
In the Circuit Court HENRY L. BURNETT, United States District Attorney for the Southern District of New York.

In the Supreme Court JOHN W. GRIGGS, Attorney General of the United States, and JOHN K. RICHARDS, Solicitor General.

The action was commenced in the Circuit Court of the United States for the Southern District of New York by the plaintiff against the defendant as collector of the port of New York to recover back duties exacted and paid under protest upon certain oranges consigned to the plaintiff to New York and brought thither from the port of San Juan in the island of Porto Rico during the month of November, 1900, after the passage of the act temporarily providing a civil government and revenues for the Island of Porto Rico, known as the "Foraker act." (31 U. S. Stat. at L. p. 77, approved April 12, 1899.)

The defendant demurred for want of jurisdiction in the court, and for insufficiency of its averments in the complaint, the Circuit Court sustained the demurrer and dismissed the complaint *pro forma;* (Ins. Cas. Rec. 725).

The plaintiff sued out in the Supreme Court of the United States a writ of error. The plaintiff in error made a motion to advance the cause which was granted (Ins. Cas. Rec. p. 731).

Two briefs were filed in the Supreme Court by F. R. COUDERT, JR., and PAUL FULLER. (Ins. Cas. Rec. pp. 733–754, and for analysis and list of authorities cited, see Table of Contents, Ins. Cas. Rec. pp. xxvii, xxviii.) The briefs for the United States filed by the Attorney General and the Solicitor General were the same as those filed in *De Lima* vs. *Bidwell.* (Ins. Cas. Rec. *contra,* p 754, and see p. 469, *ante* of this Appendix.)

The cases were argued January 8 and 9, 1901, simultaneously with the *De Lima* and other cases.

The merchandise on which the duties were paid were not imported until November 20; the case was argued in the Supreme Court of the United States in less than two months after the cause of action arose.

The Supreme Court of the United States affirmed the judgment of the Circuit Court on the ground "that the Island of Porto Rico is a territory appurtenant and belonging to the United States, but not a part of the United States within the revenue clauses of the constitution; that the Foraker act is constitutional, so far as it imposed duties on imports from such island, and that the plaintiff cannot recover back the duties exacted in this case."

There is in this case apparently no *majority opinion* of the court, the docket stating that " Mr. Justice BROWN announced the conclusion and judgment of the court." (182 U. S. Rep. 247.) None of the judges concurred, but Mr. Justice WHITE delivered an opinion concurring in result (182 U. S. Rep. 287), in which Justices SHIRAS and McKENNA joined; Mr. Justice GRAY also concurred with Mr. Justice WHITE with a brief supplementary memorandum as to his views. (182 U. S. Rep. 344.) Although the processes of reasoning by which the result is reached in the respective opinions of Mr. Justice BROWN and Mr. Justice WHITE are in many respects diametrically opposed to each other, as the same conclusion was reached by five justices the judgment became that of the Court.

Chief Justice FULLER delivered a dissenting opinion in which Justices HARLAN, BREWER and PECKHAM concurred. (182 U. S. Rep. 347.) Mr. Justice HARLAN also delivered a separate dissenting opinion. (182 U. S. Rep. 375.)

OPINION BROWN, J., IN DOWNES VS. BIDWELL.

In all the opinions the history of the congressional government of the territories is discussed and numerous cases are cited. Mr. Justice BROWN holds, as in the *De Lima* case, that Porto Rico became territory of the United States on the ratification of the treaty; he also holds that Congress has plenary power to govern all the territories, and in doing so is not bound by the limitations affecting congressional action in regard to States, so far as the uniformity of duties and imports is concerned.

In regard to congressional government of the territories, after citing numerous cases, he says (182 U. S. Rep. 270), "Eliminating, then, from the opinions of this court all expressions unnecessary to the disposition of the particular case, and gleaning therefrom the exact point decided in each, the following propositions may be considered as established:

"1. That the District of Columbia and the territories are not States, within the judicial clause of the Constitution giving jurisdiction in cases between citizens of different States;

"2. That territories are not States, within the meaning of Revised Statutes, sec. 709, permitting writs of error from this court in cases where the validity of a *State* statute is drawn in question;

"3. That the District of Columbia and the territories are States, as that word is used in treaties with foreign powers, with respect to the ownership, disposition and inheritance of property;

"4. That the territories are not within the clause of the Constitution providing for the creation of a Supreme Court and such inferior courts as Congress may see fit to establish;

"5. That the Constitution does not apply to foreign countries or to trials therein conducted, and that Congress may lawfully provide for such trials before consular tribunals, without the intervention of a grand or petit jury;

"6. That where the Constitution has been once formally extended by Congress to territories, neither Congress nor the territorial legislature can enact laws inconsistent therewith."

The opinion then refers to the *Dred Scott* case (19 Howard, 393), stating that it is not of great authority and that much of the opinion, which otherwise might be applicable to this case, was *obita dicta*. Further commenting upon it he says: " It must be admitted that this case is a strong authority in favor of the plaintiff, and if the opinion of the chief justice be taken at its full value it is decisive in his favor. We are not, however, bound to overlook the fact that, before the chief justice gave utterance to his opinion upon the merits, he had already disposed of the case adversely to the plaintiff upon the question of jurisdiction, and that, in view of the excited political condition of the country at the time, it is unfortunate that he felt compelled to discuss the question upon the merits, particularly so in view of the fact that it involved a ruling that an act of Congress, which had been acquiesced in for thirty years, was declared unconstitutional. It would appear from the opinion of Mr. Justice Wayne that the real reason for discussing these constitutional questions was that ' there had become such a difference of opinion' about them 'that the peace and harmony of the country required the settlement of them by judicial decision.' (p. 455.) The attempt was not successful. It is sufficient to say that the country did not acquiesce in the opinion, and that the civil war, which shortly thereafter followed, produced such changes in judicial, as well as public, sentiment, as to seriously impair the authority of this case."

In regard to the right to govern territory the opinion cites §§ 905 and 906 of the Revised Statutes of the United States, and § 6 of the Constitution; declares that uniformity as decided in *Knowlton* vs. *Moore*, in 178 U. S. 41, means geographical uniformity, and that the words "throughout the United States " are considered indistinguishable from the words "among or between the several states" and that the prohibitions of the Constitution " were intended to apply only to commerce between ports of the several states as then existed or should thereafter be admitted to the Union." The opinion concluded as follows (182 U. S. pp. 279, *et seq.*) :

" We are also of opinion that the power to acquire territory by treaty implies not only the power to govern such territory, but to prescribe upon what terms the United States will receive its inhabitants, and what their *status* shall be in what Chief Justice Marshall termed the 'American Empire.' There seems to be no middle ground between this position and the doctrine that if their inhabitants do not become, immediately upon annexation, citizens of the United States, their children thereafter born, whether savages or civilized, are such, and entitled to all the rights, privileges and immunities of citizens. If such be their *status*, the consequences will be extremely serious. Indeed, it is doubtful if Congress would ever assent to the annexation of territory upon the condition that its inhabitants, however foreign they may be to our habits, traditions and modes of life, shall become at once citizens of the United States. In all its treaties hitherto the treaty-making power has made special provision for this subject; in the cases of Louisiana and Florida, by stipulating that ' the inhabitants shall be incorporated into the Union of the United States and admitted as soon as possible . . . to the enjoyment of all rights, advantages and immunities of citizens of the United States;' in the case of Mexico, that they should 'be incorporated into the Union, and be admitted at the proper time, (to be judged of by the Congress of the United States,) to the enjoyment of all the rights of the citizens of the United States;' in the case of Alaska, that the inhabitants who remain three years, 'with the exception of uncivilized native tribes, shall be admitted to the enjoyment of all the rights,' etc.; and in the case of Porto Rico and the Philippines, 'that the civil rights and political *status* of the native inhabitants . . . shall be determined by Congress.' In all these cases there is an implied denial of the right of the inhabitants to American citizenship until Congress by further action shall signify its assent thereto. Grave apprehensions of danger are felt by many eminent men—a fear lest an unrestrained possession of power on the part of Congress may lead to unjust and oppressive legislation, in which the natural rights of territories, or their inhabitants, may be engulfed in a centralized despotism. These fears, however, find no justification in the action of Congress in the past century, nor in the conduct of the British Parliament toward its outlying possessions since the American revolution. Indeed, in the only instance in which this court has declared an act of Congress unconstitutional as trespassing upon the rights of territories, (the Missouri Compromise), such action was dictated by motives of humanity and justice, and so far commanded popular approval as to be embodied in the Thirteenth Amendment to the Constitution. There are certain principles of natural justice inherent in the Anglo-Saxon character which need no expression in constitutions or statutes to give them effect or to secure dependencies against legislation manifestly hostile to their real interests. Even in the Foraker act itself, the constitutionality of which is so vigorously assailed, power was given to the legislative assembly of Porto Rico to repeal the very tariff in question in this case, a power it has not seen fit to exercise. The words of Chief Justice Marshall in *Gibbons* vs. *Odgen*, (9 Wheat. 1,) with respect to the power of Congress to regulate commerce, are pertinent in this connection: 'This power,' said he, 'like all others vested in Congress, is complete in itself, and may be exercised to its utmost extent, and acknowledges no limitations other than are prescribed in the Constitution. . . . The wisdom and discretion of Congress, their identity with the people, and the influence which their constituents possess at elections are in this, as in many other instances, as that, for example, of declaring war, the sole restraints on which they have relied to secure them from its abuse. They are the restraints on which the people most often rely on solely in all representative governments.'" Citing *Johnson* vs. *McIntosh*, 8 Wheat. 543, 589, and *Knowlton* vs. *Moore*, 178 U. S. 41, 109, with quotations therefrom at length.

" It is obvious that in the annexation of outlying and distant possessions grave questions will arise from differences of race, habits, laws and customs of the people, and from differences of soil, climate and production, which may require action on the part of Congress that will be quite unnecessary in the annexation of contiguous territory inhabited only by people of the same race, or by scattered bodies of native Indians.

"We suggest, without intending to decide, that there may be a distinction between certain natural rights, enforced in the Constitution by prohibitions against interference with them. and what may be termed artificial or remedial rights, which are peculiar to our own system of jurisprudence. Of the former class are the rights to one's own religious opinion and to a public expression of them, or, as sometimes said, to worship God according to the dictates of one's own conscience; the right to personal liberty and individual property; to freedom of speech and of the press; to free access to courts of justice, due process of law and to an equal protection of the laws; to immunities from unreasonable searches and seizures, as well as cruel and unusual punishments; and to such other immunities as are indispensable to a free government. Of the latter class, are the rights to citizenship, to suffrage (*Minor* vs. *Happersett*, 21 Wall. 162,) and to the particular methods of procedure pointed out in the Constitution, which are peculiar to Anglo-Saxon jurisprudence, and some of which have already been held by the States to be unnecessary to the proper protection of individuals.

"Whatever may be finally decided by the American people as to the *status* of these islands and their inhabitants—whether they shall be introduced into the sisterhood of States or be permitted to form independent governments—it does not follow that, in the meantime, awaiting that decision, the people are in the matter of personal rights unprotected by the provisions of our Constitution, and subject to the merely arbitrary control of Congress. Even if regarded as aliens, they are entitled under the principles of the Constitution to be protected in life, liberty and property. This has been frequently held by this Court in respect to the Chinese, even when aliens, not possessed of the political rights of citizens of the United States. (*Yick Wo* vs. *Hopkins*, 118 U. S. 356; *Fong Yue Ting* vs. *United States*, 149 U. S. 698; *Lem Moon Sing* vs. *United States*, 158 U. S. 538, 547; *Wong Wing* vs. *United States*, 163 U. S. 228.) We do not desire, however, to anticipate the difficulties which would naturally arise in this connection, but merely to disclaim any intention to hold that the inhabitants of these territories are subject to an unrestrained power on the part of Congress to deal with them upon the theory that they have no rights which it is bound to respect.

"Large powers must necessarily be intrusted to Congress in dealing with these problems, and we are bound to assume that they will be judicially exercised. That these powers may be abused is possible. But the same may be said of its powers under the Constitution as well as outside of it. Human wisdom has never devised a form of government so perfect that it may not be perverted to bad purposes. It is never conclusive to argue against the possession of certain powers from possible abuse of them. It is safe to say that if Congress should venture upon legislation manifestly dictated by selfish interests, it would receive quick rebuke at the hands of the people. Indeed, it is scarcely possible that Congress could do a greater injustice to these islands than would be involved in holding that it could not impose upon the States taxes and excises without extending the same taxes to them. Such requirement would bring them at once within our internal revenue system, including stamps, licenses, excises and all the paraphernalia of that system, and applying it to territories which have had no experience of this kind, and where it would prove an intolerable burden.

"This subject was carefully considered by the Senate committee in charge of the Foraker bill, which found, after an examination of the facts, that property in Porto Rico was already burdened with a private debt amounting probably to $30,000,000; that no system of property taxation was or ever had been in force in the island, and that it probably would require two years to inaugurate one and secure returns from it; that the revenues had always been chiefly raised by duties on imports and exports, and that our internal revenue laws, if applied in that island, would prove oppressive and ruinous to many people and interests; that to undertake to collect our heavy internal revenue tax, far heavier than Spain ever imposed upon their products and vocations, would be to invite violations of the law so innumerable as to make prosecutions impossible, and to almost certainly alienate and destroy the friendship and good will of that people for the United States.

"In passing upon the questions involved in this and kindred cases, we ought not to overlook the fact that, while the Constitution was intended to establish a permanent form of government for the States which should elect to take advantage of its conditions, and continue for an indefinite future, the vast possibilities of that future could never have entered the mind of its framers. The States had but recently emerged from a war with one of the most powerful nations of Europe; were disheartened by the failure of the confederacy, and were doubtful as to the feasibility of a stronger union. Their territory was confined to a narrow strip of land on the Atlantic coast from Canada to Florida, with a somewhat indefinite claim to territory beyond the Alleghenies, where their sovereignty was disputed by tribes of hostile Indians supported, as was popularly believed, by the British, who had never formally delivered possession under the treaty of peace. The vast territory beyond the Mississippi, which formerly had been claimed by France, since 1762 had belonged to Spain, still a powerful nation, and the owner of a great part of the Western Hemisphere. Under these circumstances it is little wonder that the question of annexing these territories was not made a subject of debate. The difficulties of bringing about a union of States were so great, the objections to it seemed so formidable, that the whole thought of the convention centered upon surmounting these obstacles. The question of territories was dismissed with a single clause, apparently applicable only to the territories then existing, giving Congress the power to govern and dispose of them.

"Had the acquisition of other territories been contemplated as a possibility, could it have been foreseen that, within little more than one hundred years, we were destined to acquire not only the whole of the vast region between the Atlantic and Pacific Oceans, but the Russian possessions in America and distant islands in the Pacific, it is incredible that no provision should have been made for them, and the question of whether the Constitution should or should not extend to them had been definitely settled. If it be once conceded that we are at liberty to acquire foreign territory, a presumption arises that our power with respect to such territories is the same power which other nations have been accustomed to exercise with respect to territories acquired by them. If, in limiting the power which Congress was to exercise within the United States, it was also intended to limit it with regard to such territories as the people of the United States should thereafter acquire, such limitations should have been expressed. Instead of that, we find the Constitution speaking only to States, except in the territorial clause, which is absolute in its terms, and suggestive of no limitations upon the power of Congress in dealing with them. The States could only delegate to Congress such powers as they themselves possessed, and as they had no power to acquire new territory they had none to delegate in that connection. The logical inference from this is, that if Congress had power to acquire new territory, which is conceded, that power was not hampered by the constitutional provisions. If, upon the other hand, we assume that the territorial clause of the Constitution was not intended to be restricted to such territory as the United States then possessed, there is nothing in the Constitution to indicate that the power of Congress in dealing with them was intended to be restricted by any of the other provisions.

"There is a provision that ' new States may be admitted by the Congress into this Union.' These words, of course, carry the Constitution with them, but nothing is said regarding the acquisition of new territories or the extension of the Constitution over them. The liberality of Congress in legislating the Constitution into all our contiguous territories has undoubtedly fostered the impression that it went there by its own force, but there is nothing in the Constitution itself, and little in the interpretation put upon it, to confirm that impression. There is not even an analogy to the provisions of an ordinary mortgage for its attachment to after-acquired property, without which it covers only property existing at the date of the mortgage. In short, there is absolute silence upon the subject. The executive and legislative departments of the government have for more than a century interpreted this silence as precluding the idea that the Constitution attached to these territories as soon as acquired, and unless such interpretation be manifestly contrary to the letter or spirit of the Constitution, it should be followed by the judicial department. (Cooley's Const. Lim., secs. 81 to 85; *Lithographic Co.* vs. *Sarony*, 111 U. S. 53, 57; *Field* vs. *Clark*, 143, U. S. 649, 691.)

"Patriotic and intelligent men may differ widely as to the desirableness of this or that acquisition, but this is solely a political question. We can only consider this aspect of the case so far as to say that no construction of the Constitution should be adopted which would prevent Congress from considering each case upon its merits, unless the language of the instrument imperatively demand it. A false step at this time might be fatal to the development of what Chief Justice Marshall called the American Empire. Choice in some cases, the natural gravitation of small bodies towards large ones in others, the result of a successful war

31

in still others, may bring about conditions which would render the annexation of distant possessions desirable.   If those possessions are inhabited by alien races, differing from us in religion, customs, laws, methods of taxation and modes of thought, the administration of government and justice, according to Anglo-Saxon principles, may for a time be impossible; and the question at once arises whether large concessions ought not to be made for a time, that, ultimately, our own theories may be carried out, and the blessings of a free government under the Constitution extended to them.   We decline to hold that there is anything in the Constitution to forbid such action.

"We are therefore of opinion that the Island of Porto Rico is a territory appurtenant and belonging to the United States, but not a part of the United States within the revenue clauses of the Constitution; that the Foraker act is constitutional, so far as it imposes duties on imports from such island, and that the plaintiff cannot recover back the duties exacted in this case."   The judgment of the Circuit Court was affirmed.

OPINION WHITE, J., IN DOWNES VS. BIDWELL.

Mr. Justice BROWN announced the conclusion and judgment of the Court; Mr. Justice WHITE, however, delivered an opinion uniting in the judgment and the conclusion, but differing as to the process of reasoning by which the conclusion was reached.   Justices SHIRAS and McKENNA concurred in the whole opinion while Mr. Justice GRAY practically concurred although he added a few words in a separate opinion.   (See p. 488, *post*, of this appendix.)

Mr. Justice WHITE's opinion, (182 U. S. pp. 287–344) which is the longest of all the opinions delivered on May 27th, is a lengthy review of historical and legal precedents regarding the application of the treaty-making power to the acquisition of territory and the subsequent government of the territory acquired.   Inasmuch as four members of the court united in this opinion, and as some of the members uniting in the other opinions coincide to some extent with Mr. Justice WHITE, this opinion in so far as it relates to the treaty-making power is of equal if not greater weight than any other opinion rendered in the Insular Cases. The view is taken that the treaty-making power cannot incorporate territory into the domain of the United States without subsequent congressional action, but that it has the power to purchase territory, and that the ultimate disposition of it rests with Congress.

There is an exhaustive *résumé* of the instances in which the treaty-making power has been exercised and of the subsequent government of territory obtained in this opinion.

At the outset (182 U. S. p. 288) he states eight propositions of law as to the application of constitutional provisions to territory of the United States, from which he deduces the following (182 U. S. p. 293):

"From these conceded propositions it follows that Congress in legislating for Porto Rico was only empowered to act within the Constitution and subject to its applicable limitations, and that every provision of the Constitution which applied to a country situated as was that island, was potential in Porto Rico.

"And the determination of what particular provision of the Constitution is applicable, generally speaking, in all cases, involves an inquiry into the situation of the territory and its relations to the United States."

After discussing the relations of Porto Rico to the United States and whether the uniformity provisions of the Constitution are applicable thereto, he says (182 U. S. p. 299): "This is to be resolved by answering the inquiry, Had Porto Rico, at the time of the passage of the act in question, been incorporated into and become an integral part of the United States?"

Mr. Justice WHITE then devotes a large part of his opinion to the general rules of international law, and to the right of the United States to acquire territory, and from that point takes up the question of whether the provisions of the Constitution apply to the new territory as soon as it is acquired, in which respect he declares it would be but to "admit the power to acquire and immediately to deny its beneficial existence"; he refers to a number of instances in which the United States has acquired territory for particular purposes, such as the Guano Islands, and cites numerous cases relating thereto. At p. 307, he says:

"And these considerations concerning discovery are equally applicable to ownership resulting from conquest. A just war is declared and in its prosecution the territory of the enemy is invaded and occupied. Would not the war, even if waged successfully, be fraught with danger if the effect of occupation was to necessarily incorporate an alien and hostile people into the United States? Take another illustration. Suppose at the termination of a war the hostile government had been overthrown and the entire territory or a portion thereof was occupied by the United States, and there was no government to treat with or none willing to cede by treaty, and thus it became necessary for the United States to hold the conquered country for an indefinite period, or at least until such time as Congress deemed that it should be either released or retained because it was apt for incorporation into the United States. If holding was to have the effect which is now claimed for it, would not the exercise of judgment respecting the retention be so fraught with danger to the American people that it could not be safely exercised?

"Yet, again. Suppose the United States, in consequence of outrages perpetrated upon its citizens, was obliged to move its armies or send its fleets to obtain redress, and it came to pass that an expensive war resulted and culminated in the occupation of a portion of the territory of the enemy, and that the retention of such territory—an event illustrated by examples in history—could alone enable the United States to recover the pecuniary loss it had suffered. And suppose further that to do so would require occupation for an indefinite period, dependent upon whether or not payment was made of the required indemnity. It being true that incorporation must necessarily follow the retention of the territory, it would result that the United States must abandon all hope of recouping itself for the loss suffered by the unjust war, and, hence, the whole burden would be entailed upon the people of the United States. This would be a necessary consequence, because if the

United States did not hold the territory as security for the needed indemnity it could not collect such indemnity, and on the other hand if incorporation must follow from holding the territory the uniformity provision of the Constitution would prevent the assessment of the cost of the war solely upon the newly acquired country. In this, as in the case of discovery, the traditions and practices of the government demonstrate the unsoundness of the contention. Congress, on May 13, 1846, declared that war existed with Mexico. In the summer of that year New Mexico and California were subdued by the American arms and the military occupation which followed continued until after the treaty of peace was ratified, in May, 1848. Tampico, a Mexican port, was occupied by our forces on November 15, 1846, and possession was not surrendered until after the ratification. In the spring of 1847 President Polk, through the Secretary of the Treasury, prepared a tariff of duties on imports and tonnage which was put in force in the conquered country. (1 Senate Documents, First Session, 30th Congress, pp. 562, 569.) By this tariff, *duties were laid as well on merchandise exported from the United States* as from other countries, except as to supplies for our army, and ou May 10, 1847, an exemption from tonnage duties was accorded to ' all vessels chartered by the United States to convey supplies of any and all descriptions to our army and navy, and actually laden with supplies.' (Ib. 583.) An interesting debate respecting the constitutionality of this action of the President is contained in 18 Cong. Globe, First Session, 30th Congress, at pp. 478, 479, 484-489, 495, 498, etc."

After reviewing *Fleming* vs. *Page*, (9 Howard, 603,) and *Cross* vs. *Harrison*, (16 Howard, 164), he continues (182 U. S. p. 310):

"This further argument, however, is advanced. Granting that Congress may regulate without incorporating, where the military arm has taken possession of foreign territory, and where there has been or can be no treaty, this does not concern the decision of this case, since there is here involved no regulation but an actual cession to the United States of territory by treaty. The general rule of the law of nations, by which the acquiring government fixes the *status* of acquired territory, it is urged, does not apply to the government of the United States, because it is incompatible with the Constitution that that government should hold territory under a cession and administer it as a dependency without its becoming incorporated. This claim, I have previously said, rests on the erroneous assumption that the United States under the Constitution is stripped of those powers which are absolutely inherent in and essential to national existence. The certainty of this is illustrated by the examples already made use of in the supposed cases of discovery and conquest.

"If the authority by treaty is limited as suggested, then it will be impossible to terminate a successful war by acquiring territory through a treaty, without immediately incorporating such territory into the United States. Let me, however, eliminate the case of war and consider the treaty-making power as subserving the purposes of the peaceful evolution of national life. Suppose the necessity of acquiring a naval station or a coaling station on an island inhabited with people utterly unfit for American citizenship and totally incapable of bearing their proportionate burden of the national expense. Could such island, under the rule which is now insisted upon, be taken? Suppose again the acquisition of territory for an interoceanic canal, where an inhabited strip of land on either side is essential to the United States for the preservation of the work. Can it be denied that, if the requirements of the Constitution as to taxation are to immediately control, it might be impossible by treaty to accomplish the desired result?"

In speaking of the extent of the treaty-making power Justice WHITE says (182 U. S. p. 312):

"Let me come, however, to a consideration of the express powers which are conferred by the Constitution to show how unwarranted is the principle of immediate incorporation, which is here so strenuously insisted on. In doing so it is conceded at once that the true rule of construction is not to consider one provision of the Constitution alone, but to contemplate all, and therefore to limit one conceded attribute by those qualifications which naturally result from the other powers granted by that instrument, so that the whole may be interpreted by the spirit which vivifies, and not by the letter which killeth. Undoubtedly, the power to carry on war and to make treaties implies also the exercise of those incidents which ordinarily inhere in them. Indeed, in view of the rule of construction which I have just conceded—that all powers conferred by the Constitution must be interpreted with reference to the nature of the government and be construed in harmony with related provisions of the Constitution—it seems to me impossible to conceive that the treaty-making power by a mere cession can incorporate an alien people into the United States without the express or implied approval of Congress. And from this it must follow that there can be no foundation for the assertion that where the treaty-making power has inserted conditions which preclude incorporation until Congress has acted in respect thereto, such conditions are void and incorporation results in spite thereof. If the treaty-making power can absolutely, without the consent of Congress, incorporate territory, and if that power may not insert conditions against incorporation, it must follow that the treaty-making power is endowed by the Constitution with the most unlimited right, susceptible of destroying every other provision of the Constitution; that is, it may wreck our institutions. If the proposition be true, then millions of inhabitants of alien territory, if acquired by treaty, can, without the desire or consent of the people of the United States speaking through Congress, be immediately and irrevocably incorporated into the United States, and the whole structure of the government be overthrown. While thus aggrandizing the treaty-making power on the one hand, the construction at the same time minimizes it on the other, in that it strips that authority of any right to acquire territory upon any condition which would guard the people of the United States from the evil of immediate incorporation. The treaty-making power then, under this contention, instead of having the symmetrical functions which belong to it from its very nature, becomes distorted—vested with the right to destroy **upon the one hand and deprived of all power to protect the government on the other. . . ."**

The opinion then takes up the question of the right of this Government to sell, and the extent of the treaty-making power to acquire, territory, and in doing so demonstrates that the treaty-making power must be sufficient to acquire territory conditionally without incorporating it at once as a part of the Union.   He says (182 U. S. p. 315):

"The reasoning which has sometimes been indulged in by those who asserted that the Constitution was not at all operative in the territories is that, as they were acquired by purchase, the right to buy included the right to sell.   This has been met by the proposition that if the country purchased and its inhabitants became incorporated into the United States, it came under the shelter of the Constitution, and no power existed to sell American citizens.   In conformity to the principles which I have admitted it is impossible for me to say at one and the same time that territory is an integral part of the United States protected by the Constitution, and yet the safeguards, privileges, rights and immunities which arise from this situation are so ephemeral in their character that by a mere act of sale they may be destroyed.   And applying this reasoning to the provisions of the treaty under consideration, to me it seems indubitable that if the treaty with Spain incorporated all the territory ceded into the United States, it resulted that the millions of people to whom that treaty related were, without the consent of the American people as expressed by Congress, and without any hope of relief, indissolubly made a part of our common country.

"Undoubtedly, the thought that under the Constitution power existed to dispose of people and territory and thus to annihilate the rights of American citizens was contrary to the conceptions of the Constitution entertained by Washington and Jefferson.   In the written suggestions of Mr. Jefferson, when Secretary of State, reported to President Washington in March, 1792, on the subject of proposed negotiations between the United States and Spain, which were intended to be communicated by way of instruction to the commissioners of the United States appointed to manage such negotiations, it was observed, in discussing the possibility as to compensation being demanded by Spain 'for the ascertainment of our right' to navigate the lower part of the Mississippi, as follows:

"'We have nothing else' (than a relinquishment of certain claims on Spain) 'to give in exchange.   For as to territory, we have neither the right nor the disposition to alienate an inch of what belongs to any member of our Union.   Such a proposition therefore is totally inadmissible, and not to be treated for a moment.' (Ford's Writings of Jefferson, vol. V, p. 476.)

"The rough draft of these observations were submitted to Mr. Hamilton, then Secretary of the Treasury, for suggestions, previously to sending it to the President, some time before March 5, and Hamilton made the following (among other) notes upon it:

"'Page 25.   Is it true that the United States have no right to *alienate an inch* of the territory in question, except in the case of necessity intimated in another place? Or will it be useful to avow the denial of such a right? It is apprehended that the doctrine which restricts the alienation of territory to cases of *extreme necessity* is applicable rather to *peopled* territory than to waste and uninhabited districts. Positions restraining the right of the United States to accommodate to exigencies which may arise ought ever to be advanced with great caution,' (Ford's Writings of Jefferson, vol. V, p. 443.)

"Respecting this note, Mr. Jefferson commented as follows: 'The power to alienate the *unpeopled* territories of any State is not among the enumerated powers, given by the Constitution to the general government, and if we may go out of that instrument and *accommodate to exigencies which may arise* by alienating the *unpeopled* territory of a State, we may accommodate ourselves a little more by alienating that which is *peopled*, and still a little more by selling the *people* themselves. A shade or two more in the degree of exigency is all that will be requisite, and of that degree we shall ourselves be the judges. However, may it not be hoped that these questions are forever laid to rest by the Twelfth Amendment once made a part of the Constitution, declaring expressly that 'the powers not delegated to the United States by the Constitution are reserved to the States respectively?' And if the general government has no power to alienate the territory of a State, it is too irresistible an argument to deny ourselves the use of it on the present occasion." (Ib.)

"The opinions of Mr. Jefferson, however, met the approval of President Washington. On March 18, 1792, in inclosing to the commissioners to Spain their commission, he said, among other things:

"'You will herewith receive your commission; as also observations on these several subjects reported to the President and approved by him, which will therefore serve as instructions for you. These expressing minutely the sense of our government, and what they wish to have done, it is unnecessary for me to do more here than desire you to pursue these objects unremittingly,' &c. (Ford's Writings of Jefferson, vol. V, p. 456.)

"When the subject matter to which the negotiation related is considered it becomes evident that the word 'State' as above used related merely to territory which was either claimed by some of the States, as Mississippi Territory was by Georgia, or to the Northwest Territory embraced within the ordinance of 1787, or to the territory south of the Ohio (Tennessee), which had also been endowed with all the rights and privileges conferred by that ordinance, and all which territory had originally been ceded by States to the United States under express stipulations that such ceded territory should be ultimately formed into States of the Union. And this meaning of the word 'State' is absolutely in accord with what I shall hereafter have occasion to demonstrate was the conception entertained by Mr. Jefferson of what constituted the United States.

"True, from the exigency of a calamitous war or the necessity of a settlement of boundaries, it may be that citizens of the United States may be expatriated by the action of the treaty-making power, impliedly or expressly ratified by Congress.

"But the arising of these particular conditions cannot justify the general proposition that territory which is an integral part of the United States may, as a mere act of sale, be disposed of. If however the right to dispose of an incorporated American territory and citizens by the mere exertion of the power to sell be conceded, *arguendo*, it would not relieve the dilemma. It is ever true that where a malign principle is adopted, as long as the error is adhered to it must continue to produce its baleful results. Certainly, if there be no power to acquire subject to a condition, it must follow that there is no authority to dispose of subject to conditions, since it cannot be that the mere change of form of the transaction could bestow a power which the Constitution has not conferred. It would follow then that any conditions annexed to a disposition which looked to the protection of the people of the United States or to enable them to safeguard the disposal of territory would be void; and thus it would be that either the United States must hold on absolutely or must dispose of unconditionally.

" A practical illustration will at once make the consequences clear. Suppose Congress should determine that the millions of inhabitants of the Philippine Islands should not continue appurtenant to the United States, but that they should be allowed to establish an autonomous government, outside of the Constitution of the United States, coupled, however, with such conditions providing for control as far only as essential to the guarantee of life and property and to protect against foreign encroachment. If the proposition of incorporation be well founded, at once the question would arise whether the ability to impose these conditions existed, since no power was conferred by the Constitution to annex conditions which would limit the disposition. And if it be that the question of whether territory is immediately fit for incorporation when it is acquired is a judicial and not a legislative one, it would follow that the validity of the conditions would also come within the scope of judicial authority, and thus the entire political policy of the government be alone controlled by the judiciary.

" The theory as to the treaty-making power upon which the argument which has just been commented upon rests, it is now proposed to be shown, is refuted by the history of the government from the beginning. There has not been a single cession made from the time of the Confederation up to the present day, excluding the recent treaty with Spain, which has not contained stipulations to the effect that the United States through Congress would either not disincorporate or would incorporate the ceded territory into the United States. There were such conditions in the deed of cession by Virginia when it conveyed the Northwest Territory to the United States. Like conditions were attached by North Carolina to the cession whereby the territory south of the Ohio, now Tennessee, was transferred. Similar provisions were contained in the cession by Georgia of the Mississippi territory, now the States of Alabama and Mississippi. Such agreements were also expressed in the treaty of 1803, ceding Louisiana; that of 1819, ceding the Floridas, and in the treaties of 1848 and 1853, by which a large extent of territory was ceded to this country, as also in the Alaska treaty of 1867. To adopt the limitations on the treaty-making power now insisted upon would presuppose that every one of these conditions thus sedulously provided for were superfluous, since the guaranties which they afforded would have obtained, although they were not expressly provided for.

"When the various treaties by which foreign territory has been acquired are considered in the light of the circumstances which surrounded them, it becomes to my mind clearly established that the treaty-making power was always deemed to be devoid of authority to incorporate territory into the United States without the assent, express or implied, of Congress, and that no question to the contrary has ever been even mooted."

The *Dred Scott* case, (19 How. 438,) is discussed at some length, and the history of territorial government and of acquisitions by the United States, with extracts from the treaties with France ceding Louisiana, with Spain ceding Florida, are referred to, as well as the debates in the Senate and the correspondence relating to the acquisition of Louisiana. The Mexican and Alaskan cessions are also discussed at some length with the effect thereof on citizenship of the inhabitants.

The articles in the Spanish treaty relating to citizenship and status of the ceded territory are then quoted, and the effect of those stipulations discussed, in regard to which the opinion says (182 U. S. p. 340):

"It is to me obvious that the above quoted provisions of the treaty do not stipulate for incorporation, but on the contrary expressly provide that the ' civil rights and political *status* of the native inhabitants of the territories hereby ceded,' shall be determined by Congress. When the rights to which this careful provision refers are put in juxtaposition with those which have been deemed essential from the foundation of the government to bring about incorporation, all of which have been previously referred to, I cannot doubt that the express purpose of the treaty was not only to leave the *status* of the territory to be determined by Congress but to prevent the treaty from operating to the contrary. Of course, it is evident that the express or implied acquiescence by Congress in a treaty so framed cannot import that a result was brought about which the treaty itself—giving effect to its provisions—could not produce. And, in addition, the provisions of the act by which the duty here in question was imposed, taken as a whole, seem to me plainly to manifest the intention of Congress that for the present at least Porto Rico is not to be incorporated into the United States."

OPINION OF GRAY, J., IN DOWNES VS. BIDWELL.

The whole opinion is as follows (182 U. S. pp. 344–347):

"Concurring in the judgment of affirmance in this case, and in substance agreeing with the opinion of Mr. Justice WHITE, I will sum up the reasons for my concurrence in a few propositions, which may also indicate my position in other cases now standing for judgment.

"The cases now before the court do not touch the authority of the United States over the Territories, in the strict and technical sense, being those which lie within the United States, as bounded by the Atlantic and Pacific Oceans, the Dominion of Canada and the Republic of Mexico, and the Territories of Alaska and Hawaii; but they relate to territory, in the broader sense, acquired by the United States by war with a foreign State.

"As Chief Justice MARSHALL said: 'The Constitution confers absolutely on the Government of the Union the powers of making war, and of making treaties; consequently, that government possesses the power of acquiring territory, either by conquest or by treaty. The usage of the world is, if a nation be not entirely subdued, to consider the holding of conquered territory as a mere military occupation, until its fate shall be determined at the treaty of peace. If it be ceded by the treaty, the acquisition is confirmed, and the ceded territory becomes a part of the nation to which it is annexed; either on the terms stipulated in the treaty of cession, or on such as its new master shall impose.' *American Insurance Co.* vs. *Canter*, (1828) 1 Pet. 511, 542.

"The civil government of the United States cannot extend immediately, and of its own force, over territory acquired by war. Such territory must necessarily, in the first instance, be governed by the military power under the control of the President as commander in chief. Civil government cannot take effect at once, as soon as possession is acquired under military authority, or even as soon as that possession is confirmed by treaty. It can only be put in operation by the action of the appropriate political department of the government, at such time and in such degree as that department may determine. There must, of necessity, be a transition period.

"In a conquered territory, civil government must take effect, either by the action of the treaty-making power, or by that of the Congress of the United States. The office of a treaty of cession ordinarily is to put an end to all authority of the foreign government over the territory; and to subject the territory to the disposition of the Government of the United States.

"The government and disposition of territory so acquired belong to the Government of the United States, consisting of the President, the Senate, elected by the States, and the House of Representatives, chosen by and immediately representing the people of the United States. Treaties by which territory is acquired from a foreign State usually recognize this.

"It is clearly recognized in the recent treaty with Spain, especially in the ninth article, by which 'The civil rights and political *status* of the native inhabitants of the territories hereby ceded to the United States shall be determined by the Congress.'

"By the fourth and thirteenth articles of the treaty, the United States agree that, for ten years, Spanish ships and merchandise shall be admitted to the ports of the Philippine Islands on the same terms as ships and merchandise of the United States, and Spanish scientific, literary and artistic works, not subversive of public order, shall continue to be admitted free of duty into all the ceded territories. Neither of the provisions could be carried out if the Constitution required the customs regulations of the United States to apply in those territories.

"In the absence of Congressional legislation, the regulation of the revenue of the conquered territory, even after the treaty of cession, remains with the executive and military authority.

"So long as Congress has not incorporated the territory into the United States, neither military occupation nor cession by treaty makes the conquered territory domestic territory, in the sense of the revenue laws. But those laws concerning 'foreign countries' remain applicable to the conquered territory until changed by Congress. Such was the unanimous opinion of this court, as declared by Chief Justice TANEY, in *Fleming* vs. *Page*, 9 How. 603, 617.

"If Congress is not ready to construct a complete government for the conquered territory, it may establish a temporary government, which is not subject to all the restrictions of the Constitution.

"Such was the effect of the act of Congress of April 12, 1900, c. 191, entitled 'An act temporarily to provide revenues and a civil government for Porto Rico, and for other purposes.' By the third section of that act, it was expressly declared that the duties thereby established on merchandise and articles going into Porto Rico from the United States, or coming into the United States from Porto Rico, should cease in any event on March 1, 1902, and sooner if the legislative assembly of Porto Rico should enact and put into operation a system of local taxation to meet the necessities of the government established by that act.

"The system of duties, temporarily established by that act during the transition period, was within the authority of Congress under the Constitution of the United States."

DISSENTING OPINIONS IN DOWNES VS. BIDWELL.

Mr. Chief Justice FULLER delivered a dissenting opinion (182 U. S. 347–375) in which Justices HARLAN, BREWER and PECKHAM concurred, Justice HARLAN also wrote a separate opinion.

The Chief Justice considered that the Foraker act created a civil government in Porto Rico and placed it on a par with other organized territories, so far as constitutional provisions are concerned, including such as relate to uniformity of taxation and imposts.

The opinion quotes the 2d, 3d, 4th, 5th and 38th sections of the act (182 U. S. pp. 349, *et seq.*, and see pp. 513, *et seq. post*, of this appendix), and declares that "this act on its face does not comply with the [constitutional] rule of uniformity," and says (182 U. S. 352):

"The uniformity required by the Constitution is a geographical uniformity, and is only attained when the tax operates with the same force and effect in every place where the subject of it is found. *Knowlton* vs. *Moore*, 178 U. S. 41; *Head Money Cases*, 112 U. S. 580, 594. But it is said that Congress in attempting to levy these duties was not exercising power derived from the first clause of section 8, or restricted by it, because in dealing with the territories Congress exercises unlimited powers of government, and, moreover, that these duties are merely local taxes.

"This court, in 1820, when MARSHALL was Chief Justice, and WASHINGTON, WILLIAM JOHNSON, LIVINGSTON, TODD, DUVALL and STORY were his associates, took a different view of the power of Congress in the matter of laying and collecting taxes, duties, imposts and excises in the territories, and its ruling in *Loughborough* vs. *Blake*, 5 Wheat. 317, has never been overruled.

"It is said in one of the opinions of the majority that the Chief Justice 'made certain observations which have occasioned some embarrassment in other cases.' Manifestly this is so in this case, for it is necessary to overrule that decision in order to reach the result herein announced."

These expressions of Chief Justice MARSHALL, in his opinion, were not *obiter*. During a discussion of many of the cases cited in the briefs and arguments, as to the extension of the Constitution over territory acquired by the United States and the status of such territory, the opinion says (182 U. S. 358):

"I repeat that no satisfactory ground has been suggested for restricting the words 'throughout the United States,' as qualifying the power to impose duties, to the States, and that conclusion is the more to be avoided when we reflect that it rests, in the last analysis, on the assertion of the possession by Congress of unlimited power over territories."

The keynote of this opinion is that all powers of Congress, and in fact all governmental powers of the United States, are necessarily limited by the Constitution, and that the Constitution applies to all territory owned by the United States.

As to the extent of the treaty-making power the opinion says (182 U. S. p. 369) after referring to *Railway Co.* vs. *McGlinn*, (114 U. S. 546) and *Cross* vs. *Harrison*, (16 Howard, 198): "The power of the United States to acquire territory by conquest, by treaty, or by discovery and occupation, is not disputed, nor is the proposition that in all international relations, interests, and responsibilities the United States is a separate, independent, and sovereign nation; but it does not derive its powers from international law, which, though a part of our municipal law, is not a part of the organic law of the land. The source of national power in this country is the Constitution of the United States; and the government, as to our internal affairs, possesses no inherent sovereign power not derived from that instrument, and inconsistent with its letter and spirit.

"Doubtless the subjects of the former sovereign are brought by the transfer under the protection of the acquiring power, and are so far forth impressed with its nationality, but it does not follow that they necessarily acquire the full *status* of citizens. The ninth article of the treaty ceding Porto Rico to the United States provided that Spanish subjects, natives of the Peninsula, residing in the ceded territory, might remain or remove, and in case they remained might preserve their allegiance to the crown of Spain by making a declaration of their decision to do so, 'in default of which declaration they shall be held to have renounced it and to have adopted the nationality of the territory in which they reside.'

"The same article also contained this paragraph: 'The civil rights and political *status* of the native inhabitants of the territories hereby ceded to the United States shall be determined by Congress.' This was nothing more than a declaration of the accepted principles of international law applicable to the *status* of the Spanish subjects and of the native inhabitants. It did not assume that Congress could deprive the inhabitants of ceded territory of rights to which they might be entitled. The grant by Spain could not enlarge the powers of Congress, nor did it purport to secure from the United States a guaranty of civil or political privileges.

" Indeed a treaty which undertook to take away what the Constitution secured or to enlarge the Federal jurisdiction would be simply void.

" ' It need hardly be said that a treaty cannot change the Constitution or be held valid if it be in violation of that instrument. This results from the nature and fundamental principles of our government.' *The Cherokee Tobacco*, 11 Wall. 620. (Citing also Mr. Justice Field in *Geofroy* vs. *Riggs*, 133 U. S. 258, p. 267. See § 335, p. 23, vol. II). . . .

" And it certainly cannot be admitted that the power of Congress to lay and collect taxes and duties can be curtailed by an arrangement made with a foreign nation by the President and two-thirds of a quorum of the Senate. See 2 Tucker on the Constitution, §§ 354, 355, 356."

The opinion concludes by attempting to refute the views expressed in Justice White's opinion as follows (182 U. S. p. 373):

" The concurring opinion recognizes the fact that Congress, in dealing with the people of new territories or possessions, is bound to respect the fundamental guarantees of life, liberty, and property, but assumes that Congress is not bound, in those territories or possessions, to follow the rules of taxation prescribed by the Constitution. And yet the power to tax involves the power to destroy, and the levy of duties touches all our people in all places under the jurisdiction of the government.

" The logical result is that Congress may prohibit commerce altogether between the States and territories, and may prescribe one rule of taxation in one territory, and a different rule in another.

" That theory assumes that the Constitution created a government empowered to acquire countries throughout the world, to be governed by different rules than those obtaining in the original States and territories, and substitutes for the present system of republican government, a system of domination over distant provinces in the exercise of unrestricted power.

" In our judgment, so much of the Porto Rican act as authorized the imposition of these duties is invalid, and plaintiffs were entitled to recover.

" Some argument was made as to general consequences apprehended to flow from this result, but the language of the Constitution is too plain and unambiguous to permit its meaning to be thus influenced. There is nothing 'in the literal construction so obviously absurd, or mischievous, or repugnant to the general spirit of the instrument, as to justify those who expound the Constitution' in giving it a construction not warranted by its words.

" Briefs have been presented at this bar, purporting to be on behalf of certain industries, and eloquently setting forth the desirability that our government should possess the power to impose a tariff on the products of newly acquired territories so as to diminish or remove competition. That, however, furnishes no basis for judicial judgment, and if the producers of staples, in the existing States of this Union, believe the Constitution should be amended so as to reach that result, the instrument itself provides how such amendment can be accomplished. The people of all the States are entitled to a voice in the settlement of that subject.

" Again, it is objected on behalf of the government that the possession of absolute power is essential to the acquisition of vast and distant territories, and that we should regard the situation as it is to-day rather than as it was a century ago. ' We must look at the situation as comprehending a possibility—I do not say a probability, but a possibility—that the question might be as to the powers of this government in the acquisition of Egypt and the Soudan, or a section of Central Africa, or a spot in the Antarctic Circle, or a section of the Chinese Empire.'

" But it must be remembered that, as Marshall and Story declared, the Constitution was framed for ages to come, and that the sagacious men who framed it were well aware that a mighty future waited on their work. The rising sun to which Franklin referred at the close of the convention, they well knew, was that star of empire, whose course Berkeley had sung sixty years before.

" They may not indeed have deliberately considered a triumphal progress of the nation, as such, around the earth, but, as Marshall wrote: ' It is not enough to say, that this particular case was not in the mind of the convention, when the article was framed, nor of the American people, when it was adopted. It is necessary to go farther, and to say that, had this particular case been suggested, the language would have been so varied as to exclude it, or it would have been made a special exception.'

" This cannot be said, and, on the contrary, in order to the successful extension of our institutions, the reasonable presumption is that the limitations on the exertion of arbitrary power would have been made more rigorous.

" After all, these arguments are merely political, and ' political reasons have not the requisite certainty to afford rules of judicial interpretation.'

" Congress has power to make all laws which shall be necessary and proper for carrying into execution all the powers vested by the Constitution in the government of the United States, or in any department or officer thereof. If the end be legitimate and within the scope of the Constitution, then, to accomplish it, Congress may use ' all means which are appropriate, which are plainly adapted to that end, which are not prohibited, but consistant with the letter and spirit of the Constitution.'

" The grave duty of determining whether an act of Congress does or does not comply with these requirements is only to be discharged by applying the well settled rules which govern the interpretation of fundamental law, unaffected by the theoretical opinions of individuals.

" Tested by those rules our conviction is that the imposition of these duties cannot be sustained."

Mr. Justice Harlan concurred in this opinion of Chief Justice Fuller, but he also wrote a brief dissenting opinion (182 U. S. 375–391). The concluding sentence of this opinion (182 U. S. p. 391), is as follows:

"In my opinion Porto Rico became, at least after the ratification of the treaty with Spain, a part of and subject to the jurisdiction of the United States in respect of all its territory and people, and Congress could not thereafter impose any duty, import or excise, with respect to that island and its inhabitants, which departed from the rule of uniformity established by the Constitution."

. V.

HENRY W. DOOLEY, LOUIS G. SMITH, AND CHARLES W. OGDEN, TRADING AS COPARTNERS UNDER THE FIRM NAME OF DOOLEY, SMITH & COMPANY, PLAINTIFFS IN ERROR, VS. THE UNITED STATES, ACTION No. 1.

In error to the Circuit Court of the United States for the Southern District of New York.

No. 501, October term, 1900, Transcript filed December 10, 1900 (Ins. Cas. Rec. p. 755).

For Dooley, Smith & Co.:
HENRY M. WARD, 45 William Street, New York City, Attorney, JOHN G. CARLISLE (formerly Secretary of Treasury of the United States), WILLIAM G. CHOATE, JOSEPH LAROCQUE, WILLIAM EDMOND CURTIS, of counsel.

For the United States:
In the Circuit Court: HENRY L. BURNETT, United States District Attorney for the Southern District of New York.

In the Supreme Court, JOHN W. GRIGGS, Attorney-General of the United States, and JOHN K. RICHARDS, Solicitor-General.

The *Goetze, De Lima* and *Downes* cases were brought to recover duties paid in New York on goods brought from Porto Rico; the *Dooley, Smith & Company* cases were brought to recover duties paid on goods brought into Porto Rico from New York. There were two actions; one to recover duties collected prior to, and the other for duties collected after, May 1, 1900, under the provisions of the Foraker act. This action related to duties prior to the Foraker act and the complaint prayed judgment for the return of duties paid during three separate periods as stated in the opinion (182 U. S. Rep. 222):

"1. From July 26, 1898, until August 19, 1898, under the terms of the proclamation of General Miles, directing the exaction of the former Spanish and Porto Rican duties.

"2. From August 19, 1898, until February 1, 1899, under the customs tariff for Porto Rico, proclaimed by order of the President.

"3. From February 1, 1899, to May 1, 1900, under the amended tariff customs promulgated January 20, 1899, by order of the President."

For Petition and Complaint, see Ins. Cas. Rec. p. 757.

A demurrer was interposed upon the ground of the want of jurisdiction, and the insufficiency of the complaint. The Circuit Court, LACOMBE, J., sustained the demurrer upon the second ground, and dismissed the petition following the decision of TOWNSEND, J., in the *Goetze* case, p. 21, Ins. Cas. Rec., and 103 Fed. Rep. 73. (*Pro forma*, November 30, 1900, Ins. Cas. Rec. p. 764.)

A writ of error was allowed and the cases were advanced on the Supreme Court calendar. (Motion papers not included in Ins. Cas. Rec.)

Briefs were filed in Supreme Court for the plaintiffs in error by HENRY M. WARD, Attorney, and J. G. CARLISLE, and WILLIAM EDMOND CURTIS of counsel; (Ins. Cas. Rec. pp. 771–802 and for analysis and list of authorities cited, see Table of Contents, Ins. Cas. Rec. pp. xxix–xxx.) An oral argument on jurisdictional questions was made before the Supreme Court by Mr. WARD on January 9, 1901 (Ins. Cas. Rec. pp. 803–815,) and an oral argument on the general questions involved by MR. CARLISLE in this case, the second *Dooley* case, and the *Armstrong* case referred to at p. 500 *post* of this Appendix. (Ins. Cas. Rec. pp. 817–845. For analysis of these arguments, see Table of Contents, Ins. Cas. Rec. pp. xxx.) The briefs filed with, and arguments before, the Supreme Court on behalf of the United States were the same as those used in other Porto Rican cases argued in January, 1901, by the Attorney General and Solicitor General. (Ins. Cas. Rec. *contra*. p. 846.) This case was decided May 27, 1901.

OPINION BROWN, J., IN DOOLEY VS. UNITED STATES.

Mr. Justice BROWN delivered the opinion in this case (182 U. S. 223–236), Chief Justice FULLER and Justices HARLAN, BREWER and PECKHAM concurring with him. Mr. Justice WHITE delivered a dissenting opinion in which Justices GRAY, SHIRAS and McKENNA concurred. (182 U. S. 236–243.)

A large part of Mr. Justice Brown's opinion relates to procedure and whether or not the action should be brought in the Court of Claims or in the Circuit Court; it was held that the action was properly brought. That part of the opinion which relates to the exaction of duties in Porto Rico prior to the Foraker act is as follows (182 U. S. 230):

"2. In their legal aspect, the duties exacted in this case were of three classes: (1) the duties prescribed by General Miles under order of July 26, 1898, which merely extended the existing regulations; (2) the tariffs of August 19, 1898, and February 1, 1899, prescribed by the President as Commander-in-Chief, which continued in effect until April 11, 1899, the date of the ratification of the treaty and the cession of the island to the United States; (3) from the ratification of the treaty to May 1, 1900, when the Foraker act took effect.

"There can be no doubt with respect to the first two of these classes, namely, the exaction of duties under the war power, prior to the ratification of the treaty of peace. While it is true the treaty of peace was signed December 10, 1898, it did not take effect upon individual rights, until there was an exchange of ratifications. (*Haver* vs. *Yaker*, 9 Wall. 32.) Upon the occupation of the country by the military forces of the United States, the authority of the Spanish Government was superseded, but the necessity for a revenue did not cease. The government must be carried on, and there was no one left to administer its functions but the military forces of the United States. Money is requisite for that purpose, and money could only be raised by order of the military commander. The most natural method was by the continuation of existing duties. In adopting this method, General Miles was fully justified by the laws of war. The doctrine upon this subject is thus summed up by Halleck in his work on International Law, (vol. 2, page 444): 'The right of one belligerent to occupy and govern the territory of the enemy while in its military possession, is one of the incidents of war, and flows directly from the right to conquer. We, therefore, do not look to the Constitution or political institutions of the conqueror, for authority to establish a government for the territory of the enemy in his possession, during its military occupation, nor for the rules by which the powers of such government are regulated and limited. Such authority and such rules are derived directly from the laws of war, as established by the usage of the world, and confirmed by the writings of publicists and decisions of courts—in fine, from the law of the nations. . . . The municipal laws of a conquered territory, or the laws which regulate private rights, continue in force during military occupation, except so far as they are suspended or changed by the acts of the conqueror. . . . He, nevertheless, has all the powers of a *de facto* government, and can at his pleasure either change the existing laws or make new ones.'

"In *New Orleans* vs. *Steamship Co.*,(20 Wall. 387, 393,) it was said, with respect to the powers of the military government over the city of New Orleans after its conquest, that it had 'the same power and rights in territory held by conquest as if the territory had belonged to a foreign country and had been subjugated in a foreign war. In such cases the conquering power has the right to displace the pre-existing authority, and to assume to such extent as it may deem proper the exercise by itself of all the powers and functions of government. It may appoint all the necessary officers and clothe them with designated powers, larger or smaller, according to its pleasure. It may prescribe the revenues to be paid, and apply them to its own use or otherwise. It may do anything necessary to strengthen itself and weaken the enemy. There is no limit to the powers that may be exerted in such cases, save those which are found in the laws and usages of war. These principles have the sanction of all publicists who have considered the subject.' See also *Thirty Hogsheads of Sugar* vs. *Boyle*, (9 Cr. 191); *Fleming* vs. *Page*, (9 How. 603); *American Ins. Co.* vs. *Canter*, (1 Pet. 511).

"But it is useless to multiply citations upon this point, since the au-

32

thority to exact similar duties was fully considered and affirmed by this court in *Cross* vs. *Harrison*, (16 How. 164). This case involved the validity of duties exacted by the military commander of California upon imports from foreign countries, from the date of the treaty of peace, February 3, 1848, to November 13, 1849, when the collector of customs appointed by the President entered upon the duties of his office. Prior to the treaty of peace, and from August, 1847, duties had been exacted by the military authorities, the validity of which does not seem to have been questioned. Page 189: " That war tariff, however, was abandoned as soon as the military govenor had received from Washington information of the exchange and ratification of the treaty with Mexico, and duties were afterwards levied in conformity with such as Congress had imposed upon foreign merchandise imported into other ports of the United States, Upper California having been ceded by the treaty to the United States. The duties were held to have been legally exacted.' Speaking of the duties exacted before the treaty of peace, Mr. Justice Wayne observed (p. 190): 'No one can doubt that these orders of the President, and the action of our Army and Navy commanders in California, in conformity with them, was according to the law of arms and the right of conquest, or that they were operative until the ratification and exchange of a treaty of peace. Such would be the case upon general principles in respect to war and peace between nations.' It was further held that the right to collect these duties continued from the date of the treaty up to the time when official notice of its ratification and exchange were received in California. Owing to the fact that no telegraphic communication existed at that time, the news of the ratification of this treaty did not reach California until August 7, 1848, during which time the war tariff was continued. The question does not arise in this case, as the ratifications of the treaty appear to have been known as soon as they were exchanged.

" The court further held in *Cross* vs. *Harrison* that the right of the military commander to exact the duties prescribed by the tariff laws of the United States continued until a collector of customs had been appointed. Said the court: ' The government, of which Colonel Mason was the executive, had its origin in the lawful exercise of a belligerent right over a conquered territory. It had been instituted during the war by a command of the President of the United States. It was the government when the territory was ceded as a conquest, and it did not cease, as a matter of course, or as a necessary consequence, of the restoration of peace. The President might have dissolved it by withdrawing the army and navy officers who administered it, but he did not do so. Congress could have put an end to it, but that was not done. The right inference from the inaction of both is, that it was meant to be continued until it had been legislatively changed. . . . We think it was continued over a ceded conquest, without any violation of the Constitution or laws of the United States, and that, until Congress legislated for it, the duties upon foreign goods, imported into San Francisco, were legally demanded and lawfully received by Mr. Harrison, the collector of the port, who received his appointment, according to instructions from Washington, from Governor Mason.'

"Upon this point that case differs from the one under consideration only in the particular that the duties were levied in *Cross* vs. *Harrison*, upon goods imported from foreign countries into California, while in the present case they were imported from New York, a port of the conquering country. This, however, is quite immaterial. The United States and Porto Rico were still foreign countries with respect to each other, and the same right which authorized us to exact duties upon merchandise imported from Porto Rico to the United States authorized the military commander in Porto Rico to exact duties upon goods imported into that island from the United States. The fact that, notwithstanding the military occupation of the United States, Porto Rico remained a foreign country within the revenue laws is established by the case of *Fleming* vs. P*age*, (9 How. 603,) in which we held that the capture and occupation of a Mexican port during our war with that country did not make it a part of the United States, and that it still remained a foreign country within the meaning of the revenue laws. The right to exact duties upon goods imported into Porto Rico from New York arises from the fact that New York was still a foreign country with respect to Porto Rico, and from the correlative right to exact at New York duties upon merchandise imported from that island.

"3. Different considerations apply with respect to duties levied after the ratification of the treaty and the cession of the island to the United States. Porto Rico then ceased to be a foreign country, and, as we have just held in *De Lima* vs. *Bidwell*, the right of the collector of New York to exact duties upon imports from that island ceased with the exchange of ratifications. We have no doubt, however, that, from the necessities of the case, the right to administer the government of Porto Rico continued in the military commander after the ratification of the treaty, and until further action by Congress. (*Cross* vs. *Harrison*, above cited.) At the same time, while the right to administer the government continued, the conclusion of the treaty of peace and the cession of the island to the United States were not without their significance. By that act Porto Rico ceased to be a foreign country, and the right to collect duties upon imports from that island ceased. We think the correlative right to exact duties upon importations from New York to Porto Rico also ceased. The spirit as well as the letter of the tariff laws admit of duties being levied by a military commander only upon importations from foreign countries; and while his power is necessarily despotic, this must be understood rather in an administrative than in a legislative sense. While in legislating for a conquered country he may disregard the laws of that country, he is not wholly above the laws of his own. For instance, it is clear that while a military commander during the civil war was in the occupation of a Southern port, he could impose duties upon merchandise arriving from abroad, it would hardly be contended that he could also impose duties upon merchandise arriving from ports of his own country. His power to administer would be absolute, but his power to legislate would not be without certain re-

strictions—in other words, they would not extend beyond the necessities of the case. Thus in the case of *The Admittance; (Jecker* vs. *Montgomery,* 13 How. 498,) it was held that neither the President, nor the
military commander, could establish a court of prize, competent to
take jurisdiction of a case of capture, whose judgments would be conclusive in other admiralty courts. It was said that the courts established in Mexico during the war 'were nothing more than agents of
the military power, to assist in preserving order in the conquered territory, and to protect the inhabitants in their persons and property,
while it was occupied by the American arms. They were subject to the
military power, and their decisions under its control, whenever the
commanding officer thought proper to interfere. They were not courts
of the United States, and had no right to adjudicate upon a question of
prize or no prize,' although Congress, in the exercise of its general
authority in relation to the national courts, would have power to validate
their action. (*The Grapeshot,* 9 Wall. 129, 133.)

"So, too, in *Mitchell* vs. *Harmony,* (13 How. 115,) it was held that, where
the plaintiff entered Mexico during the war with that country, under a
permission of the commander to trade with the enemy and under the
sanction of the executive power of the United States, his property was
not liable to seizure by law for such trading, and that the officer directing the seizure was liable to an action for the value of the property
taken. To the same effect is *Mostyn* vs. *Fabrigas,* (1 Cowp. 161).

"In *Raymond* vs. *Thomas,* (91 U. S. 712,) a special order, by the officer
in command of the forces in the State of South Carolina, annulling a
decree rendered by a court of chancery in that State, was held to be void.
In delivering the opinion, Mr. Justice SWAYNE observed: 'Whether
Congress could have conferred the power to do such an act is not the
question we are called upon to consider. It is an unbending rule of law,
that the exercise of military power, where the rights of the citizens are
concerned, shall never be pushed beyond what the exigency requires.'

"Without questioning at all the original validity of the order imposing
duties upon goods imported into Porto Rico from foreign countries, we
think the proper construction of that order is, that it ceased to apply
to goods imported from the United States from the moment the United
States ceased to be a foreign country with respect to Porto Rico, and
that until Congress otherwise constitutionally directed, such merchandise was entitled to free entry.

"An unlimited power on the part of the Commander-in-Chief to exact
duties upon imports from the States might have placed Porto Rico in a
most embarrassing situation. The ratification of the treaty and the cession of the island to us severed her connection with Spain, of which the
island was no longer a colony, and with respect to which she had become a foreign country. The wall of the Spanish tariff was raised against
her exports, the wall of the military tariff against her imports, from
the mother country. She received no compensation from her new relations with the United States. If her exports, upon arriving there, were
still subject to the same duties as merchandise arriving from other foreign
countries, while her imports from the United States were subjected to

duties prescribed by the Commander-in-Chief, she would be placed in a position of practical isolation, which could not fail to be disastrous to the business and finances of an island. It had no manufactures or markets of its own, and was dependent upon the markets of other countries for the sale of her productions of coffee, sugar and tobacco. In our opinion the authority of the President as Commander-in-Chief to exact duties upon imports from the United States ceased with the ratification of the treaty of peace, and her right to the free entry of goods from the ports of the United States continued until Congress should constitutionally legislate upon the subject."

The judgment of the Circuit Court was reversed.

DISSENTING OPINIONS DOOLEY VS. UNITED STATES.

The four Justices who dissented did so wholly in so far as the court decided that the duties collected *after* the ratification were illegal, following the reasoning laid down in Mr. Justice WHITE's opinion in *Downes* vs. *Bidwell*, and following the doctrine laid down in *Fleming* vs. *Page*. The view was also taken that the tariff laws of the United States did not apply to Porto Rico without congressional action; in fact, he said (182 U. S. p. 242): "I cannot conceive that under the provisions of the Constitution conferring upon Congress the power to raise revenue that consequences such as would flow from immediately putting in force in Porto Rico the revenue laws of the United States could constitutionally be brought about without affording to the Congress the opportunity to adjust the revenue laws of the United States to meet the new situation."

VI.

HENRY W. DOOLEY, LOUIS C. SMITH, AND CHARLES W. OGDEN, TRADING AS COPARTNERS UNDER THE FIRM NAME OF DOOLEY, SMITH & CO., PLAINTIFFS IN ERROR, VS. THE UNITED STATES, ACTION NO. 2.

In error to the Circuit Court of the United States for the Southern District of New York.

No. 502, October Term, 1900. Tanscript filed December 10, 1900. (Ins. Cas. Rec. p. 847.)

Same counsel as in action No. 1. See p. 494, *ante*, of this Appendix, and same procedure followed. The only difference between this case and action No. 1, is that the duties were exacted after the Foraker Act went into effect, while the duties in other cases were exacted prior thereto. One of the legal questions raised in the argument of this case was whether the collection of duties in Porto Rico on goods brought there from a State was equivalent to an export tax and therefore prohibited by the Constitution.

The same briefs that were filed in action No. 1, were also filed in this action. An additional brief for the plaintiff in error was filed in this action by WM. G. CHOATE and JOSEPH LACROCQUE, JR., of counsel

(Ins. Cas. Rec. pp. 861–870, and for analysis see Table of Contents, Ins. Cas. Rec. p. xxxi).

This case has not yet been decided, November 30, 1901.

VII.

CARLOS ARMSTRONG, APPELLANT, VS. THE UNITED STATES, APPELLEE.

Appeal from the United States Court of Claims.

No. 509, October 1900. Transcript filed December 15, 1900. (Ins. Term Cas. Rec. p. 871.)

For the plaintiff, Appellant, JOHN C. CHANEY and ALPHONZO HART, Attorneys, Washington, D. C.   JOHN G. CARLISLE and CHARLES C. LEEDS, of counsel, New York.

For the United States in the Court of Claims, L. A. PRADT, Assistant Attorney General.

In the Supreme Court, JOHN W. GRIGGS, Attorney General, and JOHN K. RICHARDS, Solicitor General.

This action was commenced November 13, 1900, by petition in the Court of Claims to recover duties paid in Porto Rico on merchandise brought from United States ports. The petition is on p. 871, and the schedule of duties paid is on p. 875, of the Ins. Cas. Rec. The duties were paid between August 22, 1898, and December 5, 1899.

The United States demurred on the grounds of lack of jurisdiction of the Court of Claims to try the cause, and because the petition did not allege facts sufficient to constitute a cause of action.

The demurrer was sustained and judgment entered December 15, 1900 (Ins. Cas. Rec. p. 876), dismissing the petition. An appeal was allowed to the Supreme Court.

The appeal was advanced and argued simultaneously with De Lima vs. Bidwell, and on the same briefs and arguments for the United States. (See pp. 409, et seq., ante, of this Appendix.)

Two separate briefs for the appellants were filed in the Supreme Court. (Ins. Cas. Rec., pp. 879–930. For analysis and list of authorities cited see Table of Contents Ins. Cas. Rec., pp. xxxi–xxxiii.) A large part of these briefs was devoted to the questions of jurisdiction of the Court of Claims to hear cases of this nature.

The decision in this case was controlled by the decision in Dooley vs. United States, (182 U. S. 222,) and no separate opinion was delivered.

On May 27, 1901, Mr. Justice BROWN delivered the opinion of the court as follows (182 U. S. 244):

" This case is controlled by the case of Dooley vs. United States, (No. 501,) just decided. So far as the duties were exacted upon goods imported prior to the ratification of the treaty of April 11, 1899, they were properly exacted. So far as they were imposed upon importations after that date and prior to December 5, 1899, plaintiff is entitled to recover them back.

"The judgment of the Court of Claims is therefore reversed and the case remanded to that court for further proceedings not inconsistent with this opinion."

VIII.

CHRISTIAN HUUS, APPELLANT, VS. NEW YORK AND PORTO RICO STEAMSHIP COMPANY.

The Porto Rico Pilotage Case.

On a certificate for the United States Circuit Court of Appeals for the Second Circuit.

No. 514. October Term, 1900. Transcript filed December 18, 1900. (Ins. Cas. Rec. p. 931.)

For the libellant, appellant.
LINDSAY, KREMER, KALISH & PALMER, 27 William St., New York, Proctors, for libellants. WILLIAM LINDSAY, of counsel, in the Supreme Court.

For the respondents, appellee.
CURTIS, MALLET-PREVOST and COLT, 30 Broad St., New York City. WILLIAM EDMOND CURTIS and F. KINGSBURY CURTIS, of counsel.

In this case a pilot libeled an American built steamship belonging to a New York corporation for the amount of his pilotage, his services having been refused on the ground that he was entitled to pilotage as the vessel was not engaged in a coastwise trade and was therefore required to take pilot. The vessel was enrolled and licensed for the coasting trade between New York and Porto Rico. The libel was dismissed by the District Court (105 Fed. Rep. 74); an appeal was taken to the Circuit Court of Appeals which certified the following questions to the Supreme Court for instructions (182 U. S. 392):

"1. Since the proclamation of the treaty of peace between the United States and the Kingdom of Spain, and the passage of the act of Congress entitled 'An act temporarily to provide revenues and civil government for Porto Rico, and for other purposes,' (approved April 12, 1900,) do Porto Rican ports remain foreign ports in the sense in which those words are used in the statutes of the State of New York regulating pilotage ?

"2. Are vessels engaged in trade between Porto Rican ports and ports of the United States engaged in the coasting trade in the sense in which those words are used in the statutes of the State of New York regulating pilotage?

"3. Are steam vessels engaged in trade between Porto Rican ports and ports of the United States coastwise steam vessels in the sense in which those words are used in section 4444 of the Revised Statutes of the United States ? "

The case was advanced in the Supreme Court and argued January 11, 1901. WILLIAM LINDSAY argued for the appellants and W. F. KINGSBURY CURTIS, for the appellee.

For briefs in this case see Ins. Cas. Rec. pp. 937–1013, and for analysis and list of authorities cited, See Table of Contents Ins. Cas. Rec. pp. xxxiv–xxxvii. This case was decided May 27, 1901.

OPINION BROWN, J., IN PILOTAGE CASE.

Mr. Justice BROWN delivered the opinion of the court and answered the second and third questions in the affirmative which rendered an answer to the first question unnecessary.

The opinion is brief and defines the expressions "foreign ports," "foreign commerce" and "coastwise trade," holding that the words "coasting trade" are intended to include domestic trade in the United States upon other than interior waters, and that vessels engaged in trade between New York and Porto Rico are in the coasting trade, and not subject to pilotage laws relating to foreign vessels.

After discussing the pilotage laws the opinion says (182 U. S. p. 395): " As the statement of facts connected with the question certified shows that the Ponce was an American built steamship, sailing from New York, belonging to a New York corporation, enrolled and licensed for the coasting trade, navigated by a master duly licensed to act as pilot in the bay and harbor of New York, under the laws of the United States, and was engaged in trade between the Island of Porto Rico and the port of New York, the only question remaining to be considered is whether she was a *coastwise seagoing steam vessel* under Rev. Stat. sec. 4401, and actually employed in the coasting trade by way of Sandy Hook under sec. 2111 of the New York Consolidation Act.

"Under the commercial and navigation laws of the United States merchant vessels are divisible into two classes: First, vessels registered pursuant to Rev. Stat., sec. 4131. These must be wholly owned, commanded and officered by citizens of the United States, and are alone entitled to engage in foreign trade; and, second, vessels enrolled and licensed for the coasting trade or fisheries. Rev. Stat. sec. 4311. These may not engage in foreign trade under penalty of forfeiture. Sec. 4337. This class of vessels is also engaged in navigation upon the Great Lakes and the interior waters of the country—in other words, they are engaged in domestic instead of foreign trade.

"The words ' coasting trade,' as distinguishing this class of vessels, seem to have been selected because at that time all the domestic commerce of the country was either interior commerce, or coastwise, between ports upon the Atlantic or Pacific coasts, or upon islands so near thereto, and belonging to the several States, as properly to constitute a part of the coast. Strictly speaking Porto Rico is not such an island, as it is not only situated some hundreds of miles from the nearest port on the Atlantic coast, but had never belonged to the United States, or any of the States composing the Union. At the same time trade with that island is properly a part of the domestic trade of the country since the treaty of annexation, and is so recognized by the Porto Rican or Foraker act. By section 9 the Commissioner of Navigation is required to ' make such regulations . . . as he may deem expedient for the nationalization of all vessels owned by the inhabitants of Porto Rico on April 11, 1899, . . . and for the admission of the same to all the benefits of the coasting trade of the United States; and the coasting trade between Porto Rico and the United States shall be regulated in accordance with the provisions of law applicable to such trade between any two great coasting districts of the United States.' By this act it was evidently intended, not only to nationalize all Porto Rican vessels as vessels of the United States, and to admit them to the benefits of their coasting trade, but to place Porto Rico substantially upon the coast of the United States, and vessels engaged in trade between that island and the continent, as engaged in the coasting trade. This was the view taken by the executive officers of the government in issuing an enrollment and license to the Ponce, to be employed in carrying on the coasting trade, instead of treating her as a vessel engaged in foreign trade.

" That the words ' coasting trade ' are not intended to be strictly limited to trade between ports in adjoining districts is also evident from Rev. Stat. sec. 4358, wherein it is enacted that ' the coasting trade between the territory ceded to the United States by the Emperor of Russia, and any other portion of the United States, shall be regulated in accordance with the provisions of law applicable to such trade between any two great districts.' These great districts were, for the more convenient regulation of the coasting trade, divided by the act of March 2, 1819, (3 Stat. 492, c. 48) as amended by act of May 7, 1822, (3 Stat. 684; Rev. Stat. sec. 4348,) as follows: ' The first to include all the collection districts on the seacoast and navigable rivers between the eastern limits of the United States and the southern limits of Georgia; the second to include all the collection districts on the seacoast and navigable rivers between the river Perdido and the Rio Grande; and the third to include all the collection districts on the seacoast and navigable rivers between the southern limits of Georgia and the river Perdido.' A provision similar to that for the admission of the Territory of Alaska was also adopted in the act to provide a government for the Territory of Hawaii, (31 Stat. 141, sec. 98,) which provides that all vessels carrying Hawaiian registers on August 12, 1888, and owned by citizens of the United States or citizens of Hawaii, ' shall be entitled to be registered as American vessels, . . . and the coasting trade between the islands aforesaid and any other portion of the United States shall be regulated in accordance with the provisions of law applicable to such trade between any two great coasting districts.'

" This use of the words ' coasting trade ' indicates very clearly that the words were intended to include the domestic trade of the United States upon other than interior waters. The District Court was correct in holding that the Ponce was engaged in the coasting trade, and that the New York pilotage laws did not apply to her.

"The second and third questions are therefore answered in the affirmative. An answer to the first question becomes unnecessary."

IX.

GEORGE W. CROSSMAN ET AL., APPELLANTS, vs. THE UNITED STATES.

The Hawaiian Islands Case.

Appeal from the Circuit Court of the United States for the Southern District of New York.

No. 515. October Term, 1900. Transcript filed December 18, 1900. (Ins. Cas. Rec. p. 1015.)

For the appellants:

CURIE, SMITH & MAXWELL, 20 William St., New York City. CHARLES CURIE, W. WICKHAM SMITH, of counsel.

For the United States:

In the Circuit Court, HENRY L. BURNETT, United States District Attorney, and HENRY C. PLATT, Assistant. In the Supreme Court, JOHN W. GRIGGS, Attorney General, and JOHN K. RICHARDS, Solicitor General.

The action was brought to recover duties paid in New York on merchandise brought from the Hawaiian Islands after July 7, 1898, the date of the joint resolution of Congress annexing the Hawaiian Islands.

The protest of the importers was first heard and decided adversely to them by the Board of General Appraisers, July 27, 1900, SOMERVILLE Gen'l App'r, writing the opinion (Ins. Cas. Rec. p. 1021).

From this decision the importers appealed to the Circuit Court of the United States under the Customs Administrative Act. The decision was affirmed, TOWNSEND. J., December 13, 1900 (Ins. Cas. Rec. p. 1023, opinion in full, also reported in 105 Fed. Rep. 608).

An appeal was taken to the Supreme Court (Ins. Cas. Rec. p. 1027) a motion to advance the cause was granted and the case was argued January 14 and 15, 1901.

The briefs and arguments for the United States were the same as those in *De Lima* vs. *Bidwell*, (see pp. 469, et seq., ante, of this Appendix. For Solicitor-General's argument, see Ins. Cas. Rec. p. 1063. For the brief and arguments for appellants, see Ins. Cas. Rec. pp. 1033–1061, and for analysis and list of authorities cited, see Table of Contents, Ins. Cas. Rec. pp. xxviii–xxxix).

This case was decided on May 27, 1901 (182 U. S. 221). The opinion which is only ten lines was delivered by Mr. Justice BROWN and is also entitled in the case of *Goetze* vs. *United States*, (see pp. 465, et seq., ante, of this appendix) as follows:

"As the sole question presented by the record in these cases was whether Porto Rico and the Hawaiian Islands were foreign countries within the meaning of the tariff laws, we must hold, for the reasons stated in *De Lima* vs. *Bidwell*, just decided, that the board of general appraisers had no jurisdiction of the cases.

" The judgments of the Circuit Court are therefore reversed, and the cases remanded to that court with instructions to reverse the action of the board of general appraisers."

PROTOCOL OF AGREEMENT BETWEEN THE UNITED STATES AND SPAIN, EMBODYING THE TERMS OF A BASIS FOR THE ESTABLISHMENT OF PEACE BETWEEN THE TWO COUNTRIES.

[Signed at Washington in English and French, August 12, 1898. 30 U. S. Stat. at Large, 1742.] The English text is as follows:

PROTOCOL.

William R. Day, Secretary of State of the United States, and His Excellency Jules Cambon, Ambassador Extraordinary and Plenipotentiary of the Republic of France at Washington, respectively possessing for this purpose full authority from the Government of the United States and the Government of Spain, have concluded and signed the following articles, embodying the terms on which the two Governments have agreed in respect to the matters hereinafter set forth, having in view the establishment of peace between the two countries, that is to say:

ARTICLE I.

Spain will relinquish all claim of sovereignty over and title to Cuba.

ARTICLE II.

Spain will cede to the United States the island of Porto Rico and other islands now under Spanish sovereignty in the West Indies, and also an island in the Ladrones to be selected by the United States.

ARTICLE III.

The United States will occupy and hold the city, bay and harbor of Manila, pending the conclusion of a treaty of peace which shall determine the control, disposition and government of the Philippines.

ARTICLE IV.

Spain will immediately evacuate Cuba, Porto Rico and other islands now under Spanish sovereignty in the West Indies; and to this end each Government will, within ten days after the signing of this protocol, appoint Commissioners, and the Commissioners so appointed shall, within thirty days after the signing of this protocol, meet at Havana for the purpose of arranging and carrying out the details of the aforesaid evacuation of Cuba and the adjacent Spanish islands; and each Government will, within ten days after the signing of this protocol, also appoint other Commissioners, who shall, within thirty days after the signing of this protocol, meet at San Juan, in Porto Rico, for the purpose of arranging and carrying out the details of the aforesaid evacuation of Porto Rico and other islands now under Spanish sovereignty in the West Indies.

ARTICLE V.

The United States and Spain will each appoint not more than five commissioners to treat of peace, and the commissioners so appointed shall meet at Paris not later than October 1, 1898, and proceed to the negotiation and conclusion of a treaty of peace, which treaty shall be subject to ratification according to the respective constitutional forms of the two countries.

ARTICLE VI.

Upon the conclusion and signing of this protocol, hostilities between the two countries shall be suspended, and notice to that effect shall be given as soon as possible by each Government to the commanders of its military and naval forces.

Done at Washington in duplicate, in English and in French, by the Undersigned, who have hereunto set their hands and seals, the 12th day of August, 1898.

[SEAL]   WILLIAM R. DAY.

[SEAL]   JULES CAMBON.

TREATY OF PEACE BETWEEN THE UNITED STATES OF AMERICA AND THE KINGDOM OF SPAIN.

Signed at Paris, December 10, 1898; ratification advised by the Senate, February 6, 1899; ratified by the President February 6, 1899; ratified by her Majesty the Queen Regent of Spain, March 19, 1899; ratifications exchanged at Washington April 11, 1899; proclaimed, Washington, April 11, 1899; (U. S. Stats. Vol. 30, p. 1754, U. S. Treaties in Force, 1899, p. 595).

This treaty is in English and Spanish; the English text is as follows:

The United States of America and Her Majesty the Queen Regent of Spain, in the name of her august son Don Alfonso XIII, desiring to end the state of war now existing between the two countries, have for that purpose appointed as plenipotentiaries:

The President of the United States,

William R. Day, Cushman K. Davis, William P. Frye, George Gray, and Whitelaw Reid, citizens of the United States;

And Her Majesty the Queen Regent of Spain,

Don Eugenio Montero Ríos, president of the senate, Don Buenaventura de Abarzuza, senator of the Kingdom and ex-minister of the Crown; Don José de Garnica, deputy to the Cortes and associate justice of the supreme court; Don Wenceslao Ramirez de Villa-Urrutia, envoy extraordinary and minister plenipotentiary at Brussels, and Don Rafael Cerero, general of division;

Who, having assembled in Paris, and having exchanged their full powers, which were found to be in due and proper form, have, after discussion of the matters before them, agreed upon the following articles:

ARTICLE I.

Spain relinquishes all claim of sovereignty over and title to Cuba.

And as the island is, upon its evacuation by Spain, to be occupied by the United States, the United States will, so long as such occupation shall last, assume and discharge the obligations that may under international law result from the fact of its occupation, for the protection of life and property.

ARTICLE II.

Spain cedes to the United States the island of Porto Rico and other islands now under Spanish sovereignty in the West Indies, and the island of Guam in the Marianas or Ladrones.

ARTICLE III.

Spain cedes to the United States the archipelago known as the Philippine Islands, and comprehending the islands lying within the following line:

A line running from west to east along or near the twentieth parallel of north latitude, and through the middle of the navigable channel of Bachi, from the 118th to the 127th degree meridian of longitude east of Greenwich, thence along the 127th degree meridian of longitude east of Greenwich to the parallel of 4° 45′ north latitude, thence along the parallel of 4° 45′ north latitude to its intersection with the meridian of longitude 119° 35′ east of Greenwich, thence along the meridian of longitude 119° 35′ east of Greenwich to the parallel of latitude 7° 40′ north; thence along the parallel of latitude of 7° 40′ north to its intersection with the 116th degree meridian of longitude east of Greenwich, thence by a direct line to the intersection of the 10th degree parallel of north latitude with the 118th degree meridian of longitude east of Greenwich, and thence along the 118th degree meridian of longitude east of Greenwich to the point of beginning.

(In the original the numerals are written out in full.)

The United States will pay to Spain the sum of twenty million dollars ($20,000,000) within three months after the exchange of the ratifications of the present treaty.

ARTICLE IV.

The United States will, for the term of ten years from the date of the exchange of the ratifications of the present treaty, admit Spanish ships and merchandise to the ports of the Philippine Islands on the same terms as ships and merchandise of the United States.

ARTICLE V.

The United States will, upon the signature of the present treaty, send back to Spain, at its own cost, the Spanish soldiers taken as prisoners of war on the capture of Manila by the American forces. The arms of the soldiers in question shall be restored to them.

Spain will, upon the exchange of the ratifications of the present treaty, proceed to evacuate the Philippines, as well as the island of Guam, on terms similar to those agreed upon by the Commissioners appointed to arrange for the evacuation of Porto Rico and other islands in the West Indies, under the Protocol of August 12, 1898, which is to continue in force till its provisions are completely executed.

The time within which the evacuation of the Philippine Islands and Guam shall be completed shall be fixed by the two Governments. Stands of colors, uncaptured war vessels, small arms, guns of all calibres, with their carriages and accessories, powder, ammunition, live-stock, and materials and supplies of all kinds, belonging to the land and naval forces of Spain in the Philippines and Gaum, remain the property of Spain. Pieces of heavy ordnance, exclusive of field artillery, in the fortifications and coast defences, shall remain in their emplacements for the term of six months, to be reckoned from the exchange of ratifications of the treaty; and the United States may, in the meantime, purchase such material from Spain, if a satisfactory agreement between the two Governments on the subject shall be reached.

Article VI.

Spain will, upon the signature of the present treaty, release all prisoners of war, and all persons detained or imprisoned for political offences, in connection with the insurrections in Cuba and the Philippines and the war with the United States.

Reciprocally, the United States will release all persons made prisoners of war by the American forces, and will undertake to obtain the release of all Spanish prisoners in the hands of the insurgents in Cuba and the Philippines.

The Government of the United States will at its own cost return to Spain and the Government of Spain will at its own cost return to the United States, Cuba, Porto Rico, and the Philippines, according to the situation of their respective homes, prisoners released or caused to be released by them, respectively, under this article.

Article VII.

The United States and Spain mutually relinquish all claims for indemnity, national and individual, of every kind, of either Government, or of its citizens or subjects, against the other Government, that may have arisen since the beginning of the late insurrection in Cuba and prior to the exchange of ratifications of the present treaty, including all claims for indemnity for the cost of the war.

The United States will adjudicate and settle the claims of its citizens against Spain relinquished in this article.

Article VIII.

In conformity with the provisions of Articles I, II, and III of this treaty, Spain relinquishes in Cuba, and cedes in Porto Rico and other islands in the West Indies, in the island of Guam, and in the Philippine Archipelago, all the buildings, wharves, barracks, forts, structures, public highways and other immovable property which, in conformity with law, belong to the public domain, and as such belong to the Crown of Spain.

And it is hereby declared that the relinquishment or cession, as the case may be, to which the preceding paragraph refers, cannot in any respect impair the property or rights which by law belong to the peaceful possession of property of all kinds, of provinces, municipalities, public or private establishments, ecclesiastical or civic bodies, or any other associations having legal capacity to acquire and possess property in the aforesaid territories renounced or ceded, or of private individuals, of whatsoever nationality such individuals may be.

The aforesaid relinquishment or cession, as the case may be, includes all documents exclusively referring to the sovereignty relinquished or ceded that may exist in the archives of the Peninsula. Where any document in such archives only in part relates to said sovereignty, a copy of such part will be furnished whenever it shall be requested. Like rules shall be reciprocally observed in favor of Spain in respect of documents in the archives of the islands above referred to.

In the aforesaid relinquishment or cession, as the case may be, are also included such rights as the Crown of Spain and its authorities possess in respect of the official archives and records, executive as well as judicial, in the islands above referred to, which relate to said islands or the rights and property or their inhabitants. Such archives and records shall be carefully preserved, and private persons shall without distinction have the right to require, in accordance with law, authenticated copies of the contracts, wills and other instruments forming part of notorial protocols or files, or which may be contained in the executive or judicial archives, be the latter in Spain or in the islands aforesaid.

ARTICLE IX.

Spanish subjects, natives of the Peninsula, residing in the territory over which Spain by the present treaty relinquishes or cedes her sovereignty, may remain in such territory or may remove therefrom, retaining in either event all their rights of property, including the right to sell or dispose of such property or of its proceeds; and they shall also have the right to carry on their industry, commerce and professions, being subject in respect thereof to such laws as are applicable to other foreigners. In case they remain in the territory they may preserve their allegiance to the Crown of Spain by making, before a court of record, within a year from the date of the exchange of ratifications of this treaty, a declaration of their decision to preserve such allegiance; in default of which declaration they shall be held to have renounced it and to have adopted the nationality of the territory in which they may reside.

The civil rights and political status of the native inhabitants of the territories hereby ceded to the United States shall be determined by the Congress.

ARTICLE X.

The inhabitants of the territories over which Spain relinquishes or cedes her sovereignty shall be secured in the free exercise of their religion.

ARTICLE XI.

The Spaniards residing in the territories over which Spain by this treaty cedes or relinquishes her sovereignty shall be subject in matters civil as well as criminal to the jurisdiction of the courts of the country wherein they reside, pursuant to the ordinary laws governing the same; and they shall have the right to appear before such courts, and to pursue the same course as citizens of the country to which the courts belong.

ARTICLE XII.

Judicial proceedings pending at the time of the exchange of ratifications of this treaty in the territories over which Spain relinquishes or cedes her sovereignty shall be determined according to the following rules:

1. Judgments rendered either in civil suits between private individuals, or in criminal matters, before the date mentioned, and with respect to which there is no recourse or right of review under the Spanish law, shall be deemed to be final, and shall be executed in due form by competent authority in the territory within which such judgments should be carried out.

2. Civil suits between private individuals which may on the date mentioned be undetermined shall be prosecuted to judgment before the court in which they may then be pending or in the court that may be substituted therefore.

3. Criminal actions pending on the date mentioned before the Supreme Court of Spain against citizens of the territory which by this treaty ceases to be Spanish shall continue under its jurisdiction until final judgment; but, such judgment having been rendered, the execution thereof shall be committed to the competent authority of the place in which the case arose.

ARTICLE XIII.

The rights of property secured by copyrights and patents acquired by Spaniards in the Island of Cuba and in Porto Rico, the Philippines and other ceded territories, at the time of the exchange of the ratifications of this treaty, shall continue to be respected. Spanish scientific, literary and artistic works, not subversive of public order in the territories in question, shall continue to be admitted free of duty into such territories, for the period of ten years, to be reckoned from the date of the exchange of the ratifications of this treaty.

ARTICLE XIV.

Spain shall have the power to establish consular officers in the ports and places of the territories, the sovereignty over which has been either relinquished or ceded by the present treaty.

ARTICLE XV.

The Government of each country will, for the term of ten years, accord to the merchant vessels of the other country the same treatment in respect of all port charges, including entrance and clearance dues, light dues, and tonnage duties, as it accords to its own merchant vessels, not engaged in the coastwise trade.

This article may at any time be terminated on six months' notice given by either Government to the other.

ARTICLE XVI.

It is understood that any obligations assumed in this treaty by the United States with respect to Cuba are limited to the time of its occupancy thereof; but it will upon the termination of such occupancy, advise any Government established in the islands to assume the same obligations.

ARTICLE XVII.

The present treaty shall be ratified by the President of the United States, by and with the advice and consent of the Senate thereof, and by Her Majesty the Queen Regent of Spain; and the ratifications shall be exchanged at Washington within six months from the date hereof, or earlier if possible.

In faith whereof, we, the respective Plenipotentiaries, have signed this treaty and have hereunto affixed our seals.

Done in duplicate at Paris, the tenth day of December, in the year of Our Lord one thousand eight hundred and ninety-eight.

[SEAL]	WILLIAM R. DAY,	[SEAL]	EUGENIO MONTERO RIOS,
[SEAL]	CUSHMAN K. DAVIS,	[SEAL]	B. DE ABARZUZA,
[SEAL]	WILLIAM P. FRYE,	[SEAL]	J. DE GARNICA,
[SEAL]	GEO. GRAY,	[SEAL]	W. R. DE VILLA URRUTIA,
[SEAL]	WHITELAW REID,	[SEAL]	RAFAEL CERERO.

See Foreign Relations Report of United States, 1898, for correspondence relating to the foregoing Protocol (pp. 819, *et seq.*), and to the Treaty (pp. 904, *et seq.*)

JOINT RESOLUTION TO PROVIDE FOR ANNEXING THE HAWAIIAN ISLANDS TO THE UNITED STATES (30 U. S. Statutes at Large, 750).

Whereas, the government of the Republic of Hawaii having, in due form, signified its consent, in the manner provided by its constitution, to cede absolutely and without reserve to the United States of America all rights of sovereignty of whatsover kind in and over the Hawaiian Islands and their dependencies, and also to cede and transfer to the United States the absolute fee and ownership of all public, government, or crown lands, public buildings or edifices, ports, harbors, military equipment, and all other public property of every kind and description belonging to the government of the Hawaiian Islands, together with every right and appurtenance thereunto appertaining: Therefore,

Resolved by the Senate and House of Representatives of the United States of America in Congress assembled, That said cession is accepted ratified and confirmed, and that the said Hawaiian Islands and their dependencies be, and they are hereby, annexed as a part of the territory

33

of the United States and are subject to the sovereign dominion thereof, and that all and singular the property and rights hereinbefore mentioned are vested in the United States of America.

The existing laws of the United States relative to public lands shall not apply to such lands in the Hawaiian Islands; but the Congress of the United States shall enact special laws for their management and disposition: Provided, That all revenue from or proceeds of the same, except as regards such part thereof as may be used or occupied for the civil, military or naval purposes of the United States, or may be assigned for the use of the local government, shall be used, solely for the benefit of the inhabitants of the Hawaiian Islands for educational and other public purposes.

Until Congress shall provide for the government of such islands all the civil, judicial and military powers exercised by the officers of the existing government in said islands shall be vested in such person or persons and shall be exercised in such manner as the President of the United States shall direct; and the President shall have power to remove said officers and fill the vacancies so occasioned.

The existing treaties of the Hawaiian Islands with foreign nations shall forthwith cease and determine, being replaced by such treaties as may exist, or as may be hereafter concluded, between the United States and such foreign nations. The municipal legislation of the Hawaiian Islands, not enacted for the fulfillment of the treaties so extinguished, and not inconsistent with this joint resolution nor contrary to the Constitution of the United States nor to any existing treaty of the United States, shall remain in force until the Congress of the United States shall otherwise determine.

Until legislation shall be enacted extending the United States customs laws and regulations to the Hawaiian Islands the existing customs relations of the Hawaiian Islands with the United States and other countries shall remain unchanged.

The public debt of the Republic of Hawaii, lawfully existing at the date of the passage of this joint resolution, including the amounts due to depositors in the Hawaiian Postal Savings Bank, is hereby assumed by the Government of the United States; but the liability of the United States in this regard shall in no case exceed four million dollars. So long, however, as the existing Government and the present commercial relations of the Hawaiian Islands are continued as hereinbefore provided, said Government shall continue to pay the interest on said debt.

There shall be no further immigration of Chinese into the Hawaiian Islands, except upon such conditions as are now or may hereafter be allowed by the laws of the United States; and no Chinese, by reason of anything herein contained, shall be allowed to enter the United States from the Hawaiian Islands.

The President shall appoint five commissioners, at least two of whom shall be residents of the Hawaiian Islands, who shall, as soon as reasonably practicable, recommend to Congress such legislation concerning the Hawaiian Islands as they shall deem necessary or proper.

SEC. 2. That the commissioners hereinbefore provided for shall be appointed by the President, by and with the advice and consent of the Senate.

SEC. 3. That the sum of one hundred thousand dollars, or so much thereof as may be necessary, is hereby appropriated, out of any money in the Treasury not otherwise appropriated, and to be immediately available, to be expended at the discretion of the President of the United States of America, for the purpose of carrying this joint resolution into effect.

Approved, July 7, 1898.

TARIFF PROVISIONS OF THE FORAKER ACT.

Act of April 12, 1900, chapter 191 of the 56th Congress, 1st session. 31 U. S. Stat. at Large, pp 77–86.

An Act Temporarily to provide revenues and a civil government for Porto Rico, and for other purposes.

Be it enacted etc., That the provisions of this Act shall apply to the Island of Porto Rico and to the adjacent islands and waters of the islands lying east of the seventy-fourth meridian of longitude west of Greenwich, which were ceded to the United States by the Government of Spain by treaty entered into on the tenth day of December, eighteen hundred and ninety-eight; and the name Porto Rico, as used in this Act, shall be held to include not only the island of that name, but all the adjacent islands as aforesaid. (This act consists of forty-one sections. The tariff provisions only were involved in the Insular cases; they are here quoted at length as in the opinion of Chief Justice FULLER in *Downes* vs. *Bidwell*, 182 U. S. pp. 349 *et seq.*

SEC. 2. That on and after the passage of this Act the same tariffs, customs, and duties shall be levied, collected, and paid upon all articles imported into Porto Rico from ports other than those of the United States which are required by law to be collected upon articles imported into the United States from foreign countries: P*rovided*, That on all coffee in the bean or ground imported into Porto Rico there shall be levied and collected a duty of five cents per pound, any law or part of law to the contrary notwithstanding: *And provided further*, That all Spanish scientific, literary, and artistic works, not subversive of public order in Porto Rico, shall be admitted free of duty into Porto Rico for a period of ten years, reckoning from the eleventh day of April, eighteen hundred and ninety-nine, as provided in said treaty of peace between the United States and Spain: *And provided further*, That all books and pamphlets printed in the English language shall be admitted into Porto Rico free of duty when imported from the United States.

Sec. 3. That on and after the passage of this act all merchandise coming into the United States from Porto Rico and coming into Porto Rico from the United States shall be entered at the several ports of entry upon payment of fifteen per centum of the duties which are required to be levied, collected, and paid upon like articles of merchandise imported from foreign countries; and in addition thereto upon articles of merchandise of Porto Rican manufacture coming into the United States and withdrawn for consumption or sale upon payment of a tax equal to the internal-revenue tax imposed in the United States upon the like articles of merchandise of domestic manufacture; such tax to be paid by internal-revenue stamp or stamps to be purchased and provided by the Commissioner of Internal Revenue and to be procured from the collector of internal revenue at or most convenient to the port of entry of said merchandise in the United States, and to be affixed under such regulations as the Commissioner of Internal Revenue, with the approval of the Secretary of the Treasury shall prescribe; and on all articles of merchandise of United States manufacture coming into Porto Rico in addition to the duty above provided upon payment of a tax equal in rate and amount to the internal-revenue tax imposed in Porto Rico upon the like articles of Porto Rican manufacture: *Provided*, That on and after the date when this Act shall take effect, all merchandise and articles, except coffee, not dutiable under the tariff laws of the United States, and all merchandise and articles entered in Porto Rico free of duty under orders heretofore made by the Secretary of War, shall be admitted into the several ports thereof, when imported from the United States, free of duty, all laws or parts of laws to the contrary notwithstanding; and whenever the legislative assembly of Porto Rico shall have enacted and put into operation a system of local taxation to meet the necessities of the government of Porto Rico, by this act established, and shall by resolution duly passed so notify the President, he shall make proclamation thereof, and thereupon all tariff duties on merchandise and articles going into Porto Rico from the United States or coming into the United States from Porto Rico shall cease, and from and after such date all such merchandise and articles shall be entered at the several ports of entry free of duty; and in no event shall any duties be collected after the first day of March, nineteen hundred and two, on merchandise and articles going into Porto Rico from the United States or coming into the United States from Porto Rico.

Sec. 4. That the duties and taxes collected in Porto Rico in pursuance of this Act, less the cost of collecting the same, and the gross amount of all collections of duties and taxes in the United States upon articles of merchandise coming from Porto Rico, shall not be covered into the general fund of the Treasury, but shall be held as a separate fund, and shall be placed at the disposal of the President to be used for the government and benefit of Porto Rico until the government of Porto Rico herein provided for shall have been organized, when all moneys theretofore collected under the provisions hereof, then unexpended, shall be transferred to the local treasury of Porto Rico, and the Secretary of the Treasury shall designate the several ports and sub-ports of entry into Porto Rico and shall make such rules and regulations and appoint such agents as may be necessary to collect the duties and taxes authorized to be levied, collected, and paid in Porto Rico by the provisions of this Act, and he shall fix the compensation and provide for the payment thereof of all such officers, agents, and assistants as he may find it necessary to employ to carry out the provisions hereof; *Provided, however,* That as soon as a civil government for Porto Rico shall have been organized in accordance with the provisions of this Act and notice thereof shall have been given to the President he shall make proclamation thereof, and thereafter all collections of duties and taxes in Porto Rico under the provisions of this Act shall be paid into the treasury of Porto Rico, to be expended as required by law for the government and benefit thereof instead of being paid into the Treasury of the United States.

Sec. 5. That on and after the day when this act shall go into effect all goods, wares, and merchandise previously imported from Porto Rico, for which no entry has been made, and all goods, wares, and merchandise previously entered without payment of duty and under bond for warehousing, transportation, or any other purpose, for which no permit of delivery to the importer or his agent has been issued, shall be subjected to the duties imposed by this Act, and to no other duty, upon the entry or the withdrawal thereof: *Provided*, That when duties are based upon the weight of merchandise deposited in any public or private bonded warehouse said duties shall be levied and collected upon the weight of such merchandise at the time of its entry.

Sec. 38. That no export duties shall be levied or collected on exports from Porto Rico; but taxes and assessments on property, and license fees for franchises, privileges, and concessions may be imposed for the purposes of the insular and municipal governments, respectively, as may be provided and defined by act of the legislative assembly; and where necessary to anticipate taxes and revenues, bonds and other obligations may be issued by Porto Rico or any municipal government therein as may be provided by law to provide for expenditures authorized by law, and to protect the public credit, and to reimburse the United States for any moneys which have been or may be expended out of the emergency fund of the War Department for the relief of the industrial conditions of Porto Rico caused by the hurricane of August eighth, eighteen hundred and ninety-nine: *Provided, however,* That no public indebtedness of Porto Rico or of any municipality thereof shall be authorized or allowed in excess of seven per centum of the aggregate tax valuation of its property.

EXECUTIVE ORDERS OF THE PRESIDENT AS TO TARIFF IN PORTO RICO.

I.

EXECUTIVE MANSION,
August 19, 1898.

By virtue of the authority invested in me as Commander in Chief of the Army and Navy of the United States of America, I do hereby order and direct that upon the occupation and possession of any ports and any places in the island of Porto Rico by the forces of the United States the following tariff of duties and taxes to be levied and collected as a military contribution, and regulations for the administration thereof shall take effect and be in force in the ports and places so occupied.

Questions arising under said tariff and regulations shall be decided by the general in command of the United States forces in that island. Necessary and authorized expenses for the administration of said tariff and regulations shall be paid from the collections thereunder.

Accurate accounts of collections and expenditures shall be kept and rendered to the Secretary of War.

WILLIAM McKINLEY.

II.

EXECUTIVE MANSION,
September 9th, 1898.

Article XIV of customs tariff and regulations for ports in Porto Rico in possession of the United States is hereby amended so as to read as follows:

Any goods, wares, and merchandise not duty entered for payment of duty within ninety days after importation shall be sold at auction, by order of the officer in command of the United States forces, after five days' public notice conspicuously posted at the port, provided that the period of ninety days may be extended by said officer not exceeding a period of six months from the date of importation, when good and sufficient reasons therefor are presented to him, if, in his judgment, the interests of the Government will permit such extension. The proceeds of such sale will be kept for ten days subject to the demand of the importer, after the deduction of the proper duties on the goods and all expenses of storage and sale.

WILLIAM McKINLEY.

III.

EXECUTIVE MANSION, January 20, 1899.

By virtue of the authority vested in me as Commander in Chief of the Army and Navy of the United States of America, I do hereby order and direct that the following tariff of duties and taxes shall be levied and collected, and the regulations for the administration thereof shall take effect and be in force in all ports and places in the island of Porto Rico and all islands in the West Indies east of the 74th degree, west longitude, evacuated by Spain on and after February 1, 1899.

All questions arising in the administration of customs shall be referred to the collector at the port of San Juan for decision, and there shall be no appeal from such decisions except in cases where the collector may find it expedient to ask for special instructions of the War Department on the points involved.

Necessary and authorized expenses for the administration of said tariff and regulations shall be paid from the collections thereunder.

Accurate account of collections and expenditures shall be kept and rendered to the Secretary of War.

WILLIAM McKINLEY.

CONSTITUTION OF THE UNITED STATES.

WE THE PEOPLE of the United States, in Order to form a more perfect Union, establish Justice, insure domestic Tranquility, provide for the common defence, promote the general Welfare, and secure the Blessings of Liberty to ourselves and our Posterity, do ordain and establish this CONSTITUTION for the United States of America.

ARTICLE I.

SECTION 1. All legislative Powers herein granted shall be vested in a Congress of the United States, which shall consist of a Senate and House of Representatives.

SECTION 2. [1] The House of Representatives shall be composed of Members chosen every second Year by the People of the several States, and the Electors in each State shall have the Qualifications requisite for Electors of the most numerous Branch of the State Legislature.

In May, 1785, a committee of Congress made a report recommending an alteration in the Articles of Confederation, but no action was taken on it, and it was left to the State Legislatures to proceed in the matter. In January, 1786, the Legislature of Virginia passed a resolution providing for the appointment of five commissioners, who, or any three of them, should meet such commissioners as might be appointed in the other States of the Union, at a time and place to be agreed upon, to take into consideration the trade of the United States; to consider how far a uniform system in their commercial regulations may be necessary to their common interest and their permanent harmony; and to report to the several States such an act, relative to this great object, as, when ratified by them, will enable the United States in Congress effectually to provide for the same. The Virginia commissioners, after some correspondence, fixed the first Monday in September as the time, and the city of Annapolis as the place for the meeting, but only four other States were represented, viz: Delaware, New York, New Jersey, and Pennsylvania; the commissioners appointed by Massachusetts, New Hampshire, North Carolina, and Rhode Island failed to attend. Under the circumstances of so partial a representation, the commissioners present agreed upon a report, (drawn by Mr. Hamilton, of New York,) expressing their unanimous conviction that it might essentially tend to advance the interests of the Union if the States by which they were respectively delegated would concur, and use their endeavors to procure the concurrence of the other States, in the appointment of commissioners to meet at Philadelphia on the second Monday of May following, to take into consideration the situation of the United States; to devise such further provisions as should appear to them necessary to render the Constitution of the Federal Government adequate to the exigencies of the Union; and to report such an act for that purpose to the United States in

519

² No Person shall be a Representative who shall not have attained to the Age of twenty-five Years, and been seven Years a Citizen of the United States, and who shall not, when elected, be an Inhabitant of that State in which he shall be chosen.

³ * [Representatives and direct Taxes shall be apportioned among the several States which may be included within this Union, according to their respective Numbers, which shall be determined by adding to the whole Number of free Persons, including those bound to Service for a Term of Years, and excluding Indians not taxed, three fifths of all other Persons.] The actual Enumeration shall be made within three Years after the first Meeting of the Congress of the United States, and within every subsequent Term of ten Years. in such Manner as they shall by Law direct. The Number of Representatives shall not exceed one for every thirty Thousand, but each State shall have at Least one Representative; and until such enumeration shall be made, the State of New Hampshire shall be entitled to chuse three, Massachusetts eight, Rhode-Island and Providence Plantations one, Connecticut five, New-

---

Congress assembled as, when agreed to by them and afterwards confirmed by the Legislatures of every State, would effectually provide for the same.

Congress, on the 21st of February, 1787, adopted a resolution in favor of a convention, and the Legislatures of those States which had not already done so (with the exception of Rhode Island) promptly appointed delegates. On the 25th of May, seven States having convened, George Washington, of Virginia, was unanimously elected President, and the consideration of the proposed constitution was commenced. On the 17th of September, 1787, the Constitution as engrossed and agreed upon was signed by all the members present, except Mr. Gerry, of Massachusetts, and Messrs. Mason and Randolph, of Virginia. The president of the convention transmitted it to Congress, with a resolution stating how the proposed Federal Government should be put in operation, and an explanatory letter. Congress, on the 28th of September, 1787, directed the Constitution so framed. with the resolutions and letter concerning the same, to "be transmitted to the several Legislatures in order to be submitted to a convention of delegates chosen in each State by the people thereof, in conformity to the resolves of the convention."

On the 4th of March, 1789, the day which had been fixed for commencing the operations of Government under the new Constitution, it had been ratified by the conventions chosen in each State to consider it, as follows: Delaware, December 7, 1787; Pennsylvania, December 12, 1787; New Jersey, December 18, 1787; Georgia, January 2, 1788; Connecticut, January 9, 1788; Massachusetts, February 6, 1788; Maryland, April 28, 1788; South Carolina, May 23, 1788; New Hampshire, June 21, 1788; Virginia, June 26, 1788; and New York, July 26, 1788.

The President informed Congress, on the 28th of January, 1790, that North Carolina had ratified the Constitution November 21, 1789; and he informed Congress on the 1st of June, 1790, that Rhode Island had ratified the Constitution May 29, 1789. Vermont, in convention, ratified the Constitution January 10, 1791, and was, by an act of Congress approved February 18, 1791, "received and admitted into this Union as a new and entire member of the United States."

* The clause included in brackets is amended by the 14th amendment, 2d section. (See p. 532, *post*.)

York six, New Jersey four, Pennsylvania eight, Delaware one, Maryland six, Virginia ten, North Carolina five, South Carolina five, and Georgia three.

[4] When vacancies happen in the Representation from any State, the Executive Authority thereof shall issue Writs of Election to fill such Vacancies.

[5] The House of Representatives shall chuse their Speaker and other Officers; and shall have the sole Power of Impeachment.

SECTION 3. [1] The Senate of the United States shall be composed of two Senators from each State, chosen by the Legislature thereof, for six Years; and each Senator shall have one Vote.

[2] Immediately after they shall be assembled in Consequence of the first Election, they shall be divided as equally as may be into three Classes. The Seats of the Senators of the first Class shall be vacated at the Expiration of the second Year, of the second Class at the Expiration of the fourth Year, and of the third Class at the Expiration of the sixth Year, so that one-third may be chosen every second Year; and if Vacancies happen by Resignation, or otherwise, during the Recess of the Legislature of any State, the Executive thereof may make temporary Appointments until the next Meeting of the Legislature, which shall then fill such Vacancies.

[3] No Person shall be a Senator who shall not have attained to the Age of thirty Years, and been nine Years a Citizen of the United States, and who shall not, when elected, be an Inhabitant of that State for which he shall be chosen.

[4] The Vice President of the United States shall be President of the Senate, but shall have no Vote, unless they be equally divided.

[5] The Senate shall chuse their other Officers, and also a President pro tempore, in the Absence of the Vice President, or when he shall exercise the Office of President of the United States.

[6] The Senate shall have the sole Power to try all Impeachments. When sitting for that Purpose, they shall be on Oath or Affirmation. When the President of the United States is tried, the Chief Justice shall preside: And no Person shall be convicted without the Concurrence of two thirds of the Members present.

[7] Judgment in Cases of Impeachment shall not extend further than to removal from Office, and disqualification to hold and enjoy any Office of honor, Trust or Profit under the United States: but the Party convicted shall nevertheless be liable and subject to Indictment, Trial, Judgment and Punishment, according to Law.

SECTION 4. [1] The Times, Places and Manner of holding Elections for Senators and Representatives, shall be prescribed in each State by the Legislature thereof; but the Congress may at any time by Law make or alter such Regulations, except as to the Places of chusing Senators.

[2] The Congress shall assemble at least once in every Year, and such Meeting shall be on the first Monday in December, unless they shall by Law appoint a different Day.

SECTION 5. [1] Each House shall be the Judge of the Elections, Returns and Qualifications of its own Members, and a Majority of each shall constitute a quorum to do business; but a smaller Number may adjourn from day to day, and may be authorized to compel the Attendance of absent Members, in such Manner, and under such Penalties as each House may provide.

² Each House may determine the Rules of its Proceedings, punish its Members for disorderly Behaviour, and, with the Concurrence of two thirds, expel a Member.

³ Each House shall keep a Journal of its Proceedings, and from time to time publish the same, excepting such Parts as may in their Judgment require Secrecy; and the Yeas and Nays of the Members of either House on any question shall, at the Desire of one fifth of those Present, be entered on the Journal.

⁴ Neither House, during the Session of Congress, shall, without the Consent of the other, adjourn for more than three days, nor to any other Place than that in which the two Houses shall be sitting.

SECTION 6. ¹ The Senators and Representatives shall receive a Compensation for their Services, to be ascertained by Law, and paid out of the Treasury of the United States. They shall in all Cases, except Treason, Felony and Breach of the Peace, be privileged from Arrest during their Attendance at the Session of their respective Houses, and in going to and returning from the same; and for any Speech or Debate in either House, they shall not be questioned in any other Place.

² No Senator or Representative shall, during the Time for which he was elected, be appointed to any civil Office under the Authority of the United States, which shall have been created, or the Emoluments whereof shall have been encreased during such time; and no Person holding any Office under the United States, shall be a Member of either House during his Continuance in Office.

SECTION 7. ¹ All Bills for raising Revenue shall originate in the House of Representatives; but the Senate may propose or concur with Amendments as on other Bills.

² Every Bill which shall have passed the House of Representatives and the Senate, shall, before it become a Law, be presented to the President of the United States; If he approve he shall sign it, but if not he shall return it, with his Objections to that House in which it shall have originated, who shall enter the Objections at large on their Journal, and proceed to reconsider it. If after such Reconsideration two thirds of that House shall agree to pass the Bill, it shall be sent, together with the Objections, to the other House, by which it shall likewise be reconsidered, and if approved by two-thirds of that House, it shall become a Law. But in all such Cases the Votes of both Houses shall be determined by Yeas and Nays, and the Names of the Persons voting for and against the Bill shall be entered on the Journal of each House respectively. If any Bill shall not be returned by the President within ten Days (Sundays excepted) after it shall have been presented to him, the Same shall be a Law, in like Manner as if he had signed it, unless the Congress by their Adjournment prevent its Return, in which Case it shall not be a Law.

³ Every Order, Resolution, or Vote to which the Concurrence of the

Senate and House of Representatives may be necessary (except on a question of Adjournment) shall be presented to the President of the United States; and before the Same shall take Effect, shall be approved by him, or being disapproved by him, shall be repassed by two thirds of the Senate and House of Representatives, according to the Rules and Limitations prescribed in the Case of a Bill.

SECTION 8. The Congress shall have Power [1] To lay and collect Taxes, Duties, Imposts and Excises, to pay the Debts and provide for the common Defence and general Welfare of the United States; but all Duties, Imposts and Excises shall be uniform throughout the United States;

[2] To borrow Money on the credit of the United States;

[3] To regulate Commerce with foreign Nations, and among the several States, and with the Indian Tribes;

[4] To establish an uniform Rule of Naturalization, and uniform Laws on the subject of Bankruptcies throughout the United States;

[5] To coin Money, regulate the Value thereof, and of foreign Coin, and fix the Standard of Weights and Measures;

[6] To provide for the Punishment of counterfeiting the Securities and current Coin of the United States;

[7] To establish Post Offices and post Roads;

[8] To promote the Progress of Science and useful Arts, by securing for limited Times to Authors and Inventors the exclusive Right to their respective Writings and Discoveries;

[9] To constitute Tribunals inferior to the supreme Court;

[10] To define and punish Piracies and Felonies committed on the high Seas, and Offences against the Law of Nations;

[11] To declare War, grant Letters of Marque and Reprisal, and make Rules concerning Captures on Land and Water;

[12] To raise and support Armies, but no Appropriation of Money to that Use shall be for a longer Term than two Years;

[13] To provide and maintain a Navy;

[14] To make Rules for the Government and Regulation of the land and naval Forces;

[15] To provide for calling forth the Militia to execute the Laws of the Union, suppress Insurrections and repel Invasions;

[16] To provide for organizing, arming, and disciplining, the Militia, and for governing such Part of them as may be employed in the Service of the United States, reserving to the States respectively, the Appointment of the Officers, and the Authority of training the Militia according to the discipline prescribed by Congress;

[17] To exercise exclusive Legislation in all Cases whatsoever, over such District (not exceeding ten Miles square) as may, by Cession of particular States, and the Acceptance of Congress, become the Seat of the Government of the United States, and to exercise like Authority over all Places purchased by the Consent of the Legislature of the State in which the Same shall be, for the Erection of Forts, Magazines, Arsenals, dock-Yards, and other needful Buildings;—And

[18] To make all Laws which shall be necessary and proper for carrying

into Execution the foregoing Powers, and all other Powers vested by this Constitution in the Government of the United States, or in any Department or Officer thereof.

Section 9.   ¹ The Migration or Importation of such Persons as any of the States now existing shall think proper to admit, shall not be prohibited by the Congress prior to the Year one thousand eight hundred and eight, but a Tax or duty may be imposed on such Importation, not exceeding ten dollars for each Person.

² The Privilege of the Writ of Habeas Corpus shall not be suspended, unless when in Cases of Rebellion or Invasion the public Safety may require it.

³ No Bill of Attainder or ex post facto Law shall be passed.

⁴ No Capitation, or other direct, tax shall be laid, unless in Proportion to the Census or Enumeration herein before directed to be taken.

⁵ No Tax or Duty shall be laid on Articles exported from any State.

⁶ No Preference shall be given by any Regulation of Commerce or Revenue to the Ports of one State over those of another: nor shall Vessels bound to, or from, one State, be obliged to enter, clear, or pay Duties in another.

⁷ No Money shall be drawn from the Treasury, but in Consequence of Appropriations made by Law; and a regular Statement and Account of the Receipts and Expenditures of all public Money shall be published from time to time.

⁸ No Title of Nobility shall be granted by the United States: And no Person holding any Office of Profit or Trust under them, shall, without the Consent of the Congress, accept of any present, Emolument, Office, or Title, of any kind whatever, from any King, Prince, or foreign State.

Section 10.   ¹ No State shall enter into any Treaty, Alliance, or Confederation; grant Letters of Marque and Reprisal; coin Money; emit Bills of Credit; make any Thing but gold and silver Coin a Tender in Payment of Debts; pass any Bill of Attainder, ex post facto Law, or Law impairing the Obligation of Contracts, or grant any Title of Nobility.

² No State shall, without the Consent of the Congress, lay any Imposts or Duties on Imports or Exports, except what may be absolutely necessary for executing it's inspection Laws: and the net Produce of all Duties and Imposts, laid by any State on Imports or Exports, shall be for the Use of the Treasury of the United States; and all such Laws shall be subject to the Revision and Controul of the Congress.

³ No State, shall without the Consent of Congress, lay any Duty of Tonnage, keep Troops, or Ships of War in time of Peace, enter into an Agreement or Compact with another State, or with a foreign Power, or engage in War, unless actually invaded, or in such imminent Danger as will not admit of delay.

ARTICLE II.

Section 1.   ¹ The executive Power shall be vested in a President of the United States of America.   He shall hold his Office during the Term of four Years, and, together with the Vice President, chosen for the same Term, be elected, as follows:

2 Each State shall appoint, in such Manner as the Legislature thereof may direct, a Number of Electors, equal to the whole Number of Senators and Representatives to which the State may be entitled in the Congress: but no Senator or Representative, or Person holding an Office of Trust or Profit under the United States, shall be appointed an Elector.

3 The Congress may determine the Time of chusing the Electors, and the Day on which they shall give their Votes; which day shall be the same throughout the United States.

4 No person except a natural born Citizen, or a Citizen of the United States, at the time of the Adoption of this Constitution, shall be eligible to the Office of President; neither shall any Person be eligible to that Office who shall not have attained to the Age of thirty-five Years, and been fourteen Years a Resident within the United States.

5 In Case of the Removal of the President from Office, or of his Death, Resignation, or Inability to discharge the Powers and Duties of the said Office, the same shall devolve on the Vice President, and the Congress may by Law provide for the Case of Removal, Death, Resignation or Inability, both of the President and Vice President, declaring what Officer shall then act as President, and such Officer shall act accordingly, until the Disability be removed, or a President shall be elected.

6 The President shall, at stated Times, receive for his Services, a Compensation, which shall neither be encreased nor diminished during the Period for which he shall have been elected, and he shall not receive within that Period any other Emolument from the United States, or any of them.

7 Before he enter on the Execution of his Office, he shall take the following Oath or Affirmation:—" I do solemnly swear (or affirm) that I will faithfully execute the Office of President of the United States, and will to the best of my Ability, preserve, protect and defend the Constitution of the United States."

SECTION 2. 1 The President shall be Commander in Chief of the Army and Navy of the United States, and of the Militia of the several States, when called into the actual Service of the United States; he may require the Opinion, in writing, of the principal Officer in each of the executive Departments, upon any Subject relating to the Duties of their respective Offices, and he shall have power to grant Reprieves and Pardons for Offences against the United States, except in Cases of Impeachment.

2 He shall have Power, by and with the Advice and Consent of the Senate, to make Treaties, provided two thirds of the Senators present concur; and he shall nominate, and by and with the Advice and Consent of the Senate, shall appoint Ambassadors, other public Ministers and Consuls, Judges of the supreme Court, and all other Officers of the United States, whose Appointments are not herein otherwise provided for, and which shall be established by Law: but the Congress may by Law vest the Appointment of such inferior Officers, as they think proper,

in the President alone, in the Courts of Law, or in the Heads of Departments.

³ The President shall have Power to fill up all Vacancies that may happen during the Recess of the Senate, by granting Commissions which shall expire at the End of their next Session.

SECTION 3. He shall from time to time give to the Congress Information of the State of the Union, and recommend to their Consideration such Measures as he shall judge necessary and expedient; he may, on extraordinary Occasions, convene both Houses, or either of them, and in Case of Disagreement between them, with Respect to the Time of Adjournment, he may adjourn them to such Time as he shall think proper; he shall receive Ambassadors and other public Ministers; he shall take Care that the Laws be faithfully executed, and shall Commission all the Officers of the United States.

SECTION 4. The President, Vice President and all civil Officers of the United States, shall be removed from Office on Impeachment for, and Conviction of, Treason, Bribery, or other high Crimes and Misdemeanors.

ARTICLE III.

SECTION 1. The judicial Power of the United States, shall be vested in one supreme Court, and in such inferior Courts as the Congress may from time to time ordain and establish. The Judges, both of the supreme and inferior Courts, shall hold their Offices during good Behaviour, and shall, at stated Times, receive for their Services, a Compensation, which shall not be diminished during their Continuance in Office.

SECTION 2. ¹ The judicial Power shall extend to all Cases, in Law and Equity, arising under this Constitution, the Laws of the United States, and Treaties made, or which shall be made, under their Authority;— to all Cases affecting Ambassadors, other public Ministers and Consuls; —to all Cases of admiralty and maritime Jurisdiction;—to Controversies to which the United States shall be a Party;—to Controversies between two or more States;—between a State and Citizens of another State;—between Citizens of different States,—between Citizens of the same State claiming Lands under Grants of different States, and between a State, or the Citizens thereof, and foreign States, Citizens or Subjects.

² In all Cases affecting Ambassadors, other public Ministers and Consuls. and those in which a State shall be Party, the supreme Court shall have original Jurisdiction. In all the other Cases before mentioned, the supreme Court shall have appellate Jurisdiction, both as to Law and Fact. with such Exceptions, and under such Regulations as the Congress shall make.

³ The Trial of all Crimes, except in Cases of Impeachment, shall be by Jury; and such Trial shall be held in the State where the said Crimes shall have been committed; but when not committed within any State, the Trial shall be at such Place or Places as the Congress may by Law have directed.

SECTION 3. ¹ Treason against the United States, shall consist only in levying War against them, or in adhering to their Enemies, giving them Aid and Comfort. No Person shall be convicted of Treason unless on the Testimony of two Witnesses to the same overt Act, or on Confession in open Court.

2 The Congress shall have Power to declare the Punishment of Treason, but no Attainder of Treason shall work Corruption of Blood, or Forfeiture except during the Life of the Person attainted.

ARTICLE IV.

SECTION 1. Full Faith and Credit shall be given in each State to the public Acts, Records, and judicial Proceedings of every other State. And the Congress may by general Laws prescribe the Manner in which such Acts, Records and Proceedings shall be proved, and the Effect thereof.

SECTION 2. 1 The Citizens of each State shall be entitled to all Privileges and Immunities of Citizens in the several States.

2 A person charged in any State with Treason, Felony, or other Crime, who shall flee from Justice, and be found in another State, shall on Demand of the executive Authority of the State from which he fled, be delivered up, to be removed to the State having Jurisdiction of the Crime.

3 No Person held to Service or Labour in one State, under the Laws thereof, escaping into another, shall, in Consequence of any Law or Regulation therein, be discharged from such Service or Labour, but shall be delivered up on Claim of the Party to whom such Service or Labour may be due.

SECTION 3. 1 New States may be admitted by the Congress into this Union; but no new State shall be formed or erected within the Jurisdiction of any other State; nor any State be formed by the Junction of two or more States, or Parts of States, without the Consent of the Legislatures of the States concerned as well as of the Congress.

2 The Congress shall have Power to dispose of and make all needful Rules and Regulations respecting the Territory or other Property belonging to the United States; and nothing in this Constitution shall be so construed as to Prejudice any Claims of the United States, or of any particular State.

SECTION 4. The United States shall guarantee to every State in his Union a Republican Form of Government, and shall protect each of them against Invasion; and on Application of the Legislature, or of the Executive (when the Legislature cannot be convened) against domestic Violence.

ARTICLE V.

The Congress, whenever two thirds of both Houses shall deem it necessary, shall propose Amendments to this Constitution, or, on the Application of the Legislatures of two thirds of the several States, shall call a Convention for proposing Amendments, which, in either Case, shall be valid to all Intents and Purposes, as Part of this Constitution, when ratified by the Legislatures of three fourths of the several States, or by Conventions in three fourths thereof, as the one or the other Mode of Ratification may be proposed by the Congress; Provided that no Amendment which may be made prior to the Year One thousand eight hundred and eight shall in any Manner affect the first and fourth Clauses in the Ninth Section of the first Article; and that no State, without its Consent, shall be deprived of its equal Suffrage in the Senate.

ARTICLE VI.

[1] All Debts contracted and Engagements entered into, before the Adoption of this Constitution, shall be as valid against the United States under this Constitution, as under the Confederation.

[2] This Constitution, and the Laws of the United States which shall be made in Pursuance thereof; and all Treaties made, or which shall be made, under the Authority of the United States, shall be the supreme Law of the Land; and the Judges in every State shall be bound thereby, any Thing in the Constitution or Laws of any State to the Contrary notwithstanding.

[3] The Senators and Representatives before mentioned, and the Members of the several State Legislatures, and all executive and judicial Officers, both of the United States and of the several States, shall be bound by Oath or Affirmation, to support this Constitution; but no religious Test shall ever be required as a Qualification to any Office or public Trust under the United States.

ARTICLE VII.

The Ratification of the Conventions of nine States, shall be sufficient for the Establishment of this Constitution between the States so ratifying the Same.

Done in Convention by the Unanimous Consent of the States present the Seventeenth Day of September in the Year of our Lord one thousand seven hundred and Eighty seven, and of the Independance of the United States of America the Twelfth. **In Witness** whereof We have hereunto subscribed our Names,

Go. Washington—
Presidt. and Deputy from Virginia.

New Hampshire.

JOHN LANGDON,   NICHOLAS GILMAN.

Massachusetts.

NATHANIEL GORHAM,   RUFUS KING.

Connecticut.

WM. SAML. JOHNSON,   ROGER SHERMAN.

New York.

ALEXANDER HAMILTON.

New Jersey.

WIL.: LIVINGSTON,   WM. PATERSON,
DAVID BREARLEY,   JONA. DAYTON.

Pennsylvania.

B. FRANKLIN,
ROBT. MORRIS,
THO: FITZSIMONS,
JAMES WILSON,

THOMAS MIFFLIN,
GEO: CLYMER,
JARED INGERSOLL,
GOUV: MORRIS.

Delaware.

GEO: READ,
JOHN DICKINSON,
JACO: BROOM,

GUNNING BEDFORD, Jun'r,
RICHARD BASSETT.

Maryland.

JAMES M'HENRY,
DANL CARROLL.

DAN: OF ST. THOS. JENIFER.

Virginia.

JOHN BLAIR,

JAMES MADISON, Jr.

North Carolina.

WM. BLOUNT,
HU. WILLIAMSON.

RICH'D DOBBS SPAIGHT,

South Carolina.

J. RUTLEDGE,
CHARLES PINCKNEY,

CHARLES COTESWORTH PINCKNEY,
PIERCE BUTLER.

Georgia.

WILLIAM FEW,
Attest:

ABR. BALDWIN.
WILLIAM JACKSON, Secretary.

ARTICLES IN ADDITION TO, AND AMENDMENT OF, THE CONSTITUTION OF THE UNITED STATES OF AMERICA, PROPOSED BY CONGRESS, AND RATIFIED BY THE LEGISLATURES OF THE SEVERAL STATES PURSUANT TO THE FIFTH ARTICLE OF THE ORIGINAL CONSTITUTION.

(The first ten amendments to the Constitution of the United States were proposed to the legislatures of the several States by the First Congress, on the 25th of September, 1789. They were ratified by the following States, and the notifications of ratification by the governors thereof were successively communicated by the President to Congress: New Jersey, November 20, 1789; Maryland, December 19, 1789; North Carolina, December 22, 1789; South Carolina, January 19, 1790; New Hampshire, January 25, 1790; Delaware, January 28, 1790; Pennsylvania, March 10, 1790; New York, March 27, 1790; Rhode Island, June 15, 1790; Vermont, November 3, 1791; and Virginia, December 15, 1791. There is no evidence on the journals of Congress that the legislatures of Connecticut, Georgia, and Massachusetts ratified them.)

ARTICLE I.

Congress shall make no law respecting an establishment of religion, or prohibiting the free exercise thereof; or abridging the freedom of speech, or of the press; or the right of the people peaceably to assemble, and to petition the Government for a redress of grievances.

34

ARTICLE II.

A well regulated Militia, being necessary to the security of a free State, the right of the people to keep and bear Arms, shall not be infringed.

ARTICLE III.

No Soldier shall, in time of peace be quartered in any house, without the consent of the Owner, nor in time of war, but in a manner to be prescribed by law.

ARTICLE IV.

The right of the people to be secure in their persons, houses, papers, and effects, against unreasonable searches and seizures, shall not be violated, and no Warrants shall issue, but upon probable cause, supported by Oath or affirmation, and particularly describing the place to be searched, and the persons or things to be seized.

ARTICLE V.

No person shall be held to answer for a capital, or otherwise infamous crime, unless on a presentment or indictment of a Grand Jury, except in cases arising in the land or naval forces, or in the Militia, when in actual service in time of War or public danger; nor shall any person be subject for the same offence to be twice put in jeopardy of life or limb; nor shall be compelled in any Criminal Case to be a witness against himself, nor be deprived of life, liberty, or property, without due process of law; nor shall private property be taken for public use, without just compensation.

ARTICLE VI.

In all criminal prosecutions, the accused shall enjoy the right to a speedy and public trial, by an impartial jury of the State and district wherein the crime shall have been committed, which district shall have been previously ascertained by law, and to be informed of the nature and cause of the accusation; to be confronted with the witnesses against him; to have compulsory process for obtaining Witnesses in his favor, and to have the Assistance of Counsel for his defence.

ARTICLE VII.

In suits at common law, where the value in controversy shall exceed twenty dollars, the right of trial by jury shall be preserved, and no fact tried by a jury shall be otherwise re-examined in any Court of the United States, than according to the rules of the common law.

ARTICLE VIII.

Excessive bail shall not be required, nor excessive fines imposed, nor cruel and unusual punishments inflicted.

ARTICLE IX.

The enumeration in the Constitution, of certain rights, shall not be construed to deny or disparage others retained by the people.

ARTICLE X.

The powers not delegated to the United States by the Constitution, nor prohibited by it to the States, are reserved to the States respectively, or to the people.

ARTICLE XI.

The Judicial power of the United States shall not be construed to extend to any suit in law or equity, commenced or prosecuted against one of the United States by Citizens of another State, or by Citizens or Subjects of any Foreign State.

(The eleventh amendment to the Constitution of the United States was proposed to the legislatures of the several States by the Third Congress, on the 5th September, 1794; and was declared in a message from the President to Congress, dated the 8th of January, 1798, to have been ratified by the legislatures of three-fourths of the States.)

ARTICLE XII.

The Electors shall meet in their respective states, and vote by ballot for President and Vice-President, one of whom, at least, shall not be an inhabitant of the same state with themselves; they shall name in their ballots the person voted for as President, and in distinct ballots the person voted for as Vice-President, and they shall make distinct lists of all persons voted for as President, and of all persons voted for as Vice-President, and of the number of votes for each, which lists they shall sign and certify, and transmit sealed to the seat of the government of the United States, directed to the President of the Senate; —The President of the Senate shall, in presence of the Senate and House of Representatives, open all the certificates and the votes shall then be counted;—The person having the greatest number of votes for President, shall be the President, if such number be a majority of the whole number of Electors appointed; and if no person have such majority, then from the persons having the highest numbers not exceeding three on the list of those voted for as President, the House of Representatives shall choose immediately, by ballot, the President. But in choosing the President, the votes shall be taken by states, the representation from each state having one vote; a quorum for this purpose shall consist of a member or members from two-thirds of the states, and a majority of all the states shall be necessary to a choice. And if the House of Representatives shall not choose a President whenever the right of choice shall devolve upon them, before the fourth day of March next following, then the Vice-President shall act as President, as in the case of the death or other constitutional disability of the President. The person having the greatest number of votes as Vice-President, shall be the Vice-President, if such number be a majority of the whole number of Electors appointed, and if no person have a ma-

jority, then from the two highest numbers on the list, the Senate shall
choose the Vice-President; a quorum for the purpose shall consist of
two-thirds of the whole number of Senators, and a majority of the
whole number shall be necessary to a choice. But no person constitutionally ineligible to the office of President shall be eligible to that of
Vice-President of the United States.

(The twelfth amendment to the Constitution of the United States was proposed to the legislatures of the several States by the Eighth Congress, on the
12th of December, 1803, in lieu of the original third paragraph of the first section of the second article; and was declared in a proclamation of the Secretary
of State, dated the 25th of September, 1804, to have been ratified by the legislatures of three-fourths of the States.)

ARTICLE XIII.

SECTION 1. Neither slavery nor involuntary servitude, except as a
punishment for crime whereof the party shall have been duly convicted, shall exist within the United States, or any place subject to
their jurisdiction.

SECTION 2. Congress shall have power to enforce this article by appropriate legislation.

(The thirteenth amendment to the Constitution of the United States was
proposed to the legislatures of the several States by the Thirty-eighth Congress, on the 1st of February, 1865, and was declared, in a proclamation of the
Secretary of State, dated the 18th of December, 1865, to have been ratified by
the legislatures of twenty-seven of the thirty-six States, viz: Illinois, Rhode
Island, Michigan, Maryland, New York, West Virginia, Maine, Kansas, Massachusetts, Pennsylvania, Virginia, Ohio, Missouri, Nevada, Indiana, Louisiana,
Minnesota, Wisconsin, Vermont, Tennessee, Arkansas, Connecticut, New
Hampshire, South Carolina, Alabama, North Carolina, and Georgia.)

ARTICLE XIV.

SECTION 1. All persons born or naturalized in the United States, and
subject to the jurisdiction thereof, are citizens of the United States
and of the State wherein they reside. No State shall make or enforce
any law which shall abridge the privileges or immunities of citizens of
the United States; nor shall any State deprive any person of life, liberty, or property, without due process of law; nor deny to any person
within its jurisdiction the equal protection of the laws.

SECTION 2. Representatives shall be apportioned among the several
States according to their respective numbers, counting the whole number of persons in each State, excluding Indians not taxed. But when
the right to vote at any election for the choice of electors for President
and Vice President of the United States, Representatives in Congress,
the Executive and Judicial officers of a State, or the members of the
Legislature thereof, is denied to any of the male inhabitants of such
State, being twenty-one years of age, and citizens of the United States,
or in any way abridged, except for participation in rebellion, or other
crime, the basis of representation therein shall be reduced in the proportion which the number of such male citizens shall bear to the whole
number of male citizens twenty-one years of age in such State.

SECTION 3. No person shall be a Sen tor or Representative in Con-gress, or elector of President and Vice President, or hold any office, civil or military, under the United States, or under any State, who, having previously taken an oath, as a member of Congress, or as an officer of the United States, or as a member of any State legislature, or as an executive or judicial officer of any State, to support the Con-stitution of the United States, shall have engaged in insurrection or rebellion against the same, or given aid or comfort to the enemies thereof. But Congress may by a vote of two-thirds of each House, re-move such disability.

SECTION 4. The validity of the public debt of the United States, au-thorized by law, including debts incurred for payment of pensions and bounties for services in suppressing insurrection or rebellion, shall not be questioned. But neither the United States nor any State shall assume or pay any debt or obligation incurred in aid of insurrection or rebel-lion against the United States, or any claim for the loss or emancipa-tion of any slave; but all such debts, obligations and claims shall be held illegal and void.

SECTION 5. The Congress shall have power to enforce, by appropriate legislation, the provisions of this article.

(The fourteenth amendment to the Constitution of the United States was proposed to the legislatures of the several States by the Thirty-ninth Congress, on the 16th of June, 1866. On the 21st of July, 1868, Congress adopted and transmitted to the Department of State a concurrent resolution, declaring that "the legislatures of the States of Connecticut, Tennessee, New Jersey, Oregon, Vermont, New York, Ohio, Illinois, West Virginia, Kansas, Maine, Nevada, Missouri, Indiana, Minnesota, New Hampshire, Massachusetts, Nebraska, Iowa, Arkansas, Florida, North Carolina, Alabama, South Carolina, and Louisiana, being three-fourths and more of the several States of the Union, have ratified the fourteenth article of amendment to the Constitution of the United States, duly proposed by two-thirds of each House of the thirty-ninth Congress: There-fore Resolved, That said fourteenth article is hereby declared to be a part of the Constitution of the United States, and it shall be duly promulgated as such by the Secretary of State." The Secretary of State accordingly issued a proclama-tion, dated the 28th of July, 1868, declaring that the proposed fourteenth amend-ment had been ratified, in the manner hereafter mentioned, by the legislatures of thirty of the thirty-six States, viz: Connecticut, June 30, 1866; New Hamp-shire, July 7, 1866; Tennessee, July 19, 1866; New Jersey, September 11, 1866, (and the legislature of the same State passed a resolution in April, 1868, to withdraw its consent to it;) Oregon, September 19, 1866; Vermont, November 9, 1866; Georgia rejected it November 13, 1866, and ratified it July 21, 1868; North Carolina rejected it December 4, 1866, and ratified it July 4, 1868; South Caro-lina rejected it December 20, 1866, and ratified it July 9, 1868; New York rati-fied it January 10, 1867; Ohio ratified it January 11, 1867, (and the legislature of the same State passed a resolution in January, 1868, to withdraw its consent to it;) Illinois ratified it January 15, 1867; West Virginia, January 16, 1867; Kansas, January 18, 1867; Maine, January 19, 1867; Nevada, January 22, 1867; Missouri, January 26, 1867; Indiana, January 29, 1867; Minnesota, February 1, 1867; Rhode Island, February 7, 1867; Wisconsin, February 13, 1867; Pennsyl-vania, February 13, 1867; Michigan, February 15, 1867; Massachusetts, March 20, 1867; Nebraska, June 15, 1867; Iowa, April 3, 1868; Arkansas, April 6, 1868; Florida, June 9, 1868; Louisiana, July 9, 1868; and Alabama, July 13, 1868.

Georgia again ratified the amendment February 2, 1870. Texas rejected it November 1, 1866, and ratified it February 18, 1870. Virginia rejected it January 19, 1867, and ratified October 8, 1869. The amendment was rejected by Kentucky January 10, 1867; by Delaware February 8, 1867; by Maryland March 23, 1867; and was not afterward ratified by either State.)

ARTICLE XV.

SECTION 1. The right of citizens of the United States to vote shall not be denied or abridged by the United States or by any State on account of race, color, or previous condition of servitude.

SECTION 2. The Congress shall have power to enforce this article by appropriate legislation.

(The fifteenth amendment to the Constitution of the United States was proposed to the legislatures of the several States by the Fortieth Congress on the 27th of February, 1869, and was declared, in a proclamation of the Secretary of State, dated March 30, 1870, to have been ratified by the legislatures of twenty-nine of the thirty-seven States. The dates of these ratifications (arranged in the order of their reception at the Department of State) were: from North Carolina, March 5, 1869; West Virginia, March 3, 1869; Massachusetts, March 9–12, 1869; Wisconsin, March 9, 1869; Maine, March 12, 1869; Louisiana, March 5, 1869; Michigan, March 8, 1869; South Carolina, March 16, 1869; Pennsylvania, March 26, 1869; Arkansas, March 30, 1869; Connecticut, May 19, 1869; Florida, June 15, 1869; Illinois, March 5, 1869; Indiana, May 13–14, 1869; New York, March 17–April 14, 1869, (and the legislature of the same State passed a resolution January 5, 1870, to withdraw its consent to it;) New Hampshire, July 7, 1869; Nevada, March 1, 1869; Vermont, October 21, 1869; Virginia, October 8, 1869; Missouri, January 10, 1870; Mississippi, January 15–17, 1870; Ohio, January 27, 1870; Iowa, February 3, 1870; Kansas, January, 18–19, 1870; Minnesota, February 19, 1870; Rhode Island, January 18, 1870; Nebraska, February 17, 1870; Texas, February 18, 1870. The State of Georgia also ratified the amendment February 2, 1870.)

ANALYSIS AND CLASSIFICATION OF CASES CITED IN BRIEFS, ARGUMENTS AND OPINIONS IN INSULAR CASES.

There were about three hundred cases cited in the briefs, arguments and opinions in the Insular Cases, (exclusive of those relating to the form of action, construction of the Customs Administrative Act as to procedure, and to the Jurisdiction of United States Circuit Courts and the United States Court of Claims). An effort has been made to classify the cases cited on constitutional points under the following headings (for a consecutive list of these headings I–XXV, see Table of Contents of Insular Cases, pp. 462, 463, *ante.*)

The analysis is necessarily imperfect, many of the cases having been cited on so many points that it has been impossible to make a perfect classification.

I.

Nationality and Sovereignty of the United States and Sovereign Powers of Central Government.

Ableman vs. *Booth,* U. S. Sup. Ct. 1858, 21 Howard, 506, Taney, Ch. J.

American Ins. Co. vs. *Canter (Florida Case),* U. S. Sup. Ct. 1828, 1 Peters, 511, Marshall, Ch. J.

Amy Warwick, The, U. S. Dist. Ct. Mass. 1862; 2 Sprague, 123, 150, Sprague, J.

Antelope, The, U. S. Sup. Ct. 1825, 10 Wheaton, 66, Marshall, Ch. J.

Barron vs. *Baltimore,* U. S. Sup. Ct. 1833, 7 Peters, 243, Marshall, Ch. J.

Briscoe vs. *Bank,* U. S. Sup. Ct. 1837, 11 Peters, 257, McLean, J.

Buckner vs. *Finley,* U. S. Sup. Ct. 1829, 2 Peters, 586, Washington, J.

Chae Chan Ping vs. *United States (Chinese Exclusion Case),* U. S. Sup. Ct. 1889, 130 U. S. 581, Field, J.

Charkieh, The, High Court of Adm. 1873, L. R., 4 A & E. 59, and Corbett's Cas. Int. Law, p. 9, Sir Robert Phillimore.

Chew Heong vs. *United States,* U. S. Sup. Ct. 1884, 112 U. S. 536, Harlan, J.

Chicago, etc., Ry. Co. vs. *Tompkins,* U. S. Sup. Ct. 1900, 176 U. S. 167, Brewer, J.

Chisholm vs. *Georgia,* U. S. Sup. Ct. 1793, 2 Dallas, 419, Jay, Ch. J., Iredell, Blair, Wilson, Cushing, JJ.

Cohens vs. *Virginia,* U. S. Sup. Ct. 1821, 6 Wheaton, 264, Marshall, Ch. J.

Coleman vs. *Tennessee,* U. S. Sup. Ct. 1878, 97 U. S. 509, Field, J.

535

Cooper, In re, (Bering Sea Cases) U. S. Sup. Ct. 1891, 138 U. S. 404, and 1892, 143 U. S. 472, FULLER, Ch. J.

Crandall vs. *Nevada*, U. S. Sup. Ct. 1867, 6 Wallace, 35, MILLER, J.

Debs, In re, U. S. Sup. Ct. 1895, 158 U. S. 564, BREWER, J.

Dodge vs. *Woolsey*, U. S. Sup. Ct. 1855, 18 Howard, 331, WAYNE, J.

Dow v. *Johnson*, U. S. Sup. Ct. 1879, 100 U. S. 158, FIELD, J.

Ekiu, Nishimura, vs. *United States*, U. S. Sup. Ct. 1891, 142 U. S. 651, GRAY, J.

Exchange, Schooner, vs. *McFadden*, U. S. Sup. Ct. 1812, 7 Cranch, 116, MARSHALL, Ch. J.

Fong Yue Ting vs. *United States (Chinese Exclusion Case)*, U. S. Sup. Ct. 1893, 149 U. S. 698, GRAY. J.

Georgia vs. *Stanton*, U. S. Sup. Ct. 1867, 6 Wallace, 50, NELSON, J.

Gibbons vs. *Ogden*, U. S. Sup. Ct. 1824, 9 Wheaton, 1, MARSHALL, Ch. J.

Gibbons vs. *United States*, U. S. Sup. Ct. 1868, 8 Wallace, 269, MILLER, J.

Gilman vs. *Philadelphia*, U. S. Sup. Ct. 1865, 3 Wallace, 713, SWAYNE, J.

Hamilton vs. *Dillin*, U. S. Sup. Ct. 1874, 21 Wall. 73, BRADLEY, J.

Hepburn vs. *Griswold*, U. S. Sup. Ct. 1869, 8 Wallace, 603, CHASE, Ch. J.

Jones vs. *United States (Navassa Islands Case)*, U. S. Sup. Ct. 1890, 137 U. S. 202, GRAY, J.

Kennett vs. *Chambers*, U. S. Sup. Ct. 1852, 14 Howard, 38, TANEY, Ch. J.

Kilbourn vs. *Thompson*, U. S. Sup. Ct. 1880, 103 U. S. 168, MILLER, J.

Lane vs. *Oregon*, U. S. Sup. Ct. 1868, 7 Wallace, 71, CHASE, Ch. J.

Legal Tender Cases, U. S. Sup. Ct. 1869, 8 Wallace, 603, CHASE, Ch. J.; 1870, 12 Wallace, 457, STRONG, J.; 1884, 110 U. S. 421, GRAY, J.

Livingstone vs. *Moore*, U. S. Sup. Ct. 1833, 7 Peters, 469, JOHNSON, J.

Luther vs. *Borden*, U. S. Sup. Ct. 1849, 7 Howard, 1, TANEY, Ch. J.

McCulloch vs. *Maryland*, U. S. Sup. Ct. 1819, 4 Wheaton, 316, MARSHALL, Ch. J.

McDaniel vs. *McMeekin*, Ct. of App. So. Car. 1834, 2 Hill S. C. Law, Part I, p. 1, O'NEALL, JOHNSON, HARPER, JJ.

McPherson vs. *Blacker*, U. S. Sup. Ct. 1892, 146 U. S. 1, FULLER, Ch. J.

Marbury vs. *Madison*, U. S. Sup. Ct. 1803, 1 Cranch, 137, MARSHALL, Ch. J.

Martin vs. *Waddell*, U. S. Sup. Ct. 1842, 16 Peters, 367, TANEY, Ch. J.

Miller vs. *United States*, U. S. Sup. Ct. 1870, 11 Wallace, 268, STRONG, J.

Mormon Church vs. *United States*, U. S. Sup. Ct. 1890, 136 U. S. 1, BRADLEY, J.

Munn vs. *Illinois*, U. S. Sup. Ct. 1876, 94 U. S. 113, WAITE, Ch. J.

Neagle, In re, U. S. Sup. Ct. 1890, 135 U. S. 1, MILLER, J.

New Orleans vs. *United States*, U. S. Sup. Ct. 1836, 10 Peters, 662, McLEAN, J.

Penhallow vs. *Doane*, U. S. Sup. Ct. 1795, 3 Dallas, 54, PATERSON, BLAIR, CUSHING, JJ.

Phillips vs. *Payne*, U. S. Sup. Ct. 1875, 92 U. S. 130, SWAYNE, J.

Prigg vs. *Pennsylvania (Fugitive Slave Law Case)*, U. S. Sup. Ct. 1842, 16 Peters, 539, STORY, J.

Quarles, In re, U. S. Sup. Ct. 1895, 158 U. S. 532, GRAY, J.

Republic vs. *Sweers,* Sup. Ct. Penna. 1779, 1 Dallas, 45, MCKEAN, Ch. J.

Rhode Island vs. *Massachusetts,* U. S. Sup. Ct. 1838, 12 Peters, 657, BALDWIN, J.

Rose vs. *Himeley,* U. S. Sup. Ct. 1808, 4 Cranch, 241, MARSHALL, Ch. J.

Ross, In re, U. S. Sup. Ct. 1891, 140 U. S. 453, FIELD, J.

Scott vs. *Sandford (Dred Scott Case),* U. S. Sup. Ct. 1857, 19 Howard, 393, TANEY, Ch. J.

Siebold, Ex parte, U. S. Sup. Ct. 1879, 100 U. S. 371, BRADLEY, J.

Slaughterhouse Cases, U. S. Sup. Ct. 1872, 16 Wallace, 36, MILLER, J.

Swan, The, U. S. Dist. Ct. Washington, 1892, 50 Fed. Rep. 108, HANFORD, J.

Tennessee vs. *Davis,* U. S. Sup. Ct. 1879, 100 U. S. 257, STRONG, J.

Texas vs. *White,* U. S. Sup. Ct. 1868, 7 Wallace, 700, CHASE, Ch. J.

United States vs. *Holliday,* U. S. Sup. Ct. 1865, 3 Wallace, 407, MILLER, J.

United States vs. *Palmer,* U. S. Sup. Ct. 1818, 3 Wheaton, 610, MARSHALL, Ch. J.

United States vs. *Williams,* U. S. Dist. Ct. Penna. 1852, Fed. Cas. 16,705, 4 Hall's Am. L. J. 486, KANE, J.

United States vs. *Yorba,* U. S. Sup. Ct. 1863, 1 Wallace, 412, FIELD, J.

Ware vs. *Hylton,* U. S. Sup. Ct. 1796, 3 Dallas, 199, CHASE, WILSON, PATERSON, CUSHING, IREDELL, JJ.

Williams vs. *Suffolk Ins. Co.,* U. S. Sup. Ct. 1839, 13 Peters, 415, MCLEAN, J.

Wong Wing vs. *United States,* U. S. Sup. Ct. 1896, 163 U. S. 228, SHIRAS, J.

II.

POWER OF UNITED STATES TO ACQUIRE TERRITORY.

American Ins. Co. vs. *Canter (Florida Case),* U. S. Sup. Ct. 1828, 1 Peters, 511, MARSHALL, Ch. J.

Boyd &c. vs. *Nebraska,* U. S. Sup. Ct. 1892, 143 U. S. 135, FULLER, Ch. J.

Clinton vs. *Englebrecht,* U. S. Sup. Ct. 1871, 13 Wallace, 434, CHASE, Ch. J.

Delassus vs. *United States,* U. S. Sup. Ct. 1835, 9 Peters, 117, MARSHALL, Ch. J.

Doe (Clark) vs. *Braden,* U. S. Sup. Ct. 1853, 16 Howard, 635, TANEY, Ch. J.

Endleman vs. *United States,* U. S. Cir. Ct. App. 9th Cir. 1898, 57 U. S. App. 1, MORROW, J.

Fleming vs. *Page (Tampico Duty Case),* U. S. Sup. Ct. 1850, 9 Howard, 603, TANEY, Ch. J.

Foster vs. *Neilson,* U. S. Sup. Ct. 1829, 2 Peters, 253, MARSHALL, Ch. J.

Garcia vs. *Lee,* U. S. Sup. Ct. 1838, 12 Peters, 511, TANEY, Ch. J.

Holden vs. *Hardy,* U. S. Sup. Ct. 1898, 169 U. S. 366, BROWN, J.

Johnson vs. *McIntosh*, U. S. Sup. Ct. 1823, 8 Wheaton, 543, MARSHALL, Ch. J.

Jones vs. *United States* (*Navassa Island Case*), U. S. Sup. Ct. 1890, 137 U. S. 202, GRAY, J.

Leitensdorfer vs. *Webb*, U. S. Sup. Ct. 1857, 20 Howard, 176, DANIEL, J.

McKay vs. *Campbell*, U. S. Dist. Ct. Oregon, 1871, 2 Sawyer, 118, DEADY, J.

Mitchel vs. *United States*, U. S. Sup. Ct. 1835, 9 Peters, 711, BALDWIN, J.

Mormon Church vs. *United States*, U. S. Sup. Ct. 1890, 136 U. S. 1, BRADLEY, J.

Morris vs. *United States*, U. S. Sup. Ct. 1899, 174 U. S. 196, SHIRAS, J.

Neeley vs. *Henkel*, U. S. Sup. Ct. 1901, 180 U. S. 109, HARLAN, J.

Ortiz, Ex parte, U. S. Cir. Ct. Minn. 1900, 100 Fed. Rep. 955, LOCHBAN, J.

Pollard vs. *Hagan*, U. S. Sup. Ct. 1845, 3 Howard, 212, McKINLEY, J.

Pollard's Heirs vs. *Kibbe*, U. S. Sup. Ct. 1840, 14 Peters, 353, THOMPSON, J.

Scott vs. *Sandford* (*Dred Scott Case*), U. S. Sup. Ct. 1857, 19 Howard, 393, TANEY, Ch. J.

Shively vs. *Bowlby*, U. S. Sup. Ct. 1894, 152 U. S. 1, GRAY, J.

Soulard vs. *United States*, U. S. Sup. Ct. 1830, 4 Peters, 511, MARSHALL, Ch. J.

Stearns vs. *United States*, U. S. Sup. Ct. 1867, 6 Wallace, 589, SWAYNE, J.

Strother vs. *Lucas*, U. S. Sup. Ct. 1832, 6 Peters, 763, THOMPSON, J.

United States vs. *Arredondo*, U. S. Sup. Ct. 1832, 6 Peters, 691, BALDWIN, J.

United States vs. *Castillero*, U. S. Sup. Ct. 1862, 2 Black. 1, CLIFFORD, J.

United States vs. *Gratiot*, U. S. Sup. Ct. 1840, 14 Peters, 526, THOMPSON, J.

United States vs. *The Nancy*, U. S. Cir. Ct. Penna. 1814, 3 Wash. 281, WASHINGTON, J.

United States vs. *Percheman*, U. S. Sup. Ct. 1833, 7 Peters, 51, MARSHALL, Ch. J.

United States vs. *Repentigny*, U. S. Sup. Ct. 1866, 5 Wallace, 211, NELSON, J.

United States vs. *Reynes*, U. S. Sup. Ct. 1850, 9 Howard, 127, DANIEL, J.

III.

THE CONSTITUTION OF THE UNITED STATES; ITS OPERATION IN, AND EXTENSION OVER, TERRITORY OF THE UNITED STATES.

Alexander vs. *Roulet*, U. S. Sup. Ct. 1871, 13 Wallace, 386, DAVIS, J.

American Ins. Co. vs. *Canter* (*Florida Case*), U. S. Sup. Ct. 1828, 1 Peters, 511, MARSHALL, Ch. J.

American Publishing Co. vs. *Fisher* (*Utah Jury Case*), U. S. Sup. Ct. 1897, 166 U. S. 464, BREWER, J.

Baumann vs. *Ross*, U. S. Sup. Ct. 1896, 167 U. S. 548, GRAY, J.

Benner vs. *Porter*, U. S. Sup. Ct. 1850, 9 Howard, 235, NELSON, J.

Black vs. *Jackson*, U. S. Sup. Ct. 1899, 177 U. S. 349, HARLAN, J.

Boyd vs. *Nebraska*, U. S. Sup. Ct. 1892, 143 U. S. 135, FULLER, Ch. J.

City of Panama, The, U. S. Sup. Ct. 1879, 101 U. S. 453, CLIFFORD, J.

Clinton vs. *Englebrecht*, U. S. Sup. Ct. 1871, 13 Wallace, 434, CHASE, Ch. J.

Cross vs. *Harrison* (*San Francisco Duty Case*), U. S. Sup. Ct. 1853, 16 Howard, 164, WAYNE, J.

Endleman vs. *United States*, U. S. Cir. Ct. App. 9th Cir. 1898, 57 U. S. App. 1, MORROW, J.

Fleming vs. *Page* (*Tampico Duty Case*), U. S. Sup. Ct. 1850, 9 Howard, 603, TANEY, Ch. J.

Holden vs. *Hardy*, U. S. Sup. Ct. 1898, 169 U. S. 366, BROWN, J.

Hornbuckle vs. *Toombs*, U. S. Sup. Ct. 1873, 18 Wallace, 648, BRADLEY, J.

Leitensdorfer vs. *Webb*, U. S. Sup. Ct. 1857, 20 Howard, 176, DANIEL, J.

Loughborough vs. *Blake*, U. S. Sup. Ct. 1820, 5 Wheaton, 317, MARSHALL, Ch. J.

McAllister vs. *United States*, U. S. Sup. Ct. 1891, 141 U. S. 174, HARLAN, J.

Miners' Bank vs. *Iowa*, U. S. Sup. Ct. 1851, 12 Howard, 1, DANIEL, J.

Mitchel vs. *United States*, U. S. Sup. Ct. 1835, 9 Peters, 711, BALDWIN, J.

Mormon Church vs. *United States*, U. S. Sup. Ct. 1890, 136 U. S. 1, BRADLEY, J.

Murphy vs. *Ramsey*, U. S. Sup. Ct. 1885, 114 U. S. 15, MATTHEWS, J.

National Bank vs. *County of Yankton*, U. S. Sup. Ct. 1879, 101 U. S. 129, WAITE, Ch. J.

Ortiz Ex parte, U. S. Cir. Ct. Minn. 1900, 100 Fed. Rep. 955, LOCHRAN, J.

Pollard vs. *Hagan*, U. S. Sup. Ct. 1845, 3 Howard, 212, McKINLEY, J.

Pollard's Heirs vs. *Kibbe*, U. S. Sup. Ct. 1840, 14 Peters, 353, THOMPSON, J.

Reynolds vs. *United States*, U. S. Sup. Ct. 1878, 98 U. S. 145, WAITE, Ch. J.

Roberts vs. *Reilly*, U. S. Sup. Ct. 1885, 116 U. S. 80, MATTHEWS, J.

Scott vs. *Sandford* (*Dred Scott Case*), U. S. Sup. Ct. 1857, 19 Howard, 393, TANEY, Ch. J.

Sere vs. *Pitot*, U. S. Sup. Ct. 1810, 6 Cranch, 332, MARSHALL, Ch. J.

Shively vs. *Bowlby*, U. S. Sup. Ct. 1894, 152 U. S. 1, GRAY, J.

Snow vs. *United States*, U. S. Sup. Ct. 1873, 18 Wallace, 317, BRADLEY, J.

Springville vs. *Thomas*, U. S. Sup. Ct. 1897, 166 U. S. 707, FULLER, Ch. J.

Strader vs. *Graham*, U. S. Sup. Ct. 1850, 10 Howard, 82, TANEY, Ch. J.

Strother vs. *Lucas*, U. S. Sup. Ct. 1832, 6 Peters, 763, THOMPSON, J.

Talbott vs. *Silver Bow Co.*, U. S. Sup. Ct. 1891, 139 U. S. 438, BREWER, J.

Thomas vs. *Gay*, U. S. Sup. Ct. 1898, 169 U. S. 264, SHIRAS, J.

Thompson vs. *Utah*, U. S. Sup. Ct. 1898, 170 U. S. 343, HARLAN, J.

United States vs. *Forty-three Gallons, etc.*, U. S. Sup. Ct. 1876, 93 U. S. 188, DAVIS, J., and 1883, 108 U. S. 491, FIELD, J.

United States vs. *Gratiot*, U. S. Sup. Ct. 1840, 14 Peters, 526, THOMPSON, J.

United States vs. *Kagama*, U. S. Sup. Ct. 1886, 118 U. S. 375, MILLER, J.

United States vs. *The Nancy*, U. S. Cir. Ct. Penna. 1814, 3 Wash. 281, WASHINGTON, J.

Webster vs. *Reid*, U. S. Sup. Ct. 1850, 11 Howard, 437, McLEAN, J.

IV.

STATUS OF THE DISTRICT OF COLUMBIA.

Barnes vs. *District of Columbia*, U. S. Sup. Ct. 1875, 91 U. S. 542, HUNT, J.

Barney vs. *Baltimore City*, U. S. Sup. Ct. 1867, 6 Wallace, 280, MILLER, J.

Callan vs. *Wilson*, U. S. Sup. Ct. 1887, 127 U. S. 540, HARLAN, J.

Capital Traction Co. vs. *Hof*, U. S. Sup. Ct. 1899, 174 U. S. 1, GRAY, J.

Geofroy vs. *Riggs*, U. S. Sup. Ct. 1890, 133 U. S. 258, FIELD, J.

Gibbons vs. *District of Columbia*, U. S. Sup. Ct. 1886, 116 U. S. 404, GRAY, J.

Hepburn vs. *Ellzey*, U. S. Sup. Ct. 1805, 2 Cranch, 445, MARSHALL, Ch. J.

Hooe vs. *Jamieson*, U. S. Sup. Ct. 1897, 166 U. S. 395, FULLER, Ch. J.

Kendall vs. *United States*, U. S. Sup. Ct. 1838, 12 Peters, 524, THOMPSON, J.

Loughborough vs. *Blake*, U. S. Sup. Ct. 1820, 5 Wheaton 317, MARSHALL, Ch. J.

Mattingly vs. *District of Columbia*, U. S. Sup. Ct. 1878, 97 U. S. 687, STRONG, J.

Metropolitan R. R. Co. vs. *District of Columbia*, U. S. Sup. Ct. 1889, 132 U. S. 1, BRADLEY, J.

Stoutenbergh vs. *Hennick*, U. S. Sup. Ct. 1889, 129 U. S. 141, FULLER, Ch. J.

V.

CONSTRUCTION OF THE CONSTITUTION OF THE UNITED STATES.

Boyd vs. *United*, U. S. Sup. Ct. 1886, 116 U. S. 616, BRADLEY, J.

Chisholm vs. *Georgia*, U. S. Sup. 1793, 2 Dallas, 419, JAY, Ch. J., IREDELL, BLAIR, WILSON, CUSHING, JJ.

Brown vs. *Maryland*, U. S. Sup. Ct. 1827, 12 Wheaton, 419, MARSHALL, Ch. J.

Cohens vs. *Virginia*, U. S. Sup. Ct. 1821, 6 Wheaton, 264, MARSHALL, Ch. J.

County of Wilson vs. *National Bank*, U. S. Sup. Ct. 1880, 103 U. S. 770, WOOD, J.

Dartmouth College vs. *Woodward*, U. S. Sup. Ct. 1819, 4 Wheaton, 518, MARSHALL, Ch. J.

Field vs. *Clark*, U. S. Sup. Ct. 1892, 143 U. S. 649, HARLAN, J.

Fletcher vs. *Peck*, U. S. Sup. Ct. 1810, 6 Cranch 87, MARSHALL, Ch. J.

Genessee Chief, The, U. S. Sup. Ct. 1851, 12 Howard, 443, TANEY, Ch. J.

Gibbons vs. *Ogden,* U. S. Sup. Ct. 1824, 9 Wheaton, 1, MARSHALL, Ch. J.

Hepburn vs. *Griswold,* (*Legal Tender Case*) U. S. Sup. Ct. 1869, 8 WALLACE, 603, CHASE, Ch. J.

Interstate Com. Comm. vs. *Brimson,* U. S. Sup. Ct. 1894, 154 U. S. 447, HARLAN, J.

Johnson vs. *McIntosh,* U. S. Sup. Ct. 1823, 8 Wheaton, 543, MARSHALL, Ch. J.

Kennard vs. *Louisiana,* U. S. Sup. Ct. 1875, 92 U. S. 480, WAITE, Ch. J.

Knowlton vs. *Moore* (*War Revenue Inheritance Tax Case*), U. S. Sup. Ct. 1900, 178 U. S. 41, WHITE, J.

McCulloch vs. *Maryland,* U. S. Sup. Ct. 1819, 4 Wheaton 316, MARSHALL, Ch. J.

McPherson vs. *Blacker,* U. S. Sup. Ct. 1892, 146 U. S. 1, FULLER, Ch. J.

Marbury vs. *Madison,* U. S. Sup. Ct. 1803, 1 Cranch, 137, MARSHALL, Ch. J.

Milligan, Ex parte, U. S. Sup. Ct. 1866, 4 Wallace, 2, DAVIS, J.

Missouri vs. *Lewis,* U. S. Sup. Ct. 1879, 101 U. S. 22, BRADLEY, J.

Monongahela Nav. Co. vs. *United States,* U. S. Sup. Ct. 1893, 148 U. S. 312, BREWER, J.

Mormon Church vs. *United States,* U. S. Sup. Ct. 1890, 136 U. S. 1, BRADLEY, J.

Murphy vs. *Ramsey,* U. S. Sup. Ct. 1885, 114 U. S. 15, MATTHEWS, J.

Neely vs. *Henkel,* U. S. Sup. Ct. 1901, 180 U. S. 109, HARLAN, J.

New York vs. *Miln* (*Passenger Case*), U. S. Sup. Ct. 1837, 11 Peters, 102, BARBOUR, J.

Permoli vs. *Municipality,* U. S. Sup. Ct. 1845, 3 Howard, 589, CATRON, J.

Pollock vs. *Farmers' L. & T. Co.* (*Income Tax Case*), U. S. Sup. Ct. 1895, 157 U. S. 429, FULLER, Ch. J.

Prigg vs. *Pennsylvania* (*Fugitive Slave Law Case*), U. S. Sup. Ct. 1842, 16 Peters, 539, STORY, J.

Robertson vs. *Baldwin,* U. S. Sup. Ct. 1897, 165 U. S. 275, BROWN, J.

Ross, In re, U. S. Sup. Ct. 1891, 140 U. S. 453, FIELD, J.

Scott vs. *Sandford* (*Dred Scott Case*), U. S. Sup. Ct. 1857, 19 Howard, 393, TANEY, Ch. J.

Shively vs. *Bowlby,* U. S. Sup. Ct. 1894, 152 U. S. 1, GRAY, J.

Slaughterhouse Cases, U. S. Sup. Ct. 1872, 16 Wallace, 36, MILLER, J.

Stuart vs. *Laird,* U. S. Sup. Ct. 1803, 1 Cranch, 299, PATERSON, J.

Texas vs. *White,* U. S. Sup. Ct. 1868, 7 Wallace, 700, CHASE, Ch. J.

United States vs. *Joint Traffic Ass'n.,* U. S. Sup. Ct. 1898, 171 U. S. 505, PECKHAM, J.

United States vs. *Wong Kim Ark,* (*Chinese Baby Case*) U. S. Sup. Ct. 1898, 169 U. S. 649, GRAY, J.

Ware vs. *Hylton,* U. S. Sup. Ct. 1796, 3 Dallas, 199, CHASE, WILSON, PATERSON, CUSHING, IREDELL, JJ.

Yick Wo vs. *Hopkins,* U. S. Sup. Ct. 1886, 118 U. S. 356, MATTHEWS, J.

VI.

DIVISION OF SOVEREIGNTY BETWEEN THE FEDERAL GOVERNMENT AND STATE GOVERNMENTS.

Ableman vs. *Booth*, U. S. Sup. Ct. 1858, 21 Howard, 506, TANEY, Ch. J.

Chae Chan Ping vs. *United States* (*Chinese Exclusion Case*), U. S. Sup. Ct. 1889, 130 U. S. 581, FIELD, J.

Chew Heong vs. *United States*, U. S. Sup. Ct. 1884, 112 U. S. 536, HARLAN, J.

Chisholm vs. *Georgia*, U. S. Sup. Ct. 1793, 2 Dallas, 419, JAY, Ch. J., IREDELL, BLAIR, WILSON, CUSHING, JJ.

Cohens vs. *Virginia*, U. S. Sup. Ct. 1821, 6 Wheaton, 264, MARSHALL, Ch. J.

Coleman vs. *Tennessee*, U. S. Sup. Ct. 1878, 97 U. S. 509, FIELD, J.

Cook vs. *United States*, U. S. Sup. Ct. 1891, 138 U. S. 157, HARLAN, J.

Cooley vs. *Board of Port Wardens*, U. S. Sup. Ct. 1851, 12 Howard, 299, CURTIS, J.

Crutcher vs. *Kentucky*, U. S. Sup. Ct. 1891, 141 U. S. 47, BRADLEY, J.

Dartmouth College vs. *Woodward*, U. S. Sup. Ct. 1819, 4 Wheaton, 518. MARSHALL, Ch. J.

Emert vs. *Missouri*, U. S. Sup. Ct. 1894, 156 U. S. 296, GRAY, J.

Georgia vs. *Stanton*, U. S. Sup. Ct. 1867, 6 Wallace, 50, NELSON, J.

Gibbons vs. *Ogden*, U. S. Sup. Ct. 1824, 9 Wheaton, 1, MARSHALL, Ch. J.

Gibbons vs. *United States*, U. S. Sup. Ct. 1868, 8 Wallace, 269, MILLER, J.

Gillespie vs. *Winberg*, N. Y. Ct. Com. Pleas, 1872, 4 Daly, 318, DALY, Ch. J.

Gilman vs. *Philadelphia*, U. S. Sup. Ct. 1865, 3 Wallace, 713, SWAYNE J.

Griswold vs. *Atlantic Dock Co.*, N. Y. Sup. Ct. 1855, 21 Barbour, 225, STRONG, J.

Interstate Commerce Comm. vs. *Brimson*, U. S. Sup. Ct. 1894, 154 U. S. 447, HARLAN, J.

Kilbourn vs. *Thompson*, U. S. Sup. Ct. 1880, 103 U. S. 168, MILLER, J.

Lane vs. *Oregon*, U. S. Sup. Ct. 1868, 7 Wallace, 71, CHASE, Ch. J.

Livingstone vs. *Moore*, U. S. Sup. Ct. 1833, 7 Peters, 469, JOHNSON, J.

Loan Ass'n vs. *Topeka*, U. S. Sup. Ct. 1874, 20 Wall. 655, MILLER, J.

McCulloch vs. *Maryland*, U. S. Sup. Ct. 1819, 4 Wheaton, 316, MARSHALL, Ch. J.

McNeil, *Ex parte*, U. S. Sup. Ct. 1871, 13 Wallace, 236, SWAYNE, J.

Martin vs. *Waddell*, U. S. Sup. Ct. 1842, 16 Peters, 367, TANEY, Ch. J.

Maxwell vs. *Dow*, U. S. Sup. Ct. 1900, 176 U. S. 581, PECKHAM, J.

May vs. *New Orleans*, U. S. Sup. Ct. 1900, 178 U. S. 496, HABLAN, J.

Milligan, *Ex parte*, U. S. Sup. Ct. 1866, 4 Wallace, 2, DAVIS, J.

Minor vs. *Happersett* (*Woman's Rights Case*), U. S. Sup. Ct. 1874, 21 Wallace, 162, WAITE, Ch. J.

Munn vs. *Illinois*, U. S. Sup. Ct. 1876, 94 U. S. 113, WAITE, Ch. J.

New Hampshire vs. *Louisiana*, U. S. Sup. Ct. 1883, 108 U. S. 76, WAITE, Ch. J.

New Orleans vs. *United States*, U. S. Sup. Ct. 1836, 10 Peters, 662, McLEAN, J.

New York vs. *Miln* (*Passenger Case*) U. S. Sup. Ct. 1837, 11 Peters, 102, BARBOUR, J.

O'Neill vs. *Vermont*, U. S. Sup. Ct. 1892, 144 U. S. 323, BLATCHFORD, J.

Penhallow vs. *Doane*, U. S. Sup. Ct. 1795, 3 Dallas, 54, BLAIR, PATERSON, CUSHING, JJ.

Permoli vs. *Municipality*, U. S. Sup. Ct. 1845, 3 Howard, 589, CATRON, J.

Pervear vs. *Commonwealth*, U. S. Sup. Ct. 1866, 5 Wallace, 475, CHASE, Ch. J.

Prigg vs. *Pennsylvania* (*Fugitive Slave Law Case*), U. S. Sup. Ct. 1842, 16 Peters, 539, STORY, J.

Republica vs. *Sweers*, Sup. Ct. Penna. 1779, 1 Dallas, 45, McKEAN, Ch. J.

Shanks vs. *Dupont*, U. S. Sup. Ct. 1830, 3 Peters, 242, STORY, J.

Siebold, Ex parte, U. S. Sup. Ct. 1879, 100 U. S. 371, BRADLEY, J.

Slaughterhouse Cases, U. S. Sup. Ct. 1872, 16 Wallace, 36, MILLER, J.

Spies vs. *Illinois* (*Chicago Anarchist Case*), U. S. Sup. Ct. 1887, 123 U. S. 131, WAITE, Ch. J.

Tennessee vs. *Davis*, U. S. Sup. Ct. 1879, 100 U. S. 257, STRONG, J.

Texas vs. *White*, U. S. Sup. Ct. 1868, 7 Wallace, 700, CHASE, Ch. J.

United States vs. *Osborne*, U. S. Dist. Ct. Oregon, 1880, 6 Sawyer, 406, DEADY, J.

United States vs. *Joint Traffic Ass'n*, U. S. Sup. Ct. 1898, 171 U. S. 505, PECKHAM, J.

United States vs. *Wong Kim Ark* (*Chinese Baby Case*), U. S. Sup. Ct. 1898, 169 U. S. 649, GRAY, J.

Vance vs. *Vandercook Co.*, U. S. Sup. Ct. 1898, 170 U. S. 438, WHITE, J.

Walker vs. *Sauvinet*, U. S. Sup. Ct. 1875, 92 U. S. 90, WAITE, Ch. J.

Wood vs. *Wood*, Sup. Ct. Arkansas, 1891, 54 Ark. 172, HEMINGWAY, J.

VII.

SEPARATE DEPARTMENTS OF THE GOVERNMENT OF THE UNITED STATES, EXECUTIVE, LEGISLATIVE AND JUDICIAL, AND THE FUNCTIONS OF EACH.

Amiable Isabella, The, U. S. Sup. Ct. 1821, 6 Wheaton, 1, STORY J.

Castro vs. *DeUriarte*, U. S. Dist. Ct. S. D. N. Y. 1883, 16 Fed. Rep. 93, BROWN, J.

Chae Chan Ping vs. *United States*, (*Chinese Exclusion Case*), U. S. Sup. Ct. 1889, 130 U. S. 581, FIELD, J.

Chew Heong vs. *United States*, U. S. Sup. Ct. 1884, 112 U. S. 536, HARLAN, J.

Chouteau vs. *Eckhart*, U. S. Sup. Ct. 1844, 2 Howard, 344, CATRON, J.

Clinton Bridge, The, U. S. Cir. Ct. Iowa, 1867, 1 Woolworth, 150, MILLER, J.

Coffee vs. *Groover*, U. S. Sup. Ct. 1887, 123 U. S. 1, BRADLEY, J.

In re Cooper, (*Behring Sea Cases*), U. S. Sup. Ct. 1891, 138 U. S. 404; and 1892, 143 U. S. 472, FULLER, Ch. J.

Dodge vs. *Woolsey*, U. S. Sup. Ct. 1855, 18 Howard, 331, WAYNE, J.

Field vs. *Clark*, U. S. Sup. Ct. 1892, 143 U. S. 649, HARLAN, J.

Foster vs. *Neilson*, U. S. Sup. Ct. 1829, 2 Peters, 253, MARSHALL, Ch. J.

Frelinghuysen vs. *Key*, U. S. Sup. Ct. 1884, 110 U. S. 63, WAITE, Ch. J.

Garcia vs. *Lee*, U. S. Sup. Ct. 1838, 12 Peters, 511, TANEY, Ch. J.

Georgia vs. *Stanton*, U. S. Sup. Ct. 1867, 6 Wallace, 50, NELSON, J.

Great Western Ins. Co. vs. *United States*, U. S. Sup. Ct. 1884, 112 U. S. 193, MILLER, J.

Head Money Cases, U. S. Sup. Ct. 1884, 112 U. S. 580, MILLER, J.

Holmes vs. *Jennison*, U. S. Sup. Ct. 1840, 14 Peters, 540, THOMPSON, J.

Jones vs. *United States*, U. S. Sup. Ct. 1890, 137 U. S. 202, GRAY, J.

Kansas Indians, The, U. S. Sup. Ct. 1866, 5 Wallace, 737, DAVIS, J.

Kennett vs. *Chambers*, U. S. Sup. Ct. 1852, 14 Howard, 38, TANEY, Ch. J.

Luther vs. *Borden*, U. S. Sup. Ct. 1849, 7 Howard, 1, TANEY, Ch. J.

McPherson vs. *Blacker*, U. S. Sup. Ct. 1892, 146 U. S. 1, FULLER, Ch. J.

Marbury vs. *Madison*, U. S. Sup. Ct. 1803, 1 Cranch, 137, MARSHALL, Ch. J.

Miller vs. *United States*, U. S. Sup. Ct. 1870, 11 Wallace, 268, STRONG, J.

Mormon Church vs. *United States*, U. S. Sup. Ct. 1890, 136 U. S. 1, BRADLEY, J.

Morrill vs. *Jones*, U. S. Sup. Ct. 1882, 106 U. S. 466, WAITE, Ch. J.

Munn vs. *Illinois*, U. S. Sup. Ct. 1876, 94 U. S. 113, WAITE, Ch. J.

Neeley vs. *Henkel*, U. S. Sup. Ct. 1901, 180 U. S. 109, HARLAN, J.

Phillips vs. *Payne*, U. S. Sup. Ct. 1875, 92 U. S. 130, SWAYNE, J.

Pollard's Heirs vs. *Kibbe*, U. S. Sup. Ct. 1840, 14 Peters, 353, THOMPSON, J.

Pollock vs. *Farmers' L. & T. Co.*, (*Income Tax Case*), U. S. Sup. Ct. 1895, 157 U. S. 429, FULLER, Ch. J.

Rhode Island vs. *Massachusetts*, U. S. Sup. Ct. 1838, 12 Peters, 657, BALDWIN, J.

Rose vs. *Himeley*, U. S. Sup. Ct. 1808, 4 Cranch, 241, MARSHALL, Ch. J.

Taylor vs. *Morton*, U. S. Cir. Ct. Mass. 1855, 2 Curtis, 454, CURTIS, J., (aff'd U. S. Sup. Ct. 1862, 2 Black, 481, CLIFFORD, J.).

United States vs. *Holliday*, U. S. Sup. Ct. 1865, 3 Wallace, 407, MILLER, J.

United States vs. *Johnson*, U. S. Sup. Ct. 1888, 124 U. S. 236, HARLAN, J.

United States vs. *Palmer*, U. S. Sup. Ct. 1818, 3 Wheaton, 610, MARSHALL, Ch. J.

United States vs. *Rauscher*, U. S. Sup. Ct. 1886, 119 U. S. 407, MILLER, J.

United States vs. *Reynes*, U. S. Sup. Ct. 1850, 9 Howard, 127, (cited as 50 U. S.) DANIEL, J.

United States vs. *Yorba*, U. S. Sup. Ct. 1863, 1 Wallace, 412, FIELD, J.

Whitney vs. *Robertson*, U. S. Sup. Ct. 1888, 124 U. S. 190, FIELD, J.

Whiton vs. *Albany County Ins. Co.*, Sup. Ct. Mass. 1871, 109 Mass. 24, GRAY, J.

Williams vs. *Suffolk Ins. Co.*, U. S. Sup. Ct. 1839, 13 Peters, 415, Mc-Lean, J.

VIII.

POWERS OF THE JUDICIAL DEPARTMENT OF THE UNITED STATES GOVERNMENT, INCLUDING THOSE OF TERRITORIAL COURTS.

American Ins. Co. vs. *Canter* (*Florida Case*), U. S. Sup. Ct. 1828, 1 Peters, 511, MARSHALL, Ch. J.

American Publishing Co. vs. *Fisher*, U. S. Sup. Ct. 1897, 166 U. S. 464, BREWER, J.

Amy Warwick, The, U. S. Dist. Ct. Mass. 1862, 2 Sprague, 123, 150, SPRAGUE, J.

Castro vs. *DeUriarte*, U. S. Dist. Ct. S. D. N. Y. 1883, 16 Fed. Rep. 93, BROWN, J.

Clawson vs. *United States*, U. S. Sup. Ct. 1885, 114 U. S. 477, BLATCHFORD, J.

Clinton vs. *Englebrecht*, U. S. Sup. Ct. 1871, 13 Wallace, 434, CHASE, Ch. J.

Charkieh, The, High Ct. of Adm. 1873, 4 L. R. A. & E. 59, and Cobbett's Cas. Int. Law, p. 9, Sir ROBERT PHILLIMORE.

Cruikshank vs. *Bidwell*, U. S. Sup. Ct. 1900, 176 U. S. 73, FULLER, Ch. J.

Debs, In re, U. S. Sup. Ct. 1895, 158 U. S. 564, BREWER, J.

Genessee Chief, The, U. S. Sup. Ct. 1851, 12 Howard, 443, TANEY, Ch. J.

Godson vs. *United States*, Sup. Ct. Oklahoma, 1898, BURFORD, Ch. J.

Good vs. *Martin*, U. S. Sup. Ct. 1877, 95 U. S. 90, CLIFFORD, J.

Grapeshot, The, U. S. Sup. Ct. 1869, 9 Wallace, 129, CHASE, Ch. J.

Jecker vs. *Montgomery*, U. S. Sup. Ct. 1851, 13 Howard, 498, TANEY, Ch. J.

Lascelles vs. *Bidwell*, U. S. Cir. Ct. S. D. N. Y. 1900, 102 Fed. Rep. 1004, LACOMBE, J.

Leitensdorfer vs. *Webb*, U. S. Sup. Ct. 1857, 20 Howard, 176, DANIEL, J.

Lyons vs. *Woods*, U. S. Sup. Ct. 1894, 153 U. S. 649, FULLER, Ch. J.

McAllister vs. *United States*, U. S. Sup. Ct. 1891, 141 U. S. 174, HARLAN, J.

Marbury vs. *Madison*, U. S. Sup. Ct. 1803, 1 Cranch, 137, MARSHALL, Ch. J.

Milligan, Ex parte, U. S. Sup. Ct. 1866, 4 Wallace, 2, DAVIS, J.

Missouri vs. *Lewis*, U. S. Sup. Ct. 1879, 101 U. S. 22, BRADLEY, J.

Neagle, In re, U. S. Sup. Ct. 1890, 135 U. S. 1, MILLER, J.

Ortiz, Ex parte, U. S. Cir. Ct. Minn. 1900, 100 Fed. Rep. 955, LOCHRAN, J.

Postmaster General vs. *Early*, U. S. Sup. Ct. 1827, 12 Wheaton, 136, MARSHALL, Ch. J.

Ross In re, U. S. Sup. Ct. 1891, 140 U. S. 453, FIELD, J.

Thompson vs. *Utah*, U. S. Sup. Ct. 1898, 170 U. S. 343, HARLAN, J.

United States vs. *Hill*, U. S. Cir. Ct. Virginia, 1 Brockenbrough, 156, MARSHALL, Ch. J.

35

United States, Lyon et al. **vs.** *Huckabee*, U. S. Sup. Ct. 1872, 16 **Wall.** 414, CLIFFORD, J.

Walker vs. *Saucinet*, U. S. Sup. Ct. 1875, 92 U. S. 90, WAITE, Ch. J.

Wilburn vs. *State*, Sup. Ct. Arkansas, 1860, 21 Ark. 198, CAMPTON, J.; 1895, 60 Ark. 141, WOOD, J.

IX.

CONSTRUCTION OF UNIFORMITY AND COMMERCE CLAUSES OF THE CON-STITUTION OF THE UNITED STATES; FEDERAL AND STATE POWERS OF TAXATION AND CONTROL OF COMMERCE.

Almy vs. *California*, U. S. Sup. Ct. 1860, 24 Howard, 169, TANEY, Ch. J.

Asher vs. *Texas*, U. S. Sup. Ct. 1888, 128 U. S. 129, BRADLEY, J.

Brennan vs. *Titusville*, U. S. Sup. Ct. 1894, 153 U. S. 289, BREWER, J.

Briscoe vs. *Bank*, U. S. Sup. Ct. 1837, 11 Peters, 257, McLEAN, J.

Brown vs. *Maryland*, U. S. Sup. Ct. 1827, 12 Wheaton, 419, MARSHALL, Ch. J.

Clinton Bridge, The, U. S. Cir. Ct. Iowa, 1867, 1 Woolworth, 150, MILLER, J.

Cohens vs. *Virginia*, U. S. Sup. Ct. 1821, 6 Wheaton, 264, MARSHALL, Ch. J.

Cooley vs. *Board of Port Wardens*, U. S. Sup. Ct. 1851, 12 Howard, 299, CURTIS, J.

Crandall vs. *Nevada*, U. S. Sup. Ct. 1867, 6 Wallace 35, MILLER, J.

Crutcher vs. *Kentucky*, U. S. Sup. Ct. 1891, 141 U. S. 47, BRADLEY, J.

Fairbank vs. *United States*, U. S. Sup. Ct. 1901, 181 U. S. 283. BROWN, J.

Field vs. *Clark*, U. S. Sup. Ct. 1892, 143 U. S. 649, HABLAN, J.

Gibbons vs. *Ogden*. U. S. Sup. Ct. 1824, 9 Wheaton, 1, MARSHALL, Ch. J.

Gibbons vs. *United States*, U. S. Sup. Ct. 1868, 8 Wallace, 269, MILLER. J.

Head Money Cases, U. S. Sup. Ct. 1884, 112 U. S. 580, BLATCHFORD, J.

Kennard vs. *Louisiana*, U. S. Sup. Ct. 1875, 92 U. S. 480, WAITE, Ch. J.

Knowlton vs. *Moore* (*War Revenue Inheritance Tax Case*), U. S. Sup. Ct. 1900, 178 U. S. 41, WHITE, J.

License Tax Cases, U. S. Sup. Ct. 1866, 5 Wallace, 462, CHASE, Ch. J.

Loughborough vs. *Blake*, U. S. Sup. Ct. 1820, 5 Wheaton, 317, MARSHALL, Ch. J.

McCall vs. *California*, U. S. Sup. Ct. 1890, 136 U. S. 104, LAMAR, J.

May vs. *New Orleans*, U. S. Sup. Ct. 1900, 178 U. S. 496, HARLAN, J.

Monongahela Nav. Co. vs. *United States*, U. S. Sup. Ct. 1893, 148 U. S. 312, BREWER, J.

Munn vs. *Illinois*, U. S. Sup. Ct. 1876, 94 U. S. 113, WAITE, Ch. J.

New York vs. *Miln* (*Passenger Cases*), U. S. Sup. Ct. 1837, 11 Peters, 182, BARBOUR, J.

Penna. vs. *Wheeling Bridge Co.*, U. S. Sup. Ct. 1855, 18 Howard, 421, NELSON, J.

Pervear vs. *Commonwealth*, U. S. Sup. Ct. 1866, 5 Wallace, 475, CHASE, Ch. J.

Pittsburg and Southern Coal Co. vs. *Bates*, U. S. Sup. Ct. 1895, 156 U. S. 577, FIELD, J.

Pollock vs. *Farmers' L. & T. Co.* (*Income Tax Case*), U. S. Sup. Ct. 1895, 157 U. S. 429, FULLER, Ch. J.

Rhodes vs. *Iowa*, U. S. Sup. Ct. 1898, 170 U. S. 412, WHITE, J.

Robbins vs. *Shelby Taxing District*, U. S. Sup. Ct. 1897, 120 U. S. 489, BRADLEY, J.

Sherman vs. *United States*, U. S. Sup. Ct. 1900, 178 U. S. 150, SHI-RAS, J.

Stoulenbergh vs. *Hennick*, U. S. Sup. Ct. 1889, 129 U. S. 141, FULLER, Ch. J.

Talbott vs. *Silver Bow Co.*, U. S. Sup. Ct. 1891, 139 U. S. 438, BREWER, J.

Thomas vs. *Gay*, U. S. Sup. Ct. 1898, 169 U. S. 264, SHIRAS, J.

United States vs. *Fisher*, U. S. Sup. Ct. 1805, 2 Cranch, 358, MAR-SHALL, Ch. J.

United States vs. *Joint Traffic Ass'n*, U. S. Sup. Ct. 1898, 171 U. S. 505, PECKHAM, J.

Vance vs. *Vandercook Co.*, U. S. Sup. Ct. 1898, 170 U. S. 438, WHITE, J.

X.

CONSTRUCTION OF TARIFF AND OTHER LAWS OF THE UNITED STATES.
(See also TREATIES AND STATUTES.)

Adams vs. *Bancroft*, U. S. Cir. Ct. Mass. 1838, 3 Sumner, 384, STORY, J.

American Net and Twine Co. vs. *Worthington*, U. S. Sup. Ct. 1891, 141 U. S. 468, BROWN, J.

Asher vs. *Texas*, U. S. Sup. Ct. 1888, 128 U. S. 129, BRADLEY, J.

Barney vs. *Baltimore City*, U. S. Sup. Ct. 1867, 6 Wallace, 280, MIL-LER, J.

Conqueror, The (*Vanderbilt Yacht Case*), U. S. Sup. Ct. 1896, 166 U. S. 110, BROWN, J.

Cruikshank vs. *Bidwell*, U. S. Sup. Ct. 1900, 176 U. S. 73, FUL-LER, Ch. J.

Good vs. *Martin*, U. S. Sup. Ct. 1877, 95 U. S. 90, CLIFFORD, J.

Hartranft vs. *Wiegman*, U. S. Sup. Ct. 1887, 121 U. S. 609, BLATCH-FORD, J.

Lascelles vs. *Bidwell*, U. S. Cir. Ct. S. D. N. Y. 1900, 102 Fed. Rep. 1004, LACOMBE, J.

Phila. & Reading R. R. Co. vs. *Kenney*, U. S. Cir. Ct. Penna. 1873, 18 Int. Rev. Rec. 92, MCKENNA, J.

Powers vs. *Barney*, U. S. Cir. Ct. S. D. N. Y. 1863, 5 Blatchford, 202, NELSON, J.

United States vs. *Dickson*, U. S. Sup. Ct. 1841, 15 Pet. 141, STORY, J.

United States vs. *Isham*, U. S. Sup. Ct. 1873, 17 Wallace, 496, HUNT, J.

United States vs. *Rice*, U. S. Sup. Ct. 1819, 4 Wheat. 246, STORY, J.

United States vs. *Ullman*, U. S. Dt. Ct. N. Y. 1871, 4 Ben. 547, BLATCH-FORD, J.

United States vs. *Union Pacific Ry. Co.*, U. S. Sup. Ct. 1875, 91 U. S. 72, DAVIS, J.

United States vs. *Wigglesworth*, U. S. Cir. Ct. Mass. 1842, 2 Story, 369, STORY, J.

United States vs. *Weed*, U. S. Sup. Ct. 1866, 5 Wallace, 62, MILLER, J.

Woodruff vs. *Parham*, U. S. Sup. Ct. 1868, 8 Wallace, 123, MILLER, J.

XI.

JUDICIAL DEFINITIONS OF TERMS USED IN THE CONSTITUTION OF THE UNITED STATES, AND IN TARIFF AND OTHER LAWS.

Adventure and Cargo, The, U. S. Cir. Ct. Virginia, 1812, 1 Brockenbrough, 235, MARSHALL, Ch. J.

Alameda vs. *Neal*, U. S. Cir. Ct. Cal. 1887, 32 Fed. Rep. 331, FIELD, J.

Asher vs. *Texas*, U. S. Sup. Ct. 1888, 128 U. S. 129, BRADLEY, J.

Brown vs. *Houston*, U. S. Sup. Ct. 1885, 114 U. S. 622, BRADLEY, J.

Brown vs. *Maryland*, U. S. Sup. Ct. 1827, 12 Wheaton, 419, MARSHALL, Ch. J.

Cherokee Nation vs. *Georgia*, U. S. Sup. Ct. 1831, 5 Peters, 1, MARSHALL, Ch. J.

Coe vs. *Errol*, U. S. Sup. Ct. 1886, 116 U. S. 517, BRADLEY, J.

Cohens vs. *Virginia*, U. S. Sup. Ct. 1821, 6 Wheaton, 264, MARSHALL, Ch. J.

Conqueror, The (*Vanderbilt Yacht Case*), U. S. Sup. Ct. 1896, 166 U. S. 110, BROWN, J.

Davidson vs. *McKibben*, Ct. of Com. Pleas, 2 Geo. IV. 1821, 3 Broderip & Bingham, 112, DALLAS, Ch. J.

Dixon vs. *United States*, U. S. Cir. Ct. Virginia, 1811, 1 Brockenbrough, 177, MARSHALL, Ch. J.

Eliza and Cargo, The, U. S. Cir. Ct. Mass. 1813, 2 Gallison, 4, STORY, J.

Fairbank vs. *United States*, U. S. Sup. Ct. 1901, 181 U. S. 283, BREWER, J.

Fleming vs. *Page* (*Tampico Duty Case*), U. S. Sup. Ct. 1850, 9 Howard, 603, TANEY, Ch. J.

Hornbuckle vs. *Toombs*, U. S. Sup. Ct. 1873, 18 Wallace, 648, BRADLEY, J.

King vs. *Parks*, N. Y. Sup. Ct. 1822, 19 Johnson, 375, SPENCER, Ch. J.

Lark and Cargo, The, U. S. Cir. Ct. Mass. 1812, 1 Gallison, 55, STORY, J.

Loughborough vs. *Blake*, U. S. Sup. Ct. 1820, 5 Wheaton, 317, MARSHALL, Ch. J.

Marbury vs. *Madison*, U. S. Sup. Ct. 1803, 1 Cranch, 137, MARSHALL, Ch. J.

Murray vs. *Clark*, N. Y. Com. Pleas 1873, 4 Daly 468, DALY, Ch. J.

Ravesies vs. *United States*, U. S. Cir. Ct. Alabama, 1889, 37 Fed. Rep. 447, PARDEE, J.

Rhodes vs. *Iowa*, U. S. Sup. Ct. 1898, 170 U. S. 412, WHITE, J.

Sally and Cargo, The, U. S. Cir. Ct. Mass. 1812, 1 Gallison, 58, STORY, J.

Sprague vs. *Thompson*, U. S. Sup. Ct. 1886, 118 U. S. 90, MATTHEWS, J.

Stairs vs. *Peaslee*, U. S. Sup. Ct. 1855, 18 Howard, 521, TANEY, Ch. J.

Steamboat Co. vs. *Livingston,* Ct. Errors N. Y. 1825, 3 Cowan, 713, SANDFORD, Chan.

Sturges vs. *Crowninshield,* U. S. Sup. Ct. 1819, 4 Wheaton, 122, MARSHALL, Ch. J.

Tuber vs. *United States,* U. S. Cir. Ct. Mass. 1839, 1 Story 1, STORY, J.

Turpin vs. *Burgess,* U. S. Sup. Ct. 1886, 117 U. S. 504, BRADLEY, J.

United States vs. *Hayward,* U. S. Cir. Ct. Mass. 1815, 2 Gallison, 485, STORY, J.

United States vs. *Patten,* U. S. Ct. Maine, 1 Holmes, 421, SHEPLEY, J.

Veazie vs. *Moor,* U. S. Sup. Ct. 1852, 14 Howard. 568, DANIEL, J.

Woodruff vs. *Parham,* U. S. Sup. Ct. 1868, 8 Wallace, 123, MILLER, J.

XII.

APPLICATION OF THE FIRST TEN AMENDMENTS (BILL OF RIGHTS) OF THE CONSTITUTION OF THE UNITED STATES; THEIR EFFECT ON THE STATES AND ON FEDERAL LAWS.

Brown vs. *New Jersey,* U. S. Sup. Ct. 1899, 175 U. S. 172, BREWER, J.

Cook vs. *United States,* U. S. Sup. Ct. 1891, 138 U. S. 157, HARLAN, J.

Mitchell vs. *Harmony,* U. S. Sup. Ct. 1851, 13 Howard, 115, TANEY, Ch. J.

Monongahela Nav. Co. vs. *United States,* U. S. Sup. Ct. 1893, 148 U. S. 312, BREWER, J.

O'Neill vs. *Vermont,* U. S. Sup. Ct. 1892, 144 U. S. 323, BLATCHFORD, J.

Spies vs. *Illinois* (*Chicago Anarchist Case*), U. S. Sup. Ct. 1887, 123 U. S. 131, WAITE, Ch. J.

United States vs. *Cruikshank,* U. S. Sup. Ct. 1875, 92 U. S. 542, WAITE, Ch. J.

XIII.

FUNDAMENTAL LIMITATIONS OF GOVERNMENT, AND THEIR EFFECT UPON THE CONGRESSIONAL GOVERNMENT OF TERRITORY OF THE UNITED STATES.

American Publishing Co. vs. *Fisher* (*Utah Jury Case*), U. S. Sup. Ct. 1897, 166 U. S. 464, BREWER, J.

Bank of Columbia vs. *Okely,* U. S. Sup. Ct. 1819, 4 Wheaton, 235, JOHNSON, J.

Briscoe vs. *Bank,* U. S. Sup. Ct. 1837, 11 Peters, 257, McLEAN, J.

Chicago, etc., Ry. Co. vs. *Tompkins,* U. S. Sup. Ct. 1900, 176 U. S. 167, BREWER, J.

Cummings vs. *Missouri,* U. S. Sup. Ct. 1866, 4 Wallace, 277, FIELD, J.

Dartmouth College vs. *Woodward,* U. S. Sup. Ct. 1819, 4 Wheaton, 518, MARSHALL, Ch. J

Kemmler, In re, U. S. Sup. Ct. 1890, 126 U. S. 436, FULLER, Ch. J.

Legal Tender Cases, U. S. Sup. Ct. 1869, 8 Wallace, 603, CHASE, Ch. J.; 1870, 12 Wallace, 467, STRONG, J.; 1884, 110 U. S. 421, GRAY, J.

Loan Ass'n vs. *Topeka,* U. S. Sup. Ct. 1874, 20 Wallace, 655, MILLER, J.

Maxwell vs. *Dow,* U. S. Sup. Ct. 1900, 176 U. S. 581, PECKHAM, J.

Missouri vs. *Lewis*, U. S. Sup. Ct. 1879, 101 U. S. 22, BRADLEY, J.

Mormon Church vs. *United States*, U. S. Sup. Ct. 1890, 136 U. S. 1, BRADLEY, J.

Murphy vs. *Ramsey*, U. S. Sup. Ct. 1885, 114 U. S. 15, MATTHEWS, J.

O'Neill vs. *Vermont*, U. S. Sup. Ct. 1892, 144 U. S. 323, BLATCH-FORD, J.

Slaughter House Cases, U. S. Sup. Ct. 1872, 16 Wallace, 36, MILLER, J.

Thompson vs. *Utah*, U. S. Sup. Ct. 1898, 170 U. S. 343, HARLAN, J.

United States vs. *Hill*, U. S. Cir. Ct. 1809, Virginia, 1 Brockenbrough, 156, MARSHALL, Ch. J.

Weimer vs. *Bunbury*, Sup. Ct. Michigan, 1874, 30 Mich. 201, COOLEY, J.

XIV.

SUABILITY OF THE UNITED STATES, AND OF STATES, BY CITIZENS AND BY ALIENS.

Carlisle vs. *United States*, U. S. Sup. Ct. 1872, 16 Wallace, 147, FIELD, J.

Cherokee Nation vs. *Georgia*, U. S. Sup. Ct. 1831, 5 Peters, 1, MARSHALL, Ch. J.

Chisholm vs. *Georgia*, U. S. Sup. Ct. 1793, 2 Dallas, 419, JAY, Ch. J., IREDELL, BLAIR, WILSON, CUSHING, JJ.

Ficheras Case, U. S. Ct. of Claims, 1873, 9 Ct. of Claims, 254, NOTT, J.

Gibbons vs. *United States*, U. S. Sup. Ct. 1868, 8 Wallace, 269, MILLER, J.

Hill vs. *United States*, U. S. Sup. Ct. 1893, 149 U. S. 593, GRAY, J.

New Hampshire vs. *Louisiana*, U. S. Sup. Ct. 1883, 108 U. S. 76, WAITE, Ch. J.

Scott vs. *Jones*, U. S. Sup. Ct. 1847, 5 Howard, 343, WOODBURY, J.

United States vs. *O'Keefe*, U. S. Sup. Ct. 1870, 11 Wallace, 178, DAVIS, J.

Worcester vs. *Georgia*, U. S. Sup. Ct. 1832, 6 Peters, 515, MARSHALL, Ch. J.

XV.

MILITARY POWERS AND GOVERNMENT; MILITARY OCCUPANCY; PRIZE AND CONQUEST.

Alexander vs. *Roulet*, U. S. Sup. Ct. 1871, 13 Wallace, 386, DAVIS, J.

American Ins. Co. vs. *Canter* (*Florida Case*), U. S. Sup. Ct. 1828, 1 Peters, 511, MARSHALL, Ch, J.

Amiable Isabella, The, U. S. Sup. Ct. 1821, 6 Wheaton, 1, STORY, J.

Amy Warwick, The, U. S. Dist. Ct. Mass. 1862, 2 Sprague, 123, 150, SPRAGUE, J.

Blankard vs. *Galdy*, King & Queen's Bench, 5 Wm. & Mary, 4 Mod. 222, PER CURIAM.

Calvin's Case, Ct. Exchequer Chamber, 6 James I., 4 Coke, 1.

Campbell vs. *Hall*, King's Bench, 15 Geo. III. Cowper, 204, LORD MANSFIELD.

Coleman vs. *Tennessee*, U. S. Sup. Ct. 1878, 97 U. S. 509, FIELD, J.

Cross vs. *Harrison* (*San Francisco Duty Case*), U. S. Sup. Ct. 1853. 16 Howard, 164, WAYNE, J.

Dow vs. *Johnson*, U. S. Sup. Ct. 1879, 100 U. S. 158, FIELD, J.

Elphinstone vs. *Bedreechund,* Privy Council 1830, 1 Knapp's P. C. Rep. 316, LORD TENTERDEN.

Exchange (Schooner) vs. *McFadden,* U. S. Sup. Ct. 1812, 7 Cranch, 116, MARSHALL, Ch. J.

Fleming vs. *Page (Tampico Duty Case),* U. S. Sup. Ct. 1850, 9 Howard, 603, TANEY, Ch. J.

Georgia vs. *Stanton,* U. S. Sup. Ct. 1867, 6 Wallace, 50, NELSON, J.

Grapeshot, The, U. S. Sup. Ct. 1869, 9 Wallace, 129, CHASE, Ch. J.

Hamilton vs. *Dillin,* U. S. Sup. Ct. 1874, 21 Wallace, 73, BRADLEY, J.

Jecker vs. *Montgomery,* U. S. Sup. Ct. 1851, 13 Howard, 498, TANEY, Ch. J.

Legal Tender Cases, U. S. Sup. Ct. 1869, 8 Wallace, 603, CHASE, Ch. J.; 1870, 12 Wallace, 457, STRONG, J.; 1884, 110 U. S. 421, GRAY, J.

Leitensdorfer vs. *Webb,* U. S. Sup. Ct. 1857, 20 Howard, 176, DANIEL, J.

Liverpool Hero, The, U. S. Cir. Ct. Mass. 1814, 2 Gallison, 184, STORY, J.

Luther vs. *Borden,* U. S. Sup. Ct. 1849, 7 Howard, 1, TANEY, Ch. J.

Mechanics' Bank vs. *Union Bank,* U. S. Sup. Ct. 1874, 22 Wallace, 276, STRONG, J.

Milligan, Ex parte, U. S. Sup. Ct. 1866, 4 Wallace, 2, DAVIS, J.

Mitchell vs. *Harmony,* U. S. Sup. Ct. 1851, 13 Howard, 115, TANEY, Ch. J.

Mostyn vs. *Fabrigas,* King's Bench, 1774, Cowper, 180, LORD MANSFIELD.

Neely vs. *Henkel,* U. S. Sup. Ct. 1901, 180 U. S. 109, HARLAN, J.

New Orleans vs. *Steamship Co.,* U. S. Sup. Ct. 1874, 20 Wallace, 387, SWAYNE, J.

Ortiz, Ex parte, U. S. Cir. Ct. Minnesota, 1900, 100 Fed. Rep. 955, LOCHRAN, J.

Paquette Habana, The, U. S. Sup. Ct. 1900, 175 U. S. 677, GRAY, J.

Pizarro, The, U. S. Sup. Ct. 1817, 2 Wheaton, 227, STORY, J.

Raymond vs. *Thomas,* U. S. Sup. Ct. 1875, 91 U. S. 712, SWAYNE, J.

Rose vs. *Himeley,* U. S. Sup. Ct. 1808, 4 Cranch, 241, MARSHALL, Ch. J.

Siebold, Ex parte, U. S. Sup. Ct. 1897, 100 U. S. 371, BRADLEY, J.

Stearns vs. *United States,* U. S. Sup. Ct. 1867, 6 Wallace, 589, SWAYNE, J.

Tennessee vs. *Davis,* U. S. Sup. Ct. 1879, 100 U. S. 257, STRONG, J.

Texas vs. *White,* U. S. Sup. Ct. 1868, 7 Wallace 700, CHASE, Ch. J.

Thirty Hogsheads of Sugar vs. *Boyle,* U. S. Sup. Ct. 1815, 9 Cranch, 191, MARSHALL, Ch. J.

United States vs. *Castillero,* U. S. Sup. Ct. 1862, 2 Black, 1, CLIFFORD, J.

United States, Lyon et al., vs. *Huckabee,* U. S. Sup. Ct. 1872, 16 Wall. 414, CLIFFORD, J.

United States vs. *Repentigny,* U. S. Sup. Ct. 1866, 5 Wallace, 211, NELSON, J.

United States vs. *Rice (The Castine Case),* U. S. Sup. Ct. 1819, 4 Wheaton, 246, STORY, J.

Vallandigham, Ex parte, U. S. Cir. Ct. Ohio, 1863, Fed. Cas. 16,816; (pamphlet Rickey & Carroll, Cincinnati,) LEAVITT, J.

Williams vs. *Suffolk Ins. Co.,* U. S. Sup. Ct. 1839, 13 Peters, 415, McLEAN, J.

XVI.

NATIONAL UNITY AND THE CONTROL OF FOREIGN RELATIONS OF THE UNITED STATES BY THE CENTRAL GOVERNMENT.

Chae Chan Ping vs. *United States*, U. S. Sup. Ct. 1889, 130 U. S. 581, FIELD, J.

Chew Heong vs. *United States*, U. S. Sup. Ct. 1884, 112 U. S. 536, HARLAN, J.

Cooper, In re (Bering Sea Cases), U. S. Sup. Ct. 1891, 138 U. S. 404, and 1892, 143 U. S. 472, FULLER, Ch. J.

Ekiu, Nishimura vs. *United States*, U. S. Sup. Ct. 1891, 142 U. S. 651, GRAY, J.

Exchange (Schooner) vs. *McFadden*, U. S. Sup. Ct. 1812, 7 Cranch, 116, MARSHALL, Ch. J.

Fong Yue Ting vs. *United States*, U. S. Sup. Ct. 1893, 149 U. S. 698, GRAY, J.

Geofroy vs. *Riggs*, U. S. Sup. Ct. 1890, 133 U. S. 258, FIELD, J.

Jones vs. *United States*, U. S. Sup. Ct. 1890, 137 U. S. 202, GRAY, J.

Neely vs. *Henkel*, U. S. Sup. Ct. 1901, 180 U. S. 109, HARLAN, J.

New York vs. *Miln (Passenger Cases)*, U. S. Sup. Ct. 1837, 11 Peters, 102, BARBOUR, J.

Paquette Habana, The, U. S. Sup. Ct. 1900, 175 U. S. 677, GRAY, J.

Pizarro, The, U. S. Sup. Ct. 1817, 2 Wheaton, 227, STORY, J.

Quarles, In re, U. S. Sup. Ct. 1895, 158 U. S. 532, GRAY, J.

Rose vs. *Himeley,* U. S. Sup. Ct. 1808, 4 Cranch, 241, MARSHALL, Ch. J.

Ross, In re, U. S. Sup. Ct. 1891, 140 U. S. 453, FIELD, J.

United States vs. *Rauscher,* U. S. Sup. Ct. 1886, 119 U. S. 407, MILLER, J.

United States vs. *Wong Kim Ark (Chinese Baby Case),* U. S. Sup. Ct. 1898, 169 U. S. 649, GRAY, J.

Wong Wing vs. *United States,* U. S. Sup. Ct. 1896, 163 U. S. 228, SHIRAS, J.

XVII.

EXTENT OF THE TREATY-MAKING POWER OF THE UNITED STATES.

American Ins. Co. vs. *Canter (Florida Case),* U. S. Sup. Ct. 1828, 1 Peters, 511, MARSHALL, Ch. J.

Amiable Isabella, The, U. S. Sup. Ct. 1821, 6 Wheaton, 1, STORY. J.

Boyd vs. *Nebraska,* U. S. Sup. Ct. 1892, 143 U. S. 135, FULLER, Ch. J.

Chae Chan Ping vs. *United States (Chinese Exclusion Case),* U. S. Sup. Ct. 1889, 130 U. S. 581, FIELD, J.

Chew Heong v. *United States,* U. S. Sup. Ct. 1884, 112 U. S. 536, HARLAN, J.

Davis vs. *Police Jury, etc.,* U. S. Sup. Ct. 1850, 9 Howard, 280, WAYNE, J.

Doe (Clark) vs. *Braden,* U. S. Sup. Ct. 1853, 16 Howard, 635, TANEY, Ch. J.

Fleming vs. *Page (Tampico Duty Case),* U. S. Sup. Ct. 1850, 9 Howard, 683, TANEY, Ch. J.

Fong Yue Ting vs. *United States (Chinese Exclusion Case),* U. S. Sup. Ct. 1893, 149 U. S. 698. GRAY, J.

Foster vs. *Neilson*, U. S. Sup. Ct. 1829, 2 Peters, 253, MARSHALL, Ch. J.

Geofroy vs. *Riggs*, U. S. Sup. Ct. 1890, 133 U. S. 258, FIELD, J.

Head Money Cases, U. S. Sup. Ct. 1884, 112 U. S. 580, MILLER, J.

La Abra, etc., Co. vs. *United States*, U. S. Sup. Ct. 1899, 175 U. S. 423, HARLAN, J.

Mitchel vs. *United States*, U. S. Sup. Ct. 1835, 9 Peters, 711, BALD-WIN, J.

New Orleans vs. *United States*, U. S. Sup. Ct. 1836, 10 Peters, 662, MCLEAN, J.

New York vs. *Miln* (*Passenger Cases*), U. S. Sup. Ct. 1837, 11 Peters, 102, BARBOUR, J.

Ortiz, Ex parte, U. S. Cir. Ct. Minnesota, 1900, 100 Fed. Rep. 955, LOCHRAN, J.

Pollard vs. *Hagan*, U. S. Sup. Ct. 1845, 3 Howard, 212, McKINLEY, J.

Ross, In re, U. S. Sup. Ct. 1891, 140 U. S. 453, FIELD, J.

Scott vs. *Sandford* (*Dred Scott Case*), U. S. Sup. Ct. 1857, 19 Howard, 393, TANEY, Ch. J.

Strother vs. *Lucas*, U. S. Sup. Ct. 1832, 6 Peters, 763, THOMPSON, J.

United States vs. *Arredondo*, U. S. Sup. Ct. 1832, 6 Peters, 691, BALD-WIN, J.

United States vs. *Forty-three gallons, etc.*, U. S. Sup. Ct. 1876, 93 U. S. 188, DAVIS, J.; and 1883, 108 U. S. 491, FIELD, J.

United States vs. *Gratiot*, U. S. Sup. Ct. 1840, 14 Peters, 526, THOMP-SON, J.

United States vs. *Nelson*, U. S. Dist. Ct. Alaska, 1886, 29 Fed. Rep. 202, DAWSON, J., and affirmed 30 Fed. Rep. 112, DEADY, J.

United States vs. *Percheman*, U. S. Sup. Ct. 1833, 7 Peters, 51, MAR-SHALL, Ch. J.

United States vs. *Rauscher*, U. S. Sup. Ct. 1886, 119 U. S. 407, MIL-LER, J.

United States vs. *Reynes*, U. S. Sup. Ct. 1850, 9 Howard, 127, DANIEL, J.

United States vs. *Repentigny*, U. S. Sup. Ct. 1866, 5 Wallace, 211, NELSON, J.

Ware vs. *Hylton*, U. S. Sup. Ct. 1796, 3 Dallas, 199, CHASE, WILSON, PATERSON, CUSHING, IREDELL, JJ.

Whitney vs. *Robertson*, U. S. Sup. Ct. 1888, 124 U. S. 190, FIELD, J.

XVIII.

EFFECT OF CESSION OF TERRITORY, BY TREATY AND BY CONQUEST, ON PRIVATE RIGHTS OF THE INHABITANTS AND ON THE CONTINUANCE OF LOCAL LAWS OF THE CEDED TERRITORY.

Alexander vs. *Roulet*, U. S. Sup. Ct. 1871, 13 Wallace, 386, DAVIS, J.

American Ins. Co. vs. *Canter* (*Florida Case*), U. S. Sup. Ct. 1828, 1 Peters, 511, MARSHALL, Ch. J.

Blankard vs. *Galdy*, King & Queen's Bench, 5 Wm. & M. 4 Modern 222, PER CURIAM.

Calvin's Case, Court Exch. Cham. 6 James I, 4 Coke, 1.

Campbell vs. *Hall*, Kings' Bench, 15 Geo. III., Cowper, 204, LORD MANS-FIELD.

Chicago, etc., Ry. Co., vs. *McGlinn*, U. S. Sup. Ct. 1885, 114 U. S. 542, FIELD, J.

Chouteau vs. *Eckhart*, U. S. Sup. Ct. 1844, 2 Howard, 344, CATRON, J.

Cross vs. *Harrison* (*San Francisco Duty Case*), U. S. Sup. Ct. 1853, 16 Howard, 164, WAYNE, J.

Delassus vs. *United States*, U. S. Sup. Ct. 1835, 9 Peters, 117, MAR-SHALL, Ch. J.

Fama, The, High Ct. Admiralty 1804, 5 Ch. Robinson, 106, SIR W. SCOTT.

Foster vs. *Neilson*, U. S. Sup. Ct. 1829, 2 Peters, 253, MARSHALL, Ch. J.

Garcia vs. *Lee*, U. S. Sup. Ct. 1838, 12 Peters, 511, TANEY, Ch. J.

Hallet vs. *Hunt*, Sup. Ct. Alabama, 1845, 7 Ala. Rep. 882, COLLIER, Ch. J.

Holden vs. *Hardy*, U. S. Sup. Ct. 1898, 169 U. S. 366, BROWN, J.

Inglis vs. *Sailors' Snug Harbor*, U. S. Sup. Ct. 1830, 3 Peters, 99, THOMP-SON, J.

Keene vs. *McDonough*, U. S. Sup. Ct. 1834, 8 Peters, 308, THOMPSON, J.

Leitensdorfer vs. *Webb*, U. S. Sup. Ct. 1857, 20 Howard, 176, DANIEL, J.

Lord Bishop of Natal, Privy Council, 1864, 3 Moore P. C. N. S. 115. WESTBURY, Ld. Chan.

McKay vs. *Campbell*, U. S. Dist. Ct. Oregon, 1871, 2 Sawyer, 118, DEADY, J.

Mitchel vs. *United States*, U. S. Sup. Ct. 1835, 9 Peters, 711, BALD-WIN, J.

Neely vs. *Henkel*, U. S. Sup. Ct. 1901, 180 U. S. 109, HARLAN, J.

New Orleans vs. *Armas*, U. S. Sup. Ct. 1835, 9 Peters, 224, MAR-SHALL, Ch. J.

New Orleans vs. *Steamship Co.*, U. S. Sup. Ct. 1874, 20 Wallace, 387, SWAYNE, J.

Ortiz, Exparte, U. S. Cir. Ct. Minnesota, 1900, 100 Fed. Rep. 955, LOCH-RAN, J.

Penn vs. *Lord Baltimore*, High Ct. of Chancery, 1750, 1 Vesey, Sr., 445, HARDWICKE, Ld. Chan.

Pollard vs. *Hagan*, U. S. Sup. Ct. 1845, 3 Howard, 212, McKINLEY, J.

Pollard's Heirs vs. *Kibbe*, U. S. Sup. Ct. 1840, 14 Peters, 353, THOMP-SON, J.

Sah Quah's Case, U. S. Dist. Ct. Alaska, 1886, 31 Fed. Rep. 327, DAW-SON, J.

Scott vs. *Sandford* (*Dred Scott Case*), U. S. Sup. Ct. 1857, 19 Howard, 393, TANEY, Ch. J.

Soulard vs. *United States*, U. S. Sup. Ct. 1330, 4 Peters 511, MAR-SHALL, Ct. J.

Stearns vs. *United States*, U. S. Sup. Ct. 1867, 6 Wallace, 589, SWAYNE, J.

Strother vs. *Lucas*, U. S. Sup. Ct. 1832, 6 Peters, 763, THOMPSON, J.

United States vs. *Arredondo*, U. S. Sup. Ct. 1832, 6 Peters, 691, BALD-WIN, J.

United States vs. *Castillero*, U. S. Sup. Ct. 1812, 2 Black, 1, CLIF-FORD, J.

United States vs. *Gratiot,* U. S. Sup. Ct. 1840, 14 Peters, 526, THOMP-
SON, J.

United States vs. *Percheman,* U. S. Sup. Ct. 1833, 7 Peters, 51, MAR-
SHALL, Ch, J.

United States vs. *Repentigny,* U. S. Sup. Ct. 1866, 5 Wallace, 211, NEL-
SON, J,

United States vs. *Reynes,* U. S. Sup. Ct. 1850, 9 Howard, 127, DAN-
IEL, J.

United States vs. *Rice (The Castine Case),* U. S. Sup. Ct. 1819, 4
Wheaton, 246, STORY, J.

XIX.

PERSONAL AND INDIVIDUAL RIGHTS AND LIBERTIES GUARANTEED BY THE CONSTITUTION OF THE UNITED STATES.

American Publishing Co. vs. *Fisher (Utah Jury Case),* U. S. Sup. Ct.
1897, 166 U. S. 464, BREWER, J.

Bank of Columbia vs. *Okely,* U. S. Sup. Ct. 1819, 4 Wheaton, 235,
JOHNSON, J.

Barnes vs. *Dist. of Col.,* U. S. Sup. Ct. 1875, 91 U. S. 542, HUNT, J.

Boyd vs. *Nebraska,* U. S. Sup. Ct. 1892, 143 U. S. 135, FULLER, Ch. J.

Boyd vs. *United States,* U. S. Sup. Ct. 1886, 116 U. S. 616, BRAD-
LEY, J.

Callan vs. *Wilson,* U. S. Sup. Ct. 1887, 127 U. S. 540, HARLAN, J.

Calvin's Case, Court Exch. Cham. 6 James I, 4 Coke, 1.

Campbell vs. *Hall,* King's Bench, 15 Geo. III, Cowper, 204, LORD MANS-
FIELD.

Capital Traction Co. vs. *Hof,* U. S. Sup. Ct. 1899, 174 U. S. 1, GRAY, J.

Cummings vs. *Missouri,* U. S. Sup. Ct. 1866, 4 Wallace, 277, FIELD, J.

Delassus vs. *United States,* U. S. Sup. Ct. 1835, 9 Peters, 117, MAR-
SHALL, Ch. J.

Doe (Clark) vs. *Braden,* U. S. Sup. Ct. 1853, 16 Howard, 635, TANEY,
Ch. J.

Foster vs. *Neilson,* U. S. Sup. Ct. 1829, 2 Peters, 253, MARSHALL,
Ch. J.

Garcia vs. *Lee,* U. S. Sup. Ct. 1838, 12 Peters, 511, TANEY, Ch. J.

Geofroy vs. *Riggs,* U. S. Sup. Ct. 1890, 133 U. S. 258, FIELD, J.

Great Western Ins. Co. vs. *United States,* U. S. Sup. Ct. 1884, 112
U. S. 193, MILLER, J.

Haver vs. *Yaker,* U. S. Sup. Ct. 1869, 9 Wallace, 32, DAVIS, J.

Head Money Cases, U. S. Sup. Ct. 1884, 112 U. S. 580, MILLER, J.

Inglis vs. *Sailors' Snug Harbor,* U. S. Sup. Ct. 1830, 3 Peters, 99,
THOMPSON, J.

La Abra, etc., Co. vs. *United States,* U. S. Sup. Ct. 1899, 175 U. S.
423, HARLAN, J.

Lem Moon Sing vs. *United States,* U. S. Sup. Ct. 1895, 158 U. S. 538,
HARLAN, J.

Lord Bishop of Natal, Privy Council, 1864, 3 Moore, P. C. N. S. 115,
WESTBURY, Ld. Chan.

McKay vs. *Campbell*, U. S. Dist. Ct. Oregon, 1871, 2 Sawyer, 118, DEADY, J.

Marbury vs. *Madison*, U. S. Sup. Ct. 1803, 1 Cranch, 137, MARSHALL, Ch. J.

Maxwell vs. *Dow*, U. S. Sup. Ct. 1900, 176 U. S. 581, PECKHAM, J.

Milligan, Ex parte, U. S. Sup. Ct. 1866, 4 Wallace, 2, DAVIS, J.

Minor vs. *Happersett* (*Woman's Rights Case*), U. S. Sup. Ct. 1874, 21 Wallace, 162, WAITE, Ch. J.

Murphy vs. *Ramsey*, U. S. Sup. Ct. 1885, 114 U. S. 15, MATTHEWS, J.

Neagle, In re, U. S. Sup. Ct. 1890, 135 U. S. 1, MILLER, J.

Neely vs. *Henkel*, U. S. Sup. Ct. 1901, 180 U. S. 109, HARLAN, J.

O'Neill vs. *Vermont*, U. S. Sup. Ct. 1892, 144 U. S. 323, BLATCHFORD, J.

Ortiz, Ex parte, U. S. Cir. Ct. Minn. 1900, 100 Fed. Rep. 955, LOCHRAN, J.

Ross, In re, U. S. Sup. Ct. 1891, 140 U. S. 453, FIELD, J.

Sah Quah's Case, U. S. Dist. Ct. Alaska, 1886, 31 Fed. Rep. 327, DAWSON, J.

Scott vs. *Sanford* (*Dred Scott Case*), U. S. Sup. Ct. 1857, 19 Howard, 393, TANEY, Ch. J.

Siebold, Ex parte, U. S. Sup. Ct. 1879, 100 U. S. 371, BRADLEY, J.

Slaughter House Cases, U. S. Sup. Ct. 1872, 16 Wallace, 36, MILLER, J.

Spies vs. *Illinois* (*Chicago Anarchist Case*), U. S. Sup. Ct. 1887, 123 U. S. 131, WAITE, Ch. J.

Tennessee vs. *Davis*, U. S. Sup. Ct. 1879, 100 U. S. 257, STRONG, J.

Thompson vs. *Utah*, U. S. Sup. Ct. 1898, 170 U. S. 343, HARLAN, J.

United States vs. *Morris*, U. S. Cir. Ct. Mass. 1851, 1 Curtis, 23, CURTIS, J.

United States vs. *Rauscher*, U. S. Sup. Ct. 1886, 119 U. S. 407, MILLER, J.

Vallandigham, Ex parte, U. S. Cir. Ct. Ohio, 1863, Fed. Cas. 16,816 (pamphlet Rickey & Carroll, Cincinnati), LEAVITT, J.

Weimer vs. *Bunbury*, Sup. Ct. Michigan, 1874, 30 Mich. 201' COOLEY, J.

Yick Wo vs. *Hopkins*, U. S. Sup. Ct. 1886, 118 U. S. 356, MATTHEWS, J.

XX.

CITIZENSHIP, BIRTH AND ALLEGIANCE AS AFFECTED BY TREATIES, STATUTES AND THE CONSTITUTION.

American Ins. Co. vs. *Canter* (*Florida Case*), U. S. Sup. Ct. 1828, 1 Peters, 511, MARSHALL, Ch. J.

Barnes vs. *District of Columbia*, U. S. Sup. Ct. 1875, 91 U. S. 542, HUNT, J.

Boyd vs. *Nebraska*, U. S. Sup. Ct. 1892, 143 U. S. 135, FULLER, Ch. J.

Calvin's Case, Court of Exch. Chamber, 6 James I, 4 Coke, 1.

Campbell vs. *Hall*, King's Bench, 15 Geo. III, Cowper, 204, LORD MANSFIELD.

Cherokee Nation vs. *Georgia*, U. S. Sup. Ct. 1831, 5 Peters, 1, MARSHALL, Ch. J.

Cooper, In re (*Bering Sea Cases*), U. S. Sup. Ct. 1891, 138 U. S. 404, and 1892, 143 U. S. 472, FULLER, Ch. J.

Elk vs. *Wilkins*, U. S. Sup. Ct. 1884, 112 U. S. 94, GRAY, J.

Fong Yue Ting vs. *United States* (*Chinese Exclusion Case*), U. S. Sup. Ct. 1893, 149 U. S. 698, GRAY, J.

Geofroy vs. *Riggs*, U. S. Sup. Ct. 1890, 133 U. S. 258, FIELD, J.

Head Money Cases, U. S. Sup. Ct. 1884, 112 U. S. 580, MILLER, J.

Hepburn vs. *Ellzey*, U. S. Sup. Ct. 1805, 2 Cranch, 445, MARSHALL, Ch. J.

Inglis vs. *Sailors' Snug Harbor*, U. S. Sup. Ct. 1830, 3 Peters, 99, THOMPSON, J.

Lynch vs. *Clark*, N. Y. Court of Chancery, 1844, 1 Sanford Ch. 583, SANDFORD, V. Chan.

McKay vs. *Campbell*, U. S. Dist. Ct. Oregon, 1871, 2 Sawyer, 118, DEADY, J.

Martin vs. *Hunter*, U. S. Sup. Ct. 1816, 1 Wheaton, 304, STORY, J.

Minor vs. *Happersett* (*Woman's Rights Case*), U. S. Sup. Ct. 1874, 21 Wallace, 162, WAITE, Ch. J.

Moore vs. *Illinois*, U. S. Sup. Ct. 1852, 14 Howard, 13, GRIER, J.

O'Neill vs. *Vermont*, U. S. Sup. Ct. 1892, 144 U. S. 323, BLATCHFORD, J.

Ortiz, Ex parte, U. S. Cir. Ct. Minnesota, 1900, 100 Fed. Rep. 955, LOCHRAN, J.

Penn vs. *Lord Baltimore*, High Ct. of Chancery, 1750, 1 Vesey, Sr., 445, HARDWICKE, Lord Chan.

Pizarro, The, U. S. Sup. Ct. 1817, 2 Wheaton, 227, STORY, J.

Ross, In re, U. S. Sup. Ct. 1891, 140 U. S. 453, FIELD, J.

Sah Quah's Case, U. S. Dist. Ct. Alaska, 1886, 31 Fed. Rep. 327, DAWSON, J.

Scott vs. *Sandford* (*Dred Scott Case*), U. S. Sup. Ct. 1857, 19 Howard, 393, TANEY, Ch. J.

Shanks vs. *Dupont*, U. S. Sup. Ct. 1830, 3 Peters, 242, STORY, J.

Slaughter House Cases, U. S. Sup. Ct. 1872, 16 Wallace, 36, MILLER, J.

Smith vs. *Maryland*, U. S. Sup. Ct. 1810, 6 Cranch, 286, WASHINGTON, J.

Spies vs. *Illinois* (*Chicago Anarchist Cases*), U. S. Sup. Ct. 1887, 123 U. S. 131, WAITE, Ch. J.

Swan, The, U. S. Dist. Ct. Washington, 1892, 50 Fed. Rep. 108, HANFORD, J.

Tennessee vs. *Davis*, U. S. Sup. Ct. 1879, 100 U. S. 257, STRONG, J.

Texas vs. *White*, U. S. Sup. Ct. 1868, 7 Wallace, 700, CHASE, Ch. J.

Thirty Hogsheads of Sugar vs. *Boyle*, U. S. Sup. Ct. 1815, 9 Cranch, 191, MARSHALL, Ch. J.

United States vs. *Forty-three Gallons, etc.*, U. S. Sup. Ct. 1876, 93 U. S. 188, DAVIS, J., and 1883, 108 U. S. 491, FIELD, J.

United States vs. *Kagama*, U. S. Sup. Ct. 1886, 118 U. S. 375, MILLER, J.

United States vs. *Osborne*, U. S. Dist. Ct. Oregon, 1880, 6 Sawyer, 406, DEADY, J.

United States vs. *Repentigny*, U. S. Sup. Ct. 1866, 5 Wallace, 211, NELSON, J.

United States vs. *Rhodes*, U. S. Cir. Ct. Kentucky, 1866, 1 Abb. U. S. Rep. 28, SWAYNE, J.

United States vs. *Rogers*, U. S. Sup. Ct. 1846, 4 Howard, 567, TANEY, Ch. J.

United States vs. *Wong Kim Ark* (*Chinese Baby Case*), U. S. Sup. Ct. 1898, 169 U. S. 649, GRAY, J.

Wong Wing vs. *United States*, U. S. Sup. Ct. 1896, 163 U. S. 228, SHIRAS, J.

Worcester vs. *Georgia*, U. S. Sup. Ct. 1832, 6 Peters, 515, MARSHALL, Ch. J.

Yick Wo vs. *Hopkins*, U. S. Sup. Ct. 1886, 118 U. S. 356, MATTHEWS, J.

XXI.

CONSTRUCTION OF TREATIES AND GENERAL RULES APPLICABLE THERETO. EXECUTIVE AND JUDICIAL CONSTRUCTION, CONGRESSIONAL POWER THEREOVER.

Amiable Isabella, The, U. S. Sup. Ct. 1821, 6 Wheaton, 1, STORY, J.

Boyd vs. *Nebraska,* U. S. Sup. Ct. 1892, 143 U. S. 135, FULLER, Ch. J.

Castro vs. *DeUriarte,* U. S. Dist. Ct. S. D. N. Y. 1883, 16 Fed. Rep. 93, BROWN, J.

Chae Chan Ping vs. *United States* (*Chinese Exclusion Case*), U. S. Sup. Ct. 1889, 130 U. S. 581, FIELD, J.

Cherokee Tobacco, The, U. S. Sup. Ct. 1870, 11 Wallace, 616, SWAYNE, J.

Chew Heong vs. *United States,* U. S. Sup. Ct. 1884, 112 U. S. 536, HARLAN, J.

Clinton Bridge, The, U. S. Cir. Ct. Iowa, 1867, 1 Woolworth, 150, MILLER, J.

Coffee vs. *Groover,* U. S. Sup. Ct. 1887, 123 U. S. 1, BRADLEY, J.

Elk vs. *Wilkins,* U. S. Sup. Ct. 1884, 112 U. S. 94, GRAY, J.

Fong Yue Ting vs. *United States* (*Chinese Exclusion Case*), U. S. Sup. Ct. 1893, 149 U. S. 698, GRAY, J.

Foster vs. *Neilson,* U. S. Sup. Ct. 1829, 2 Peters, 253, MARSHALL, Ch. J.

Frelinghuysen vs. *Key,* U. S. Sup. Ct. 1884, 110 U. S. 63, WAITE, Ch. J.

Garcia vs. *Lee,* U. S. Sup. Ct. 1838, 12 Peters, 511, TANEY, Ch. J.

Geofroy vs. *Riggs,* U. S. Sup. Ct. 1890, 133 U. S. 258, FIELD, J.

Great Western Ins. Co. vs. *United States,* U. S. Sup. Ct. 1884, 112 U. S. 193, MILLER, J.

Griswold vs. *Atlantic Dock Co.,* N. Y. Sup. Ct. 1855, 21 Barbour, 225, STRONG, J.

Haver vs. *Yaker,* U. S. Sup. Ct. 1869, 9 Wallace, 32, DAVIS, J.

Head Money Cases, U. S. Sup. Ct. 1884, 112 U. S. 580, MILLER, J.

Holmes vs. *Jennison,* U. S. Sup. Ct. 1840, 14 Peters, 540, THOMPSON, J.

Inglis vs. *Sailors' Snug Harbor,* U. S. Sup. Ct. 1830, 3 Peters, 99, THOMPSON, J.

Jecker vs. *Magee* (*Haver* vs. *Yaker*), U. S. Sup. Ct. 1869, 9 Wallace, 32, DAVIS, J.

Kansas Indians, The, U. S. Sup. Ct. 1866, 5 Wallace, 737, DAVIS, J.

La Abra, etc., Co. vs. *United States,* U. S. Sup. Ct. 1899, 175 U. S. 423, HARLAN, J.

McKay vs. *Campbell,* U. S. Dist. Ct. Oregon, 1871, 2 Sawyer, 118, DEADY, J.

Martin vs. *Waddell,* U. S. Sup. Ct. 1842, 16 Peters, 367, TANEY, Ch. J.

Martin vs. *Hunter,* U. S. Sup. Ct. 1816, 1 Wheaton, 304, STORY, J.

Mitchel vs. *United States,* U. S. Sup. Ct. 1835, 9 Peters, 711, BALDWIN, J.

Neely vs. *Henkel,* U. S. Sup. Ct. 1901, 180 U. S. 109, HARLAN, J.

New Orleans vs. *Armas,* U. S. Sup. Ct. 1835, 9 Peters, 224, MARSHALL, Ch. J.

New Orleans vs. *United States,* U. S. Sup. Ct. 1836, 10 Peters, 662, MCLEAN, J.

New York vs. *Miln (Passenger Cases),* U. S. Sup. Ct. 1837, 11 Peters, 102, BARBOUR, J.

Pollard vs. *Hagan,* U. S. Sup. Ct. 1845, 3 Howard, 212, MCKINLEY, J.

Pollard's Heirs vs. *Kibbe,* U. S. Sup. Ct. 1840, 14 Peters, 353, THOMPSON, J.

Ross, In re, U. S. Sup. Ct. 1891, 140 U. S. 453, FIELD, J.

Sah Quah's Case, U. S. Dist. Ct. Alaska, 1886, 31 Fed. Rep. 327, DAWSON, J.

Shanks vs. *Dupont,* U. S. Sup. Ct. 1830, 3 Peters, 242, STORY, J.

Soulard vs. *United States,* U. S. Sup. Ct. 1830, 4 Peters, 511, MARSHALL, Ch. J.

Strothers vs. *Lucas,* U. S. Sup. Ct. 1832, 6 Peters, 763, THOMPSON, J.

Taylor vs. *Morton,* U. S. Cir. Ct. Mass. 1855, 2 Curtis, 454, CURTIS, J., (aff'd U. S. Sup. Ct. 1862, 2 Black, 481, CLIFFORD, J.).

United States vs. *Arredondo,* U. S. Sup. Ct. 1832, 6 Peters, 691, BALDWIN, J.

United States vs. *Castillero,* U. S. Sup. Ct. 1862, 2 Black, 1, CLIFFORD, J.

United States vs. *Forty-three Gallons, etc.,* U. S. Sup. Ct. 1876, 93 U. S. 188, DAVIS, J., and 1883, 108 U. S. 491, FIELD, J.

United States vs. *Gratiot,* U. S. Sup. Ct. 1840, 14 Peters, 526, THOMPSON, J.

United States vs. *Kagama,* U. S. Sup. Ct. 1886, 118 U. S. 375, MILLER, J.

United States vs. *Percheman,* U. S. Sup. Ct. 1833, 7 Peters, 51, MARSHALL, Ch. J.

United States vs. *Rauscher,* U. S. Sup. Ct. 1886, 119 U. S. 407, MILLER, J.

United States vs. *Repentigny,* U. S. Sup. Ct. 1866, 5 Wallace, 211, NELSON, J.

United States vs. *Reynes,* U. S. Sup. Ct. 1850, 9 Howard, 127, DANIEL, J.

United States vs. *Rogers,* U. S. Sup. Ct. 1846, 4 Howard, 567, TANEY, Ch. J.

United States vs. *Texas*, U. S. Sup. Ct. 1896, 102 U. S. 1, HARLAN, J.
United States vs. *Tobacco Factory*, U. S. Cir. Ct. Arkansas, 1871, 1 Dillon, 264, CALDWELL, J.
Ware vs. *Hylton*, U. S. Sup. Ct. 1796, 3 Dallas, 199, CHASE, WILSON, PATERSON, CUSHING, IREDELL, JJ.
Whitney vs. *Robertson*, U. S. Sup. Ct. 1888, 124 U. S. 190, FIELD, J.
Wong Wing vs. *United States*, U. S. Sup. Ct. 1896, 163 U. S. 228, SHIRAS, J.
Yick Wo vs. *Hopkins*, U. S. Sup. Ct. 1886, 118 U. S. 356, MATTHEWS, J.

XXII.

RELATIVE EFFECTS OF TREATIES AND UNITED STATES STATUTES.

Bates vs. *Clark*, U. S. Sup. Ct. 1877, 95 U. S. 204, MILLER, J.
Chae Chan Ping vs. *United States* (*Chinese Exclusion Case*), U. S. Sup. Ct. 1889, 130 U. S. 581, FIELD, J.
Cherokee Tobacco, The, U. S. Sup. Ct. 1870, 11 Wallace, 616, SWAYNE, J.
Chew Heong vs. *United States*, U. S. Sup. Ct. 1884, 112 U. S. 536, HARLAN, J.
Doe (*Clark*) vs. *Braden*, U. S. Sup. Ct. 1853, 16 Howard, 635, TANEY Ch. J.
Fong Yue Ting vs. *United States* (*Chinese Exclusion Case*), U. S. Sup Ct. 1893, 149 U. S. 698, GRAY, J.
Foster vs. *Neilson*, U. S. Sup. Ct. 1829, 2 Peters, 253, MARSHALL, Ch. J.
Frelinghuysen vs. *Key*, U. S. Sup. Ct. 1884, 110 U. S. 63, WAITE, Ch. J.
Great Western Ins. Co. vs. *United States*, U. S. Sup. Ct. 1884, 112 U. S. 193, MILLER, J.
Griswold vs. *Atlantic Dock Co.*, N. Y. Sup. Ct. 1855, 21 Barbour, 225, STRONG, J.
Head Money Cases, U. S. Sup. Ct. 1884, 112 U. S. 580, MILLER, J.
Kansas Indians, The, U. S. Sup. Ct. 1866, 5 Wallace, 737, DAVIS, J.
La Abra, etc., Co. vs. *United States*, U. S. Sup. Ct. 1899, 175 U. S. 423, HARLAN, J.
Mobile vs. *Eslava*, U. S. Sup. Ct. 1842, 16 Peters, 234, McLEAN, J.
New York vs. *Miln* (*Passenger Cases*), U. S. Sup. Ct. 1837, 11 Peters, 102, BARBOUR, J.
Ross, In re, U. S. Sup. Ct. 1891, 140 U. S. 453, FIELD, J.
Taylor vs. *Morton*, U. S. Cir. Ct. Mass. 1855, 2 Curtis, 454, CURTIS, J., (aff'd U. S. Sup. Ct. 1862, 2 Black, 481, CLIFFORD, J.).
United States vs. *Forty-three Gallons, etc.*, U. S. Sup. Ct. 1876, 93 U. S. 188, DAVIS, J., and 1883, 108 U. S. 491, FIELD, J.
United States vs. *Rauscher*, U. S. Sup. Ct. 1886, 119 U. S. 407, MILLER, J.
Whitney vs. *Robertson*, U. S. Sup. Ct. 1888, 124 U. S. 190, FIELD, J.
Wong Wing vs. *United States*, U. S. Sup. Ct. 1896, 163 U. S. 228 SHIRAS, J.
Yick Wo vs. *Hopkins*, U. S. Sup. Ct. 1886, 118 U. S. 356, MATTHEWS, J.

XXIII.

RELATIVE EFFECTS OF TREATIES MADE BY THE UNITED STATES AND STATE LAWS.

Cherokee Nation vs. *Georgia*, U. S. Sup. Ct. 1831, 5 Peters, 1, MARSHALL, Ch. J.

Clinton Bridge, The, U. S. Cir. Ct. Iowa, 1867, 1 Woolworth, 150, MILLER, J.

Geofroy vs. *Riggs*, U. S. Sup. Ct. 1890, 133 U. S. 258, FIELD, J.

Haver vs. *Yaker*, U. S. Sup. Ct. 1869, 9 Wallace, 32, DAVIS, J.

Holmes vs. *Jennison*, U. S. Sup. 1840, 14 Peters, 540, THOMPSON, J.

Hurltado vs. *California*, U. S. Sup. 1884, 143 U. S. 570, BLATCHFORD, J.

Inglis vs. *Sailors' Snug Harbor*, U. S. Sup. Ct. 1830, 3 Peters, 99, THOMPSON, J.

Jecker vs. *Magee*, same as *Haver* vs. *Yaker*, *supra*.

Martin vs. *Waddell*, U. S. Sup. Ct. 1842, 16 Peters, 367, TANEY, Ch. J.

Martin vs. *Hunter*, U. S. Sup. Ct. 1816, 1 Wheaton, 304, STORY, J.

New York vs. *Miln (Passenger Cases)*, U. S. Sup. Ct. 1837, 11 Peters, 102, BARBOUR, J.

Shanks vs. *Dupont*, U. S. Sup. Ct. 1830, 3 Peters, 242, STORY, J.

United States vs. *Forty-three Gallons, etc.*, U. S. Sup. Ct. 1876, 93 U. S. 188, DAVIS, J.; 1883, 108 U. S. 491, FIELD, J.

Ware vs. *Hylton*, U. S. Sup. Ct. 1796, 3 Dallas, 199, CHASE, WILSON, PATERSON, CUSHING, IREDELL, JJ.

Yick Wo vs. *Hopkins*. U. S. Sup. Ct. 1886, 118 U. S. 356, MATTHEWS, J.

XXIV.

WHEN TREATIES TAKE EFFECT AS TO THE CONTRACTING GOVERNMENTS AND AS TO THE RIGHTS OF INDIVIDUALS AFFECTED THEREBY.

Chouteau vs. *Eckhart*, U. S. Sup. Ct. 1844, 2 Howard, 344, CATRON, J.

Davis vs. *Police Jury, etc.*, U. S. Sup. Ct. 1850, 9 Howard, 280, WAYNE, J.

Doe (Clark) vs. *Braden*, U. S. Sup. Ct. 1853, 16 Howard, 635, TANEY, Ch. J.

Haver vs. *Yaker*, U. S. Sup. Ct. 1869, 9 Wallace, 32, DAVIS, J.

Head Money Cases, U. S. Sup. Ct. 1884, 112 U. S. 580, MILLER, J.

Inglis vs. *Sailors' Snug Harbor*, U. S. Sup. Ct. 1830, 3 Peters, 99, THOMPSON, J.

Jecker vs. *Magee*, same as *Haver* vs. *Yaker*, *supra*.

Ortiz, Ex parte, U. S. Cir. Ct. Minn. 1900, 100 Fed. Rep. 955, LOCHRAN, J.

Taylor vs. *Morton*, U. S. Cir. Ct. Mass. 1855, 2 Curtis, 454, CURTIS, J. (aff'd U. S. Sup. Ct. 1862, 2 Black. 481. CLIFFORD, J.).

United States vs. *Reynes*, U. S. Sup. Ct. 1850, 9 Howard, 127, DANIEL, J.

Whitney vs. *Robertson*, U. S. Sup. Ct. 1888, 124 U. S. 190, FIELD, J.

XXV.

STATUS OF INDIAN TRIBES AND THE CONSTRUCTION OF INDIAN TREA-
TIES; THE RELATIVE EFFECT OF INDIAN TREATIES AND STATE AND
FEDERAL LAWS.

Bates vs. *Clark*, U. S. Sup. Ct. 1877, 95 U. S. 204, MILLER, J.

Cherokee Nation vs. *Georgia*, U. S. Sup. Ct. 1831, 5 Peters, 1, MAR-
SHALL, Ch. J.

Cherokee Tobacco, The, U. S. Sup. Ct. 1870, 11 Wallace, 616, SWAYNE, J.

Crow Dog, Ex parte, U. S. Sup. Ct. 1883, 109 U. S. 556, MATTHEWS, J.

Elk vs. *Wilkins*, U. S. Sup. Ct. 1884, 112 U. S. 94, GRAY, J.

Johnson vs. *McIntosh*, U. S. Sup. Ct. 1823, 8 Wheaton, 543, MAR-
SHALL, Ch. J.

Kansas Indians, The, U. S. Sup. Ct. 1866, 5 Wallace, 737, DAVIS, J.

Sah Quah's Case, U, S. Dist. Ct. Alaska, 1886, 31 Fed. Rep. 327, DAW-
SON, J.

Taltan vs. *Mayes*, U. S. Sup. Ct. 1896, 163 U. S. 376, WHITE, J.

United States vs. *Forty-three Gallons, etc.*, U. S. Sup. Ct. 1876, 93
U. S. 188, DAVIS, J., and 1883, 108 U. S. 491, FIELD, J.

United States vs. *Kagama*, U. S. Sup. Ct. 1886, 118 U. S. 375, MIL-
LER, J.

United States vs. *Osborne*, U. S. Dist. Ct. Oregon, 1880, 6 Sawyer, 406,
DEADY, J.

United States vs. *Rogers*, U. S. Sup. Ct. 1846, 4 Howard, 567, TANEY,
Ch. J.

United States vs. *Tobacco Factory*, U. S. Cir. Ct. Arkansas, 1871, 1
Dillon, 264, CALDWELL, J.

Worcester vs. *Georgia*, U. S. Sup. Ct. 1832, 6 Peters, 515, MAR-
SHALL, Ch. J.

INSULAR CASES APPENDIX.

DECISIONS OF DECEMBER 2, 1901.

After the foregoing APPENDIX was completed and this volume was in press, the Supreme Court decided the two cases known as the *Fourteen Diamond Rings* (*Pepke*) *Case*, (see pages 467, *et seq.*, of this APPENDIX, *ante*,) involving the status of the Philippine Islands as to tariff laws, and the *Second Dooley Case*, (see pages 501, *et seq.*, of this APPENDIX, *ante*,) involving the right to collect duties *in* Porto Rico on merchandise *from* other ports of the United States. As it was too late to include those decisions in their proper places in the foregoing APPENDIX, they have been added as a supplement thereto, and they appear in full in the following pages.

THE FOURTEEN DIAMOND RINGS.

In error to the District Court of the United States for the Northern District of Illinois. No. 158. October term, 1901.

[Decided December 2, 1901.]

For appearances, abstract of record, briefs and arguments, see p. 467, *ante*, of this appendix.

Mr. Chief Justice FULLER delivered the opinion of the court as follows:

"Emil J. Pepke, a citizen of the United States and of the State of North Dakota, enlisted in the First Regiment of the North Dakota United States Volunteer Infantry, and was assigned for duty with his regiment in the island of Luzon, in the Philippine Islands, and continued in the military service of the United States until the regiment was ordered to return, and, on arriving at San Francisco, was discharged September 25, 1899.

"He brought with him from Luzon fourteen diamond rings, which he had there purchased, or acquired through a loan, subsequent to the ratification of the treaty of peace between the United States and Spain, February 6, 1899, and the proclamation thereof by the President of the United States, April 11, 1899.

"In May, 1900, in Chicago, these rings were seized by a customs officer as having been imported contrary to law, without entry, or declaration,

563

or payment of duties, and an information was filed to enforce the forfeiture thereof.

"To this Pepke filed a plea setting up the facts, and claiming that the rings were not subject to customs duties; the plea was held insufficient; forfeiture and sale were decreed; and this writ of error was prosecuted.

"The tariff act of July 24, 1897, (30 Stat. 151,) in regulation of commerce with foreign nations, levied duties 'upon all articles imported from foreign countries.'

"Were these rings, acquired by this soldier after the ratification of the treaty was proclaimed, when brought by him from Luzon to California, on his return with his regiment to be discharged, imported from a foreign country?

"This question has already been answered in the negative, in respect of Porto Rico in De Lima vs. Bidwell, 182 U. S. 1, and unless the cases can be distinguished, which we are of opinion they cannot be in this particular, that decision is controlling.

"The Philippines, like Porto Rico, became, by virtue of the treaty, ceded conquered territory or territory ceded by way of indemnity. The territory ceased to be situated as Castine was when occupied by the British forces in the war of 1812, or as Tampico was when occupied by the troops of the United States during the Mexican war, ' cases of temporary possession of territory by lawful and regular governments at war with the country of which the territory so possessed was part.' Thorington vs. Smith, 8 Wall. 10. The Philippines were not simply occupied but acquired, and having been granted and delivered to the United States, by their former master, were no longer under the sovereignty of any foreign nation.

"In Cross vs. Harrison,16 How. 164, the question was whether goods imported from a foreign country into California after the cession were subject to our tariff laws, and this court held that they were.

"In De Lima vs. Bidwell the question was whether goods imported into New York from Porto Rico, after the cession, were subject to duties imposed by the act of 1897 on 'articles imported from foreign countries,' and this court held that they were not. That act regulated commerce with foreign nations, and Porto Rico had ceased to be within that category; nor could territory be foreign and domestic at the same time.

"Among other things it was there said: ' The theory that a country remains foreign with respect to the tariff laws until Congress has acted by embracing it within the customs union, presupposes that a country may be domestic for one purpose and foreign for another. It may undoubtedly become necessary for the adequate administration of a domestic territory to pass a special act providing the proper machinery and officers, as the President would have no authority, except under the war power, to administer it himself; but no act is necessary to make it domestic territory if once it has been ceded to the United States. . . . This theory also presupposes that territory may be held indefinitely by the United States; that it may be treated in every particular, except for tariff purposes, as domestic territory; that laws may be enacted and enforced by officers of the United States sent there for that purpose; that insurrections may be suppressed, wars carried on, revenues collected, taxes imposed; in short, that everything may be done which a government can do within its own boundaries, and yet that the territory may still remain a foreign country. That this state of things may continue for years, for a century even, but that until Congress enacts otherwise, it still remains a foreign country. To hold that this can be done as matter of law we deem to be pure judicial legislation. We find no warrant for it in the Constitution or in the powers conferred upon this court. It is true the nonaction of Congress may occasion a temporary inconvenience; but it does not follow that courts of justice are authorized to remedy it by inverting the ordinary meaning of words.'

'' No reason is perceived for any different ruling as to the Philippines. By the third article of the treaty Spain ceded to the United States 'the archipelago known as the Philippine Islands,' and the United States agreed to pay to Spain the sum of twenty million dollars within three months. The treaty was ratified; Congress appropriated the money; the ratification was proclaimed. The treaty-making power; the executive power; the legislative power, concurred in the completion of the transaction.

'' The Philippines thereby ceased, in the language of the treaty, 'to be Spanish.' Ceasing to be Spanish, they ceased to be foreign country. They came under the complete and absolute sovereignty and dominion of the United States, and so became territory of the United States over which civil government could be established. The result was the same although there was no stipulation that the native inhabitants should be incorporated into the body politic, and none securing to them the right to choose their nationality. Their allegiance became due to the United States and they became entitled to its protection.

'' But it is said that the case of the Philippines is to be distinguished from that of Porto Rico because on February 14, 1899, after the ratification of the treaty, the Senate resolved, as given in the margin,* that it was not intended to incorporate the inhabitants of the Philippines into citizenship of the United States, nor to permanently annex those islands.

'' We need not consider the force and effect of a resolution of this sort, if adopted by Congress, not like that of April 20, 1898, in respect of Cuba,

---

* '' ' Resolved by the Senate and House of Representatives of the United States of America in Congress assembled, That by the ratification of the treaty of peace with Spain it is not intended to incorporate the inhabitants of the Philippine Islands into citizenship of the United States, nor is it intended to permanently annex said islands as an integral part of the territory of the United States; but it is the intention of the United States to establish on said islands a government suitable to the wants and conditions of the inhabitants of said islands to prepare them for local self-government, and in due time to make such disposition of said islands as will best promote the interests of the United States and the inhabitants of said islands.' Cong. Rec. 55th Cong. 3d Sess. vol. 32, p. 1847.''

preliminary to the declaration of war, but after title had passed by ratified cession. It is enough that this was a joint resolution; that it was
adopted by the Senate by a vote of 26 to 22, not two thirds of a quorum;
and that it is absolutely without legal significance on the question before us. The meaning of the treaty cannot be controlled by subsequent
explanations of some of those who may have voted to ratify it. What
view the House might have taken as to the intention of the Senate in
ratifying the treaty we are not informed, nor is it material; and if any
implication from the action referred to could properly be indulged, it
would seem to be that two thirds of a quorum of the Senate did not
consent to the ratification on the grounds indicated.

"It is further contended that a distinction exists in that while complete possession of Porto Rico was taken by the United States, this was
not so as to the Philippines, because of the armed resistance of the native inhabitants to a greater or less extent.

"We must decline to assume that the government wishes thus to disparage the title of the United States, or to place itself in the position
of waging a war of conquest.

"The sovereignty of Spain over the Philippines and possession under
claim of title had existed for a long series of years prior to the war with
the United States. The fact that there were insurrections against her
or that uncivilized tribes may have defied her will did not affect the
validity of her title. She granted the islands to the United States, and
the grantee in accepting them took nothing less than the whole grant.

"If those in insurrection against Spain continued in insurrection
against the United States, the legal title and possession of the latter remained unaffected.

"We do not understand that it is claimed that in carrying on the pending hostilities the government is seeking to subjugate the people of a
foreign country, but, on the contrary, that it is preserving order and
suppressing insurrection in territory of the United States. It follows
that the possession of the United States is adequate possession under
legal title, and this cannot be asserted for one purpose and denied for
another. We dismiss the suggested distinction as untenable.

" But it is sought to detract from the weight of the ruling in De Lima
vs. Bidwell because one of the five justices concurring in the judgment
in that case concurred in the judgment in Downes vs. Bidwell, 182 U. S.
244.

"In De Lima vs. Bidwell, Porto Rico was held not to be a foreign country after the cession, and that a prior act exclusively applicable to foreign countries became inapplicable.

"In Downes vs. Bidwell, the conclusion of a majority of the court was
that an act of Congress levying duties on goods imported from Porto
Rico into New York, not in conformity with the provisions of the Constitution in respect to the imposition of duties, imposts and excises, was
valid. Four of the members of the court dissented from and five concurred, though not on the same grounds, in this conclusion. The justice
who delivered the opinion in De Lima's case was one of the majority,
and was of opinion that although by the cession Porto Rico ceased to

be a foreign country, and became a territory of the United States and domestic, yet that it was merely 'appurtenant' territory, and 'not a part of the United States within the revenue clauses of the Constitution.'

"This view placed the territory, though not foreign, outside of the restrictions applicable to interstate commerce, and treated the power of Congress, when affirmatively exercised over a territory, situated as supposed, as uncontrolled by the provisions of the Constitution in respect of national taxation. The distinction was drawn between a special act in respect of the particular country, and a general and prior act only applicable to countries foreign to ours in every sense. The latter was obliged to conform to the rule of uniformity, which was wholly disregarded in the former.

"The ruling in the case of *De Lima* remained unaffected, and controls that under consideration. And this is so notwithstanding four members of the majority in the *De Lima* case were of opinion that Porto Rico did not become by the cession subjected to the exercise of governmental power in the levy of duties unrestricted by constitutional limitations.

"*Decree reversed and cause remanded with directions to quash the information.*"

"Mr. Justice BROWN delivered a concurring opinion as follows:

"I concur in the conclusion of the court in this case, and in the reasons given therefor in the opinion of the Chief Justice.

"The case is distinguishable from *De Lima* vs. *Bidwell* in but one particular, viz., the Senate resolution of February 6, 1899. With regard to this, I would say that in my view the case would not be essentially different if this resolution had been adopted by a unanimous vote of the Senate. To be efficacious such resolution must be considered either (1) as an amendment to the treaty, or (2) as a legislative act qualifying or modifying the treaty. It is neither.

"It cannot be regarded as part of the treaty, since it received neither the approval of the President nor the consent of the other contracting power. A treaty in its legal sense is defined by Bouvier as 'a compact made between two or more independent nations with a view to the public welfare,' (2 Law Dic. 1136,) and by Webster as 'an agreement, league or contract between two or more nations or sovereigns, formally signed by commissioners properly authorized, and solemnly ratified by the sovereigns or the supreme power of each state.' In its essence it is a contract. It differs from an ordinary contract only in being an agreement between independent states instead of private parties. (*Foster* vs. *Neilson*, 2 Pet. 253, 314; *Head Money Cases*, 112 U. S. 580.) By the Constitution, (art. 2, sec. 2,) the President 'shall have power, by and with the advice and consent of the Senate, to make treaties, provided two-thirds of the Senators present concur.' Obviously the treaty must contain the whole contract between the parties, and the power of the Senate is limited to a ratification of such terms as have already been agreed upon between the President, acting for the United States, and the commissioners of the other contracting power. The

Senate has no right to ratify the treaty and introduce new terms into it, which shall be obligatory upon the other power, although it may refuse its ratification, or make such ratification conditional upon the adoption of amendments to the treaty. If, for instance, the treaty with Spain had contained a provision instating the inhabitants of the Philippines as citizens of the United States, the Senate might have refused to ratify it until this provision was stricken out. But it could not, in my opinion, ratify the treaty and then adopt a resolution declaring it not to be its intention to admit the inhabitants of the Philippine Islands to the privileges of citizenship of the United States. Such resolution would be inoperative as an amendment to the treaty, since it had not received the assent of the President or the Spanish commissioners.

"Allusion was made to this question in the *New York Indians* vs. *United States*, (170 U. S. 1, 21,) wherein it appeared that, when a treaty with certain Indian tribes was laid before the Senate for ratification, several articles were stricken out, several others amended, a new article added, and a proviso adopted that the treaty should have no force or effect whatever until the amendment had been submitted to the tribes, and they had given their free and voluntary assent thereto. This resolution, however, was not found in the original or in the published copy of the treaty, or in the proclamation of the President, which contained the treaty without the amendments. With reference to this the court observed: ' The power to make treaties is vested by the Constitution in the President and the Senate, and, while this proviso was adopted by the Senate, there was no evidence that it ever received the sanction or approval of the President. It cannot be considered as a legislative act, since the power to legislate is vested in the President, Senate and House of Representatives. There is something, too, which shocks the conscience in the idea that a treaty can be put forth as embodying the terms of an arrangement with a foreign power or an Indian tribe, a material provision of which is unknown to one of the contracting parties, and is kept in the background to be used by the other only when the exigencies of a particular case may demand it. ' The proviso appears never to have been called to the attention of the tribes, who would naturally assume that the treaty embodied in the Presidential proclamation contained all the terms of the arrangement.'

" In short, it seems to me entirely clear that this resolution cannot be considered a part of the treaty.

" I think it equally clear that it cannot be treated as a legislative act, though it may be conceded that under the decisions of this court Congress has the power to disregard or modify a treaty with a foreign state. This was not done.

" The resolution in question was introduced as a *joint* resolution, but it never received the assent of the House of Representatives or the signature of the President. While a joint resolution, when approved by the President, or, being disapproved, is passed by two-thirds of each house, has the effect of a law, (Const. art. 1, sec. 7,) no such effect can be given to a resolution of either house acting independently of the other. Indeed, the above clause expressly requires concurrent action upon a resolution 'before the same shall take effect.'

"This question was considered by Mr. Attorney General Cushing in his opinion on certain Resolutions of Congress, (6 Ops. Atty. Gen. 680,) in which he held that while joint resolutions of Congress are not distinguishable from bills, and have the effect of law, separate resolutions of either house of Congress, except in matters appertaining to their own parliamentary rights, have no legal effect to constrain the action of the President or Heads of Departments. The whole subject is there elaborately discussed.

"In any view taken of this resolution it appears to me that it can be considered only as expressing the individual views of the Senators voting upon it.

"I have no doubt the treaty might have provided, as did the act of Congress annexing Hawaii, that the existing customs relations between the Spanish possessions ceded by the treaty and the United States should remain unchanged until legislation had been had upon the subject; but in the absence of such provision the case is clearly controlled by that of *De Lima* vs. *Bidwell*."

Mr. Justice GRAY, Mr. Justice SHIRAS, Mr. Justice WHITE and Mr. Justice McKENNA dissented, for the reasons stated in their opinions in *De Lima* vs. *Bidwell*, 182 U. S. 1, 200–220, in *Dooley* vs. *United States*, 182 U. S. 222, 236–243, and in *Downes* vs. *Bidwell*, 182 U. S. 244, 287–347.

HENRY W. DOOLEY ET AL., PLAINTIFFS IN ERROR, *vs.* THE UNITED STATES.

In error to the Circuit Court of the United States for the Southern District of New York for abstract of record, appearance, briefs and cases cited see p. 501 of this APPENDIX, *ante*. No. 207, October term, 1901.

[Decided December 2, 1901.]

This was an action begun in the Circuit Court as a Court of Claims by the firm of Dooley, Smith & Co., to recover duties exacted of them and paid under protest to the collector of the port of San Juan, Porto Rico, upon merchandise imported into that port from the port of New York after May 1, 1900, and since the Foraker act. This act requires all merchandise 'coming into Porto Rico from the United States' to be 'entered at the several ports of entry upon payment of fifteen per centum of the duties which are required to be levied, collected and paid upon like articles of merchandise imported from foreign countries.'

A demurrer was interposed by the District Attorney upon the ground that the court had no jurisdiction of the subject of the action, and also that the complaint did not state facts sufficient to constitute a cause of action. The demurrer to the complaint for insufficiency was sustained, and the petition dismissed.

Mr. Justice BROWN delivered the opinion of the court as follows:

"This case raises the question of the constitutionality of the Foraker act, so far as it fixes the duties to be paid upon merchandise imported into Porto Rico from the port of New York. The validity of this requirement is attacked upon the ground of its violation of that clause of the Constitution (Art. 1, sec. 9) declaring that ' no tax or duty shall be laid on articles exported from any State.'

" While the words ' import ' and ' export ' are sometimes used to denote goods passing from one State to another, the word ' import,' in connection with the provision of the Constitution that ' no State shall levy any imposts or duties on imports or exports,' was held in *Woodruff* vs. *Parham*, (8 Wall. 123,) to apply only to articles imported from foreign countries into the United States.

" That was an action to recover a tax imposed by the city of Mobile for municipal purposes, upon sales at auction. Defendants, who were auctioneers, received in the course of their business for themselves, or as consignees or agents for others, large amounts of goods and merchandise, the products of other States than Alabama, and sold the same in Mobile to purchasers, in unbroken and original packages. The Supreme Court of Alabama decided the case in favor of the tax, and the case came here for review.

" The question, as stated by Mr. Justice Miller, was ' whether merchandise brought from other States and sold, under the circumstances stated, comes within the prohibition of the Federal Constitution, that no State shall, without the consent of Congress, levy any imposts or duties on imports or exports.' Defendants relied largely upon a dictum in *Brown* vs. *Maryland*, (12 Wheat. 419,) to the effect that the principles laid down in that case as to the non-taxability of imports from foreign countries might perhaps apply equally to importations from a sister State.

" In discussing this question, and particularly of the power of Congress to levy and collect taxes, duties, imposts and excises, Mr. Justice MILLER observed: ' Is the word, ' impost,' here used, intended to confer upon Congress a distinct power to levy a tax upon all goods or merchandise carried from one State into another? Or is the power limited to duties on foreign imports? If the former be intended, then the power conferred is curiously rendered nugatory by the subsequent clause of the ninth section, which declares that no tax shall be laid on articles exported from any State, for no article can be imported from one State into another which is not at the same time exported from the former. But if we give to the word ' imposts ' as used in the first mentioned clause, the definition of Chief Justice Marshall, and to the word ' export ' the corresponding idea of something carried out of the United States, we have, in the power to lay duties on imports from abroad, and the prohibition to lay such duties on exports to other countries the power and its limitations concerning imposts.'

" ' It is not too much to say that, so far as our research has extended, neither the word ' export,' ' import ' or ' impost ' is to be found in the discussion on this subject, as they have come down to us from that time, in reference to any other than foreign commerce, without some special form of words to show that foreign commerce is not meant. Whether we look, then, to the terms of the clause of the Constitution in question, or to its relation to other parts of that instrument, or to the history of its formation and adoption, or to the comments of the eminent men who took part in those transactions, we are forced to the conclusion that no intention existed to prohibit, by this clause,' (that no State shall, without the consent of Congress, levy any impost or duty upon any export or import,) 'the right of one State to tax articles brought into it from another.' This definition of the word impost was afterwards approved in *Brown* vs. *Houston,* (114 U. S. 623). See also *Fairbank* vs. *United States* (181 U. S. 283).

"It follows, and is the logical sequence of the case of *Woodruff* vs. *Parham,* that the word 'export' should be given a correlative meaning, and applied only to goods exported to a foreign country. (*Muller* vs. *Baldwin,* L. R. 9 Q. B. 457.) If, then, Porto Rico be no longer a foreign country under the Dingley act, as was held by a majority of this court in *De Lima* vs. *Bidwell,* (182 U. S. 1,) and *Dooley* vs. *United States,* (182 U. S. 222,) we find it impossible to say that goods carried from New York to Porto Rico can be considered as 'exported' from New York within the meaning of that clause of the Constitution. If they are neither exports nor imports, they are still liable to be taxed by Congress under the ample and comprehensive authority conferred by the Constitution 'to lay and collect taxes, duties, imposts and excises.' (Art. 1, sec. 8.)

"In another view, however, the case presented by the record is, whether a duty laid by Congress upon goods arriving at Porto Rico from New York is a duty upon an export from New York, or upon an import to Porto Rico. The fact that the duty is exacted upon the arrival of the goods at San Juan certainly creates a presumption in favor of the latter theory. At the same time it is possible that it may also be a duty upon an export. The mere fact that the duty is not laid at the port of departure is by no means decisive against its being such. It is too clear for argument that if vessels bound for a foreign country were compelled to stop at an intermediate port and pay into the Treasury of the United States a duty upon their cargoes, such duty would be a tax upon an export, and the place of its exaction would be of little significance. The manner in which and the place at which the tax is levied are of minor consequence. Thus in *Brown* vs. *Maryland,* (12 Wheat. 419,) it was held that an act of a State legislature requiring importers of foreign goods to take out a license was a violation of the Constitution declaring that no State shall, without the consent of Congress, lay any impost or duty on imports or exports; and in the recent case of *Fairbank* vs. *United States,* (181 U. S. 283,) we held that a discriminating stamp tax upon bills of lading, covering goods to be carried to a foreign country, was a tax upon exports within the same provision of the Constitution.

"One thing, however, is entirely clear. The tax in question was imposed upon goods imported into Porto Rico, since it was exacted by the collector of the port of San Juan after the arrival of the goods within the limits of that port. From this moment the duties became payable as upon imported merchandise. (*United States* vs. *Howell,* 5 Cranch, 368; *Arnold* vs. *United States,* 9 Cranch, 104; *Meredith* vs. *United States,* 13 Pet. 486.) Now while an import into one port almost necessarily in-

volves a prior export from another, still, in determining the character
of the tax imposed, it is important to consider whether the duty be laid
for the purpose of adding to the revenues of the country from which
the export takes place, or for the benefit of the territory into which they
are imported.   By the third section of the Foraker act imposing duties
upon merchandise coming into Porto Rico from the United States, it
is declared that 'whenever the legislative assembly of Porto Rico shall
have enacted and put into operation a system of local taxation to meet
the necessities of the government of Porto Rico, by this act established,
and shall by resolution duly passed so notify the President, he shall
make proclamation thereof, and thereupon all tariff duties on merchandise and articles going into Porto Rico from the United States or coming into the United States from Porto Rico shall cease, and from and
after such date all such merchandise and articles shall be entered at the
several ports of entry free of duty.'   And by section four, 'the duties
and taxes collected in Porto Rico in pursuance of this act, less the cost
of collecting the same, and the gross amount of all collections and taxes
in the United States upon articles of merchandise coming from Porto
Rico, shall not be covered into the general fund of the Treasury, but
shall be held as a separate fund, and shall be placed at the disposal of
the President to be used for the government and benefit of Porto Rico
until the government of Porto Rico, herein provided for, shall have been
organized, when all moneys theretofore collected under the provisions
hereof, then unexpended, shall be transferred to the local treasury of
Porto Rico.'

" Now, there can be no doubt whatever that, if the legislative assembly
of Porto Rico should, with the consent of Congress, lay a tax upon goods
arriving from ports of the United States, such tax, if legally imposed,
would be a duty upon imports to Porto Bico, and not upon exports from
the United States; and we think the same result must follow, if the duty
be laid by Congress in the interest and for the benefit of Porto Rico.
The truth is, that, in imposing the duty as a temporary expedient, with
a proviso that it may be abolished by the legislative assembly of Porto
Rico at its will, Congress thereby shows that it is undertaking to legislate for the island for the time being and only until the local government
is put into operation.   The mere fact that the duty passes through the
hands of the revenue officers of the United States is immaterial, in view
of the requirement that it shall not be covered into the general fund of
the Treasury, but be held as a separate fund for the government and
benefit of Porto Rico.

" The action is really correlative to that of *Downes* vs. *Bidwell*, (182
U. S. 244,) in which we held that Congress could lawfully impose a duty
upon imports from Porto Rico, notwithstanding the provision of the Constitution that all duties, imposts and excises shall be uniform throughout the United States.   It is true that this conclusion was reached by a
majority of the court by different processes of reasoning, but it is none
the less true that in the conclusion that certain provisions of the Constitution did apply to Porto Rico, and that certain others did not, there
was no difference of opinion.

"It is not intended by this opinion to intimate that Congress may lay an export tax upon merchandise carried from one State to another. While this does not seem to be forbidden by the express words of the Constitution, it would be extremely difficult, if not impossible, to lay such a tax without a violation of the first paragraph of Art. 1, sec. 8, that 'all duties, imposts and excises shall be uniform throughout the United States.' There is a wide difference between the full and paramount power of Congress in legislating for a territory in the condition of Porto Rico and its power with respect to the States, which is merely incidental to its right to regulate interstate commerce. The question, however, is not involved in this case, and we do not desire to express an opinion upon it.

"These duties were properly collected, and the action of the Circuit Court in sustaining the demurrer to the complaint was correct, and it is therefore

"Affirmed."

Mr. Justice WHITE delivered a concurring opinion as follows:

"Whilst agreeing to the judgment of affirmance and in substance concurring in the opinion of the court just announced, by which the affirmance is sustained, I propose to summarize in my own language the reasoning which the opinion embodies as it is by me understood.

"In my judgment the opinion of the court in the cases of *De Lima* vs. *Bidwell*, (182 U. S. 1,) and *Dooley* vs. *United States*, (182 U. S. 222,) decided in the last term, and that just announced in the case of *The Diamond Rings*, as well as the opinions of the majority of the members of the court in *Downes* vs. *Bidwell*, (182 U. S. 244,) also decided at the last term, when considered in connection with the previous adjudications of this court, are conclusive in favor of the affirmance of the judgment in this cause. The question is, whether a tax imposed by authority of the act of April 12, 1900, (31 Stat. 77,) in Porto Rico, on merchandise coming into that island from the United States, is repugnant to clause 5, section 9, of article I of the Constitution of the United States, which provides that 'no tax or duty shall be laid on articles exported from any State.' Is the tax here assailed an export tax within the meaning of the Constitution? If it is, the judgment sustaining it should be reversed; if it is not, affirmance is required.

"In *Woodruff* vs. *Parham*, (1870) 8 Wall. 123, the validity of a tax on auction sales levied by the city of Mobile pursuant to authority conferred by the laws of the State of Alabama was called in question. One of the contentions was that as the tax was on sales at auction of goods in the original packages brought into the State of Alabama from other States, it was repugnant to that clause of section 9 of article I of the Constitution, which forbids any State, without the consent of Congress, from laying imposts or duties on imports or exports, except what may be absolutely necessary for executing its inspection laws. In approaching the consideration of the question thus presented, the court, in its opinion, which was announced by Mr. Justice Miller, said (p. 131):

"'The words imposts, imports and exports are frequently used in the

Constitution.   They have a necessary co-relation, and when we have a
clear idea of what either word means in any particular connection in
which it may be found, we have one of the most satisfactory tests of
its definition in other parts of the same instrument.   . . .   Leaving,
then, for a moment, the clause of the Constitution under consideration,' (forbidding a State to lay an import or an export tax,) ' we find
the first use of these co-relative terms in that clause of the eighth section of the first article which begins the enumeration of the powers
confided to Congress, ' that Congress shall have power to levy and collect taxes, duties, imposts and excises. . . .   But all duties, imposts
and excises shall be uniform throughout the United States.'   Is the
word impost, here used, intended to confer upon Congress a distinct
power to levy a tax upon all goods or merchandise carried from one
State into another ? or is the power limited to duties on foreign imports ? If the former be intended, then the power conferred is curiously
rendered nugatory by the subsequent clause of the ninth section, which
declares that no tax shall be laid on articles exported from any State,
for no article can be imported from one State into another which is not,
at the same time, exported from the former.   But if we give to the word
imposts, as used in the first mentioned clause, the definition of Chief
Justice Marshall, and to the word export the corresponding idea of
something carried out of the United States, we have, in the power to
lay duties on imports from abroad and the prohibition to lay such duties
on exports to other countries, the power and its limitation concerning
imposts.'

  " The opinion then proceeded to elaborately consider the meaning of
the words imports, exports and imposts in the Constitution, with reference to the powers of Congress, and concluded that they related only
to the bringing in of goods from a country foreign to the United States
or the taking out of goods from the United States to such a country.
From this conclusion the deduction was drawn that the words imports
and exports, when used in the Constitution with reference to the power
of the several States, had a similar meaning, and hence the tax levied
by the city of Mobile was decided not to be repugnant to the clause of
the Constitution heretofore referred to, prohibiting a State ' from laying imposts or duties on imports or exports.'   In the course of the
opinion an intimation of Mr. Chief Justice Marshall in *Brown* vs. *Maryland*, that the words imports and exports might relate to the movement
of goods between the States, was referred to, and it was expressly said
that this was a mere suggestion on the part of the Chief Justice, not
involved in the cause, and not therefore decided.   So, also, the attention of the court was directed to the case of *Almy* vs. *California*, (1860)
24 How. 169.   That case involved the validity of a stamp tax imposed
in California on all bills of lading for the shipment of gold from California to a point without the State.   The particular bill of lading which
was in question was for the shipment of gold from California to New
York.   It was held that this stamp tax was at least an indirect burden
on exports, and hence was void, because an export tax within the meaning of the Constitution.   In the opinion in *Woodruff* vs. *Parham* it was

expressly decided that although the conclusion in *Almy* vs. *California,* that the tax was void, was sustained by the commerce clause of the Constitution which had been referred to in the argument of that case, it had been erroneously held that import or export within the constitutional sense of the words related to the movement of goods between the States and not exclusively to foreign commerce. To the extent therefore that *Almy* vs. *California* held or intimated that an export or import tax within the meaning of the Constitution embraced anything but foreign commerce, it was expressly overruled.

"In *Brown* vs. *Houston,* (114 U. S. 622,) decided in 1884, fourteen years after the decision in *Woodruff* vs. *Parham,* the question which arose in the latter case was again presented. A tax levied by the State of Louisiana on certain coal which had come down the Ohio River was assailed on the ground that it amounted to both an export and import tax within the meaning of the constitution. The court, speaking through Mr. Justice Bradley, said (p. 628):

"'It was decided by this court in the case of *Woodruff* vs. *Parham,* (8 Wall. 123,) that the term imports as used in that clause of the Constitution which declares that ' no State shall without the consent of Congress lay any imposts or duties on imports or exports,' does not refer to articles carried from one State into another, but only to articles imported from foreign countries into the United States.'

"The opinion, after stating the facts which were presented in *Woodruff* vs. *Parham,* and the contention which was in that case based upon them, said (pp. 628, 629):

"'This court, however, after an elaborate examination of the question, held that the terms ' imports ' and ' exports' in the clause under consideration had reference to goods brought from or carried to foreign countries alone and not to goods transported from one State to the other. It is unnecessary, therefore, to consider further the question raised by the plaintiffs in error under their assignment of error so far as it is based on the assumption that the tax complained of was an impost or duty on imports.'

"Thus treating the meaning of the words imports and exports as having been conclusively determined by *Woodruff* vs. *Parham,* the court passed to the consideration of the contention that the tax levied in the State of Louisiana was an export tax within the meaning of the Constitution, because some of the coal was intended for export to a foreign country, or had been, as it was claimed, in part actually exported to such country.

"Again, in *Fairbank* vs. *United States,* (1900) 181 U. S. 283, the court was called upon to determine whether the requirement in an act of Congress that a revenue stamp be affixed to every bill of lading for goods shipped to a foreign country was a tax on exports. In the course of the opinion, in considering the question, the court referred to *Almy* vs. *California, supra,* as authority for the proposition that a tax on the bill of lading was a tax on the movement of the goods which the bill of lading evidenced. But, in referring to the *Almy* case, the court was careful to say (p. 294):

" ' It is true that thereafter in *Woodruff* vs. P*arham*, (8 Wall. 123,) it was held that the words ' imports ' and ' exports,' as used in the Constitution, were used to define the shipment of articles between this and a foreign country and not that between the States, and while therefore that case is no longer an authority as to what is or what is not an export, the proposition that a stamp duty on a bill of lading is in effect a duty on the article transported remains unaffected.'

" A consideration of the opinions in *Woodruff* vs. P*arham* and *Brown* vs. *Houston*, so recently in effect approved by this court in the case of *Fairbank* vs. *United States*, will make it clear that an adherence to the interpretation of the words export and import which was expounded in those cases is essential to the preservation of the necessary powers of taxation of the several States, as well as of those of the government of the United States. And, by implication, in a number of cases decided by this court since the decision in *Woodruff* vs. P*arham*, the doctrine of export and import there defined has been, if not expressly, at least tacitly, approved in many ways. Indeed, it may be safely assumed that many State statutes levying taxes and much legislation of Congress has been enacted upon the express or implied recognition of the settled construction of the Constitution hitherto affixed to the import and export clauses by this court in the cases referred to. And this will be made obvious when it is considered that if the words export and import as used in the Constitution be applied to the movement of goods between the States, then it amounts to not only an express prohibition on the States to impose any direct but also any indirect burden, and, therefore, under the doctrine of *Brown* vs. *Maryland*, any state tax law which would indirectly burden the coming of goods from one State to the other would be wholly void. So also, as to the government of the United States, if the provision as to the laying and collection of imposts be not construed as a ' distinct ' provision relating to foreign commerce and co-related with the clause as to exports, it would follow, as was clearly pointed out in *Woodruff* vs. P*arham*, that the Constitution had granted on the one hand a power and immediately denied it. Besides, it would follow that all the general powers of taxation conferred upon Congress would be limited by the export clause, and thus any domestic tax, although fulfilling the requirements of uniformity and not violating the prohibition against preferences which indirectly burdened the ultimate export, would be void, a doctrine which would manifestly cause to be invalid methods of taxation exercised by Congress from the beginning without question.

" It being then beyond doubt that this court has, in a line of well-considered cases, determined that the words export and import when employed in the Constitution relate to the bringing in of goods from a country foreign to the United States and to the carrying out of goods from the United States to such a country, the only question remaining is, Is Porto Rico a country foreign to the United States? In answering this question it is manifest, from the entire reasoning of the court, in the cases in which it was decided that the terms export and import relate to a foreign country alone, that the words foreign country, as used in those opinions, signified a country outside the sovereignty of the United States and beyond its legislative authority, and that such meaning of those words was absolutely essential to the process of reasoning by which the conclusion in the cases referred to was reached.

"Is Porto Rico a country foreign to the United States in the sense that it is not within the sovereignty and not subject to the legislative authority of the United States? is then the issue. In *De Lima* vs. *Bidwell* and *Dooley* vs. *United States, supra*, it was held that instantly upon the ratification of the treaty with Spain, Porto Rico ceased to be a foreign country within the meaning of the tariff laws of the United States. In the case of *The Diamond Rings*, it has just been held that the Philippine Islands immediately upon the ratification of the treaty ceased to be foreign country within the meaning of the tariff laws; and of course, as these islands were acquired by the same treaty by which Porto Rico was acquired, this ruling is predicated on the decisions in *De Lima* and *Dooley*, above referred to. It is true that both in the *De Lima* and the *Dooley* cases, as well as in the case of *The Diamond Rings*, just decided, dissents were announced. None of the dissents rested, however, upon the theory that Porto Rico or the Philippine Islands had not come under the sovereignty and become subject to the legislative authority of the United States, but were based on the ground that legislation by Congress was necessary to bring the territory within the line of the tariff laws in force at the time of the acquisition; and especially was this the case where the new territory had not, as the result of the acquisition, been incorporated into the United States as an integral part thereof, though coming under its sovereignty and subject, as a possession, to the legislative power of Congress.

"In *Downes* vs. *Bidwell, supra*, the question was whether a tax imposed by Congress on goods coming into the United States from Porto Rico was repugnant to that clause of the Constitution requiring uniformity 'throughout the United States' of all 'duties, imposts and excises.' The contention on the one hand was, that as Porto Rico had by the treaty with Spain been acquired by the United States, Congress could not impose a burden on goods coming from Porto Rico, in disregard of the requirement of uniformity 'throughout the United States.' On the other hand, it was contended that although Porto Rico had become territory of the United States and was subject to the legislative authority of Congress, it had not been so made a part of the United States as to cause Congress to be subject, in legislating with regard to that island, to the uniformity provision of the Constitution. The court maintained the latter view. Whilst it is true the members of the court who agreed in this conclusion did so for different reasons, nevertheless, in all the opinions delivered by the justices who formed the majority of the court, it was declared that Porto Rico had come under the sovereignty and was subject to the legislative authority of the United States. Indeed, this was controverted by no one, since the members of the court who dissented did so because they deemed that Porto Rico had so entirely ceased to be foreign country and had so completely been made a part of the United States, that Congress could not, in legislating for that

37

island, disregard the provision of uniformity throughout the United
States.

"It having been thus affirmatively repeatedly determined that the export and import clauses of the Constitution refer only to commerce
with foreign countries, that is, to a country or countries without the
sovereignty and entirely beyond the legislative authority of the United
States, and it having been conclusively settled that Porto Rico is not
such a country, it seems to me the claim here made that the tax imposed by Congress in Porto Rico is an export or an import within the
meaning of the Constitution, is untenable.   But, it is said, if Porto Rico
is not foreign, and, therefore, the tax laid on goods in that island on
their arrival from the United States is not within the purview of the
import and the inhibition of the export clauses of the Constitution,
then Porto Rico is domestic, and the tax is void because repugnant to
the first clause of section 8 of article I of the Constitution conferring
upon Congress 'the power to lay and collect taxes, duties, imposts and
excises, . . . but all duties, imposts and excises shall be uniform
throughout the United States.'   This contention, however, is but a re-
statement of the proposition which the court held to be unsound in
Downes vs. *Bidwell*, for, in that case, it was expressly decided that a provision of the statute now in question which imposes a tax on goods
coming to the United States from Porto Rico was valid because that
island occupied such a relation to the United States as empowered Congress to exact such a tax since the requirement of uniformity throughout the United States was inapplicable.   I do not propose to recapitu-
late the grounds of the conclusion so elaborately expressed by the opinions of the majority of the court in that case, since it suffices to say,
for the purposes of the uniformity clause, that decision is controlling
in this case.   If the contention be that because the impost clause of the
Constitution refers only to foreign commerce, therefore there was no
power in Congress to impose the tax in question, or that such power is
impliedly denied, the contention is unfounded, and really but amounts
to an indirect attack upon the doctrines announced in *Woodruff* vs. *Parham*, *Brown* vs. *Houston* and *Fairbank* vs. *United States*.   As held in
Woodruff vs. *Parham*, the impost clause and the export clause are co-
related and refer to a distinct subject, that is, foreign commerce.   By
what process of reasoning it can be said that because a special enumeration on a particular subject of taxation and a particular limitation as to
that subject is expressed in the Constitution, therefore other and general
powers of taxation not relating to the subject in question are taken
away, is not by me perceived.   Certainly the argument cannot be that
because a power has been conferred on Congress by the Constitution
to levy a tax on foreign commerce, therefore the Constitution has
taken away from Congress power to tax even indirectly domestic commerce.   Because the grant of power as to imposts contained in the first
clause of section 8 of article I of the Constitution relates to foreign
commerce there arises no limitation on the general authority to tax as to
all other subjects, which flow from the other provisions of the same
clause.   Referring to such power—the authority to levy and collect

taxes, duties, imposts and excises—the court, in the *License Tax Cases*,
(1866) 5 Wall. 462, 471, said:

"'The power of Congress to tax is a very extensive power. It is
given in the Constitution, with only one exception and only two qualifications. Congress cannot tax exports, and it must impose direct taxes
by the rule of apportionment, and indirect taxes by the rule of uniformity. Thus limited, and thus only, it reaches every subject, and
may be exercised at discretion.'

"Of course, the Constitution contemplates freedom of commerce between the States, but it also confers upon Congress the powers of taxation to which I have referred, and safeguarded the freedom of commerce and equality of taxation between the States by conferring upon
Congress the power to regulate such commerce, by providing for the
apportionment of direct taxes, by exacting uniformity throughout the
United States in the laying of duties, imposts and excises, and by prohibiting preferences between ports of different States. Indeed, when
the argument which I am considering is properly analyzed, it amounts
to a denial, as I have said, of the substantial powers of Congress with
regard to domestic taxation, and, as I understand it, overthrows the
settled interpretation of the Constitution, long since announced and
consistently adhered to."

Mr. Chief Justice FULLER, with whom concurred Mr. Justice Harlan,
Mr. Justice Brewer and Mr. Justice Peckham, delivered a dissenting
opinion as follows:

"This is an action brought to recover back duties levied and collected
under the Porto Rican act of April 12, 1900, (31 Stat. 77,) at San Juan,
on articles shipped to that port by citizens of New York from the State
of New York. Plaintiffs were engaged in the business of commission
merchants, having their main office in the city of New York and a
branch office at San Juan.

"The second section of the act provides that, from the time of its passage, 'the same tariffs, customs, and duties shall be levied, collected,
and paid upon all articles imported into Porto Rico from ports other
than those of the United States which are required by law to be collected upon articles imported into the United States from foreign countries,' with some exceptions not material here.

"The third section, by which these duties are imposed, reads: 'That
on and after the passage of this act all merchandise coming into the
United States from Porto Rico and coming into Porto Rico from the
United States shall be entered at the several ports of entry upon payment of fifteen per centum of the duties which are required to be levied,
collected, and paid upon like articles of merchandise imported from
foreign countries; and in addition thereto upon articles of merchandise
of Porto Rican manufacture coming into the United States and withdrawn for consumption or sale upon payment of a tax equal to the internal revenue tax imposed in the United States upon the like articles
of merchandise of domestic manufacture;' and it was further provided
that articles of merchandise manufactured in the United States coming

into Porto Rico should, after entry, be subject to whatever internal revenue taxes might be in force on the island. And also that whenever the legislative assembly of Porto Rico should have enacted and put into operation a system of local taxation, and proclamation thereof had been made, 'all tariff duties on merchandise and articles going into Porto Rico from the United States or coming into the United States from Porto Rico shall cease.'

"Assuming that 'the United States' as referred to is the United States as constituted at the date of the proclamation of the treaty, the act, explicitly recognizing the distinction between tariff duties and internal taxes, is in respect of such duties an act to raise revenue by taxing the commerce of the people of every State and territory.

"The fact that the net proceeds of the duties are appropriated by the act for use in Porto Rico does not affect their character any more than if so appropriated by another and separate act. The taxation reaches the people of the States directly, and is national and not local, even though the revenue derived therefrom is devoted to local purposes.

"Customs duties are duties imposed on imports or exports, and, according to the terms of this act, these are customs duties, not levied according to the rule of uniformity, and laid on exports as well as imports.

" By the first clause of section 8 of Article I of the Constitution, Congress is empowered to lay and collect duties, imposts and excises, subject to the rule of uniformity, but this court has held that customs duties are only leviable on foreign commerce, *Woodruff* vs. *Parham*, 8 Wall. 123, and that the uniformity required is geographical merely, *Knowlton* vs. *Moore*, 178 U. S. 41. By the third clause of the same section, Congress is empowered 'to regulate commerce with foreign nations, and among the several States, and with the Indian tribes.' The power to tax and the power to regulate commerce are distinct powers, yet the power of taxation may be so exercised as to operate in regulation of commerce.

"Clauses 5 and 6 of section 9 provide: ,

" ' No tax or duty shall be laid on articles exported from any State.

' "No preference shall be given by any regulation of commerce or revenue to the ports of one State over those of another; nor shall vessels bound to or from one State be obliged to enter, clear or pay duties in another.'

" These provisions were intended to prevent the application of the power to lay taxes or duties, or the power to regulate commerce, so as to discriminate between one part of the country and another. The regulation of commerce by a majority vote and the exemption of exports from duties or taxes were parts of one of the great compromises of the Constitution.

" If, after the cession, Porto Rico remained a foreign country, the prohibition of clause 5 would be fatal to these duties; while if Porto Rico became domestic, then, as they are customs duties, they could not be sustained, according to *Woodruff* vs. *Parham*, under the first clause of section 8; and were also prohibited by clause 5 of section 9, whether customs duties or not, if the application of that clause is not limited to foreign commerce.

"The prohibition, that 'no tax or duty shall be laid on articles exported from any State,' negatives the existence of any power in Congress to lay taxes or duties in any form on articles exported from a State, *irrespective of their destination*, and, this being so, the act in imposing the duties in question is invalid, whether Porto Rico, after its passage, was a foreign or reputed foreign territory, a domestic territory, or a territory subject to be dealt with at the will of Congress regardless of constitutional limitations.

"Confessedly the prohibition applies to foreign commerce, and the question is whether it is confined to that. In other words, whether language which embraces all articles exported can be properly restricted to particular exports. On what ground can the insertion in this comprehensive denial of power of the words 'to foreign countries,' thereby depriving it of effect on commerce other than foreign, be justified?

"If the words 'exported from any State' apply only to articles exported from a State to foreign country, it would seem to follow that then broad power granted to Congress 'to lay and collect taxes,' for the purposes specified in the Constitution, may be exerted in the way of taxation on articles exported from one State to another. The right to carry legitimate articles of commerce from one State to another State without interference by National or State authority was, it has always been supposed, firmly established and secured by the Constitution. But that right may be destroyed or greatly impaired if it be true that articles may be taxed by Congress by reason of their being carried from one State to another.

"Undoubtedly the clause confines the power to lay customs duties or imposts to imports only. This was so stated by Mr. Hamilton in the thirty-second number of The Federalist: "The first clause of the same section [§ 8] empowers Congress '*to lay and collect taxes, duties, imposts, and excises;*' and the second clause of the tenth section of the same article declares that '*no State shall, without the consent of Congress, lay ang imposts or duties on imports or exports*, except for the purpose of executing its inspection laws.' Hence would result an exclusive power in the Union to lay duties on imports and exports, with the particular exception mentioned. But this power is abridged by another clause, which declares that no tax or duty shall be laid on articles exported from any State; in consequence of which qualification it now only extends to the *duties on imports.*'

"Nevertheless because the clause secured that object, it is not to be assumed that it was not also intended to secure unrestrained intercourse between the different parts of a common country.

"As was said in *Gibbons* vs. *Ogden*, the right of intercourse between State and State was derived 'from those laws whose authority is acknowledged by civilized man throughout the world. The Constitution found it an existing right, and gave to Congress the power to regulate it.' 9 Wheat. 211. From this grant, however, the power to regulate by the levy of any tax or duty on articles exported from any State was expressly withheld.

" In *Woodruff* vs. P*arham*, 8 Wall. 132, Mr. Justice Miller, in support of the conclusion that clause 1 of section 8 was confined as to customs duties to foreign commerce, said: ' Is the word impost, here used, intended to confer upon Congress a distinct power to levy a tax upon all goods or merchandise carried from one State into another? Or is the power limited to duties on foreign imports ? If the former be intended, then the power conferred is curiously rendered nugatory by the subsequent clause of the ninth section, which declares that no tax shall be laid on articles exported from any State, for no article can be imported from one State into another which is not, at the same time, exported from the former.'

" In that case, clause 2 of section 10 was under consideration: ' No State shall, without the consent of Congress, lay any imposts or duties on imports or exports, except what may be absolutely necessary for executing its inspection laws; and the net produce of all duties and imposts, laid by any State on imports or exports, shall be for the use of the Treasury of the United States; and all such laws shall be subject to the revision and control of the Congress.'

" It was held that this referred to foreign commerce only, and ' that no intention existed to prohibit, by *this clause*, the right of one State to tax articles brought into it from another.' This was reaffirmed in *Brown* vs. *Houston*, 114 U. S. 622, 630, and Mr. Justice Bradley said: ' But in holding, with the decision in *Woodruff* vs. *Parham*, that goods carried from one State to another are not imports or exports within the meaning of the clause which prohibits a State from laying any impost or duty on imports or exports, we do not mean to be understood as holding that a State may levy import or export duties on goods imported from or exported to another State. We only mean to say that the clause in question does not prohibit it. Whether the laying of such duties by a State would not violate some other provision of the Constitution, that, for example, which gives to Congress the power to regulate commerce with foreign nations, among the several States, and with the Indian tribes, is a different question.'

" That question has been repeatedly answered by this court to the effect ' that no State has the right to lay a tax on interstate commerce in any form, whether by way of duties laid on the transportation of the subjects of that commerce, or on the receipts derived from that transportation, or on the occupation or business of carrying it on, for the reason that such taxation is a burden on that commerce, and amounts to a regulation of it, which belongs solely to Congress.' *Lyng* vs. *Michigan*, 135 U. S. 166. But if that power of regulation is absolutely unrestricted as respects interstate commerce, then the very unity the Constitution was framed to secure can be set at naught by a legislative body created by that instrument.

" Such a conclusion is wholly inadmissible. The power to regulate interstate commerce was granted in order that trade between the States might be left free from discriminating legislation and not to impart the power to create antagonistic commercial relations between them.

"The prohibition of preference of ports was coupled with the prohibition of taxation on articles exported. The citizens of each State were declared 'entitled to all privileges and immunities of citizens in the several States,' and that included the right of ingress and egress, and the enjoyment of the privileges of trade and commerce. (*Slaughterhouse Cases*, 16 Wall. 36.)

"And so the court, in *Woodruff* vs. P*arham*, as the quotation from its opinion by Mr. Justice MILLER demonstrates, did not put upon the absolute and general prohibition of power to lay any tax or duty on articles exported from any State that narrow construction which would limit it to exports to a foreign country, and would concede the power to Congress to impose duties on exports from one State to another in regulation of interstate commerce.

"The power to lay duties in regulation of commerce with foreign nations is relied on as the source of power to pass laws for the protection and encouragement of domestic industries, and except for this clause the same effect would be attributed to the power to regulate commerce among the States. This, however, the clause, literally read, prevents, and to limit its application to foreign commerce, as the power to lay customs duties under the first clause of section 8 has been limited, would defeat the manifest purpose of the constitution by enabling discriminating taxes and duties to be laid against one section of the country as distinguished from another.

"And if the prohibition be not confined to foreign commerce then it applies to all commerce, not wholly internal to the respective States, and the destination of articles exported from a State cannot affect, or be laid hold of to affect, the result.

"In short, clause 5 operates, and was intended to operate, to except the power to lay any tax or duty on articles exported from the general power to regulate commerce whether interstate or foreign. And this is equally true in respect to commerce with the territories, for the power to regulate commerce includes the power to regulate it not only as between foreign countries and the territories, but also by necessary implication as between the States and territories. *Stoutenburgh* v. *Hennick*, 129 U. S. 141.

"Nothing is better settled than that the States cannot interfere with interstate commerce, yet it is easy to see that if the exclusive delegation to Congress of the power to regulate commerce did not embrace commerce between the States and territories, the interference by the States with such commerce might be justified.

"Again, if, in any view, these duties could be treated as other than custom duties, the result would be the same, inasmuch as the goods were articles exported from New York, and there was a total lack of power to lay *any* tax or duty on such articles.

"The prohibition on Congress is explicit, and noticeably different from the prohibition on the States. The State is forbidden to lay 'any imposts or duties;' Congress is forbidden to lay 'any tax or duty.'

The State is forbidden from laying imposts or duties 'on imports or exports' that is, articles coming into or going out of the United States. Congress is forbidden to tax 'articles exported *from any State.*'

" The plain language of the Constitution should not be made 'blank paper by construction,' and its specific mandate ought to be obeyed.

" As said in *Marbury* vs. *Madison*, ' It is declared that " no tax or duty shall be laid on articles exported from any State." Suppose a duty on the export of cotton, of tobacco, or of flour; and a suit instituted to recover it. Ought judgment to be rendered in such a case? Ought the judges to close their eyes on the Constitution, and only see the law ? ' 1 Cranch, 178.

" Nor is the result affected by the fact that the collection of these duties was at Porto Rico.

" In *Brown* vs. *Maryland*, 12 Wheat. 437, Chief Justice Marshall said: ' An impost, or duty on imports, is a custom or a tax levied on articles brought into a country, and is most usually secured before the importer is allowed to exercise his rights of ownership over them, because evasions of the law can be prevented more certainly by executing it while the articles are in its custody. It would not, however, be less a duty or impost on the articles, if it were to be levied on them after they were landed. The policy and consequent practice of levying or securing the duty before, or on entering, the port, does not limit the power to that state of things, nor, consequently, the prohibition, unless the true meaning of the clause so confines it. What, then, are 'imports?' The lexicons inform us they are 'things imported.' If we appeal to usage for the meaning of the word, we shall receive the same answer. They are the articles themselves which are brought into the country, ' A duty on imports,' then, is not merely a duty on the act of importation, but is a duty on the thing imported. It is not, taken in its literal sense, confined to a duty levied while the article is entering the country, but extends to a duty levied after it has entered the country.'

" And so of exports. They are the things exported—the articles themselves. A duty on exports is not merely a duty on the act of exportation, but it is a duty on the article exported, and the article exported remains such until it has reached its final destination. The place of collection is purely incidental, and immaterial on the question of power.

" But we are told that these duties were laid, not on articles exported from the State of New York, but on articles imported into Porto Rico. The language used, however, precludes this contention, and there is nothing in the act to indicate that at some particular point on a voyage articles exported were to cease to be such and to become imports, and nothing in the facts in this case to indicate a sea change of that sort as to these goods. The geographical origin of the shipment controls, and, as heretofore said, it is not material whether the duties were collectible at the place of exportation or at Porto Rico. They were imposed on articles exported from the State of New York, and before the articles had reached their ultimate destination and been mingled with the common mass of property on the island.

" Chief Justice Marshall disposed of the suggested evasion thus: 'Suppose revenue cutters were to be stationed off the coast for the purpose of levying a duty on all merchandise found in vessels which were leaving the United States for foreign countries; would it be received as an excuse for this outrage were the government to say that exportation meant no more than carrying goods out of the country, and as the prohibition to lay a tax on imports, or things imported, ceased the instant they were brought into the country, so the prohibition to tax articles exported ceased when they were carried out of the country.' 12 Wheat. 445.

" There is no difference in principle between the case supposed and that before us. The course of transportation is arrested until the exaction is paid.

" The proposition that because the proceeds of these duties were to be used for the benefit of Porto Rico they might be regarded as if laid by Porto Rico itself with the consent of Congress, and were, therefore, lawful, will not bear examination. No moneycan be drawn from the Treasury except in consequence of appropriations made by law. This act does not appropriate a fixed sum for the benefit of Porto Rico, but provides that the money collected, and collected from citizens of the United States in every port of the United States, shall be placed in a separate fund or subsequently in the treasury of Porto Rico, to be expended for the government and benefit thereof. And although the destination of the proceeds in this way were lawful, it would not convert duties on articles exported from the States into local taxes.

" States may, indeed, under the Constitution, lay duties on foreign imports and exports, for the use of the Treasury of the United States, with the consent of Congress, but they do not derive the power from the general government. The power pre-existed, and it is its exercise only that is subjected to the discretion of Congress.

" Congress may lay local taxes in the territories, affecting persons and property therein, or authorize territorial legislatures to do so, but it cannot lay tariff duties on articles exported from one State to another, or from any State to the territories, or from any State to foreign countries, or grant a power in that regard which it does not possess. But the decision now made recognizes such powers in Congress as will enable it, under the guise of taxation, to exclude the products of Porto Rico from the States as well as the products of the States from Porto Rico; and this notwithstanding it was held in *De Lima* vs. *Bidwell*, 182 U. S. 1, that Porto Rico after the ratification of the treaty with Spain ceased to be foreign and became domestic territory.

" My Brothers HARLAN, BREWER and PECKHAM concur in this dissent.

" We think it clear on this record that plaintiffs were entitled to recover and that the judgment should be reversed."

Lightning Source UK Ltd.
Milton Keynes UK
UKHW020214091118
331957UK00012B/1581/P